OLD
TESTAMENT
THEOLOGY

OLD TESTAMENT THEOLOGY

ITS HISTORY,
METHOD,
AND MESSAGE

RALPH L. SMITH

BROADMAN
& HOLMAN
PUBLISHERS

Nashville, Tennessee

© Copyright 1993 Broadman & Holman Publishers
All Rights Reserved
4216-06
ISBN 0-8054-1606-4
Dewey Decimal Classification: 230
Subject Headings: THEOLOGY // BIBLE. OLD TESTAMENT
Library of Congress Catalog Number: 92-29516
Printed in the United States of America

Library of Congress-in-Publication Data

Smith, Ralph L. (Ralph Lee), 1918-

Old Testament theology: its history, method, and message / Ralph L. Smith.

p.   cm.

Includes bibliographical references and index.

ISBN 0-8054-1606-4

1. Bible. O.T. — Theology. I. Title.

BS1192.5.S65   1993

230 — dc20   92-29516

CIP

*For
Dorothy*

Table of Contents

Abbreviations

AJSL	*American Journal of Semitic Languages*
BA	*Biblical Archaeologist*
BAR	*Biblical Archaeologist Reader*
BASOR	*Bulletin of American Schools of Oriental Research*
BBC	Broadman Bible Commentary
BDB	Brown, Driver, and Briggs, *Hebrew and English Lexicon of the Old Testament*
BJRL	*Bulletin of the John Rylands University Library of Manchester*
BTB	*Biblical Theology Bulletin*
BWANT	Beitrage zur Wissenschaft vom Alten und Neuen Testament
BZAW	Beihefte zur ZAW
CBQ	*Catholic Biblical Quarterly*
EJ	*Encyclopedia Judaica*
ET	*Expository Times*
HBT	*Horizons in Biblical Theology*
HTR	*Harvard Theological Review*
HUCA	*Hebrew Union College Annual*

IB	*Interpreter's Bible*
ICC	*International Critical Commentary*
IDB	*Interpreter's Dictionary of the Bible*
JAOS	*Journal of American Oriental Society*
JBL	*Journal of Biblical Literature*
JBR	*Journal of Bible and Religion*
JR	*Journal of Religion*
JSOT	*Journal for the Study of the Old Testament*
JTS	*Journal of Theological Studies*
NICOT	*New International Commentary on the Old Testament*
OTMS	*Old Testament and Modern Study*
RSPhTH	*Revue des sciences philosophiques et theologiques*
SBL	Society of Biblical Literature
SBT	*Studies in Biblical Theology*
SJT	*Scottish Journal of Theology*
SVT	*Supplements to Vetus Testamentum*
SWJT	*Southwestern Journal of Theology*
TB	*Tyndale Bulletin*
TDOT	*Theological Dictionary of the Old Testament*
THAT	*Theologisches Handwörterbuch zum Alten Testament*
ThLZ	*Theologische Literaturzeitung*
TOTC	Tyndale Old Testament Commentary
TWAT	*Theologisches Wörterbuch zum Alten Testament*
TTZ	*Trierer theologische Zeitschrift*
VT	*Vetus Testamentum*
WMANT	Wissenschaftliche Monographien zum Alten und Neuen Testament
WBC	Word Bible Commentary
ZAW	*Zeitschrift für die altestamentliche Wissenschaft*
ZTK	*Zeitschrift für Theologie und Kirche*

Preface

Old Testament theology has lived a charmed life. It has been in crisis since birth. Some scholars have spoken of its demise and rebirth. However, it continues to survive. James Barr, J. J. Collins, and others are skeptical about its future. [See Gerhard Hasel, *Old Testament Theology: Basic Issues in the Current Debate* (Grand Rapids: Eerdmans, 1991), 37, 94-95]. Scholars cannot agree on its definition, methodology, value, and content; yet, the debate goes on. This volume is not intended to be a part of the debate although it addresses most of the issues in the debate. This is an elementary introduction to the study of Old Testament theology. It began as a "Handbook" on Old Testament theology and was switched in midstream to the purpose expressed in the present title: *Old Testament Theology: Its History, Method, and Message.* It is directed toward students, pastors, and interested lay people. The large number of quotes from "authorities" is part of a design to familiarize the reader with a basic bibliography in the field and to allow the authorities to express their thoughts in their own words. Most of the biblical quotations are from the New Revised Standard Version.

I am debtor to countless people (teachers, students parents, family, and friends) and institutions (schools, colleges, and seminaries) for helping in my preparation. I want to thank especially Dr. Trent C. Butler at Broadman & Holman Publishers for his invaluable helpfulness in this project, and Mrs. Denise Hess for supreme patience, commitment, and unusual gifts and skills in preparing the manuscript. I could not have written and published this book without them. Thanks go also to my colleagues and administration for their support and encouragement. Most of all I want to thank my wife Dorothy for being the dearest spouse any human ever had. She learned many of her graces by reading the Old Testament.

Ralph L. Smith
Southwestern Baptist Theological Seminary
August, 1992

Introduction

What is Old Testament theology?

How should we do Old Testament theology?

What is the relationship of the Old Testament to the New Testament and to the Christian faith?

Why is the Old Testament an integral part of the Christian Bible?

Should Christians continue to call the first part of their Bible "The Old Testament" as they have through most of their history, or should they join a growing number of scholars in calling it "The Hebrew Bible"?

Who are some major writers in this field? How did they do Old Testament theology? What is the current state of this discipline, and what is its future?

Does the Old Testament have a message for us today?

These are some of the questions I will address in *Old Testament Theology: Its History, Method, and Message.*

The purpose of this book is to explore, not to argue or debate. It does not set out any radically new method of doing Old Testament theology or of interpreting the Old Testament. Its aim is to provide university and seminary students a textbook that gives a partial report of what others have said and done about Old Testament theology and then suggests ways the theological materials in the Old Testament may be organized, interpreted, and appropriated.

Chapter 1 traces the story of Old Testament theology from Old Testament times to the present. Chapter 2 deals in some detail with the nature and method of Old Testament theology.

I have not chosen some central theme, such as the covenant, to serve as a stack-pole around which to organize all of the material. Nor have I selected some broad topic such as "the promise" or "salvation-history" which may be traced chronologically through the Old Testament. I have chosen, instead, a modified systematic-thematic approach. Therefore, chapters 3 through 11 present a model of how one may do Old Testament theology using the following major theological themes: The Knowledge of God; Election and Covenant; Who Is a God Like Yahweh?; What Is Mankind?; Sin and Redemption; Worship; The Good Life; Death and Beyond; and In That Day.

The dangers of this approach are well documented. Perhaps the greatest danger is that in picking and choosing themes to include and to omit and in systematizing the materials used to discuss each theme, I will put my own "spin" on the organization and interpretation of each subject. In that case the result is in danger of being commensurate with what I bring to the discussion and not what the Old Testament itself actually says. However, this danger is inherent in any presentation of Old Testament theology.

This discipline in its modern form began in the late 1700s as an attempt to free the theological study of the Bible from the shackles of dogmatic theology and its misuse of the Bible to support its own beliefs. (See the section "The Germination and Growth of Old Testament Theology" in chap. 1.) Every presentation of Old Testament theology is colored by the author's viewpoint, background, and preparation. We must be aware of the dangers of subjectivity and strive to permit the Old Testament materials to speak for themselves.

One source of subjectivity in this field may be the religious affiliation and/or commitment of the author. Historically, Old Testament theologies have been written by Christians primarily for Christians. The term "Old Testament" is a Christian term. Jews do not use that term; they use "Hebrew Bible," "The Bible," "the Scripture," or "Tanach." *Tanach* is an acronym for the three parts of the Hebrew Bible: *Torah, Nebi'im,* and *Kethubim* (Law, Prophets, and Writings).

The term *theology* has been used largely by Christians. The early church adopted the Greek word *theologia* when they penetrated the western world. The Greeks used *theologia* for stories and teaching about their gods. "The church applied it to the God of Israel who is finally revealed in Jesus Christ. For Christians 'theology' means teaching about God. Old Testament theology, then, is teaching about God in Israel's scripture" (Christoph Barth, *God With Us,* 2).

Jewish writers have never produced a comprehensive theology of the Old Testament or of Judaism. The Old Testament itself is unsystematic in form, as are the Mishnah and the Talmud. Rabbinic literature is notoriously unholistic in its approach. Samuel Sandmel, a well-known Jewish New Testament scholar, said that although Jews have produced eminent philosophers, religious scholars, and brilliant homileticians, they have produced precious few theologians. "We have provided men who have done good work on theological themes, but not a single first rate systematic theologian" ("Reflection on the Problem of Theology for Jews," 111).

M. H. Goshen-Gottstein addressed the lack of Jewish "theologies of the Old Testament" in a paper read before the Eighth Congress of the International Organization for the Study of the Old Testament, which met in Edinburgh in August 1974. Goshen-Gottstein advanced his belief that the failure of Jews to produce an Old Testament theology is a direct result of Jews having no real part in European academic Bible studies until the twentieth century. "From the point of view of academic establishment, Biblical studies were pursued in the framework of 'Theological Faculties' or their equivalent. . . . No nineteenth-century Jew could think of becoming a 'Bible scholar' in the European sense, which almost of necessity entailed moving back and forth between the testaments" ("Christianity, Judaism and Modern Bible Study," 77).

Those Jewish scholars who could be called theologians of sorts (Heschel, Gordis, Sandmel, and Jon D. Levenson) have functioned almost exclusively in the context of American theological seminaries. If we add the names of some non-American Jewish philosophers (like Buber, Neher), the list is almost exhaustive. Goshen-Gottstein may be the first Professor of Bible at an Israeli University to insist on teaching a graduate course on biblical theology.

Goshen-Gottstein concluded that if we assume that "theology is by necessity" an exclusively Christian branch of study, we had better realize that only the belated entry of Jews into twentieth-century biblical scholarship has prevented until now the development of a Jewish biblical theology.

Jewish scholars are now entering the field of biblical theology in a big way. Jacob Neusner and Jon D. Levenson are two "bright lights" among contemporary Jewish scholars in this field (See Brooks and Collins, 1-29, 109-146). Jon D. Levenson of Harvard Divinity School wrote an article, "Why Jews Are Not Interested in Biblical Theology," (See Neusner, *Judaic Perspectives of Biblical Studies,* 281-307), in which he said that biblical theology had been a Protestant preoccupation and was not free from Protestant presuppositions about the Torah.

Old Testament theology is essentially a Christian discipline, not because of the use of the term "Old Testament" or because Christians are more apt to systematize or theologize biblical materials, but because Jesus saw Himself and the early church saw Him as the fulfillment of the hopes and promises in the Old Testament. Because Jesus used the Old Testament theologically to refer to Himself, Christians who follow Him have used it theologically. In contrast, Jews, who have had little interest in theology historically, have not written theologies of the Hebrew Bible.

Most Old Testament theologies have been christological in some sense. Edmond Jacob said that a theology of the Old Testament that is not founded on isolated verses but on the Old Testament as a whole "can only be a Christology, for what was revealed under the old covenant, through a long and varied history, in events, persons and institutions is, in Christ, gathered together and brought to perfection" (*Theology of the Old Testament,* 12). At the end of his second volume on Old Testament theology, von Rad said that "all these writings of ancient Israel were seen by Jesus Christ, and certainly by the Apostles and the early Church, as a collection of predictions which pointed to Him as the Savior of the world" (*Old Testament Theology II,* 319). Von Rad used the traditio-historical method of interpretation in trying to understand the theological implications of the Old Testament. With the use of this method, he concluded that the Old Testament must be read as a book in which "expectation keeps mounting up to vast proportions."

The Old Testament is absorbed in the New as "the logical end of a process initiated by the Old Testament itself" (*Old Testament Theology II*, 321).

Walther Eichrodt believed that "covenant" was the central theme of the Old Testament. Covenant formed "the very deepest layer of the foundation of Israel's faith." He assumed that the idea of a covenant was present whether the word was used or not. "Covenant" was not a dogmatic concept but the *"typical description of a living process* which began at a particular time and place, and which was designed to make manifest a divine reality quite unique in the whole history of religion" (*Theology of the Old Testament I*, 18).

Eichrodt also asserted that anyone who studies the historical development of the Old Testament will find throughout the materials a powerful and purposive movement which forces itself on one's attention. Sometimes the religion may appear static and harden into a rigid system, but every time this happens the forward drive breaks through the impasse and continues the movement. "This movement does not come to rest until the manifestation of Christ, in whom the noblest powers of the Old Testament find their fulfillment. Negative evidence in support of this statement is afforded by the torso-like appearance of Judaism in separation from Christianity" (*Theology of the Old Testament I*, 26).

Assertions like these by Eichrodt—that the "noblest" powers of the Old Testament have their fulfillment in Christ and that Judaism has a torso-like appearance in separation from Christianity—have sparked a heated response. Some recent Old Testament scholars contend that Old Testament theology should not be considered as only pointing to or ending with Jesus Christ, since this denigrates modern Judaism.

John H. Hayes has severely criticized Eichrodt and von Rad for their "anti-Judaism" bias. Hayes said, "This anti-Judaism bias has its roots in the New Testament and has been a cancerous sore on the church throughout (Hayes and Prussner, *Old Testament Theology: Its History and Development*, 276). Hayes argued that "Judaism must be seen as just as legitimate a continuation of the Hebrew scriptures as is Christianity. They are both legitimate daughters of the same earlier mother" (*Old Testament Theology*, 279).

Therein lies the rub. The New Testament and historical Christianity both claim that the fulfillment of the Old Testament is in Christ. Most Jews and many Christian Old Testament scholars argue that the Jews have as much right to believe that the Old Testament is fulfilled in modern Judaism as Christians have to believe that the Old Testament is fulfilled only in Christ. Can we resolve this issue? Is there a "center," or "heart," or "core" in the Old Testament that points inevitably to Christ?

Is Old Testament theology a uniquely Christian discipline? It is if Eichrodt, von Rad, the New Testament, and perhaps the Old Testament itself are right in asserting that there is a process or movement working itself out through the Old Testament which finds its goal or fulfillment in Jesus Christ. Does this mean that Old Testament theology should focus only on that process or movement and not consider all of the Old Testament materials such as history, law, cult, and wisdom in their own setting in the Old Testament? The answer to this question will have some bearing on whether Old Testament theology is a normative or descriptive discipline. These and other questions will be addressed in chapter 2, "The Nature and Method of Old Testament Theology."

First we should consider the story of Old Testament theology. How did it begin? How has it fared as a separate discipline? What is the present state of the study?

The Story of
Old Testament Theology

1. Old Testament Theology:
A Modern Discipline with Ancient Roots

The story of Old Testament theology is long, fascinating, and tortuous. Although this discipline in its modern form is barely two hundred years old, its roots go back to the Old Testament itself. Many Old Testament scholars date the beginning of the modern study of Old Testament theology with Johann Philipp Gabler's inaugural address at the University of Altdorf in 1787. (See Hayes and Prussner, 2; Hasel, *Basic Issues,* 15; Ollenburger, Martens, and Hasel, *The Flowering of Old Testament Theology,* 489, 507, 527; Martin H. Woudstra, "The Old Testament in Biblical Theology and Dogmatics," 47-51). Until Gabler's time the church had not distinguished between dogmatic theology and biblical theology or between New Testament theology and Old Testament theology. Gabler thought such distinctions should be made. Although he did not write an Old Testament theology, he set out the basic principles and method by which a biblical theology and an Old Testament theology could be written. Gabler was a rationalist and probably chafed under what he considered a stranglehold the church had on exegesis and the interpretation of Scripture.

At that time perhaps only a rationalist could or would have called for a separation of dogmatic and biblical theology. The separation that followed had a wrenching effect. Rather than setting out the doctrines of the Old Testament more clearly, the first Old Testament theologies filtered the theological materials of the Old Testament through the lens of rationalism.

The first book to carry the title *Old Testament Theology* was probably G. L. Bauer's *Theologie des Alten Testaments* published in Leipzig in 1796. Bauer also was a rationalist; Hayes and Prussner said that "again and again" Bauer judged Old Testament materials by the standards of his rationalistic interpretation of religion. He went out of his way "to point out the mythological, legendary, or miraculous elements in the Hebrew scriptures and dismiss them as the superstitions of a primitive race." (Hayes and Prussner, 69). Joseph Blenkinsopp said that Bauer achieved the distinction of writing the first Old Testament theology and at the same time dismissing about four-fifths of the content of the Old Testament as unworthy of serious attention. (Blenkinsopp, "Old Testament Theology and the Jewish-Christian Connection," 3).

2. Sowing the Seed for Old Testament Theology

To understand the problems of and debates about Old Testament theology, one needs to begin not with Gabler but with the Old Testament itself. Then one should trace the history of the theological use various groups have made of the Old Testament through the centuries.

Later writers in the Old Testament used some of its earlier writings theologically. Zechariah referred to the teachings of the "former prophets" several times (see Zech. 1:4; 7:7,12). Haggai must have known about Jeremiah's prophecy that God would remove His "signet ring" from the hand of Coniah (Jer. 22:24-25) when he said God would make Zerubbabel, Coniah's grandson, like a signet ring (Hag. 2:23). Jeremiah spoke about a *new* covenant (Jer. 31:31-34). Other prophets spoke of a *new* Exodus (Isa. 43:14-21; 48:20; 52:12) and a *new* David (Jer.

23:5-6; Ezek. 34:23-24; 37:24-27). The forerunner of the Messiah would be a "coming" of Elijah (Mal. 4:5-6).

The Qumran community interpreted the Old Testament materials theologically. They wrote commentaries on some Old Testament books and sang hymns based on Old Testament themes. They saw themselves as living in the last days and believed the Old Testament was being fulfilled in some of their experiences.

Similarities and contrasts exist between the Qumran method of interpretation and that used in the New Testament. They both reinterpreted the Old Testament in light of their own situation. Both believed the Old Testament prophecies contained something mysterious whose meaning was revealed to their leaders (the teacher of righteousness to the Qumran community and Jesus to the first-century Christians). Neither community created events to fit the Scriptures, but both interpreted the Scriptures to fit with their contemporary events.

The primary difference between Qumran's interpretation of the Old Testament and that of New Testament writers is that the Qumran people were still looking for the Messiah. New Testament people said He had already come. Also, New Testament writers understood that the Gentiles were included in the Abrahamic promise (Rom. 9:24-26; 1 Pet. 2:10). Such an application of the Old Testament Scriptures—extending to the Gentiles equal privileges within the Abrahamic covenant— would have been unacceptable to the Qumran sect. (For a discussion of how the Qumran community used the Old Testament, see Ralph L. Smith, *Micah-Malachi*, WBC 32, 179-180; and F. F. Bruce, *Biblical Exegesis in the Qumran Texts*.)

The New Testament used the Old Testament theologically. Of the twenty-seven books of the New Testament, only Philemon shows no direct relation to the Old Testament. Henry Shires said that if all the Old Testament influences were removed from the New Testament it would "consist of little but meaningless shreds" (*Finding the Old Testament in the New*, 15). New Testament writers never question the scriptural nature of the Old Testament; neither do they make a system of theology out of it (see C. H. Dodd, *According to the Scriptures*, 12).

Jesus spoke with authority, originality, freshness, and freedom in dealing with the Old Testament Scriptures. He set himself above them; He did not regard the Old Testament as complete or as God's last word, but He accepted it as God's first words. Jesus said "Do not think that I have come to abolish the law or the prophets; I have come not to abolish but to fulfill" (Matt. 5:17). In five examples in the Sermon on the Mount, Jesus set His authority over the Law, not to nullify or abrogate the Law but to fill it with a higher and fuller meaning (Matt. 5:21-22,27-28,33-35,38-39,43-45).

Paul used the Old Testament theologically. He supported his doctrine of justification by faith by referring to Habakkuk 2:4 (see Rom. 4:3; Gal. 3:6). He quoted from a number of Psalms as evidence that "all have sinned" (Rom. 3:10-18). Other New Testament writers used the Old Testament theologically (1 Pet. 1:10-12; Heb. 1:1; 10:1), but nowhere do they present a theology of the Old Testament.Matthew, for example, referred to many Old Testament passages to try to convince the Jews that Jesus was the Messiah.

The early church overthrew Marcionism and retained all of the Old Testament as their Scriptures, but they did not focus all of their attention on it. The church continued to search the Scriptures but did not write commentaries on it as the Qumran community did. Jesus, not the Old Testament, was the center of the faith of the early church.

When Paul became the apostle for the Gentiles, a dispute arose over whether Gentile converts should be required to observe all the Jewish laws in the Old Testament. The council of Jerusalem decided that the laws of the covenant of Moses should not apply to Gentile Christians. "For it has seemed good to the Holy Spirit and to us to impose on you no further burden than these essentials: that you abstain from what has been sacrificed to idols and from blood and from what is strangled and from fornication. If you keep yourselves from these, you will do well. Farewell" (Acts 15:28-29).

Many early church fathers did not maintain the New Testament perspective on the Old Testament. They became embroiled in bitter controversies with some Jews and with early heretical groups. They used the Old Testament to defend their faith and as a source for their teaching, but in doing so they often resorted to excessive use of allegory and typology.

The author of the Epistle of Barnabas (about A.D. 130) regarded the Old Testament as a book of parables and a store of mysteries which were impossible for Jews in Old Testament times to understand. Barnabas saw the scapegoat (Lev. 16:10) as a type of Christ. The scarlet wool with which it was crowned pointed to the scarlet robe of Christ at his trial. Barnabas saw the red heifer in Numbers 19:2-3 as a type of Christ. For him, the 318 men in Abraham's army pointed to the crucifixion because the number three hundred in Greek is represented by the letter *tau* which is made in the form of a cross when written. The numbers ten and eight, equaling eighteen, are represented by the letters *iota* and *eta*, the first two letters in Jesus' name.

Such extremes in interpreting the Old Testament were characteristic of the early centuries of the Christian church. Only a few places, such as the school of Antioch (and there for only a little while), saw any real effort made to interpret the Old Testament in light of its own historical background. Old Testament theology in its modern sense could not exist in such a religious climate.

The Old Testament fared no better in the Middle Ages than it had in earlier times. In fact, it was almost completely overlooked or forgotten. Greek and Hebrew texts no longer formed the basis of Bible study. Even scholars read only the Old Latin version (the Vulgate). The Middle Ages emphasized the authority of the church, not of the Bible. Schoolmen simply systematized what the church fathers had said, giving little attention to the Scriptures. The church did nothing to encourage investigation or search for new truth in the Word. The medieval world was a static world. The slightest departure from any teaching of the church in that day would have brought upon the head of the innovator the condemnation of the church, condemnation medieval Christians dreaded as nothing else.

In the Middle Ages the schoolmen taught that every passage of Scripture had four meanings: the literal or historical; the allegorical or theological—what we are to believe; the moral or tropological—what we are going to do; and the spiritual or

anagogical—where we are going. An example of the four meanings is found in the various meanings attached to the word
manna. Literally, manna was the food God miraculously provided the Israelites in the wilderness. Allegorically, it was the
blessed sacrament in the Eucharist. Tropologically, it was the
spiritual substance of the soul day by day through the indwelling Spirit of God. And anagogically, it became the food of
blessed souls in heaven—the "beatific vision" and perfect
union with Christ. Such was the status in the Roman church
from about 800 to 1500. This kind of hermeneutic could not
produce an Old Testament theology.

The long, dark night of the medieval period ended with the
dawn of the Renaissance. The Renaissance probably began in
Italy shortly after 1300 as a revival of learning about the arts,
sciences, and classical literature of the ancient Greek and
Latin worlds. It spread to other countries during the succeeding centuries (1400 to 1600) and marked the transition from
the medieval to the modern world.

One distinguishing mark of the Renaissance was the rediscovery of the worth and individuality of persons. In the Middle
Ages the individual was a cog in the machinery of mass
humanity.Reventlow reports that for some, the Renaissance
was the climax in the history of the human spirit. Brought to
life by the rediscovery of antiquity, the Renaissance found the
forces of a new individualism everywhere—in politics, art, and
education. Enthusiasm flowed for aesthetics, independence of
thought, moral earnestness, unbridled passion, the desire for
bloody vengeance, and asceticism—all together in inimitable
juxtaposition. We may also find in these attitudes the germ of
a deep-seated alienation from traditional religion (see H. G.
Reventlow, *The Authority of the Bible,* 10).

Where was the Old Testament in all of this? It was rediscovered as one of the "classics." Some Jewish scholars had maintained an acquaintance with the Hebrew Bible. A converted
Jew, Nicolaus de Lyra (about 1340), advocated a new method
of interpreting Scripture. Lyra said that the literal or historical meaning was the one true meaning of Scripture. Lyra
seems to have influenced Martin Luther in his break with the
four-fold view of the interpretation of the Bible. Luther, how-

ever, started with a principle quite different from the one which sought the literal sense of each passage of Scripture.

John Wycliffe probably influenced Luther's view of the Bible more than Lyra. Wycliffe (1328-1384), an Oxford graduate and an Augustinian monk, followed Augustine's teaching that the true church was composed of those God picked for salvation and *not* necessarily those in the Roman Catholic Church. Based on this teaching, membership in the visible church and participating in its sacraments had nothing to do with salvation. This rendered the whole Catholic system unnecessary. Wycliffe's bitter denunciation of the pope as the Antichrist and of the sins of the clergy paved the way for revolt. So did his appeal to the Bible as an ultimate authority.

Luther, like Wycliffe, emphasized not so much Scripture's literal meaning but the Scripture's authority above that of the pope and the church. Luther continued to use allegory in interpreting the Old Testament and made no distinction between the authority of the two Testaments. For him the Old Testament contained the full revelation of Christ. In the preface to the 1523 edition of his translation he said:

> Here (in the OT) shalt thou find the swaddling-clothes and the manger in which Christ lies—Poor and of little value are the swaddling-clothes, but dear is Christ, the treasure that lies in them (quoted by G. F. Oehler, *Theology of the Old Testament,* 24).

Again, in the same work, he wrote:

> Moses is the fountain of all wisdom and understanding, out of which welled all that was known and told by all the prophets. The New Testament also flows from it, and is grounded therein.—If thou wilt interpret well and surely, take Christ for thee; for He is the man to whom alone all refers. So, then, in the high priest Aaron see no one, but Christ alone (quoted by Oehler, 2).

This sounds like allegory or typology, and so it is. But by his claim to let the Bible speak for itself, Luther made an advance over those who were before him.

John Calvin went further than Luther in applying the principle that every Scripture has only one literal meaning. Calvin laid the foundation for historical exegesis by insisting that every Scripture be interpreted in light of its own background.

In fact, Calvin was so much of an historical expositor of the prophets that his opponents often referred to him as "the Judaizing Calvin." In the doctrinal treatment of the Old Testament, however, he took a position as rigid as that of Luther.

For Calvin the difference in the Testaments lay not in their doctrines but in their form. Calvin so Christianized the Old Testament that he almost lost sight of the newness of the Gospel. The difference between the two revelations for Calvin was only one of degree of clarity. Since even the Reformation did not detect the true relationship between the Testaments, no reformer attempted to write an Old Testament theology.

A period of Protestant scholasticism immediately followed the Reformation. In their vigorous disputes with the Roman Catholics, Protestants developed as rigid an authoritarianism as had the Roman Church, except that the Protestants found the ultimate authority in the Bible. They strongly contested anyone or any movement that challenged their view of Scripture, claiming even that every word and every letter of the original text was inspired—including the Hebrew vowel points.

In 1538 a Jewish scholar, Elias Levita, challenged this view and claimed that the vowel points were not a part of the original Hebrew texts. Johann Buxtorf and his son, of the University of Basel, argued long and hard to defend the orthodox view but in the end lost their cause. We now know from discoveries such as the Dead Sea Scrolls that the original Hebrew text *did not* have vowel points. They were invented by the Massoretes between A.D. 500 and 800.

For Catholics, the "argument from Scripture" began shortly after A.D. 1500, about the time of the Council of Trent. It started mostly as an answer to the controversy with Protestants or in controversies between Jesuits and Dominicans. Joseph Blenkinsopp suggested that one reason the Bible was divided into verses in this period evidently was "for the purpose of providing ready-made ammunition for controversial ends" (*A Sketchbook of Biblical Theology*, 6).

In addition to Luther and Calvin, other groups challenged the traditional view of Scripture, including the Anabaptists and Socinians. Anabaptists in general rejected the Old Testament as authoritative for Christians, claiming it was a book given only to the Jews. They also believed the Old Testament did *not* contain any belief in individual immortality (see Emil G. Kraeling, *The Old Testament Since the Reformation,* 22). The Socinians conceded the divine character of the Old Testament but maintained that *now* it only had an historical interest and was not essential for Christian doctrine (Kraeling, 40).

The Anabaptists and Socinians were the first of many to attempt to break through the shell of tradition to a more objective approach to the Old Testament—an approach which ultimately led to a true Old Testament theology. Shortly after 1600 George Calixtus denied that the Old Testament contained the doctrine of the trinity. Others attempted to return to the Bible as the primary source of their theology. The most prominent of these were Cocceius (1603-1669), the leader of the pietists, and G. C. Storr, founder of the "Older Tübingen School" (Dentan, *Preface to Old Testament Theology,* 16-17).

Along with these men and movements, the universities became centers for publishing collections of prooftexts— (*dicta probantia*) taken from all parts of the Bible to support orthodox doctrine. Dentan said that although most of the books written from this viewpoint were wooden and artificial in their treatment of the Bible, they "contained the seed of interest from which the study of biblical theology was to develop, and the last of them, a treatise by Carl Haymann (1768), was actually entitled *Biblische Theologie* (*Preface to Old Testament Theology,* 418).

3. The Germination and Growth of Old Testament Theology

If the seed of interest in biblical theology is seen in the works of those who used prooftexts to support orthodox doctrine, it was nurtured by those who used prooftexts to criticize orthodoxy. The prooftext method could never produce a true Old Testament theology. Old Testament theology is basically an historical and descriptive discipline. Only after the discovery of the historical-grammatical principles of interpretation could a true Old Testament theology be written. That did not come until the Age of Reason.

The Age of Reason was an outgrowth of the Renaissance and the Reformation. The crusaders had rediscovered the Greek classics in science and philosophy. The pioneers of modern science, taking their clue from the old Greek classics, began to challenge the traditional theories about the universe. Copernicus (1473-1543) insisted that the sun, not the earth, was the center of the universe; and Sir Isaac Newton (1642-1727) saw the world as a machine run by natural laws. The English deists, such as Lord Herbert of Cherbury and Thomas Hobbes (1588-1679), did not deny the existence of God but did rule out revelation, miracles, and the supernatural in history and nature.

English deism did not survive, but German rationalism did. J. D. Michaelis (1717-1791) and J. D. Semler (1725-1792) were key figures in applying the principles of rationalism to the Bible. The Age of Reason discovered the historical-grammatical principle of interpretation of the Scriptures, developed proper skills and tools for research, and freed biblical scholars and theologians from the authority of the church and the state.

Johann Philipp Gabler was the first rationalist to call for a separate discipline of biblical theology. He believed that much of the confusion in the Christian world was due largely to an improper use of the Bible and to the failure of churchmen to distinguish between dogmatic theology and the simple historical religion of the Bible. In his inaugural address at the University of Altdorf, March 30, 1787, entitled *"De iuso discrimine theologiae biblicae et dogmaticae regundisque recte utriusque finibus"* ("On the correct distinction between biblical and dogmatic theology and the proper determination of the goals of each"), Gabler called for the separation of the two disciplines. Thus he is often called the father of biblical theology.

For Gabler, dogmatic theology is didactic and normative in character and teaches what a particular theologian decides about a matter in accordance with his character, time, age, place, sect, or school. Biblical theology is historical and descriptive in character, transmitting what the sacred writers thought about sacred matters.

Gabler set out principles for doing biblical theology. He said that the biblical theologian should first study each passage of Scripture separately according to the historical-grammatical principles of interpretation. Second, he should compare the individual passages of Scripture with each other, noting differences and similarities. Third, he should systematize or formulate general ideas without distorting materials or obliterating distinctions.

Gabler inspired a number of scholars to write biblical theologies. G. L. Bauer (1755-1806) was the first to publish an Old Testament theology (*Theologie des Alten Testaments,* Leipzig, 1796). This book's arrangement into three sections—theology, anthropology, and christology—showed Bauer's continued dependence on the rubrics of dogmatic theology. His interpretation of the biblical materials, however, was naively rationalistic. "Any idea of supernatural revelations of God through theophanies, miracles, or prophecies is to be rejected, since such things are contrary to sound reason and can easily be paralleled amongst other peoples" (Dentan, *Preface to Old Testament Theology,* 27).

The field of biblical theology was occupied almost exclusively by rationalists for fifty years after Gabler's address. The rationalists delivered biblical theology from the inordinate influence of dogmatic theology but immediately placed it under the tyranny of rationalism.

The influence of philosophy on Old Testament theology can be seen in W. M. L. de Wette's turning away from extreme rationalism. With the publication of *Biblische Dogmatick* in 1813, he attempted to rise above both rationalism and orthodoxy to a higher unity of faith and religious feeling. De Wette was greatly influenced by his teacher and colleague at the University of Jena, Jacob Fries. Fries, like Schleiermacher, was brought up by the Moravian Brethren and had strong religious feelings. Fries' thought, however, was more Kantian. Kant's influence can be seen in de Wette's work, too. To de Wette, revelation meant "any true religious idea expressed in language or symbol" (*Biblische Dogmatick,* 25). Such true ideas, according to de Wette, cannot appear without the Spirit of God working through reason. The thinker, therefore, must always be conscious of dependence on that higher power.

Three outstanding philosophers working in Europe during the first part of the nineteenth century had a tremendous effect on Old Testament theology. They were Friedrich Schleiermacher (1768-1834), the father of modern theology; George Wilhelm Hegel (1770-1831); and Søren Kierkegaard

(1813-1855). Schleiermacher was an influential pastor in Berlin who made the feeling of dependence the basis of the Christian faith. Schleiermacher had a low view of the Old Testament. "For him it was merely a historical accident that Christianity developed from the soil of Judaism" (Dentan, *Preface to Old Testament Theology,* 35).

Hegel was a colleague of Schleiermacher and de Wette at the University of Berlin. The most significant feature of Hegel's philosophy was its dialectical character. For Hegel, everything in the world had its opposite, every thesis its antithesis. Each thesis and antithesis came together to form a synthesis which became a new thesis for a higher stage of thought or being. Thus, according to Hegel, the idea of development from a lower to a higher stage was the key to comprehending the secret of the universe. The effect of such a philosophy revolutionized our understanding of almost every area of life, including the study of Old Testament theology.

Hegel's theory of development was almost immediately applied to the Old Testament by his student and colleague, Wilhelm Vatke, who published *Biblische Theologie* in 1835. Because of its philosophical style and terminology and its extremely novel and critical view of the Old Testament, the work did not find general acceptance. Though its influence was dormant for almost a quarter of a century, this application of Hegelian philosophy to the study of the Old Testament led to Wellhausen's establishment of the modern documentary hypothesis of the Pentateuch and eventually to the death of Old Testament theology.

Søren Kierkegaard, the "Melancholy Dane," rejected Hegel's dialectic with its emphasis on rationalism for an existential emphasis on experience. The central issue for Kierkegaard was: "What does it mean to be a Christian—in Christendom?" He saw in Christianity the truth which humans cannot discover for themselves. Kenneth Scott Latourette said of Kierkegaard:

> He rejected vehemently Hegelianism with its attempts to reach truth through human reason. To him to speak of the reasonableness of Christianity was treason, because it subjected the self-revelation of the infinite God to human standards. Christianity, he held, cannot be verified by the human mind; it is a scandal, a

stumbling block, to our intellectual faculties. He emphasized the paradoxical character of Christianity. The central note of the Christian faith is God in time, yet this, he declared, is a pure contradiction, for God is by definition eternal. Before God man is always a sinner and his best as well as his worst stands under the judgment of God and needs divine pardon. Between the sinless God and sinful man a vast abyss yawns. Yet the paradox is resolved in God and by God. What to human reason is impossible has been done by God. The Eternal enters time: the Son of God becomes incarnate, uniting the two irreconcilable elements, God and man. He does this incognito and in weakness. The cross is an offense both to man's reason and to his moral sense. By the leap of faith we sacrifice our intellects and accept what God has done for us. Kierkegaard was struck by the contrast between 'Christendom' and the demands of Christ. To him Christendom was a prodigious illusion: it had done away with Christianity (*Nineteenth Century in Europe,* 143-144).

Conservatives entered the field of biblical theology about fifty years after Gabler's address. The first conservative in the field of Old Testament theology was E. W. Hengstenberg. Hengstenberg was brought up in the Reformed tradition and was exposed to strong rationalistic influences as a student at the University of Bonn. Reacting to the University's extreme rationalism, he experienced a marked change in his views in 1823 when he entered the Missionary school at Basel. In 1824 he went from the Missionary school to the University of Berlin. He was already deeply pious, "full of zeal for orthodoxy, and ready to smite with a heavy hand every form of error" (A. H. Newman, *A Manual of Church History II,* 556).

Pietism was in favor at the royal court of Frederick William III (1770-1840), so Hengstenberg's promotion was rapid and easy. In 1825 he became a member of the faculty of Berlin, opposing his colleagues Vatke, Schleiermacher, Bleek, Hegel, and Neander. In 1827 he began publishing the "Evangelical Church Review." He was a staunch supporter of the king and other conservative causes. His hatred of democracy and constitutional government caused him to support the Southern states in their defense of slavery and bitterly denounce President Lincoln (Newman, *A Manual of Church History II,* 558).

Hengstenberg did not write an Old Testament theology, but he published the four-volume *Christology of the Old Testament,* a commentary on the messianic prophecies of the Old

Testament. The publication of this work marked a vigorous reawakening of the strictly orthodox view of the Bible. Hengstenberg rejected any idea of real progress in revelation, hardly distinguishing between the Testaments, and giving a spiritual" interpretation to Old Testament prophecies "which almost ignores any consideration of their original reference (Dentan, *Preface to Old Testament Theology,* 41).

H. A. C. Havernick, a student of Hengstenberg and a young professor at Königsberg, wrote *Vorlesungen über die Theologie des Alten Testaments* (1848), a very conservative work with some fresh and stimulating insights. He demanded the use of objective historical methods in the study of the materials but acknowledged that these by themselves would not give adequate results. The student must have a "theological aptitude" which comes through belief and experience. Havernick said that God reveals Himself not in abstract ideas but in a series of acts which form an organic, developing whole.

In this last point Havernick was very close to another outstanding conservative scholar of this period, J. C. K. von Hofmann (1810-1877) of Erlangen. Von Hofmann was one of the founders of the salvation-history, or *Heilsgeschichte*, school of the 1800s. According to von Hofmann, the Bible is a linear record of saving history in which the active Lord of history is the triune God whose purpose and goal is to redeem mankind. In his book *Promise and Fulfillment,* von Hofmann argued that the Old and New Testaments are related as prophecy and fulfillment, but stressed that Christ was the fulfillment of the whole history of Israel. The salvation-history approach to biblical faith has had tremendous influence through the years and can be seen in the work of such modern scholars as G. E. Wright and Gerhard von Rad.

Gustav Friedrich Oehler (1812-1872) of Tübingen dominated the study of Old Testament until 1875. A pupil of Steudel, a rationalist, he was strongly influenced by Hegel. He criticized his teacher for not seeing that the Hebrew religion had displayed organic growth. He published his *Prolegomena to Old Testament Theology* in 1845, but his full-length book on Old Testament theology was published posthumously by his son, Theodor Oehler, in 1873. He presented the material in three parts: Mosaism, Prophetism, and Wisdom. Oehler's *Old*

Testament Theology was the first such work to be translated into English (1874-1875).

4. The Death of Old Testament Theology and the Triumph of *Religionsgeschichteschule*

The year 1878 marks the beginning of the period of the failure of Old Testament theology. In that year Julius Wellhausen published his *Prolegomena zur Geschichte Israels,* which was the logical culmination of the genetic and developmental approach to the history of Israel's literature and religion. Basing his work on that of Graf and Keunen before him, Wellhausen argued that the Old Testament prophets lived before the giving of the Law. He came to this conclusion partly through his study of the Old Testament, finding that the Books of Joshua, Judges, Samuel, and Kings show little knowledge of the laws of the Pentateuch, and partly because of his presupposition that everything moves from the simple to the complex and from freedom to authoritarianism.

Wellhausen believed that Old Testament religion grew out of nature religion. Behind the sacrifices and rituals of Israel lay the agricultural feasts of her pagan neighbors. He thought that the old agricultural stage of Israel's religion could still be seen in the earliest sources of Israel's literature (*Prolegomena to the History of Israel,* 83-120). Deuteronomy historicized these agricultural festivals and tied them to redemptive history, according to Wellhausen.

He found not one theology in the Old Testament, but many different theologies, all following the line of development. The theology presently in the Pentateuch is a retrojection of the late faith of Israel onto that earlier period. Although some Old Testament theologies continued to be published after Wellhausen's work, they were largely a carryover from the earlier period.

In English-speaking countries very little had been done in biblical theology before Wellhausen. The first extensive work on Old Testament theology in English was A. B. Davidson's *The Theology of the Old Testament* published in 1904. Although it has some undesirable features, largely due to its being edited post humously by a former student, it has remained a useful work. Had Davidson edited his own book, he might have given it another form. He hints as much when he says in the opening chapter:

> though we speak of Old Testament *theology,* all that we can attempt is to present the religion or the religious ideas of the Old Testament. As held in the minds of the Hebrew people, and as exhibited in their Scriptures, these ideas form as yet no theology. There is no system in them of any kind. . . . We do not find a *theology* in the Old Testament; we find a *religion.* . . . It is we ourselves that create the theology when we give to these religious ideas and convictions a systematic or orderly form. Hence our subject is really the History of the Religion of Israel as represented in the Old Testament (*The Theology of the Old Testament,* 11).

Still, Davidson presented his lectures in the form of systematic theology and arranged his book the same way.

Two other significant works on Old Testament theology were published in this "dormant" period. H. Wheeler Robinson's *The Religious Ideas of the Old Testament,* and A. C. Knudson's *The Religious Teachings of the Old Testament* were released in 1913 and 1918 respectively. Neither of these works is comprehensive, and neither carries the title "Old Testament Theology." Each follows the rubrics of systematic theology in presenting the material.

A number of volumes on the religion of Israel were published during this period, such as those written by R. L. Ottley, *The Religion of Israel* (Cambridge: The University Press, 1905, 3rd ed. 1926); Karl Marti, *The Religion of the Old Testament,* trans. G. A. Bienmann (New York: G. P. Putnam's Sons, 1907); W. O. E. Oesterley and Theodore E. Robinson, *Hebrew Religion: Its Origin and Development* (London: SPCK, 1930); and Harry Emerson Fosdick, *A Guide to Understanding the Bible* (New York: Harper and Brothers, 1938). All of these volumes followed Wellhausen's developmental approach until the movement reached its logical conclusion. Walther Eichrodt said that Fosdick's book represented the end of an era.

> The author has, to speak candidly, written the obituary of a whole scholarly approach and method of investigation. . . . While no trained scholar of today would deny the great importance of the evolutionary principle in history, much less its

value in clearing up many seemingly enigmatic phenomena of biblical literature, we are today acutely conscious of the danger of assuming unilinear evolution of institutions or ideas (Eichrodt, "Review: *A Guide to Understanding the Bible*," 205).

James Smart said that Old Testament theology "sickened and died and was quietly buried as the twentieth century began ("The Death and Rebirth of Old Testament Theology," 1). The causes of the death or failure of Old Testament theology are varied. The work of Wellhausen, one of the main causes, emphasized the variety of theologies in the Old Testament and de-emphasized its unity. Another cause was the reaction against earlier scholars who read too many of their theological presuppositions into the text. In this new age scholars attempted to be totally objective in their approach to Scripture. A third factor in the death of Old Testament theology was the general lack of interest in theology *per se* in the early twentieth century. Old Testament scholars had turned their attention instead to the study of archaeology, Semitic languages, and comparative religions.

For almost twenty-five years after Davidson published his *Old Testament Theology* in 1904, very little work was done in this field. But in the early 1930s a new stream of materials began to appear, a stream that became a veritable flood by 1950.

5. The Revival of Old Testament Theology

What caused this sudden shift in Old Testament theology? What brought it back to life? The major cause of the shift in theology and biblical studies was the "fall-out" from World War I. Prior to 1917 the prevailing attitude of the western world was one of confidence in inevitable progress. People could lift themselves by their own bootstraps out of any crisis and turn it into a stepping-stone to a higher standard of living.

Then two world wars, with their destruction, devastation, cruelty, hatred, and alienation occurred in one generation. Confidence in inevitable progress and in humanity's inherent goodness and ability was shattered. People began to search for a source of strength and a word of guidance outside themselves. Some rediscovered such strength and guidance in the Word of God.

Karl Barth described the change in theology after 1918:

> The actual end of the 19th century as the 'good old days' came for theology as for everything else with the fateful year of 1914. Accidentally or not, a significant event took place during that very year. Ernst Troeltsch, the well-known professor of systematic theology and the leader of the then most modern school, gave up his chair in theology for one in philosophy. One day in early August 1914 stands out in my personal memory as a black day. Ninety-three German intellectuals impressed public opinion by their proclamation in support of the war policy of Wilhelm II and his counselors. Among these intellectuals I discovered to my horror almost all of my theological teachers who I had greatly venerated. In despair over what this indicated about the signs of the time I suddenly realized that I could not any longer follow either their ethic and dogmatics or their understanding of the Bible and of history. For me at least, 19th century theology no longer held any future. For many, if not for most people, this theology did not become again what it had been, once the waters of the flood descending upon us at that time had somewhat receded *(The Humanity of God,* 14-15).

James Smart said that Karl Barth's commentary on Romans, published in 1919, was "like the explosion of a bomb or better, like the introduction of a chemical substance that had the effect of separating the divergent elements that had been mingled together in New Testament scholarship (Smart, *The Interpretation of Scripture,* 276). Smart said that the origin of the commentary on Romans was the frustration of two Swiss pastors, Barth and Thurneysen, as they tried to fulfill their ordination vows to be ministers of the Word of God to their people. Both had been trained in historical criticism but not in how to understand the Word of God as a unique revelation of God to people. Yet this was the point at which, as ministers of God, they had to speak.

Barth and Thurneysen turned to Luther, Calvin, Kierkegaard, and others for help. They challenged the conclusions of a century of New Testament scholarship. Readers immediately found many flaws in the commentary (it was so rough-hewn that Barth began to rewrite it as soon as it was finished), but New Testament scholars were forced to recognize the legitimacy of the theological approach (Smart, *The Interpretation of Scripture,* 278).

Karl Barth led the way to a new dogmatic theology which affected biblical theology almost immediately. The fortunes of these two disciplines have often gone hand in hand. Biblical theology has lived and died in the shadow of dogmatic theology. A renewed interest in Old Testament theology began in 1921 when Rudolph Kittel spoke at Leipzig to a group of Old Testament scholars on "The Future of Old Testament Science." Kittel emphasized the inadequacy of the literary and historical investigation and called for the "elucidation of the specifically religious values in the Old Testament." Kittel said that scholars must make a systematic presentation of the essence of Old Testament religion and delve into the secret of divine power in which it has its ground ("Die Zukunft der alttestamentlichen Wissenschaft," 84-99).

The question of whether Old Testament theology was an historical discipline was hotly debated by O. Eissfeldt and W. Eichrodt from 1926 to 1929. Eissfeldt argued that the history of Israel's religion and Old Testament theology were two separate disciplines and must use different methods and goals. Eichrodt insisted that Old Testament theologians could get to the "essence" of Old Testament religion by means of the same historical-critical methods investigators of the history of religion used (see articles by Eichrodt and Eissfeldt in Ollenburger, et. al., *The Flowering of Old Testament Theology*, 3-39).

One reason for renewed interest in the Old Testament after World War I was the fact that many theologians and politicians in Germany began attacking the Old Testament as part of an anti-Semitism campaign. During the late twenties and especially the thirties, the church's struggle in Germany focused attention on the Old Testament and began to provoke radical thought on its nature and relevance.

That radical thought was expressed in such works as Adolph von Harnack's *Marcion, Das Evangelium vom Fremden* (Gott, Leipzig, 1924); Friedrich Delitzsch's "The Great Deception" (*Die grosse Täuschung*) I and II; Houston S. Chamberlain's *Foundations of the 19th Century* (Munich, 1898); Hitler's *Mein Kampf* (1925-1927), and Alfred Rosenberg's *Myth of the 20th Century* (1930). Von Harnack said that the Old Testament should be removed from the Christian canon and placed at the head of the Apocrypha (see Bright, *The Authority of the Old Testament*, 65).

Friedrich Delitzsch, son of the famous conservative Lutheran Old Testament scholar, Franz Delitzsch, was strongly anti-Semitic. He considered the Old Testament a very dangerous book for Christians and also taught that Jesus was a Gentile.

Houston Stewart Chamberlain was born in 1855 of a family high in the English military. Poor health prevented him from entering military service and ended the possibility of his fighting the Germans. Early in his life, Chamberlain became enamored of German art, with the result that he spent his life in Germany and Austria. During World War I he became a German citizen and a friend of Adolf Hitler in the early twenties. Chamberlain saw Germany's salvation coming in Hitler's movement, but he died in 1927, six years before Hitler became Chancellor [see Tanner, *The Nazi Christ,* 2; Andrew J. Krzesinski, *National Cultures, Nazism, and the Church* (Bruce Humphries, 1945); D. L. Baker, *Two Testaments One Bible* (Downers Grove: InterVarsity Press, 1976), 79-85; H. G. Reventlow, *Problems of Old Testament Theology,* 28-43].

Chamberlain's *Foundations* was a two-volume work in which he argued that the history of Europe is a record of the struggle between Indo-Europeans and Semites. The attack of Carthage on Rome and the Mohammedan invasions of Europe were two examples of this struggle. Chamberlain saw in Christ a person of utmost importance for world history but thought he was non-Jewish. Chamberlain's work was widely read in Germany from the time it was published (1889-1901) until 1918. The Kaiser personally donated ten thousand marks to purchase copies for German libraries. After the war its popularity declined; but by 1938 the Nazis were publishing it in an inexpensive paperback edition, and it went through eight editions under Hitler. In one of the popular editions the announcement was made that over 200,000 copies had been sold.

The Nazi regime (1933-1945) was characterized by racism (the purity and superiority of the German race), nationalism (the supremacy of the German state), and emphasis on soil (the sanctity of the German Fatherland). Therefore everything non-German or non-Aryan had to be isolated from and subjected to the control of the German state. The Jews, with their Hebrew Bible (Old Testament), were targeted for extermination. Even some Christian scholars lent their influence to the elimination of the Jews and the Old Testament. W. F. Albright wrote that Gerhard Kittel, youngest son of the outstanding Hebrew scholar Rudolph Kittel and the editor of the *Theological Word Book of the New Testament* "became the mouthpiece of the most vicious Nazi anti-Semitism, sharing with Emanuel Hirsch of Gottingen the grim distinction of making extermination of the Jews theologically respectable" (Albright, *History, Archaeology, and Christian Humanism,* 229).

According to S. J. De Vries, the Nazi regime in Germany was made possible largely because modern biblical scholars before 1933

> were wont to regard the Old Testament faith, and that of the New Testament as well, as an infantile expression of emergent humanism—no more. Now the Old Testament seemed remote; the Jews were scorned, along with traditionalistic Christians.... Modernity had reshaped the Old Testament to its taste; its ancient sovereign word could no longer be heard in its ears. If this had not been so, perhaps the European, and especially German, church might have retained sufficient prophetic zeal to have withstood the monstrous claims of National Socialism. But it was so; because the Old Testament was dead, the Jews had to die *(The Achievements of Biblical Religion,* 12-13).

The Nazi attack on the Jews also involved an attack on the Old Testament and Christianity. This attack led to a reaction on the part of many sensitive biblical scholars and Christian leaders, who defended the Old Testament as an integral part of the Christian canon and began again to focus on the message of the Old Testament for ancient Israel and for modern people.

Ironically, the first complete works on Old Testament theology after its revival were published in 1933, the same year Hitler became chancellor of Germany. They were Ernst Sellin's two-volume work, *Alttestamentliche Theologie auf religionsgeschtlicher Grundlage* and Walther Eichrodt's first volume of his three-volume work, *Theologie des Alten Testaments.*

Sellin (1867-1945) was a professor at the University of Berlin and editor of the *KAT* commentary series on the Old Testament. Sellin's view of Old Testament theology was that it should present in systematic form the religious teachings and faith of the Jewish community based on the writings collected and canonized during the period from 500 to 100 B.C. Sellin said that (1) the Old Testament canon is significant for the Old Testament theologian only as far as it was accepted by Jesus and the apostles; (2) Old Testament theology is interested only in the passages fulfilled in the Gospels; (3) Christianity was based on the Old Testament but added something new to it; and (4) Christian Old Testament theology must be selective, leaving aside the Canaanite influence and also the whole national-cultic side of Israel's religion.

One of the most important Old Testament theologies is Walther Eichrodt's three-volume work, *Theologie des Alten Testaments* (1933-1939, edited and translated 1961-67). Walther Eichrodt was born in Gernsback, Germany, in August 1890. His studies included work at the theological school, Bethel-Bielefeld, and the University of Griefswald and Heidelberg. In 1917 Otto Procksch appointed him *privatdozent* at Erlangen. In 1922 he succeeded Albrecht Alt in an endowed chair of biblical studies at Basel. In 1934 he was named full professor at Basel, and in 1953 he was elected chancellor of the University.

Norman Gottwald called Eichrodt's Old Testament theology "the single most important work of its genre in the twentieth century" (Norman Gottwald, "W. Eichrodt, Theology of the Old Testament," *Contemporary Old Testament Theologians*, edited by Robert B. Laurin, 25]. Robert C. Dentan called it "incomparably the greatest work ever to appear in the field of Old Testament theology, in terms of both sheer magnitude and depth of insight" *(Preface to Old Testament Theology, 66).* John Baker, the English translator of Eichrodt's *Theology of the Old Testament,* wrote that "this is incomparably the greatest work in its field—a work in which burning faith and scientific precision combine to give the reader a living experience of that new reality of God of which it so often speaks" (Eichrodt, *Theology of the Old Testament I,* 21).

Eichrodt wrote in the preface of his first edition (1933):

> The spiritual situation in general and that of theology in particular is impressing ever more peremptorily on everyone concerned with Old Testament theology. There are quite enough historical descriptions of Israelite and Judaistic religion: but by contrast only the most rudimentary attempts have been made

to present the religion of which the records are to be found in the Old Testament as a self-contained entity exhibiting, despite ever-changing historical conditions, a constant basic tendency and character (*Theology of the Old Testament I*, 11).

Eichrodt's concerns were apparent in the preceding statement. He was concerned with his spiritual and cultural climate. He was concerned with changing from a history of Israel's religion to "the self-contained entity" in the Old Testament that has a basic tendency and a constancy in the midst of historical changes. Eichrodt suggested that the "self-contained entity" is the covenant between Yahweh and Israel.

For him the covenant was the central concept which illuminates the structural unity and the unchanging basic tendency of the message of the Old Testament. The idea of the covenant was broader than the use of the Hebrew term *berit*. It was a convenient symbol of a description of a living process which began at a particular place and time in order to reveal a divine reality unique in the whole history of religion (*Theology of the Old Testament I*, 13-14).

Eichrodt said that the theology of the Old Testament is concerned with a complete picture of the Old Testament realm of belief in order to comprehend its immensity and uniqueness. The uniqueness of Old Testament faith can be seen most clearly in its contrasts with ancient Near Eastern religions and in the powerful and purposive movement toward the New Testament. The thing that binds the two testaments together is "the irruption of the Kingship of God into this world and its establishment here" (*Theology of the Old Testament I*, 26). The same God pursues the same purpose in both Testaments.

Eichrodt borrowed his overall outline, which presumably follows the Old Testament's dialectic, from his teacher, Otto Procksch. Volume 1 is concerned with the "God of the People," volume 2 with the "God of the World," and volume 3 with "God and Man" (i.e., the individual). In the English translations, volumes 2 and 3 are combined into volume 2.

Hermann Schultz's second volume of the second English edition (1895) used an outline similar to that of Procksch and Eichrodt. Schultz's outline was "God and People," "God and the World," "God and Man," and "the Hope of Israel."

Ludwig Köhler (1880-1956), professor at Zurich, was primarily a linguistic scholar. He and W. Baumgartner published an extensive Hebrew lexicon (Brill, 1953). His *Old Testament Theology* is brief and without documentation. It is organized around the rubrics of systematic theology: theology, anthropology, and soteriology. Köhler dealt with the cult at the end of his section on man. He said that the cult does not belong to the realm of soteriology (it is not part of the divine plan of salvation) or to the realm of anthropology. Köhler placed his discussion of the cult at the end of the section on anthropology because it deals with people's efforts to save themselves (*Old Testament Theology*, 9). A whole new view of the cult has arisen since Köhler's work, and it is now seen as the institution that transmitted much of the Old Testament tradition.

The significance of Köhler's work is in the fact that he, a linguist and historian, stopped his work to produce a brief but useful handbook on Old Testament theology. One of its strong points is its discussions of at least seventy Hebrew words. Although Köhler used the broad outline of systematic theology, he stated that a book may be called "Old Testament Theology if it manages to bring together and relate those ideas, thoughts, and concepts of the Old Testament which are or can be important." Köhler believed that the central theme or the one fundamental statement in the theology of the Old Testament is: God is the ruling Lord. "Everything else leans on it. Everything else can be understood with reference to it and only to it. Everything else subordinates itself to it" (*Old Testament Theology*, 30).

One of the most influential Old Testament scholars in Germany during the first part of the twentieth century was Artur Weiser. He never wrote an Old Testament theology, but he discussed the subject frequently. [See Artur Weiser, *Glaube und Geschichte im Alten Testament* (Göttingen, 1961); Weiser, "Vom Verstehen des Alten Testaments," *ZAW* 61 (1945), 17-30]. Weiser saw exegesis as a theological as well as a historical and critical task. According to Weiser, a person does not adequately understand an Old Testament passage by determining the grammatical, syntactical, and historical meaning. The real life of the passage lies in its religion (or faith) and its distinctive character.

Weiser argued that a dynamic view of reality runs through the Old Testament with a theological way of looking at people and events in the text itself. Weiser believed that to systematize the theology of the Old Testament was contrary to the dynamic understanding in the Old Testament itself, although he conceded a certain pedagogical value in marshalling scattered facts. Weiser followed Barth in arguing that exegesis should bear the theological task. Although Weiser did not write an Old Testament theology, he founded and edited one of the most significant series of commentaries on the Old Testament, *Das Alte Testament Deutsch* (ATD). One of the distinctive features of this series is its emphasis on the theological message of each section. Scholars such as Gerhard von Rad, Martin Noth, Walther Eichrodt, Norman Porteous, Karl Elliger, and Weiser himself contributed to the series. Many of the volumes have been translated into English as a part of the "Old Testament Library Series."

Undoubtedly one of the leading men in the field of Old Testament theology was Gerhard von Rad (1901-1971). After extensive studies at Erlangen and Tübingen, von Rad became the pastor of a Lutheran church in Bavaria in 1925. His daily struggle with a growing anti-Semitism caused him to return to academic studies in Old Testament at Leipzig. Otto Procksch and Albrecht Alt guided him in his studies and his dissertation, *Das Gottesvolk in Deuteronomium, BWANT*, 47 (Stuttgart: W. Kohlhammer Verlag, 1929).

In 1930 von Rad joined Alt on the faculty at Leipzig. In 1934 he moved to Jena, where national socialism flourished. Here von Rad was an unpopular teacher, but he managed to engage many who had not surrendered to the anti-Semitism of the day in illegal church discussions. (Compare James L. Crenshaw, *Gerhard von Rad*, 21).

From the summer of 1944 until June of 1945, von Rad was forced into the German military and became a POW in 1945. After the war he taught briefly at Bethel, Bonn, and Erlangen before moving to Göttingen. In 1949 he moved to Heidelberg, where he taught until his retirement in 1967 and continued to live until his death in 1971.

Von Rad took an entirely different approach to Old Testament theology than all his predecessors. He saw a very close relationship between Old Testament theology and Old Testament criticism. Anyone desiring to understand von Rad's *Old Testament Theology* should be familiar with his views concerning the origin and transmission of the Old Testament literature. One of his earliest works was *The Form-Critical Problem of the Hexateuch*, published in 1938, in which he laid the groundwork for his later *Old Testament Theology*.

Von Rad argued that the Hexateuch (Genesis—Joshua) was built on an ancient cultic creed now found in Deuteronomy 26:5b-9; 6:20-24; Joshua 24:2-13; and 1 Samuel 12:7-8. The Yahwist took a number of different traditions that had once been connected to various tribal shrines in Israel and arranged them in the order that constituted the framework of the Pentateuch. Von Rad posited a lengthy period of time between the original "event" (of the patriarchal promise, exodus, and conquest) and the writing of the document in which the account of the event is preserved. During that period the "story" was transmitted orally, often at a tribal altar in a cultic setting. According to von Rad, the Yahwist was a theologian.

One of the problems von Rad's successors have had with his approach is the vast difference in his view of "holy history" (Israel's own account of her history) and the scientific historical account of Israel's history as reconstructed by modern Old Testament scholars. Although von Rad said that Old Testament theology is based on history, he appeared very skeptical about the authenticity of some of the personalities and events in the Old Testament. Other scholars have criticized von Rad's work for its lack of a systematic arrangement. Some have said that his major work is really a history of Israel's traditions rather than an Old Testament theology (Dentan, *Preface to Old Testament Theology,* 79).

Joseph W. Groves wrote a doctoral dissertation on von Rad's (and others') method of interpretation: "Actualization and Interpretation in the Old Testament" (Atlanta: *SBL Dissertation Series* 86, 1987) in which he declared that "the goal of an inner-Biblical base for a theological-historical interpretation (like that of von Rad) is yet to be achieved" (Groves, 162-163; see also Hasel, *Basic Issues,* 75-77).

Th. C. Vriezen of the Netherlands published his *Hoofdinjnen der theologie von het Oude Testament* in 1949.

That work was almost completely revised in the third Dutch edition (1966) and published as the second English edition in 1970. The first 150 pages of Vriezen's book are introductory. They deal with the place of the Old Testament in the Christian church, how it should be interpreted, and the task and method of Old Testament theology. The main part of the book is divided into four lengthy chapters: (1) the knowledge of God; (2) the intercourse between God and Man; (3) the community of God; and (4) the future. Vriezen saw communion, or the relationship between God and man, as central in the Old Testament.

The Strasbourg professor Edmond Jacob wrote a substantial but popular Old Testament theology in 1955. Jacob's *Theologie de l'Ancien Testament* was translated into English in 1958. It served as a popular college and seminary textbook in this field for twenty years. It is clear and concise, yet treats adequately almost every facet of Old Testament theology. It has an excellent introduction. The main part of the book follows a modified systematic approach.

It is surprising that no British scholar has written a full-length Old Testament theology since A. B. Davidson (1904). H. Wheeler Robinson and Norman Porteous have written a number of books and essays about Old Testament theology. H. H. Rowley wrote a slim volume, *The Faith of Israel* in 1956, and another on *The Biblical Doctrine of Election* in 1948. Ronald E. Clements published his *Old Testament Theology, A Fresh Approach* in 1978, but this work was actually based on a series of lectures at Spurgeon's College in 1976 and is admittedly representative of only a tentative essay.

H. Wheeler Robinson (1872-1945), a British Baptist scholar, was able to combine solid critical scholarship with a warm evangelical faith. He stated that the Old Testament did not consist of a system of doctrine, but was mainly a divine drama acted out in the arena of history, where God revealed Himself and His will through His acts. Robinson acknowledged that to speak of a "historical revelation is a paradox. History implies dynamic movement of some kind, whether or not it can be called progress; revelation implies static and permanent truth" (*Record and Revelation,* 305). The resolution of the paradox of the relation between the timeless revelation and changing history is found in the "actuality of living" where revelation and history form a blended unity. (Compare Max Polley, "H. Wheeler Robinson and the Problem of Organizing an Old Testament Theology," in *The Use of the Old Testament in the New,* ed. James M. Efird, 157.)

One can see from an overview of Robinson's works on Old Testament theology that he was trying to think the thoughts of God after Him. For him the key to Old Testament theology was the idea of revelation, an idea that appears in the titles of many of his books. Robinson wanted to let the Old Testament speak for itself. He knew the danger of imposing some outside system on its message, but he also knew that some organizing principle was necessary to present the Old Testament materials to the modern interpreter. He believed that the Old Testament materials kept close to life and that anyone who hoped to understand them must be at least a "resident alien" (*Inspiration and Revelation in the Old Testament,* 281-282). He divided Old Testament theology into three parts: God and Nature, God and Man, and God and History, and presented the characteristic doctrines in propositions. He wrote:

> It is inevitable that we should state this in a series of propositions to constitute a "Theology of the Old Testament," even if they are arranged in a historical order. . . . If they are stated topically and not chronologically, as a "theology" requires, they become still more abstract and remote from the once-living, vibrating, and dynamic religion of Israel (*Inspiration and Revelation,* 281).

Eric Rust, one of Wheeler Robinson's students, came to the United States in 1952 as professor of Biblical Theology at Crozier Theological Seminary and became professor of Christian Apologetics at The Southern Baptist Theological Seminary in Louisville, Kentucky, in 1953. Rust made several contributions to the field of Old Testament theology. In 1953 he published *Nature and Man in Biblical Thought.* In the October 1953 issue of *The Review and Expositor,* Rust dealt with "The Nature and Problems of Biblical Theology" (63-64). In 1964 he published his full-length book, *Salvation History* (Atlanta: John Knox Press), dedicated to H. Wheeler Robinson and T. W. Manson. In 1969 Rust wrote his article on "The Theology of the

Old Testament" in the *Broadman Bible Commentary* (vol. 1, 71-86).

Another British Old Testament scholar who worked in the field of Old Testament theology but who never published a full-length book in the field is Norman Porteous. He was a pastor and teacher at St. Andrews and Edinburgh, principal of New College from 1964 until his retirement in 1968. Porteous published a number of essays on Old Testament theology in various theological journals. Some of them were reprinted in a volume, *Living the Mystery*. His important essays are: "Towards a Theology of the Old Testament," *SJT* 2 (1948); "Semantics and Old Testament Theology," *Oudtestamentische Studien* 8 (1950); "Old Testament Theology," *OTMS*, ed. H. H. Rowley (1951); "The Old Testament and Some Theological Thought Forms," *SJT* 7 (1954); "The State of Old Testament Studies Today: Old Testament Theology," *The London Quarterly and Holborn Review* (1959); "The Present State of Old Testament Theology," *ET* 75 (1963); "The Theology of the Old Testament," in *Peake's Commentary on the Bible* (1962); "*Magnalia Dei*," in von Rad's *Festschrift*, ed. H. W. Wolff, *Probleme biblischer Theologie* (1971), 417-427; and with Ronald E. Clements, "Old Testament Theology," in *The Westminster Dictionary of Christian Theology,* eds. A. Richardson and J. Bowden (Philadelphia: Westminster, 1983), 398-403, 406-413.

Porteous saw Old Testament theology as a science of Israel's religion based on the use of the modern techniques of archaeology, comparative religions, and historical and literary analysis. Its method may be as systematic as the subject matter permits. Beyond this it has a normative function and can thus claim the right to be regarded as theology. (See Porteous, "The Theology of the Old Testament" in *Peake's Commentary on the Bible,* 151.) After dealing with preliminary matters, Porteous outlined his approach in *Peake's Commentary* as: (1) the knowledge of God; (2) the saving acts of God; (3) the covenant; (4) Yahweh, the God of the covenant; (5) Israel and the nations; (6) royal theology; (7) the prophets; (8) the institutions of Judaism; (9) wisdom and hope.

The works of other British scholars who have dealt with Old Testament theology recently (G. A. F. Knight, F. F. Bruce, W.

J. Harrelson, and Ronald E. Clements) will be discussed in section 7.

6. The Biblical Theology Movement

Robert Dentan spoke of the period beginning in 1949 as "the Golden Age" of Old Testament theology. Dentan saw this Golden Age beginning with Otto Baab's *The Theology of the Old Testament* (1949), Otto Procksch's *Theologie des Alten Testaments* (1949), and Th. C. Vriezen's *An Outline of Old Testament Theology* (1949; edited and translated from the Dutch in 1958). Roman Catholic scholars contributed to the field as Paul Heinisch's *Theology of the Old Testament* appeared (in English) in 1950, and Paul van Imschoot, a French Catholic scholar, published an extensive two-volume work on Old Testament theology in 1954 and 1956.

A new monograph series, *Studies in Biblical Theology,* began in 1950. By 1963, thirty-seven titles had appeared, twelve of them concerned with the Old Testament.

What Dentan called "the Golden Age" of Old Testament theology was discussed as the "Biblical Theology Movement" by Brevard Childs (*Biblical Theology in Crisis*). Childs saw the biblical theology movement beginning near the end of World War II. H. H. Rowley's *The Relevance of the Bible* (1942) and *Rediscovery of the Old Testament* (1946), Alan Richardson's *A Preface to Bible Study* (1943), and Norman Snaith's *The Distinctive Ideas of the Old Testament* (1944) led the way in England. In America, G. Ernest Wright's *The Challenge of Israel's Faith* (1944), Paul Minear's *Eyes of Faith* (1946), and B. W. Anderson's *Rediscovering the Bible* (1951) were in the vanguard of the new movement.

New journals were started to support the movement: *Theology Today* (1944), *Interpretation* (1947), *The Scottish Journal of Theology* (1948); and numerous articles on Old Testament theology were published in other journals: James Smart, "The Death and Rebirth of Old Testament Theology," *JR* 23 (1943), 1-11, 125-136; Clarence T. Craig, "Biblical Theology and the Rise of Historicism," *JBL 62* (1943), 281-294; Muriel S. Curtis, "The Relevance of Old Testament Today, *JBR* 9 (1943), 81-87; W. A. Irwin, "The Reviving Theology of the Old Testament," *JR* 25 (1945), 235-247); W. A. Irwin, "The Nature and Function of

Old Testament Theology," *JBR* 14 (1946), 16-21; W. F. Albright, "Return to Biblical Theology," *The Christian Century* 75 (1958), 1328-1331.

Childs believed that the biblical theology movement reached a consensus around five major themes: (1) the rediscovery of the theological dimension (the concern was to penetrate to the heart of the Bible to recover its message and mystery that had been lost by the previous generation); (2) the unity of the whole Bible; (3) the idea that revelation is historical; (4) the distinctiveness of biblical (Hebrew) thought; and (5) the uniqueness of the biblical faith over against other religions.

Childs said that cracks began to appear in the wall of the consensus of the biblical theology movement when a group of scholars such as James Barr, Langdon Gilkey, and Bertil Albrektson began to raise questions about the revelation, history, and uniqueness of Israel's faith. Gerhard von Rad used an entirely new method in writing his Old Testament theology, which raised serious questions for the earlier consensus. The dominance of Barth's and Brunner's ideas subsided even before their deaths. New interests and concerns and social and political issues took the spotlight off theology. Childs dated the end of the biblical theology movement to May 1963 with the publication of J. A. T. Robinson's *Honest to God*. Robinson popularized the skeptical views about God and institutional religions being voiced by philosophers and theologians such as Tillich, Bonhoeffer, and Bultmann and by some modern scientists and secularists.

Childs claimed the biblical theology movement ceased, but that a need for a biblical theology remains. He proposed a new shape, beginning with the establishment of a proper context. He made the whole canon of the Bible the context, and one sees immediately that for Childs, the two Testaments belong together, with little room for separate disciplines of Old Testament and New Testament theology (*Biblical Theology in Crisis,* 6).

James Smart, a Presbyterian pastor, teacher, author, and developer of church curricula, responded to Childs. According to Smart, Childs created a false picture of the development of biblical interpretation (Smart, *The Past, Present, and Future of Biblical Theology,* 7). Smart objected to Childs' use of the term "movement," saying that it is not appropriate for the study of biblical theology. Movements come and go. The "death of God" movement, the "secular city" movement, or the "liberation theology" movements are issue-centered and are temporary "fads" of theology. Smart said that biblical theology is no more a movement than is the development of literary, historical, and/or form criticism (*Past, Present and Future,* 11).

Smart argued that biblical theology is international in its concern. He suggested that Childs was correct in speaking of a crisis but wrong in locating it with biblical theology. Smart saw the crisis in the whole vast enterprise of biblical scholarship (*Past, Present, and Future,* 22). Smart believed that the problem is a hermeneutical one. The solution to the problem is to acknowledge the double nature of the Scriptures, historical and theological, and the impossibility of separating the two (*Past, Present and Future,* 145).

7. The Present State
of Old Testament Theology

A. Continued Interest in and Flow of Literature
of Old Testament Theology to 1985

Biblical theology may be in crisis, but that has not stemmed the flow of Old Testament theologies, articles, and essays dealing with important aspects of the subject. A number of new Old Testament theologies have appeared since 1970. A Catholic scholar, A. Deissler, wrote *Die Grundbotshaft des Alten Testaments* ("The Basic Message of the Old Testament") in 1972. Deissler saw the center of Old Testament faith as God's relationship to the world and persons.

Walther Zimmerli published his *Old Testament Theology in Outline* in 1972. Zimmerli considered the Old Testament a "book of address" in contrast to von Rad's concept of the Old Testament as a "history book." Zimmerli made the First Commandment his starting point and the center of his discussion. He said: "Obedience to Yahweh, the one God, who delivered Israel out of slavery and is jealous of his own uniqueness, defines the fundamental nature of the Old Testament faith" (*Old Testament Theology in Outline,* 116).

Georg Fohrer, the editor of *ZAW,* published his *Theologische Grundstructuren des Alten Testaments* in 1972. The first chapter dealt with the problem of interpreting the Old Testament. Chapter 2 dealt with revelation and the Old Testament. Fohrer, as an existentialist, saw revelation in the hearer's decision of life and death. Chapter 3 spoke about the multiplicity of attitudes toward life in the Old Testament. Chapter 4 discussed the question of a center or midpoint in the Old Testament which Fohrer considered the sovereignty of God and the community of God. Chapter 5 dealt with the transforming power and the potential of Old Testament faith. Chapter 6 described certain basic elements within the Old Testament such as the hiddenness of God and His acts in history and nature. Chapter 7 made application, dealing with such matters as the crisis of man, the state and politics, poverty and social measure, man and technology, and the future in prophecy and apocalyptic literature. (See G. E. Wright's review in *Interpretation* 28 (1974), 460-462; and G. F. Hasel, *Old Testament Theology: Basic Issues,* 63-66.)

In 1974 John L. McKenzie, a leading Catholic Old Testament scholar, published *A Theology of the Old Testament.* In his preface McKenzie said that an Old Testament theology or a history of Israel offers an author an opportunity to summarize his entire work. However, there is a hidden obstacle: Old Testament theology has no accepted structure or style. McKenzie said that he read most of the other books on the subject, the major fruit of which was to learn what not to do. He quoted James Barr as saying that "Biblical theology is now out of date," then remarked that he was determined to show that Barr was "out of date" (McKenzie, *A Theology of the Old Testament,* 10)." McKenzie criticized von Rad's approach as being "a theology of development" (McKenzie, 20). McKenzie defined theology as "God-talk" and said that if anyone collects all the God-talk in the Old Testament, a fairly clear personal reality emerges which is seemingly not entirely consistent with itself, but is also not to be identified with any other personal reality. McKenzie's book is a theology of the Old Testament—not an exegesis, a history of Israel's religion, or a theology of the Bible. Its interest is not in "religious experience"; it is directed toward the documents of the Old Testament. "Presumably something emerges from the totality which does not emerge from any single utterance" (McKenzie, 21). A theology of the Old Testament should articulate that reality in the language of academic discussion.

After an introduction, McKenzie's book has seven chapters: (1) cult; (2) revelation; (3) history; (4) nature; (5) wisdom; (6) political and social institutions; and (7) the future of Israel, ending with an epilogue.

In 1978 Walter C. Kaiser, Jr. of the Trinity Evangelical Divinity School published his *Toward An Old Testament Theology*. Kaiser contended that Old Testament theology functions best "as a handmaiden of exegetical theology rather than in its traditional role of supplying data for systematic theology" (p. viii). Kaiser's main starting point is his assumption that the Old Testament writers themselves "cast their messages against the backdrop of an accumulated theology which they, their hearers, and now their readers must recollect if they are ever to capture the precise depth of the message they had originally intended" (p. viii). Kaiser seems to claim that the Old Testament writers wrote with a knowledge of a body of theological materials. He also seems to think that we can discover the original "intent" of those writers. "Intent" is always difficult to discover and prove.

After reviewing the history of Old Testament theology from 1933 to 1978, Kaiser asserted that the discipline is in a state of confusion—if not crisis—because scholars have not been able to "restate and reapply" the *authority* of the Bible. For Kaiser the authority of the Bible was closely related to the normative type of theology (*Toward an Old Testament Theology*, 6). Kaiser saw the norm of Old Testament theology in its center, which he identified with the promise. Like Eichrodt, Kaiser believed that the "quest for a center, a unifying conceptuality, was at the very heart of the concern of the receivers of the divine Word" (*Toward an Old Testament Theology*, 6-7).

Kaiser's concept of Old Testament theology was that it must be "a theology in conformity with the whole Bible, described and contained *in* the Bible, and consciously joined from era to era. The previous antecedent context becomes the base for theology which followed in each era" (*Towards an Old Testament*

Theology, 9). It is not surprising, given Kaiser's assumptions, that his method was the tracing of the "promise" through the Old Testament. In concentrating on promise and blessing, however, Kaiser almost totally ignored such topics as creation, cult, and wisdom.

Another conservative writer, William Dyrness, dean of the School of Theology at Fuller Theological Seminary, said that his *Themes in Old Testament Theology* grew out of his teaching experience in the Asian Theological Seminary in Manila. He felt the need for such a book for his Asian students and was unable to find an adequate recent theological survey of the Old Testament to put into their hands. He said that his book is "more an acknowledgment of that gap than an attempt to fill it."

Elmer A. Martens, president and professor of Old Testament at Mennonite Brethren Biblical Seminary, wrote *God's Design: A Focus on Old Testament Theology.* Martens, an informed conservative Old Testament scholar, co-edited *The Flowering of Old Testament Theology* (1992). Martens claimed that the overarching theme of the Old Testament is God's design found in Exodus 5:22–6:8. "Design" may mean "center." This design incorporates four components: deliverance, community, knowledge of God, and the abundant life. Martens tried to take a synthetic (the four themes) and a diachronic approach to the three periods of Old Testament history. The three periods are: premonarchy, monarchy, and post-Exilic era. He also attempted both a descriptive and a normative approach to Old Testament theology.

Ronald Clements is one of the more creative contemporary Old Testament scholars in England. His interest in Old Testament theology is reflected in "The Problem of Old Testament Theology." [See *The London Quarterly and Holborn Review* 190 (1965), 11-17; *God's Chosen People; One Hundred Years of Old Testament Interpretation,* chapter 7; *Old Testament Theology: A Fresh Approach;* and "Old Testament Theology" with N. Porteous in *The Westminster Dictionary of Christian Theology* (1983), 398-403, 406-413.] Clements, writing against the backdrop of the variety of other Old Testament theologies, argues that there is a need for a fresh approach—which is in reality an old approach. Clements' new approach is to pay closer attention to the way in which Christians, and to some extent Jews also, actually hear the Old Testament speaking to them theologically (*Old Testament Theology*, 4). Clements believes that the idea of the canon is significant in Old Testament theology. It determines the limits, authority, and shape of such a study.

Clements' *Old Testament Theology* is a slender volume of two hundred pages organized into eight chapters. The first chapter deals with the problems of Old Testament theology: what it is and how to do it. Chapter 2 discusses the dimensions of faith in the Old Testament: literary, historical, cultic, and intellectual. Chapters 3 and 4 constitute the heart of the study: Israel's idea of God and of herself as the people of God. Chapters 5 and 6 show Clements' idea of the canon. Chapter 5 deals with the Old Testament as Law (Torah), and 6 deals with Prophecy or Promise. He has no separate section on Psalms or Wisdom. The last two chapters (7 and 8) deal with the relevance of the Old Testament and Old Testament theology to contemporary religion and theology.

Samuel Terrien, a Frenchman and an American, a graduate of the University of Paris (1933) and Union Seminary in New York (1941), taught in Wooster College (1936-40) and Union Seminary (1941-1976). Terrien was trained in the classics, archaeology, Semitics, and the history of religions. His interests in Semitics and comparative religions helped him focus his attention on Old Testament Wisdom literature and the Book of Job. His interest in Job led to his quest for the divine presence in absence, a quest that culminated in his book, *The Elusive Presence: Toward a New Biblical Theology.*

Terrien believed that the reality of the presence of God stands at the center of biblical faith, but this presence is always elusive (*The Elusive Presence*, xxvii). Only a handful of ancestors, prophets, and poets had actually perceived the immediacy of God. The rank and file of the people experienced divine closeness by cultic procuration or mediation (*The Elusive Presence*, 1-2). However, the cult did not always bring God close to the people. It often produced stagnation and corruption.

Terrien called his book "a prolegomena" to a genuinely biblical theology which can deal with the similarities and differences between the idea of the presence of God in Israel's faith and that of her neighbors (*The Elusive Presence,* 27). The idea of the presence of God can provide the unifying link across the centuries between the patriarchs and Jesus and a basis for a dialogue between Jews and Christians. It can incorporate all kinds of Old Testament literature (Wisdom and Psalms) into an Old Testament theology.

After rejecting Eichrodt's covenant idea and von Rad's history of salvation method of organizing biblical theology, Terrien asked, "Does the Hebrew theology of Presence provide a legitimate approach to a genuine theology of the whole Bible?" He suggested that "this may well be the case" (*The Elusive Presence,* 473). This book should be considered as a prolegomena to a description of the specific characteristics of biblical faith. It puts too much emphasis on the "elusiveness" of God's presence and not enough on the reality of His presence. The method deals too much with a discussion of different types of literature and is not "systematic" or "theological." It is addressed too much to the secular society and not enough to the church, emphasizing God as Creator above God as Redeemer. A glance at the index of Terrien's book reveals how little is said in the book about sin or guilt (*The Elusive Presence,* 510).

One of the most prolific writers in the field of Old Testament studies has been Claus Westermann. Westermann retired as professor of Old Testament at Heidelberg in 1978. He has written commentaries on Genesis and Isaiah 40—66, extensive essays on the Psalms and the Prophets, and two books on Old Testament theology: *What Does the Old Testament Say About God?* and *Elements of Old Testament Theology.* The latter book is a translation of *Theologie des Alten Testaments in Grundzügen* (Göttingen, 1978). These two books are very similar and have essentially the same outline. The 1979 book is based on a series of lectures delivered at Union Theological Seminary in Richmond, Virginia, in 1977.

Westermann insisted that the task of Old Testament theology is to summarize and view together what the Old Testament as a whole says about God (*Elements of Old Testament Theology,* 9). The Old Testament has no theological center as the New Testament does. We must present Old Testament the-

ology the way the Old Testament does it, in the form of a narrative or story, based on events rather than concepts.

Westermann used the threefold division of the Hebrew
canon (Torah, Prophets, and Writings) as a guide to the theology of the various parts of the Old Testament. The Torah contains history or the saving acts of God; the Prophets represent
the word of God; and the Writings (Wisdom and Psalms) represent human response. All three of these elements are necessary to an Old Testament theology. Chapter 1 deals primarily
with definition and methodology. Chapters 2 and 3 speak of
God as the saving God and the blessing God. Chapter 4 (the
Prophets) represents the word of God speaking in judgment
and compassion. Chapter 5 is human response to God's saving
acts and word. People respond in praise and lament, as well as
in actions, to commandments and laws in everyday life and in
worship.

Undoubtedly the idea of tradition or traditions occupies center stage in Old Testament studies today, especially in the area
of Old Testament theology. In 1977 a volume of essays, *Tradition and Theology in the Old Testament,* was published by Fortress Press. The editor was Douglas A. Knight of Vanderbilt
University. In the Introduction Knight spoke about the positive and negative effects traditions have on all of us. The term
tradition can be applied as readily to oral and written literature as to customs, habits, beliefs, moral standards, cultural
attitudes, and standards. Knight defined tradition as anything in the heritage from the past that is delivered down to
the present and can contribute to the makeup of the new ethos
(*Tradition and Theology,* 2).

Tradition can refer to the process of transmission as well as
the content of the materials handed down. Walter Harrelson,
in the same volume, referred to a narrow definition of tradition
which refers to the passing on of what one (or a group) has
received as they have received it (*Tradition and Theology,* 15).
Traditions may change or grow in the course of their transmis-
sions, but the handing down process must keep *intact* what
has been received. The essential elements of the traditions
must be there and recognizable. Some traditions passed were
nonweighty in the sense that they were not decisive for self-
understanding. Other traditions were passed along because

they had genuine weight. The group recognized in them something of decisive importance for the maintenance of its life and faith. [For an interesting example of the tradition tracing, see Trent C. Butler, *Joshua,* xxii-xxiii. "There was Tradition and there were traditions" (Knight, *Tradition and Theology,* 17).] Harrelson saw a core tradition made up of four parts that functioned orally and accounted for the origins of Israel. (1) Yahweh was Israel's God (this begins in mystery); (2) He accompanied them in their movements; (3) He was particularly concerned with the oppressed and mistreated among them; and (4) He was leading them into a future, the features of which remained open. Harrelson argued that these core traditions lie near the beginning of the community and have the character of the fundamental revelatory disclosure or discovery (Knight, *Tradition and Theology,* 22-28).

The last essay in *Tradition and Theology* is "Tradition and Biblical Theology" by Hartmut Gese. Gese, professor of Old Testament at Tübingen, has followed von Rad's approach to the history of Israel's traditions. It is Gese's conviction that the Old Testament and New Testament should not be separated as Christians have done in the past. He says there is only one canon. The same process of forming the Old Testament canon continued through the New Testament and apostolic period (Knight, *Theology and Tradition,* 322). Gese argued that a unity exists between the Old Testament and New Testament. The death and resurrection of Jesus marks the goal, end, *telos* of the path of the biblical tradition. Therefore, with the death and resurrection of Jesus, the canon is closed where it was not closed previously.

Gese continued his work on biblical theology using the history of tradition approach. In a collection of *Essays on Biblical Theology,* (edited and translated, 1981), Gese explained his method of doing biblical theology and treats six biblical themes historically and theologically. The six themes are: Death, the Law, the Atonement, the Lord's Supper, the Messiah, and the Prologue to John's Gospel. Gese saw all of these themes beginning in te Old Testament and continuing into the New Testament. The origin of the Lord's Supper, for example, is found in the Old Testament psalms of thanksgiving (see Hartmut Gese, *Zur Biblische Theologie: Altestamentliche Vor-*

träge [Chr. Kaiser Verlag Munchen], 1977; edited and translated, 1981).

John Goldingay has evaluated the new history of traditions approach to Old Testament theology and to canon criticism in his book, *Approaches to Old Testament Interpretation*. He acknowledged that the biblical canon is the result of a long process (*Approaches to Old Testament Interpretation,* 122). About the history of tradition, Goldingay said, "The traditio-historical approach is suggestive, though it makes too exclusive a claim. The New Testament is a selective actualization of the Old Testament, rather than the inevitable goal to which the whole Old Testament is manifestly aimed" (*Approaches to Old Testament Interpretation,* 131).

Most Old Testament theologians have made "salvation history" the major emphasis in Old Testament theology, but now there is a growing concern with Wisdom as a major subject. (Compare Walther Zimmerli, "The Place and Limit of Wisdom in the Framework of Old Testament Theology," 165-181). In 1962 von Rad said that Israel knew neither our concept of nature nor the Greek concept of cosmos. "For her the world was not a stable and harmoniously ordered organism" (*Old Testament Theology I,* 426).

H. H. Schmid has taken an entirely different approach to the basic category of thought in the Old Testament. Schmid argued that in Israel, as in the entire Ancient Near East, world order is the basic category of thought. He asserted that the Hebrew word *sedeq* is equivalent to the Egyptian word *maat* and Sumerian *me*. World order includes Law, Wisdom, nature, war, cult, and history. According to Schmid, Hebrew terms such as *'emet, shalom*, and *chesed* belong to the same semantic field. This terminology is deeply rooted in wisdom thinking; therefore, "wisdom is not a backwater but a central element in the Bible" ("Creation, Righteousness, and Salvation," *Creation in the Old Testament,* 102-117; compare H. Graf Reventlow, "Basic Problems in Old Testament Theology," 10; Roland E. Murphy, "Wisdom—Theses and Hypotheses," in *Israelite Wisdom*, edited by John Gammie and others, 37).

In 1983 Simon J. De Vries published *The Achievements of Biblical Religion*. This book approaches biblical understanding from a strictly historical and exegetical standpoint, stressing particular themes that distinguished Israel from their neighbors. De Vries claimed that these distinctive elements account for the survivability and contemporary relevance of the Old Testament (*The Achievements of Biblical Religion*, vii). The particular themes that distinguished Israel were: (1) The Transcendence of God; (2) The Divine Image Mirrored in Human Personhood; (3) A Life of Fulfilling Integrity Within a Covenant Community; (4) History as Responsible Dialogue with God; and (5) A Meaning and Purpose in Finite Existence. These five themes furnish the headings to the five chapters of his book.

De Vries concluded that there is a unity within the whole Bible; and "from Genesis to Revelation there is a witness to one and the same God, working onward age by age, bringing his works to ever greater perfection" (*The Achievements of Biblical Religion*, 28). De Vries believes that the reason Judaism and Christianity have survived, grown, and expanded over the world in face of opposition and persecution was that "they had something dear to hold on to, something that made their lives different from those of their pagan neighbors, something worth dying for and transcending death" (*The Achievements of Biblical Religion*, 29).

In 1983 Martin H. Woudstra wrote an article on "The Old Testament in Biblical Theology and Dogmatics," in which he addressed the current interest in the Old Testament and its place in dogmatics. Before he discussed the place of the Old Testament in dogmatics, he traced the history of the biblical theology movement from Gabler's work to the present. Woudstra believed that Gabler's work was much more influential than simply a call for a separation of dogmatics and biblical theology. Gabler was a key figure in the development of biblical scholarship in Germany. Woudstra thought that Gabler was influenced primarily by four men: Eichhorn, Semler, Lessing, and Herder. The influence of these four men was more negative than positive as far as the Christian view of the Bible and theology was concerned.

Woudstra noted that Gabler was the first to entertain the notion of "myth" as a suitable term for understanding the nature of the biblical narrative. Gabler undermined the authority of the church creeds and made the scholarly study of the Bible an "esoteric pursuit" ("The Old Testament in Biblical Theology," 49).

Woudstra held up Abraham Kuyper, Charles Hodge, and B. B. Warfield as models of dogmatic theologians and seemed to approve their use of the Old Testament over against the work of such modern scholars as K. H. Miskotte, A. A. van Ruler, K. Barth, and H. Berkhof. Woudstra thought the latter scholars make too much of the "Jewishness" of the Old Testament, which seriously jeopardizes the unity and continuity of the Testaments ("The Old Testament in Biblical Theology," 53). Woudstra believed that the whole Barthian approach blurs the line of division between Judaism and the church. He objected to Miskotte's and William Temple's use of the term *schism* to refer to the division between Jews and Christians because the term suggests a separation between those of a common faith. Woudstra said, "This does no justice to the full depth of the biblical view" ("The Old Testament in Biblical Theology," 57, n. 39). The bottom line for Woudstra is the New Testament's use of the Old Testament.

> The present writer believes that the messianic identity of Jesus, and hence the nature and mission of his earthly ministry from birth to ascension, stands or falls with the believing acceptance, also from the exegetical point of view, of the New Testament insights into the meaning of the Old Testament ("The Old Testament in Biblical Theology," 58).

Ideally what is needed, according to Woudstra, is a better version of Miskotte, van Ruler, Berkhof, and Ernst Block.

> This is a great task, and the people available to do it from a consistently biblical viewpoint are scarce and sometimes overburdened. . . . In the meantime, Old Testament scholarship itself should also attempt to so 'digest' and expound the biblical material that the systematician can use it without the need of a complete re-orientation ("The Old Testament in Biblical Theology," 60-61).

A recent book on the history of Old Testament theology, Hayes and Prussner's *Old Testament Theology: Its History and Development,* takes this "Jewish" stance of which Woudstra spoke. This is Hayes' expansion, revision, and updating of Prussner's doctoral dissertation at the University of Chicago in 1952. The book is made up of five chapters: (1) The Earliest

Developments in Old Testament Theology; (2) Old Testament Theology in the Eighteenth Century (3) Old Testament Theology in the Nineteenth Century; (4) The Rebirth of Old Testament Theology; and (5) Recent Developments in Old Testament Theology.

Excellent, up-to-date bibliographies mark the beginning of each major section. Twenty-one extensive current bibliographies appear in the book, and about fifty major works on Old Testament theology are reviewed and evaluated.

However, a "hidden" agenda seems to lie behind much of Hayes and Prussner's book. It may begin with the dedication, "To Sidney Isenberg, who knows all the reasons why." Unlike most works on Old Testament theology, which conclude with some reference to its completion or "fulfillment" in the New Testament and the Christian faith, Hayes and Prussner conclude their book with an abrupt apology for Judaism being a legitimate continuation and interpretation of the Hebrew Scriptures. Then we are told that "throughout this volume" the authors have noted the low esteem in which post-Exilic and early Judaism have been held by biblical theologians (*Old Testament Theology,* 276). Hayes spoke of the deprecation of Judaism and said that it is unfortunate that the negative trend toward Judaism was continued by Eichrodt and von Rad.

Actually, Hayes and Prussner's work reflects the trend among some contemporary Old Testament scholars to try to correct what they feel is a wrong against Jews by Christian Old Testament scholars. James Barr delivered the seventh Montefiore lecture on *Judaism: Its Continuity with the Bible* at the University of Southampton in 1968. Barr said that Claude Montefiore felt, and Barr agreed, that Christians, especially educated and cultured Christians, customarily looked down on Judaism as a religion lacking in spirituality and true morality. They saw it as a set of practices followed without inward conviction. Such views were supposed to be in accord with the basic and original criticism of Judaism, exemplified in the teaching of Jesus Himself, and supported and encouraged by the depiction of Judaism in the Gospels and Pauline letters (Barr, *Judaism: Its Continuity with the Bible,* 5).

To counteract this negative image of Judaism, Montefiore set out to present the rabbinic materials from the time of Jesus in a way that would display its spirituality, its moral nobility, and its fundamental values. Montefiore emphasized the positive *teachings* of Judaism and Christianity without making value-judgments regarding the person, office, and miraculous deeds of Jesus (Barr, *Judaism: Its Continuity,* 6).

However, after World War II and the Nazi attack on the Old Testament, their attempt to exterminate the Jews led to a philo-semitic atmosphere in academic theology. The Old Testament was valued very highly, and many scholars and theologians echoed the words of Jesus, "Salvation is from the Jews" (John 4:22). The emphasis was not expressed in terms of spirituality or morality but in terms of continuity and difference.

Christians have a great appreciation for their Jewish heritage, but their emphasis on the redemptive acts of God found in the Old Testament led naturally and biblically, according to the New Testament, to Christ. Since many Jews reject Christians' claim about Jesus, Barr thought a tendency to despise Judaism was built into the structure of Christianity (*Judaism: Its Continuity,* 9). It seems that Hayes and Prussner felt strongly that Judaism had been wronged by biblical theologians, so they made an effort to correct the situation.

Excursus: The Jewish-Christian Relationship and Old Testament Theology

Martin Woudstra touched a sensitive nerve when he said K. H. Miskotte, A. A. van Ruler and Karl Barth made too much of the "Jewishness" of the Old Testament. (Woudstra, The Old Testament in Biblical Theology and Dogmatics, 53). Until recently no Jew had participated in the writing of an Old Testament theology, and Jews generally did not participate in the discipline. But the Nazi regime (1933-1945) changed all that. The slaying of six million Jews in the Holocaust left many Christian leaders with a sense of shame and guilt because they felt they might have contributed to the rise and conduct of Adolf Hitler.

Jewish-Christian relations has been the subject of a vast amount of writings and vigorous debates since 1945. R. W. L. Moberly said, "The growth of Jewish-Christian dialogue has been one of the striking features of recent theological debate in the Western world" (*The Old Testament of the Old Testament,* 147). Many Christians risked their lives protecting Jews and opposing Hitler. Bonhoeffer, K. Barth, Miskotte, G. von Rad, and other Christian leaders were actively and publicly involved in the anti-Nazi resistance.

Karl Barth saw a close relationship between the role of Israel and the role of Jesus. He said that Jesus' mission was Israel's mission.

> In this Jesus Christ we are dealing with the man in whom the mission of this one people, the people of Israel, the Jewish people, is set forth and revealed. Christ, the Servant of God who came from it, the future of God's Servant for all peoples, as well as this one people of Israel, are two realities inseparable from each other, not only at that time but for the whole of history, indeed for all eternity. Israel is nothing apart from Jesus Christ; but we also have to say that Jesus Christ would not be Jesus Christ apart from Israel (*Dogmatics In Outline*, 74).

For Barth there was little redemptive progress from the Old to the New Testament. He tended to regard them as "two concentric circles which revolve around an identical circle" (K. H. Miskotte, *When the Gods are Silent,* x). The Church and the synagogue together constitute a congregation of God. They are one yet separate. A person cannot belong to the church and the synagogue at the same time (Miskotte, 77-78, 81). Israel in the Old Testament is presented as unique and distinctive in its election and calling. In its folly, perversity, and weakness it is the object of the "ever new love and goodness of God, but also . . . the judgments of God—this nation embodies in history the free grace of God for us all" (Barth, *Dogmatics in Outline,* 74). Barth claimed the picture the Old Testament gives of the Israelite is "in an utterly shattering way that of a man who *resists* his own election and consequently the mission given him, who proves himself unworthy and incapable of the mission, and who in consequence, since he is the subject of God's grace, is continually struck down and broken by the judgment which afflicts him just because he withdraws from grace" (*Dogmatics In Outline,* 78).

Israel's mission must be understood as a mission fulfilled, revealed, and accomplished in Jesus Christ; but, according to Barth, Israel still has a mission to demonstrate human unworthiness and at the same time to become a demonstration of God's free grace. Miskotte bought K. Barth's theology "wholesale" and wrote probably the first theological work in post-biblical times that concerns Judaism and Christianity (Miskotte, *When the Gods Are Silent,* ix-x, 76-77).

The Roman Catholic Church was severely criticized for its involvement or lack of involvement in the Nazi terror against the Jews. Pope John XXIII called a meeting of one of the rare ecumenical councils (Vatican II) in 1964-65. The Pope wanted the council to make a statement on the Jews and asked Cardinal Bea to see to it. "Between that beginning and the outcome there is perhaps the most dramatic story of the council" (Robert A. Graham, S. J., "Non-Christians," in *The Documents of Vatican II,* ed. Walter M. Abbot, S. J. [New York: Guild Press, 1966], 656).

The Vatican II document on non-Christians says the Church of Christ acknowledges that the beginnings of her faith and election are already found among the patriarchs, Moses, and the prophets. The Church cannot forget that she received the revelation of the Old Testament from the people through whom

God established the ancient covenant. From the Jewish people sprang the apostles and most of the early disciples; but Jerusalem did not recognize the time of her visitation (see Luke 19:44), nor did the Jews in large numbers accept the gospel. Nevertheless, the Jews still remain most dear to God (Rom. 11:28-29). "The Church awaits that day, known to God alone, on which all people will address the Lord in a single voice and 'serve him with one accord'" (*Documents of Vatican II,* 664-665). Vatican II documents absolve Jews of any charge of deicide and deplore the hatred, persecutions, and display of anti-Semitism directed against the Jews at any time and any place.

The statements of Vatican II sparked a great number of dialogues between Christians and Jews. At first Jews were charged with rejecting Jesus and of not believing the gospel. However, in recent years it seems that many Christian leaders excuse Jews of not believing the gospel and of rejecting Jesus as the Christ on the grounds that Jews are still God's covenant people and they have the right of self-definition and self-interpretation of who they are in the light of the Hebrew Bible. The old theological view that Christianity superseded Judaism has been cast aside by many Christian theologians. In the introduction to a volume of papers read at the University of Notre Dame in 1989, the editors said the traditional supersessionist claim that biblical religion finds its true fulfillment in Christianity has undeniably led to the denigration of Judaism, ancient, medieval, and modern and cannot be held innocent of the outrage of anti-Semitism and holocaust in our century. "It is a pre-supposition of the dialogue presented in this volume that a supersessionist view of the Old Testament is no longer tenable" (Roger Brooks and John J. Collins, eds., *Hebrew Bible or Old Testament,* 1).

Many Christian writers are making other concessions to Jews by trying to change the name "Old Testament" to "Hebrew Bible," "Prime Testament," or "First Testament" as suggested by James Sanders ("First Testament and Second," 47-49). Sanders said the thinking world at large seems to be settling on the expression "Hebrew Bible." One sees it now in Christian seminary catalogues and in the names of books and articles. One recent major publication of the Society for Biblical Literature was called *The Hebrew Bible and Its Modern Interpreters* (D. A. Knight and G. M. Tucker; See also Norman K. Gottwald, *The Hebrew Bible: A Socio-Literary Introduction.*)

Some Christians have become uncomfortable with the term "Old Testament" because they think the Jews are uncomfortable with it (Sanders, *The Hebrew Bible or Old Testament,* 41). However, Jacob Neusner has persuaded many students and scholars that it is not the "Old Testament" or the Hebrew Bible that is the real canon of Judaism; it is the rabbinic corpus of Formative Judaism, primarily the Mishnah and Talmuds (*Formative Judaism,* 2 vols.).

The term "Old Testament" has been referred to as "improper," "anti-Semitic," and "pejorative" (see Moberly, *The Old Testament of the Old Testament,* 159). M. Braybrooke said it is best to avoid the use of the terms "Old" and "New" Testaments because it carries with it, especially to Jewish ears, "the implication that the Church has replaced the Jewish people and that God abandoned them because they killed Jesus" (*Time To Meet,* 171, n. 16; see C. M. Williamson and R. J. Allen, *Interpreting Difficult Texts: Anti-Judaism and Christian Preaching,* 115). J. F. A. Sawyer of Newcastle University consistently referred to the Christian use of the term "Old Testament" as anti-Semitic, saying it "is damaging, arrogant, oppressive, symbolic of a rejection of the Jews, and theologically indefensible" ("Combating Prejudices About the Bible and Judaism," 269-78; see Moberly, *The Old Testament of the Old Testament,* 160).

All scholars do not agree with the claim that the term "Old Testament" must be abandoned. Roland Murphy has continued to use "Old Testament" because it is traditional (see 2 Cor. 3:14) and because old does not necessarily mean "out of date" or "outworn." The value of the Old Testament is that it is a source of the Christian's "knowledge of God" ("Canon and Interpretation" in *Hebrew Bible or Old Testament,* 11, n.1).

One reason Christians should not abandon the term "Old Testament" is that no other term is available to express adequately the biblical meaning of "Old" and "New" covenants. R. W. L. Moberly suggested that before Christians abandon the use of the terms "Old" and "New" Testaments they should ask two questions. First, do the terms express such essential insights that the integrity of the Christian faith would be threatened by their abandonment? Second, if the terms are essential to the Christian faith, do they necessarily imply a negative assessment of Jews or Judaism?

Moberly concluded that the language "Old" and "New" Testaments is essential. "It is as necessary for the Christian that the faith centered on Jesus in some ways supersedes the religion of the Old Testament as it was for the adherents of Mosaic Yahwism that their faith in some ways supersede patriarchal religion" (*The Old Testament of the Old Testament,* 161). There is a sense of continuity with what went before for Mosaic Yahwism and Christianity, but there is also a sense of a new beginning which gives normative status to the adherents of the new and relativizes the significance of the old or the former. It is no longer possible for the adherents of the "new age" to continue in the old as it once was. Whatever the apparent attraction to abandon the language, "Old Testament," "it is simply not possible for the Christian to do so and still explain the logic of a Christian as distinct from a Jewish position" (R.W.L. Moberly, 161).

Moberly's second question is: Do the terms "Old" and "New" (Testaments) necessarily imply a negative assessment of the Jewish faith? Moberly answered, "No." Moberly supported his answer by his analogy between Mosaic Yahwism's treatment of patriarchal religion and the church's treatment of Mosaic Yahwism. Patriarchal religion worshiped only one God, but there is no implied opposition to the worship of other gods. In Mosaic Yahwism exclusive worship of Yahweh was required of all Israel in the First Commandment. Genesis depicts no patriarchal antagonism or opposition to the "pagan" religious practices of the inhabitants of Canaan. However, Mosaic Yahwism prohibited the practice of idol worship in the Second Commandment. Patriarchs worshiped wherever God appeared to them. In Mosaic Yahwism eventually only one place was legitimate as a place of worship and to offer sacrifice. Elaborate and strict rules regulated priestly privileges and responsibilities in Mosaic Yahwism. Patriarchal religion had few such rules.

We could list other differences between patriarchal and Mosaic religions, but Mosaic Yahwism did not denigrate patriarchal religion when it superseded it. It respected and preserved the distinctiveness of patriarchal religion as the foundation of its own faith and included it in its "creed" in the recital of the great acts of God (Deut. 26:5-9).

In the same way Christians should respect patriarchal religion and Mosaic Yahwism as part of their religious foundation and "creed," but in itself Christianity is something new. Some things in the old are left behind. Fundamental differences lie behind the church's and Judaism's use of the Old Testament. The Old Testament is a part of the Christian Bible, but Christians interpret it in the light of Jesus Christ. His teachings burst the old wineskins (Matt. 9:17). His blood was the blood of the new covenant (Matt. 26:28).

There is a difference between Mosaic Yahwism's treatment of patriarchal religion and Christian treatment of Mosaic Yahwism. Mosaic Yahwism absorbed the patriarchs and their descendants (with the possible exception of the Rechabites, 2 Kings 10:15; Jer. 35:2-11). Patriarchal religion did not survive as a separate institution. Mosaic Yahwism did not survive in Judaism without some basic changes. Actually both Judaism and Christianity are grounded in the Old Testament. The apostle Paul said, "If some of the branches were broken off, and you, a wild olive shoot, were grafted in their place to share the rich root of the olive tree, do not boast over the branches. . . . They were broken off because of their unbelief, but you stand only through faith" (Rom. 11:17-20).

Mosaic Yahwism did not cease when Jesus came. It was absorbed and changed into rabbinic Judaism which used the Mishnah and Talmud to interpret the old forms. A lively debate continues about the proper relationship between Jewish-Christian relations. Joseph Blenkinsopp said, "No theology of the Old Testament is therefore likely to be successful which perpetuates a prejudicial and false understanding of the developments during the second commonwealth, one of which was of course the emergence and consolidation of the Christian movement" ("Old Testament Theology and the Jewish-Christian Connection," 11). It might be said also that a successful Old Testament theology will probably not be written without a proper understanding of New Testament theology.

Bruce Corley, dean of the School of Theology at Southwestern Baptist Theological Seminary, began an article in the SWJT with a reference to K. L. Schmidt's address to the Confessing Church at the height of the Nazi terror. Schmidt appealed to Romans 9—11 as the key to faith in such perilous times. Paul's hope for Israel was proclaimed as a light in foreboding darkness, not a trickle of revelation but a disclosure of God's presence. Corley said, "His [Schmidt's] climactic point reads, 'The God question, the future question, the Jewish question are the same question'" (Corley, "The Jews, the Future, and God," 42). Corley considered Schmidt's statement a carefully balanced summary of Romans 9–11. "Indeed, when Paul contemplates the question of unbelief, his eye finally turns to future hope for the salvation of Israel. But the entire reasoning proceeds from a standpoint well within history: the present situation of hardened Israel genuinely magnifies the faithfulness of God" (Corley, 42]. God has been faithful from the beginning of His work of salvation. He is not unjust (Rom. 9:14), and He has not rejected His people (11:1). Although Israel as a people have not believed the gospel, their rejection of the gospel is partial (Rom. 11:1-10) and temporary (vv.11-27). Paul believed a time will come when all Israel will be saved when and if they believe the gospel (Rom. 11:23).

Corley cautioned the reader against reading particularism, dispensationalism, or universalism into this passage. Nothing is said about "a restored theocracy in the land of Palestine or the automatic salvation of every Jew living and dead!" ("The Jews, the Future, and God," 55).

The length of this excursus underscores the importance of the issues involved in Jewish-Christian relations. So far the debates and dialogues have raised many more questions than they have answered. The search for answers and solutions must continue.

B. Interest in and Flow of Literature of Old Testament Theology Since 1985

In 1985 Thomas E. McComiskey of Trinity Evangelical Seminary wrote *The Covenants of Promise: A Theology of the Old Testament Covenants*. This book sees the covenant as the center of God's acts in history from creation to the end of time. Although the author uses modern principles of exegesis, the book is essentially uncritical. It makes much use of the New Testament and is greatly influenced by covenant theology. However, it reflects a continuing interest in Old Testament theology.

Quite different from McComiskey's *The Covenants of Promise* is Brevard Childs' latest work, *Old Testament Theology in a Canonical Context*. This is a slender volume of 250 pages. It is, therefore, only a summary or outline of Childs' understanding of what the form and content of an Old Testament theology should be. The treatment of the various topics in his twenty chapters is very sketchy. He was consistent in carrying on his emphasis on the canonical approach to Scripture, which he has used since the late 1960s. [His first two works, *Myth and Reality in the Old Testament* (1960) and *Memory and Tradition in Israel* (1962), do not mention canon.]

One can detect in Childs' latest work the influence of Eichrodt, von Rad, and Zimmerli, but he has gone beyond them. He has a strong emphasis on the Old Testament as revelation. The Decalogue has held a significant place in Old Testament theology for Childs. He dealt with election and covenant, the institutions of Israel and their officials, Old Testament ethics, judgment, and promise. He concluded with a section on the Messiah, the land, and eternal life. He followed a modified systematic approach, and the book contains excellent, relevant bibliographies at the end of each chapter.

Most recently Childs has offered his framework of a full-blown biblical theology (*Biblical Theology of the Old and New Testaments*). He shows "the Discrete Witness" of first the Old and then the New Testament; then he exemplifies exegesis in the context of biblical theology, working with Genesis 22:1-19 as the Akedah and Matthew 21:33-46.

Finally he does theological reflection on the Christian Bible, tracing the Old Testament witness, early Judaism's understanding, and the New Testament understanding on important themes. He then reflects on and traces the line from biblical theology to dogmatics.

In 1988 Jesper Høgenhaven published a small monograph on *Problems and Prospects of Old Testament Theology* (JSOT Press, 1988). This work grew out of a seminar in Queen's College in Oxford in 1983 and was originally published in Danish. Høgenhaven proposed to make the principal literary categories of the Old Testament (Wisdom, Psalmic literature, Narrative literature, Law, and Prophetic literature) the structure of an Old Testament theology.

Christoph Barth (1917-1986), late second son of Karl Barth, spent much of his life in Indonesia in theological education but served twelve years as professor of Old Testament at Mainz, Germany. We are told in the Foreword to his *God With Us* (Eerdmans, 1991) that he intended to write a textbook "sharpening his student's ears, so that in listening to what God had said and done in the past, they would be open to what God's Spirit says and does now" (viii).

Actually, the book is the product of the editorial work of Geoffrey W. Bromiley of Fuller Seminary. With the consent of Mrs. Christoph Barth, Bromiley took the collected notes and lectures of Dr. Barth and edited them for publication. The world of Old Testament scholarship owes Bromiley and William B. Eerdmans, Jr. for making this material available.

The method is an attempt to expound the message of the Old Testament in a manner faithful to the Old Testament itself—namely, as an account of the mighty acts of God rather than abstract doctrines. The titles to the nine chapters are: (1) God Created Heaven and Earth; (2) God Chose the Fathers of Israel; (3) God Brought Israel Out of Egypt; (4) God Led His People through the Wilderness; (5) God Revealed Himself at Sinai; (6) God Granted Israel the Land of Canaan; (8) God Chose Jerusalem; (9) God Sent His Prophets. This is an inspiring and helpful work.

Another major work on Old Testament theology is a compilation of twenty-two previously published articles. Ben C. Ollenburger, Elmer A. Martens, and Gerhard F. Hasel selected, introduced, and, in some cases, translated these articles from recognized international Old Testament scholars. The book is called *The Flowering of Old Testament Theology* (1992).

Perhaps a book that is not called an "Old Testament theology," but which deals with many themes of Old Testament theology, should be mentioned here. It is *The World of Ancient Israel,* edited by R. E. Clements. It deals with Israel's historical and cultural setting, kingship, law, prophecy, wisdom, apocalyptic, holiness, covenant, women, and life and death.

Studies in Old Testament Theology (1992) is a festschrift for David A. Hubbard, edited by his nephew, Robert L. Hubbard, Jr., Robert K. Johnston, and Robert P. Meye. This compilation contains fourteen articles relating to Old Testament study.

We began this chapter saying the story of Old Testament theology "is long, fascinating, and tortuous." It has been long. It is fascinating in the sense that it intrigues and captures the mind of the serious reader. It raises life and death issues. It is tortuous at times; we get bogged down in minutiae and sometimes become lost in various twists and turns. But we cannot stop. We must go on to the question of the nature and method of Old Testament theology.

2

The Nature and Method Of Old Testament Theology

8. The Nature of Old Testament Theology

A. No Generally Accepted Definition

What is Old Testament theology? A review of the basic books on Old Testament theology written in the last fifty years shows little agreement on the nature, task, and methodology of this discipline. John McKenzie said, "Biblical theology is the only discipline or sub-discipline in the field of theology that lacks generally accepted principles, methods, and structure. There is not even a general definition of its purpose and scope" (*A Theology of the Old Testament*, 15). Gerhard von Rad wrote that "there is no agreement up to now as to what really is the proper subject of . . . the theology of the Old Testament" (*Old Testament Theology I*, v).

Scholars cannot agree on whether to call this subject "the theology of the Old Testament" or "Old Testament theology." Although the two terms have been used interchangeably, there is a basic difference. The theology of the Old Testament places the primary emphasis on the theology contained in or confined to the Old Testament. The study is descriptive and historical, and there is some question about calling the result "theology" at all. If Old Testament theology is the subject, "theology" is primary, and Old Testament theology is that branch of modern theology concerned primarily with the Old Testament.

B. Does the Old Testament Contain "Theology"?

Some scholars are reluctant to call any study a *theology* if it confines itself to the Old Testament or even to the whole Bible. James Barr said that *theology* means the study of God, but the study of God should not be limited to the Old Testament or to the Bible. For Barr *theology* should include the study of history, philosophy, psychology, and the natural world along with the Bible.

For some, biblical theology is not really theology because it limits itself to the biblical materials and organizes its materials in a descriptive way. For most systematic theologians, theology is a modern critical construct, and "a refining of *our* concepts of God in Christ and in the Church" (Barr, "The Theological Case Against Biblical Theology," in *Canon, Theology and Old Testament Interpretation,"* 9).

For most Old Testament theologians today, Old Testament theology "derives from theological reflection on a received body of scripture" (Childs, *Old Testament Theology in a Canonical Context,* 6). Old Testament theology is a normative discipline rather than a merely descriptive one.

The word *theology* can in itself be a source of confusion because it has been used in many different ways. The word does not occur in the Old or New Testament. Plato and Aristotle used it in the sense of the "science of divine things," an idea that might suggest that divine things can be understood with the intellect alone. Terrien objected to this definition by Plato and Aristotle. He said the nearest expression in the Old Testament to theology is "the knowledge of God." This expression points to a reality that *induces* and *transcends* intellectual investigation and discussion. "It designates the presence of Yahweh" (*The Elusive Presence,* 41).

In the Hebraic sense of "the knowledge of God," theology does not refer to an objective science of divine things, but it does use the critical faculties of the mind. It proceeds from both an *inner commitment* to faith and a *participation* in the destiny of a people.

C. Must Theology Be Normative?

Can the term *theology* be used to designate a descriptive, phenomenological study of the religion of Israel? Or must *theology* be normative and correlated to the New Testament and dogmatic theology? James L. Mays asked, "Is a comprehensive description of the Old Testament yet theology apart from a correlation with the New Testament or a coordination with the rubrics of dogmatics? Or can the subject matter of theology be clarified from within the Old Testament itself?" (James L. Mays, "Historical and Canonical: Recent Discussion About the Old Testament and the Christian Faith," *Magnalia Dei*, ed. F. M. Cross, Lemke, and Miller, 510-530). Both Eichrodt and von Rad limited their discussions of the theology of the Old Testament primarily to the materials in the Old Testament.

Some scholars still refuse to relate the term *theology* to any descriptive and historical study. They insist that theology implies experience, commitment, and faith. Norman Porteous would limit theology to a normative science. He said, "It is, of course, possible and in its own way legitimate to use the word 'theology' in a perfectly harmless way as a name for the systematic statement of beliefs held by the adherents . . . of some particular religion. Any scholar with the requisite knowledge might write such a theology, and the result might very well be valuable and illuminating for certain purposes" (*Living the Mystery*, 22-23).

Porteous argued also that theology is a discipline that "has to do with the knowledge of God." He asserted that in the biblical view, the knowledge of God does not mean mere cognition but involves the emotions and the will no less than the intellect. Therefore, if the biblical theologian does not himself have the knowledge of God, "then, strictly speaking, the object of his study disappears from view" (*Living the Mystery*, 23).

Porteous also asked:

> Is it the task of the Old Testament theologian to determine as accurately as he can and set forth with whatever system he can contrive what the Hebrews in Old Testament times believed

about God and about themselves in relation to God, and what were the ways in which they gave concrete expression to what they believed? There is no doubt at all about the importance of performing such a task. It represents an indispensable step toward the right appropriation of the Old Testament. Yet what the accomplishment of this task would provide us with is, strictly speaking, a religious Phenomenology of the Old Testament rather than a Theology (*Living the Mystery*, 36-37).

For Porteous, then, any study that bears the name *Old Testament Theology* must be considered in some sense normative for the one making the study. That would seem to limit those who could write an Old Testament theology to Christians and Jews. H. Wheeler Robinson said, "Let us constantly remind ourselves that this religion, like any other, can be understood only from within, or through a sympathy that makes us its 'resident aliens' *(gerim)*" (*Inspiration and Revelation in the Old Testament*, 281-282). According to this view Old Testament theology is normative, relevant, and contemporary.

Recently John Goldingay strongly supported this view. Goldingay said that the task of writing an Old Testament theology is not

merely a reconstructive task but a constructive one. We are not merely reformulating the faith explicitly expressed or implicitly presupposed by a believing community of Old Testament times, in order to understand Old Testament faith for its own sake, but formulating the theological implications of that faith in a way that brings them home to us as members of a believing community in our own time" (*Theological Diversity and the Authority of the Old Testament*, 111).

This viewpoint is not unanimous among biblical scholars. It might surprise some readers to hear a conservative scholar such as F. F. Bruce say that "a systematic Old Testament theology need not be distinctively Christian; it may equally well be Jewish, and the norm could then be rabbinical tradition rather than New Testament fulfillment" ("The Theology and Interpretation of the Old Testament," *Tradition and Interpretation*, 386).

Is the task of Old Testament theology to contemporize and normalize the theological message of the Old Testament? If so, this represents a major shift from the purpose perceived by Gabler and many who followed him. A. B. Davidson said, "Biblical theology is the knowledge of God's great operation in introducing His kingdom among men, presented to our view exactly as it lies presented in the Bible" (*Old Testament Theology*, 1). G. E. Wright said that biblical theology is the confessional recital of the redemptive acts of God in a particular history (*God Who Acts*, 13). John Bright wrote:

> The task of biblical theology is essentially descriptive. It does not, as biblical theology, have the task of defending the validity of the biblical faith or of setting forth its contemporary significance—although the individual biblical theologian as a teacher and minister of the church may well be, and indeed must be, vitally and unceasingly concerned with just these things (*The Authority of the Old Testament*, 115).

We must admit that our interest in the Old Testament message is more than a passing curiosity. We want to know what the people of the Old Testament believed about God, His relation to themselves, and the world because we believe that the Old Testament is God's revelation about such matters in that time frame. We agree that theology deals with revelation and the knowledge of God and that the Old Testament revelation is valid as far as it goes. Vriezen was right in agreeing with Haitjema's definition of theology as "the thought of faith springing from revelation" (*An Outline of Old Testament Theology*, 145, n. 6).

Roland de Vaux said:

> The Bible is accounted sacred Scripture not just because it contains sacred history but principally because it is written under the inspiration of God to express, preserve, and transmit God's revelation to men. The object of a theology cannot therefore be restricted, as Von Rad would have it, to the definition of the ways in which Israel conceived of its relationship with God and the awareness of Israel that God intervened in history. The theologian, accepting the Old Testament as the Word of God, searches there for what God himself wished to teach, by means of history and also to ourselves (*The Bible and the Ancient Near East*, 58).

Old Testament theology is hard to define. It is descriptive in the sense that it describes and is based on what God and the people did and said as recorded in the Old Testament. It must include all of the Old Testament materials. For Protestants these materials are limited primarily to the Masoretic text. For Catholics they may include the Apocrypha. Old Testament theology is theological. It is not concerned merely with reciting the history of Israel or with retelling what God did with and for Israel. The Old Testament is inspired Scripture and has a message from God for all times. Old Testament theology is a "reflection on," a "construal," and a "construct" of the theological materials in the Old Testament that are relevant to us.

9. The Method of Old Testament Theology

A. No Natural or Obvious Single Method

How should we do Old Testament theology? Most academic disciplines have a "natural" or "built-in" way of presenting their own subject matter. Dogmatic theologies usually follow some kind of logical systematic treatment. Old Testament introductions follow the same natural outline of treating general subjects such as canon and text, followed by treatments of each book in the Old Testament. Old Testament theology, however, does not seem to have a natural method of presenting its subject matter.

The earliest biblical or Old Testament theologies used the systematic method in following the rubrics of dogmatic theology: theology, anthropology, and soteriology. The systematic method was still being used in 1935 when Ludwig Köhler published his *Old Testament Theology*, but many different methods have been used since.

In 1975 Gerhard Hasel said five clearly distinguishable major methods were in vogue, but they were not mutually exclusive (*Old Testament Theology: Basic Issues*, 35). According to Hasel, the five major methods for doing Old Testament theology were: (1) The Descriptive Method, (2) The Confessional Method, (3) The Cross-Section Method, (4) The Diachronic Method, and (5) The New Biblical Theology Method. Hasel's five major methods overlap each other and are not sharply distinguished. In his 1982 revised edition Hasel enlarged the number of major methods in vogue to nine. In 1991 Hasel published his fourth edition of *Old Testament Theology: Basic Issues in the Current Debate*, expanding his treatment fourteen pages from the third edition. He added one new method, "Recent Critical Old Testament Theology Methods" (p. 94), bringing the number of methods to ten.

Hasel's ten methods, along with representatives of each method, are:

(1) The Dogmatic-Didactic Method is the traditional method of organizing Old Testament theology with systematic rubrics, theology, anthropology, and soteriology. Ludwig Köhler's *Old Testament Theology* is a good example of the use of this method.

(2) The Genetic-Progressive Method presents the unfolding of God's revelation as the Bible presents it. Geerhardus Vos' and Chester K. Lehman's works use this method.

(3) The Cross-Section Method is an attempt to combine the thematic and the diachronic approaches. Walther Eichrodt was the cardinal example of this approach. He took the idea of the covenant and treated its occurrences throughout the Old Testament as he talked about the God of the covenant, people of the covenant, and institutions of the covenant.

(4) The Topical Method uses topics drawn from the Old Testament alone to organize a discussion of its theology. John L. McKenzie's *A Theology of the Old Testament* is the best example of this method.

(5) The Diachronic Method is dependent upon the traditio-historical method of interpretation developed in the 1930s by von Rad and his associates. It is a retelling of the *kerygma,* "the saving acts of God" as set out in Israel's confessions. It penetrates the successive layers of recited traditions and traces the growth of Israel's faith from period to period. Von Rad was the only writer of a full-fledged diachronic Old Testament theology.

(6) The Formation-of-Tradition Method is represented in the work of Hartmut Gese. Gese insisted that there is only one biblical theology realized by means of the Old Testament formation of tradition which is brought to an end in the New Testament ("Tradition and Biblical Theology," in Knight, *Tradition and Theology,* 322).

(7) The Thematic-Dialectic Method is represented by three prominent Old Testament scholars: Samuel Terrien, Claus Westermann, and Paul Hanson. These three scholars have suggested a governing dialectic of "ethic/aesthetic" (Terrien), "deliverance/blessing" (Westermann), and "teleological/cosmic" (Hanson). This method has been helpful in that it makes

it possible for the reader to see how opposite emphases can be related to enlarge one's understanding of a larger problem.

(8) Recent "Critical" Old Testament Theology Methods. This is Hasel's newest category. This method is the work of scholars such as James Barr and John J. Collins, who have not written an Old Testament theology and who have grave doubts about the future of the discipline.

(9) The New Biblical Theology Method. This method deals with the problem of the relationship between the Old and New Testaments. Brevard Childs believes that one should do an Old Testament theology and a New Testament theology separately, then put them together. He has done an Old Testament theology and a separate biblical theology. Childs insists that only the final form of the biblical text in the canon we now have is Scripture and authoritative. (For a good summary of Child's approach see Hasel [1991], 103-111.)

(10) Multiplex Canonical Old Testament Theology is a summary of Hasel's conception of Old Testament theology. First, Hasel thinks Old Testament theology should be tied to the final canonical form of the Old Testament. This rules out a history of religions and a history of traditions approach. Second, an Old Testament theology should be thematic rather than dealing with a center or a key concept. Third, the structure should be multiplex, which avoids the pitfalls of the cross-section, genetic, and topical methods. Fourth, the final aim of an Old Testament theology is to penetrate through the various theologies of individual books and groups of writings to the dynamic unity that binds all theologies and themes together.

Finally, according to Hasel, the Christian theologian understands that Old Testament theology is a part of a larger whole. Old Testament theology is not the same as the theology of ancient Israel and implies the larger whole of the entire Bible made up of both Testaments.

> These proposals for a canonical Old Testament theology seek to take seriously the rich theological variety of the Old Testament texts in their final form without forcing the manifold witnesses into a single structure, unilinear point of view, or even a compound approach of a limited nature. It allows full sensitivity for both similarity and change as well as old and new, without in the least distorting the texts (*Old Testament Theology: Basic Issues,* 4th ed., 114).

Why have so many Old Testament theologians used such a variety of methods to present Old Testament theology? Because no inherent or "natural" method is suggested in the Old Testament itself, and because each Old Testament theologian approaches the task from a different perspective and may have different goals.

B. Methodological Clues from the Old Testament

Does the Old Testament have any clues about how to do Old Testament theology? Claus Westermann answered yes and said:

> If we wish to describe what the Old Testament as a whole says about God, we must start by looking at the way the Old Testament presents itself . . . 'The Old Testament tells a story' (G. von Rad). With that statement we have reached our first decision about the form of an Old Testament theology: If the Old Testament narrates what it has to say in the form of a story (understood here in the broader sense of event), then the structure of an Old Testament theology must be based on events rather than concepts (*Elements of Old Testament Theology*, 9).

Is telling a story really the only way the Old Testament has to present its message? Is Old Testament theology merely the retelling of Israel's story? Neither of these is true, and yet the narrative form of much of the Old Testament gives us a clue to the nature and form of Old Testament theology. The Hebrews knew what God was like by what He had done.

Walter Kaiser claimed that he found the "biblical" way to do Old Testament theology, although that way must exclude all the "assured results" of source criticism. This criticism has deleted the textual connectors of each advance in "word, event, and time" of a unifying central theme (the Promise) running through much of the Old Testament. Kaiser further asserted that in listening to the canon as a canonical witness to itself, one finds that each antecedent event or meaning was handed on from one key figure, generation, country, or crisis to another by connectors which criticism has deleted or assigned to "pious or misguided redactors." He concluded by saying that "Biblical theology will always remain an endangered species until the heavy handed methodology of imaginary source criticism, history of tradition, and certain types of form criticism are arrested" (*Toward an Old Testament Theology*, 7).

Most Old Testament theologians have not been convinced by Kaiser's claims. They are not ready to abandon the use of source, form, history of tradition, or canonical criticism in doing Old Testament theology. However, Kaiser's claims have not yet been disproved.

Are there other clues in the Old Testament about how to do Old Testament theology? Some clues may be found in certain "creeds" or "confessions of faith" contained in the Old Testament. Some of these creeds are historical, and some are non-historical. The form of the canon (Torah, Prophets, and Writings) may also provide a clue about the method of Old Testament theology.

Gerhard von Rad was the first Old Testament scholar to call attention to the historical creeds in the Old Testament. In his *The Problem of the Hexateuch and Other Essays* (1966) and in *Old Testament Theology, I* (1962), von Rad argued that the Hexateuch has as its core an early confession of the faith of Israel, found in Deuteronomy 26:5-9:

> A wandering Aramean was my ancestor; he went down into Egypt and lived there as an alien, few in number, and there he became a great nation, mighty and populous. When the Egyptians treated us harshly and afflicted us, by imposing hard labor on us, we cried to the LORD, the God of our ancestors; the LORD heard our voice and saw our affliction, our toil, and our oppression. The LORD brought us out of Egypt with a mighty hand and an outstretched arm, with a terrifying display of power, and with signs and wonders; and he brought us into this place and gave us this land, a land flowing with milk and honey.

This historical confession has as its setting the offering of the tithe (Deut. 26:1-4) and contains three basic elements: (1) the call of the patriarchs (26:5*b*), (2) the exodus from Egypt (26:8), and (3) the gift of the land of Canaan (26:9).

Von Rad argued that this historical creed, which recites the great redemptive acts of God, was expanded later to include creation and God's covenant with David. Different forms of this historical creed are found in many places in the Old Testament (Deut. 6:20-24; Josh. 24:2-13; 1 Sam. 12:7-8; Neh. 9:6-37; Ps. 77:12-20; 78; 105; 136). These creeds reciting the great redemptive acts of God were one of the primary ways Israel had to confess her faith. Unlike the New Testament and the early Christian movement, which expressed faith with nouns representing absolute and abstract ideas from the Greek language, the Old Testament expressed its faith primarily with action verbs such as *save, deliver, judge,* and *bless.* (Compare Westermann, *Elements of Old Testament Theology,* 10.)

G. Ernest Wright said, "An event is expressed by means of a subject conjugating a verb. . . . Universals are not declined; they are not in historical movement; they are defined and related to one another as nouns and adjectives, chiefly by the copula 'is'" (*The Old Testament and Theology,* 44-45]. The language of the Old Testament is verb-centered not noun-centered; there is no noun in the Old Testament for revelation, election, or eschatology.

In many places in the Old Testament, great emphasis is placed on handing on the tradition of God's great saving acts. At cultic festivals children were taught to ask the meaning of the rituals, and the parents would reply by reciting the great acts of God (Ex. 13:14-16; Deut. 6:20-24; Josh. 4:6-7, 21-24). The Psalms refer often to the retelling in worship of these great redemptive acts:

> Posterity will serve him;
> future generations will be told
> about the Lord, and proclaim
> his deliverance to a people yet unborn,
> saying that he has done it.
> (Ps. 22:30-31)

> Walk about Zion, go all around it,
> count its towers,
> consider well its ramparts;
> go through its citadels,
> that you may tell the next
> generation that this is God,
> our God forever and ever.
> He will be our guide forever.
> (Ps. 48:12-14)

> We will not hide them from their children;
> we will tell to the coming generation
> the glorious deeds of the LORD, and his might,
> and the wonders that he has done.
> He established a decree in Jacob,
> and appointed a law in Israel,
> which he commanded our ancestors
> to teach to their children;

> that the next generation might know them,
> the children yet unborn,
> and rise up and tell them to their children,
> so that they should set their hope in God,
> and not forget the works of God,
> but keep his commandments;
> and that they should not be like
> their ancestors,
> a stubborn and rebellious generation,
> a generation whose heart was not steadfast,
> whose spirit was not faithful to God.
> (Ps. 78:4-8)

> O give thanks to the LORD, call on his name,
> make known his deeds among the peoples.
> Sing to him, sing praises to him;
> tell of all his wonderful works.
> Glory in his holy name;
> let the hearts of those who seek
> the LORD rejoice.
> Seek the LORD and his strength;
> seek his presence continually.
> Remember the wonderful works he has done,
> his miracles, and the judgments he uttered.
> (Ps. 105:1-5)

This form of reciting the saving acts of God became the basis of the apostles' preaching. They added the last climactic saving act of God to the list, namely the death and resurrection of Jesus (compare Acts 7:2-53; 13:16-41).

Another remarkable, yet altogether different, confession or creed is found in Exodus 34:6-7 (author's translation):

> Yahweh, Yahweh, a God compassionate and gracious, slow of anger and great in devotion and faithfulness, maintaining devotion, forgiving iniquity and transgression and sin but by no means acquitting (the guilty), visiting the iniquity of the fathers upon the children and upon the children of the children unto the third and fourth (generation).

This passage, which we call nonhistorical, is quoted or echoed in many other places in the Old Testament (Num. 14:18; 2 Chron. 30:9; Neh. 9:17,31; Ps. 86:15; 103:8; 111:4; 112:4; Jer. 30:11b; 32:18; Joel 2:13; Jonah 4:2). G. Ernest Wright said, "The nearest the Bible comes to an abstract presentation of the nature of God by means of his 'attributes' is an old liturgical confession embedded in Exodus 34:6-7. . . . This confession is one of the very few in the Bible which is not a recital of events" (*God Who Acts,* 85).

As the Pentateuch now stands, this confession is a part of a theophany account in which Yahweh's name is proclaimed or disclosed. Undoubtedly the reference to God's graciousness (Ex. 34:6) is related to the earlier promise, "I will be gracious to whom I will be gracious" (Ex. 33:19). The reference to God visiting the iniquity of the fathers on their children (Ex. 34:7) is surely related to the threat of judgment, "When the day comes for punishment, I will punish them for their sin" (Ex. 32:34*b*).

This passage (Ex. 34) stands out from its context and from most of the theological formularies of the Old Testament by its "propositional" nature. It is not kerygmatic, but descriptive; it is not concerned with God's acts, but with His character. This passage holds in tension "God the lover and God the punisher." So we have some biblical basis for doing Old Testament theology by using modified "propositional" statements about the nature and character of God.

This nonhistorical creed concludes by saying that "God visits the iniquity of the parents upon their descendants for several generations," a statement that is omitted in all of the quotations of or later references to this passage. This last part of the passage does point out the inescapable fact that children commonly suffer from the failings of their parents, which is evidence that sin does not flourish unrequited. Whatever else this last part of the confession means, it is intended to prevent those who recited it from supposing that God's love meant that He was indifferent to wrongdoing.

Other nonhistorical "creeds" or portions of creeds in the Old Testament include the Shema (Deut. 6:4), the First Commandment, and certain doxologies (Amos 4:13; 5:8-9; 9:5-6; 1 Chron. 29:10; Zech. 12:1*b*). Judaism knows no more important devotional tradition than the reading of the Shema. The faithful recite the passage upon rising in the morning and before retiring at night, thus acknowledging God's sovereignty over themselves and the world.

We do not know how early the Shema became a part of the individual Jew's daily devotion. The Mishnah *Tamid* (4:3-5:1) indicates that four Old Testament passages were included in the reading: the Decalogue, the Shema, Deuteronomy 11:13-21, and Numbers 15:37-41. The Nash Papyrus, which was discovered in Egypt, dates from about 150 B.C. and contains the Decalogue and the Shema. This papyrus was probably a part of the contents of a *mezuzah* of a synagogue or Jewish home. A mezuzah was a metal container attached to a door or gate containing several passages of Scripture called the *Shema.* Soon after the beginning of the Christian era, the Jews dropped the reading of the Decalogue from their creed because the "heretics" argued that the Decalogue was the only part of the Torah that was still authoritative.

The Shema says that Yahweh is one—that is, He is undivided in His nature. He alone is sovereign over people and the world. In the context of Deuteronomy, Israel was an apostate people whose single focus on Yahweh was blurred by the enticements of foreign cults and idolatrous practices. The Shema may be a positive restatement of the First Commandment, yet the formulation has a "liturgical aura about it, the feel of having been shaped through long usage in the cult" (McBride, "The Yoke of the Kingdom" 296-297). Reflections of the Shema are found in 2 Kings 23:25 and Zechariah 14:9. Echoes of it may be seen in Deuteronomy 4:29; 10:12; 11:13; 13:3; 26:16; 30:2,6,10; Joshua 22:5; 23:14; 1 Kings 2:4; 8:48; 2 Kings 23:3; 2 Chronicles 15:12; Jeremiah 32:41.

The doxologies in Amos are very similar in content and structure and may serve as a clue to the method of Old Testament theology.

> For lo, the one who forms the mountains,
>   creates the wind,
>   reveals his thoughts to mortals,
>   makes the morning darkness,
>   and treads on the heights of the earth—
>   the LORD, the God of hosts, is his name!
>   (Amos 4:13)

> The one who made the Pleiades and Orion,
>   and turns deep darkness into the morning,
>   and darkens the day into night,
>   who calls for the waters of the sea,
>   and pours them out on the
>   surface of the earth,
>   the LORD is his name,

> who makes destruction flash out
>   against the strong,
> so that destruction comes upon the fortress.
>   (Amos 5:8-9)

> The Lord, GOD of hosts,
> he who touches the earth and it melts,
>   and all who live in it mourn,
>   and all of it rises like the Nile,
> and sinks again, like the Nile of Egypt;
> who builds his upper chambers in the heavens,
>   and founds his vault upon the earth;
>   who calls for the waters of the sea,
>   and pours them out upon the
>   surface of the earth—
>   the LORD is his name.
>   (Amos 9:5-6)

All of these doxologies use predicative participles and have a hymnlike refrain, "Yahweh, God of hosts, is his name." They depict the majesty and power of Yahweh. He is the Creator and sustainer of creation. He gives the rain; controls the wind, the light, and the darkness; walks on the high places; communicates His purpose to people; and judges human works.

Two other doxologies or creedal fragments are found in 1 Chronicles 29:10*b*-12 and Zechariah 12:1*b*.

> Blessed are you, O LORD, the God of our ancestor Israel, forever and ever. Yours, O LORD, are the greatness, the power, the glory, the victory, and the majesty; for all that is in the heavens and on the earth is yours; yours is the kingdom, O LORD, and you are exalted as head above all. Riches and honor come from you, and you rule over all. In your hand are power and might; and it is in your hand to make great and to give strength to all (1 Chron. 29:10-12).

This passage is the doxology in David's prayer near the end of his life before the Temple was built. Five different Hebrew words are used in verse 11 to attribute to Yahweh "glory" and "might." His sovereignty and preeminence are acknowledged by all. The expression "The Lord, who stretched out the heavens and founded the earth and formed the human spirit within" (Zech. 12:1*b*) appears to be a fragment of a hymn or a "creed." Similar ideas may be found in Isaiah 42:5; 44:24; 45:12; 51:13.

So we see tucked away, often in remote places, evidence of Israel's theological statements. These provide many theological clues, but are any of them comprehensive enough to form the framework for a presentation of Old Testament theology? Many scholars have tried to construct Old Testament theologies on these clues from the Old Testament. Walther Eichrodt wrote an Old Testament theology using the covenant as a central theme. Von Rad found his clue in the repetitions or the recitals of the great acts of God (Deut. 26:5-9; Josh. 24; 1 Sam. 12:7-8). Zimmerli's clue is the First Commandment. Martens' clue is "God's design" in Exodus 5:22—6:8. Terrien's clue is the "presence of God," and Westermann's clue is the shape of the canon (Torah, Prophets, and Writings; the saving, blessing, creating God; God's judgment and love; and the response of the people). H. H. Schmid's clue is "creation faith," and James Crenshaw's clue is "wisdom" or "theodicy."

John Goldingay said that the search for the right structure of an Old Testament theology "has been fruitless (or overfruitful!)" (*Approaches to Old Testament Interpretation,* 27). Goldingay did not think that the overfruitful search is bad. Actually, many starting points present themselves to help us understand the theology of the Old Testament. "No one solution to the problem of structuring an Old Testament theology will illuminate the whole; a multiplicity of approaches will lead to a multiplicity of insights" (*Approaches to Old Testament Interpretations,* 29).

Anyone who attempts to write an Old Testament theology should certainly be familiar with all of the various models produced in recent years. (See G. Hasel, *Old Testament Theology: Basic Issues,* 4th ed., 29-114.) Rather than using one of Hasel's ten methods (see the list cited earlier), it is probably best to consider one or more of the following six major models: the systematic model; the central theme model; the recital, diachronic, or *Heilsgeschichte* model; the key word model; the history of tradition model; and the canonical model. Perhaps some combination of all these models is necessary to deal with all of the theological materials in the Old Testament.

1. Old Testament theology began by using the *systematic model* of orthodox theology. G. L. Bauer's *Theologie des Alten Testaments* (1796) had the threefold structure of theology, anthropology, and christology. A. B. Davidson and Otto Baab followed the systematic model. Edmond Jacob's *Theology of*

the Old Testament (1955) used a modified systematic method. Dentan argued for a systematic model:

> The fact is that any method of arrangement we may adopt will be imposed from the outside. . . . Consequently we are forced to seek for some method which (1) will be simple, and (2) will present the material in a form meaningful to *us*. For this purpose it seems difficult to think of a better outline than that which is used in systematic theology, since its outline arose from an attempt to answer the basic questions concerning human life: What is the nature of God . . . ? (theology); What is the nature of man . . . ? (anthropology); What is the nature of that dynamic process by which man's weakness becomes reconciled with God's perfection? (soteriology) (*Preface to Old Testament Theology*, 119-120).

Dentan added that this simple and obvious outline in no way distorts the material on which it is imposed and has the obvious advantage of making clear the relevance of Old Testament religion to contemporary thought. The questions it attempts to answer are not always asked by a professor in a lecture hall but by all people in their existential situation.

We must modify Dentan's argument by admitting that imposing any system on the Old Testament materials runs the risk of changing the meaning of the original texts simply by altering their context. By explicating, articulating, and defining Old Testament concepts, the Old Testament theologian may not be merely describing Old Testament faith but may be creating new concepts of God and the world through the interaction of what the Old Testament says and what the theologian brings to it. An outsider faces the danger of "underplaying" such distinctive Old Testament themes as law, Israel, the land, and worship. However, a modified systematic model may be still the best one to use in doing Old Testament theology.

2. The *central theme method,* such as Eichrodt's use of the covenant, tries to highlight the central theme of the Old Testament; but it is not comprehensive enough to cover all Old Testament materials. Wisdom literature makes no use of the idea of the covenant.

3. The *recital, diachronic, or salvation-history model* has as its strengths that its clue comes directly from the Old Testament "creeds" and that it traces the history of Israel's theology

from period to period. Its weaknesses are that it consists mainly of retelling Israel's story of salvation and has no place in its system for wisdom literature.

4. The *"key word"* model supported by theological word books suffers from the problem of the unrelatedness of each key word to another and to its original context. Much can be gleaned about a theological concept by studying the etymology and use of a Hebrew or Greek word, but the "key word" method is inadequate for presenting Old Testament theology.

James Barr noted that the expectations of a theological dictionary reached an apogee of repute in the heyday of Kittel's *Theological Word Book of the New Testament,* but now those expectations are gone forever. Why? Because the method provides no straightforward or necessary alignment between the patterns of biblical vocabulary and the structure of biblical theology. (For a critique of Kittel's New Testament *Wordbook,* see James Barr, *The Semantics of Biblical Language,* 206-262).

5. The *history of tradition model* is the outgrowth of von Rad's "salvation history" method, but it puts much more emphasis on the period of the oral transmission of the texts and the supposed *Sitz im Leben* in which the traditions moved. Harmut Gese said:

> Tradition history in the narrower sense describes the preliterary, oral transmission of the text or its contents; in a broader sense, tradition history describes a text's formal and substantial presuppositions, taken from tradition. So ascertained, this formation of the text is of decisive importance. . . . The reason for this great importance is that the biblical texts grow out of *life processes* and exist in *life contexts* ("Tradition and Biblical Theology" in Knight, *Tradition and Theology,* 308).

The basic thrust of the history of traditions approach is that Israel reinterpreted and reapplied her tradition to meet the needs of each succeeding generation and its situation. There can be no question that the covenant was supposed to be renewed periodically (Deut. 31:10-13). Some evidence indicates that each generation of Israelites thought of themselves as being in Egypt, at the Red Sea, and at Sinai (Ex. 13:8; Deut. 5:3; 26:5-9).

Still, the history of tradition method is very subjective since the Old Testament itself does not explain when and how it reinterprets its traditions. The presuppositions of the scholars who use this method often determine their conclusions. Their conclusions rest more on theoretical reconstructions than on the biblical text. Old Testament theology finds its authoritative foundation in literature, not in tradition.

6. The *canonical method* has appeared in recent years with the renewal of interest in the canon as a guide to doing Old Testament and/or biblical theology. The idea of a canon lends support to the authoritativeness of the biblical materials and can be an objective guide on methodology. B. S. Childs argued that a new biblical theology should be written using both Old Testament and New Testament materials. The clue to the use of Old Testament materials would be how and when the New Testament uses them (*Biblical Theology in Crisis*, 97-122). On the other hand, John Bright said that the authority of the Old Testament or the Bible does not reside in a mechanically determined list of books called the canon but in the structure of its theology. "In establishing the canon the church did not create a new authority, but rather acknowledged and ratified an existing one" (*The Authority of the Old Testament*, 38, 156-160).

Claus Westermann has taken the threefold structure of the Old Testament canon (Law, Prophets, and Writings) as the key to his presentation of Old Testament theology. Westermann said, "The structure of the Old Testament in its three parts indicates that the narrative in the Old Testament is determined by the word of God occurring in it and by the response of those for whom and with whom this story unfolds" (*Elements of Old Testament Theology*, 10). Hartmut Gese also ties the shape of biblical theology to the shape of the canon. But because he does not believe that the Old Testament canon was ever closed in pre-Christian times, he sees not two canons (the Old Testament and New Testament canons) but one, covering the whole Bible (*Essays on Biblical Theology*, 10). For Gese there is no Old Testament theology or New Testament theology—only biblical theology.

Such an argument ignores the differences between the Old Testament faith and that of the New Testament. The understanding of God or the understanding of the identity of the people of God is essentially the same in both Testaments. However, the Old Testament is a pre-Christian book and in one sense should be studied "as if the New Testament did not exist" (Goldingay, *Approaches to Old Testament Interpretation,* 19). The Old Testament is also a Christian book because Christians received it from Jesus. It was the only Bible the early church had. All of the Hebrew Old Testament is canonical and authoritative. The question in the early Christian era seems to have been not "Is the Old Testament Christian?" but "Is the New Testament biblical?" (Goldingay, *Approaches to Old Testament Interpretation,* 34).

Should Old Testament theology be a separate discipline, apart from New Testament theology? If the aim or task of Old Testament theology is historical and descriptive, the answer is yes. If the task is perceived as a normative one, the answer will probably be no. Even though the Old Testament is an integral part of the Christian Bible and looks forward to something beyond itself, it is not to be read as if it contains the complete knowledge of God. H. H. Rowley said:

> In a real sense they [the Old Testament and New Testament] belong to one another and form a single whole; the Old Testament is not to be read as a Christian book. It is an essential part of the Christian Bible, but it is not a part in which the meaning of the whole is to be found. A doctor may take a sample of our blood and test it, and form sound conclusions about the blood that is left in our veins; but the Bible is not to be treated in that way. This unity is of a wholly different order. There is a unity in the life of an individual; yet it is impossible from the most careful study of the child to know the future course of his life. The unity of the Bible is of this latter kind. It is the unity of growth, and not a static unity, and each stage of the growth must be considered in relation to the whole, as well as in its uniqueness (*The Faith of Israel,* 14).

John Bright concurred with Rowley's view. "The entire perspective of the Old Testament is B.C. Every word of it was spoken before Christ, by and to men living before Christ and caught up in a history that was moving toward a destination the nature of which was not yet clear" (*The Authority of the Old Testament,* 206).

How, then, shall we present the theology of the Old Testament? First, we should acknowledge our presuppositions. We use the term *Old Testament theology* advisedly. By *Old Testament* we confess that this part of the Bible is an integral part of the inspired record of the revelation of God, which culminates in the full and final revelation of God in Jesus Christ. By the use of the term *theology* we understand that the contents of the Old Testament are both human and divine.

Second, we must be alert to the difficulties in doing Old Testament theology. In fact, some scholars have argued that it is an impossible task. F. F. Bruce called attention to P. Wernberg-Moller's article in the *Hibbert Journal* entitled, "Is There an Old Testament Theology?" in which a real question was raised as to the validity of that task (Bruce, *New Testament Development,* 11).

The task of doing Old Testament theology is replete with all kinds of difficulties: textual, historical, literary, hermeneutical, and theological. But the task is necessary and can be rewarding. An Old Testament theology should be biblical in content and in form as far as possible. It should be limited primarily to the Old Testament materials. It should include all of the Old Testament in its scope but concentrate on the persistent, pervasive, normative features of Israel's faith (Bright, *Authority of the Old Testament,* 115). It should use all of the modern hermeneutical tools available to a student of the Old Testament: textual, literary, form, history of tradition, and canonical criticism. The findings of archaeology may often be helpful in reconstructing the life and religion of Israel and their neighbors.

Some kind of "grid" or structure must be supplied to present the theological materials of the Old Testament in an orderly fashion. The warning against a rational systematizing of these materials is appropriate, but it cannot keep us from thinking systematically about God. Eichrodt and Barth were grand systemizers. One central theme is not broad enough to include all of the theological variety and diversity in the Old Testament.

To do a comprehensive Old Testament theology, one must give consideration to what the various Old Testament books and sources have in common, but also what they mean collectively. John Goldingay said, "In studying Old Testament theology, we are concerned not merely with the beliefs actually expressed by individual Old Testament writers . . . or with the assumptions which underlie these beliefs, or with the Old Testament faith as 'an entity given in finished form at the start and merely unfolding itself in history,' but with the total perspective" (*Theological Diversity and the Authority of the Old Testament,* 183).

For Goldingay doing Old Testament theology is a constructive task. The Old Testament provides the building blocks which were collected by Jews, who arranged them in a canon. It is not necessarily their vision of the building that is to be implemented, according to Goldingay. The building must be appropriate to the materials themselves, even though they may have been taken from different quarries and are of different shapes. The blocks must not be cut down to the same size and shape, but each block should be used to maximize its distinctiveness. Alone, each block might seem unusable. But together, as a whole, they may present a theology that does not correspond to any one writer's views but does justice to what each writer knew.

Such a task is overwhelming and almost impossible, but the task must be attempted if we are to comprehend the full reality expressed in its various aspects in unsystematic ways in the Old Testament. (See Goldingay, *Theological Diversity and the Authority of the Old Testament,* 184.)

This volume makes no attempt to present a comprehensive treatment of the whole of Old Testament theology. What follows is a *model* of how to do Old Testament theology and a discussion of some major themes that should be included. It will attempt to show that a modified systematic model is still the best one to use in doing Old Testament theology. It will provide students a foundation of methodology, reflection, and content they can use to build their own theology of the Old Testament.

Before starting to do this, the student needs to stop at this point to reflect on the six methodological options presented in this chapter. Should something be adopted from each of them or only from a few? What must be rejected? What shape would each give to a full-blown theology? Do the clues from the Bible itself give sufficient information to give form to an Old Testament theology?

The Knowledge Of God

10. Old Testament Theology Begins with Revelation

Where does one begin a study of Old Testament theology? Do we begin where the Bible begins—with God as Creator—or with God's call of Abraham and the beginning of "salvation history" (Deut. 26:5-15)? We could begin with a systematized reflection on the theological materials in the Old Testament about God or humanity. Systematic theologians often begin with "revelation." It may not even be correct to speak about Israel's "view" of revelation because the Israelites did not even have a word for revelation, much less a systematic treatment of the subject.

In selecting revelation as the necessary starting point for theology, we follow a modern emphasis. As James Barr said, an affirmation of revelation is absolutely necessary for the Christian faith; otherwise, it "would be a series of ideas we have thought up for ourselves" (*Old and New in Interpretation,* 83). Karl Barth, Emil Brunner, Paul Tillich, D. M. Baillie, Wheeler Robinson, Rudolph Bultmann, and Wolfhart Pannenberg all emphasized revelation. (Note that otherwise their theological positions were quite different. Emphasis on revelation does not lead to theological unity or agreement.)

Why do we moderns place so much emphasis on revelation if our source of revelation does not seem to do so? James Barr said that in modern theology, the idea of revelation works against two particular problems that did not exist or were unimportant in the ancient world. The first problem is the denial that God exists or that any true knowledge of Him exists. The second is that of demarcating the knowledge God has given of Himself from the methods and contents of human sciences as they work apart from this revelation. "In the Bible, apart from some quite limited concessions, there is no stage at which God is not known. . . . The problems in relation to which revelation functions do not appear to exist in the Bible, or are not central in it. In Israel God is known" (Barr, *Old and New in Interpretation,* 89).

Not all modern theologians begin with revelation. James Crenshaw would not begin a study of Old Testament theology with revelation. He believes that one should begin with humanity. Crenshaw elevates anthropology or sociology to at least an equal position with theology in Old Testament understanding (*Studies in Ancient Israelite Wisdom,* 291). He maintains that the question of meaning is more basic than that of God. The biblical point of departure was not God but self. The God question is secondary to self-understanding, according to Crenshaw.

"This suggests that Old Testament theology should begin with man rather than God as is common in the works adopting the systematic principle" (*Studies in Ancient Israelite Wisdom,* 291). One wonders if Crenshaw's intense study of wisdom literature had led to this conclusion.

Two other contemporary authors who start with humanity rather than God in their study of the Old Testament are Norman Gottwald, *The Tribes of Yahweh,* and Peter L. Berger, *A Rumor of Angels.* Gottwald started with a sociological approach and explained the religious ideology of the Old Testament in terms of a cultural-materialistic mutant. There is no place for the theme of revelation in Gottwald's work. The term does not appear in the index of his book. Brevard Childs said that "Gottwald's position results in a massive theological reductionism" (*Old Testament Theology,* 25). Gottwald's devotion to sociological methodology steers him away from revelation.

Peter Berger in *A Rumor of Angels* looked for a way of starting with humans in doing theology without glorying in humanity as secular "theology" does. Berger saw "signals of transcendence" in some human behavior. People's attitudes presuppose an underlying order in the universe. A curse or tragedy of supernatural dimensions may be due to grossly outrageous behavior. Even atheists may sometimes feel grateful for life and the world, though they may say they have no one to thank for such blessings. The point is that they presuppose a belief in the transcendent. (See John Goldingay, *Theological Diversity,* 211, for a critique of Berger's view.)

G. Ernest Wright took a strong stance for beginning a study of Old Testament theology with God, not humanity. Wright said:

> Since for both Jews and Christians the Bible is believed by faith to be revelation from him who otherwise in the world would have been the unknown God, I am not entitled to begin the discussion with the existential question, "What does the Old Testament mean for me? What basic possibility does it present for new existence now?" I am called upon instead to transcend myself and my existence, in so far as I can, to labor for comprehension of a new reality external to myself. It is not mine to command; it is instead itself, separated from me and from my community as regards it [sic] original setting and time (*Reflections,* 380).

Gerhard von Rad said that one does not stumble onto the transcendent. Human understanding of God or of humanity does not start from self and then ask from that starting point about contact with God. It begins with God and affirms that a person can only be understood at all if one begins with God. Every other way to understand humanity can lead only to distortions or diminutions.

Humanity finds its origin in God's heart. At creation God took the model for humans from the upper divine world, something He did not do for His other creative works. "Man is thus a creature who can be understood only from above and who, having severed his relationship with God, can regain and maintain his humanity only by hearkening to the divine word" (*God At Work in Israel,* 91-92).

Hans W. Wolff asked how the Old Testament person is initiated into knowledge of self. A reliable doctrine of humanity is an imperative in Old Testament theology; however, human self-understanding does not begin with earthly people but with the

Creator God. Wolff said, "Just as it is impossible for a man to confront himself and see himself from all sides . . . just so certainly does man fundamentally need the meeting with another, who investigates and explains him. But where is the other to whom the being man can put the question: Who am I?" Wolff's answer was that the Other has already shown Himself through His bond with man in word and deed recorded in the Old Testament (*Anthropology of the Old Testament,* 1-2).

One should begin a study of Old Testament theology with God and not humanity. But how do I do that? B. S. Childs raised this question at the beginning of his *Old Testament Theology* (p. 28). For him the canonical context made a difference. To speak of the Old Testament as canon means that it is Scripture and authoritative. The Old Testament bears witness that God revealed Himself to Abraham, and we confess that He has broken into our lives.

"I do not come to the Old Testament to be informed about some strange religious phenomenon, but in faith I strive for knowledge as I seek to understand ourselves in the light of God's self-disclosure. In the context of the church's scripture I seek to be pointed to our God who has made himself known, is making himself known, and will make himself known" (Childs, *Old Testament Theology,* 28). Childs also said that the term *revelation* is only "a shorthand formula pointing to the whole enterprise of theological reflection on the reality of God" (*Old Testament Theology,* 25-26).

One may deny an absolute starting point for doing Old Testament theology. John Goldingay said, "Many starting points, structures, and foci can illuminate the landscape of the Old Testament; a multiplicity of approaches will lead to a multiplicity of insights" (*Theological Diversity and Authority,* 115). Still, we will begin with revelation because we do not discover God, God finds us. In fact, God knows all about us (Ps. 139:1-18).

11. The Existence of God Is Assumed in the Old Testament

Ancient Israel did not argue for or attempt to prove the existence of God; they simply assumed that God is and that He reveals Himself to humans. God is assumed in the Old

Testament. A. B. Davidson asserted that it never occurred to any prophet or writer of the Old Testament to prove the existence of God. "To do so might well have seemed an absurdity" (*Old Testament Theology,* 30).

Edmond Jacob said that the affirmation of the sovereignty of God gives the Old Testament its force and unity. God is the basis of all things, and all that exists only exists by His will. Moreover, the existence of God is never questioned. The knowledge of God in the sense of divine reality is to be found everywhere. The entire world knows God. Nature has been created to proclaim His power (Ps. 148:9-13). Even sin proclaims the existence of God by contrast. "The fact of God is so normal that we have no trace of speculation in the Old Testament about the origin or the evolution of God. Whilst neighboring religions present a theogony as the first step in the organization of chaos, the God of the Old Testament is there from the beginning" (Jacob, *Theology of the Old Testament,* 37-38).

G. Ernest Wright noted that "the proposition which is Israel's great gift to humanity is simply this: *God is.* His existence for the Israelite writer is completely self-evident, always presupposed, and never placed in question" (*The Challenge of Israel's Faith,* 55). The biblical doctrine of God is not the achievement of the philosopher, arguing back to a first cause, or the personification of nature. The biblical doctrine rests on the belief that "the God who is veiled from our sight has revealed himself to man" (Rowley, *The Faith of Israel,* 23).

Agnosticism in the modern sense has no place in Hebrew thought. R. E. Clements believes that the "idea of God . . . remains an indispensable presupposition" in all Old Testament writings. Ideas of creation, natural order, social order, time, and the spatial realm are all established in relation to a belief in God. The notion of a "secular" society simply did not arise. Ancient Israel's cosmology was fundamentally religious in its character so that the fundamental institutes of society—kingship, law, culture, and education—were all founded on religious assumptions (R. E. Clements, "Israel In Its Historical and Cultural Setting," in *The World of Ancient Israel,* 9).

12. To Know God Means More
Than Intellectual Knowledge

The Old Testament not only assumes that God can be known. It also states clearly that God has made Himself known.

> He made known his ways to Moses,
>   his acts to the people of Israel.
>   (Ps. 103:7)

> I appeared to Abraham, Isaac, and Jacob as God Almighty,
>   but by my name 'The LORD' I did not
>   make myself known to them.
>   (Ex. 6:3)

> And he said, 'Hear my words:
> When there are prophets among you,
>   I the LORD make myself known
>   to them in visions;
>   I speak to them in dreams.
> Not so with my servant Moses;
> he is entrusted with all my house.
> With him I speak face to face—
>   clearly, not in riddles;
> and he beholds the form of the LORD.
>   (Num. 12:6-8)

> On the day when I chose Israel,
> I swore to the offspring of the house of Jacob—
> making myself known to them in the land of Egypt.
>   (Ezek. 20:5)

A. The Vocabulary of Revelation

These passages use the passive or reflexive forms of the verbs *yādaʿ* "know," *rāʾâ* "see," and the intensive form of the verb *dābar* "speak." All of these verbs are cognitive words. Hebrew does not have a noun for "revelation." It does have the verb *gālâ* "to reveal." The root occurs about 180 times in the Old Testament. It contains two basic concepts: "to uncover," "to reveal"; and "to emigrate," "to go away (into exile)." It is not easy to understand how the same root can mean "reveal," "uncover," and "go into exile" unless the thought was, "with the people's going into exile the land was uncovered." (Compare Hans-Jürgen Zobel, *galah* in *TDOT,* 478.)

The word *gālâ* is used predominantly in the Old Testament in the everyday sense, "to go away," "to be open" (Jer. 32:11,14).

In some instances it refers to the revelation of Yahweh Himself. It is used in Genesis 35:7 to refer to the time God appeared to Jacob at Bethel when he was fleeing from Esau. "And there he built an altar and called the place El-bethel, because it was there that God had revealed himself [niphal perf.] to him when he fled from his brother."

The niphal participial form of *gālâ* is used in Deuteronomy 29:29 (Heb. v. 28) to refer to the Torah as "the revealed things": "The secret things belong to the LORD our God, but the revealed things belong to us and to our children forever, to observe all the words of this law." This verse indicates that some things were revealed which they were responsible for doing and some things were secret (not revealed). They had no knowledge of them. They were not responsible for things that had not been revealed. Verses 21-27 of Deuteronomy 29 refer to a time when Israel would break the covenant by worshiping other gods and would be taken into exile. They had been warned that this would happen if they did not obey the revealed words of the law.

Peter Craigie said that it would be presumptuous for people to assume that revelation gives them total knowledge of God. "It may never be possible to *know* all things, the *secret things,* for man's mind is bound by the limits of his finitude . . . and it is possible to know God in a profound and living way, through his grace, without ever having grasped or understood the *secret things*" (*The Book of Deuteronomy,* 361).

The word *gālâ* is used to refer to a time when Samuel did not know the Lord. "Now Samuel did not yet know the LORD, and the word of the LORD had not yet been revealed [niphal imperf.] to him" (1 Sam. 3:7).

gālâ is used in 2 Samuel 7:27 when David claimed that the Lord of Hosts "uncovered his ear" and revealed to him that God would build him a house—that is, a dynasty. Isaiah claimed that God had "uncovered himself" or "revealed himself" in Isaiah's ear that the sin the prophet had identified would not be forgiven (Isa. 22:14). The term *gālâ* is used to speak of revealing Yahweh's word (1 Sam. 2:27), His glory (Isa. 40:5), His arm (Isa. 53:1), His salvation (Isa. 56:1), secret things (Deut. 29:29; Amos 3:7), and mystery (Dan. 2:19,22,28,29,30,47). The people in the Old Testament believed God had revealed Himself many times, but in ways, places, and times that He chose.

B. The Meaning of Revelation

The Old Testament speaks often about "knowing" (yd^c) or "not knowing" Yahweh (compare Isa. 1:3; Jer. 2:8; 4:22; 31:34; Hos. 2:20; 4:1,6; 5:3-4; 6:6; 13:4). Knowledge in the Old Testament is quite different from our understanding of that term. For us, knowledge implies grasping things by reason, analyzing, and seeing the relationships of cause and effect. In the Old Testament, knowledge means "communion," "an intimate acquaintance with someone or something."

Speaking for God to Israel, Amos said:

> You only have I known
> of all the families of the earth;
> therefore I will punish you
> for all your iniquities.
> (Amos 3:2)

Vriezen said that the Old Testament makes "knowing God" the first demand of life, but it never explains what it means by the term. The purpose of God's revelation is not specifically stated in the Old Testament. Revelation is not grounded in some need of God. God did not create the world or reveal Himself in order to have someone observe the Sabbath, as some earlier rabbis said. The knowledge of God is more than a mere intellectual knowledge; it concerns the whole of human life.

> It is essentially a communion with God, and it is also faith; it is a knowledge of the heart demanding man's love (Deut. vi); its vital demand is that man should act in accordance with God's will and walk humbly in the ways of the Lord (Micah vi. 8). It is the recognition of God as God, the total surrender to God as Lord (*Outline of Old Testament Theology,* 154).

Gerhard von Rad suggested that "the knowledge of God" means "commitment to," "confidence in," "obedience to the divine will." Effective knowledge about God is the only thing that puts a person in a right relationship with the objects of his perception. "Faith does not—as is popularly believed today—hinder knowledge; on the contrary, it liberates knowledge" (*Wisdom in Israel,* 67-68).

Thus "to know Yahweh" is to be obedient to Him, to have a commitment to Him. "Not to know God" meant "to rebel against Him," "to deny one's commitment to Him." In Hosea the meaning of the term "knowledge of God" was extended to include the morality of the individual Israelite. The knowledge of God can be identified with the practice of traditional Hebrew morality, moral integrity (Hos. 4:1-2).

The Hebrew expression "the knowledge of God" thus carries at least three connotations: (1) the intellectual sense, (2) the emotional sense, and (3) the volitional sense. The verb "to know" *yādaᶜ* refers basically to what we call intellectual, cognitive activity; but Hebrew psychology knew no special faculty for the intellect or reason.

The Hebrew has no word for "brain." The word most commonly used for "mind" in Hebrew is "heart" *lēb* (1 Sam. 9:20; Isa. 46:8). The heart is regarded as the seat of the intellect, as well as the seat of the will and the emotions. The ancient Hebrew did not suppose that people thought with their minds, felt with their emotions, and made decisions with their wills. All these activities were carried on by the whole person. (See chapter 6, pp. 268-271, for a fuller discussion of "heart.")

"To know God" meant to have an intellectual understanding of who He was, to be related to Him personally and emotionally, and to be obedient to His covenant and commandments. A true knowledge of God always issued in ethical behavior. Jeremiah said to the wicked king Jehoiakim concerning his righteous father Josiah,

> Did not your father eat and drink
> and do justice and righteousness?
> Then it was well with him.
> He judged the cause of the poor and needy;
> then it was well.
> Is not this to know me?
> says the LORD.
> (Jer. 22:15-16)

"Not to know God" in the Old Testament does not necessarily mean ignorance about God; sometimes it means an unwillingness to obey him.

C. The Inflation of Revelation

Karl Barth and some other modern theologians inflated the role of revelation in theology by denying any knowledge of God to people apart from special revelation. Carl Braaten challenged Barth's view of making revelation the dominant idea in theology. Braaten said, "If the ignorance of man stands in the center, the fact of revelation relieves that plight; but if man's *guilt* is the problem then not revelation but reconciliation must become the theological centrum" (*History and Hermeneutics,* 14). Barth denied all other means of revelation except that of Jesus Christ because of his conviction that Christ is unique and stands alone. Braaten believed in the uniqueness of Christ but said:

> By distinguishing revelation and reconciliation, however, it is possible to maintain both the duality of revelation and the uniqueness of Christ. Jesus is the sole Savior, not the sole revealer. The idea of revelation suggests that something is disclosed that was previously hidden. The Christ event is not a disclosure of something that has always been but that has hitherto remained hidden and shrouded in mystery. That is a completely Platonic view of revelation. Rather something new *happens* in Christ, the act of reconciliation. Reconciliation is not merely revealed, as if it were there but only hidden; it is acted out in history, a unique event, something absolutely new under the sun. . . . The act of reconciliation brings about an objectively new situation, not just for the believer but for the cosmos. The *world* was reconciled to God in Christ (*History and Hermeneutics,* 15).

To "know the Lord" means to be "reconciled" to Him. He does that for us through the death and life of His Son for us (see Rom. 5:10-11; 2 Cor. 5:15-21).

13. The Hiddenness of God

Although the Old Testament knows that in one sense the whole world is aware of the divine or "the holy," it often speaks of the hiddenness of God. Job believed in God, but he could not find Him.

> Look, he passes by me, and I do not see him;
> he moves on, but I do not perceive him.
> He snatches away; who can stop him?
> Who will say to him, 'What are you doing?'
> (Job 9:11-12)

The prophet of the exile said:

> Truly, you are a God who hides himself,
> O God of Israel, the Savior.
> (Isa. 45:15)

On the flyleaf of his *The Elusive Presence,* Samuel Terrien quoted Blaise Pascal, "A religion which does not affirm that God is hidden is not true." (Compare Blaise Pascal, *Pensees,* no. 584.) Pascal continued his saying about the hiddenness of God: "A religion which does not offer a reason (for this hiddenness) is not illuminating (Terrien, *The Elusive Presence,* 474). Terrien suggested that it was because Jesus would be in agony until the end of the world that Pascal could appropriate with assurance the words of the prophet, *Vere tu es Deus Absconditus* (Isa. 45:15).

The truth is that God is never totally visible or completely known in the Old Testament. If God were completely known, He would be limited by or to human capacity to comprehend and would not be God at all. Only a handful of ancestors, prophets, and poets actually perceived the immediacy of God; and, then, God's disclosure was mediated.

B. W. Anderson said, "The presupposition of Revelation is that God is hidden from man's sight. Revelation, therefore, is God's unveiling or uncovering of himself and his purposes" ("The Old Testament View of God," 419). The Old Testament speaks often of the "hiddenness" of God. Twenty-six times we are told that God hides His face (Deut. 31:17,18; 32:20; Job 13:24; 34:29; Pss. 10:11; 13:1; 22:24; 27:9; 30:7; 44:24; 51:19; 69:17; 88:14; 102:2; 104:29; 143:7; Isa. 8:17; 54:8; 59:2; 64:5; Jer. 33:5; Ezek. 39:23,24,29; Mic. 3:4). God hides His eyes (Isa. 1:15) and His ears (Lam. 3:56). God hides Himself (Ps. 10:1; 55:1; 89:46; Isa. 45:15). (For a discussion of the Hebrew words for "hide," see the works of Samuel E. Ballentine listed in the Bibliography.)

What does the Old Testament mean when it speaks of Yahweh hiding Himself? Vriezen said that it is God's Being that remains hidden. "The knowledge of God does not imply a theory about His nature, it is not ontological, but existential . . . knowledge of God and communion with Him are possible, but the secret of God's Being is never encroached upon" (*An Outline of Old Testament Theology,* 155).

This may be true, but when the Old Testament speaks of God hiding Himself, it refers primarily to His inactivity on behalf of His worshipers and to the fact that God seems to give no response to their prayers. Many of the expressions concerning God's hiding His face are in the laments (in Psalms and Lamentations). Psalm 44 is an example of a community lamenting because God is hidden. Israel had been defeated, and God did not rescue them as He had at other times. Therefore the psalmist asks:

> Why do you hide your face?
> Why do you forget our
> affliction and oppression?
> (Ps. 44:24)

Why did God seem to act differently on some occasions than He did at other times? That was a mystery. The speakers in Psalm 44 claimed that God had not helped them as He had helped their fathers, even though they had not sinned (Ps. 44:9-22). Ecclesiastes says that people cannot find the reason God does what He does (Eccl. 8:17).

Many of the psalms speak of "waiting for God" (25:3; 37:9; 40:17; 62:1; Isa. 8:17) and of God being far away (10:1; 22:1,11,19). They claim that God has forgotten (13:1). The psalmists believed that God was consistent in His purpose and true to His word. In the complexities and ambiguities of historical existence, however, God's purpose can be seen only dimly.

The psalms of lament lead us to the deepest dimension of the witness of the Bible: faith's acknowledgment that the God who reveals Himself in history often remains hidden. He is not the prisoner of human thoughts or the captive of their schemes. Nor is His purpose easily discernible in the unfolding dramas of human history. God permitted the Philistines to capture the ark of the covenant, which produced consternation on the part of Israel and the Philistines (1 Sam. 4:18-19; 6:9).

Vriezen agreed that God's purpose cannot always be seen even in the history of salvation. He said that if we compare this history with a line, only certain points of it are visible. No one can copy the line itself because it is God's secret and because He Himself remains a miraculous and essentially hidden God (*Outline of Old Testament Theology,* 152).

The prophets never presumed to know precisely what God was going to do. God is free to do what He wills. His purposes, plans, and ways are often hidden. The prophets refrained from saying exactly what God would or would not do.

> For my thoughts are not your thoughts,
> nor are your ways my ways, says the LORD.
> For as the heavens are higher than the earth,
> so are my ways higher than your ways
> and my thoughts than your thoughts.
> (Isa. 55:8-9)

> Hate evil and love good,
> and establish justice in the gate;
> it may be that the LORD, the God of hosts,
> will be gracious to the remnant of Joseph.
> (Amos 5:15)

> Seek the LORD, all you humble of the land,
> who do his commands;
> seek righteousness, seek humility;
> perhaps you may be hidden
> on the day of the LORD's wrath.
> (Zeph. 2:3)

The king of Nineveh said, "Let man and beasts cry mightily to God; yea, let every one turn from his evil way and from the violence which is in his hands. Who knows, God may yet repent and turn from his fierce anger, so that we perish not" (Jonah 3:8-9, author's translation).

The repentance of God in the Old Testament is anchored in the concept of His freedom.

> The pagan gods of the nations surrounding Israel lacked this freedom. Once they had spoken or issued a decree, they were powerless to alter this in any way. It was different with Israel's God. He always remained Lord of his own purposes. He kept open the option of changing his decrees whenever the situation warranted such a change (Kelley, "The Repentance of God," 13).

This changing of God's stated course of action frustrated Jonah but revealed God's grace. The Hebrews believed God could "repent" of His stated purpose if human attitudes and actions changed, but He was also free not to repent. Kelley said, "The repentance of God saves us from both despair and presumption" ("The Repentance of God," 13). The repentance of God is consistent with His hiddenness. So not only is the

Being of God hidden in the Old Testament; His purposes and ways are only partially known.

> These are indeed but the outskirts
> of his ways;
> and how small a whisper do we
> hear of him!
> But the thunder of his power
> who can understand?
> (Job 26:14)

14. Means of Revelation

How does God reveal Himself in the Old Testament? The ways are many and varied. John Goldingay noted the wide range of means by which Yahweh revealed Himself to Israel:

> She experienced his presence and activity and heard his voice in the story of her past as a nation and she expected to experience it in her future. Thus she was aware of living in history. But she also experienced it in her present, in nature, in personal experience, in worship, in the theophany, in the hearing and uttering of the prophetic word, in her moral awareness, in the law, in her institutions and ordinances (*Approaches to Old Testament Interpretation,* 69).

A. Theophanies and Epiphanies

In a model of Old Testament theology we can only touch on some of the ways God makes Himself known. One of the ways God reveals Himself in the Old Testament is through His appearances (theophanies/epiphanies). Adam and Eve heard the sound of the Lord God walking in the garden in the cool of the day (Gen. 3:8). The Lord appeared to the patriarchs Abraham, Isaac, and Jacob (Gen. 15:1-21; 17:1-21; 18:33; 26:2-5,24; 28:12-16; 32:24-32).

Some scholars refer to all appearances of God in the Old Testament as theophanies. Others distinguish between theophanies and epiphanies. Terrien referred to God's appearances to the patriarchs as "epiphanic visitations" because they usually lack the accompaniment of the outburst of nature such as earthquake, fire, cloud, wind, thunder, and/or smoke which other notable theophanies have. The most notable theophanies in the Old Testament are the burning bush (Ex. 3), the shaking of Sinai (Ex. 19-24), the calls of Isaiah (Isa. 6) and

Ezekiel (Ezek. 1), and the whirlwind (Job 38) (*The Elusive Presence,* 63-66).

Claus Westermann isolated a number of passages which he called epiphanies (Deut. 33; Judg. 5:4-5; Pss. 18:7-15; 29; 50:1-3; 68:7-8,33; 77:16-19; 97:2-5; 114; Isa. 30:27-33; 59:15b-20; 63:1-6; Mic. 1:3-4; Nah. 1:3b-6; Hab. 3:3-15; Zech. 9:14). According to Westermann, epiphanies refer only to God's appearances to help, rescue, or save His people. A theophany is an appearance of God for the purpose of conveying a message—call of a prophet, making a covenant, or giving a promise (*Elements of Old Testament Theology,* 25-26, 57-61).

Closely related to the theophanies and/or epiphanies are the accounts of God appearing to people in visions and dreams, in the angel of the Lord, in His face, His name, or His glory. Kuntz said that deity's appearance has no consistent *form.* The theophanic description may mention some of the divinely appointed instruments through which the deity might be represented. Biblical theologians usually identify four: the *kābôd* (glory), *maPāk* (messenger or angel), *pānîm* (face), and *šem* (name). These vehicles, technically known as *theologoumena,* are the "representations" of the deity in His real yet never fully revealed nature (Kuntz, *The Self-Revelation of God,* 37).

B. History

For centuries Christian theologians spoke of revelation in terms of "the word of God." Most systematic theologians have spoken of revelation as propositional, but in 1952 G. Ernest Wright attempted to recover the biblical view of revelation from the dogmatic theologians. In *God Who Acts* he said, "The purpose of this monograph is to describe the special and characteristic nature of the biblical presentation of faith and to defend the use of the word 'theology' for it" (*God Who Acts,* 11). Wright claimed that, for most people, revelation has been propositional, stated as abstractly and universally as possible, and arranged in accordance with a preconceived and coherent system. Obviously, the Bible contains nothing of the sort. Christian theology has tended to think of the Bible chiefly as "the Word of God," though in fact a more accurate title would be "the Acts of God." "The Word is certainly present in the Scripture, but it is rarely, if ever, dissociated from the Act;

instead it is the accompaniment of the Act" (*God Who Acts,* 12). Wright defined biblical theology as "the confessional recital of the redemptive acts of God in a particular history because history is the chief medium of revelation" (*God Who Acts,* 13).

Wright probably overreacted against the propositional form of systematic theology, but his was a sincere effort to allow the Old Testament to speak in its own terms. Wright was influenced at this point by von Rad's treatment of the Old Testament "creeds" which recited the great acts of God (Deut. 26:5-12).

The idea that revelation is historical is closely associated with the ideas of the salvation history school, which can be traced back to the mid-nineteenth-century "Erlangen school" of J. C. K. von Hofmann. "Revelation is historical" was also one of the five key ideas in the biblical theology movement in America, according to B. S. Childs (*Biblical Theology in Crisis,* 39-44).

We can conclude, then, that revelation in the Old Testament is primarily historical. It is historical in the sense that:

(1) God revealed Himself in events and in the milieu of Old Testament history.

(2) The revelatory events, experiences, and encounters occurred over a long span of time.

(3) The knowledge of God in the Old Testament must be a mediated knowledge, because God is presented in the Old Testament as a consuming fire. No one can see God and live (Ex. 33:20).

God exists on one level, and humans on a lower level. Job acknowledged this gulf between God and humanity and asked for an umpire to bridge it (Job 9:33). One way to bridge the gulf between God and persons is to mediate revelation through historical means. Kierkegaard saw the idea that biblical revelation is historical as a paradox, for revelation is a vision of the eternal, the unchanging, the divine, but history is human, mediate, time-bound. Kierkegaard spoke of biblical revelation in these terms: "Who grasps this contradiction of sorrows? Not to reveal oneself is the death of love; to reveal oneself is the death of the beloved" (see Frank M. Cross, "Creation and History").

Frank M. Cross paraphrased Kierkegaard's parable illustrating the nature of revelation.

> There was a great king who loved a humble, rustic maiden. At first it seemed simple to the great king to go to his beloved's cottage and declare his love for the maiden. But the great king was wise and knew that he could not win the maiden's love by his declaration of his love for she would be overwhelmed. His glory would strike her down, and she could do nothing other than to marry the great king. Then the king thought that he would make her a princess, that is he would exalt her to his equal. But again the king knew that in exalting her he would change her so that she would no longer be the humble maiden he loved. Therefore he decided that if he were to woo and win her as she was he must give up his power and glory as king and become a shepherd. He could only win her by coming down to her level. That is what God did in revealing himself in history and in the incarnation (Cross, "Creation and History").

In recent years the concept of revelation as history has come under increasing attack. James Barr predicted that the time will come when the concept will be neither clear nor useful. The concept does have problems; it has been too one-sided and too ambiguous.

It has been one-sided in the sense that it does not allow for revelation through nature, wisdom, or word. It has been ambiguous in the sense that the term *history* can be and has been used in many different ways.

The concept *can* continue to function as a viable and meaningful theological concept and as an essential ingredient of any biblical theology. The concept of revelation through history is not simply a passing theological fad or aberration; it belongs to "the core of biblical religion" (Lemke, *Interpretation* 36 [1982]). Goldingay said, "It is not 'time to say goodbye to *Heilsgeschichte*,' but the critique has certainly indicated points at which the idea needs clarifying and seeing in perspective" (*Approaches to Old Testament Interpretation,* 67).

Greek philosophers speculated about being, essence, and eternity. They identified reality in terms of static "being." The Scriptures of Judaism and Christianity were the product of history and are essentially concerned with God and humans in history. Scripture is not concerned with so-called secular history but with history as a revelation of God.

C. Words

If revelation is primarily historical in the Old Testament, how do God's words (speeches) relate to His acts in history? In the Old Testament words have a prominent place as God's means of communicating with His people. Edmond Jacob said the fact that God reveals Himself by His word is a truth confirmed by every book in the Old Testament (*Old Testament Theology*, 127). The phrase most commonly used in this regard is "the word of the LORD came to . . ."(Gen. 15:1; 2 Sam. 7:4; 1 Kings 6:11; 17:2 and in most of the Prophets). The primary Hebrew term for "word" is *dābār*. The verbal form, according to Jacob, can mean "to be behind and to push." A word, then, is the projection forward of that which lies behind—that is, the transition into act of that which is in the heart (Jacob, 128). (For a modification of this definition of *dābār* "word," see James Barr, *The Semantics of Biblical Language*, 129-140.)

A *word* in the Old Testament is dynamic, powerful, a force that "happens" or overtakes one. It is a destroying fire (Jer. 5:14); it lasts forever (Isa. 40:8). The Ten Commandments are called the "ten words" (Ex. 20:1; 24:3,4,8; 34:1,27,28). These "words" constitute a revelation of God; in them Yahweh affirms that He is Lord. They take on the authority of God Himself so that no true prophet ever dreamed of questioning their authority.

True prophets also spoke the word of God, but the difference between the prophetic word and the ten words was that the ten words "have a lasting value for all generations, whilst the word of the prophet . . . has no bearing after its fulfillment" (Jacob, 130).

Claus Westermann distinguished three kinds of words in the Old Testament: (1) announcement or proclamation—either of salvation or judgment; (2) instruction or directive—either law or commandment; and (3) the cultic word in worship—either blessing or curse. The announcement is usually thought of as the word of the prophet, but priests and Levites could also proclaim the word of God in the pronouncement of a blessing or a curse. Haggai asked his people to go to the priests to ask about holiness and uncleanness (Hag. 2:11-14).

The three kinds of words are interrelated. When one function of the word is overemphasized to the neglect of the others, misunderstandings may arise. For example, Christians have often emphasized the promise function of prophecy to the exclusion of the law or instruction. In this case the Old Testament becomes a book whose chief value is the prediction of the coming of Christ. Jews, on the other hand, have made the law the most important aspect of the Old Testament.

Westermann said that no one of these functions of the word of God in the Old Testament can be absolutized apart from the others. Every one-sided view of the word of God in the Old Testament can be countered by the fact that only together can the three functions of the word (announcement, instruction, and cultic) express what the word of God is in the Old Testament (*Elements of Old Testament Theology,* 24).

In speaking about the word of God in the Old Testament, we need to remember that the Old Testament often asserts that God "speaks" to mankind, but it does not explain how He speaks. When we read that God spoke to Abraham, Moses, or one of the prophets, we should not assume that He spoke in an audible voice. The word *speak* can simply mean "to communicate," "to reveal," or "to manifest" oneself in various ways. The Hebrew word "voice" *qôl]* can also mean "thunder" (Gen. 3:8; 1 Sam. 12:17; Ps. 29:3,4,5,7,8,9).

Did God speak audibly in the Old Testament? Both the Old and New Testaments speak about certain people hearing a voice from heaven. When the people of Israel came to Sinai, the mountain was wrapped in cloud and smoke because Yahweh had descended upon it in fire. Moses spoke to Yahweh, and God answered him in thunder (Ex. 19:18-19). Then God spoke the ten words to all the people. They were so afraid when they heard His voice that they asked if in the future Moses might be the mediator between themselves and God, so that they would not have to hear His voice again (Ex. 20:18-19).

Later the writer of Deuteronomy said of this event, "Then the LORD spoke to you out of the fire. You heard the sound [*qol*] of words but saw no form; there was only a voice" [*qôl*]" (Deut. 4:12). A reference to an audible voice may appear in Numbers 7:89: "When Moses went into the tent of meeting to speak with the LORD, he would hear the voice speaking to him from above the mercy seat that was on the ark of the covenant from between the two cherubim; thus it spoke to him." This language may mean that Moses received his revelation of God from the very dwelling place of God on earth.

Wheeler Robinson said that in the Law and the Prophets, the revelation is usually described as "spoken" by God to people.

> This externalization of the process was inevitable, with the given psychological limitations, in order to express the authority of the revelation. But the historic form of the event, the actual way in which it came about, must have been much more intimate than an actual voice in order to secure the necessary nucleus of conviction. Even if an external voice was sometimes "heard" by the prophet (as is quite possible), this would not dispense us from psychological analysis of the constituent experience (*Inspiration and Revelation*, 274).

D. Relationship of Words and History

Is revelation to be found in events or in words? We should let word and event interact and not subsume one to the other. There needs to be a matching of theological concept with historical fact. "Facts without words (interpretation) are blind; words without facts are empty" (Goldingay, *Approaches to Old Testament Interpretation,* 77). If interpretation (words) is involved, can we speak of the "history" in the Old Testament as "facts"? It must be admitted that the facts in the Old Testament are interpreted. They are writers' descriptions of what happened between God, people, and the world. Nineteenth-century historians considered only that which could be documented and verified by scientific methods as "history." They ruled out any acts of God as an integral part of history. (See B. Stade, *Geschichte des Volkes Israel I,* [1887]; compare E. W. Nicholson, *God and His People,* 7-8.)

In the Old Testament that which moves history takes place between God and people. The question remains: Did history in the Old Testament happen, or is the Old Testament story of the acts of God merely human inferences or deductions from certain events? Do we have interpretation, not history?

R. J. Blaike has called for "those who no longer believe that God is a living, personal agent to stop using the terms *acts of God, God in action,* and the like, when referring to something other than purposeful and deliberate acts of such a God" (*Secular Christianity and God Who Acts,* cited by Lemke, "Revelation Through History," 41).

Lemke argued that unless we are able and willing to affirm the activity of a divine agent at work in the minds of Israel's leaders or helping deliver Israel from Egypt through natural or extraordinary means, "all talk about acts of God or revelation through history is meaningless and misleading and basic honesty should compel us to refrain from doing so" ("Revelation Through History," 41).

Scholars continue to debate the difference between the Old Testament's story of Israel's history and the reconstruction of that history by modern critical scholars. Gerhard von Rad argued that a vast difference exists between what the Old Testament says happened and what modern scientific historians say happened. Again, we need to remember that Old Testament writers and modern historians have very different presuppositions. Even with that difference, a recognized Old Testament scholar can say, "Today we have no good reason to doubt that there is a significant measure of congruence between the actual events of Israel's history as critically reconstructed and the way they were remembered in her sacred traditions" (Lemke, 45-46).

E. History and Faith

In the final analysis, whether Old Testament salvation history happened is a matter of faith. While faith is impossible if it has no historical grounds, the historian cannot prove or disprove the historicity of the early acts of God in Israel's history. So on the bases of personal experiences with God and the message of the Bible, we can say, "I may maintain the conviction that salvation history happened" (Goldingay, *Approaches to Old Testament Interpretation,* 74). Still, faith-convictions cannot make historical investigation irrelevant. If Old Testament writers were seeking to write pure "history" and failed, "it is difficult to take their work seriously. But if they were telling a story with a message, it is their story we have to interpret" (Goldingay, *Approaches to Old Testament Interpretation,* 74).

We believe that biblical history is true to God's purpose of showing us who He is by what He has done and showing us how to respond to Him. George L. Kelm recently published his understanding of the biblical account of Israel's exodus from Egypt and their conquest of Canaan. Kelm rejected the "simplistic understanding of the biblical text that seems to disregard completely the possibility of a far more complex historical event than a casual reading would suggest." He also rejected the historical-critical method that subjects the biblical text to rigorous internal analysis to determine the historical reliability through "the subjective prejudice of the critic" (*Escape to Conflict,* xxiii).

Kelm acknowledged that "the biblical record does present a major problem. Some of the historical evidence appears clearly contradictory, and reconciliation of biblical details, even apart from extra-biblical data, is not simple" (*Escape to Conflict,* xx). He looked to the role of the scribes in transmitting the texts to explain many problems and complexities of the present biblical texts. Kelm agreed with many Jewish scholars that as the scribes copied the texts, generation after generation, they may have added to or commented on the texts "to give sense" to them or to make them understandable to their generation. They possibly changed, revised, or restated the texts to clarify and help interpret them. So-called "anachronisms" (language of a later age applied in a text about an earlier age) may be attributed to the scribes as their way of updating the texts (*Escape to Conflict,* xxv).

These scribal changes may also account for many inconsistencies, duplications, contradictions, and especially differences in style and vocabulary. The scribes' modernization of the text assured a constant transition of meaning, ultimately short-circuited by canonization. At that point the sanctity of the texts precluded the interpretative process of the scribes. Its meaning was fixed in the literary concepts of that time and place, far removed from the twentieth century mind (Kelm, xxv-xxvi).

Kelm may be right in what he said about the role of the scribes, but all the textual or historical problems of the Old Testament cannot be attributed to the work of the scribes. Trent C. Butler discussed the historical problem and faith as it applies to the Old Testament's treatment of the conquest of Canaan. Butler said the problem starts with one's theological and faith presuppositions. The believer does not go to the biblical narratives to validate their truth qualities. The narratives have already proved themselves true for the life of faith long before the believer learns to raise the historical issue. The historical question becomes "a means to buttress one's faith or to validate one's doctrine" (*Joshua,* xxxix).

All of us seek knowledge and understanding, so we pursue the historical question. We believe that the biblical tradition is historically based. "The biblical tradition was not invented from thin air" (Butler, xli). Many theories have been advanced to explain the historical version of Israel's conquest. So far no scholarly consensus on any one theory has been established. Our theological presuppositions may incline us to go beyond the rules of the objective historian to a statement of faith concerning the historical situation. "If this is the case, we must be consciously aware of the nature of the statements we are making" (Butler, xli-xlii).

15. The Name of God - אהיה אשר אהיה

A. A Name Denotes Essence

The knowledge of God in the Old Testament comes not only through history, word, creation, and theophany, but also through the revelation of the name Yahweh. It is generally agreed that "among primitive peoples, and throughout the ancient East, the name denotes the essence of a thing: to name it is to know it, and, consequently, to have power over it" (de Vaux, *Ancient Israel,* 43).

The Israelites were no exception to this general law of primitive peoples. They supposed that a person's sum total was concentrated in one's personal name (Jacob, 43). The name was related to the nature of the character of the person. Eve's name, "life," related her to man (Gen. 2:18-23). Esau said that Jacob's actions reflected his name (Gen. 27:36). Nabal was like his name, "a fool" (1 Sam. 25:25).

Von Rad and Jacob argued that the name of a god in the ancient world carried a power and could be either dangerous or beneficent. It was thus important to know the god's name.

B. Invocation of the Name

In the Old Testament, invocation of the name of Yahweh was necessary in approaching Him. The first word of many of the prayers in the Psalms is an invocation, "Yahweh" (3:1; 6:1; 7:1;

8:1; 12:1). However, in some prayers Elohim, "God," is used instead. David's doxology begins with the word Yahweh (1 Chron. 29:10-11). Invocation of the name was still important in New Testament times. Jesus taught His disciples to begin their prayers, "Our Father . . . hallowed be your name" (Matt. 6:9).

When God took the initiative to reveal Himself, He started by uttering His name, "I am Yahweh" (Gen. 35:11; Ex. 6:2; 20:1; 34:5-6). But revelation of the name did not make Yahweh easily accessible and familiar. Israel considered Yahweh's name holy and insisted that it not be profaned (Lev. 22:2,32; Pss. 103:1; 105:3; 111:9; 145:21; Ezek. 20:39; 36:20-23; 39:7; 43:7; Amos 2:7). Yahweh's name was a surrogate for Himself, representing all His holy presence.

Invocation of the name was an important part of the cult. If Yahweh had not revealed His name, the worshiper could not invoke it, and there would be no worship. Childs acknowledged that the connection between the name and the cult is valid. But when God gave His name to Moses (Ex. 3:14), the issue was one of relating Moses' commission to the name in terms of God's authority rather than to the cult (*The Book of Exodus*, 67).

C. Meaning and Significance of the Name of Israel's God

The name Yahweh seems to come from an imperfect form of the Hebrew verb *hāyâ* "to be" or "to become." Albright argued that the name comes from the hifil (causative) form of the verb, hence it means "the one who causes to be," therefore "the creator." Many of Albright's students made similar proposals. David Noel Freedman suggested that the tetragrammaton *YHWH* be translated "he creates" ("The Name of the God of Moses," 155). Frank Cross thought that Yahweh was originally a cultic name for El. The cultic phrase "El who creates" later became "Yahweh the creator" ("Yahweh and the God of the Fathers," 225-259).

Philip Hyatt argued that rather than seeing Yahweh as originally a creator deity, He should be understood as the patron deity of one of Moses' ancestors. His name could have meant "he causes (the ancestor) to exist" or "he sustains (the ancestor)" ("Was Yahweh Originally a Creator Deity?", 376).

William Brownlee, a specialist in the Qumran materials, suggested on the basis of the *Manual of Discipline*'s use of 1 Samuel 2:3 and other evidence that the meaning of Yahweh should be "the one who makes things happen" ("The Ineffable Name of God," 39-45). Brownlee said that this name fit Moses' announcement of Yahweh's deliverance of the Hebrews from bondage. Their situation seemed hopeless. What they needed was the assurance that their God, Yahweh, could make things happen and fulfill the promises he had made to them through Moses ("The Ineffable Name of God," 45).

The idea that Yahweh means "the creator" may be seriously questioned because it is based on the assumption that the name Yahweh comes from the hifil (causative) form of the verb "to be." The hifil form of this verb never occurs in the Old Testament (Jacob, *Theology of the Old Testament,* 50). Both Jacob and von Rad believed that the primary meaning of Yahweh is "presence," "I will be with you" (Ex. 3:12; compare Gen. 28:20; Josh. 3:7; Judg. 6:12) (Jacob, *Theology of the Old Testament,* 53; von Rad, *Old Testament Theology I,* 180).

Terrien said, "To the vacillating Moses, Yahweh first gave assurance by affirming, 'I shall be with you'" (*The Elusive Presence,* 118). By revealing His name, Yahweh, "I am" or "I will be," God was promising His presence to Moses. He would be with him. In the Great Commission Jesus promised to be with His disciples always, even to the end of the age (Matt. 28:20).

Was God revealing Himself when He gave Moses His name? Or was He being evasive by refusing to give Moses an answer when He said, "I AM WHO I AM"? (Ex. 3:14). God refused to give his name to Jacob (Gen. 32:30) and to Manoah (Judg. 13:17-18). A. M. Dubarle concluded that God refuses to reveal His name to Moses in Exodus 3:14 because that would compromise His liberty to be God. Dubarle understood God to be saying, "My name does not concern you" ("La signification du nom de Jahweh," 3-21). Ludwig Köhler also interpreted Exodus 3:14 as an evasion of the question. God is the *deus absconditus* (*Old Testament Theology,* 242, n. 38).

Some ambivalence appears in the text, but the primary purpose is to reveal what God will do rather than the essence of His being. So, although Yahweh revealed His name to Moses and to Israel and allowed Himself to be "invoked" by them, or "gave Himself away" in commitment and trust to Israel alone, He still maintained His freedom.

Zimmerli said that the freedom of Yahweh means that He is never simply an object. Even though He revealed His name freely, He gave the Third Commandment of the Decalogue to protect that freedom against "religious abuse" (*Old Testament Theology in Outline,* 21).

D. Origin of the Name

Is the name Yahweh older than Moses? Yahweh appears as God's name beginning with the second chapter of Genesis. However, Exodus 6:3 says, "I appeared to Abraham, Isaac, and Jacob, as God Almighty, but by my name 'The LORD' [Yahweh] I did not make myself known to them." On biblical and extra-biblical evidence, it is probable that the divine name Yahweh existed outside Israel before Moses; but we have as yet no conclusive proof of this. The "Jo" element in Jochabed, Moses' mother's name, suggests a biblical use of Yah before Moses. Concerning extrabiblical evidence, P. D. Miller said, "The name 'Yahweh' itself is now widely attested in Judean inscriptions (over thirty examples) and there are no references to other deities" ("Israelite Religion," 206, 217).

Childs said that we should recognize the Ancient Near Eastern cognates of the divine name and even reckon with a long prehistory of the name before its entrance into Israel, but he remained open to the possibility that Israel attached a totally new meaning to the name (*The Book of Exodus,* 64). Walter Harrelson believed that the appearance of belief in God under "the personal name Yahweh antedated the period of Moses" ("Life, Faith, and the Emergence of Tradition," 21).

W. H. Schmidt went so far as to say, "The name Yahweh is not restricted to Israel, and furthermore is older than the Old Testament, that is, it is quite probably originally not Israelite" (*The Faith of the Old Testament,* 58). R. W. L. Moberly has recently argued vigorously that the name of Yahweh was first revealed to Moses, and earlier uses of the name in Genesis were anachronistic (see R. W. L. Moberly, *The Old Testament of the Old Testament,* 5-6). We can only conclude that the question of the origin of the name Yahweh is still unanswered.

E. God's Name and His Presence

Deuteronomy speaks often of making God's name "inhabit" or "dwell in" a certain place (Deut. 12:5,11). Obviously, Israel could not presume on God's presence in worship. Only God could ensure His presence. Yahweh's name stands for His presence, power, and authority. Perhaps this is the reason the name Yahweh occurs so often (about 6700 times) in the Old Testament, while Elohim occurs only 2500 times. Yahweh rather than Elohim was the name of the God to be worshiped. Through much of Old Testament history the name Yahweh seems to have been used freely by each and every Israelite. But in the post-Exilic period the name was withdrawn from general usage, probably from fear of God's judgment if the name was mispronounced. In Jesus' time the name was used only on certain occasions in the Temple, but no longer in the synagogue services. This hesitation to pronounce the name is reflected in the way the name appears in the Masoretic text. It usually appears as four consonants, YHWH, along with the vowels of the word *ădonay*, creating a combination ("Yehowah") that no Israelite ever pronounced. In pre-Exilic Israel the name was probably pronounced Yahweh.

The English word "Jehovah" reflects the German pronunciation, since the German *J* is used for *Y* and *W* is pronounced *V* in German. The pronunciation of Jehovah was never used by Jews. They read and pronounced the word as "*ădonay.*" However, when the word appears before the tetragrammaton in the Hebrew Bible (310 times), the vowels of the word *elohim* are used with the four consonants; and the word is pronounced "Elohim."

F. Summary

Yahweh was Israel's special name for her God. By revealing His name to Moses, and in turn to Israel, God chose to be described as "the definable, the distinctive, the individual. In this way the faith of Israel sets its face against both an abstract concept of deity and a nameless 'ground of being.' Both the intellectualist and the mystical misunderstandings of God are rejected" (Eichrodt, *Theology of the Old Testament I,* 206).

This is quite different from Paul Tillich's abstract description of God as the one who is the ultimate mystery, the infinite depth, the ground, the power, and the source of all being (see G. Ernest Wright, *The Rule of God*, 16). This definition comes nowhere near the Definite One, the Living God, the Coming Savior of the Old Testament. The name Yahweh is a *personal* name, not an abstract noun. Based on a form of the verb "to be," it is in some way related to the idea of being: past, present, and future.

It is connected with the past as far as Moses was concerned. Yahweh is the same as the God of the fathers Abraham, Isaac, and Jacob (Ex. 3:16). He is also the God of the future: "This is my name forever, and this my title for all generations" (Ex. 3:15b). The name even has an eschatological dimension in the Old Testament. There may be a connection between the name Yahweh and the origin of eschatology, "for a God who defines himself as 'I am' does not rest until that being and that presence are actualized in their perfection" (Jacob, 54).

The prophet of the Exile could refer to Yahweh as "the first and the last, Creator, Lord of history and only Savior" (Isa. 41:4; 43:10; 44:6; 48:12-13; 49:6,26; compare Rev. 22:13). By Yahweh's mighty acts in history Pharaoh, the Egyptians, the nations, and Israel would know that Yahweh was God ("I am Yahweh," Ex. 7:5; 8:10,22; 9:14; 10:2; Ezek. 20:26,38; 24:24,27; 34:27; 35:9,15; 36:11,23, 38; 38:23; 39:6,28).   This definable, distinctive *one* God (Yahweh) chose *one* man (Abraham) and *one* people (Israel) and entered into a special covenant with them. Through them He would bless all nations.

4

I Will Be Your God; You Shall Be My People (Election and Covenant)

16. You Shall Be My People (Election)

A. Recent Trends in the Study of Election

In 1950 H. H. Rowley lamented the fact that in modern biblical studies the doctrine of election had received little attention (*The Biblical Doctrine of Election,* 15). Actually, a number of articles and books on election in the Old Testament had been written before Rowley's work, and the reviving Old Testament theology of the day gave much attention to it.

In 1928 K. Galling wrote a monograph, "Die Erwählungstraditionen Israels," in which he suggested that the Old Testament has two traditions of God's election of Israel, one in the time of Abraham and the other in the time of Moses. Galling argued that the latter is the older tradition. Rowley acknowledged two election traditions in the Old Testament but defended the early choice of Abraham as substantially reliable. Rowley said that Israel was elected in Abraham, but that election was revealed through Moses (*The Biblical Doctrine of Election,* 30-31).

In 1929, J. M. P. Smith argued that Israel's faith in her election rested on a natural pride of nation and race and on the Israelite faith in Yahweh, whom she represented among the nations ("The Chosen People," 73-82). Rowley rejected Smith's view, saying, "If it had no deeper basis than this it would have little validity in itself, and would possess no more than a historical interest" (*The Biblical Doctrine of Election,* 16).

Walther Eichrodt did not give a separate section to a discussion of election. He was so engrossed in the covenant idea that the idea of election was almost forgotten, but he did consider the two closely related. Eichrodt said, "There can be no escaping the fact that in the Old Testament *divine love is absolutely free and unconditioned in its choices*; it is directed to one man out of thousands and lays hold on him with jealous exclusiveness despite all his deficiencies" (*Theology of the Old Testament I,* 286). Eichrodt emphasized that even where the word *election* was not used, the people and the prophets understood that Israel had a special position among the nations (*Theology of the Old Testament I,* 269).

G. Ernest Wright saw election as one of the chief clues for understanding Israel and the faith of the Old Testament. "Here is the focal point of the literature" (*The Old Testament Against Its Environment,* 47). Two years later (1952) Wright disagreed with Eichrodt's view that covenant is the chief unifying element in the Old Testament, insisting that election is more primary than covenant. "While the two go together, the latter is a conceptual language for expressing the meaning of the former and it makes considerable difference as to which receives the primary emphasis" (*God Who Acts,* 36, n. 1). Wright said that the initial and fundamental theological inference of the Exodus event was the doctrine of the chosen people. However, near the end of his life Wright seems to have modified his position on the relationship of election to covenant, agreeing more with Eichrodt that the covenant is central (*The Old Testament and Theology,* 62).

In 1938 Wheeler Robinson noted that the Old Testament describes "the divine choice of Abraham as an individual, and follows the fortunes of his family until it becomes a nation. Then the nation is delivered from Egypt and settles in the Promised Land. Much later, the doctrine of a righteous remnant emerges (Isa. 7:3; 8:16-18)." Robinson said that it is difficult to see how any revealed religion can dispense with the doctrine of election, for it is the mandate to a minority to persist in their purpose as the people of God. The particularism it involves belongs to every high mission and is no mark of provincialism in religion (*Record and Revelation,* 327). In 1946 Robinson wrote that the doctrine of election opens into the whole development of Israelite and Jewish religion and can be taken as the most comprehensive principle of unity in it, next to the primary emphasis on the unity of God. He disagreed with Eichrodt that the doctrine of election should be subordinate to the covenant (*Inspiration and Revelation,* 153).

In 1953 John Bright emphasized the importance of the doctrine of election in the Old Testament saying, "We find no period in her history when Israel did not believe that she was the chosen people of Yahweh. . . . The Bible story traces this history of election back to Abraham, but it was in the Exodus event that Israel saw her real beginnings as a people" (*The Kingdom of God,* 27). Bright believed that this was no esoteric notion advanced by spiritual leaders. The people were saturated with it. In 1967 Bright wrote that among the complex of beliefs in the Old Testament, the word *election* stands out.

> Whenever one looks in the Old Testament, one encounters the stubbornly held conviction that Yahweh has in his sovereign grace called Israel to himself, delivered her from bondage, and given her the Promised Land, and that Israel therefore occupies a peculiar position among the nations of the earth as his chosen people. . . . Belief in Israel's election is one that pervades the whole of the Old Testament, both early and later. Nowhere in the Old Testament is it not tacitly assumed or confidently asserted that Yahweh has called Israel out of all the nations of the earth to be his chosen people (*The Authority of the Old Testament,* 132).

In 1953 Th. C. Vriezen published a monograph on election in the Old Testament in which he limited the full meaning of election to the Hebrew term *bāhar,* "choose." Therefore, he arrived at a narrow meaning of election, secondary to covenant and dating from the seventh century ("Die Erwählung Israels," 35). He agreed that most of the Old Testament is concerned with the relationship between Yahweh and Israel, although other voices such as Ruth, Jonah, and (Second) Isaiah are heard to remind Israel that God's grace extends to the other nations as well (*Outline of Old Testament Theology,* 314). Vriezen said, "In the Old Testament the choice is always the action of God, of his grace, and always contains a mission for man; and only out of this mission can man comprehend the choice of God" ("Die Erwählung Israels," 109).

Vriezen saw God's election of Israel as His own possession as a source of tension and a paradox in the Old Testament. On one hand, God chose Israel and warned her to have nothing to do with other nations. On the other hand, God chose Israel for service to Him and to other nations. If we concentrate on one aspect of this doctrine, we will misunderstand it, and it becomes untrue.

> For instance, the truth of Israel's election is unacceptable if it is rationally understood to mean that *for that reason* God has rejected the nations of the world, that *for that reason* Israel is of more importance to God than those other nations, for Israel was only elected in order to serve God in the task of leading those other nations to God. In Israel God sought the world. Israel was God's point of attack on the world. When from the knowledge that it is God's people Israel derived the certainty of its special election, and because of that considered itself to be superior to the other nations, the prophets must contradict this and recall the people to the living God, whose mercy is great for Israel but also for the world. For in His mercy He has called Israel to the service of His kingdom among the nations of the earth (*Outline of Old Testament Theology,* 88).

Election, according to Vriezen, is the manifestation of the majesty and holiness of God and implies the right to make decisions that transcend humanity (*Outline of Old Testament Theology,* 316). Vriezen distinguished between *Erwählung,* "election," and *Erwählheit,* "electness," "choiceness," the feeling of pride in being elected. Election is legitimate; electness is not ("Die Erwählung Israels," 115).

In a lengthy section on election Edmond Jacob said that election is one of the central realities of the Old Testament.

> Even though it is less frequently mentioned than the covenant it is however the initial act by which Yahweh comes into relation with his people and the permanent reality which assumes the constancy of that bond. Every intervention of God in history is an election (*Theology of the Old Testament,* 201).

Jacob agreed with Rowley that election in the Old Testament is only for service. He believed that the fact of election in Abraham and Moses is older than the theology of election in the Yahwist and Deuteronomist. Jacob said, "There was in the movement that brought them [the Patriarchs] from Haran to Canaan something which corresponded to an election and it seems impossible to see in the religion of the patriarchs a simple projection into the past forms of belief that were only current five centuries later" (*Theology of the Old Testament,* 205).

Von Rad spoke of election in the Old Testament often, although he did not devote a separate section to it in his *Old Testament Theology.* Very early in his work he asserted that the later belief in Israel's election is already implicit in the "pre-Jahwistic cult of the ancestors" of Israel (*Old Testament Theology I,* 7). The concept of election is used first on a broad theological basis by Deuteronomy at a relatively late date, but "the belief that Jahweh took Israel as his own peculiar people is, of course, very very old" (*Old Testament Theology I,* 178).

One of the things that interested von Rad about the Old Testament's view of election is its relationship to the law or the Ten Commandments. He clarified the Old Testament view that election or the saving act came before the law and Ten Commandments. Keeping the law was not a condition of her salvation but a further expression of God's grace to her as an elect people. "Now there can be no doubt that it is the proclamation of the Decalogue over her which puts Israel's election into effect . . . those addressed are thus the ransomed of Jahweh" (*Old Testament Theology I,* 192).

There is always a close connection between Commandments and covenant,

> but in no case were these commandments prefixed to the covenant in a conditional sense, as if the covenant would only come into effect once obedience had been rendered. The situation is rather reverse. The covenant is made, and with it Israel receives the revelation of the commandments. . . . It [the Decalogue] was the guarantee of her election (*Old Testament Theology I,* 194).

Von Rad did recognize certain passages in which the blessings of salvation are conditional and are dependent on Israel's obedience (Deut. 6:18; 7:12; 8:1; 11:8-9; 16:20; 19:8-9; 28:9).

But even with these, "Deuteronomy's great offer of grace is not in any way annulled and a legal way of salvation proclaimed. Even the cases which seem to make salvation conditional, and dependent upon Israel's achievement, are prefaced by a declaration of Jahweh's election and his love" (*Old Testament Theology I,* 230).

Von Rad believed that the concept of the election of Israel dissolved before the time of the Chronicler. The Chronicler used the verb *bāhar* "choose" eleven times, but the objects of this divine election are the king, the place for the cult, or the tribe of Levi. "The Chronicler says nothing at all about the election of Israel—he does not even know of a Covenant theology" (*Old Testament Theology I,* 353).

The prophets made some earlier election traditions normative. However, the election traditions were not always the same for all the prophets. Hosea and Jeremiah stood in the Exodus traditions, while Isaiah stood in the Davidic traditions (von Rad, *Old Testament Theology II,* 117). The pre-Exilic prophets, according to von Rad, believed that Israel had broken the covenant with God and was about to experience His judgment, sealing the end of Israel's present existence. Her guilt canceled the security these election traditions gave Israel.

In the Exile the prophet was familiar with three old election traditions: the Exodus (Isa. 41:27; 46:13; 49:13; 51:3,11,16; 52:1,7-8); Abraham and Jacob (Isa. 41:8; 43:22,28; 51:1-2;); and David (Isa. 55:3) and Zion (Isa. 46:13; 49:14-21; 52:1-2). The prophet turned his eyes to the future and saw a new exodus, a new David, and a new Zion.

Finally, the Book of Daniel does not base its predictions about the future on earlier election traditions. The Exodus and Zion seem to lie outside Daniel's mental world. "The speaker's religious horizon has almost no connexion with the actual events of history; he extols the greatness of God's power, which can make and unmake kings, deliver men and set them free. God's enlightening wisdom is also praised, and so is the indestructibility of his kingdom" (*Old Testament Theology II,* 309).

The two main election traditions in the Old Testament are the Exodus and the Davidic traditions, which were preserved and maintained primarily in the Northern and Southern Kingdoms respectively. At times these traditions were combined. The prophets reinterpreted the traditions as no longer in effect, but God would act again on behalf of His people in a new exodus, a new David, and a new Jerusalem.

Hans Wildberger suggested in an article, "Auf dem Wege zu einer biblischen Theologie," that the central concept of the Old Testament is Israel's election as the people of God. He expanded his treatment of election in the Old Testament in his article "bchr, erwählen."

Walther Zimmerli noted that Yahweh was not the God of Israel from the beginning of the world. Israel does not appear as a people until the Book of Exodus (*Old Testament Theology In Outline,* 14). Even though the theology of election was formulated later (the use of *bāhar,* in the sense of God choosing Israel, does not occur before Deuteronomy), the account of the call of Abraham in Genesis 12 contains the roots of Israel's life as the people of God (*Old Testament Theology,* 27, 44).

Zimmerli acknowledged that the terminology of election includes Hebrew words other than *bāhar* "choose." *Qara'* "call," *yādaᶜ* "know," *bādal* "separate," and *hāzaq* "seize" are also used in the context of election, although no Hebrew noun for "election" is found in the Old Testament (*Old Testament Theology,* 44). Zimmerli discussed the question of why God chose Israel and pointed to the Old Testament's answer that God loved the fathers (Deut. 7:8). Then he asked what this divine election meant for the elect. It meant honor, holiness, mediation, and service (*Old Testament Theology,* 45). Zimmerli noted that election was applied to the king in the predeuteronomistic period (1 Sam. 8:18). It was also applied to the priests, especially the tribe of Levi (Num. 16:5; 17:2-10), and to the Temple.

Finally, Zimmerli raised the question of why the pre-Exilic prophets almost never speak of the election of Israel. Only Amos (3:2) and Jeremiah (1:5) use such terminology. Zimmerli believed that this silence was not because the pre-Exilic prophets did not know the election traditions, as Galling claimed. Instead, their silence "shows how critical the prophets are of all self-satisfied claims on the part of Israel to be a 'chosen people'" (*Old Testament Theology in Outline,* 47).

Ronald Clements said that when we ask why Israel is the people of God in a unique way, the Old Testament answers with a theology of election. Deuteronomy 7:6-8 is the classic passage of that theology. The form of this theology is Deutero-nomic, but "the main ideas of such a theology are certainly very much older" (*Old Testament Theology,* 88). For Clements the Book of Deuteronomy is normative for the Old Testament theology of election. He sees Israel's relationship to the other nations from the perspective of crisis and threat rather than that of a mission. In Deuteronomy Israel has no role of service to the nations (*Old Testament Theology,* 95). However, the Yah-wist said that Abraham (and by implication, Israel) would be a blessing to the nations. In the servant songs of Isaiah, Israel is to be a light and a servant to the nations.

Samuel Terrien said:

> The separation of Israel from all other peoples points to the idea of election, although the word is not yet used. To be the object of a unique love means 'to be chosen.' Election is predicated on the emotional awareness of 'predilection.' Israel, however, is not loved in a historical vacuum. Yahweh is not a dilettante. Israel is loved so as to become Yahweh's priestly kingdom in the history of the world (*The Elusive Presence,* 124).

We detect in Terrien's book a retreat from a strong emphasis on election on the part of some biblical scholars.

The diminishing role of the doctrine of election in Old Testament theologies is in further evidence in the work of Claus Westermann. He said that for a long time the idea of election played an important role in the theology of the Old Testament. It designated the entirety of God's actions concerning Israel. Westermann limited the idea of election to the technical use of *bāḥar* "choose," which, he claimed, is never used of the patriarchs or the Exodus and always has a subsequent, interpretative function. "It was not God's election which made Israel into his people, but rather his saving deed at the beginning. This act of God was explained by subsequent reflection such that God elected Israel" (*Elements of Old Testament Theology,* 41). Westermann asserted that one misunderstands the concept of election if any claims are made concerning it. We are not to generalize the concept of election or speak in an abstract sense "about the election tradition, the condition of election, or about an elect people" (*Elements of Old Testament Theology,* 42).

Byron Shafer argued that God chose Israel as His people according to Deuteronomy 7:7-8 simply because He loved them and had made a promise to their fathers (compare Deut. 4:37; 10:15; 2 Kings 19:34; Isa. 37:35). Election in the Old Testament is not necessarily a rational choice for a verifiable reason. Sometimes the only explanation given is "because God loves you" ("The Root *bḥr*," 20).

Shafer objected to a late dating of Israel's election and cites four bits of evidence which support an early date for Israel's election. (1) The pattern of divine royal election in Ancient Near Eastern literature is not sufficient to explain Israel's use of *bāḥar* "choose." (2) Evidence of theophoric names using the root *bhr* goes back to 1900 B.C. in the Ancient Near East. (Names such as Ibhar occur in 2 Sam. 5:15; 1 Chron. 3:6; 14:5.) (3) The Old Testament idea of the election of Israel did not move from the mythic realm of divine royal election to the historical choice of Israel because in the earliest passages in Deuteronomy (10:14-15,17-18,21-22; 11:3-7,10-12) and in Psalm 47, Yahweh is a cosmic or universal God. (4) The idea that the election of the patriarchs is a late retrojection is disputed because all the key passages in Deuteronomy (4:32-40; 7:7-8; 14:1-2) tie the election of Israel to the promise to the patriarchs. The study of the old Psalms such as 47 supports the priority of the election of the patriarchs.

Shafer was influenced by Frank M. Cross's ideas about El being the God of the Fathers. Cross cited Genesis 28:10-22 as the fullest remaining example in the Hebrew Bible of the ancient patriarchal pattern of covenant. (Compare Cross, *Canaanite Myth and Hebrew Epic,* 244-245; Shafer, 36.)

Shafer's thesis is that the ancient root *bhr* can be associated with the gods of the fathers in the Ancient Near Eastern tribal societies. Moreover, he asserted that the chosen people concepts in Deuteronomy and Psalms can be interpreted as "survivals, extensions, developments, and/or revisions of patriarchal religious concepts" ("The Root *bḥr*," 30, 33). Shafer and Frank Cross believed that the concept of election goes back to the days when the patriarch and his God made reciprocal covenants. Such covenants were conditional, but the God of the patriarchs was also seen as a cosmic and agrarian deity who promised to give the land to the patriarchs and their seed. Therefore, two views of election and covenant survive from patriarchal times: conditional and promissory (or unconditional).

Shafer followed Cross in seeing a radical shift taking place in Solomonic times from the conditional election to the pattern of an "eternal, unconditional covenant" with David's dynasty. After Solomon's death and the division of the kingdom, the old idea of a conditional election surfaced again in the North. The unconditional idea continued in the South (Shafer, 38-39). After the fall of Jerusalem in 586 B.C., the tensions between the two ideas of election continued throughout the periods of the Exile and the second Temple (Shafer, 42). Shafer used Psalms 47, 78, and 89 to trace the patriarchal and Davidic traditions in Israel.

Election is an important topic in Christoph Barth's last work, *God With Us* (1991). The election of the patriarchs is a basic article in Israel's creed. The stories of the patriarchs are told only in Genesis. Little is said about them in other Old Testament books. The election of the fathers is, however, an article in many of Israel's creeds. In some creeds it stands first (Deut. 26:5-9; Josh. 24:2-13; 1 Sam. 12:8). Creation comes before it in Nehemiah 9:6-31. The fathers are left out of several recitations of the creed (Deut. 32:6-14; Pss. 135; 136; Jer. 32:17-23). Christoph Barth said that the essential parts of the creed were the Exodus and the gift of the land. "Neither creation nor the election of the fathers has the same priority" (*God With Us,* 34).

The topic of the fathers' election is complementary to the Exodus and the gift of the land. Israel did not become a nation until it came out of Egypt (Ezek. 20:5-6; Hos. 11:1; 12:9; 13:4; Amos 3:1). Christoph Barth says that it was only after the Exodus that Israel acknowledged its descent from the patriarchs. "This is the right sequence for modern readers too" (*God With Us,* 39).

Ernest Nicholson again took up the questions of election and covenant in the Old Testament. He noted that since Wellhausen, the study of the covenant (at least for some) had "run itself into the ground, leaving 'covenant' as a played-out concept for the student of the Old Testament." He said that the debate among scholars has made it possible to see more clearly "just how crucial the covenant idea was in the development of what is distinctive in the faith of ancient Israel." Covenant is a central theme and "deserves to be put back squarely on the agenda for students of the Old Testament" (*God and His People,* v).

Nicholson noted that F. Giesebrecht first challenged Wellhausen's view that Israel's early relation to Yahweh was a natural relationship—like that of son and father. This made Israel similar to other nations in the way they viewed their relationship to their gods. Giesebrecht argued that Israel's relationship was *historically* based and did not emerge as a part of a "natural religion" (*Die Geschichtlichkeit des Sinaibundes,* 25). From the beginning, it was the belief in divine election that shaped the peculiar direction. It brought with it an aggressive exclusivism and "a belief in the incomparability of Yahweh" (Nicholson, *God and His People,* 23).

B. The Vocabulary of Election

The word *bāḥar* "choose" is used of God's choosing the patriarchs (Neh. 9:7); Israel (Deut. 4:37; 7:7-8; 10:15; 14:2; Ps. 105:43; Isa. 44:1-2; Ezek. 20:5); David (2 Sam. 6:21; 1 Kings 8:16; Pss. 78:70; 89:3); the place of worship (Deut. 12:18,26; 14:25; 15:20; 16:7,16; 17:8,10; 18:6; 31:11; Josh. 9:27; Ps. 132:13); and the priests (Num. 16:5,7; 17:5 [Heb. 17:20]; Deut. 18:5; 1 Sam. 2:27-28).

Other Hebrew terms are used to express the idea of election in the Old Testament. The word *qāraʾ* "call" is used of Abraham in Isaiah 51:2 (compare Gen. 12:1-3), of Samuel   (1 Sam. 3:4-21), and of many prophets. The word *yādaʿ* "know" is used to mean "to choose" or "to elect" in Genesis 18:19 and Amos 3:2.

Herbert Huffmon demonstrated that Mesopotamian words equivalent to *yādaʿ* "know" are used in ancient Near Eastern literature of mutual legal recognition on the part of the suzerain and vassal ("The Treaty Background of Hebrew *Yada,*" 31-37). One text says to Ashurbanipal, "You are the king whom the god(s) knows." Huffmon found parallels to this language in the Old Testament references to Abraham (Gen. 18:19); Moses (Ex. 33:12,17); Cyrus (Isa. 45:3-4); David (2 Sam. 7:20; 1 Chron. 17:18); Jeremiah (1:5); and Israel (Amos 3:2; Hos. 13:4-5).

The word *bādal* "separate" or "set apart" in the sense of God separating Israel from the nations is used for election in Leviticus 20:24; Numbers 8:14; 16:9; Deuteronomy 10:8. The word *māṣaʾ* "found" is used with the sense of "election" in Deuteronomy 32:10; Psalm 89:21; Hosea 9:10; and the term *lāqaḥ* "take" is used in Exodus 6:7 and Deuteronomy 4:34. The terms "love" and "hate" in Genesis 29:31 and Malachi 1:2-3 are "election" terms (Ralph L. Smith, *Micah-Malachi*, WBC 32, 305).

C. Objections to Election

One can see from the use of these terms that the idea that God chose or elected the patriarchs and Israel is pervasive in the Old Testament. But the idea was not always properly understood by those who were "called." The pre-Exilic prophets rarely mentioned the concept; and when they did, they usually pronounced judgment on the "chosen" ones for rejecting their calling. Israel often drew conclusions from their calling that were contrary to a true understanding of God's love— the basis of their calling. Jacob said, "They stiffen into rigid exclusivism, interpreting their election, which had become a hardened conception, as a duty to hate and a matter of pride" (*Theology of the Old Testament*, 111, 204).

Amos saw that Israel misunderstood election in terms of privilege without responsibility. The majority of Amos' contemporaries confused election with privilege and favoritism. "They seemed to feel that since God had chosen them he must love them more than anyone else; therefore they could count on more of the blessings of God, and less of the stringent judgment of God" (Ralph L. Smith, *Amos*, 100). Deuteronomy 9 fiercely condemned the deadly sin of pride. The Old Testament doctrine of election allows no room for pride. When one begins to use the term "choose," the ideas of exclusiveness, arbitrariness, favoritism, or special privilege immediately arise.

Norman Snaith said there is an exclusiveness in God's love. The idea of election has been part of "the offense of the gospel" from very early times. We may not like the word "chosen" or its companion "election." Election and chosen may be abhorrent to us, "but they are firmly embedded in both Old and New Testaments" (*The Distinctive Ideas of the Old Testament*, 139).

Celsus forcefully objected to the Old Testament doctrine of election. In caricature he said:

> Jews and Christians appear to me like a host of bats or ants who come out of their hiding places, or like frogs who sit in a swamp, or worms who hold a meeting in the corner of a manure pile and say to one another: 'To us God reveals and proclaims everything. He does not trouble himself with the rest of the world; we are the only beings with whom he has dealings. . . . To us is subjected everything: the earth, the water, the air, the stars. Because it has happened that some of us have sinned, God himself will come or will send his own Son in order to destroy the wicked one with fire and to give us a share in eternal life (quoted by Cullmann, *Christ and Time,* 28).

In 1945 Paul Scherer, pastor of the Evangelical Lutheran Church of the Holy Trinity and professor of preaching at Union Seminary in New York, used shocking language to chide the Jews. His perception of their understanding of election was that they thought God's purpose in history was to benefit them, when in reality it was to manifest His glory and establish His kingdom on earth. Scherer noted that "all through the Old Testament and into the New, Israel is spoken of as an elect nation" (*Event in Eternity,* 193). The Bible insists that whatever happened did not happen just for them. "That relieves heaven of a good deal of responsibility, and throws it where it belongs!" (Scherer, 194).

Richard L. Rubenstein, a modern Jew, objected to the doctrine of election. After Auschwitz Jews

> can never again with integrity believe in the God who exercises providential control over human affairs; what occurred was too monstrous to be reconciled through the usual techniques of theodicy with the existence of such a God, despite the convictions of biblical faith. After Auschwitz, to trust in providence in the traditional sense is immoral as well as impossible, since it turns God into an accomplice of Hitler, deliberately willing the slaughter of the chosen people for no other reason than the crime of being chosen (Richard L. Rubenstein, *After Auschwitz,* quoted by Alan T. Davies, *Anti-Semitism and the Christian Mind,* 36).

Rubenstein wrote that many modern Israelites have rejected covenant theology entirely. He says that even though the biblical religion is a part of the heritage of every Jew, "many Israelis believe as little in the God of the Bible as contemporary Greeks believe in the Homeric gods. Israel became a reality when Jews stopped awaiting divine intervention and took history into their own hands" (Foreword to Davies, *Anti-Semitism and the Christian Mind,* 12). In his book *My Brother Paul,* Rubenstein said, "In the light of objective history, no religious position can be privileged" (*My Brother Paul,* 21).

Gordon D. Kaufman of Harvard Divinity School addressed the charge that God was unjust and partial when He revealed Himself in Jesus Christ to some and not to others. The argument runs that in principle, truth, particularly truth about the ultimate reality, ought to be available to all. A God who plays favorites in this fashion could hardly be regarded as loving; even a human father knows that it is wrong to discriminate without warrant among his children.

Kaufman said in his *Systematic Theology* that these common criticisms are seemingly plausible; but closer examination reveals that they are grossly misleading, for no one really believes that all people have equal access to truth and reality. The truth we can or will know is conditioned by, among other things, historical and psychological factors. All persons have not had the same opportunity to know the truth that Plato or Einstein taught because of historical or circumstantial facts.

> Truth known and knowable is always relative to the historical situation of the knower. The Christian claim, therefore, that God has specially revealed himself in and through the historical development of one community, beginning in remote antiquity and ultimately flowering into a universal church may involve no scandal at all (*Systematic Theology,* 14).

G. Ernest Wright said that the answers to the objections to election are obvious. Israel paid a terrible price for this election. The story Israel tells of themselves is a sordid, sorry tale. When Israel claimed to be the chosen people, they gave the only possible explanation of the deliverance from Egypt. It is part of Israel's explanation of their origin and is not a late idea. "Later writers take the matter for granted and look upon it as the supreme manifestation of divine grace" (*The Old Testament Against Its Environment,* 50).

D. The Purpose of Election

The Old Testament claims that God chose Israel as His special people. Does it tell us why he chose them? Yes and no. Some portions of the Old Testament seem to leave the answer to this question in the realm of mystery, and modern scholars have pondered the mystery of election. The poet A. E. Housman once wrote, "How odd/ of God/ To choose/ the Jews" (quoted from Scherer, 194),

Norman Snaith said that we may not be able to answer this question, but the teaching is there plainly enough. Why is this one chosen and not that one? "We have no answer. Calvin tried to find the answer to both parts of the question, and his answer was predestination. Luther said that Calvin went wrong because he tried to climb up into the majesty of God. The first part of the question (why one is chosen) can be answered. God chose this one because He loved him" (Snaith, *The Distinctive Ideas of the Old Testament,* 139). Snaith had no satisfactory answer to the second part of his question: why did God not choose some?

Some parts of the Old Testament answer that Israel was chosen to be a blessing to the nations. The only logical assumption is that the election of Israel must in some way be the answer to the plight of humanity. The prophet, therefore, is elaborating and deepening no newly invented doctrine when he proclaims that God called Israel to be a "light to the nations" (Isa. 42:5-7). Perhaps it should be noted that it is Israel, the surviving remnant of earlier Israel, that is to be a light to the nations. Israel's election was not what Celsus imagined it to be. The freedom and privilege which election conferred were limited by the independent purposes of God.

H. H. Rowley noted that the Old Testament cautions Israel that they were not chosen because of their goodness or greatness (Deut. 7:7-8; 9:4-6). The doctrine of election creates an unreal drama. "If God chooses the worthy, then His grace is in question; while if He chooses the unworthy, then His justice is in question" (*The Biblical Doctrine of Election,* 39). Rowley thought that viewing election teleologically removes the dilemma. God's purpose of election was revelation and service (*The Biblical Doctrine of Election,* 39, 54-68).

Israel's election, then, was not based on merit but upon God's mysterious grace; and its reality was confirmed in the Exodus from Egypt. In the Babylonian exile, at least one prophet understood that God chose Israel to be a light to the nations and the instrument of "His universal redemptive purposes" (Wright, *God Who Acts,* 20).

William LaSor said that the biblical doctrine of election is much misunderstood. A common view is that God chooses some people and gives them a free pass to heaven, consigning the rest to hell. No attempt is made to understand God's person, character, or purpose in election (*The Truth About Armageddon,* 36). "The 'elect' is a person or a community of persons to whom God has given or is giving a special revelation, and through whom God will reveal himself to other nations or peoples. . . . Election in the biblical sense always has a purpose of mission. . . . Election is never an end in itself; it is always a means to an end" (LaSor, 41-42). The words *bāḥar* and *eklegomai* are positive and do not convey the meaning of rejection of what is not chosen. They stress the idea of selection or preference with no explication of reprobation (LaSor, 37).

The basis of election in the Old Testament is God's sovereignty. Jeremiah portrayed God as the potter with absolute power to make the clay into any vessel He chooses. But in that same passage He reserves the right "to change His mind" if a nation repents (Jer. 18:1-6). LaSor said, "No statement of the doctrine of God's sovereignty can destroy his sovereignty" (*The Truth About Armageddon,* 43). God is not capricious. His will and entire purpose include His wisdom and His love.

Alongside the truth of the sovereignty of God must be placed the biblical teaching that humans were created "a little lower than God" (Ps. 8:5). Each person has a will and is completely responsible for personal decisions. Persons may be "elected," but they still must "call on the name of the Lord" to be saved (Joel 2:32; Matt. 3:5). People are not mere pawns, but God is gracious and long-suffering (Ex. 34:6-7).

Why did God choose Abram rather than Haran (Gen. 11:27)? The Old Testament does not answer this question. Christoph Barth said God does not have to give reasons for His decisions. He chooses freely. Of course, God does have reasons for doing what He does; His choices are not arbitrary. He chooses out of free compassion, but the grounds or reasons for His choices are not in the persons or objects chosen but in His purpose (*God With Us,* 41). God did not choose the fathers or Israel because they were good or faithful.

What about the nonelect? If the elect are privileged, are the nonelect nonprivileged? They may be privileged, but not in the same way as the elect. Christoph Barth said, "They have their own roles and are not put in an especially bad light. They are just as good as the elect, and sometimes better. God has not necessarily refused, rejected, or cursed them. They have a place in his plan" (*God With Us*, 44).

Election is a vital part of the biblical materials. Because God loved the world, He chose Abraham and some of his descendants to be a kingdom of priests and a light to the nations of His saving grace.

17. I Will Be Your God (Covenant)

A. Recent Trends in the Study of the Covenant

The Hebrew word *bĕrît*, "covenant" is important in the Old Testament, but it, along with the term for "election," has had a checkered theological career. At times it has stamped its name on a whole school of theological thought, while at other times it has almost completely dropped out of regular theological discussions—even though the two parts of our Bible carry this word in their titles.

The term *covenant* is used unevenly in the Old Testament. Parts of the Old Testament (Deut.) make much use of the term, while the pre-Exilic prophets and the Wisdom literature rarely use it. However, the importance of this concept does not depend on where or how often the term *berit* is used.

1) Renewed Interest in the Covenant (Eichrodt and Albright)— Earlier Old Testament scholars such as Oehler (*Theology of the Old Testament*, 175-178] and Wellhausen (*Prolegomena*, 417-419) discussed the covenant, but they did not make it central in their presentation of the Old Testament materials. In fact, Wellhausen taught that the covenant in early Israel was a "natural bond" between Israel and Yahweh, like that of a son and father. It did not rest on the observance of the conditions of a pact. It meant "help" from God to Israel, often in times of war. The name Israel means "El does battle," according to Wellhausen (*Prolegomena*, 434).

The idea of the early covenant was a "help" from God on all occasions, "not 'salvation' in the theological sense. The forgiveness of sins was a matter of subordinate importance" (*Prolegomena*, 469). Wellhausen could say this because he did not believe that the priestly legislation that dealt with the sin problem was Mosaic. The priestly Torah did not arise until after Ezra's time (*Prolegomena,* 438).

However, the eighth-century prophets, with their emphasis on God's righteousness and His demand for social justice, caused Wellhausen to see a shift from a covenant as a natural bond to one of a pact or treaty. Commandments were understood as demands or conditions on which Yahweh's continued relation to Israel depended (see Nicholson, "Israelite Religion in the Pre-exilic Period," 3). The natural bond between Yahweh and Israel was severed.

Many scholars accepted Wellhausen's covenant ideas and considered the issue settled. There was little debate among scholars on the covenant for a while. In 1900 F. Giesebrecht published his influential monograph *Die Geschichtlichkeit des Sinaibundes,* in which he challenged Wellhausen's early "natural bond" theory of the covenant. Giesebrecht argued that Israel's relationship with Yahweh was *historically* founded and did *not* emerge, as in the case of the so-called "natural" religions (Giesebrecht, 25; see Nicholson, *God and His People,* 23).

Not until 1933 did anyone write an Old Testament theology making the covenant its central theme. Walther Eichrodt was the first Old Testament scholar to write an Old Testament theology around the central theme of the covenant. Eichrodt said:

> The concept of the covenant was given this central position in the religious thinking of the OT so that, by working outward from it, the structural unity of the OT message might be made more readily visible. . . . For the concept of the covenant enshrines Israel's most fundamental conviction, namely its sense of a unique relationship with God. The crucial point is not—as an all too naive criticism sometimes seems to think— the occurrence or absence of the Hebrew word *berit,* but the fact that all the crucial statements of faith in the OT rest on the assumption, explicit or not, that a free act of God in history raised Israel to the unique dignity of the People of God, in whom his nature and purpose were to be made manifest. The actual term "covenant" is, therefore, so to speak, only the code-word for a much more far-reaching certainty, which formed the very deepest layer of the foundations of Israel's faith, and without which indeed Israel would not have been Israel at all. As epitomizing God's action in history "covenant" is not a dogmatic concept with the help of which a "corpus of doctrine" can be

evolved, but the *typical description of a living process,* which
began at a particular time and place, and which was designed to
make manifest a divine reality quite unique in the whole history of religion. The references to this living process in every
single chapter of this work will not escape the attentive reader
(*Theology of the Old Testament I,* 17-18).

W. F. Albright agreed that the idea of the covenant dominates the entire religious life of Israel and that the idea is
present often when the term *bĕrît* does not occur. In the Preface to the second edition of *From the Stone Age to Christianity,*
Albright said that even though in the first edition of this book
he emphasized briefly the pre-Mosaic origin of the covenant
between God and Israel, he failed to recognize that the concept
of covenant:

dominates the entire religious life of Israel to such an extent
that W. Eichrodt's apparently extreme position is fully justified.
We cannot understand Israelite religion, political organization,
or the institution of the Prophets without recognizing the
importance of the "Covenant." The word itself appears as a
Semitic loan-word in the fifteenth-twelfth centuries in Syria
and Egypt and clearly goes to the earliest times in Israel (*From
Stone Age to Christianity,* 16).

*2) Parallels to the Old Testament Covenant in Ancient Near
Eastern Treaties*—E. Bikerman seems to have been the first
scholar to notice a possible analogy between the treaties of the
Hittite kings and their vassals and the covenant relationship
between Yahweh and Israel ("Couper une alliance," 133-156;
see also E. W. Nicholson, God and His People, 57).

George Mendenhall took up Bikerman's suggestion and
argued that the Hittite treaty form was an early source of the
Old Testament's idea of covenant (*Law and Covenant in Israel,*
24-27). Mendenhall argued that the tribes of Israel were not
bound together by blood-ties but by a covenant based on religion and modeled after the suzerainty treaty by which the
great Hittite king bound his vassals to faithfulness and obedience to himself (*Law and Covenant in Israel,* 25-26).

Mendenhall believed that this type of international treaty
(or covenant) came only from the Hittite Empire (1450-1200
B.C.) at the approximate time of the beginning of the people of
Israel. This made the covenant form in the Old Testament date
from the Mosaic period. (Although the Hittites used the suzer-

ainty treaty form, they probably did not originate it. It seems to have been the common property of a number of states and people in the second millennium B.C. and was known and used by much later peoples. See J. J. Roberts, "Ancient Near Eastern Environment," in *The Hebrew Bible and Its Modern Interpreters*, ed. Knight and Tucker, 93-94.)

The primary purpose of the suzerainty treaty was to establish a firm relationship between the suzerain and his vassal, including military support from the suzerain. However, the interests of the suzerain were primary. Its form was unilateral. The stipulations were binding only on the vassal, although a prologue often related the suzerain's benevolent deeds in behalf of the vassal.

The Hittites or Babylonians did not have a single word for contract or covenant, but both used a phrase meaning "oaths and bonds." The specific obligations imposed upon the vassal were called "words" of the sovereign (Mendenhall, *Law and Covenant in Israel*, 31).

When empires again arose, notably Assyria, the structure of the treaty or covenant by which they bound their vassals was entirely different. Even in Israel, the older form of the covenant was no longer widely known after the united monarchy. Therefore, the idea of covenant in Israel must have been old (Mendenhall, *Law and Covenant in Israel*, 30-31).

Mendenhall agreed with V. Korosec that six elements in the Hittite covenants have parallels in the Sinai covenant form in the Old Testament. Those six elements are: (1) a preamble, the identification of the great king (compare Ex. 20: "I am Yahweh your God"); (2) the historical prologue; (3) the stipulations (compare the "ten words"); (4) depositing a copy of the treaty in the temple of the suzerain and of the vassal; (5) the list of gods as witnesses; and (6) the curses and blessings (compare Deut. 28). The motivation for the vassal's obedience is not the power of the king but the curses and blessings enforced by the gods.

The clans that came out of Egypt were of diverse background, including a mixed multitude. At Sinai they were formed into a new community by covenant. The text of that covenant was the Decalogue (Ex. 34:28; Deut. 4:13; 9:9). Israel did not bind herself to Moses, but to Yahweh. Moses was the mediator of the covenant. Mendenhall believed the covenant was the factor that unified the tribes of Israel when they took the land from the Canaanite kings.

In 1963 (rev. 1978) Dennis J. McCarthy published his "Treaty and Covenant: A Study in Form in the Ancient Oriental Documents and in the Old Testament." McCarthy translated many Hittite and Assyrian treaties and compared them with some Old Testament passages. McCarthy concluded in 1963 that the Israelite covenant form resembled that of the Hittite treaty form; but he also said we cannot be sure that the form in Israel goes back to the second millennium. "We simply do not know what might have been practiced in the way of treaties from c. 1200-850 B.C." (McCarthy, 174).

In 1972 Dennis McCarthy made a thorough study of scholarly opinions on Old Testament covenant. He agreed with Mendenhall that the evidence that Israel's use of the treaty-form "to describe its special relationship with Yahweh, is irrefragable" (*Old Testament Covenant,* 14). However, he was much more cautious than Mendenhall about using literary form to argue for an early date for Old Testament passages using the treaty forms. McCarthy also rejected Mendenhall's view that Israel was formed by the rebellious peasants of Canaan rather than by Israelite clans invading Palestine from the desert. He said that this reconstruction by Mendenhall "is interesting but hardly successful. There is simply too much evidence which makes the Hebrews, before their entrance into Palestine, something like nomads" (*Old Testament Covenant,* 22).

As early as 1930, Martin Noth advanced a view of Israel's tribal covenant society similar to Mendenhall's. Noth argued that the people to whom the laws in the Old Testament were given constituted a sacral union of twelve tribes, which he called an amphictyony. This amphictyony constituted Israel, the people of God, over against the Canaanites.

Noth said that the twelve-tribe confederacy traced back its relationship with Yahweh, and so its own existence, to the unique experience of a covenant made between Yahweh and Israel. The amphictyony also traced its personal entry into a relationship between God and people, to an image taken from a type of human judicial agreement called a covenant ("Das System der zwölf Stämme Israels"; see also Noth, *The History of Israel,* 85-109). Martin Noth's view of the covenant as the basis of Israel's amphictyony was greatly influenced by Max Weber's book, *Ancient Judaism.* (For a review of Weber's work see Nicholson, *God and His People,* 38-43.)

Noth's thesis was so ably and persuasively presented that it almost became the consensus of scholarship. However, in recent years it has become "the target of a veritable barrage of criticism from scholars who deny that such an amphictyony . . . ever existed, and who in some cases even deny that the very notion of covenant was determinative in Israel until a much later date" (Bright, *Covenant and Promise,* 33).

3) Criticisms of Parallels Between the Covenant and the Treaties—In 1962 H. M. Orlinsky ("The Tribal System of Israel," *Oriens Antiquus 1,* 11-20) pointed out that "amphictyony" was not an appropriate name for pre-monarchical Israel. The tribes were too independent; there is no evidence of a central government or of a central cultic center. Other early critics of Noth's theory were Roland de Vaux (*The Early History of Israel* 695-715; A. D. H. Mayes, *Israel in the Period of the Judges;* and C. H. J. de Geus, *The Tribes of Israel,* chap. 2).

G. W. Anderson analyzed the whole amphictyony hypothesis and rejected much of it. He found no evidence for the name "amphictyony" in the Old Testament and little evidence to support the number *twelve* for the tribal league in the Old Testament. Little evidence supports the importance of the central sanctuary in the premonarchic period ("Israel: Amphictyony," in *Translating and Understanding the Old Testament,* ed. Frank and Reed, 138, 141). Anderson denied Noth's views and argued that the basis for the unity of Israel's tribes in the settlement period was not due so much to what happened after they came into the land, but to what happened before they came into Canaan—namely, the Sinai covenant. Anderson said:

> It seems natural, therefore, to look for the establishment of this unity, not in the emergence of an amphictyony on Canaanite soil in the wake of an invasion, but rather, where so much ancient Israelite tradition would lead us to expect to find it, in the period before the settlement, and, more specifically, in the establishment of the Sinai covenant between Yahweh and the Israelite tribes ("Israel: Amphictyony," 149).

Anderson further stated, "To look for the establishment of that unity elsewhere than in the institution of the Sinai covenant is to disregard the testimony of tradition in the interests of airborne guesswork" ("Israel: Amphictyony," 150).

After acknowledging some of the objections that some scholars expressed toward the suzerainty treaty form and the early date for the Sinai covenant, John Bright continued to hold that view. He said:

> The notion of a covenant bond between God and people seems clearly to antedate the earliest of the prophets, and it was presumably much older still. . . . We may with some confidence believe that Israel did in fact come into being as a sacral confederation formed in covenant with Yahweh, and that this covenant followed broadly the pattern of those international suzerainty treaties that are known to us from the texts of the second millennium B.C. (*Covenant and Promise,* 43).

Bright concluded that the view that Israel emerged into history as a sacral covenant league accords best with the biblical evidence. "Only so, indeed, can earliest Israel be understood." (*Covenant and Promise,* 36).

Robert Davidson asked, "Can the thesis be sustained that covenant, modelled on the treaty form, played an important, and perhaps decisive, role in the formation of Israel, whether in religious or sociological terms? Or must we agree (with Nicholson that) ". . . in reality it has yielded little permanent value?" ("Covenant Ideology in Ancient Israel," in *The World of Ancient Israel,* ed. R. E. Clements, 332).

Nicholson's reasons for his conclusion that the parallels to the suzerainty treaty "yielded little that is of value are: One, Deuteronomy is not a legal document in the sense that the treaties are. Second, it is not treaty-like in its manner of presentation; rather it is a valedictory speech of Moses. Third, its laws deal with many matters not strictly pertinent to the suzerain-vassal relationship. Fourth, the fact that Deuteronomy contains two prologues unlike anything found in treaties. Fifth, conspicuously absent is the designation of "Yahweh as King" (*God and His People,* 71).

Nicholson raised another important question: Would such an analogy for their relationship with God have had any appeal of an apt or desirable nature, especially when Assyrian suzerains had subjected and despoiled the land and people? In spite of the fact that treaties referred to the "love" of suzerain for vassal and vassal for suzerain, relations of suzerains and vassals were seldom loving.

> Vassals did not as a rule 'love' those who conquered, subdued and dominated them. . . . To tell Israelites that Yahweh 'loves' them in the same way as a suzerain (e.g. Ashurbanipal or Nebuchadnezzar) 'loves' his vassals, and that they are to 'love' Yahweh as vassals love their suzerains would surely have been a bizarre depiction of Yahweh's love (*God and His People,* 78-79).

Nicholson has presented some forceful arguments against the use of parallels to suzerainty treaties to interpret the Sinai covenant. It still may be true that the model of Israel's covenant with Yahweh was based on a political analogy. The marriage model of the covenant does not begin until the time of Hosea.

Two very important works by Perlitt and Kutsch seemed to turn scholars' direction from the "treaty form" of the covenant to that of a "theological idea." Perlitt dated the "full-blown" idea of the covenant between Yahweh and Israel in the post-Exilic period. We will discuss these two works more fully in the following section "Meaning of *bĕrît.*"

In 1984 W. J. Dumbrell built a comprehensive biblical theology around the idea of covenant (*Covenant and Creation*). The five main chapters of the book center on specific covenant promises (Noah, Abraham, Sinai, David, and the "new" covenant). A brief epilogue deals with post-Exilic developments. Dumbrell saw "covenant" as implicit even in the account of creation.

Israel's failure to fulfill the covenant terms and thus to achieve the full realization of the covenant promises led to the eschatological hope of a new covenant. All eschatology is brought under the overarching expectation of this new covenant, which is even yet not completely fulfilled. Dumbrell's work represents a theological construct with connections to the seventeenth-century "Federal" theology of Cocceius, finding in the Bible the idea of "one-covenant" under different dispensations. (See R. E. Clements' review in *Expository Times* 96 [1985], 345.)

In 1985 T. E. McComiskey of Trinity Evangelical Divinity School published a similar argument for the covenantal structure of redemptive history. McComiskey saw two types of covenants in the Old Testament: promissory and administrative. In the Old Testament are two promissary covenants: the Abrahamic and Davidic covenants. The promissory covenant states and guarantees the element of promise. It is unconditional. Its force never fails, although the language may be reinterpreted (*The Covenants of Promise,* 140-144, 223-231).

Three administrative covenants in the Old Testament are the covenant of circumcision, the Mosaic covenant, and the new covenant. The administrative covenants set forth stipulations of obedience and, except for the covenant of circumcision, explicate the elements of the promise in terms of the economies they govern (McComiskey, 140). McComiskey distinguished between the promise which is unconditional, for all time, and the administrative covenants, which apply only on a temporary basis.

B. The Meaning of *berit*

Since 1944 a lively debate has developed among Old Testament scholars over the meaning of the word *bĕrît* "covenant." In that year Joachim Begrich published his now famous article in which he argued that *bĕrît* referred to a relationship between two unequal partners whereby the stronger gave to the weaker the assurance of friendly behavior and protection. Only the stronger was bound by the covenant. The weaker remained completely passive. Begrich believed God's covenant with Israel was originally a covenant of promise and assurance. Only after Israel settled in Canaan and adopted Canaanite conceptions of law was the donor *bĕrît* changed into a contractual *bĕrît* with obligations on both sides. (See Joachim Begrich, "*berit,* Ein Beitrage zur Erfassung einer altestamentlichen Denkform," 1-11.)

The word *bĕrît* "covenant" is used in the Old Testament in a secular sense of agreements between individuals (Gen. 21:22-24; 26:23-33; 47:29; 1 Sam. 18:3; 23:18); between states and their representatives (1 Kings 5:1-12; 15:19; 20:34); between kings and their subjects (2 Sam. 5:3; 2 Kings 11:17); and between husband and wife (Ezek. 16:8; Mal. 2:14; Prov. 2:17). It is also used in the figurative sense of a covenant between people and animals (Job 5:23; 41:1-4), people and stones (Job

5:23), a person and his eyes (Job 31:1), and between a person and death (Isa. 28:15-18).

"Covenant," *bĕrît*, occurs approximately 275 times in the Old Testament and is found in every Old Testament book except Ruth, Esther, Ecclesiastes, Song of Songs, Lamentations, Joel, Obadiah, Jonah, Micah, Nahum, Habakkuk, and Haggai. It appears in the Pentateuch about eighty times, seventy times in the Former Prophets, seventy-five times in the Latter Prophets, and sixty times in the Writings.

Alfred Jepsen agreed that *bĕrît* carried the idea of assurance from the stronger to the weaker party. Jepsen insisted that the covenant between God and Israel was never understood in legal or contractual terms. No obligation was ever imposed on Israel except that of renouncing the worship of other gods. This was a "moral obligation," not a law. (See A. Jepsen, *Berith, Ein Beitrag zur Theologie der Exilszeit,* 161-179.)

Ernst Kutsch conducted a thorough study of the contexts of the various uses of the word *berit* in the Old Testament. He concluded that the primary meaning of the word *bĕrît* was "obligation." It never means a relationship, an alliance, or a covenant, but always an obligation. Sometimes a person took on the obligation without expectation of a return. Sometimes the obligation was laid on another without the first party's taking an obligation (*Verheissung und Gesetz*; compare THAT I [1971], 339-352).

Lothar Perlitt attacked the form-critical approach of Mendenhall and the whole comparative religions approach to the study of *bĕrît*. Perlitt insisted against Eichrodt that the theology of covenant must be tied inseparably to the actual usage of the term *bĕrît*. Perlitt reverted to the old Wellhausen view that all references to *bĕrît* in the Old Testament are late—no earlier than the Deuteronomic materials. Every mention of a *bĕrît* in the Sinai accounts is eliminated by literary-critical procedures. For Perlitt, the account of Yahweh's *bĕrît* with Abraham in Genesis 15 in its present form was an early Deuteronomic document to be dated at the beginning of the seventh century (*Bundestheologie im Alten Testament*; for a critique of Perlitt's views see Zimmerli, "The History of Israelite Religion," in *Tradition and Interpretation,* ed. G. W. Anderson, 379-380; Nicholson, *God and His People,* 109-117).

J. J. Roberts saw the discussions of Kutsch and Perlitt as a return to a narrow, biblically based discussion of the covenant on a simple syntactical study of a single Hebrew word. Roberts thought that the avoidance of comparative ancient Near Eastern materials is "a false step" and an attempt to gain a "bogus security in the constricted wombs of pure Old Testament studies." Roberts said, "If genuine progress is to be made in this area, it will come from a continued firsthand acquaintance with the extra-biblical material conjoined with careful analysis of the biblical texts" ("Ancient Near Eastern Environment" in *The Hebrew Bible and Its Modern Interpreters,* ed. Knight and Tucker, 93-94).

Scholars are still debating the meaning of the term *bĕrît.* Four theories of the etymology of *berit* among recent scholars are that it comes: (1) from the Akkadian word *biritu,* "clasp," "bind," or "fetter"; (2) from the Akkadian word *birit,* "between"; (3) from a Hebrew root *brh* "to eat"; or (4) from another Hebrew root *brh* "to see, search out, select" (compare Isa. 28:15-18; 1 Sam. 17:8). (For a thorough discussion of the etymology of *bĕrît* see Zimmerli, *Old Testament Theology in Outline,* 49; M. Weinfeld, *"berit," TDOT* 2, 253-255; Barr, "Some Semantic Notes on the Covenant," 23-38; and Nicholson, *God and His People,* 94-109.)

James Barr argued that none of these theories is completely satisfying because scholars make too much of etymology. Barr focused his study not on etymology but on the peculiar uses of the word. He discovered an unusual group of four features about the grammatical behavior of *bĕrît:* (1) its opacity, (2) its idiomaticity, (3) its nonpluralization, and (4) the peculiar shape of its semantic field.

By its opacity, Barr meant the lack of any transparent meaning in the word itself, such as the German word *Handschuh* over against the English word "glove." Barr said that *berit* is fully opaque, a simple arbitrary sign whose historical derivation was unknown ("Some Semantic Notes on the Covenant," 26).

By idiomaticity, Barr meant that the phrase "to cut a covenant," which is used eighty times in the Old Testament, is an idiomatic construction. According to the classic definition, an idiom is an expression the meaning of which is different from the independent meanings of the constituent's parts ("Some Semantic Notes on the Covenant," 27). "Cut a covenant" originally referred to the cutting of a calf to be used in the cultic ceremony sealing the covenant (see Gen. 15:5-18; Jer. 34:18). The calf was cut, not the covenant. Barr calls the expression "to cut a covenant" by far the most important and striking case of idiom in all biblical Hebrew.

Another peculiarity of covenant in the Old Testament is that it never occurs in the plural. We speak often of "covenants," but the Old Testament only speaks of "covenant." Barr did not have an adequate explanation for this phenomenon, but he rejected the suggestions that it can be explained by the notion that there is only one "covenant" with many manifestations or that the Israelites were unable to think of this entity in the plural.

A final peculiarity of the use of the word "covenant" in the Old Testament, according to Barr, is that its semantic range seems to be very wide from one perspective, yet very restricted from another. For example, in English a variety of different words such as agreement, treaty, contract, promise, obligation have been used to translate the Hebrew word *berit*. Indeed, all of these ideas seem to be included in this one Hebrew word. Barr said that the only real synonyms are very rare and marginal: perhaps *ʾămānâ* "covenant," "settled provision," in Nehemiah 10:1 (Eng. 9:38); 11:23 and *ḥozeh* and *ḥazut* "covenant" in Isaiah 28:15-18 are the only true synonyms of *bĕrît*.

In addition to these rare and marginal words, many other Hebrew words have been considered synonymous with *berit*. Such words are *dābār*, "word"; *etse*, "counsel"; *tōrâ*, "law"; *ʿēdût*, "statute"; *ʾālâ* and *šĕbûʿâ*, "oath." None of these, according to Barr, are true synonyms of *bĕrît*. Some of these terms often accompany *bĕrît* and are associated with it, but are not strict synonyms of it. Barr concluded that from the standpoint of semantic analysis, we might do better to suppose that *berit* is a primitive Hebrew noun, no more "derived" from anything else than "*ab* father," and that "it never had any other meanings than those which we find in the Old Testament" ("Some Semantic Notes on the Covenant," 35).

In 1986 E. W. Nicholson published two important works on the covenant (*God and His People*; "Israelite Religion in the

Pre-exilic Period" in *A Word in Season*). He traced the history of covenant studies and argued that the covenant may still be considered the central theme of the Old Testament. *Covenant* refers to choice. *Covenant* makes Old Testament religion unique and distinctive not because other religions did not use the idea of covenant, but because Israel's idea was not based on nature or necessity. God chose Israel freely for no expressed reason, and Israel responded freely to God's offer (*God and His People,* vii-viii).

In 1991 Christoph Barth claimed that "making a covenant" has a legal background. When God chose Abraham, God did not show him an isolated kindness which He might withdraw at His pleasure. He entered into a "lasting and regulated" relationship that could be understood only in legal terms because it was founded on God's justice. The terms *ṣĕdeqâ* "justice" and *ḥesed* "covenant-love" are a part of covenant language.

Christoph Barth said, "When the Old Testament portrays God as 'submitting' to the legal agreement that he has set up, it is speaking figuratively. After all, the covenant is simply God's Word to Abraham when he promised him his blessing. Through the covenant God laid bare his heart to Abraham and declared to him his firm intention to keep his Word" (*God With Us,* 52). A legal agreement sets rights and duties for each party, but the "rights" of the human party in the covenant are based on God's promise. Israel and Jacob were not worthy of these "rights"; nor did they earn them (Gen. 32:10).

God did not owe anyone anything. He was not a prisoner of His own act or promise. He was free to do what He pleased. He kept faith freely by His own decision (*God With Us,* 52).

One of the newest and most significant trends in Old Testament theology is associated with the name Hans H. Schmid. This trend is often referred to as "creation-theology." It is a reappraisal of creation not merely as a common theme with ancient Near Eastern religions, but as the broad horizon of Israelite faith and belief. There has been a shift to the theme of the "divine ordering of the world" as the framework for religious "givens" that Israel shared with her neighbors and within which the distinctive features of Israel's religion had to be and were worked out. According to this view, one does not begin with the "particularist" themes of election and covenant, but with the "universalist theme of creation and faith." (See Schmid, *Gerechtigkeit als Weltordnung*; Nicholson, *God and His People,* vii, 194-207; "Israelite Religion in the Pre-exilic Period," 19-29.)

Robert Davidson characterized the current state of Old Testament covenant studies by saying:

> The key questions around which the debate continues, involving the use of extra-biblical material and the relationship between traditio-historical methodology and the new literary approaches to the Old Testament, concern the provenance of these different covenant traditions and their interrelatedness. It is doubtful whether the pan-Deuteronomic thesis, or theories of exilic redaction, which have characterized much recent study, can have the last word to say on these issues ("Covenant Ideology in Ancient Israel," 343-344).

The covenant materials in the Old Testament are so massive and varied, and scholarly literature is so massive, that it will take more time to settle these issues. We now turn our attention to the Old Testament materials on the covenant.

C. Covenant in the Old Testament

1) Covenant with Noah—bĕrît "covenant" first appears in the Old Testament in Genesis 6:18. God told Noah that He was about to bring a flood upon the earth. It would destroy all flesh. Then God said, "I will establish my covenant with you, and you shall come into the ark." Does this refer to a covenant God made with Noah before he went into the ark, or is it a promise of the covenant God would make with Noah at the end of the Flood? Delitzsch and Gunkel distinguished the two covenants, taking this pre-Flood covenant as a pledge for Noah's safety during the flood. John Murray insisted that this first reference to covenant in the Old Testament was prior to the Flood; he sees the covenant as one of grace, based on the sovereignty of God ("Covenant," 264). S. R. Driver (*The Book of Genesis,* 88) took it as a promise of the covenant given in 9:8-17.

God's covenant with Noah includes his descendants and every living creature with him (9:10). It is an unconditional and everlasting covenant that promises that God will never cut off all flesh by the waters of a flood. The sign of the covenant is a bow high above all humans, between heaven and earth, as a pledge of true grace. Von Rad said:

> The Hebrew word that we translate "rainbow" usually means in
> the Old Testament "the bow of war." The beauty of the ancient
> conception thus becomes apparent: God shows the world that he
> has put aside his bow. Man knows of the blessing of this new
> gracious relationship in the stability of the orders of nature, i.e.,
> first of all in the sphere of the impersonal elements only (*Gene-
> sis,* 130).

God's covenant with Noah was His covenant with humanity
and all earth's creatures (Gen. 9:9-10) that he would never
again destroy the earth by flood; that the four seasons would
continue (Gen. 8:21-22). Mankind could eat the flesh of animals but not the blood. Anyone or anything killing a human
should die because humans are made in the image of God
(Gen. 9:6). Humans were to multiply and fill the earth. God's
power over nature and history are assumed in this covenant.
God's grace and judgment are also asserted.

2) Covenant with Adam (?)—Genesis says nothing about a
covenant with Adam. Some scholars have inferred from the
early chapters of Genesis and some New Testament passages
that God made a covenant with Adam. Julius Wellhausen
spoke of a *liber quattuor foederum,* a "Book of Four Covenants,"
between God and Adam, Noah, Abraham, and Moses (*Prolegomena,* 338-342, 357). Wellhausen said that the covenant with
Adam (Gen. 1:28—2:4) is the simplest of the four. It is not called
a covenant but is the basis of the covenant with Noah, which
modifies it (Zimmerli, *Old Testament Theology,* 55).

Some earlier biblical and systematic theologians such as
Francis Roberts in 1657 spoke of a covenant with Adam. (See
Francis Roberts, *The Mysterie and Marrow of the Bible: viz.,
God's Covenants with Man, in the first Adam, before the Fall;
and in the last Adam, Jesus Christ, after the Fall; from the
Beginning to the End of the World; Unfolded and Illustrated in
positive Aphorisms and their Explanations,* 2 vols; C. A.
Briggs, *The Study of Holy Scripture,* 465.) Roberts anticipated
Cocceius and the Dutch Federal theology. W. T. Conner said
the Federal theory teaches that:

> God made a covenant with Adam, the terms of which were that
> on condition of Adam's obedience to God his descendants should
> have eternal life; on conditions of his disobedience his sin
> should be charged to them, and hence they would be guilty and
> condemned. There is not a shred of evidence from the Bible that

> any such covenant was made with Adam. Somebody has well
> said that the covenant originated in Holland rather than in the
> Garden of Eden. Such a charging of the sins of one human indi-
> vidual to another on the ground of a covenant, with which the
> one to whom sin is charged had nothing to do, would be the
> height of injustice (*The Gospel of Redemption,* 29-30).

Even so, whole systems of Old Testament theology have
been built on the idea of a covenant of works before the fall and
a covenant of grace after the fall. Gerhard Vos, Edward J.
Young, John Murray, and J. Barton Payne, all from the Princeton and Westminster Seminary tradition, follow the Federal
theologians and argue that there were in fact these two covenants before and after the fall. The covenant of grace (after the
fall) was a monergic covenant—that is, completely the work of
God. (See Vos, *Biblical Theology*; E. J. Young, *The Study of Old
Testament Theology Today,* 61-78; J. Barton Payne, *The Theology of the Older Testament.*)

Again, the Old Testament says nothing about a covenant
between God and Adam. The first covenant in the Old Testament is between God and Noah. It is a promissory covenant
assuring the whole human race of the stability of the orders of
nature. By New Testament times, Jews and Christians had
developed the laws of Noah, which applied to the whole human
race rather than to Jews only. These Noah laws, based on Genesis 9:17 and parts of the Holiness Code (Lev. 17-26), include
such universal laws as not eating blood or an animal that had
been strangled and not permitting murder, adultery, idolatry,
or blasphemy (compare Acts 15:28-29).

3) Covenant with Abraham—The second covenant in the Old
Testament is between God and Abraham. Three different
accounts of this covenant appear in Genesis 12; 15; and 17. Genesis 12 does not contain the term "covenant," but it does have
the account of Abram's call out of Ur. God promises that Abram's
name will be great, that he will become a great nation (12:2),
that the land of Canaan will belong to his descendants (12:7),
that a divine blessing will belong to those blessing Abram, that
a curse will be upon those cursing him, and that Abram himself
will bless all the families of the earth (12:3). Nothing is said in
this chapter about any obligation on Abram other than the
implied obligation to go where God told him to go.

The word "covenant" does occur in Genesis 15:18. The promises of a land and a great posterity are repeated. Although Abram responded in faith to God's promise (15:6), no particular conditions are attached to the covenant in this chapter. The covenant-making ritual, involving dividing sacrificial animals, is described in Genesis 15:9-10. Such a ceremony is mentioned in only one other place in the Old Testament (Jer. 34:17-20), but similar rituals have been found in Mari, Alalakh, and Aslan Tash (see Cross, *Canaanite Myth and Hebrew Epic,* 265-266).

Some scholars see this "self-curse" ceremony as evidence of some obligation resting on both parties of the covenant. But John Bright argued that the ceremony assures Abraham that, after generations of hard bondage, his descendants would possess the land. John Bright believed this means that God binds himself "by a solemn self-curse to make his promises good. The patriarchal covenant thus rests in God's unconditional promises for the future, and it asks the recipient only that he trust" (*Covenant and Promise,* 26). Of course, scholars like Perlitt and Kutsch disagreed with Bright. They see obligation in almost all covenants.

The third account of a covenant between God and Abraham appears in Genesis 17. The language of this chapter is different. The word "establish," *hăqîm,* is used rather than "cut," *kārat.* "Establish" emphasizes the role of God in the process and implies some permanence to the arrangement. In fact, the word "everlasting" occurs in verses 7, 8, and 13. The promise is for a great posterity (vv. 2,5) and the land (v. 8). The only stated obligations in the passage are that Abraham is to "walk before me (*El Shaddai*) and be blameless" (v. 1) and that he keep "my covenant" by circumcising every male among them (v. 10).

Ronald Clements observed that "this rite of circumcision does not make the covenant conditional in the manner of the law covenant of Sinai, hence no difficulty was anticipated in carrying out the requirement to circumcise every male child. It must firmly be stressed that the Priestly authors intended to make circumcision a sign, and not a restrictive condition" (*Old Testament Theology,* 73). Walther Zimmerli said that once again we are dealing with a pure promise, as was the case in Genesis 15. Any individual who is not circumcised breaks the covenant and will be cut off (17:14), but the punishment affects only the disobedient individual. "The covenant as a whole remains intact" (*Old Testament Theology in Outline,* 56).

Abraham's covenant is a binding promise or a "promissory oath on God's part" (R. Davidson, "Covenant Ideology in Ancient Israel," 338). A running debate has been conducted between scholars who believe the accounts of the Abrahamic covenant are a reading back of later concepts from the Davidic, Solomonic, or even post-exilic periods, and those who see evidence of a tradition of this covenant that can be traced back to its roots in a "cultic" repetition of the account of the promise in Genesis 15:7-21 (see R. E. Clements, "Abraham and David: Genesis 15 and Its Meaning for Israelite Tradition").

I agree with the early dating. Robert Davidson said in this connection that "there is a real danger of the exilic period becoming a convenient catchment area for much of what is regarded as theologically significant in the Old Testament with too little concern to trace back to their sources the varied rivulets which flow into this catchment area ("Covenant Ideology in Ancient Israel," 342).

4) Covenant with Israel at Sinai—The covenant God made with Israel at Sinai is presented in the Old Testament as an extension or a fulfillment of the covenant God made with Abraham.

> After a long time the king of Egypt died. The Israelites groaned under their slavery, and cried out. Out of the slavery their cry for help rose up to God. God heard their groaning, and God remembered his covenant with Abraham, Isaac, and Jacob (Ex. 2:23-24).

> God also spoke to Moses and said to him: "I am the LORD. I appeared to Abraham, Isaac, and Jacob as God Almighty, but by my name 'The LORD' I did not make myself known to them. I also established my covenant with them, to give them the land of Canaan, the land in which they resided as aliens. I have also heard the groaning of the Israelites whom the Egyptians are holding as slaves, and I have remembered my covenant. Say therefore to the Israelites, 'I am the LORD, and I will free you from the burdens of the Egyptians and deliver you from slavery to them. I will redeem you with an outstretched arm and with mighty acts of judgment. I will take you as my people, and I will be your God. You shall know that I am the LORD your God, who

has freed you from the burdens of the Egyptians. I will bring you into the land that I swore to give to Abraham, Isaac, and Jacob; I will give it to you for a possession. I am the LORD ' (Ex. 6:2-8).

The primary account of the Sinai covenant is in Exodus 19—24, one of the most important passages in the Old Testament. Terrien said, "Few pages in the literature of mankind compare to this awesome description of an encounter between God and man" (*The Elusive Presence,* 119). The passage is made up of various kinds of materials (theophany, narrative, laws, cultic materials), and substantial disagreement exists among scholars concerning the exact strata which have been woven into the present text.

Childs believed that the literary tensions in Exodus 19 are such that the traditional source division (J and E) is unable to cope with them. He said that even if two literary strands, such as J and E, are present in chapter 19, they share so much of the same oral tradition that a separation is unlikely and without great significance (*The Book of Exodus,* 350). Childs said that one must be aware of the depth and the variety of forces which have been at work on this passage, but at the same time one must concentrate his efforts on interpreting the final stage of the text.

According to the passage (Ex. 19—24) as it now stands, Israel arrived at Sinai in the third month after leaving Egypt (19:1-2). God offered to make a covenant with Israel, and all the people agreed. Moses served as the mediator between God and Israel (19:3-9). The people prepared for the appearance of God (19:10-15). On the morning of the third day, God descended on Sinai with fire, smoke, clouds, thunder, and quakings (19:16-25). Then Yahweh proclaimed the Ten Commandments of the covenant (20:1-17). The people drew back in fear and trembling and asked Moses to be their mediator (20:18-21). The laws of the covenant were given (20:22—23:33), and the covenant between God and Israel was sealed with sacrificial blood and a communal meal (24:1-18).

Before Israel left Sinai, they broke their covenant with Yahweh by making a golden calf and worshiping it (Ex. 32:3-8). After God's judgment and Moses' intercession, the covenant was renewed (Ex. 34:10,27-28).

Another account of the Sinai covenant appears in Deuteronomy, a covenant book. The term *bĕrît* occurs at least twenty-seven times in Deuteronomy. Deuteronomy is concerned with renewing the Sinai covenant with the second generation of Israelites, the survivors of wilderness wanderings before they went into the land of Canaan. Succeeding generations of Israelites probably used the materials in the book as a covenant renewal document down to the time of Josiah's reform and beyond (29:14-15).

The Sinai covenant, in contrast to the Abrahamic covenant, seems to emphasize the human obligation to keep the laws and ordinances so that the covenant would continue in effect. So there arose two covenant traditions in Israel: (1) the promissory covenant tradition connected with Noah, Abraham, and David, and (2) the human obligation covenant related to the events of Sinai. It seems that the Sinai covenant became the basis for the twelve-tribe league during the time of Joshua and the Judges (Josh. 24).

5) Covenant with David—The rise of the monarchy brought a change in the idea of covenant. The king needed divine approval and support. God made a covenant with David that one of his descendants would always occupy his throne (2 Sam. 7:12-16). The word covenant does not occur in this passage, but it appears in "the last words of David" (2 Sam. 23:5). God's covenant with David was twofold: (1) David's kingdom would be established forever (Pss. 18:50; 89:3-4,35-37; Isa. 55:3), and (2) Jerusalem or Zion would be God's dwelling place forever (1 Kings 8:12-13; Pss. 78:68-69; 132:13-14).

When Solomon died, the monarchy split into the Northern and Southern Kingdoms. The Northern Kingdom, consisting of ten tribes, maintained the Sinai covenant with its seeming human obligation features. The Southern Kingdom kept its capital in Jerusalem and had a descendant of David on the throne, thus holding to the promissory Davidic covenant. It is possible that in capturing Jerusalem and making it his capital, David retained some of the religious traditions and personnel from the Jebusites. These ideas could have influenced Judah's concept of kingship and everlasting covenant. (See Bright, *Covenant and Promise,* 49-77; Cross, *Canaanite Myth and Hebrew Epic,* 229-287; Miller and Hayes, *A History of Ancient Israel and Judah,* 173.)

Of course, those scholars who hold that no clear idea of a covenant concept emerged in Israel until post-exilic times have problems with a Davidic covenant. Hayes and Miller said, "Covenant is a late motif in the patriarchal traditions (Kutsch; Perlitt)", and 2 Samuel 7 is the final product of Deuteronomistic reworking of these materials (*A History of Ancient Israel and Judah,* 142, 333).

6) The Prophets and the Covenant—The eighth-century prophets made little use of the term "covenant," perhaps because of the people's false impression that it was automatic. Amos nowhere used the term to refer to God's relationship with Israel; however, it is clear that the crimes he attacked were infractions of covenant law. Though Hosea used the word "covenant" rarely (and is the only eighth-century prophet to do so), he accused Israel of breaking her covenant with Yahweh. In one place (4:1-3) he depicted Yahweh as launching His covenant lawsuit against His people. Hosea was steeped in the traditions of the Exodus, the wilderness wanderings, and the conquest, as well as in the stipulations of Yahweh's covenant (at Sinai). But the theology of Yahweh's eternal covenant with David seems to have meant nothing to him. Hosea was the first prophet to use the metaphor of marriage for the covenant relationship between Yahweh and Israel.

In the Southern Kingdom, Isaiah was rooted in the traditions of David and the sure promise God had made to him. This was the theological basis of Isaiah's lifelong criticism of national policy. Isaiah was probably also acquainted with the Sinai covenant traditions. Jeremiah stood in the Northern Kingdom traditions and, therefore, worked from the basis of the Sinai covenant. He insisted that Israel had broken her covenant with God (11:3-10; 22:9; 31:32; 34:18).

Many people opposed Jeremiah at this point, claiming that God's covenant with Jerusalem was everlasting and the Temple was inviolable. But Jeremiah was right. Nebuchadnezzar came against Jerusalem, destroyed the city, burned the Temple, and carried many of the people into Babylon as captives. This brought a spiritual crisis to the people who believed that God would protect Jerusalem, the Temple, and the people at all costs.

John Bright said:

The foundations of faith had been shaken. Israel's very survival as a definable community was at stake. And, humanly speaking, one can say that she could not possibly have survived if she could not have found some explanation of the tragedy in terms of her faith, specifically in terms of Yahweh's sovereign power, justice, and faithfulness to his promises. One shudders to think of the outcome had the only voices of religion in her midst been those of priest and professional prophet proclaiming the inviolability of Zion and the eternity of the Davidic line. That was just not so! (*Promise and Covenant,* 189).

Jeremiah, Ezekiel, and others interpreted what happened to Jerusalem as an act of God's judgment for violating the covenant. It was a saving word that explained tragedy in terms of faith. God's action did not mean the death of Israel or of religion. It did not mean that God was unfair or unjust.

But what about the future? Was there any hope? Jeremiah wrote a letter to some people carried captive to Babylon in 597 B.C. In that letter he said:

For surely I know the plans I have for you, says the LORD, plans for your welfare and not for harm, to give you a future with hope. Then when you call upon me and come and pray to me, I will hear you. When you search for me, you will find me; if you seek me with all your heart, I will let you find me, says the LORD, and I will restore your fortunes and gather you from all the nations and all the places where I have driven you, says the LORD, and I will bring you back to the place from which I sent you into exile (Jer. 29:11-14).

Jeremiah, like most of the Old Testament prophets, believed hope beckoned beyond judgment. What form would that hope for the future take?

7) The New Covenant—The future hope for Israel would not take the form of the promise of the restoration of the state along the old lines, or even the coming of a "messianic" deliverer of the house of David. It took the form of the promise of a new covenant. We may ask, "How can there be a *new* covenant?" Israel had no power, merit, or basis to claim a new one; but God initiated the first covenant, and He would initiate a new one.

What good would a new covenant do? Would it not be quickly broken, as the former one was? God could remedy that situation also. He would forgive past sins and write His covenant law on the hearts (that is, the minds and wills) of His people, thus giving them both the desire and the ability to obey it and live as His people. When would this happen? All that Jeremiah could say was, "The days are surely coming" (31:31).

This new covenant is in some ways similar to the old one. It was given by divine initiative, and based on grace, with the expectation of obedience. The difference is that the people are made new (Bright, *Covenant and Promise,* 196; Bright, "An Exercise in Hermeneutics: Jeremiah 31:31-34," 188-210).

Does this mean that the Sinai covenant was right and the Davidic covenant wrong? Bright was probably correct in concluding that both covenants gave expression to essential features in Israel's faith. The Sinai covenant reminded Israel of God's grace and of their obligations. The Abrahamic and Davidic covenants reminded Israel that their future did not rest ultimately on what they were or what they did or did not do but upon "the immutable purpose of God which nothing could cancel" (*Covenant and Promise,* 196).

Both covenant patterns continued in the New Testament. There they are brought together in Christ and announced as fulfilled. Bright concluded that the church, like Israel, lives under both patterns of covenant. We have received from Christ unqualified promises to which no conditions have been attached. We have also received grace and stipulations: "keep my commandments" (John 14:10).

To accept the promise without the obligations would be to sink into complacency. To shoulder the burdens of Christ's commands without the promises would be to despair or to fall into self-righteous legalism. So we, like Israel, must live in tension. "It is a tension between grace and obligation: The unconditional promises in which we are invited to trust, and the obligation to obey him as the church's sovereign Lord" (Bright, *Covenant and Promise,* 198).

In addition to the term "new covenant," other expressions such as "everlasting covenant" and "the covenant of peace" occur. What is the relationship between these expressions? The term "new covenant" occurs only once in the Old Testament (Jer. 31:31) and seven times in the New Testament (Matt. 26:28; Mark 14:24; Luke 22:20; 1 Cor. 11:25; Heb. 8:8; 9:15; 12:24), while the expression "everlasting covenant" occurs nineteen times in the Old Testament and only once in the New Testament (Heb. 13:20). The new covenant in Jeremiah 31:31-34 is not described as an everlasting covenant, and the everlasting covenant in the Old Testament is never called a new covenant. This, however, does not mean that the two concepts are unrelated. Some references to an everlasting covenant in the Old Testament are to covenants made in the past: once to the covenant with Noah (Gen. 9:16); four times to the covenant with Abraham (Gen. 17:7,13; Ps. 105:8-10; 1 Chron. 16:15-17); once to sabbath observance (Ex. 31:16); once to the shewbread (Lev. 24:8); once to the priesthood of Phinehas (Num. 25:13); once to Israel's breaking the everlasting covenant (Isa. 24:5). Six references to the "everlasting covenant" are to a covenant to be made in the future. Yahweh says on five occasions that he will make an everlasting covenant with Israel (Isa. 55:3; 61:8; Jer. 32:40; Ezek. 16:60; 37:26). Once He predicts that Israel will join with Judah in weeping and seeking Yahweh their God, asking to be joined to the LORD by an "everlasting covenant that will never be forgotten" (Jer. 50:5).

On two occasions, the future covenant between Yahweh and Israel is called a "covenant of peace" (Ezek. 34:25; 37:26). This covenant of peace is also to be an everlasting covenant (Ezek. 37:26; compare Isa. 54:4-10).

Is the new covenant to be completely new, with no continuity to the old covenant? If not, what will be new about it? Is the everlasting covenant of the future to be unbreakable? The old one was breakable on the part of Israel (Isa. 24:5; Jer. 31:32; 34:18; Ezek. 17:19; 44:7) and even on the part of Yahweh. Although Yahweh says He will not break His covenant (Lev. 26:44; Judg. 2:1; Ps. 89:34), He is accused of renouncing it (Ps. 89:39) and of annulling it (Zech. 11:10). These last two references could be understood as temporary actions.

Does the word "everlasting," *ʿōlām* mean "unending," "eternal" in a philosophical sense? Holladay says it does not (*ʿōlām, Concise Hebrew-Aramaic Lexicon,* 267). G. A. F. Knight said:

> *Everlasting, 'olam,* is a word that is not primarily connected with life beyond the grave. It comes from the root meaning "hidden." And so it speaks of the mists of the past, hidden from the thoughts of man, and it looks toward the mists of the future, into which man's mind cannot even begin to pry. And so it

> speaks of the God who is Lord even of the hidden realities that human beings can envisage only in terms of infinite time (*A Christian Old Testament Theology,* 45).

E. Jenni argued that the word *ʿōlām* basically means "the remotest time" ("Das Wort *'Olam* im Alten Testament," 246-247). The remotest time may refer to the past or to the future. Nothing in the word itself specifies how remote the time referred to is. Such specification may be derived from the context (Barr, *Biblical Words for Time,* 70). Thus in Joshua 24:2, *mēʿōlām* means "from remote time." Jeremiah 28:8 speaks of "the prophets who preceded you and me," *min-haʿōlām,* "from the remote time." Barr said that such cases could be translated "from eternity," but they would have to be understood as referring to the remote past within time. The word *ʿōlām* is ambiguous and should not be understood as "eternity" in a philosophical sense. In postbiblical Hebrew *ʿōlām* is used for this age, *hazeh ʿōlām,* and the age to come, *haʿōlām habaʾ.* "Everlasting" in the Old Testament means "as far as one can see or comprehend and beyond." D. F. Payne said that the term *bĕrît ʿōlām* may be translated "covenant of indefinite duration and may imply nothing more than the contracts so described, though concluded with a specific individual (or generation), affected his (or its) posterity as well" ("The Everlasting Covenant," 10-16). However, Payne hastened to say that we cannot accept this interpretation in every case.

Marten H. Woudstra said, "It is not true that a covenant which is called 'everlasting' cannot be broken" ("The Everlasting Covenant in Ezekiel 16:59-63," 32). "No one, it seems ever made a *bĕrît* for a limited period, or if they did so no instances of it found their way into the biblical text" (Cross, *Canaanite Myth and Hebrew Epic,* 35; see Nicholson, *God and His People,* 103).

Moshe Weinfeld, on the basis of his study of the "royal grants" in the Ancient Near East, suggested that Yahweh's covenants with Abraham and David in the Old Testament were patterned on those old royal grants. These royal grants of land and dynasty were given by the emperor to a loyal vassal. They were unconditional and could not be taken away ("The Covenant of Grant in the Old Testament and in the Ancient Near East," 189-192).

Since the covenants with Abraham, David, and Israel are said in some sense to be everlasting, how are we to understand their fulfillment? Have they been fulfilled in Christ and the church, or are they still to be fulfilled in the nation Israel? Dispensationalists argue that the new covenant is primarily for Israel. Some argue for two new covenants: one for the church and one for Israel. (See *The Ryrie Study Bible,* Heb. 8:6.) For a critique of this view see McComiskey, *The Covenants of Promise,* 157-161).

This subject is outside the limits of a descriptive study of Old Testament theology, and there is much disagreement about how Old Testament passages on the covenant are to be understood today. One's theological understanding of these passages and their meaning for today will be determined largely by one's hermeneutical understanding and methodology. Most Jews and Christians understand these passages differently. But all Jews do not agree with each other on matters of eschatology, and certainly all Christians do not agree with one another on these matters.

Robert D. Culver, a staunch premillenialist, discussed the issue of the fulfillment of these Old Testament passages. He reviewed the viewpoints of Augustine, Calvin, Luther, Arminianism, covenant theologians, premillenialists, amillenialists, postmillentialists, and dispensationalists. He then concluded that these matters should be treated as a question of eschatology and "be permitted to remain so" (*Daniel and the Latter Days,* 20). He advocated not taking a polemical partisan attitude, but commended the subject with affection and humility to the attention of his brethren in the ministry and fellow Christians of every persuasion, attempting to keep an open mind toward being shown a more excellent way (*Daniel and the Latter Days,* 22).

For a concise treatment of this issue in the New Testament, see Bruce Corley ("The Jews, the Future and God," 42-56).

5

Who Is a God Like Yahweh?

When Moses and Aaron commanded Pharaoh in the name of Yahweh to let Israel go, Pharaoh asked with a note of sarcasm or contempt, "Who is the LORD that I should heed him and let Israel go? I do not know the LORD, and I will not let Israel go" (Ex. 5). Because Pharaoh did not know who Yahweh was, he refused to let Israel go. His refusal resulted in the plagues of Egypt. By the time the plagues were over, everyone in Egypt, including Pharaoh and the Israelites, knew who Yahweh was (Ex. 7:5,17; 8:10, 22; 9:14-16,29; 10:2; 11:7; 12:31-32; 14:4,18,30). Yahweh revealed who He was by what He did. He delivered a group of slaves from bondage by His mighty hand and His outstretched arm. He showed himself to be a God of compassion, power, and purpose.

It is one thing to ask out of ignorance or contempt, "Who is Yahweh?" It is another to ask out of commitment and faith, "Who is a god like Yahweh?"—suggesting that there is none comparable to him. (For a thorough discussion see C. J. Labuschagne's *The Incomparability of Yahweh in the Old Testament*.) The Old Testament often asserts that Yahweh is incomparable. In the Song of the Sea the question is:

> Who is like you, O Lord, among the gods?
> Who is like you, majestic in holiness,
> awesome in splendor, doing wonders?
> (Ex. 15:11)

The psalmists said:

> Your way, O God, is holy.
> What god is so great as our God?
> You are the God who works wonders;
> you have displayed your might
> among the peoples.
> With your strong arm you
> redeemed your people,
> the descendants of Jacob and Joseph.
> Ps. 77:13-15)

> For who in the skies can be
> compared to the LORD?
> Who among the heavenly beings
> is like the LORD?
> Ps. 89:6)

Micah asked:

> Who is a God like you, pardoning iniquity
> and passing over the transgression
> of the remnant of your possession?
> (Micah 7:18)

These rhetorical questions assert that no God is as great, powerful, holy, majestic, awesome, inspiring, and forgiving as Yahweh. These terms are only a few of a multitude of words used in the Old Testament to describe him. He is a God of wrath, jealousy, judgment, and vengeance (2 Sam. 22:48; Ps. 94:1; Nah. 1:2-6). He is good and a God of love, mercy, and compassion (Ex. 34:6; Hos. 11:8; Nah.1:7). He is gracious, glorious, and awesome. He is holy, faithful, and true. He is from everlasting to everlasting (Ps. 90:1). He is the God of heaven who dwells on earth. (Ezek 43:7,9; Dan. 2:18-19; Jonah 1:9). He regrets (Gen. 6:6) but does not change (Mal. 3:6).

God walks in the garden in the cool of the day (Gen. 3:8,10). He appears to Abraham as a man, eats with him, and announces the birth of Isaac and the destruction of Sodom (Gen. 18:1-8,16-21). He speaks with Moses "face to face" (Ex. 33:11; compare Gen. 32:30; Deut. 5:4; 34:10), yet no one can see

God and live (Ex. 33:20). He is not human (Num. 23:19), but He has a face, hands, feet, eyes, nostrils, and ears. He is like fire (Ex. 19:18; Deut. 4:24; Ezek. 1:27-28), light (Ps. 104:2); a lion (Amos 1:2).

Yahweh's name occurs over 6500 times in the Old Testament, and the word *ĕlohîm* (God) appears more than 2500 times. In the Old Testament the single overwhelmingly emphasized concept is of God. Yahweh is the central character. The name of God appears in every Old Testament book except Esther and Song of Songs.

How are we to present what the Old Testament says about God? Are we to deal with the topic chronologically, according to the different literary genres, or according to the different theological perspectives (Prophets, priests, Wisdom)? Should we try to present a systematic arrangement of the material from the entire Old Testament in its final canonical form? It would be interesting and informative to show the characteristics of Israel's God set forth in the written records chronologically arranged, as these vary in emphasis from century to century.

For an Old Testament theology, the question "Who is a God like Yahweh?" should be answered in a systematic manner from a study of the final canonical form of the Old Testament. The Old Testament is consistent in its description of God. Ronald Clements said, "In its preserved canonical form the Old Testament certainly intends to present God as one unique supernatural being who has revealed himself to Abraham, Moses and other great figures of Israel's life, and who is the Lord and sole creator of the universe" (*Old Testament Theology*, 53).

A quick survey of the basic books on Old Testament theology shows no single way to present the Old Testament materials on the doctrine of God. A few basic themes appear in almost all of them. It would be practically impossible to deal with all the Old Testament says about God. A presentation of such material must be selective and represent the most significant and unique concepts about God in the Old Testament. We will present what the Old Testament says about God around nine themes: a saving God, a blessing God, a creating God, a holy

God, a loving God, a wrathful God, a judging God, a forgiving God, and the one and only God.

18. A Saving God

A. Why Begin with God as Savior?

We begin this discussion of the Old Testament view of God with the theme of God as savior because Israel knew God as savior before they knew Him as Lord. The Exodus (salvation) precedes the making of the covenant between Yahweh and Israel at Sinai (law). Israel also knew Yahweh as savior before they knew Him as creator. "The history of Israel began with the saving action of God which was motivated by compassion" (Westermann, *Elements of Old Testament Theology,* 35). Yahweh was Israel's God "from the land of Egypt" (Hos. 12:9).

> Yet I have been the LORD your God
> ever since the land of Egypt;
> you know no God but me,
> and besides me there is no savior.
> (Hos. 13:4)

B. Meaning of Salvation in the Old Testament

The words "save," "savior," and "salvation" in Hebrew are all related to the root *yš'*, which has the fundamental meaning of "to be broad," "to become spacious," "to have plenty of room" (Richardson, "Salvation, Savior," 169; Scherer, *Event in Eternity,* 154-155). Salvation is a term with a wide range of meanings. It can refer to salvation from enemies, disease, sin, destruction, and/or death. It is used with people as its subject—that is, human saviors—but in the Old Testament God is most often the subject. It is used of past, present, and future deliverances. It is used primarily for the salvation of Israel, but can be used for the salvation of the human race and/or of an individual.

Most of the Old Testament is concerned with Israel as a nation or group; therefore, the primary role of Yahweh as a saving God was to deliver Israel from their enemies. Sometimes the enemies were other nations, such as the Egyptians, Amalekites, Philistines, and Babylonians. Sometimes Israel needed to be saved from their own sin of idolatry or the worship of Baal, which was tantamount to breaking the covenant with Yahweh. Alan Richardson said that the Old Testament is not concerned primarily with asking in what salvation consists or in the techniques by which it might be attained. Instead, it is concerned primarily with the proclamation of what God has done and what He will do.

> This is the theme both of the Old Testament and of the New Testament. God is a God of salvation: this is the gospel of both Jewish and Christian faith. He has saved his people and will save them; in the Bible salvation is both a historical and an eschatological reality. God is often called "Savior," and "Salvation" is in some parts of the Bible a name for God. It is therefore wholly appropriate that the Son of God, by whom the divine purpose of salvation was achieved, should have been called Jesus, which means "Savior." Thus salvation is the central theme of the whole Bible ("Salvation, Savior," 168).

Claus Westermann traced the work of God as Savior through the Pentateuch, the historical books, the Prophets and the Psalms, pointing out that often God is presented not only as the savior of Israel but of individuals and nations as well. Westermann concluded that because the dangers and threats to human beings and their need for deliverance are so great and diverse, the acts of saving can be diverse also. Yet God is the savior in every circumstance. "The Old and New Testaments . . . agree in the statement that God is the savior. The fact that God is the savior is an aspect of his divinity in the Old as well as the New Testament." That God is the savior in both the Old and New Testaments "cannot be disputed . . . the saving God is of central significance" (*Elements of Old Testament Theology,* 46).

Westermann believed that God's saving acts in the Old Testament involve a process. The basic structure of the process of salvation is: need, cry for help, word of hearing, divine deliverance, and response of the saved. Westermann saw this structure behind the Books of Exodus and Judges. Salvation must be related to a conscious need. Without a need there would be no salvation. To be saved, one needs to recognize personal helplessness and cry out to God. God hears the cries of the needy and delivers them. Then the people praise the Lord for His steadfast love and mighty acts.

The Old Testament proclaimed, "Deliverance (salvation) belongs to the Lord" (Ps. 3:8, Jonah 2:9). "Save is the constant prayer, 'salvation' the constant desire, of the Psalmist" (Kirkpatrick, *The Book of Psalms,* 16). But are the people of Israel the only people to be saved? Is Yahweh concerned with the needs of the nations? The Old Testament is primarily the story of Yahweh's special relationship with Israel. From the first chapter of Exodus to the end of Malachi, the primary focus is on Yahweh and Israel. Occasionally a larger picture of the world emerges, and other nations come into view. Even then, the concern with other nations is directly related to Yahweh's relation to Israel.

The first eleven chapters of Genesis are concerned with all nations, but these chapters are a prologue or backdrop to the drama of redemption that begins in Genesis 12 with Abraham. Genesis 12:3 provides a clue that God called Abraham in order to bless the families of the earth in a special way. The idea that the nations will be blessed reappears in Genesis 18:18; 22:18; 26:4; 28:14; Deuteronomy 29:19; Psalm 72:17; Isaiah 65:16; Jeremiah 4:2.

At times other nations are to be put under the ban (*herem*) and destroyed (Num. 31:17-18; Deut. 7:1-5; 20:16-18), or they are to become the slaves of Israel (Isa. 49:22-23; 60:14; Mic. 7:16-17). The foreign prophecies of Amos, Isaiah, and Jeremiah and the apocalyptic woes of Ezekiel and Zechariah speak of defeat and destruction of the nations. However, a ray of hope for the other peoples of the world shines periodically throughout the Old Testament (Ps. 22:27; Isa. 2:1-4; Jer. 12:14-16; 16:19-21; Mic. 4: 1-4; Zech. 2:11; 8:20-23; 14:16).

> I will give you as a light to the nations,
> that my salvation may reach to
> the end of the earth.
> (Isa. 49:6b)

> Turn to me and be saved,
> all the ends of the earth!
> For I am God, and there is no other.
> (Isa. 45:22)

> Before me no god was formed,
> nor shall there be any after me.
> I, I am the LORD,
> and besides me there is no savior.
> (Isa. 43:10-11; compare 43:3;
> 45:15,21; 49:26; 60:16; 63:8-9)

Many people think of salvation in the Bible only in terms of salvation from sin. Edward J. Young argued that the only true Old Testament theology is one that does "full justice to the Fall" (*The Study of Old Testament Theology Today*, 42). Young also said:

> There is one interpretation only which does justice to the Scriptural data, and that is the one which takes seriously the claims of the Bible that God truly entered into covenant with unfallen Adam, and that He again entered into a covenant with the fallen Adam. This fact is basic to a proper understanding of all Old Testament revelation. Upon it, indeed, subsequent revelation builds. In fact, the further revelation given in the Old Testament is based upon the presupposition that man is a fallen creature, estranged from God, and that he needs reconciliation to God. The breach which sin has introduced into the relations existing between man and God must be healed, and this work of healing is of God alone (*The Study of Old Testament Theology Today*, 69).

Salvation from sin is a cardinal doctrine in the Scriptures, but Young seems to have taken his theology to a study of the Scriptures rather than allowing the Scriptures to determine his theology. The Old Testament never mentions a covenant between God and Adam, either before or after the fall. The terms "save" and "salvation" are used in the Old Testament more often of deliverance from physical evils than from sin. Salvation in the Old and New Testaments is a broad term. It is used of deliverance from evil, whether that evil be physical (national defeat, famine, poverty, fear, illness), moral, or spiritual.

F. J. Taylor said that "nearly a third of the New Testament references to salvation denote deliverance from specific ills, such as captivity, disease, and demon possession (Matt. 9:21; Luke 8:36), eschatological terrors (Mark 13:20), or physical death (Matt. 8:28; Acts 7:20)" ("Save, Salvation," 219-220).

Otto Baab asked:

> How does the conception of salvation depend on the nature of sin? Sin, we have seen is man's refusal to recognize his creaturehood, and his proud assertion of his spiritual uniqueness and freedom. He pretends he is God and proceeds to create images of himself in the form of economic or political power, intellectual systems that are sacrosanct, and moral codes replacing the divine righteousness, thus seeking to prove to himself and his fellows that he is God rather than a creature of

> God. He uses his freedom idolatrously and unethically,
> encroaching upon the freedom of others whom he may exploit
> and enslave. This is sin. In view of this, what is salvation? (*The*
> *Theology of the Old Testament,* 119).

Baab said that salvation is the arrival of a sense of humility
and dependence on God. It requires a person to admit creatureliness, weakness, and limitation. This is not a kind of psy-
chosomatic therapy to restore the health of mind and body.
Such a restoration can come only as the result of God's work,
and not of a psychiatrist's. "Nothing less than the penetrating
light of God's condemning and illuminating holiness can
reveal man to himself and show him his sin" (*The Theology of*
the Old Testament, 119-120).

This kind of salvation from sin can occur only on the individual level. Some Old Testament passages describe individuals'
experiencing salvation from sin. The psalmists' testimonies in
Psalms 32 and 51 and Isaiah's experience in the Temple (Isa. 6)
are classic examples of individual experiences of salvation from
sin in the Old Testament. In each case God is the savior. However, the Old Testament speaks mostly of cleansing or forgiveness of sins for the group through proper observances of rituals.
Yet proper observation of rituals did not save by themselves.
Only God could save (Ps. 3:8; Jonah 2:9).

19. A Blessing God

More than any other modern scholar, Claus Westermann
emphasized the differences between the ideas of "saving" and
"blessing" in the Old Testament. Perhaps his extensive studies
in the Psalms with their laments and praise led him to this
point of view. Westermann traced the history of the study of
blessing through the works of Dillman, Schultz, Stade,
Eichrodt, von Rad, Köhler, Vriezen, Pedersen, and Mowinckel
(*Blessing in the Bible,* 15-23). He credited Johannes Pedersen
and Ludwig Köhler as being the first to see a basic difference
in meaning between deliverance and blessing. Von Rad subsumed the concept of blessing under that of salvation.

A. The Meaning of Blessing

The meaning of "blessing" changes according to the literary
source and form in the Old Testament. The widest concept of

blessing is in the first creation narrative (Gen. 1:1—2:3). There, God as Creator bestows upon the whole human race and every living creature the blessing of fertility, "be fruitful and multiply" (Gen. 1:22,28); of space, by filling the waters, air, and earth (Gen. 1:22,28); and of food (Gen. 1:29-30). Humans received the special blessing of dominion (Gen. 1:28). God also blessed the seventh day and made it holy because He rested on that day from His creation work. In the first biblical reference "blessing" is something God does for all people, all living things, and for the sabbath day (Gen. 1:1-2:3). It is universal in its scope and continuous in its effects. Genesis 5:2 and 9:1 repeat fertility and continuance.

B. Old Testament Passages Dealing with Blessing

The idea of blessing often appears with its counterpart, "curse" in Genesis 1—11. "Bless" occurs five times (1:22,28; 2:3; 5:1; 9:1), and "curse" occurs six times. God pronounces a curse on the serpent for tempting the woman (3:14), on Cain for killing his brother (4:11), and on the ground (3:17; 5:29). Noah curses his youngest son and blesses Shem and Japheth (9:25). In 8:21 God promises He will never again curse the ground because of humankind. The curses are related to acts of wrongdoing.

The idea of blessing as God's continually regular provision of care for the world changes in the patriarchal stories (Gen. 12—36). It is combined with the Abrahamic promise. In Genesis 12:1-3 the word *bārak*, "bless," occurs five times. Yahweh is the speaker, and the blessing becomes a part of the seemingly unconditional promise. The blessing (promise) involves a great name and a great nation for Abraham. Wolff pointed out that the gift of the land is never the object of the blessing. It is the object of an "oath" of Yahweh (compare Gen. 24:7; 26:3; 50:24; Num. 11:12). (See "The Kerygma of the Yahwist," 141.)

Genesis 12 joins two different theological ideas: blessing and promise. One (promise) makes salvation the delivering act of God central; the other makes the constant blessing of God central. From this point on, the promise of blessing is included in the history of the promise (P. D. Miller, "The Blessing of God," 247).

Balaam (Num. 22—24) seems to have been a well-known professional "blesser" and "curser." Threatened by Israel, Balak, the king of Moab, sent to Pethor on the Euphrates to hire Balaam to curse Israel. Reluctantly, Balaam came to Moab and attempted to curse Israel. Each time he opened his mouth he blessed them instead of cursing them. Yahweh is shown to be firmly in control of all blessing and cursing, at least as far as the fortunes of His people are concerned. Balaam said:

> How can I curse whom God has
> not cursed?
> How can I denounce those
> whom the LORD has not denounced?
> (Num. 23:8)

> See, I received a command to bless;
> he has blessed, and I cannot revoke it.
> (Num. 23:20)

> Blessed is everyone who blesses you,
> and cursed is everyone who curses you.
> (Num. 24:9*b*)

The Balaam incident shows how Yahweh could take a well-known and widespread phenomenon of the ancient world—the ability of certain persons to bless and/or curse—and use it to teach Israel that He controls all would-be professional "cursers and blessers." Any power-laden word outside of God's will is both powerless and meaningless (Westermann, *Blessing in the Bible,* 50). Here the power of the blessing is Yahweh's power to protect, secure, and defend.

Deuteronomy promises God's blessing. For Deuteronomy obedience was the way to blessing.

> He will love you, bless you, and multiply you; he will bless the fruit of your womb and the fruit of your ground, your grain and your wine and your oil, the increase of your cattle and the issue of your flock, in the land that he swore to your ancestors to give you. You shall be the most blessed of peoples, with neither sterility nor barrenness among you or your livestock. The LORD will turn away from you every illness; all the dread diseases of Egypt that you experienced, he will not inflict on you, but he will lay them on all who hate you. You shall devour all the peoples that the LORD your God is giving over to you, showing them no pity; you shall not serve their gods, for that would be a snare to you (Deut. 7:13-16).

Blessings were to be read on Mount Gerizim and curses on Mount Ebal when Israel came into the land of Canaan (Deut.

11:29; 27:12-13). Deuteronomy contains curses as well as blessings. The covenant blessings and curses are given their fullest expression in Deuteronomy 28 (compare Lev. 26). Here the saving God has become the blessing God (giver of fertility of body, field, and cattle).

The pronouncing of blessings and curses has little place in the historical books and in the Prophets. There the idea of a saving/judging God is prominent. The Psalms and Wisdom literature have more to say about God's blessing because of wisdom's emphasis on creation and the Psalms' connection with worship. The (Wisdom) Book of Job is concerned from first to last with God's bestowal of His blessings (Job 1:10; 42:12). The Psalms played a large part in Israel's worship. Since the cult (worship) was the one place where God's blessing could be transmitted to the people by priests, we are not surprised by the abundance of blessing in the Psalms.

Cultic blessing began quite early. Soon after the institution of worship at Sinai, the priestly blessing was given:

> The LORD bless you and keep you;
> the LORD make his face to shine upon you,
> and be gracious to you;
> the LORD lift up his countenance upon you,
> and give you peace.
> So they shall put my name on the Israelites,
> and I will bless them.
> (Num. 6:24-27)

G. B. Gray said that the priestly blessing gives a terse and beautiful expression to the thought that Israel owes everything to Yahweh, who shields His people from all harm and supplies everything necessary for their welfare, including peace (*Numbers*, 71).

"Bless" may refer primarily to the physical necessities of life, while "keep" emphasizes the protecting work of Yahweh. Experiencing Yahweh's shining face was a friendly feeling of God's presence for help and favor (Pss. 31:16; 67:1; 80:3,7). "Gracious" means to reach down to help. Lifting the face instead of hiding His face or letting it fall represents God's gracious attention to personal need. Peace (*šālôm*) became the common Jewish blessing or greeting. It is more than the absence of discord. It expresses the positive well-being (welfare) and security of one "whose mind is stayed on thee [God]" (compare Isa. 26:3, RSV). *šālôm* can indicate cessation of conflict and bodily health, *rāpā'* (Ps. 38:3; Isa. 53:5; 57:19; Jer. 6:14).

By pronouncing the blessing, the priests "put Yahweh's name on the people of Israel." That is, the people will be called, identified, and protected by Yahweh's name. The passage closes with the emphatic statement, "And I (pronoun is emphatic) will bless you." The rabbis said that the pronoun was expressed to make it clear that it was Yahweh, not the priests, who blessed the people.

Closely related to the cultic use of pronouncing a blessing on other people, and perhaps growing out of that use, is the blessing employed as a greeting in the Old Testament and New Testament. A common form of greeting in ancient Israel appears in Ruth 2:4, "Just then Boaz came from Bethlehem. He said to the reapers, 'The LORD be with You.' They answered, 'The LORD bless you.' " The blessing as a benediction for parting friends, loved ones, or acquaintances can be seen in David's departure from Jonathan (1 Sam. 20:42) and in Pharaoh's request that Moses bless him as Israel left (Ex. 12:32).

The priestly blessing was not some magic conferral of power, health, or wealth through the priest's power. It is a prayer to lift up to God the hope and confidence that He will continue His ongoing provision for humankind. Albert Outler's treatment of Providence comes close to the Old Testament view of blessing as the presence of God in history and nature and with community and individuals. Outler said that Providence has been more often associated with miracles, angelic visitations, and interventions than with the constant presence of God (*Who Trusts in God,* 72). Providence and blessing mean that God is in control of history and nature, and He is always near.

20. The Creating God

In the Old Testament the saving God and the blessing God is also the creating God. Many scholars assert that Israel knew God as savior (in the Exodus experience) before they knew Him as creator. Zimmerli says it is hardly possible to overlook the fact that when the Old Testament refers to the "deliverance of Israel from Egypt," it furnishes the primary orientation and the starting point of Israel's faith (*Old Testament Theology in Outline*, 32). G. Ernest Wright said that mankind came to an understanding of creation through an understanding of the covenant.

> Man's will committed and obedient to the Creator-Lord involved a much deeper and personal relation between man and his Lord than is customary in the religions of the world. Biblical man learned this from the covenant relation, that most profound of all Biblical relationships. In it he also confronted the mystery of his creation (*The Old Testament and Theology*, 73).

A. Creation Not Primary But Subservient to "Holy History"

Until recently the prevailing opinion among Old Testament scholars was that "Creation is not a primary datum of Israel's faith, but plays a subservient role to redemption . . . [it] occupies a place on the periphery [or sidelines] of Israelite thought, rather than the center" (Crenshaw, *Studies in Ancient Israelite Wisdom*, 27). Karl Barth put covenant before creation in his dogmatics.

Christoph Barth said that creation for Israel is a salvific fact, not just an objective general truth. However, it does not have a leading role among the topics of Israel's faith (*God With Us*, 9). Creation as an act of God is a complementary topic in Israel's creed. Creation is not an element in most of Israel's "creeds" in the Old Testament. Creation does not occur in the "creeds" of Exodus 34:6; Deuteronomy 6:20-23; 26:5-9; Joshua 24:3-13; or 1 Samuel 12:8. Creation is in the "creeds" in Nehemiah 9:6-25 and Psalm 136. Westermann probably went too far in saying:

> The Old Testament never speaks of belief in the Creator. . . . Creation was not an article of faith because there was simply no alternative. In other words, the Old Testament had a different understanding of reality from ours, in as much as there was no other reality than that established by God. They had no need expressly to *believe* that the world was created by God because that was a presupposition of their thinking (*Creation*, 5; compare *Elements of Old Testament Theology*, 72, 85).

In this regard the development of the church's creed par–alleled that of Israel's creed. The early church creeds made no reference to creation. Creation became a creedal topic only from around 150 A. D. and received additional stress only at

Nicea in A. D. 325 (Christoph Barth, *God With Us,* 11; compare Jacob, *Theology of the Old Testament,* 136).

Creation's secondary relationship to covenant has been challenged in recent years. H. H. Schmid's studies of "order in the Ancient Near East" led him to conclude that creation is the framework within which historical views move. Schmid argued that the dominant background of Old Testament thinking is the comprehensive idea of world order and creation faith in the wide sense. Therefore, creation faith is not a peripheral idea but the essence of all Old Testament thinking ("Creation, Righteousness, and Salvation," 1-19; see Reventlow, *Problems of Old Testament Theology in the Twentieth Century,* 34-185; Nicholson, "Israelite Religion in the Pre-exilic Period," 20-29).

T. M. Ludwig also challenged the idea that creation is secondary to salvation history. Ludwig studied the traditions of the establishing of the earth in Isaiah 40—66 and concluded that "creation faith in Deutero-Isaiah is not merely subsumed under election or redemption faith" ("The Traditions of the Establishing of the Earth," 345-357). Crenshaw contested the prevailing view on the basis of his study of chaos within a discussion of creation. Crenshaw emphasized three things: (1) the threat of chaos in the cosmic, political, and social realms evokes a response in creation theology; (2) in wisdom thought, creation functions primarily as a defense of divine justice; (3) the centrality of the question of God's integrity in Israelite literature places creation theology at the center of the theological enterprise (*Studies in Ancient Israelite Wisdom,* 27).

Crenshaw agreed that creation plays a secondary role in the Old Testament, but not to salvation history, as von Rad taught. Crenshaw argued that the function of creation theology is to undergird the belief in divine justice. Therefore, he asserted that "creation belongs to the fundamental question of human existence, namely the integrity of God" (*Studies in Ancient Israelite Wisdom,* 34).

B. Kinds of Creation Language

Everything the Old Testament says about salvation history is remarkably uniform and unambiguous, but what it says about Yahweh as Creator is more varied and is formulated in terms of different creation language (Zimmerli, *Old Testament*

Theology in Outline, 33). The Old Testament employs four clearly defined types of creation language common in the Ancient Near East: (1) creation by means of making (*ʿāśâ*), or some sort of activity; (2) creation by means of conception and birth; (3) creation by means of battle; and (4) creation by means of word (John H. Stek, "What Says the Scriptures," in *Portraits of Creation,* ed. van Till, 207). In addition to these four kinds of creation language that Israel shared *with* her neighbors, she used one unique word for creation, *bārāʾ*—a word unknown in the ancient world outside Israel.

The first kind of creation language the Old Testament uses is of God "making" *ʿāśâ* something or someone (Gen. 1:7, 26; 2:2,4,18,22; 3:1; 6:6). It also speaks of God "forming" *yāṣār* someone or something (Gen. 2:7,8,19; Isa. 43:1,21; 44:2,21,24; 45:7,9,11,18; 49:5; Jer. 1:5; Amos 4:13). Another term the Old Testament uses for "create" similar to *ʿāśâ* is *qānâ*, "to get," "to prepare," or "to possess."*qānâ* refers to that work on which God has expended care and concern. He makes Himself the possessor of that which He has made (Gen. 14:19,22; Ex. 15:16; Deut. 32:6; Pss. 74:2; 78:54; 104:24; 139:13; Prov. 8:22).

Other terms used of God creating in the sense of "making" are: stretching out (*nāṭâ*) the heavens like a tent (Isa. 40:22; 44:24; Zech. 12:1); spreading out (*tāpah*) the heavens (Isa. 48:13); laying the foundations (*yāsad*) of the world (Pss. 24:2; 78:69; 89:11; Prov. 3:19; Isa. 14:32; Amos 9:6); establishing (*cōnĕn*) the earth (Pss. 24:2; 119:90; Isa. 45:18); building (*bānâ*) someone or something (Gen. 2:22; Amos 9:6).

The second kind of creation language Israel used was that of birth or begetting. Other peoples around Israel spoke of creation in terms of sex, begetting, and births. Von Rad said that "in the Canaanite cult, copulation and procreation were mythically regarded as a divine event; consequently, the religious atmosphere was as good as saturated with mythic sexual conceptions. But Israel did not share in the divinisation of sex. Yahweh stood absolutely beyond the polarity of sex" (*Old Testament Theology I,* 27, 146).

Although Israel took a polemical attitude toward the deification of sex and excluded the idea and practice from the whole sphere of worship and sacred seasons, some of the old language remains, depicting creation in terms of begetting (*yālad*) or birth (Job 38:8; Ps. 90:2). Westermann said that the word *tôlēdôt* "generations of" the heavens and the earth, reflects this idea (Gen. 2:4). The terms *yaṣaʾ* "bring forth" and *ḥûl* "brought forth" (Prov. 8:24) may also have that connotation (Gen. 1:20,24). The fact that Israel was able to use the birth language for creation at all suggests that a very positive doctrine of creation existed in Israel at an early period (von Rad, *Old Testament Theology I,* 28).

A third kind of language Israel and her neighbors used for creation accounts was that of a battle between the gods. Perhaps the most famous account of such a battle is the Enuma Elish, in which Marduk killed the old dragon, Tiamat, and cut her into two parts. Out of her top half he made the heavens, and out of the bottom half he made the earth (see Heidel, *The Babylonian Genesis*). Although the Old Testament does not indicate that Israel ever thought of creation as the result of a struggle of Yahweh with any god, the language of that old battle occurs from time to time. Chaos represented by the Sea, waters, the deep, Rahab, or Leviathan seems to be an enemy which Yahweh defeated and continues to keep in bounds (Job 3:8; 9:13; 26:12; 38:10-11; Pss. 46:1-3; 74:12-17; 89:9-13; 93:1-5; 104:5-9; Isa. 27:1; Jer. 5:22).

Similar stories of creation in terms of a battle among the gods have been found in the Ras Shamra texts. Frank Cross described and translated some of these Canaanite texts from Ras Shamra and pointed out similarities and differences to some Old Testament passages ("The Song of the Sea and Canaanite Myth," 1-25; compare F. F. Bruce, *The New Testament Development of Old Testament Themes,* 40-50).

The Old Testament uses one other type of creation language similar to that of her neighbors. It is the language of creation by a word. Eight times in Genesis 1 we read, "And God said, 'Let be . . . '" (vv. 3,6,9,11,14,20, 24,26). Von Rad noted that creation by the word of God reflects the "absolute effortlessness of the divine creative action" (*Old Testament Theology I,* 142). It also denotes that creation is sharply separated in its nature from God Himself. The created world is no emanation. It is God's very own possession because He called it into existence. He is its Lord. Outside Genesis 1 the Old Testament rarely refers to creation by the word (Pss. 33:6; 148:5; Isa. 41:4; 48:13; Amos 9:6).

The concept of creation by the word is not unique to the Old Testament. In the Enuma Elish (see Heidel, *The Babylonian Genesis*) Marduk proves his divine power by calling an object into existence and making it vanish in the same way. Also in the old temple texts at Memphis (see John A. Wilson, "The Theology of Memphis," in *Ancient Near Eastern Texts,* ed. James B. Pritchard), Ptah, the god of the universe, exercised his creative activity with the aid of "heart and tongue"—that is, by means of his word. "He created nine gods (the primeval water, the sun-god Re, etc.) by his word" (Von Rad, *Old Testament Theology I,* 143; Westermann, *Creation,* 10; Westermann, *Genesis 1—11,* 26-41).

The Old Testament has its own special word for create—the word *bārāʾ* is a unique Hebrew word meaning "he created." *bārāʾ* is used eleven times in Genesis (1:1,21,27 (three times); 2:3,4; 5:1,2 (twice); 6:7; once in Exodus (34:10), Numbers (16:30), Deuteronomy (4:32), Ecclesiastes (12:1), Amos (4:13), Jeremiah (31:22), Malachi (2:10), and in Isaiah 1—39 (4:5); twenty times in Isaiah 40—66 (40:26,28; 41:20; 42:5; 43:1,7,15; 45:7 (twice), 8,12,18 (twice); 48:7; 54:16 (twice); 57:18; 65:17,18 (twice); three times in Ezekiel (21:30; 28:13,15); six times in Psalms (51:10; 89:12,47; 102:18; 104:30; 148:5). As yet this word has not been found in the older Semitic languages outside the Old Testament. (See *bārāʾ* in *TDOT* II, eds. Botterweck and Ringgren, 245.) The word is used forty-eight times in the Old Testament in the qal and nifal stems to mean "create." It is used once in the hifil stem, "to fatten oneself" (1 Sam. 2:29) and four times in the piel, "to cut down timber" (Josh. 17:15,18; Ezek. 21:24; 23:27). When *bārāʾ* is used to mean "create," God is always the subject. To speak of a human "creating" using *bārāʾ* would sound blasphemous in the Old Testament. Also, the Old Testament never mentions any material from which God creates something. Although creation *ex nihilo* (out of nothing) first appears explicitly in 2 Maccabees 7:28, the meaning may be implied in Genesis 1 (Zimmerli, *Old Testament Theology in Outline,* 35; von Rad, *Old Testament Theology, I,* 143).

C. References to Creation in the Old Testament

The Old Testament begins with two unique and profound accounts of the creation of the universe and humanity (Gen. 1:1—2:4*a*; 2:4*b*-25).

Westermann said:

> The first chapter of the Bible is one of the great pieces of world
> literature. All questions which have been directed to this first
> chapter of the Bible, all doubts as to whether what is there is
> "right," all emotional explanations that it is utterly outmoded,
> in nowise affect the validity of what is there. When one hears
> that chapter read aloud and in an appropriate context, one real-
> izes that something has been expressed that has never really
> been said before nor since (*Creation,* 36).

Genesis 1 asserts that God created (*bārā'*) the whole universe and all that is in it in an effortless way. The first verse
of Genesis should be understood as a summary statement of
everything that is described in the following verses. It is an
independent sentence and should not be taken as an introductory subordinate clause to verses 2 and 3, as some modern versions (NEB, NRSV and NJB) do (von Rad, *Genesis,* 48—49; for
a thorough discussion of the problems in translating Gen.
1:1—3 see Lane, "The Initiation of Creation," 63—73). Genesis
1:2 speaks of the primeval condition of the earth before its final
shaping (creation) in one seven-day period (a week). The earth
was in a state of chaos after the initial act of creation reported
in verse 1. The chaos is indicated by *tĕhôm,* "the deep," *ḥošĕk,*
"darkness," and *tohû wābohû,* "without form and empty." Several new translations (NEB, NRSV and NJB) read "wind"
rather than "spirit" for *rûaḥ* in Genesis 1:2. Robert Luyster
defended this new translation: "An analysis of Yahweh's long-
standing conflict with the rebellious sea (*tĕhôm*) reveals that
the characteristic emblem of His sovereignty is His wind (or
breath, or voice, but *not* spirit). Any other rendering of Gen.
1:2 would be inconsistent with all that follows" ("Wind and
Water," 10). Either reading, "wind" or "spirit," is possible. The
traditional reading is "Spirit." *tĕhôm* ("deep") often refers to the
rebellious sea. It is parallel to "waters" in this verse.

Following the summary statement in 1:1 and the word-pic-
ture of the primeval state of the world in 1:2, creation is
described in a way totally unique in the ancient world. It is
presented as the work of God in six successive days, followed
by the rest of the seventh day. The first day witnessed the creation of light (1:3-5). Before light, all was darkness and damp-

ness. Here light is related to darkness and not to the light-bearers (sun, moon, and stars).

We moderns try to understand light in terms of astronomy and physics. Old Testament people thought in terms of observable phenomena. Light did not dispel all darkness. Light was pronounced "good" in verse 4 and separated from the darkness. Darkness may carry an implication of "evil" opposite the "good light." When God called the light "day" and the darkness "night," He exercised His sovereignty over them. In the ancient world, the power to name indicated a power to rule.

On the second day (1:6-8), God made the "firmament," thought of as a vault or metal dome across the heavens. The verb *rāqaʿ* can mean "stamp" (Ezek. 6:11), "spread out" (Isa. 42:5; 44:24; Ps. 136:6); "hammer out," or "beat into plates" (Ex. 39:3; Job 37:18; Jer. 10:9). The firmament separated the waters in the heavens from the waters on the earth. The word "made" is used here of God's creative activity rather than the word "create." Nothing is said about the firmament being "good."

The third day of creation (1:9-13) witnesses a further separation of the waters on earth from the dry land. The collection of waters on the earth is named "seas." Again, the naming reflects God's sovereignty over the waters. The dry land in turn was commanded to produce vegetation in the form of grass, herbs, and fruit-bearing trees. The account recognized that plants have the ability to reproduce themselves, yet they are not spoken of as "living" in the fullest sense. Again, God saw that His work was "good."

The fourth day (1:14-19) tells of the creation of the two great light-bearers and the stars in the firmament. The entire section is strongly polemical. The unmistakable message is that the sun, moon, and stars are the creation of God. They are not gods, as Israel's neighbors believed. They are not to be worshiped. They have no power other than that which God gave them to rule over the day, the night, and the seasons (see Hasel, "The Polemic Nature of the Genesis Cosmology," 81-102). The Hebrew names "sun" and "moon" are deliberately not used, perhaps because Israel's neighbors used them as names for the other gods. Von Rad thought that the words "luminaries," "lamps," or "light-bearers" are meant to be prosaic and degrading (*Genesis,* 53).

> To comprehend the significance of these statements, one must remember that they were formulated in a cultural and religious atmosphere that was saturated with all kinds of astrological false belief. All ancient Oriental (not Old Testament!) thinking with regard to time was determined by the cyclical course of the stars. Man's world, down to each individual destiny, was determined by the working of sidereal powers (*Genesis,* 54).

The modern significance of the Bible's desacralization of nature, including the heavenly bodies, cannot be overstated. The whole basis of modern science, medicine, space probes, and space travel rests upon the fact that nature is not divine. God and humans have dominion over it. This chapter in Genesis and our landing on the moon are connected (Westermann, *Creation,* 44-45).

The fifth day of creation (1:20-23) saw the creation of animal life in the sea and in the air. Although plants were created on the third day, they did not have *nepeš* "life," like the animals. The animals are divided into three groups: (1) the "swarmers" in the waters—probably the swarms or schools of fish, small water animals, and "creepers," likely reptiles; (2) the "fowl" that fly in the heavens; and (3) the great "sea-monsters."

Excursus: Great Sea-Monsters

Were these great sea-monsters whales (KJV), crocodiles, snakes, or mythological animals thought by the ancients to inhabit the sea and to be the symbols of evil? Such creatures are mentioned in other Old Testament passages. John Gammie said that contemporary scholars are divided as to whether the author of Job understood the creatures in Job 40:15-32; 41:1-34 as mythical monsters or natural animals ("Behemoth and Leviathan," 217). Nicolas K. Kiessling said "The most fearsome dragons of the Old Testament *tanin,* levitan, rahab are horrible but vague incarnations of evil, darkly outlined opponents of both God and man. They inhabit the depths of the seas and are often employed as apt metaphors of heathen kings hostile to the children of Israel" ("Antecedents," 167).

The word *tanin* occurs fifteen times in the Old Testament and refers to different kinds of creatures: a sea-monster that God has destroyed or will destroy (Ps. 74:13; Isa. 27:1; 51:9); sea-monsters in general (Gen. 1:21; Job 7:12; Ps. 148:7); a metaphor for either Babylon (Jer. 51:34) or Egypt (Ezek. 29:3; 32:3) as an enemy of Israel; and serpents (Ex. 7:9,10,12; Ps. 91:13). In Lamentations 4:3 the reference is ambiguous. "Leviathan" (Job 3:8; 41:1; Pss. 74:14; 104:26; Isa. 27:1) and "Rahab" (Job 9:13; 26:12; Ps. 87:4; 89:10; Isa. 30:7; 51:9) are used in the Old Testament parallel to *tanin.*

When Genesis 1:21 says that God created the "sea monsters," *tannîn*, it means that God created and controls everything in the universe, even that which other people regarded as symbols of evil. People have nothing to fear in the world. God has the powers of evil in His hands. He made them and named them. Two other features of this passage (1:20-23) are significant: (1) The word *bārā'* "create" is used only for the second time in the chapter. This is probably because animal life was considered a step above the rest of creation to this point. (2) The word "blessing" is used for the first time in this chapter (1:22).

Westermann noted that the "blessing" here includes the power to propagate one's kind. "That is the basic meaning of the word *bless:* the power to be fertile. The life of the living being, whether man or beast, clearly includes the capacity to propagate. Without it there would be no real life" (*Creation,* 46).

The sixth day of creation (1:24-31) sees the creation of the land animals and humans with a noticeable difference in the description of the origin of these two. The land animals come from the earth: "Let the earth bring forth . . ." (v. 24). But humans are the intimate and direct objects of God's creative work: "Let us make humankind in our image" (v. 26). The word "create" *bārā'* occurs three times in verse 27 to make clear that the high point and goal of God's creation is reached in the creation of humans. People and the animals were created on the same day, and both are uniquely called *nepeš ḥāyâ,* "living being." Each has the power of propagation of its kind. Still, humans stand out as unique, made in God's image. They receive dominion over every other created being. (We will discuss the terms *image, dominion, male,* and *female* in chap. 6 on humanity.)

On the seventh day (2:1-3), God finished His work of creation. He blessed and hallowed the seventh day because on it He rested from His work of creation. The seventh day of creation is special, different from the previous six workdays. The word "finished" in 2:1,2 suggests that the universe is complete, finished, everything that God intended it to be. God set the seventh day apart from the other days. The word for "rest" is *šābāt,* which is the basis of the word "sabbath."

Westermann said there is more here than "a reference to the Sabbath as it was later instituted in Israel. There is an order established for mankind according to which time is divided into the everyday and the special, and the everyday reaches its goal in the special" (*Creation,* 65). However, we should not read the whole sabbath institution into this passage. Von Rad said to do so "would be a complete misapprehension of the passage. For there is no word here of this rest being imposed on man or assigned to him" (*Old Testament Theology I,* 148). The universe belongs to God because He made it and continues to control it.

Von Rad said, "It would be sheer folly to regard this resting of God which concluded the creation as something like a turning away from the world by God; it is in fact a particularly mysterious gracious turning toward his Creation" (*Old Testament Theology I,* 148; compare Westermann, *Creation,* 41). God did not turn away from the world after He created it. The "rest" is more than a cessation of labor for God. It expresses God's concern for the world and perhaps hints that history will end in God's eternal rest (von Rad, *Genesis,* 60).

The second account of creation (2:4*b*-25) is usually considered older than the first (1:2—2:4*a*). As it now stands, it supplements and extends the first account's picture of creation. The first account begins with the creation of the universe and makes mankind the top step of the cosmological pyramid. The second account starts with mankind as the center and objective of creation. Mankind is made by God out of the dust. Life is the result of God's breath being breathed into persons. This breath of God belongs to no other creature.

God was not done with mankind after that initial act of creation. God provided space and pleasant environment (the garden of Eden), food (the trees of the garden), work ("till it and keep it"), community or society (man and woman), and language. God also gave them a command, "You may freely eat of every tree of the garden; but of the tree of the knowledge of good and evil you shall not eat, for in the day that you eat of it you shall die" (2:16-17).

In their original state, mankind was completely subject to God's command. God gave them perfect freedom in every area except one (only *one* tree was singled out of many for prohibition), but precisely at this point they wanted to exercise their freedom. They chose an action which God had forbidden. The outcome of the story shows that God's command was best, for eating the forbidden fruit brought sorrow, suffering, and, eventually, death. Von Rad said, "How simple and sober is our narrative, compared to the sensual myths of the nations, in letting the meaning of life in Paradise consist completely in the question of obedience to God and not in pleasure and freedom from suffering" (*Genesis*, 79).

These two accounts of creation stand at the beginning of the Old Testament to indicate that God is the Lord of the whole world and not just the God of Israel. The two creation accounts should also be viewed as a vital part of the prologue to God's saving history with Israel, which begins in Genesis 12. Direct theological statements about creation in the form of large complexes occur only in these two accounts at the beginning of our Bible.

The Old Testament contains numerous scattered and nontheological passages concerning creation. Genesis 14:18-20 preserves what is probably one of the earliest references to creation in the Old Testament. In this passage Abraham recognized El Elyon, the God of Melchizedek, as the same as his God, Yahweh, "Maker of heaven and earth." The idea of creation occurs again in the Pentateuch (Gen. 5:2; 24:3; Deut. 4:32; 32:6-8,18), in the historical books (1 Sam. 2:8; 1 Kings 8:12 (Septuagint); 2 Kings 19:15; Neh. 9:6); and in the Prophets (Isa. 37:14-20; Jer. 5:22-24; 10:12-16; 27:5; 31:35; 32:17; 33:2; 51:15,19; Hos. 2:8-9; 8:14; Amos 4:13; 5:8; 9:5-8; Zech. 12:1; Mal. 2:10).

Aside from Genesis 1—2, Isaiah 40—66 has more references to Yahweh as the Creator than any other extensive passage in the Old Testament (Isa. 40:22-31; 41:20; 42:5; 43:1,7,15; 44:2,24; 45:7-12,18; 48:13; 49:5; 51:13,16; 54:5,16; 65:17-18; 66:22). These chapters contain a variety of words for creation: *bārā²* "create" (40:26,28; 42:5); *yāṣār* "form" (45:18); *ᶜāsâ* "made" (44:24; 45:12,18); *mātaḥ* "stretched out" (40:22; 42:5); *rāqaᶜ* "hammered down" (42:5; 44:24); *qārā²* "called forth" (40:26); and *hammoṣî²* "cause to go forth or to be born" (40:26).

The stress on Yahweh as Creator in Isaiah 40—66 was due to the prophet's desire to help his people (in Babylonian exile) to realize that their suffering did not indicate the supremacy of the Babylonian gods over Yahweh. Their suffering in exile was due to their sins (40:2). Yahweh, their God, was sovereign over the whole world; therefore, He had the power to redeem them (40:27-31).

Creation is a prominent theme in Wisdom Literature. Proverbs 3:19 says, "The LORD by wisdom founded the earth; /by understanding he established the heavens." Proverbs 8:22-31 is a major passage on creation and wisdom's role in it. (See Landes, "Creation Tradition in Proverbs 8:22-31," 279-293; Whybray, "Proverbs 8:22-31 and Its Supposed Prototypes," 390-400; John Stek, "What Says the Scriptures?" in *Portraits of Creation,* ed. van Till, 203-265.)

> The LORD created me at the
> beginning of his work,
> the first of his acts of long ago.
> Ages ago I was set up,
> at the first, before the beginning
> of the earth.
> When there were no depths I was
> brought forth,
> when there were no springs
> abounding with water.
> Before the mountains had been shaped,
> before the hills, I was brought forth—
> when he had not yet made earth and fields,
> or the world's first bits of soil.
> When he established the heavens, I was there,
> when he drew a circle on the
> face of the deep,
> when he made firm the skies above,
> when he established the
> fountains of the deep,
> When he assigned to the sea its limit,
> so that the waters might not
> transgress his command,
> when he marked out the
> foundations of the earth,
> then I was beside him, like a
> master worker;
> and I was daily his delight,
> rejoicing before him always,
> rejoicing in his inhabited world
> and delighting in the human race.
> (Prov. 8:22-31)

Derek Kidner captured the overall significance of Proverbs 8 in his commentary on Proverbs. He said the increasing praise of wisdom breaks out in full force in verses 22-31. It "is not designed to preoccupy the reader with metaphysics but to stir him to decision: the true climax is the 'Now Therefore' passage of 32-36" (*Proverbs,* 76).

The origin of wisdom is described three ways in verses 22-24. Wisdom says, "God created me" (v. 22); "ages ago I was set up" (v. 23); and "I was brought forth" (v. 24). The meaning of these three expressions is subject to debate. In fact, the word translated "created" (v. 22) is not *bārā'* but *qānâ,* "to get" or "to possess." This verse was involved in the debate of hypostasis or personification. Is wisdom deified here? The Arians, who denied the deity of Christ, appealed to the Septuagint's translation "created" to deny that Christ was eternal (Kidner, *Proverbs,* 79). But wisdom is not a hypostasis of Yahweh here. It is a personification of one of His attributes.

Wisdom was an attribute of Yahweh from the beginning, before creation began (v. 25-29). God did nothing without wisdom. Yet it was not wisdom that created the world. "He established the heavens. . . . He drew a circle . . . He made firm the skies . . ." Wisdom was beside Yahweh in all of this "as a masterworker" or "little child" (v. 30). The Hebrew word is *'āmôn.* "Master worker" is supported by the principal ancient version of Jeremiah 52:15 and perhaps Song of Solomon 7:1. "Little child" is supported by Aquila. Even though we cannot solve all of the language problems, the main meaning of the passage is clear. Yahweh as Creator considered wisdom primary and indispensable. Wisdom is older than the universe and fundamental to it. Not a speck of matter, not a trace of order (v. 29) came into existence without wisdom. Wisdom is the spring of joy. The joy of creating and the joy of existence flow from the exercise of divine wisdom— "that is, from God's perfect workmanship" (Kidner, *Proverbs,* 78).

In a magnificent passage in the Book of Job Yahweh presents Job with a series of rhetorical questions about his part in the creation of the inanimate and animate world. Yahweh asks in 38:4:

> Where were you when I laid the
> foundation of the earth?
> Tell me, if you have understanding.

The implication is that Job was not there. He had neither the wisdom nor the power to create or control the universe (39:10-12). Job was a part of God's creation just as the Behemoth (40:15). Yahweh is both wise and sovereign, because He not only made the world but sustains it (Job 38:2—39:30; Ps. 104:27-30).

Old Testament creation faith is broad, bold, and significant. For years it was kept on the margin or periphery of Old Testament theology because salvation-history (von Rad) or covenant theology (Eichrodt) occupied center stage. Because the Old Testament makes relatively few references to creation and because it is often associated with wisdom and universal concepts, creation was often neglected. However, the Old Testament begins with two significant creation stories. The Old Testament canon makes creation basic and foundational to Old Testament theology. It is true that the Old Testament is not about creation. It is about salvation and deliverance, but there would have been no salvation without creation. God is the Creator of everything and everyone. How He made the universe is described in various kinds of creation language. There is order in creation, and there are enemies of creation. Creation has been affected by human sin (Hos. 4:1-3). The sense of "righteousness" and "justice" may be related to creation. (See the section "A Judging God" in this chap. and the discussion of sin in chap.7.)

Creation theology broadens and deepens one's view of God, humanity, and the world. Creation faith is not prominent in the New Testament. The New Testament says less about creation than the Old Testament. Perhaps the New Testament did not need to say as much because the Old Testament had said enough so well.

21. A Holy God

Holiness (*qōdeš*) is an intimately divine word. "It has to do ... with the very Nature of Deity; no word more so, nor indeed any other as much" (Snaith, *The Distinctive Ideas of the Old Testament,* 21). "Holiness is the quality most typical of the belief in God in the Old Testament" (Vriezen, *Outline of Old Testament Theology,* 297). "Of all the qualities attributed to the divine nature there is one which, in virtue both of the frequency and the emphasis with which it is used, occupies a position of unique importance—namely, that of holiness" (Eichrodt, *Old Testament Theology I,* 270). Johannes Hanel made holiness the center of his Old Testament theology (*Die Religion der Heiligkeit,* iii), and Edmond Jacob suggested *qdš* as the grammatical center of the Old Testament, just as the idea is the theological center (*Theology of the Old Testament,* 87).

God is not a creature, consequently, He is holy. The "attribute" of holiness refers to that mystery in the divine being which distinguishes Him as God. Creatures and objects possess holiness only in a derived sense when they are designated by God to serve a special function. G. Ernest Wright said:

> Of all the Divine "attributes," holiness comes the nearest to describing God's being rather than his activity. Yet it is no static, definable "quality" like the Greek truth, beauty and goodness, for it is that indefinable mystery in God which distinguishes him from all that he created; and its presence in the world is the sign of his active direction of its affairs (*God Who Acts,* 75).

The etymology of the word *qodeš* is not clear (Kornfeld, TWAT 6, 1181-1185). Eichrodt, Jacob, and Muilenburg believed the root *qdš* derives from a hypothetical primitive root, *qd(d),* meaning "to cut," "to mark off," "to separate." Bunzen and Vriezen took it from the Arabic and Ethiopic root *qd'* or *qdw,* "to be bright" or "to be pure." The uses of the root in the Old Testament seem to favor the meaning "to be marked off," or "separated from common use." The separation of the sacred from the profane is the basic meaning of the Greek word *temenos,* the Latin word *sanctus,* and the Hebrew word *ḥerem.* The antonym of the word *qōdeš* is *ḥôl,* which means "common" or "profane."

With the root *qdš* we are dealing with a person's primary, elemental reactions to that mystery with which in the first days he or she felt surrounded. Von Rad called the experience of the holy a primeval religious datum which cannot be deduced from other human values. Holiness is not the elevation of any other thing to the highest degree; nor is it associated with anything by way of addition. The holy could much more aptly be designated "the great stranger" in the human world. It is a datum experience over against which a person initially feels fear rather than trust. It is in fact "the wholly other" (von Rad, *Old Testament Theology I,* 205; see Otto, *The Idea of the Holy*).

Perhaps the best way to see that holiness and deity are equated in the Old Testament is to compare Amos 4:2 and 6:8: "The Lord God has sworn by his holiness" and "The Lord God has sworn by himself (*nepeš*)." The same idea is expressed in Psalm 89:35, "Once and for all I have sworn by my holiness;/ I will not lie to David." God and the holy one are synonyms in the parallel lines of Habakkuk 3:3: "God came from Teman, the Holy One from Mount Paran."

God is called "holy" three times in two places in the Old Testament. The seraphim sang, "Holy, holy, holy is the LORD of hosts;/ the whole earth is full of his glory" (Isa. 6:3). In one of the enthronement psalms, the psalmist proclaimed three times that God is Holy (Ps. 99:3,5,9). Hosea underscored the idea that God's holiness distinguishes Him from people: "For I am God and no mortal, the Holy One in your midst" (Hos. 11:9). The term "the holy one of Israel" occurs thirty times in the Book of Isaiah in reference to the God of Israel.

To say that God is holy is to say that God is God. Holiness suggests the power, the mystery, and the transcendence—but not the remoteness—of God. The Old Testament often uses anthropomorphisms in speaking of God. It speaks of His eyes, face, feet, arm, and hand. Such language could lead to the humanizing of God were it not for His holiness. God's holiness separates Him from everything else in the universe, including the universe itself. The word "holy," used to describe God, makes any thought of a humanly created God impossible. God is not a person deified.

B. The History of Holiness

Holiness has a history in the Old Testament and in the Ancient Near East. The term is probably older than Israel. It is found in several Semitic languages, including the Phoenician inscription Yehimilk (about 1200 B.C.) and the Ugaritic texts Aqhat I.27, II.16 (also about 1200 B.C.). Qadesh was the name of certain cities and places in the Near East before Israel came into Canaan. Qadesh on the Orontes River was the capital of a Hittite province and the scene of a fierce battle between Ramses II and the Hittite king. A Qadesh goddess, worshiped in Syria about 1500 B.C., probably had prior Mesopotamian associations. These names of places and of a goddess lead to the conclusion that "holiness" was a very ancient idea connected with gods.

The early concept of holiness included some primitive (materialistic) and negative connotations. At first, holiness was understood in terms of mysterious power that was dangerous, unapproachable, and fearsome. Objects that belonged to God were holy and threatened death to any humans who touched them. Nadab and Abihu died because they offered unholy fire before the Lord (Lev. 10:1-3). The Lord slew many people of Beth-shemesh for looking on the ark. Their fellows said, "Who is able to stand before the LORD, this holy God?" (1 Sam. 6:19-20). Uzzah died when he touched the ark (2 Sam. 6:6-7).

Holiness did not always have a moral or ethical connotation in the Old Testament. The word *qādēš*, "prostitute," comes from the root *qdš*, "holy." Both the masculine and feminine forms, *qādēš* and *qedešâ*, are used in the Old Testament to refer to male and female prostitutes (Deut. 23:18; 1 Kings 14:24; 15:12; 22:46; 2 Kings 23:7; Job 36:14; compare feminine forms in Gen. 38: 21-22; Deut. 23:18; Hos. 4:14). All these references are to cult prostitutes except those in Genesis 38.

Such usage suggests some influence of pagan religions on Israel's vocabulary and perhaps on the life-style of some of her people. Cult or sacred prostitution was common in the Ancient Near East, a vital part of the fertility cult. Baal worship rivaled the worship of Yahweh in Canaan after Israel came into the land. Sacred marriage or *hieros gamos* was a part of the New Year celebrations in many ancient pagan religions. Engnell found some evidence of the sacred marriage in Israel's feasts because the Song of Songs is read in the synagogue on the eighth day of the feast of Passover, but Ringgren pointed out that all evidence for reading the Song of Songs as part of the Passover celebration is late (500 A.D.) and that traces of a *hieros gamos* in the Old Testament are "disputed and precarious" (*Israelite Religion,* 188).

Marvin Pope, in his commentary on the Song of Songs, said:

> In working through the Song word for word and verse by verse, and in reviewing the interpretations that have been imposed upon it, the impression has grown to conviction that the cultic interpretation, which has been vehemently resisted from its beginnings, is best able to account for the erotic imagery (*Song of Songs*, 17).

At the end of a 228-page introduction to his commentary, Pope concluded that certain features of the Song of Songs may be understood in light of "considerable and growing evidence that funeral feasts in the Ancient Near East were love feasts celebrated with wine, women and song" (*Song of Songs*, 228).

Although the cultic view of the Song of Songs is far from being proved, ample evidence in the Prophets shows that Israel practiced "sacred" prostitution in Yahweh's name at least on some occasions (Ezek. 16:15-34; 23:12-21; Hos. 2:4-5,13; 4:12-14; Amos 2:7.

Holiness does not seem to be directly associated with morality or ethics in the Old Testament. Isaiah's reaction to his vision of Yahweh on the throne (6:5) refers primarily to the contrast between the majesty of God and human insufficiency.

Perhaps the admonishment in the Holiness Code, "You shall be holy; for I the LORD your God am holy" (Lev. 19:2), comes closest to a connection between holiness and morality in the Old Testament. Even here, however, the moral and ceremonial commandments are mixed together with nothing to distinguish them, suggesting that the basic meaning of holiness throughout the Old Testament is "separation."

C. The Spiritual Side of Holiness

Holiness in the Old Testament signifies the essence of deity. God's holiness refers to everything about God that separates Him from His creation: His mysterious power and the attraction of worshipers. In a second sense, holiness refers to God's call and demand that people be holy as He is holy, in the sense that they are to be pure, clean, just, and compassionate.

The Old Testament contains some lofty statements about the spiritual side of holiness (Ps. 51:11; Isa. 6:1-5; 57:15-16; Hos. 11:8-9). The Old Testament refers to God's holy spirit three times (Ps. 51:11; Isa. 63:10-11). Still, materialistic or cultic ideas of holiness never cease in the Old Testament. In the eschaton everything will become holy. Numbers 14:21 says that the time will come when "the earth shall be filled with the glory of the LORD." This means that in the present Yahweh's holiness, regarded as "glory," is limited to the cultic sphere. But this is temporary. Zechariah 14:20 says, "On that day there shall be inscribed on the bells of the horses, 'Holy to the LORD.' And the cooking pots in the house of the LORD shall be as holy as the bowls in the front of the altar." This means that the whole realm of the secular will be taken up into Yahweh's holiness. When that happens, Yahweh's holiness will have attained its utmost goal.

Holiness is a difficult concept to understand. Many moderns are oriented to the here and now and to the mundane affairs of the day. Their self-confidence often robs them of the fear of the divine. Profanity and vulgarity mark the spirit of too many. Walter Brueggemann captured the need of our world today:

> The holiness of God is urgent in the face of profanation, which empties life of larger passion and dignity. The holiness of God is urgent in the face of pervasive brutality, which trivializes God's purpose and abuses God's world. The holiness of God is urgent in the face of the growing authority of technique which diminishes mystery that keeps life open (Foreword to *Holiness in Israel* by John Gammie, xii).

Perhaps the cameo picture of Isaiah's call captures the essence of God's holiness as it relates to His people. Isaiah saw God on a throne, high and lifted up. He saw the glory of God represented in the cloud and felt the tremble of the earth moving. He heard the seraphim saying, "Holy, Holy, Holy, is the Lord of hosts." He was overwhelmed by his sense of sin and uncleanness and that of his people. He experienced God's cleansing with a live coal from the altar. Then he heard God's call to commitment and service.

22. A Loving God

Is the God of the Old Testament a God of love, or was Marcion right in saying that the God of the New Testament was a God of love and the God of the Old Testament was a God of wrath? (We only know about Marcion through his adversaries who quoted him to attack him.) Tertullian quoted Marcion as saying that the God of the Old Testament was "judicial, harsh, mighty in war . . . severe and . . . cruel," while the God revealed in Jesus Christ was "mild, placid, and simply good and excellent" (Roberts and Donaldson, Anti-Nicene Christian Library, vol. 7, I, 6; II, 11). For Marcion "the God of the Old Testament is another and inferior being, the Demiurge-creator, the vindictive God of the law, wholly opposed to the gracious God revealed in the gospel" (Bright, *The Authority of the Old Testament,* 62).

We still hear today that the God of the Old Testament is a God of wrath. Wrath is only one side of the Old Testament picture of God. Love is the other.

A. Hebrew Words for Love

A number of Hebrew words express various aspects of love.

1) ʾāhab "love"—The word most often translated "love" is *'ahab*. The etymology of the root is not certain. Jacob took it from a biliteral root, *hab*, meaning "to blow," "to desire, "to pant after." "Love can be defined as a desire at once violent and voluntary" (Jacob, *Theology of the Old Testament,* 108; compare Gerhard Wallis, *'ahabh, TDOT* I, 103). The word is used over two hundred times in the Old Testament. Thirty-two times it refers to God's love.

ʾāhab often expressed the love of husbands and wives (Gen. 24:67; 29:18,20,32; Judg. 16:4,15; 1 Sam. 1:5; 18:20); parents for children (Gen. 22:2; 25:28); a daughter-in-law for a mother-in-law (Ruth 4:15); and friend for friend (1 Sam. 18:1-3).

Individuals are the object of God's love: Solomon (2 Sam. 12:24; Neh. 13:26) and Cyrus (Isa. 48:14). Deuteronomy 10:18 says that the Lord loves the sojourner. He loves Jerusalem (Pss. 78:68; 87:2). God loves righteousness and those who act righteously (Pss. 11:7; 37:28; 45:7; 99:4; Prov. 3:12; 15:9; Isa. 61:8; Mal. 2:11). God loved the fathers and chose their descendants after them (Deut. 4:37; 10:15).

Several times the Old Testament speaks of God's love for Israel (Deut. 7:8-9,13; 23:5; 1 Kings 10:9; 2 Chron. 2:11; 9:8). He loved them as a husband (Ezek. 16:8; Hos. 3:1) and as a father (Hos. 11:1). He loved Jacob and hated Esau (Mal. 1:2). Because Israel was precious in His eyes, He loved, redeemed, and renewed them (Isa. 43:4; 63:9; Zeph. 3:17). Old Testament language about God's love for Israel sometimes is paradoxical, to say the least. Jeremiah 31:3 says, "I have loved you [Israel] with an everlasting love," but Hosea 9:15 says, "I will love them no more."

'āhab "love" is found in all types of literature and was in use throughout the Old Testament period. The root also occurs in Ugaratic, Aramaic, Punic, and Samaritan, but never occurs as a part of a proper name in Hebrew as it does in these dialects. The Septuagint translates it with *agapao*. Norman Snaith called 'āhabâ "election love." It is unconditional love. Election grows out of the spontaneous, "overplus" of God's love (*The Distinctive Ideas of the Old Testament*, 95, 135, 140).

2) ḥesed "devotion," "loyalty," "kindness"—A second Hebrew word related to God's love is ḥesed. Again, the etymology of ḥesed is uncertain (H.-J. Zobel, *ḥesed, TDOT* 5, 1986, 45). Gesenius suggested "keenness, ardent zeal" as the primary meaning of the root. Edmond Jacob said, "Etymology, without supplying us with an absolutely satisfactory answer to the problem, at least directs us to the primitive significance, which is that of strength" (*Theology of the Old Testament*, 103). The root *chsd* occurs only three times in the Old Testament as a verb: once in the piel in the sense of "bringing shame" (Prov. 25:10); twice in the hifil in parallel passages meaning "to show oneself loyal" (2 Sam. 22:26; Ps. 18:25). The negative side of ḥesed is present in the Old Testament in Proverbs 14:34 and Isaiah 40:6*b*.

> Righteousness exalts a nation,
> but sin is a reproach (*ḥesed*) to any
> people.
> (Prov. 14:34)

> All people are grass,
> their constancy (*ḥesed*) is like the flower
> of the field.
> (Isa. 40:6*b*)

In Arabic, Aramaic, and Syriac the bad sense of the word "shame" seems to be dominant (Snaith, *The Distinctive Ideas of the Old Testament*, 97; Jacob, *Theology of the Old Testament*, 103).

Ḥesed is difficult to translate into English. KJV translates it "mercy" 145 times; "kindness" 38 times; and "loving-kindness"

30 times. The Septuagint usually translates it *eleos*, "mercy." Twice (in Esther) it reads *karis*, "grace." The Symmachus version seems to have preferred *karis* to *eleos* (Dodd, *The Bible and The Greeks,* 61). Martin Luther used the word *Gnade,* "grace," for *hesed,* as he did for the word *karis* in the New Testament. Snaith preferred the term "covenant-love" for *hesed*; the ASV prefers "loving-kindness"; NEB prefers "loyalty"; and RSV prefers "steadfast love"; NRSV uses various words—"loyalty," "devotion," "kindness." The translation of the word *hesed* was the last word on which the RSV committee voted (Kuyper, "Grace and Truth," 8).

Edmond Jacob used "the faithfulness of God" for *hesed ʾelô-hîm,* but G. Ernest Wright criticized Jacob at this point:

> I do not think it proper to discuss *hesed* as "the faithfulness of God" and to define it theologically as "the bond uniting God to man and vice versa." . . . Indeed the LXX translation of the term by "grace" is nearer to its true meaning. It is not a bond, but the word for an action: undeserved and motivated by pure grace, by a superior to an inferior, which creates a bond and pulls a gracious response *from* the recipient. *Hesed* thus is not a synonym for the covenant (the latter is a legal term); it is a type of action which creates a bond transcending legal requirement, and pulls from the recipient an appropriate response, which is also *hesed* ("Review of Jacob's *Old Testament Theology,*" 81).

The point is that *hesed* contains two basic elements. One is the idea of strength, loyalty, and steadfastness. The other is the idea of kindness, pity, mercy, and grace. Perhaps "devotion" (Jer. 2:2) captures both elements in the word.

The word *hesed* is often used in word pairs and in parallel poetry. In forty-three cases *hesed* is joined with another noun. Twenty-two times it is joined with *ʾemet* or some form of the root *ʾaman*, "truth," in the expression "grace and truth" (Gen. 24:27,49; 47:29; Ex. 34:6; Josh. 2:14; 2 Sam. 2:6; 15:20; Pss. 25:10; 40:11; 57:3; 61:7; 85:10; 86:15; 89:14,24; 98:3; 115:1; 138:2; Prov. 3:3; 14:22; 16:6; 20:28). Seven times *hesed* is used with "covenant" (Deut. 7:9,12; 1 Kings 8:23; 2 Chron. 6:14; Neh. 1:5; 9:32; Dan. 9:4). *hesed* is used with the words *ʿōz*, "strength," and *miśgab*, "fortress," on a number of occasions (Pss. 59:9,16; 144:2).

The Old Testament speaks often of the "abundance" or "greatness" of God's *hesed* (Ex. 34:6; Num. 14:19; Neh. 9:17;

13:22; Pss. 5:7; 36:5; 69:13; 86:5,15; 103:8,11; 106:7,45; 117:2; 119:64; 145:8, Lam. 3:32; Joel 2:13; Jonah 4:2). Once the psalmist says, "The earth, O Lord, is full of your *hesed*" (119:64). Three times the psalmist says that God's *hesed* extends to the heavens, and His faithfulness, *ʾemet*, reaches the clouds (36:5; 57:10; 108:4). The idea is that His *hesed* and *ʾemet* cannot be measured. An unusual use of *hesed* appears in a psalm refrain: "O give thanks to the LORD, for he is good,/ for his steadfast love (*hesed*) endures forever."

This refrain occurs twenty-six times in 1 Chronicles 16:34,41; 2 Chronicles 5:13; 7:3,6; 20:21; Ezra 3:11; Psalms 106:1; 107:1; 118:1,2,3,4,29; 136; Jeremiah 33:11. A similar refrain appears in Psalm 107:8,15,21,31. These refrains call for God to be praised because He is "good," *tôb*, and His *hesed* is everlasting. He is not capricious as other Near Eastern gods were apt to be.

One of the most famous passages containing the word *hesed* is in Lamentations 3:22-24.

> The steadfast love (*hesed*) of the LORD
>   never ceases,
> his mercies never come to an end;
>   they are new every morning;
>   great is your faithfulness.
> "The LORD is my portion," says my soul,
>   "therefore I will hope in him."

The confession that God's *hesed* is renewed every morning is made again in Psalms 59:16; 90:14; 92:2; 143:8. In Lamentations 3:22 *hesed* actually appears in a plural form, meaning that the "mercies" of God are many acts of grace. The word is used in the plural several times (Gen. 32:10; 2 Chron. 6:21; 32:32; 35:26; Neh. 13:14; Pss. 17:7; 25:6; 89:2,49; 106:7,45; 107:43; Isa. 55:3; 63:7; Lam. 3:22). The last two references are translated "his good deeds" and "his faithful deeds," referring to the kings Hezekiah and Josiah.

If *hesed*'s primary meaning is that of "strength," "steadfastness," and "faithfulness," it also has the element of love, pity, and grace in it. *hesed* is parallel to *rāḥām*, "compassion" (Pss. 25:6; 51:1; 103:4; Isa. 54:8; Jer. 16:5; Lam. 3:22; Dan. 1:9; Hos. 2:19; Zech. 7:9) and *ḥen*, "grace" (Gen. 19:19; Esther 2:17; Pss. 77:8-9; 109:12). Once Israel is told to love *hesed* (*ʾahăbat hesed*, Mic. 6:8).

In addition to *'āhab* "love" and *hesed* "steadfast love," two other Hebrew roots *hnn* and *rhm*, often carry the idea of "love." *hānan* suggests the idea of "grace" or "unmerited love or favor." The difference between *hānan* and *hesed* is that *hesed* refers primarily to "covenant-love." That is, a tie or a relationship between the covenanting parties makes "acts of love" between them expected. But *hānan* suggests the unmerited love of a superior to an inferior. *hēn* "grace" or "favor" carries with it the idea of unmerited favor, supreme graciousness, and condescension on the part of a superior, without the slightest obligation on the superior to extend *hēn* "grace." No charge of harshness can be lodged against one who does not offer it.

Some form of the verb from the root *hnn* is used seventy-six times in the Old Testament with God or persons as the subject. The NRSV translates it variously as "Be gracious" (Pss. 4:1; 6:2; 31:9; 41:4), "gracious" (Gen. 33:5,11; 2 Kings 13:23), "will be gracious" (Ex. 33:19; Isa. 30:19). Sometimes it is translated "generous" (Ps. 37:21) or "kind" (Prov. 14:31; 19:17; 28:8). The translation "make supplication" or "plead" is found in 1 Kings 8:33,47; 9:3; 2 Chronicles 6:24,26; Job 8:5; Psalms 30:8; 142:2. The word is translated "beseech," "sought," or "entreat" in Genesis 42:21; Deuteronomy 3:23; 2 Kings 1:13; Esther 8:3; Hosea 12:4. The imperative of *hānan* is used nineteen times in the Psalms to entreat Yahweh "to be gracious" to the psalmist. So *hnn* is used as a prayer word.

The noun form *tehinah* of this root *hnn* is often parallel with *těpillâ*, "prayer" (1 Kings 8:28,38, 45,49,54; 2 Chron. 6:29; Dan. 9:3,17,18,20). Jeremiah used a noun from *hnn* as parallel with *těpillâ* in entreaties of God and human superiors such as the king (Jer. 36:7; 37:20; 38:26; 42:2,9; compare Dan. 9:17).

Another noun *hēn*, used seventy times in the Old Testament, is usually translated "favor" and appears as the object of the verbs *māsā'* "find" or *nātan* "give" (Gen. 6:8; 19:19; 30:27; Ex. 3:21; 11:3; 12:36; 33:12; Num. 11:11; Deut. 24:1; Judg. 6:17; 1 Sam. 1:18; 2 Sam. 15:25; Pss. 45:2; 84:11; Zech. 4:7; 12:10). The noun *hēn* is never used in the plural or with the article. The adjective *hānûn* "gracious" is used thirteen times in the Old Testament (Ex. 22:27; 34:6; 2 Chron. 30:9; Neh. 9:17,31; Pss. 86:15; 103:8; 111:4; 112:4; 116:5; 145:8; Joel 2:13; Jonah 4:2).

Most of these uses are part of the old nonhistorical creed often used in the cult in ancient Israel.

> The LORD, the LORD,
> a God merciful (*raḥum*) and gracious (*ḥanun*),
> slow to anger,
> and abounding in steadfast love (*ḥesed*)
> and faithfulness (*'emeth*).
> (Ex. 34:6)

The word *raḥûm*, "compassionate" or "merciful," is used in twelve of the previous references parallel to *ḥānûn*.

So the root *ḥnn* means "gracious," "favor," "generosity," "unmerited love." Even though the Septuagint translates *ḥēn* as *karis* "grace," the word does not mean what the apostle Paul meant when he used *karis*. The Septuagint follows more clearly the classical Greek meaning of *karis*. Actually, in classical Greek, *karis* has a wide range of meanings, including "that which affords joy, pleasure, delight, sweetness, charm, loveliness, grace of speech" (Thayer's *Greek-English Lexicon*, 665). Because the Septuagint used *karis* to translate *ḥēn* when it referred to God's "good-will" or to His "generosity," Paul could use *karis* in the New Testament to refer to God's "goodwill and generosity" (Reed, "Some Implications of *Hen*," 41).

Another Hebrew word sometimes used to express the "love" of God is a word rich in familial imagery, *raḥamim*. Westermann said that in its talk about God the Old Testament contains a peculiar feature, which makes God's actions at a certain point very human. In contrast to the idea of the holiness of God, which emphasizes the nonhuman aspect of God, with *raḥam* "compassion," a human emotion is attributed to God. The word actually means a "mother's womb" (*Elements of Old Testament Theology*, 138).

The plural form of the noun expands the meaning of "womb," into the abstract idea of "compassion, mercy, pity, heart, love." (See Gen. 43:14,30; Deut. 13:17; 2 Sam. 24:14; 1 Kings 3:26; 8:50; 1 Chron. 21:13; 2 Chron. 30:9; Neh. 1:11; 9:27,28,31; Pss. 25:6; 40:11; 51:1; 69:16; 77:9; 79:8; 103:4; 106:45; 119:77,156; 145:9; Prov. 12:10; Isa. 47:6; 54:7,10; Jer. 16:5; 42:12; Lam. 3:22; Dan. 1:9; 9:9,18; Hos. 2:19; Amos 1:11; Zech. 7:9.) The adjective *raḥum* "compassionate, merciful" is often used with the adjective *ḥanum* "gracious," always of God, never of persons in the Old Testament (Ex. 34:6; Deut. 4:31; 2 Chron. 30:9; Neh. 9:17,31; Pss. 78:38; 86:15; 103:8; 111:4; 112:4; 145:8; Lam. 4:10; Joel 2:13; Jon. 4:2). The verb forms of the root *rḥm* derive from the noun "womb" (Trible, *God and the Rhetoric of Sexuality*, 33). The verb occurs once in the qal meaning "love" for God (Ps. 18:1, *ʾāhab* is used for love for God in Ps. 116:1); forty-three times in the piel meaning "pity" (Ps. 102:13; 103:13; Isa. 49:10; Hos. 2:25); "compassion" (Deut. 13:8; 30:3; Lam. 3:32; Isa. 49:15; 54:8; Zech. 10:6) and "mercy" (Ex. 33:19; Deut. 13:8; Isa. 60:10; Jer. 42:12).

Phyllis Trible devoted a whole chapter to a discussion of the word *rāḥam*. She began with a study of the story of the two harlots who claimed to be the mother of the same baby in 1 Kings 3:16-28. King Solomon was able to determine the real mother by saying that he would divide the baby into two parts with his sword and give each woman half of the child. Then the true mother offered to give up her claim to the child so that the child could live.

The reason for the mother's action is given in v. 26, "because *raḥamim* 'compassion' for her son burned within her. Trible said that this woman was willing to forfeit even justice for the sake of life. *raḥam* "compassion" is a love that acts in truth and self-sacrifice. Only after this point does the word *mother* appear in this story. "Compassion" is the love of a mother for the child of her womb. It knows no demand of ego, possessiveness, or even justice. Trible said, "The womb protects and nourishes but does not possess and control. It yields its treasure in order that wholeness and well-being may happen. Truly, it is the way of compassion" (*God and the Rhetoric of Sexuality,*" 33).

The word *raḥamim* "compassion" describes Joseph's yearning for his brother, expressing a fraternal relationship (Gen. 43:30). Trible saw God's love for Israel expressed in Isaiah 46:3-4 in terms of the compassion of a mother for the child of her womb. She said that the imagery of this passage "stops just short of saying that God possesses a womb" (*God and the Rhetoric of Sexuality,*" 38).

Another significant passage that uses "compassion" terminology to speak of God's love for Israel in terms of a mother's love is Jeremiah 31:15-22. The passage begins with the note that Rachel's voice can still be heard lamenting the loss of her sons (v. 15). God comforts Rachel by promising that her children will return to their land (vv. 16-17). Ephraim (Rachel's children) repents (vv. 18-19). Then Yahweh says (v. 20):

> Is Ephraim my dear son?
> Is he my darling child?
> For as often as I speak against (of) him
> I do remember him still.
> Therefore my heart (*me'ay,* "womb") yearns for him;
> I will surely have mercy (*raḥem 'araḥamenu*) upon him,
> says Yahweh (author's translation).

Trible saw in this passage a parallel between the mother's love of Rachel for her children and God's love for Ephraim.

As Rachel mourns the loss of the fruit of her womb, so Yahweh, from the divine womb, mourns the same child. Yet there is a difference. The human mother refuses consolation; the divine mother changes grief into grace. As a result the poem has moved from the desolate lamentation of Rachel to the redemptive compassion of God (*God and the Rhetoric of Sexuality,* 45).

The last line of this poem (31:22) is its climax. Unfortunately, its meaning is obscure. It reads:

> How long will you waver,
> O faithless daughter?
> For the LORD has created a new
> thing on the earth:
> a woman encompasses a man.

The poem begins with Rachel weeping for her children who had gone into exile (vv. 15-16). Yahweh said that her children would return (v. 17). Ephraim repents (vv. 18-19). Yahweh asks Himself if Ephraim is still His darling child and answers affirmatively, promising to have mercy (*raḥam*) on him (v. 20). In verse 21 the metaphor for Ephraim changes from that of a male (son) to that of a female (virgin daughter). The five imperatives in verse 21 are all feminine. The imperatives implore Israel to return to their cities (and to their God). Still she hesitates. Verse 22 asks, "How long will you waver, O backsliding daughter?" Then, to encourage her to make one more effort, the prophet says, "For Yahweh has created (*bārā'*) a new thing in the land: female surrounds man."

What is this new thing that God has done? This is one of the most difficult sentences in the Old Testament to understand,

and it has given rise to a multitude of varied interpretations. It is something unique, significant, and unusual because the word *bārāʾ* "create" is used sparingly in the Old Testament, always with God as its subject and suggesting making something new. The word *ḥādašâ* "something new" refers to something Yahweh is about to do in bringing in the new age (compare Isa. 42:9; 43:19; 48:6; 65:17; 66:22; Jer. 31:31; Ezek. 11:19; 18:31; 36:26). Some have omitted it from the text as a gloss (Skinner, *Prophecy and Religion,* 302). John Bright translated it but put it in brackets and said, "The meaning is wholly obscure, and it might have been wiser to leave the colon blank" (Bright, *Jeremiah,* 282). B. Duhm amended the text to read "the woman is turned into a man" (see Peake, "Jeremiah," 96). Charles R. Brown amended the text to read, "A woman goes about like a man." (*Jeremiah,* 173). The Septuagint seems to read a different text: "men shall go about in safety," or "men will walk in salvation" (compare Peake, "Jeremiah," 96; Green, *Jeremiah,* 151; Septuagint, Jer. 38:22).

B. God's Love in the Future

In recent years Jeremiah 31:22 has attracted renewed attention. Some supporters of the feminist movement have seen this verse as evidence that the Old Testament speaks of God as both male and female (compare Trible, *God and the Rhetoric of Sexuality,* 47-56; Holladay, "Jer. XXXI 22b Reconsidered," 236-239). Robert P. Carroll gave an extensive discussion of this verse in which he reviewed the views of many scholars. Then Carroll said it would be wise here to admit ignorance and acknowledge that ancient texts occasionally do baffle the modern hermeneutic (*Jeremiah,* 604).

Edmond Jacob asked if this passage is feministic or messianic ("Feminisme ou Messianisme?" 179-184). Jacob noted that the messianic interpretation of this verse is as old as Jerome and has been revived by B. Kipper in a dissertation written in 1957 in which Kipper compares *neqeba* "female" with *ʿalmâ* "virgin" (Isa. 7:14) and *geber* "man" with *ʾel gebur* "mighty God" (Isa. 9:6; 10:21). Martin Luther saw the passage referring to a time when the curse of pain in childbirth would be removed from the woman (see Jacob, "Feminisme ou Messianisme?" 181).

A. W. Streane took the messianic view. "This thought is really messianic, for it attains completion only in the Incarnation of the Divine Son of God" ("Jeremiah," *Cambridge Bible,* 212).

Edmond Jacob thought that the new thing here refers to more than Israel's return from Babylonian exile. The language, "a female shall surround a man," is marriage or covenant language. He pointed to Hosea's experience with Gomer and the analogy of God's covenant (marriage) with Israel. He also cited two references where the verb "surrounds" is used as covenant language (Ps. 32:10). In light of the context of this passage (Jer. 30-31), it is probably best to understand it as referring to more than Israel's return from Babylon—perhaps to the new covenant as well.

Yahweh's love in the Old Testament may be like a mother's love, but it is also greater than a mother's love.

> Can a woman forget her nursing child,
> or show no compassion for the
> child of her womb?
> Even these may forget,
> yet I will not forget you.
> (Isa. 49:15)

Perhaps the greatest chapter on the love of God in the Old Testament is chapter 11 of Hosea. In many ways it approaches the New Testament's understanding of the nature of God. It can be outlined as: (1) electing love (11:1); (2) rejected love (11:2); (3) protecting love (11:3-4); (4) disciplining love (11:5-7); (5) suffering love (11:8-9); and (6) redeeming love (11:10-11) (Ralph L. Smith, "Major Motifs in Hosea," 27-28). B. W. Anderson said that here Hosea "strains all the resources of language in the attempt to plumb the incomprehensible depth of God's holy love, the love which includes both judgment and mercy" ("The Book of Hosea," 301).

Israel is commanded to love God several times in the Old Testament (Deut. 6:5; 11:1; 19:9; 30:16). In fact, Jesus said this is the greatest commandment (Matt. 22:37; Mark 12:30; Luke 10:27). Some scholars ask: "How can love be commanded?" It must be a part of the Hittite treaty influence. E. W. Nicholson argued that God's command to love Him is part of the familiar setting of everyday life. The Israelite is commanded to love the neighbor (Lev. 19:18, 34) and the stranger (Deut. 10:19). Hosea is commanded to love an adulteress (Hos. 3:1). People are commanded to love wisdom (Prov. 4:6), truth and peace (Zech. 8:19), and good (Amos 5:15). Why, then, should the command to love God be understood as "a strange sort of thing," explicable only when one knows suzerainty language? (Nicholson, *God and His People,* 74-80).

God's love for Israel and the world, though not often mentioned in the Old Testament, is very powerful. Deuteronomy says that because God loved (*ʾāhab*) Israel and her ancestors, He brought them out of Egyptian bondage (Deut. 4:37; 7:8; 23:5). Hosea has been called the prophet of God's love. He uses the four main words for love (*ʾāhab, ḥesed, raḥam,* and *naḥam*). In Hosea, God's love is not exhausted by a study of vocabulary. The whole concept of courtship, betrothal, and marriage in Hosea is bound up with love. An interesting courtship scene is described in 2:14: "Therefore, I will now allure her,/ and bring her into the wilderness,/ and speak tenderly to her."

The words "allure" and "speak tenderly to her heart" belong to the language of love. Shechem spoke tenderly to the heart of Dinah (Gen. 34:3); Boaz spoke to Ruth's heart (Ruth 2:11-13); the Levite spoke to the heart of his wife who had gone back to her father (Judg. 19:3). Hosea is commanded to "go, love a woman who has a lover and is an adulteress, just as the LORD loves the people of Israel, though they turn to other gods and love raisin cakes" (Hos. 3:1).

The Old Testament view of God's love is that it is deep, strong, and abiding. It serves as the background for the understanding of the love of God in the New Testament. Lester Kuyper noted that John, in the prologue to his gospel (1:14), used a New Testament phrase "full of grace and truth" to say that Jesus is God. The equivalent Old Testament phrase *ḥesed* and *ʾemet* "lovingkindness and faithfulness" is used many times of God in the Old Testament ("Grace and Truth," 3-19).

23. A Wrathful God

Wrath is one of the most frequently mentioned feelings of God in the Old Testament. The wrath of God is very real and very serious to the people of the Old Testament. What is anger? In ancient Egypt anger meant "rage," "raving," "violent reaction." The hieroglyphic signs for anger picture the "smiting of a poor person" and "a raging baboon" or "a raging panther." The Egyptians also used a word for "red" suggesting "heart" and a word for "nose" much like the Hebrew to represent anger. In Akkadian the two most frequently used words for anger are *agagu*, "to be strong momentarily," and *ezezu*, "to be wild and furious," often used of natural phenomena (J. Bergman, E. Johnson, *'anaph, TDOT* I, 350).

In the Greek religion the gods were not regarded as friends of humans. Greek writers continually decried the "vindictiveness, ill-will, and niggardliness" of the gods (Heschel, *The Prophets,* 342). Pre-Greek divinities of the earth and those which bring curses, like the Erinys, "have anger as their nature even in their names 'the furies'" (Kleinknect, Fichtner, and others, "Wrath," 3).

Punishment by the gods is not usually on moral grounds. People are punished for personal offenses against the gods. Of the few condemned to eternal torment, Ixion had assaulted Hera, an act considered an infringement on Zeus' prerogative; Sisyphus told Aesopus where Zeus had forcibly carried away his daughter Aegira; and Prometheus saved the human race by giving it the secret of fire which had been reserved for the gods. Zeus' anger was aroused because he feared for the continuance of his tyranny (Heschel, *The Prophets,* 243).

In most primitive religions, people felt threatened by the power of the gods. "Demonic dread" characterized primitive religion. It is "a horror of some power which concerns itself neither with my reason nor my morals" (Van der Leeuw, *Religion in Essence and Manifestation,* 134).

More than twenty different Hebrew words, used more than 580 times in the Old Testament, refer to God's wrath (Morris, *The Apostolic Preaching of the Cross*, 131). Morris said:

> The wrath of God is a conception which cannot be eradicated from the Old Testament without irreparable loss. It is not the monopoly of one or two writers, but pervades the entire corpus . . . the concept may need to be understood carefully, but it is so much part and parcel of the Old Testament that, if we ignore it, we cannot possibly enter into a proper appreciation of the Hebrew view of God or of man (*The Apostolic Preaching of the Cross,* 156).

E. Jacob said that wrath was so much a part of the figure of God in the Old Testament that the ancient Israelites saw no problem in it (*Theology of the Old Testament,* 114).

Many modern theologians and Bible scholars have seen the wrath of God as a problem. Abraham Heschel claimed that among those who remained open to the message of the anger of God, to which the Bible refers again and again, some have recoiled; some have treated it allegorically; and others have been repelled by it (*The Prophets,* 279). C. H. Dodd said that the wrath of God is "an archaic phrase" suiting "a thoroughly archaic idea" (*The Epistle of Paul to the Romans,* 20).

Elizabeth Achtemeier noted that Norman Snaith, in his book on the seven penitential psalms, said that it is improper to speak of God as angry. While it is good that sinners should first feel that God is angry with them, nevertheless, when they grow up spiritually and know more about the tender mercies of God, they will give up such language (Snaith, *The Seven Psalms,* 22).

Achtemeier then said, "Such a view is nonsense in the light of the biblical revelation, not only of the Old Testament, but also of the New; and it is such views which have led to the popular belief that the God and Father of Jesus Christ is a sentimental little godlet of love who winks at wrong-doing and loves us no matter what we do. Throughout the Bible God destroys Israel and mankind as a whole for its lack of reliance on his lordship and for its rebellion against his sovereign commands. Such is surely part of the meaning of the Cross of Christ—that we die for our sin against God" ("Overcoming the World," 80).

Heschel said that it is impossible to close one's eyes to the words about the wrath of God in Scripture. To interpret the wrath of God along allegorical lines or as a metonymy "is to misread the authentic meaning of the word and to misrepresent biblical thought. . . . The word about the divine anger points to a stark reality, to the power behind the facts, not to a figure of speech" (*The Prophets,* 280). The wrath of God belongs to divine holiness and must not be dismissed as a mere anthropomorphism (Robinson, *Redemption and Revelation,* 269; Robinson, *Record and Revelation,* 342). "The Israelite really believed in the wrath of Yahweh and did not project it upon God from the testings and punishments which he himself had passed through" (Jacob, *Theology of the Old Testament*, 114).

The Old Testament speaks of God's wrath or anger three times more often than it speaks of human wrath. Some terms such as *haron*, *'aph*, and *za'am* are used only of God's wrath. Most of the terms for wrath are borrowed from concrete, physiological expressions such as "get hot" or "burn" (Isa. 65:5; Jer. 15:14; 17:4); "outburst" or "overflowing" (Ezek. 13:13; 38:22); the destructive power of the "storm" (Ps. 83:15; Isa. 30:30; Jer. 23:19-20; 30:23-24); a liquid in a cup to be poured out (Ps. 69:24; Jer. 10:25; Hos. 5:10) or to be drunk (Job 21:20; Jer. 25:15-16); the stretching out of Yahweh's hand (Isa. 5:25; 9:12,17,21; 10:4). Wrath seems to be more of an activity of God than an emotion. Expressions referring to wrath are never connected with the heart (Ringgren, *Israelite Religion*, 76).

Two words closely associated with wrath in the Old Testament are "jealous" and "vengeance." God's jealousy means that He will not tolerate any other god beside Him (Ex. 20:5; 34:14; Deut. 4:24). Israel's enemies are objects of God's jealous wrath (Nah. 1:2-3; Zeph. 1:18). Sometimes the jealousy of God becomes the zeal of Yahweh for His people to establish His kingdom (Isa. 9:7; 37:32; Ezek. 39:25; Zech. 1:14).

The jealousy of God in the Old Testament is related to His holiness, His uniqueness, His unapproachableness, His self-assertion. Th. C. Vriezen said:

> We must be very accurate in our distinctions regarding this idea: it is not to be identified with what is known in heathenism as the jealousy of the gods which may be revealed not only against other gods but also against man when things are going particularly well with him. The fear of the jealousy of the gods in the higher polytheistic religions is an after-effect of a demonic belief in God which has been banished in the Old Testament. Applied to Yahweh this word has a shade of meaning different from the one it has when applied to men. The verb with which *qanna'* is connected means, besides being jealous, also to maintain one's rights to the exclusion of others (e.g. Num. xi. 29; II Sam. xxi. 2) (*Outline of Old Testament Theology*, 302).

Vriezen noted that Yahweh's jealous guarding of His right to be worshiped exclusively explains why Adam and Eve were not permitted to eat of the tree of the knowledge of good and evil. For them to do so would lead them to become like God.

This also explains why building the Tower of Babel was wrong and why all kinds of divination, magic, necromancy, and witchcraft were forbidden.

For the Bible to speak of God as jealous comes as a surprise or a shock to some people. John R. Stott noted that jealousy is condemned in the New Testament as a sin (see Gal. 5:19-20). Jealousy can denote both an attribute of God and a human sin because jealousy is neutral. "Whether it is good or evil is determined by the situation which arouses it. In essence jealousy is an intolerance of rivals; it is a virtue or a sin according to whether the rival is legitimate" (*Our Guilty Silence,* 17).

Another Hebrew word closely associated with wrath is *nāqam,* usually translated "vengeance" or "revenge." The work of W. F. Albright and his students George Mendenhall and G. E. Wright has given us a better understanding of the term in the Old Testament and in the Ancient Near East. Albright said the Hebrew word *nāqam* seldom means "avenge" but rather "save," as it does in the Mari and Amarna tablets (*History, Archaeology, and Christian Humanism,* 96).

G. Ernest Wright said that *naqam* is poorly translated "vengeance." This term refers to both the judging and redeeming activity of the sovereign Lord of history, who bears ultimate responsibility for justice and salvation. "Hence it is the prerogative of God alone" ("History and Reality," 195). Mendenhall said that *nāqam* means "exercise legitimate power," so we should translate it "sovereignty is mine" (*The Tenth Generation,* 75-76).

nāqam is often used in connection with holy war (Num. 31:1-2; 1 Sam. 14:24; 18:25; 2 Sam. 4:8; 22:48; Ps. 18:48). Individuals are not supposed to exercise this prerogative; "vengeance is mine" (Lev. 19:18; Deut. 32:35; compare Rom. 12:19). But sometimes they do (Gen. 4:24; Prov. 6:34).

"Vengeance" is often associated with the role of a judge. Yahweh is called a God of vengeance and is implored to rise up and judge the earth (Ps. 94:1-2). Perhaps the clearest passage to express the relation of *nāqam* to that of a judge is 1 Samuel 24:12. David said to Saul, "May the LORD judge between me and you, may the Lord avenge (*nāqam*) me upon you! May the LORD avenge me on you; but *my* hand shall not be against you." Jeremiah used the word *nāqam* three times in his "confessions" in the context of Yahweh judging him and "delivering him from his enemies" (11:20; 15:15; 20:12).

Jealousy and vengeance are closely associated with anger, but they are not to be identified with it. What is wrath? Some have presented it as a sinister, malignant passion, an evil force that must always be suppressed. Aristotle defined anger as the desire for retaliation or vengeance. Cicero said that anger is "the lust for revenge," and Horace called it "a brief madness" (see Heschel, *The Prophets,* 280, n. 4).

However, in the Old Testament, the conception of God's wrath receives its particular stamp from the fact that "basically Israel has to do with only one God and thus the outlet into the pantheon and the world of demons is barred" (Kleinknect, Fichtner, and others, "Wrath," 25). Eichrodt said that the wrath of God in the Old Testament never acquires the characteristics of *manis,* "that malicious hatred and envy which bulks so large in the implacability of the Greek and also of the Babylonia deities. Even if it is sometimes unintelligible, Yahweh's anger has nothing of the satanic about it; it remains simply the manifestation of the displeasure of God's unsearchable greatness" (Eichrodt, *Theology of the Old Testament I,* 261). The wrath of God is unintelligible only in some of the early stories about Jacob wrestling with the man at Jabbok and coming away limping (Gen. 32:24-32); God meeting Moses on the way to Egypt and trying to kill him (Ex. 4:24-26); or Yahweh inciting David to number the people (2 Sam. 24:1). The wrath of God was very real to Israel. Although they did not always understand God's wrath, they accepted it.

The anger of God should not be treated in insolation from other aspects of His nature or from human sin. "It is an instrument rather than a force, transitive rather than spontaneous. It is a secondary emotion, never the ruling passion" (Heschel, *The Prophets,* 282-283). Some scholars disagree with some of these assertions. Tasker said that wrath is "the permanent attitude of the holy and just God when confronted by sin and evil" ("Wrath," 1341).

Who or what are the objects of God's wrath in the Old Testament? The wrath of God in the Old Testament comes on individuals: Moses (Ex. 4:14; Deut. 1:37); Aaron (Deut. 9:20); Aaron and Miriam (Num. 12:9); Nadab and Abihu (Lev. 10:1-

2); upon Israel (Ex. 32:10 and many other references); and against the nations (Ps. 2:5; Isa. 13:3,5,13; 30:27; Jer. 50:13,15; Ezek. 25:4; 30:15; Zeph. 3:8).

The apparent reason for the anger of God is sin. Leon Morris said, "It is aroused only and inevitably by sin" (*The Apostolic Preaching of the Cross,* 131). Some of the sins that bring God's wrath are: the worship of other gods (Ex. 32; Num. 25; Deut. 2:15; 4:25-26; 9:19; Judg. 2:14; 1 Kings 11:9-10; 14:9, 15; 2 Kings 17:17-18); the shedding of blood (Ezek. 16:38; 24:7-8); adultery (Ezek. 16:38; 23:25); social injustices (Ex. 22:21-24).

What are the causes of God's wrath? It is not always possible to determine the cause of God's wrath in the Old Testament. Tragedies, national disasters, and premature deaths became an enigma to many in the Old Testament. Trouble and evil were often viewed as punishments of God (see 2 Kings 23:26-30; compare 2 Chron. 35:20-25; Job 2:10; Ps. 44:8-22).

Eichrodt said that Israel spoke of divine wrath in those cases where misfortune struck in extraordinary ways or contrary to all expectation. Amos took it for granted that every misfortune was the product of God's wrath (Amos 3:6). "Both accidental death and extraordinary public calamity are ascribed to God (Ex. 21:13; 8:15; 1 Sam. 6:5). The only reasonable attitude to incomprehensible misfortune is simply to bow to divine displeasure" (*Theology of the Old Testament I,* 260).

What are the effects of God's wrath? J. Fichtner said "the basic effect of Yahweh's wrath is intended to be annihilation, complete obliteration" (Kleinknect, Fichtner, et. al., "Wrath," 33). After Aaron and the people made the golden calf and worshiped it, the Lord said to Moses, "Now let me alone, so that my wrath may burn hot against them and I may consume them" (Ex. 32:10; compare Num. 16: 21; Deut. 7:4). Amos and Ezekiel announced that the "end" had come for Israel and Judah (Amos 8:2; Ezek. 7:2-21). The fall of Jerusalem and the exile were effects of God's wrath (2 Kings 23:26; Ezek. 7:4,9,24; 8:18; 29:12).

Wrath is not God's last word in the Old Testament. Leon Morris said, "While wrath is a dreadful reality, it must not be taken as the last word about God" (*The Apostolic Preaching of the Cross,* 135). Jacob said, "With a living God and one who bestows life, wrath cannot be the last word" (*Theology of the*

Old Testament, 116). In the Old Testament, God's wrath is modified or conditioned by his love. Amos said:

> The eyes of the Lord God are
> upon the sinful kingdom,
> and I will destroy it from the
> face of the earth
> —except that I will not utterly
> destroy the house of Jacob,
> says the Lord.
> (Amos 9:8)

Hosea said:

> How can I give you up, Ephraim?
> How can I hand you over, O Israel?
>
> ....
>
> My heart recoils within me;
> my compassion grows warm and tender.
> I will not execute my fierce anger;
> I will not again destroy Ephraim.
> (Hos. 11:8-9*a*)

Isaiah spoke of a remnant that would survive the Assyrian crisis (Isa. 10:20-23). Two verses later he announced an end to God's wrath on Judah and its redirection toward Assyria (Isa. 10:25). Jeremiah called:

> Return, faithless Israel,
> says the LORD,
> I will not look on you in anger,
> for I am merciful,
> says the LORD
> I will not be angry forever.
> (Jer. 3:12)

The psalmist said:

> "For his anger is but for a moment;
> his favor is for a lifetime."
> (Ps. 30:5; Heb.6)

The prophet of the exile said:

> For a brief moment I abandoned you,
> but with great compassion I will gather you.
> In overflowing wrath for a moment
> I hid my face from you,
> but with everlasting love I will
> have compassion on you,

> says the LORD, your Redeemer.
> (Isa. 54:7-8)

Micah said:

> Who is a God like you, pardoning iniquity
> and passing over the transgression
> of the remnant of your possession?
> He does not retain his anger forever,
> because he delights in showing clemency.
> (Mic. 7:18)

Is God's anger only a temporary, secondary part of His nature which leaves no lasting effects on His relationship or dealings with people? Eichrodt left that impression: "Unlike holiness or righteousness, *wrath never forms one of the permanent attributes of the God of Israel;* it can only be understood as, so to speak, a footnote to the will to fellowship of the covenant God" (*Theology of the Old Testament I,* 262).

Eichrodt did not understand the Old Testament to say that because God's wrath is temporary, there would be no judgment or punishment of sinners. In fact, he said that the principal and proper sphere of operation of the wrath of God in the Old Testament is in the exercise of retributive justice (*Theology of the Old Testament I,* 263). Everything that might be called punishment for sin is regarded as the operation of God's wrath on a national and an individual level. Yet the whole tone in which ancient Israel spoke of Yahweh's punishing proves that there was a "sensitive *feeling for the moral basis of punishment*" (*Theology of the Old Testament I,* 265).

It is generally recognized that God does not at once give free rein to His anger. He restrains it in order to punish at a time when the righteousness of His action will be more easily discernible and, even then, by proclaiming the coming punishment beforehand.

Christoph Barth observed that the judgment stories of Numbers introduce a new feature, "the anger of God." Exodus never speaks of God's anger except in chapter 32. Numbers refers to it often (11:1-10; 12:9; 16:46; 25:4; compare Pss. 78:21,31,38; 95:11).

> Yet the anger of God in no way contradicts his mercy, his fidelity, his patience, or his willingness to forgive. It is the same God who shows amazing patience in Exodus and who reaches the limit of

his patience in Numbers. In showing mercy, he does not let Israel do as it wants. . . . In showing anger and condemning his rebellious people, he has not totally exhausted his patience, nor is he about to sever all relations with Israel (*God With Us,* 97-98).

The Old Testament speaks often of God's patience, but patience in this case must not be understood as apathy, indifference, or indulgence. Heschel said:

The patience of God means His restraint of justifiable anger. One must not mistake divine forgiveness for indulgence. There is a limit at which forbearance ceases to be a blessing. Forgiveness is neither absolute nor unconditional. We may forgive the criminal; is it right to forgive the crime? I may forgive a wrong done to me; but do I have the right to forgive a wrong done to others? Unconditional forgiveness may be found in Pandora's box, a fine incentive to vice. Anger is a reminder that man is in need of forgiveness, and that forgiveness must not be taken for granted. The Lord is long-suffering, compassionate, loving, and faithful, but He is also demanding, insistent, terrible, and dangerous (*The Prophets,* 285).

The wrath of God is justified in the Old Testament.

> Her foes have become the masters,
> her enemies prosper,
> because the LORD has made her suffer
> for the multitude of her transgressions.
>
> ....
>
> The LORD is in the right,
> for I have rebelled against his word.
>
> ....
>
> The LORD has done what he purposed,
> he has carried out his threat;
> as he ordained long ago,
> he has demolished without pity.
> (Lam. 1:5a,18a;2:17ab)

Even though God's wrath may seem cruel at times, it is the counterpart, not the antithesis, of his love. There is a love that punishes just as there is a cruelty that pardons. "Severity must tame whom love cannot win" (Heschel, *The Prophets,* 296). Sometimes sympathy must be suppressed for love to function. A surgeon cannot indulge his natural sympathy for the patient in order to heal.

Leon Morris said the Old Testament gives us a picture of God, whose nature is merciful and who cannot be swayed by human efforts to obtain forgiveness.

> Forgiveness is always due in the last resort to God's being what He is, and not to anything man may do. Because God is God, He must react in the strongest manner to man's sin, and thus we reach the concept of the divine wrath. But because God is God, wrath cannot be the last word. "The Lord is good; his mercy endureth forever" (Ps. 5) (*The Apostolic Preaching of the Cross*, 136).

Even though anger is something that comes close to evil, it should not be identified with evil in essence. Paul paraphrased Psalm 4:4-5, "Be angry but do not sin" (Eph. 4:26). Anger is attributed to Jesus in Mark 3:5. Like fire, anger is neutral. It can be a blessing or a curse—reprehensible when associated with malice, morally necessary as resistance to malice.

24. A Judging God

A. God's Role as Judge

If God is a saving, blessing, creating, holy, loving God, is He also a judging God? Is acting as a judge consistent with saving, blessing, creating, loving, wrath, and holiness? The Old Testament speaks often of God as judge. Early in the Old Testament Abraham asked if it is right for the Judge of all the earth to destroy the righteous with the wicked. "Shall not the Judge of all the earth do what is just?" (Gen. 18:25).

The psalmist said, "The heavens declare his righteousness, for God himself is judge" (Ps. 50:6).

Isaiah said, "For the LORD is our judge, the Lord is our ruler, the LORD is our King; he will save us. (Isa. 33:22).

In the Old Testament Yahweh judges between individuals (Gen. 16:5; 31:53; 1 Sam. 24:12,15) and nations (Isa. 2:4). He also judges individuals (Gen. 30:6; Pss. 7:8; 26:1-2; 35:24-25; 43:1; 54:1); families (1 Sam. 3:13); nations (Gen. 15:14; Ps. 110:6; Joel 3:12); His people (Pss. 50:4; 67:4; Isa. 3:13; 33:22; Ezek. 36:19); the earth (Gen. 18:25; 1 Sam. 2:10; Pss. 9:8; 82:8; 94:2; 96:10); the gods and those on high (Job 21:22; Ps. 82:1-2). The fact that God could judge all these groups indicates He has authority and sovereignty over them.

Three things are essential for a good judge: authority and
sovereignty; just and equitable decisions; and the ability to
perceive and interpret properly all of the evidence. Yahweh
has all three qualities. He is sovereign over all the earth. He
judges people according to their ways (Ezek. 7:27; 24:14;
33:20). His judgments are righteous and based on equity (Gen.
18:25; Pss. 9:4,8; 67:4; 72:2; 75:2; 96:10). (Near the end of the
Old Testament some Wisdom writers raised serious questions
about the justice of God [Job 8:3; 9:2,20,22-24].) The thing that
qualified Yahweh most to be a judge was His ability to see
inside a person and to know motives and real character. The
Lord said to Samuel:

> They [mortals] look on the outward appearance,
> but the LORD looks on the heart.
> (1 Sam. 16:7)

The psalmist said:

> Prove me, O LORD, and try me;
> test my heart and mind.
> (Ps. 26:2; compare 139:23)

> If we had forgotten the name of our God,
> or spread out our hands to a strange god,
> would not God discover this?
> For he knows the secrets of the heart.
> (Ps. 44:20-21)

Jeremiah said:

> But You, O LORD of hosts, who judges righteously,
> who try the heart and the mind,
> let me see your retribution upon them:
> for to you I have committed my cause.
> (Jer. 11:20)

The role of the judge in the ancient world was more than
that of hearing the testimony of witnesses and making a decision concerning the guilt or innocence of the accused. The role
of the judge could include the discovery of the crime, hearing,
accusing, defending, sentencing, and executing the sentence
(Snaith, *Distinctive Ideas of the Old Testament,* 74; Jacob, *Theology of the Old Testament,* 97; Westermann, *Elements of Old
Testament Theology,* 120).

Laban accused Jacob of stealing his household gods. Laban
overtook Jacob on the road to Jabbok and rummaged through

his baggage. When Laban found no incriminating evidence, Jacob said, "Although you have felt about through all my goods, what have you found of all your household goods? Set it here before my kinsfolk and your kinsfolk, so that they may decide between us two" (Gen. 31:37). After sparing Saul's life in the cave at Engedi, David said to him, "May the LORD judge between me and you! May the LORD avenge me on you; but my hand shall not be against you" (1 Sam. 24:12). Later David said, "May the LORD therefore be judge and give sentence between me and you. May he see to it, and plead my cause, and vindicate me against you" (1 Sam. 24:15).

God is presented in the nonhistorical creed (Ex. 34:6) as the gracious, patient, faithful, loving, forgiving God, but also as one who will "by no means clear the guilty." He is a just Judge who will not leave unpunished the guilty ones (Ps. 9:12). He hauls them into "court" and accuses them of breaking the covenant. The Lord often has a controversy with, or "indictment" against His people (Isa. 1:18; Jer. 2:9; Hos. 4:1-3; 12:2; Mic. 6:2).

The belief that God is judge is reflected in some personal names: Jehosaphat means "Yahweh judges." Daniel means "God is judge," as does Eliphal (see 1 Chron. 11:35). Abidan means "My father is judge" (see Num. 1:11; 2:22; 7:60; 10:24).

Sometimes the word "judge" is used of God in a political role like that of earthly judges. It includes the ability to perceive the difference between good and evil and to act on that perception. Solomon prayed, "Give your servant therefore an understanding mind to govern your people, able to discern between good and evil" (1 Kings 3:9). Ludwig Köhler said that God does not so much say what is right; rather, He helps to make things right (*Old Testament Theology,* 32).

B. God's Justice and Righteousness

God's justice (*mišpaṭ*) and righteousness (*ṣĕdāqâ*) are often related to His role as judge. The terms are frequently used together. It is often difficult to distinguish the meanings of each word, but the general concept behind both words is clear and very significant. Heschel said, "There are few thoughts as deeply ingrained in the mind of biblical man as the thought of God's justice and righteousness. It is not an inference, but an *a priori* of biblical faith, self-evident; not an added attribute to His essence, but given with the very thought of God. It is inherent in His essence and identified with his ways" (*The Prophets*, 199-200). Heschel is very close to H. H. Schmid's view of righteousness as part of the world order. (See the pertinent discussion later in this chapter.)

Von Rad said there is absolutely no concept in the Old Testament with so central a significance for all the relationships of human life as that of *ṣĕdāqâ*, "righteousness" or "justice." It is the standard for a person's relationship to God, and also for relationships to other persons, reaching right to the animals and to the natural environment. *ṣĕdāqâ* can be described as "the highest value in life, that upon which all life rests when it is properly ordered" (von Rad, *Old Testament Theology I*, 370). Johnson emphasized the role of *ṣĕdāqâ* as a relationship term describing the form and operation, effects of positively ordered community relationships (B. Johnson, TWAT VI, 923).

The Old Testament often speaks of God as righteous (Ex. 9:27; Pss. 11:7; 111:3; 116:5; 129:4; 145:17; Jer. 12:1; Dan. 9:14).

> The Rock, his work is perfect,
> and all his ways are just.
> A faithful God, without deceit,
> just and upright is he.
> (Deut. 32:4)

> You are righteous, O LORD,
> and your judgments are right.
> (Ps. 119:137)

What is the difference between justice and righteousness in the Old Testament? *mišpaṭ*, "justice," is a legal term geared to the court system. *ṣĕdāqâ* "righteousness" is conformity to a norm. Often the norm is the covenant. God and Israel are righteous when they keep the covenant.

Objects can be "righteous" in the Old Testament. Balances, weights, and measures are "just" when they are what they ought to be (Lev. 19:36; Ezek. 45:10). Sacrifices are "righteous" if they are offered according to the proper rules (Deut. 33:19; Ps. 4:5; 51:19). Oak trees are "righteous" because they are always green (Isa. 61:3), and paths are "righteous" if they are fit for walking (Ps. 23:3). So *ṣĕdāqâ* "righteousness" is conformity to the norm of what each person or thing ought to be. In the Old Testament God Himself is the source of right (Deut. 1:17; compare Heschel, *The Prophets,* 200).

Heschel tried to distinguish between righteousness and justice by suggesting that righteousness is a quality of a person, while justice is a mode of action. The noun *judge* means "one who acts as a judge," but the noun *righteous* refers to a righteous person. Righteousness goes beyond justice. Justice is often "strict and exact, giving each person his due. Righteousness implies benevolence, kindness, generosity. Justice is form, a state of equilibrium; righteousness has a substantive associated meaning. Justice may be legal; righteousness is associated with a burning compassion for the oppressed" (*The Prophets,* 201; compare Deut. 24:10-13). The righteousness of God cannot be separated from the figure of God the Judge (see Jacob, *Theology of the Old Testament,* 96; Job 4:8-10; 9:13; 26:12; Pss. 74:13-14; 89:10; 96:10-13; 98:7-9; Isa. 27:1; 17:9; Nicholson, *God and His People,* 198).

Justice originally referred to the judgments or rulings of God as judge. Judgments made in the name of God by local judges became the basis of case or common law in Israel. We must not equate our view of God as judge in the Old Testament with the classical blindfolded maiden holding a balance in her hand. "The justice of God extends one arm to the wretch stretched out on the ground whilst the other pushes away the one who causes the misfortune" (Jacob, *Theology of the Old Testament,* 99). So the justice of God often has an element of grace and mercy in it. It often is biased in favor of the poor and needy.

C. Righteousness as Victory or Salvation

Almost from the beginning of the Old Testament, the "righteousness of God" was a synonym for "victory" and "salvation." The great redemptive acts of God on behalf of Israel are called "Yahweh's righteous acts" ("triumphs," Judg. 5:11; "saving deeds," 1 Sam. 12:7; "vindication," Pss. 71:15-16; 103:6; Dan. 9:16; Mic. 6:5). It is in the latter part of Isaiah and in some psalms that the blending of the ideas of righteousness, victory and salvation becomes clearest (Pss. 22:31; 35:24,27-28; 48:10; 51:1,14; 65:5; Isa. 45:8,21,25; 46:12-13; 51:1,5-6,8; 61:10; 62:1-2).

Many scholars speak of a development of meaning in the idea of God's righteousness in the Old Testament, but von Rad said that there is no discernible radical transformation or development in the ancient Israelite concept of Yahweh's righteousness. From the time of the Song of Deborah, Yahweh's righteousness was "not a norm, but acts, and it was these acts which bestow salvation" (*Old Testament Theology I*, 372-373). The individual in the Old Testament could experience these "righteous" saving acts of God as well as the nation (Pss. 22:31; 40:11; 71:2-22; 143:1). The whole idea of the justice of God in the Old Testament has been challenged by Klaus Koch and J. L. Crenshaw. (For further discussion see chapter 7, especially section 33 "The Effects of Sin," p. 286).

The noun "righteous" appears in the masculine (*ṣedîq*), feminine singular (*ṣĕdāqâ*), and feminine plural (*ṣĕdeqôt*) forms. There has been much speculation as to the difference between the masculine and feminine forms because the two forms can occur in the same sentence. Most recently Johnson has argued that the feminine form is more concrete, the masculine more abstract (TWAT 6, 912-919). There is no significant discernible difference in the employment of the masculine and feminine nouns. Jacob saw the difference as the masculine form stressing the norm of God's action, while the feminine form stresses the visible manifestation of that norm (*Theology of the Old Testament*, 98). According to Jepsen, the masculine form means "rightness," "order," while the feminine form means the "conduct that aims at right order" (cited by Zimmerli, *Old Testament Theology in Outline*, 143).

G. A. F. Knight said that until recently scholars could not fathom the difference between the masculine and feminine forms. "But again we must humbly say that since they describe aspects of the unspeakable grace and goodness of the living God, we can only fumble for words as we try to express what God is doing" (*Psalms* I, 4). In another place Knight suggested that the masculine form is used of God's saving acts from above, out of sheer grace, because in the ancient world the sky was regarded as masculine. He said that the feminine form refers primarily to the redemptive or saving acts of humans toward one another and is feminine because the earth is feminine (*A Christian Theology of the Old Testament*,

245, n. 1). In this latter sense of human redemptive or saving acts toward their peers, righteousness is synonymous with justice.

> But let justice roll down like waters,
> and righteousness an everflowing stream.
>
> (Amos 5:24)

The words "justice" and "righteousness" are used in so many different ways in the Old Testament that each use must be studied very carefully in light of its context and its meaning in other places. When "righteousness" refers to God's righteousness, it is in some way related to His "saving acts" through grace. When it refers to human righteousness, it is related either to one's standing in the covenant with God and/or how one has treated other people ethically. Walther Zimmerli noted that "righteousness," which characterizes the sphere of divine justice with specific reference to the acts of Yahweh, becomes the central term for human justice. Psalms 111—112 show how Yahweh's righteousness (Ps. 111) is reflected (Ps. 112) in the actions of a person who fears God (*Old Testament Theology in Outline,* 143). Johnson underlined the covenantal relationships, righteousness being conduct in line with the covenant (TWAT 6, 919-920).

We must admit that some passages in the Old Testament speak of God as Judge or King of the world because He created and sustains it. The world is grounded in righteousness and justice (Ps. 89:14; Isa. 28:16-17). Some passages present the Lord in a battle with the forces of evil, chaos, or enemies to keep the world established in righteousness. Sometimes these evil forces are called *Rahab,* Leviathan, *Tanin,* or dragon. In English they are called beasts, serpents, water monsters, or the rivers, floods, or oceans (Job 9:13; 26:12; 38:8-11; Pss. 74:13; 89:10; 93:3-4; 96:10-13; 98:7-9; 104:6-9; Isa. 27:1; 51:9). In Habakkuk 3:8-15 the prophet spoke of a battle between Yahweh and the seas, rivers, and waters, using metaphors from the Exodus and the crossing of the Red Sea. Old mythological language of a battle with the dragon Tiamat is evident. Waters in the Old Testament often symbolize cosmic evil. Yahweh is in control. He has power over the waters and over evil (Smith, *Word Biblical Themes: Micah—Malachi,* 35-37).

By his power he stilled the Sea;
by his understanding he struck down Rahab.
By his wind the heavens were made fair;
his hand pierced the fleeing serpent.
(Job 26:12-13)

Was your wrath against the rivers, O LORD?
Or your anger against the rivers,
or your rage against the sea,
when you drove your horses,
your chariots to victory?
You brandished your naked bow,
sated were the arrows at your
command.
Selah

You split the earth with rivers.
The mountains saw you, and writhed;
a torrent of water swept by;
the deep gave forth its voice.
The sun raised high its hands;
the moon stood still in its exalted place,
at the light of your arrows speeding by,
at the gleam of your flashing spear.
In fury you trod the earth,
in anger you trampled nations.
You came forth to save your people,
to save your anointed.
You crushed the head of the wicked house,
laying it bare from foundation
to roof.
Selah

You pierced with his own arrows
the head of his warriors,
who came like a whirlwind to scatter us,
gloating as if ready to devour
the poor who were in hiding.
You trampled the sea with your horses,
churning the mighty waters.
(Hab. 3:8-15)

At the set time that I appoint
I will judge with equity.
When the earth totters, with all its
inhabitants,
it is I who keep its pillars steady.
Selah
(Ps. 75:2-3)

Habakkuk knew that the power of evil was like a monster. Such power was too great for him, but God was sovereign over the sea. When the apostle John was a prisoner on the island of Patmos, he looked toward a day when there would be "no more sea"—meaning "no more evil" (Rev. 21:1). Revelation 12:7-12 speaks of God as sovereign over evil, as He is over the sea. War will arise in heaven between Michael and his angels and the dragon and his angels. The dragon and his angels will be defeated and cast out of heaven. The victory is attributed to the blood of Christ and the faithful witness of Christian martyrs (Rev. 12:11).

In late biblical Hebrew and Aramaic "righteousness" became almost synonymous with acts of mercy and almsgiving (Dan. 4:27; Matt. 6:1). (Compare Snaith, "Righteous, Righteousness," 202-203; Jacob, *Theology of the Old Testament,* 102; von Rad, *Old Testament Theology* I, 383; Toy, *Proverbs,* 199). The apostle Paul used "righteousness" in two ways. When he wrote of the law of righteousness, he used it in the truly ethical sense (Rom. 9:31; 10:1-6; Phil. 3:6,9). When he spoke of the "gift of righteousness" (Rom. 1:17; 3:22; 5:17), he was thinking of the great saving act of God in Christ. Here Paul is an heir of the prophet and the psalmists who made righteousness synonymous with salvation.

So Yahweh is Judge of the whole world in the Old Testament. He created it. He sustains it. He fights against the forces of evil to keep righteousness and justice in place. Eventually the "knowledge of God" will cover the earth as the "waters" (symbols of evil) cover the sea (see Isa. 11:3-9; Hab. 2:14).

25. A Forgiving God

The experience of being forgiven can be one of the most exhilarating, humbling, and healing experiences of life. The most lyrical outbursts of poetry and doxology in the Old Testament come from those who celebrate forgiveness.

Micah cried:

> Who is a God like you, pardoning iniquity
> and passing over the transgression
> of the remnant of your possession?
> He does not retain his anger forever,

because he delights in showing clemency.
(Mic. 7:18)

The psalmist said:

Happy are those whose
transgression is forgiven,
whose sin is covered.
Happy are those to whom the
LORD imputes no iniquity,
and in whose spirit there is no deceit.

....

Then I acknowledged my sin to you,
and I did not hide my iniquity;
I said, "I will confess my
transgressions to the LORD,"
and you forgave the guilt of
my sin.
Selah

....

You are a hiding place for me;
you preserve me from trouble;
you surround me with glad cries
of deliverance.
Selah
(Ps. 32:1-2,5,7)

Because we have all sinned and come short of the glory of God (Isa. 53:6), forgiveness is necessary. Only God can forgive sins (Isa. 53:4-5; see Pss. 51:3-4; 130:3-4; Mark 2:7; Luke 5:21; 7:49).

Two Hebrew roots carry the basic concept "forgive" in the Old Testament. One is *sālaḥ* and is frequently translated "forgive." In Akkadian a similar root, *salāḥu*, means "sprinkle" and is used in the medical and cultic sense. In Hebrew this concrete sense is not apparent, but this root may have come from a cultic background and could have been used in the sense of "sprinkle," then "to forgive" (Jacob, *Theology of the Old Testament*, 292; Köhler and Baumgartner, *Hebrew Lexicon*, 659). If this is true, forgiveness is a spiritual and mental cleansing and healing process that restores relationships between God and people and between persons.

The second Hebrew root meaning "forgive" is *nāśā᾿* and literally means "to take up," "to carry." *salāḥ* only occurs with God as the subject, but *nasa'* is used with God as well as people as its subject. Joseph's brothers asked him to forgive them (Gen. 50:17); Saul asked Samuel for forgiveness so that he could worship (1 Sam. 15:25); Abigail asked David to forgive her for her part in her husband's evil conduct toward David (1 Sam. 25:28).

Forgiveness is also presented in terms other than *nāśā'* and *salāḥ*. Such expressions as "be gracious," "be hidden from God's wrath," and "God may repent or turn from his anger" can indicate God's forgiveness.

The nonhistorical "creed" in Exodus 34:6-7 describes Yahweh as merciful and gracious, slow to anger, abounding in steadfast love and faithfulness, keeping steadfast love for thousands, and forgiving (*nāśā'*) iniquity, transgression, and sin. The root *slh* is used in the creed in Exodus 34:9 in the prayer, "pardon (*slh*) our iniquity and our sin." This part of the "creed" is repeated two times. A form of the root *slh* appears in Nehemiah 9:17: "You are a God ready to forgive."

Israel believed that Yahweh was a forgiving God, although in some instances God says He will not forgive (Ex. 23:21; Deut. 29:20; Josh. 24:19; 2 Kings 24:4; Job 7:21; Lam. 3:42; Hos. 1:6). Amos prayed for God to forgive Israel (Amos 7:2,5), and the Lord repented and turned away from the threatened judgment. Afterward Amos received two other visions of coming judgment, and Yahweh said that the end of God's patience on Israel had come: "I will never again pass them by" (Amos 7:8; 8:2). Yahweh commanded Jeremiah three times not to pray for his people because Yahweh would not turn away the judgment from them (Jer. 7:16; 11:14; 14:11).

God's forgiveness could not always be taken for granted. Amos said:

> Hate evil and love good,
> and establish justice in the gate;
> it may be that the LORD, the God of hosts,
> will be gracious to the remnant
> of Joseph.
> (Amos 5:15)

In the same vein, Zephaniah said:

> Seek the LORD, all you humble of the land,
> who do his commands;
> seek righteousness, seek humility;

> perhaps you may be hidden
> on the day of the LORD's wrath.
> (Zeph. 2:3)

The king of Nineveh did not take Yahweh's forgiveness for granted. He said, "All shall turn from their evil ways and from the violence that is in their hands. Who knows? God may relent and change his mind; he may turn from his fierce anger, so that we do not perish" (Jonah 3:8b-9).

In these three passages the forgiveness of God is not automatic or guaranteed. God is free to forgive or not to forgive. For the most part Israel had a strong faith in God's willingness to forgive (Neh. 9:17; Pss. 32:1-5; 65:3; 86:5; 99:8; 103:3; Is. 55:7; Mic. 7:18).

In commenting on the occasion when Israel presumed on the forgiveness of God (Isa. 48:1-2), G. A. F. Knight recalled the effrontery of Heinrich Heine's famous statement on his deathbed, "God will forgive me, for that's his job" (*Deutero-Isaiah,* 166; see Stewart's, *A Faith to Proclaim* 52). Knight saw an important evangelical truth in Isaiah 44:22 that asserts that God has already forgiven us *before* we repent, not when and *if* we repent (*Deutero-Isaiah,* 122). Later Knight said that "God offers forgiveness to man at the very moment when man is committing the fundamental sin from which all others flow. God will *abundantly pardon,* . . . or 'multiply to forgive'" (*Deutero-Isaiah,* 262).

According to the Old Testament, humanity's greatest problem is sin. Only God can deal with it effectively; and he did, and does, in Christ (see Smith, *Word Biblical Themes: Micah-Malachi,* 20). The ideas of sin and forgiveness will be discussed more fully in Chapter 7.

26. One and Only God

The Old Testament states that Yahweh is one (Deut. 6:4) and that He alone is God (Deut. 4:35,39; 2 Sam. 7:22; 1 Kings 8:60; 2 Kings 19:15; Ps. 86:10; Isa. 43:10-13; 44:6-8; 45:5-6,21-22; Joel 2:27; compare Isa. 41:4; 48:12; 64:4). These statements are few, and their dates are debatable. It is surprising that the shema (Deut. 6:4), which had become the watchword of Judaism by the beginning of the Christian era, is mentioned only one time in the Old Testament, and its precise meaning is unclear. The Hebrew text may be read, "Hear O Israel Yahweh (is) our god, Yahweh (is) one"; or "Hear O Israel Yahweh (is) our God, Yahweh alone." G. Ernest Wright said that the essential meaning is clear even though the proper English translation is not.

> The object of Israel's exclusive attention, affection, and worship (compare v. 5) is not diffuse but single. It is not a pantheon of gods, each of whose personalities has a disconcerting way of being split up by rival adherents and sanctuaries, so that the attention of the worshipper cannot be concentrated. Israel's attention is undivided; it is confined to one definite being whose name is Yahweh. . . . The word one is thus used in contradistinction to "many," but it also implies uniqueness and difference ("Deuteronomy," *IB*, 372-373).

The word translated "one" is the regular cardinal numeral *ʾĕḥad*. G. A. F. Knight suggested that this word "one" *ʾĕḥad* should not be taken here in the mathematical sense because it is often used of a unity-in-diversity, as in the example of the "one flesh" of husband and wife (Gen. 2:24). "The Person of God . . . must not be conceived in modern individualistic terms. God is no mere monad, the mere 'oneness' of being in the mathematical sense of the word 'one.' He is a 'unity-in-diversity'" (*A Christian Theology*, 58). Knight noted that another Hebrew word, *yahid*, can mean "one" in the sense of uniqueness or "the only one" (Gen. 22:2,12,16; Judg. 11:34; Pss. 22:20; 25:16; 35:17; 68:7; Prov. 4:3; Jer. 6:26; Amos 8:10; Zech. 12:10).

Christians point to the fact that Deuteronomy 6:4 uses the *united one (ʾĕḥad)* as evidence that the doctrine of the Trinity in no way contradicts or stands in opposition to the Shema. We must be careful, however, not to read the Christian doctrine of the Trinity into the Old Testament Shema. David S. Dockery has said there often is confusion as to how the Bible can affirm simultaneously the doctrine of the Trinity and monotheism. However, these two affirmations are in no way contradictory. The doctrine of the Trinity does not teach the existence of three gods. "God did not reveal Himself in clearly defined trinitarian terms in the Old Testament. However, the Old Testament prepared the faithful for the doctrine of the Trinity" (Dockery, "Monotheism in the Scriptures," 30; compare V. P. Hamilton, *Genesis 1-17*, 132-133).

The idea of the oneness of God in the Old Testament is unique and significant. Whereas other ancient peoples thought of their gods as many, with each having his or her own special sphere of influence and responsibility, ancient Israel conceived of her God as one (undivided), having all of the attributes and power of deity in His own person, ruling over all spheres of existence. There were no sexual distinctions in Yahweh. Hebrew has no word for goddess (see Excursus: Asherah, Consort of Yahweh?). There is no indication that the Yahweh of the Northern Kingdom was any different than the Yahweh of the Southern Kingdom. Westermann said:

> Because the creator is the same as the savior, because the God who blesses his creation in a universal horizon is the same who saves and judges his people, because the God whom the individual person trusts is the same who "gives to the young raven their food" (Ps. 147:9), and because there is only one to praise and only one to whom to lament—therefore there is coherency and connection in everything that happens between God and man, between God and his creation. Therefore it is a real story from beginning to end (*Elements of Old Testament Theology*, 32).

Excursus: Asherah, Consort of Yahweh?

Can Israel have lived amid her neighbors and had no female counterpart to Yahweh? Some recent evidence seems to say no.

William Dever claimed the Old Testament contains forty veiled references to the cult of the old Canaanite fertility deity Asherah, consort of El of Ugarit ("Asherah, Consort," 217). Some papyri from Elephantine, an island in the Nile River, were published early in the twentieth century (1906, 1908, 1911). They came from a Jewish military colony on the island and are dated about 450 B.C. They reveal a temple on the island where Yahweh and other gods alongside Him were worshiped. One of the goddesses mentioned in the papyri was Anath, the old Canaanite goddess (Rowley, "Papyri from Elaphantine," 256-257). John Day discussed the huge amount of material from Ugarit that treats Asherah as a goddess ("Asherah in the Hebrew Bible," 385).

Recently two archaeological excavations in the territory of Judah have yielded inscriptions from about 750 B.C. Some have interpreted the inscriptions as references to "Yahweh and his Asherah."

The texts come from two locations: one from Khirbet el-Qôm, a village almost half-way between Hebron and Lachish, and Luntillet Ajrud, a remote desert way station in the northern Sinai about forty kilometers or twenty-five miles southwest of Kadesh-Barnea. We cannot comment on all of the evidence here, but it seems that Emerton's conclusion is best at this point: "The Asherah invoked in the phrase 'Yahweh and his Asherah' is probably the wooden symbol of the goddess of that name, whose associations with the cult of Yahweh is attested in the Old Testament. She may have been regarded in some circles as the consort of Yahweh, but the inscriptions do not offer direct proof of such a relationship" ("New Light on Israelite Religion," 19).

No serious Old Testament scholar argues that any Old Testament passage gives evidence that Yahweh had a consort or shared His worship with anyone or anything. It should be said that the readings "and his Asherah" are by no means certain. If the readings were certain, there is a question whether Asherah refers to a goddess or a place, and whether the texts represent the normative Jewish religion or that of a splinter group. Baruch Margalit said although there is no "unambiguous" attestation of Asherah, meaning "wife" in the Hebrew Bible, many Old Testament references to Asherah seem to presuppose she is a goddess ("The Meaning and Significance of Asherah," 283).

It is difficult to determine when Israel came to an understanding that their God was one and that He was the only God. Israel likely knew God was one before they understood the full implications of that fact: that is, if God is one and has all of the power and prerogatives of deity in Himself, there can be no other. Israel did not reach such a conclusion through rational deduction but through observation of God's acts in history (Wright, *The Old Testament Against Its Environment,* 39).

From the beginning of her history (with Moses or with Abraham), Israel believed that God is one. Westermann said, "The fact that God is one is decisive talk about God in the Old Testament from beginning to end" (*Elements of Old Testament Theology,* 32). W. F. Albright, G. E. Wright, H. H. Rowley, Th. C. Vriezen, E. Jacob, and Dennis Baly all hold an incipient or implicit monotheism from the time of Moses. Such scholars as E. Renan, Andrew Lang, N. Soderblom, R. Pettazzoni, W. Schmidt, G. Widengren, and I. Engnell have used evidence from sociology, anthropology, and the history of religions to try to establish a "primitive monotheism" or the worship of "high gods" (compare W. F. Albright, *From the Stone Age to Christianity,* 70; Rowley, *The Old Testament and Modern Study,* 286-90; Jacob, *Theology of the Old Testament,* 44, 76).

Even though from the beginning of their history Israel thought of their God as one, they did not deny the existence of other gods until fairly late in that history (Dockery, "Monotheism in the Scriptures," 28). Eichrodt said it is easy to show that in ancient Israel, the reality of other gods besides Yahweh was still a fact to be reckoned with (*Theology of the Old Testament I*, 220-21]. The First Commandment, "Thou shalt have no other gods before me," suggests the possible reality of other gods.

Joshua called on the people to choose between Yahweh and other gods (Josh. 24:2,24). Baal worship was a constant threat to the covenant relation between Yahweh and Israel after the conquest of Canaan. The Book of Judges is a continued story of Israel's worship of other gods. Gideon made an ephod (Judg. 8:27); Micah made a graven or molten image out of the silver he had stolen from his mother (Judg. 17:3-4; 18:14,24). David believed that if he were driven out of his land, he would be forced to worship other gods (1 Sam. 26:19). Israel's history was one of apostasy (compare Deut. 9; Ps. 106; Ezek. 16; 20). Idolatry was a problem for Israel until the time of the exile.

How did Israel attempt to deal with the existence of other gods? Zimmerli says, "Yahwism did not simply eliminate the notion of alien deities, however much it considered Yahweh alone the only deity for Israel. Israel knows nothing of any theoretical monotheism. It takes for granted that there are other gods among the other nations" (*Old Testament Theology in Outline,* 42).

Israel tried to come to terms with the existence of other gods in various ways. In Deuteronomy 32:8, according to the Septuagint and the Dead Sea Scrolls, the most High God gave the nations their inheritance when he separated the sons of men. He fixed the bounds of the peoples according to the sons of God (that is, angels). The Hebrew (Masoretic) text here seems to have changed the original reading from "sons of God" to "sons of man." The "sons of God" would suggest that Israel and nations other than Israel were assigned or allotted a guardian angel or deity (compare Dan. 9:21; 10:13,20-21; 12:1). (For a discussion of the textual problem in Deuteronomy 32:8, see Craigie, "The Book of Deuteronomy," 379; J. A. Thompson, *Deuteronomy,* 299.) Deuteronomy 4:19 and 29:26 suggest that when God separated the nations He allotted other gods for the nations to worship, but Israel was strictly forbidden to worship such gods.

Psalm 82 may have a "final" solution to the problem of other gods, but admittedly it is very difficult to interpret. Is Psalm

82 talking about the death of the "gods"? Verse 1 says that God (ʾĕlōhîm) has taken his stand in the assembly (ʿādāt), "council," "congregation" of God (ʾēl) to judge whether the assembly is human or divine.

God (ʾĕlōhîm) asks, "How long will you judge unjustly/ and show partiality to the wicked?" They should judge on behalf of the weak and fatherless (v. 3). The destitute and poor should be saved (ṣādiq). The weak and the poor should be delivered from the hands of the wicked (v. 4). They (the assembly members or the poor?) do not know or understand. They walk in the dark. All of the foundations of the earth are shaken (v. 5). "I (emphatic) say, 'You are gods,/ children of the Most High, all of you./ Nevertheless, you shall die like mortals, and fall like any prince'"(v. 7). (Would the psalmist have said, "men would die like men"? Then the psalmist and the worshipers say, "Rise up, O God (ʾĕlōhîm), judge the earth;/for all the nations belong to you" (v. 8).

One should not be dogmatic about any one interpretation of this psalm. W. Stewart McCullough was probably wise to say, "In truth we do not know very much about this psalm, and we can only trust that our guesses about it are not too wide of the mark" ("Psalms," 442).

Perhaps the best way to understand Psalm 82 is to take it as a reference to Yahweh's taking His stand in the "heavenly council" to judge the members of the council for misconduct and to remove them from power and authority. The Old Testament speaks often of Yahweh being on a throne, surrounded by heavenly beings such as the seraphim, holy ones, sons of God, and even Satan. (See Deut. 32:8; 1 Kings 22:19-23; Job 1; 2; Ps. 29:1; Isa. 6:1-3; 24:21; Dan. 7:9-10.)

In line with the thought of Deuteronomy 32:8, God had given the welfare of the other nations into the hands of these subordinate divine beings, but they failed to establish justice and righteousness in the earth among the nations. Even though they were in some sense divine and supposedly had "eternal life," which in the ancient world was a possession of the gods, now they will die and fall like humans. Yahweh will take possession of all nations because they have always belonged to Him. Psalm 82 therefore is a giant step toward establishing "absolute" monotheism in ancient Israel (Tsevat, "God and the Gods in Assembly," 134; Durham, *Psalms,* 341).

What is monotheism? Monotheism has been defined as "the belief in an uncreated, Supreme Deity, wholly beneficent, omnipotent, omniscient, and omnipresent; it demands the complete exclusion of all other gods. The world in its most minute details is regarded as His work, having been created out of nothing in response to His wish" (Baly, "The Geography of Monotheism," 256). Robert L. Cate defined monotheism as "the belief in and the worship and service of one unique God existing alone as the creator and sovereign Lord of the universe" ("The Development of Monotheism," 30).

Should one speak of the faith of Israel in the Old Testament as henotheistic or monotheistic? G. E. Wright said that Old Testament scholars have generally understood henotheism to mean "the worship of one God who is confined to one people and country, but a worship which does not exclude the recognition of other deities" (*Old Testament Against Its Environment,* 37). Henotheism defined in that way certainly does not fit the universal and cosmic conception implicit in the Old Testament.

Wright prefers to use the term *monotheism* for the Old Testament faith because "it has always been used to define Judaism and Christianity in which the angelic host has survived and has been elaborated" (*The Old Testament Against Its Environment,* 37). Even later, Israel placed no abstract or metaphysical emphasis on the existence or nonexistence of the other gods. The emphasis is on their lack of power to do anything. Monotheism rather than henotheism emphasizes the most characteristic and unique feature of Israel: "the exclusive exaltation of the one source of all power, authority, and creativity" (*The Old Testament Against Its Environment,* 39). This understanding of monotheism leaves room for angelology, demonology, and the New Testament understanding of the Godhead.

Dennis Baly listed five important areas in which Israel's experience at the Exodus and Sinai laid the groundwork for Hebrew monotheism. First was the rejection of the natural world as the framework of reality and meaning. All other societies of the ancient world looked to the phenomena of nature for the clue to meaning and order, but Israel found it in God's redemptive acts and in His choosing them to be His special people. Second was the foundation of a new community by a covenant between God and Israel. Third was the non-location of God—that is, God is not bound to any one location in heaven or earth. Fourth was the concept of power as the ultimate reality. Fifth was the idea that God is a jealous God. Exclusiveness and intolerance are necessary to monotheism ("The Geography of Monotheism," 268-272).

Julius Wellhausen (see E. W. Nicholson, "Israelite Religion in the Pre-exilic Period," 3) and his followers made ethical monotheism (which they attributed to the eighth-century prophets) the high-water mark of the Old Testament faith, but ethical monotheism should not be used as the only test of a religion. Eichrodt said, "There are religions which are either monotheistic or very close to monotheism, such as the Egyptian Sun-worship or Islam, which nevertheless in respect of their inner life are inferior to non-monotheistic faiths" (*Theology of the Old Testament I,* 220), Love, grace, forgiveness, and redemption are greater concepts and actions than ethical monotheism.

God in the Old Testament is holy—One of a kind. He is personal—described by anthropomorphism and anthropathism—but He is not human or a part of His creation, as pantheism suggests. He is gracious, good, kind, faithful, dependable, and always present, although people may not be aware of His presence. He is eternal and all-powerful. He has a purpose, but we may not always perceive it or understand it. He will not fail to achieve his goal. He is truly incomparable.

What Is Mankind?

When I look at your heavens, the
work of your fingers,
the moon and the stars that you
have established:
What are human beings that you
are mindful of them,
mortals that you care for them?
(Ps. 8:3-4)

O LORD, what are human beings
that you regard them,
or mortals that you think of them?
They are like a breath;
their days are like a passing shadow.
(Ps. 144:3-4)

What are human beings, that you
make so much of them,
that you set your mind on them?
(Job 7:17)

Three times the Old Testament directs to God the question, "What are human beings?" The question itself reflects an awareness that God is mindful of people. Mankind is presented as relatively small and insignificant in comparison to the vastness of the universe and to the sovereignty of God in nature and history.

To ask the question "What is mankind?" is to exercise the gift of self-reflection. David Jenkins said that the oddest thing about human beings is that they should wonder who they are. People's awareness of themselves is unique in a two-fold sense. "First, we do not know of any other species of animal that has it, and secondly, it is an awareness of uniqueness, that is, an awareness that I am me and not anyone or anything else" (*What Is Man?* 13). It is not self-evident that people should inquire into their own nature or even that they should ask questions at all.

When people begin to inquire, they can no longer take things for granted. A mysterious movement has begun, and none can tell whither it may lead. Once the question of human nature has been raised, a second question demands to be answered: the riddle of humanity. This question cannot be shelved. It is not "the fruit of our opinions, it springs from its own inward necessity, as the question above all others" (Brunner, *Man in Revolt*, 17).

We do not know precisely when the people of the Old Testament began to ask the question, "What is mankind?" We do know the Old Testament frames the question in the context of God. Moses asked God at the burning bush, "Who am I that I should go?" (Ex. 3:11). David said, "Who am I, O Lord GOD, and what is my house, that you have brought me thus far?" (2 Sam. 7:18; compare Gen. 18:27). Such questions were not asked for a definition of the nature of mankind or for an explanation of the origin of humanity. They are questions about the value and uniqueness of human life. They address the only source with the potential for answer.

The Old Testament presents no organized systematic answer to the question "What is mankind?" The difficulties in presenting the Old Testament view of mankind include the historical varieties and the vastness of the Old Testament materials (Eichrodt, *Man in the Old Testament*, 8). Wolff said that the Old Testament does not give a unified doctrine of mankind; nor are we in a position to trace a development in the biblical image of man.

> Biblical anthropology as a scholarly task will seek its point of departure where there is a recognizable question about man within the texts themselves. The whole breadth of the context

> must be drawn upon in order to work out the specific answers.
> It will become evident that the essential contributions bear the
> character of dialogue and that the consensus in their testimony
> about man is . . . astonishing from the point of view of the his-
> tory of thought. In his dialogue with God above all, man sees
> himself as called in question, searched out and thus not so
> much established for what he is as called to new things. Man as
> he is, is anything but the measure of all things (*Anthropology of
> the Old Testament,* 3).

Although the Old Testament gives no systematic answer to
the question "What is mankind?" many implications and
assertions are made so that we may construct an answer from
the Old Testament materials. Any construct of an Old Testament view of persons is inevitably the work of the person making the construct. Selecting and arranging materials
introduces a subjective element, but the writer must be as
objective as possible in the selection, use, and interpretation
of the Old Testament materials. Wolff, in his significant work
Anthropology of the Old Testament, arranged the Old Testament materials in three parts: The Being of Man; The Time of
Man; and The World of Man. We will discuss the Old Testament view of mankind around four themes: Humans Are Created Beings; Humans Are Like God; Humans Are Social
Creatures; and Humans Are Unitary Beings.

27. Humans Are Created Beings

Old Testament writers are unanimous in saying that
humans are created beings. Both accounts of creation in Genesis explicitly mention the creation of persons (Gen. 1:27; 2:7).
The prophets knew that God made mankind (Isa. 17:7; 42:5;
43:7; 45:9,12; Jer. 1:5). The psalmists proclaimed that the Lord
has made us, and we are His (Pss. 100:3; 139:13-16). Likewise,
Job and Elihu acknowledged that God made both of them (Job
10:8-12; 36:3). The Wisdom writers asserted that God has
made everyone, including the rich and the poor (Prov. 14:31;
17:5; 20:12; 22:2).

Emil Brunner said that the biblical word *creation* means
first of all that "there is an impassable gulf between Creator
and the creature, that forever they stand over against one
another in a relation which can never be altered. There is no
greater sense of distance than that which lies in the words

Creator — creation. Now this is the first and the fundamental thing which can be said about man: He is a creature (*Man in Revolt*, 90). God is the uncreated Creator. Whatever may distinguish humans from other creatures, they have in common with all creatures that which distinguishes persons from God: they have been created.

Because humans are created beings, they share in the feebleness and limitations of all creatures. Their earthly existence is ephemeral and ends inexorably with death. Humanity's frailty is expressed in a myriad of Old Testament passages (Job 4:19; 7:7; 10:4-5; 14:1-2; Pss. 9:20; 39:5-6,11; 49:12,20; 62:9; 90:5; 103:14-16; 144:4; Isa. 2:22; 40:6; Jer. 10:23; 13:23; 51:17). Still, when God made humans, He created them with living space, nourishment, work, and companionship (Gen. 2:9-23).

In the Old Testament, God is God, and people are people. There is never a hint of any mingling of the two. Smart said that "God is never portrayed in the Old Testament as he is in Babylonia, Egypt and Greece as merely man written large and endowed with supernatural powers" (*The Interpretation of Scripture*, 137). G. Ernest Wright said of the distinction between God and humanity:

> There is today such a constant mixing of the Divine and the human that it is often difficult clearly to distinguish the two. There is a leveling process, whereby man pulls himself up until he feels himself almost on a plane with God and pulls God down until he becomes like man. But not so in the Old Testament! God is God; and man knows his place before him. Sacred things are not to be dealt with lightly. Man cannot eat of the tree of knowledge and elevate himself to the level of God. Whatever you call God, said Malachi (1:6), watch out for your attitude. If he is Father, honor him. If he is Ruler, reverence him (*The Challenge of Israel's Faith*, 57).

28. Humans Are Like God (The *Imago Dei*)

The Creator-creation relation places a great distance between God and mankind. It also binds them fast together. God made people so they might be or become what God intended. Mankind's relation to God is not something added to humanity: "it is the core and ground of his *humanitias*" (Brunner, *Man in Revolt*, 94). The created world is the world made by God. Brunner said that Paul's assertion "In Him we live and move and have our being" is a fundamental statement of Scripture. "It distinguishes the creation from the secular world. In truth there is no secular world; there is only a created world which has been secularized. The very idea of the 'secular' is an abstraction, a view of actuality apart from Him who acts" (Brunner, *Man in Revolt*, 91).

Although mankind is created, as are all other creatures, humans are different in kind from all other created beings. Psalm 8 says that God made humans just a little lower than the angels, crowned them with glory and honor, and set them over all the works of His hands (Ps. 8:5-6). G. Ernest Wright claimed that the phrase "a little lower than the angels" is precisely the same as the expression "in the image of God" in Genesis ("The Faith of Israel," 367).

Human uniqueness may be seen not only in that humans were made in the image of God, but also in that they were given dominion over the animals. The first man gave names to all of the animals (Gen. 2:19), thus exerting power over them. God breathed into the man's nostrils the breath of life (Gen. 2:7). True, the life of other creatures is ascribed to the breath or spirit of God (Job 34:14-15: Ps. 104:29-30), and the animals are described as "living souls" or "living beings" (Gen. 2:19). Still, Eichrodt said that the narrator in Genesis 2 clearly intended to mark humans off from other creatures, since only with humans did the writer relate a direct transfer of the divine breath. "Whereas the animals are produced and brought to life simply, so to speak, by the universal divine breath blowing through the whole of Nature, and therefore partake of life only as a class of beings, man receives his life by a special act of God, and is thus treated as an independent spiritual being" (*Theology of the Old Testament II*, 121).

Wolfhart Pannenberg said that the difference between humans and animals is the human "openness to the world." The needs of animals are limited to that which their environment can supply. Humans, like animals, are dependent on food, climatic and vegetative conditions for life, association with others of the same species, and the health of their own bodies. Humans are also dependent on something or Someone outside themselves.

Humans are constantly searching, investigating, and transforming the world around them, but they find no lasting rest in their own creations, which they leave behind as mere transition points in their striving (Pannenberg, *What Is Man?*, 9). In their searching and in infinite dependence, humans presuppose, with every breath they take, a corresponding, infinite, never-ending, other worldly being before whom they stand (*What Is Man?*, 10).

This dependence or restlessness is one root of all religious life, and for that reason religion is more than merely a human creation. The animal's dependence on its environment corresponds to a human's dependence on God. "What the environment is for animals, God is for man. God is the goal in which alone his striving can find rest and his destiny be fulfilled" (*What Is Man?*, 13). At this point Pannenberg sounded very much like St. Augustine, who said, "Thou has made us for Thyself, and our heart is restless until it rests in Thee (quoted by Pussey, *The Confessions of St. Augustine*, 1). The psalmist said:

> As a deer longs for flowing streams,
> so my soul longs for you, O God.
> My soul thirsts for God,
> for the living God.
> (Ps. 42:1-2*a*)

The Old Testament speaks of the distinctiveness of humanity in terms of its being created in the image of God. The importance of this concept is out of all proportion to the infrequency of its appearance in the Old Testament. Here is a case where "texts should be *weighed* not *counted* (Cook, "The Old Testament Concept of the Image of God," 85). Actually, the phrase "image of God" only occurs in four verses in the Old Testament (Gen. 1:26,27; 5:1; 9:6). It occurs twice in the Apocrypha (Ecclesiasticus 17:2-4; Wisdom of Solomon 2:23) and several times in the New Testament (1 Cor. 11:7; Col. 1:15; Jas. 3:9). The idea that kings, prophets, and priests could bear the image of the gods seems to be common in Ancient Near Eastern literature (see Jacob, *Theology of the Old Testament*, 167-169].

The earliest and clearest use of the word *dmwt* "image" outside the Old Testament was found on a basalt stone statue unearthed at Tell Fekheriyeh in Syria in February 1979 (see Millard and Bordrevil, "A Statue from Syria," 135-142). The inscription is written in two languages—Assyrian and Aramaic. The Assyrian text is on the front of the statue, written in thirty-eight vertical lines in cuneiform. On the back, twenty-three horizontal lines of Aramaic script tell essentially the same story. In the following translation the material in parentheses consists of Aramaic variations.

> To Adad (the image of Hadad-yisi which
> he set up before Hadad of Sikam),
> regulator of the waters of heaven and earth,
> who rains down abundance,
> who gives pasture and watering places to
> the people of all cities (to all lands),
> who gives portions and offerings (rest
> and vessels of food)
> to (all) the gods, his brothers,
> regulator of (all) rivers
> who enriches the regions (all lands),
> the merciful god to whom it is good to pray.
> Who dwells in Guzau (Sikau).

The word *dmwt* is translated "image" in line 1 of the inscription. Another word for "image," *ṣalam* is translated "statue" in line 1 of the second section. *Dmwt* occurs a second time in the fourth line of the second half of the inscription. It is translated "statue" ("image"). Millard and Bordrevil say:

> These two words in their Hebrew dress are the famous "image" and "likeness" in God's creation of man in Genesis 1:26; compare 5:3. Their clear application to this stone statue, the only ancient occurrence of the words as a pair outside the Old Testament, provides fuel for the debate over the meaning of the clause in Genesis 1 ("A Statue from Syria," 140).

The primary function of the image in the ancient world seems to be the dwelling-place of the spirit or fluid of the god. "This fluid was not immaterial, but was usually conceived of as a fine, rarified intangible substance which could penetrate ordinary coarse matter, so it is often spoken of as 'breath' or 'fire.' Images of gods were of two kinds: the plastic form and the living person, usually the king" (Clines, "The Image of God in Man," 81). The Old Testament vehemently denied that any spirit or breath of God resided in plastic idols (Jer. 10:14; 51:17; Hab. 2:19), but humans were created in the image of God and had the breath of God in them.

Several factors are involved in considering "the image of God" in the Old Testament. One is the "plural" factor or that of divine self-deliberation, in "Let us make man" (Gen. 1:26). The plural "us" may be one of majesty; a reference to the divine council, including angels, or the editorial "we." Eichrodt was probably correct in saying that the reference to creation as "in our image" instead of "in my image" is definitely aimed at avoiding an altogether too narrow connection with God's own form (*Theology of the Old Testament II*, 125).

The second factor in considering the Old Testament use of the "the image of God" is philological. The Hebrew expression *běṣalmēnû kîdmûtēnû* "in (as) our image, according to our likeness," is made up of two nouns—*ṣelem* "image" and *demût*—"likeness"—with the preposition *be* prefixed to *tselem* and *ke* to *demût*. The plural pronominal suffix *nu* "us" is attached to the end of each word. Numerous questions arise about the use and meaning of these terms. Are *ṣelem* and *demût* synonyms? Does *demût* soften the meaning of *ṣelem*? Does *ṣelem* refer to a physical form and *demût* a spiritual quality? Is the preposition *bě* on *ṣelem* (Gen. 1:26) the normal *bě*, "in" (RSV), or is it *be essentiae* "as," "in the capacity of"? (See *Gesenius' Hebrew Grammer*, par. 199, 1; Clines, "The Image of God in Man," 75-80; von Rad, *Genesis*, 56; V. P. Hamilton, "The Book of Genesis 1—17," 135-137; G. Wenham, *Genesis 1—15*, 26-34).

The third factor in considering "the image of God" in the Old Testament relates to dominion over the animals and all the earth (Gen. 1:26-27). Is humanity's dominion over the animals a consequence of the image (Clines, "The Image of God in Man," 96)?

A fourth factor related to "the image of God" is the fact that male and female are both included in the image (Gen. 1:27). Does this mean that sexuality is a part of the divine nature? Although most nature religions speak of male and female deities, no hint of a female counterpart to Yahweh appears in the Old Testament. (See the Excursus on Asherah in chap. 5, p. 228.) Karl Barth saw this distinction and relation between male and female as corresponding to the relation of the I and Thou in God Himself. This is a vital and thought-provoking concept. (See Karl Barth, *Church Dogmatics III*, 182-210.)

Christoph Barth spoke of the two sexes, male and female, as God's perfect creation. Adam regards Eve, one with his own flesh and bone, as the only true and authentic partner through whom he achieves his true humanity. "Creation in the image of God and in the two sexes is essential to human existence" (*God With Us*, 23).

In the Old Testament, sex is a phenomenon of the creature and not of Yahweh. "Israel did not share in the 'divinisation' of sex. Yahweh stood absolutely beyond the polarity of sex, and this meant that Israel also could not regard sex as a sacred mystery. It was excluded from the cult because it was a phenomenon of the creature (von Rad, *Old Testament Theology* I, 27-28, 146). Zimmerli said, "Since the inclusion of Yahweh in the bipolarity of sexuality is alien to the Old Testament throughout, the remark that humans are created in this bipolarity from the beginning clearly sets humanity apart from the uniqueness of God" (*Old Testament Theology in Outline*, 36; compare Eichrodt, *Theology of the Old Testament* II, 128).

However, sexuality is more than a means of reproduction and continuous progeny. The personal encounter, not progeny, is the decisive feature and mystery of our existence as male and female. Men and women are human beings on the basis of perfect equality. Clines said that Genesis 1:27 specifically denies the phenomenal distinction between male and female. "The image of God does not subsist in the male but in mankind, within which woman also belongs. Thus the most basic statement about man, according to Genesis 1, that he is the image of God, does not find its full meaning in man alone but in man and woman ("The Image of God in Man," 95).

A fifth factor in the meaning of "the image of God" is that it is passed on to succeeding generations, just as the image of a father is passed on to his son (Gen. 5:1-3). This means that all people continue to bear the image of God.

Perhaps we should acknowledge variant views about Genesis 5:3. Did Adam pass on the divine image to Seth through procreation, and then in the physical sequence to succeeding generations? Or is Genesis 5:3 simply saying that Seth was only in Adam's image? G. Henton Davies said the effect of this passage is "not to reiterate that each successive generation is also created in the image of God, but that Seth in his father's image is thus one generation away from the divine image—hence the beginning of the lessening of dominion, the lessening of vitality" (Davies, *Genesis*, 149).

Karl Barth said it is a drastic oversimplification to deduce from Genesis 5:3 that the divine likeness is passed on in the physical sequence of the generations. He refutes the idea that, in a bodily sense, what can be "passed on" is Adam's ability "to copy, confirm and repeat himself in another individual of his kind." The Father's "divine likeness" cannot be transmitted to the son "merely because he is the cause of his physical life" ("The Doctrine of Creation," *Church Dogmatics*, *III*, 199-200). Barth said this "passing on" of God's image to succeeding generations of humanity is the work of God and an act of His grace.

Claus Westermann said the phrase, "'Adam begot (a son) in his own image, corresponded to him, and named him Seth,' can only mean that the whole of humankind is God's counterpart and corresponds to him. It is something given to humans by the very fact of existence" (*Genesis 1-11*, 356).

We may not know how the divine image is transmitted from generation to generation, but it is. That is what makes humans human and not mere animals.

The sixth factor is the fact that human life is "sacred" because God made humans in His own image (Gen. 9:6). D. J. A. Clines summarized his understanding of the Old Testament's view of the image doctrine:

> Man is created not *in* [be *essentiae*], since God has no image of His own, but *as* God's image, or rather *to be* God's image, that is to deputize in the created world for the transcendent God who remains outside the world order. That man is God's image means that he is the visible corporeal representative of the invisible, bodiless God; he is representative rather than representation, since the idea of portrayal is secondary in the significance of the image. However the term "likeness" is an assurance that man is an adequate and faithful representative of God on earth. The whole man is the image of God on earth. The whole man is the image of God, without distinction of spirit and body. All mankind, without distinction, are the image of God ("The Image of God in Man," 101).

Most modern Old Testament scholars agree with Clines' understanding of the Old Testament's view of "the image of

God." However, a vastly different understanding of this doctrine has been held by different theologians at various times. The history of the interpretation of this exceedingly open-ended term "the image of God" shows that contemporary religious and philosophical ideas have greatly influenced its interpretations.

About 190 B.C. Ben Sira wrote a book of wisdom sayings called "Ecclesiasticus." Although Ecclesiasticus was not considered canonical, it was read in the churches. One account of man's creation in Ecclesiasticus says:

> The Lord created human beings out of earth,
>   and makes them return to it again.
> He gave them a fixed number of days, but granted
>   them authority over everything on the earth.
> He endowed them with strength like his own,
>   and made them in his own image.
> He put the fear of them in all living beings,
> and gave them dominion over beasts and birds.
>   (Ecclesiasticus 17:1-4)

Ecclesiasticus' view of the creation of man is essentially that of Genesis.

The Wisdom of Solomon, probably written during the latter part of the first century B.C., speaks of the incorruption of the "image," thus preparing the way for the later concept of tying the "image" to the "fall." "For God created us for incorruption, and made us in the image of his own eternity" (Wisdom of Solomon 2:23). "Incorruption" is the elevated life of the spirit for which mankind was made. It is the reward and result of obedience to wisdom, in contrast to the way of the wicked.

The Qumran materials speak about humans being formed from the dust or clay. A feeling of shame and impurity is often expressed in the creation passages, but reference to the "image of God" is not found in the Qumran materials (Ringgren, *The Faith of Qumran*, 96-97; for an excellent survey of anthropology in the Qumran materials see Brownlee, "Anthropology and Soteriology in the Dead Sea Scrolls," 210-240).

The idea that humans are made in the image of God is found also in the New Testament: "For a man ought not to have his head veiled, since he is the image and reflection of God; but woman is the reflection of man" (1 Cor. 11:7). (For a discussion of Paul's apparent implication that only the man, not woman, is "the image and glory of God" see Cook, "The Old Testament Concept of the Image of God," 92; McCasland, "The Image of God According to Paul," 85-86; Karl Barth, *Church Dogmatics III*, 203-05.)

James 3:9,10*b* says that with the same tongue "we bless the Lord and Father, and with it we curse those who are made in the likeness of God, . . . this ought not to be so." The implication is that all persons bear the "likeness" of God and have a special dignity. People should not curse other people because they are made in "the likeness of God." Jesus never used the expression "image of God" (Smart, *The Interpretation of Scripture*, 144).

Most other New Testament references to "the image of God" refer to Christ as the "image" (2 Cor. 4:4; Col. 1:15; Heb. 1:3) or to Christians who are being changed (renewed, conformed) into the image of the Son (Rom. 8:29; 1 Cor. 15:49; 2 Cor. 3:18; Col. 3:10). Neither the Old nor the New Testament refers to the loss of the "image of God" (compare 2 Cor. 4:4; Col. 1:15; Heb. 1:3). Paul spoke of people as being "changed" or "renewed" into that image or likeness of the glory of God (2 Cor. 3:18; Col. 3:10). Some church fathers understood these verses to imply the loss of the image in the fall, but Paul was speaking about sanctification rather than salvation. The Bible never explicitly relates the Fall to the loss of the image of God (Smart, *The Interpretation of Scripture*, 135, 148).

Great care should be exercised in making the *imago Dei* a basis for developing a dogmatic doctrine of the primal human condition, for the Old Testament does not do it. About 150 A.D. Irenaeus first separated the various parts of human nature on the basis of *şelem* "image" and *demût* "likeness." For Irenaeus, "image" referred to the freedom and rationality of human nature, which are inalienable and universal. It has never been lost and cannot be lost (Clements, "Claus Westermann: On Creation in Genesis," 24; Smart, *The Interpretation of Scripture*, 149; Brunner, *Man in Revolt*, 93).

For Irenaeus, "likeness" refers to a person's self-determination, which was the result of the Spirit of God's indwelling human nature. This part, according to Irenaeus, was lost in the fall and can only be restored by the redemptive work of Christ and the receiving of the Holy Spirit. Irenaeus divided persons into body, soul, and spirit. An unregenerate person consists of only body and soul, but through regeneration one can become body, soul, and spirit. Irenaeus outlined the path the church was to follow for nearly fifteen hundred years. Basically his solution is still that of the Catholic Church.

In some way Irenaeus moved the question of "the image of God" from the doctrine of creation to that of redemption. However, it is not clear what was involved for Irenaeus in the loss of the "likeness" in the fall. He conceived of the first man as a "big child" and not as an almost perfect man, as did Augustine and the Reformers (compare Brunner, *Man In Revolt*, 505).

The twofold human nature held sway in the Christian church until the time of Martin Luther. Luther's feeling for the text and exegesis of Scripture caused him to see the Hebrew parallelism between *ṣelem* "image" and *demût* "likeness." He concluded that a person is a unitary being, not one with three parts. What happened to one part of his being happened to all other parts. Therefore, if Irenaeus and church tradition were right in claiming that part of a person's being was affected by the fall, the proper conclusion is that the entire human being was affected. However, Luther and Calvin could still speak of a "relic" of the "image" that remained. It was "damaged but not destroyed, defaced but not effaced" (Creager, "The Divine Image," 117).

Karl Barth took the extreme position of saying that the bond between God and man had been completely severed in the fall. He is quoted by Brunner as saying, "The fact that man is man and not a cat is quite unimportant" (cited by Brunner, *Man in Revolt*, 95). Although Barth's statement is extreme, it should not be understood in a nihilistic sense. Leslie Weatherhead quoted two nihilistic views of humanity: "Man is a low form of cellular life on his way to the manure heap" and "Man is fighting a lone fight against a vast indifference" (*The Significance of Silence*, 114).

Recent Old Testament theologians have commented only briefly on the "image of God" in the Old Testament. Claus Westermann said, "Humans are to correspond to God so that something can happen between them and God, so that God can speak to them and they can answer" (*Elements of Old Testament Theology*, 97). Zimmerli summed up his discussion on the

"image of God" by saying, "All the many theological speculations about man's being only partially in the likeness of God at
this time are rendered nugatory" (*Outline of Old Testament
Theology*, 36; see also Thomas Finger, "Humanity," 674-75).

Humans are like God. Mankind is the only part of God's creation that is like him. We are not divine in any way. There is
no spark of the divine in our nature, but we are "like" Him. We
represent Him. We exercise some of His power on earth. We
are responsible to Him for the way we act toward Him and
toward each other.

29. Mankind: Social Beings

A. Humans (Male and Female) Are Created Social Beings

According to one account of creation man and woman were
created at the same time (Gen. 1:27), suggesting the social
nature of humans. Creation made people social beings. Man
(Adam) or mankind consists of male and female. The plural
"them," referring to male and female, is intentionally contrasted with the singular "him" and prevents one from assuming the creation of an originally androgynous man. "By God's
will, man was not created alone but designated for the 'thou'
of the other sex. The idea of man, according to P, finds its full
meaning not in the male alone but in man and woman" (von
Rad, *Genesis*, 58). The other account of human creation (Gen.
2:4*b*-25) indicates that the male was created first (Gen. 2:7)
and put in the garden to work (Gen. 2:15), but he was alone in
the midst of creation. Even the animals could not satisfy his
need for fulfillment and companionship. Therefore Yahweh
said, "It is not good that the man (*ʾādām*) should be alone; I will
make him a helper as his partner" (Gen. 2:18). The expression
ʿēzer kĕnegĕdô is difficult to translate and understand. *ʿezer* is
usually translated "helper" and suggests to some, "an assis-
tant, a subordinate, an inferior."

The idea that the Bible provides evidence that women are
inferior to men has a long history. John Skinner said, "The serpent shows his subtlety by addressing his first temptation to
the more mobile temperament of a woman (*Genesis*, 73). Jean
Higgins referred to a fragment from the writings of Irenaeus

(135-202) as an old example of such interpretation. One part of the fragment asks;

> Why did the serpent not attack the man, rather than the woman? You say he went after her because she was the weaker of the two. On the contrary. In the transgression of the commandment, she showed herself to be stronger, truly the man's "assistance" (*bœthos*) ("Anastasius Sinaita," 254).

Victor Hamilton noted that this "helper" (*ᶜezer*), for man, though masculine in gender, is a term for woman here. "Any suggestion that this particular word denotes one who has only an associate or subordinate status to a senior member is refuted by the fact most frequently this same word describes Yahweh's relationship to Israel" ("Genesis 1-17," *NICOT*, 175-176. For the word used with God as its subject see Exodus 18:4; Deuteronomy 33:7,26,29; Psalms 33:20; 115:9-11; 121:2; 124:8; 146:5).

Christoph Barth said the reference to "help" in *ᶜezer* is "in his presence," availability, relief from loneliness, therefore true and unfailing companionship and partnership. Partnership includes service, "but not in the sense of inferiority and subjection" (*God With Us*, 24). Brueggemann noted the "sharp secularization" of humans here. "God does not intend to be the *man's* helper (*Genesis, Interpretation Commentary*, 47). Bergman said, "Determinative for the meaning of the verb and the substantive is the aspect of common action or working together of subject and object where the power of one is not sufficient (Josh. 10:4-5)" (*THAT* II, 257).

The second term is a noun, *negdô* meaning "conspicuous" or "in front of," "corresponding to"—that is, "equal and adequate to himself" (*BDB*, 616, 1125). Trible said that the phrase means "identity, mutuality, and equality." "According to Yahweh God, what the earth creature needs is a companion, one who is neither subordinate nor superior; one who alleviates isolation through identity" (*God and the Rhetoric of Sexuality*, 90).

R. David Freedman recently questioned the classical translation of the Hebrew phrase *ᶜezer kĕnegdô*, "a helper fit for him." Because the first letter of the root *ᶜzr* originally had two pronunciations, the same root could have two meanings. In Akkadian the root usually meant "to be strong." On this basis

Freedman translated the Hebrew word as *gzr* (not *ʿzr*), "a power equal to man." God decided to make a power equal to him, "someone whose strength was equal to man's. Woman was not intended to be merely man's helper. She was to be instead his partner" ("Woman, A Power Equal to Man," 56). Freedman's argument alone does not carry much weight.

Walther Eichrodt expressed the Old Testament view of the relation of the sexes very well. "Because man and woman emerge at the same time from the hand of the Creator, and are created in the same way after God's image, the difference between the sexes is no longer relevant to their position before God. . . . The verse (Gen. 1:27) does away with any justification for holding the female half of the race in contempt as inferior, or in some way closer to the animals. The relationship between man and woman is placed on the same basis as that between man and God; their encounter as personal beings leads to a living for each other in a responsible co-operation which draws its strength from their common encounter with God" (*Theology of the Old Testament II*, 126-127).

B. Marriage and Family

It was not Yahweh's purpose that mankind continue to consist of only one man and one woman. Yahweh blessed man (male and female) with the power of reproduction. God's first command to man and woman was "be fruitful, and multiply, and fill the earth" (Gen. 1:28). The man and woman with their children were to live in families.

It was not Yahweh's intention for man to live alone. Marriage was the norm for the people in the Old Testament (Prov. 5:15-20). Even priests, Nazirites, and Rechabites married and had families (Lev. 21:13; Judg. 13:3-5; Jer. 35:6-10). Only Jeremiah was told not to marry (Jer. 16:1-2). Zimmerli said "that celibacy, abstinence from marriage, could be something spiritually loftier, drawing man closer to God, is quite foreign to the Old Testament" (*The Old Testament and the World*, 31).

Marriage was not automatic or fated. It was something to which a man or his parents must give an approving "yes" (see Zimmerli, *The Old Testament and the World*, 31). Samson went down to Timnah and saw one of the daughters of the Philistines. He returned home and asked his father and mother to "'get her for me as my wife,' But his father and mother said to him, 'Is there not a woman among your kin, or among all our people, that you must go to take a wife from the uncircumcised Philistines?'" (Judg. 14:1-3). His father and mother did not know that the relationship was from the Lord; for He was seeking an occasion against the Philistines (Judg. 14:4; compare Josh. 11:20; 1 Kings 11:14; 2 Chron. 22:7). For Samson marriage was not necessarily for a family or children, but an occasion for God's judgment on the Philistines.

A family in the Old Testament often included more than a father, mother, and their immediate children. A "father's house" (*bayît 'āb*) could include the extended families of children, grandchildren, servants, widows, and orphans. Extensive and very strict laws regulated the sexual conduct of all members of the extended family (see Lev. 18:1-30).

In marriage, husbands and wives were expected to produce children. Children were considered "gifts of God" (Pss. 127:3-5; 128:3). Sometimes God closed the wife's womb, and she was barren. (Note the opening of the womb of Sarah, Gen. 17:16-19; Rebekah, Gen. 25:21-26; Leah and Rachel, Gen. 29:31; 30:22-24; Hannah, 1 Sam. 1:2,5, 19-20). Children were not the only rewards of marriage. Real joy, companionship, comfort, and help were blessings of marriage. Recall the joyful exclamation of Adam at Eve's creation (Gen. 2:23). Husband and wife were to be "bone and flesh" together. They were to become one flesh and form one family. Zimmerli said, "This striking formulation, that it is the man and not the woman who leaves family, and which clearly runs quite contrary to patriarchal practice, is to stress in unmistakable terms the basic power of love" (*The Old Testament and the World*, 33). Genesis 29:20 says that Jacob worked seven years for Rachel and they seemed like a few days because he loved her.

Marriage and love border on the "secular" side of life in the Old Testament. No marriage ceremony is described, but the joy of human love is clearly presented in Song of Solomon (1:2; 8:6-8) and Ecclesiastes (9:7-9). If a young man married and was called to war, he could get a one-year deferment to enjoy the wife he had taken (Deut. 24:5).

If marriage and love are "secular" in the Old Testament, it is in the sense that they were never idealized in the name of religion or understood as part of the life of God. They were "domains of responsibility before God" (Zimmerli, *The Old Testament and the World*, 35).

The Old Testament reacts very sharply against any unnatural perversions of these God-given gifts. Sexual intercourse between people of the same sex and bestiality are strictly forbidden by Yahweh (Lev. 18:22-23; 20:13). The violation of another's marriage by adultery is prohibited in the Seventh Commandment. Zimmerli said the Old Testament is quite inexorable in this matter. "It presumes that even foreign potentates are aware that this is a boundary which none can cross (Gen. 12:10-20; 20:1-18; 26:7-11). The Old Testament never makes light of an existing marriage or adultery, as does the world today" (*The Old Testament and the World*, 36).

A wife's position in the Old Testament has created much debate. Earlier studies frequently asserted that wives were simple property in the absolute sense—chattels of their husbands. John David Michaelis said in 1814 that wives were bought and sold in ancient Israel much like bondservants and slaves (*Commentaries on the Laws of Moses I*, 450-453). Thaddaeus Engert was an extreme exponent of the wife's chattel status. He said a husband bought a wife like a cow for his herd, and she was entirely subject to his whim and despotism—treated like goods and chattel ("Ehe und Familienrecht der Hebräer," *Studien zur alttestamentlichen Einleitung und Geschichte* 3 (Munster: Aschendorfische Verlagsbuchhandlung, 1914); see Christopher J. H. Wright, *God's People in God's Land*, 184).

In recent years such views of women in the Old Testament have been challenged, modified, and denied. Millar Burrows said that the *mōhar* "purchase price" (Gen. 34:12; Ex. 22:16; 1 Sam. 18:25) should be translated "compensation gift" (*The Basis of Israelite Marriage*, 15). David Mace argued that women were regarded as persons rather than property in the Old Testament. What a husband possessed, according to Mace, was his wife's sexuality, not her very person (*Hebrew Marriage: A Sociological Study*, 186). Otto J. Baab said the *mohar* transaction was not the transfer of chattel property, but the surrender of authority over a woman by one man to another. She remained a person ("Woman," *IDB* IV, 865).

After tracing scholars' improving views of the place of women in the Old Testament, C. J. H. Wright bemoaned the fact that in recent years many scholars have reverted to the older views. He severely criticized the views of Anthony Phillips, P. A. H. de Boer, Paul K. Jewett, and Leonard Swindler for their unsatisfactory interpretations (*God's People in God's Land*, 189-190). C. J. H. Wright concluded that wives were not their husbands' property, but neither did they have independent legal status.

The wife was regarded as an extension of her husband himself. She was a part of his person so that husband and wife constituted a single legal unit. Criminal offenses of a sexual nature against a wife were regarded against the husband's person, not against his property. Malachi denounced divorce as an attack on one's own life as well as against God (Mal. 2:14-16). The wife was not specifically included as resting on the Sabbath day not because the law as not binding on her, but because she was automatically included along with her husband. Achan's wife was not named in the catalogue of his possessions (Josh. 7:24), though it is fairly certain she shared his fate.

All this may "indicate that a wife's legal status was essentially complementary to her husband's, thus constituting a legal counterpart to the theological concept of one flesh (Gen. 2:24)" (*God's People in God's Land*, 221). Wright made a strong point that the family was central in the social, economic, and religious life of Israel (*God's People in God's Land*, 1).

C. Individualism and Corporate Personality

Humans in the Old Testament were social beings. A person was an individual but at the same time a member of a family, (house), tribe, clan, and nation. The idea of the individual developed early in Israel. The Old Testament stresses the personal responsibility and personal value of a human being. "The importance of personal life is emphasized very strongly in Israel, so that we may even say that here the full conception of personality was born" (Vriezen, *Old Testament Theology in Outline*, 419). Westermann also stressed the unique emphasis on the individual in the Old Testament. Beginning with the patriarchs, God's promises are directed toward the individual as well as to the nation. "God's activity includes the personal life of the individual, his promises reach into the houses, the places of work, and into the days and nights of every individual" (*Elements of Old Testament Theology*, 67).

While the Old Testament emphasizes the value and responsibility of the individual, it does not make the individual the measure of all things. Nor does it fail to stress the individual's proper place in society. The Western world's overemphasis on the individual and a person's value, worth, rights, and freedom is a humanistic notion derived from the Renaissance and is unbiblical. G. Ernest Wright charged that even the churches have been so preoccupied with the individual's need for peace, rest, and joy in the midst of the storms of life that vigorous concern with community is excluded (*The Biblical Doctrine of Man in Society*, 21).

The law of Israel was interpreted as God's gracious gift to the nation. Although it was community law, it was by no means a tribal ethic. It was the basis of a *new society*. In this new society the individual was not lost or submerged. God's "Thou shalt" was addressed to each individual. The individual heard the word to the nation as being addressed to himself or herself. "Man was not an insignificant and unsegregated component of a tribal mass."

> . . . In the covenant with the nation God dignified each member with his personal address, so that each one understood the responsible nature of his relationship to the Divine Person. The Lord of the nation was also the Lord of each of its individuals (Wright, *The Biblical Doctrine of Man in Society*, 26).

Tensions arose when the sacred covenant community became a "state" with its borrowed form of government and an increasing tendency toward secularization and cultural accommodation. At times the individual was called upon to resist the new collective system. "State and divine kingdom were not the same, and against the former the individual was called to take his stand. What, then, *was* the community in which and for which God wished him to fulfill his election? It was the true Israel which did not yet exist in organized form but which God through his acts of judgment was bringing into being" (Wright, *The Biblical Doctrine of Man in Society*, 27).

Although the Old Testament strongly emphasized the role of the individual, "pure individualism is a modern phenomenon" (G. A. F. Knight, *A Christian Theology of the Old Testament*, 31). Israelite thinking reflected in much of the Old Testament was like that of so-called "primitive" peoples, predominantly synthetic. They grasped things in terms of their totality or wholeness rather than from their individuality. Aubrey Johnson highlighted the importance of Israel's synthetic thinking: "It is, perhaps, hardly too much to say that it is the 'Open Sesame' which unlocks the secrets of the Hebrew language and reveals the riches of the Israelite mind" (*The Vitality of the Individual*, 7-8).

This synthetic or holistic way of thinking is what H. Wheeler Robinson called "corporate personality." He noted that according to English law a corporation may function as one individual, or one individual may act as the corporation. Robinson said that in the Old Testament an individual is closely identified with his group so that an individual's sin brings punishment on his entire family (Josh. 7:24); a king may represent his nation; or the "I" speaker in the Psalms may represent his group (compare Pss. 44:1,4,6,15; 118:2-5; 144:1-2,9,12-14). (See *Corporate Personality in Ancient Israel*, 1.)

Sigmund Mowinckel followed Robinson's view, perhaps to the extreme. For Mowinckel "the basic reality in human life is, for the Israelite, not the individual, but the community. The individual had his real existence in the tribe. Outside of that he was nothing, a severed member, one without rights" (*The Psalms in Israel's Worship*, 42).

Undoubtedly the Old Testament saw a person "wrapped up" with the group (1 Sam. 25:29), but the individual was not lost or submerged in the group to the extent that he was not personally responsible for personal actions. By the time Israel appeared on the scene of history, "primitive" man, with his weakly developed consciousness of himself as a responsible person had largely disappeared from the civilized world.

J. W. Rogerson has criticized the view of H. Wheeler Robinson's *Corporate Personality in Ancient Israel*.

> In order to avoid misunderstanding, I must make it clear that if I criticize Wheeler Robinson for propounding a theory of Hebrew mentality based on what I would maintain are untenable anthropological assumptions, I also accept that parts of the Old Testament appear to imply what might be called a "corpo-

rate" sense of an individual figure or speaker. A well-known example is the 'I' of the psalms, where the speaker in the first person singular seems to be, or to represent, the whole people of Israel. I have argued elsewhere that examples of the same thing can be found in modern experience, and that in order to understand them, there is no need for a special theory of Hebrew mentality (*Anthropology and the Old Testament*, 56-57).

Rogerson was probably correct in saying that the Old Testament contains "corporate" concepts, but that does not prove the theory of a special Hebrew mentality. Also, Wheeler Robinson might have held some untenable anthropological assumptions.

D. Hebrew Terms for Units of Society

1) *Family*—The Hebrew terms for various units of society such as family, clan, tribe, and nation are often ambiguous and overlapping. The word *bêt* "house" may mean "a family," "a household," "a tribe" such as the house of Joseph (Judg. 1:22, 35), or Israel as a nation (2 Sam. 1:2). The word *mishpaʿhat* comes from a root meaning "to pour out," apparently referring to water, blood, and/or semen. The word is not a political term and means a relationship—clan or extended family. It refers to a unit not clearly defined, larger than "house" but smaller than "tribe" (Gottwald, *The Tribes of Yahweh*, 257; C. J. H. Wright, *God's People in God's Land*, 48-55).

> Another word, *'eleph*, is occasionally translated "clan" (Num. 10:36; Judg. 6:15; 1 Sam. 10:19; 23:23) and is probably a military term for "thousand." A clan (*mishpaʿhat*) consisted of about twenty families and each family furnished about fifty men to each military unit *'eleph* making a thousand (Wolff, *Anthropology of the Old Testament*, 215).

2) *Tribe*—Two major Hebrew words are translated "tribe," *šebet* and *mātteh*. Both words denote the commander's staff or the royal scepter and may refer to "all those who obeyed the same chief" (De Vaux, *Ancient Israel*, 8).

Hebrew society seems to have been made up of a pyramid of social units composed of the family, the clan, and the tribe. In two places the Old Testament speaks of these various units or strata of Israelite society (Josh. 7:14-18; 1 Sam. 10:20-21). In the first instance lots were cast over the tribes, families or clans, and houses of Israel to determine the person who was guilty of violating the ban in the battle of Jericho. In the second, lots were cast over tribes and families or clans to determine the identity of Israel's first king.

It might seem that these various terms for the different social units in Israel were used clearly and precisely, but close examination of the use of these terms reveals a different situation. Sometimes the same group is designated by different terms. The terms are never defined in the Old Testament, and the context usually has nothing to say about the number, composition, or function of the unit named (Gottwald, *The Tribes of Yahweh*, 238).

Many modern readers of these terms interpret them on the basis of their knowledge of contemporary families, clans (Scottish or West Virginian), or tribes (Indian or pagan). The subject of the spring meeting of the American Ethnological Society in 1967 was "The Problem of the Tribe." The participants did their utmost to emphasize the ambiguity of the word "tribe" in anthropology. However, one writer said, "If I had to select one word in the vocabulary of anthropology as the single most egregious case of meaninglessness, I would pass over 'tribe' in favour of 'race'" (Quoted by Rogerson, *Anthropology and the Old Testament*, 86). The American symposium on "tribe" tried to establish criteria for defining "tribe" along the lines of geographical residence, blood ties, and/or common language, but was unable to reach any solid conclusions.

3) *State*—Did Israel have any social, political, or religious organization larger than the tribes? Again, various Hebrew terms were used to refer to groups larger than tribes. The terms are *ʿam* "people"; *gôy* "nation"; *qāhal* and *ʿeda* "congregation" or "assembly"; and *māmlākâ* "kingdom." The word *ʿam* "people" is mainly a social and cultural term (Num. 23:9). It is used 1800 times in the Old Testament, while *gôy* "nation" occurs 550 times. Very rarely do *'am* and *goy* occur as parallel with *māmlākâ* "kingdom" (Ex. 19:6; 1 Kings 18:10; 2 Chron. 32:15; Jer. 18:7,9; Dan. 8:22). The idea of "kingdom" stresses the political aspect of *goy* "nation." These two terms come as close as any in the Old Testament to our word "state" in a political sense. (For a thorough discussion of these terms see Gottwald, *The Tribes of Yahweh*, 241-243; Speiser, *Oriental and Biblical Studies*, 160-170; G. W. Anderson, "Israel: Amphictyony," 135-151).

The Old Testament has no word for "state" (Clements, *Old Testament Theology*, 80). The word *gôy* can mean "nation" in a political sense, and the word *māmlākâ* may refer to a political kingdom; but it may also refer to the kingdom of Yahweh (1 Chron. 29:11). When did Israel become a state? Gottwald said that Israel only fully became a state under David (*The Tribes of Yahweh*, 297). De Vaux said that there may never have been "any Israelite idea of the state" (*Ancient Israel*, 98).

Was Israel a "state" during the period of the Judges? Martin Noth, building on the work of his predecessors Edward Meyer (1881), Georg Beer (1902), and Albrecht Alt (1929), said that Israel became a confederation of tribes, forming what he called an "amphictyony," during the days of the Judges. Noth argued that when Saul became the first king of Israel, there was already present an institution that linked the twelve tribes together in covenant with each other in the worship of Yahweh at a central sanctuary, originally located at Shechem.

Noth's ideas of an amphictyony in ancient Israel were widely accepted by a majority of Old Testament scholars, including von Rad, G. E. Wright, John Bright, and a multitude of lesser known scholars. The theory held sway over this aspect of Old Testament scholarship for about thirty years. However, almost from the time of the publication of Noth's theories objections arose. De Geus said that Emil Auerback in 1932 "hotly contested Noth's theories and rejected them" (*The Tribes of Israel*, 28, n. 129, 55).

The first serious criticism of Noth's amphictyony hypothesis came from Georg Fohrer ("Altes Testament—'Amphiktyonie' und 'Bund,'" 801-806, 893-904). Fohrer said that Noth's hypothesis was a whole conglomeration of unproven hypotheses. The number of tribes (twelve?) and the existence of a central sanctuary cannot be proved for the period of the Judges. The function of the ark of the covenant is extremely uncertain (war or cult object?). The analogy with the Graeco-Italic amphictyony is highly dubious, and the fact that Hebrew has no name in the Old Testament for such a proposed institution is very strange (de Geus, *The Tribes of Israel*, 62).

In 1970, G. W. Anderson expressed respect for Noth's "creative study" but concluded that to use the technical term "amphictyony, drawn from environments very different from those of ancient Israel, in referring to Israel begs the question rather than answers it ("Israel: Amphictyony," 148). Anderson saw a unity among the twelve tribes of Israel during the time of the Judges but sees little evidence of the distinctive features of an amphictyony. He explained the unity in Israel during the time of the Judges as due to the Sinai covenant between Yahweh and the Israelite tribes ("Israel: Amphictyony," 149).

Martin Noth's hypothesis of an Israelite amphictyony has been battered and broken by constant criticism. Whole volumes have been written reviewing and evaluating it. Many scholars agree on the weaknesses of Noth's theories, but few agree on the nature of Israel's social, political, and religious structures during the age of the Judges. John Bright, who was a supporter of Noth's hypothesis in general, said that although "Noth's reconstruction is admittedly a hypothetical one, and is subject to criticism and correction at a number of points, it seems to me that to posit a sacral league of some sort best accounts for the evidence and affords the only satisfactory explanation of the phenomenon of early Israel as we see it in the Bible" (*Covenant and Promise*, 33).

It is not accurate to call Israel a "state" in the time of the Judges if our criteria are those of modern statehood. Such a state became a reality under David (Clements, *Old Testament Theology*, 84). Deuteronomy 26:5 says that Israel became a great, mighty, and populous nation (*gôy*) in Egypt. Fluidity reigns in the structure of Israel during the Old Testament periods. Since Israel is referred to as a people, a kingdom, and/or a nation, only the context can give a definitive meaning.

4) *Kingship and Kingdom*—Israel became a state during the reigns of Saul, David, and Solomon. Israel was one of the last people in the ancient world to have a king. Egypt had a king during all of her recorded history, beginning about 3100 B.C. Egypt's king was considered to be divine.

> Pharaoh was not mortal but a god. This was the fundamental concept of Egyptian kingship, that Pharaoh was of divine essence, a god incarnate; and this view can be traced back as far as texts and symbols take us. It is wrong to speak of a deification of Pharaoh. His divinity was not proclaimed at a certain moment, in a manner comparable to the consecration of the dead emperor by the Roman senate. His coronation was not an apotheosis but an epiphany (Frankfort, *Kingship and the Gods*, 5).

Kings in Mesopotamia can be dated as early as 2600 B.C. Mesopotamian kings were not divine, but great men, members of the community (Frankfort, *Kingship and the Gods*, 6). Although Mesopotamian kings were not divine, they represented their god at the New Year festivals and other cultic events.

Israel probably knew about the institution of kingship among their neighbors but purposely resisted it. The Israelites lived for at least two centuries without having a king. Israel hesitated about establishing a monarchy, "And this hesitation may well have arisen just because, in the regions of Syria and Palestine, there was bound up with the political institutions of the monarchy precisely such a cult-function of a divinely conceived king as was unacceptable to Israel" (Noth, "God, King, and Nation," 162).

Actually kingship came late to Israel, and then not without protest and objections. Zimmerli said that anyone reading the accounts of the origin of the monarchy in 1 Samuel 8—12 "will find two different verdicts on this institution." In one, Samuel laments the people's desire to have a king, and Yahweh asserts that the people have not rejected Samuel but God (1 Sam. 8:7). The other view is that the new king will deliver the Lord's people from the Philistines (1 Sam. 9:16). Therefore, kingship was not a natural outgrowth of genuine tendencies within Yahwism, but rather a response to the challenge of the surrounding world. "In some ways the monarchy represents an assimilation to this world, in others a distinction from it" (Zimmerli, *The Old Testament and the World*, 86).

The emergence of kingship in Israel takes place as the king is the mediator of Yahweh's salvation. Kingship was different from Judgeship. Kingship "as an institution was international and inter-religious" (Westermann, *Elements of Old Testament Theology*, 76). Its own religious structure had to come into conflict with Israel's understanding of the king. The saving function receded in times of peace, and kingship became a static institution whose function was mainly that of mediator of peace and justice. The static nature of Israel's kingship is grounded in Yahweh's covenant with David (2 Sam. 7). Danger arose when the king began to abandon his role of mediator of blessing and allowed himself to be influenced by the idea of kingship in neighboring nations.

Israelite kingship never fell prey to the danger of "divine" kingship, even though the king did have social and cultic duties in Israel. Through the kings' activities and royal rituals, alien elements often made their way into the worship of Yahweh. It is possible that David maintained some Canaanite worship practices when he captured Jerusalem. Kingship in Israel was the object of criticism, primarily from the prophets, from the beginning to the end (Isa. 28:1-4; Jer. 22; Ezek. 22; Hos. 8:4). The Books of Kings present the history of the monarchy as a history of failure, basically because the kings and the nation failed to keep the covenant with Yahweh.

Many of the Psalms portray the role of the kings in a much more positive light (Pss. 2:6-7; 18:50; 21:1-2; 72; 89). The monarchy was not totally bad. The criticisms should not blind us to the good things the monarchy achieved. Even the prophets gave it an important place in their ideal picture of the future (Isa. 9:6-7). The Old Testament did not, however, identify the national life of Israel with the "kingdom of God." Clements said that the belief in Israel's special role as "the people of God" reached to a deeper level than that of a simple nationalism.

> It did not regard nationhood alone as the criterion by which the role of Israel was to be understood. The implications of this for Judaism and for Christianity have been immense, enabling each to retain a vital sense of continuity with the community of the Old Testament. At the same time the important consequences this has had upon the understanding of God are hard to over-estimate, since it has ensured that Yahweh is thought of as much more than simply a national God. Just as the "people" of Israel are constantly pressed into becoming something more than a nation, so the God of Israel was never a God whose popularity might rise and fall with the fortunes of the nation of Israel. Had this been the case then all effective regard for him would have ceased long ago, engulfed by the catastrophes that overtook the Israelite-Jewish people (*Old Testament Theology*, 87).

30. A Person, a Unitary Being

A. Holistic or Unitary Beings

The Old Testament views humans as unique in the created order. They are created beings but different from all others. Like animals, they are living beings dependent on the environment; but humans are more than a flea (1 Sam. 24:14). (See

Karl Barth's discussion of the difference between humans and animals, *Church Dogmatics III*, 185-188.) God made only them a little lower than the angels (Heb. ʾĕlōhîm, Ps. 8:5).

Scholars often contrast the Hebrew view with the Greek view that divides human nature into a dichotomy (body/soul, spirit/ flesh) or a trichotomy (body/soul/spirit) with each part in opposition to the other. The Greek view is actually Plato's view that the human soul contains two parts: reason, the immortal part, and sensuality, the mortal part. The will, energy, or courage is the combination of the two parts and constitutes the soul. Between these two, reason and sensuality, is the forceful, energetic side of human nature that Plato calls "spirit." Spirit is not, in itself, ignoble, as are the sensations and appetites. However, in itself spirit *is* unintelligent, liable to turn into blind passion. It stands on a lower level than reason, although it is a servant of the mind, helping to tame the desires of the lower nature.

A. K. Rogers said that "these three faculties (reason, sensuality and spirit) are in some real sense distinct; if man's nature were one and indivisible it would be impossible to explain how it comes to pass that reason often has to fight with all its strength against sensuous desires. On the other hand they are not separate and unrelated. Our lower faculties are intended to be subject to and used in the service of the higher; the body is for the sake of the soul (*A Student's Handbook of Philosophy*, 82-83).

Plato's view was not the same as Aristotle's. Aristotle taught that the soul was the vital principle of the body, but neither the soul nor body could exist without the other. The body exists and lives only for the sake of the soul, but the soul is a reality only insofar as it animates something. According to Aristotle, it is "as impossible to feel, to desire, and to will, without the corporeal organs, as it is to walk without feet or to make a statue out of nothing (Weber and Perry, *A History of Philosophy*, 96, n. 1). Aristotle said that the soul is to the body what cutting is to the axe. Just as cutting is impossible without an axe, so, too, the constitutive function of the soul is inseparable from the body. So the "Greek" view of humans which separates and sets the various aspects of human nature in opposition to each other is really Plato's view. The Old Testament view is radically different. Aristotle, in a sense, anticipated the modern understanding of the unity of the person.

Perhaps we have made too much of the difference between Hebrew and Greek thought. James Barr thought that the origin of the Hebrew-Greek contrast is modern. He did not find it in the church fathers or the Reformers. Both Luther and Calvin were Platonists in certain respects (Barr, *Old and New in Interpretation*, 41-42). Barr said, "The impossibility of separating body from soul, which by the twentieth century had become a 'Hebraic' insight, in the sixteenth century was Aristotelian, and was of course explicitly denied by Calvin (Inst. i. 5.5), who very emphatically states that the soul has immortal substance (i. 15.6)" (*Old and New in Interpretation*, 43).

Great care should be exercised in translating and interpreting each Hebrew term that refers to some aspect of human nature. H. W. Wolff warned that when the most frequent substantives are, as a general rule, translated by "heart," "soul," "flesh," and "spirit," misunderstandings may arise leading to important consequences. These translations go back to the Septuagint and may lead in the false direction of a dichotomic or trichotomic anthropology, in which body, soul, and spirit stand in opposition to one another (Wolff, *Anthropology of the Old Testament*, 7).

Human nature does have two sides: the inner, psychical, emotional, volitional, spiritual side; and the outer, physical and material side. The Old Testament does not sharply differentiate between these two aspects of a person's being. Terms that usually describe the physical side of a person's being also have psychical and spiritual qualities. For example, the word "flesh" not only stands for the physical or muscular part of the human body (Ezek. 37:6,8), it can refer to one's whole body (Num. 8:7), as well as to that part that "sings for joy to the living God" (Ps. 84:2). Flesh can "hope" or "trust" (Ps. 16:9); it can "long" for God (Ps. 63:1); it can "tremble" for fear of the Lord (Ps. 119:120).

Concepts such as heart, soul, flesh, and spirit are often interchangeable. At times they can be used to refer to the whole person, almost like personal pronouns.

> My soul longs, indeed it faints
> for the courts of the LORD;
> my heart and my flesh sing for joy
> to the living God.
> (Ps. 84:2)

> O God, you are my God, I seek you,
> my soul thirsts for you;
> my flesh faints for you,
> as in a dry and weary land
> where there is no water.
> (Ps. 63:1)

Wolff called this interchanging of terms for different aspects of human nature (heart, soul, flesh) "stereometric thinking." Stereometric thinking means the use of a number of words related in meaning in parallelism or in juxtaposition with each other (*Anthropology of the Old Testament*, 8). The Old Testament not only uses the various terms for the aspects of human nature interchangeably; it may use each term to refer to the whole person or to the function of one part. In this way "beautiful feet" may not refer to their graceful form but to their swift movement (Isa. 52:7; Nah. 1:15). This use of the name of the parts of the body to refer to the function of the whole body is sometimes called "synthetic" thinking (Wolff, *Anthropology of the Old Testament*, 8).

Stereometric, synthetic, and "corporate" thinking point to the Hebrew view of persons as "holistic" or "unitary"; that is, humans are made up of many aspects and parts, but these are not sharply differentiated. Each part can represent the whole and/or the function of other parts. Human nature is a unity, not a diversity. Opposition or antithesis does not characterize the various parts.

B. Hebrew Words for Persons

Five main Hebrew words are usually translated "man" in the Old Testament. *ʾadam* "Adam," "man," "humankind," or "humans" occurs 562 times, always singular in form but most often collective in meaning. It probably comes from a root meaning "dark" or "red."

ʾîš, "man," "husband," occurs 2160 times, mostly as husband opposite wife or male opposite female. It is used for male animals over against female animals (Gen. 7:2). Its etymology is uncertain (see Bratsiotis, *'Ish*, 222; Porteous, "Man," 243).

ʾĕnôš, "man" occurs 42 times and probably comes from a root meaning "to be weak" or "mortal." The word occurs most frequently in Job (18 times; see 7:1; 15:14; 25:4) and in Psalms

(13 times; for example, 103:15). *ĕnôš* often stands parallel with *ʾādām* as in the passages that ask the question: "What is man?" (Job 7:17; Ps. 8:4; 144:3). (See Maass, *'enosh*, 345-48; Porteous, "Man," 243.)

geber, "man," "strong man," "hero" occurs 65 times and carries the idea of power, strength, or excellence. The Psalms and Job often use it in the sense of a person who trusts and fears God and does what God requires (see Job 3:23; 4:17; 10:5; 14:10,15; 16:21; 22:22; 33:17,29; 34:7,9,34-35; 38:3; 40:7; Pss. 34:9; 37:23; 55:8-9; Jer. 17:7). (See Kosmala, *geber*, TDOT, II, 377-382.)

mat, "men," only appears in the plural. Sometimes it refers to man (males) in general (Deut. 2:34; 3:6; Judg. 20:48). Occasionally *matim* is used as an idiom to refer to "men few in number" (Gen. 34:30; Deut. 4:27; 26:5; 28:62; 33:6; 1 Chron. 16:19; Ps. 105:12; Jer. 44:28).

C. Hebrew Terms for Four Basic Aspects of Human Nature

In addition to the five Hebrew words for "man" in the Old Testament, four major Hebrew terms describe the primary aspects of human nature: *bāsār* or *seʾer* "flesh"; *rûaḥ* "spirit"; *nepeš* "soul"; and *lēb* "heart." The Old Testament never explains these aspects of human nature systematically. Each term has more than one meaning, often a physical and a psychical meaning. A term for one part of a person may refer to the person in the totality of individual being.

bāsār or *seʾer*, "flesh," refer to the visible, external, physical, and materialistic part of human nature. The two Hebrew words for "flesh" reveal very little difference in meaning. *Basar* occurs 273 times, while *seʾer* is found only 17 times. Both terms primarily refer to the muscular parts of people and animals. Neither term is used of God in the Old Testament. In fact, one passage explicitly states that God is not flesh (Isa. 31:3). Flesh links humans with the animal world, not the divine. Flesh in the Old Testament is weak (2 Chron. 32:8; Ps. 56:4; Jer. 17:5,7), but it is not the seat of sin. Flesh often refers to meat or food (Ex. 21:10; Lev. 4:11; 7:15-21; Ps. 78:20; Isa. 22:13; Mic. 3:2,3). Flesh can mean the visible body (Num. 8:7; Ps. 73:26). It can refer to a "blood relative" or next of kin (Gen. 29:14; 37:27; Lev. 18:6,12,13,17; 20:19; 21:2; 25:49; Num.

27:11; 2 Sam. 5:1; 19:12). Flesh may indicate a person or an individual (Lev. 13:18; Prov. 11:17). (See Johnson, *The Vitality of the Individual in the Thought of Ancient Israel*, 40-41.) Flesh also has psychical qualities in the Old Testament. It can "hope" (Ps. 16:9), "faint for God" (Ps. 63:1), "sing for joy to the living God" (Ps. 84:2).

Flesh is not identical with the human body. Hebrew has no word for body, although *gĕwiya* is translated "body" (Gen. 47:18; Neh. 9:37; Ezek. 1:11, 23; Dan. 10:6). Flesh is not used for a dead body or corpse. Hebrew terms for "corpse" or "carcass" are *nĕbēlâ* from the root *nābal* "to sink or drop down" (Deut. 21:23; 28:26; Josh. 8:29; 1 Kings 13:22,24,25,28,29,30; 2 Kings 9:37; Jer. 26:23; 36:30); *peger* from a root meaning "be exhausted, faint" (Lev. 26:30; Num. 14:29,32,33; Isa. 14:19; 34:3; 66:24; Jer. 31:40; 33:5; 41:9; Ezek. 6:5; Amos 8:3; Nah. 3:3); *gĕwiya* (Judg. 14:8,9; 1 Sam. 31:10,12; Ps. 110:6; Nah. 3:3;); *gûpâ* (1 Chron. 10:12).

rûaḥ, "wind," "spirit," "breath," occurs 378 times in the Hebrew and 11 times in the Aramaic portions of the Hebrew Bible. About 113 times (Wolff, *Anthropology of the Old Testament*, 32; Johnson, *Vitality*, 27, says 117) *rûaḥ* refers to "wind" or air in motion. In 136 places *rûaḥ* refers to the "spirit of God," leaving about 130 references to the "human spirit" and other uses.

The basic idea in *rûaḥ* as in the Greek *pneuma* is "wind." Jesus compared the work of the "Spirit" to the wind (John 3:6-8). Jesus was in the line of Old Testament prophets and writers who saw in *rûaḥ* an active power or energy, at once superhuman, invisible, mysterious, elusive. *rûaḥ* refers to east wind (Ex. 10:13; 14:21), north wind (Prov. 25:23), west wind (Ex. 10:19), four winds (Jer. 49:36; Ezek. 37:9), rushing wind (Ps. 55:8), and wind of heaven (Gen. 8:1; Ex. 15:10).

Early in the Old Testament the association is made between the "breath" of God and the "life principle" in people (Gen. 2:7; 6:17; 7:15-22). The breath that energized humans was a gift of God's spirit (Job 9:18; 19:17; 27:3; 33:4; Isa. 42:5; 57:16). This gift of God's life-giving spirit was not unique to humans. The Old Testament speaks of an animal's life or vitality as being due to God's spirit (Gen. 6:17; 7:15,22; Eccl. 3:19,21). Idols do not have "spirit" or "breath." They are lifeless and powerless

(Jer. 10:14; Hab. 2:19). The "bones" of Israel come to life again when the "spirit" comes from the four winds and breathes on them (Ezek. 37:6,8-10,14). So spirit stands for the breath and life principle in humans (and animals?).

Although the human spirit is a gift of God and the individual is never able to control it absolutely, it remains a person's own spirit (Pss. 51:10; 146:4; Ezek. 3:14; 11:5; 20:32). A person could speak of the vital energy dwelling within as "my" *rûaḥ* and attribute to it "marked deteriorations in his physical or psychic state" (see Johnson, *Vitality*, 37; compare Gen. 41:8; Judg. 8:3; 15:19; 1 Sam. 30:12; 1 Kings 10:5; Eccl. 3:21). The human spirit can grow dim (Isa. 61:3; Ezek. 21:7); become faint (Ps. 77:3; 142:3; 143:4); or vanish (Ps. 143:7). It can become disturbed (Dan. 2:3); feel distress (Job 6:4; 7:11; Prov. 15:4,13); become angry (Job 15:13; Prov. 29:11; Eccl. 10:4); rest (Zech. 6:8); feel jealousy (Num. 5:14,30); become hardened (Deut. 2:30); or become aroused (Hag. 1:14).

Some psychical qualities of *rûaḥ*, "spirit" can be seen in its relation to emotions. Spirit is sometimes associated with mental powers and can be translated "mind" (Ex. 28:3; 1 Chron. 28:12; Ps. 77:6; Isa. 29:24; Ezek. 11:5; 20:32; compare Isa. 65:17; Jer. 3:16) and "will" (Isa. 19:3; 29:24). Thus the "spirit," which began as "wind" and became "breath" and "vitality," also stands for the inner, invisible, higher aspect of human nature. Eichrodt said, "The fact that the same term was used to denote *rûaḥ* both of the deity and man, despite there being no directly religious value attached to the human *rûaḥ*, kept men continually aware that by the terms of the creation their world was linked to the supra-sensory world of God (*Theology of the Old Testament II*, 133).

nepeš, "soul," "life," "throat," is an elusive term with a wide range of meanings (Johnson, *Vitality*, 9, 26). The traditional English Bible's translation of *nepeš* as "soul" goes back to the Septuagint's translation, *anima*, but even those translations allowed other meanings in 155 out of 755 instances. Eichrodt said, "The unhappy rendering of the term by 'soul' opened the door from the start to the Greek beliefs concerning the soul (*Theology of the Old Testament II*, 135). In the KJV the word *nepeš* is translated "soul" 428 times, "life" 119 times, "self" 19 times, "person" 30 times, "heart" 15 times, "mind" 15 times, "creature" 9 times, "dead" (body) 8 times, "body" 7 times, "desire" 5 times, "will" and "pleasure" 4 times, "man" 3 times, "appetite," "beast," "ghost," "lust" 2 times. These various translations of the same word indicate extreme variations and breadth in meaning. Physical and psychical aspects of human nature may be indicated by this term in varying degrees.

The basic meaning of *nepeš* is probably "throat" or "neck." Isaiah 5:14 speaks of the underworld opening wide its *nephesh*, "throat" (compare Ps. 107:9; Hab. 2:5). Jonah (2:5) speaks of water surrounding his *nepeš*, "throat" or "neck." The meaning of *nepeš* seemingly shifted from "throat" or "neck" to "breath," indicating life and vitality. *nepeš* is not limited to the "life" of humans. Animals are also said to be "living beings" (*nepeš ḥāyâ*, Gen. 1:21,24; 2:19; 9:10,15,16; Lev. 11:46). Isaiah 10:18 speaks metaphorically of the *nepeš* and *bāsār*, "soul and body" of the forest and the land.

The verb form of the root *nps* only occurs three times in the Old Testament, meaning "exhale," "catch one's breath," "refresh oneself." David breathed a sigh of relief after arriving at the Jordan when Absalom rebelled against him (2 Sam. 16:14). Twice it explains resting on the Sabbath as "to exhale," "to breathe a breath of refreshment," once by humans (Ex. 23:12; 31:17).

The psychical qualities of the *nepeš* are numerous. It can be frightened (Job 6:4) or despondent (Ps. 42:1-2; Jonah 2:7). It can hate (2 Sam. 5:8; Isa. 1:14), love (Song of Sol. 1:7; 3:1, 2,3,4; Jer. 12:7), grieve and weep (Lev. 26:16; Deut. 28:65; Jer. 13:17). It can "think" (Esther 4:13; Prov. 2:10). Admittedly many of the passages where *nepeš* is translated as "mind" do not reflect our idea of "mind" as a reasoning entity, but they do approach it. (The Hebrew Bible uses *lēb* "heart" more often to refer to the "mind.")

nepeš not only has a physical meaning ("neck," "throat") and a psychical meaning ("loving," "hating," "fainting"). It can also stand for the whole person, approaching the English personal or reflexive pronoun. The Old Testament has no technical reflexive pronouns "himself," "herself," "themselves." It uses *nepeš* for such expressions (Johnson, *Vitality*, 19-20; Wolff, *Anthropology of the Old Testament*, 21, 23). *nepeš* is used in the Old Testament in the sense of God speaking of Himself (Jer.

5:9,29; 9:7; Amos 6:8; compare Jer. 51:14). Yahweh's nephesh (Himself) becomes indignant or impatient (Judg. 10:16; Zech. 11:8), hates (Ps. 11:5; Isa. 1:14), loves (Jer. 12:7), can be alienated (Jer. 6:8), or can become disgusted (Ezek. 23:18).

If *nepeš* could stand for the whole person, could it refer to a dead person? Is a corpse or carcass still a *nepeš*? The expression "dead nephesh" appears in Leviticus 21:11; Numbers 6:6; 19:11,13; Haggai 2:13. A. R. Johnson said that "the last passage in particular makes it quite clear that the reference must be to the *nepeš* as something with which one can come into physical contact, i.e., not the 'soul' of the dead as some sort of ghostly phenomenon" (*Vitality*, 25, n. 2). In postbiblical Hebrew, Aramaic, and Syriac *nepeš* is used to denote a funeral monument or tombstone. Jacob said, "This use takes us far from the primitive meaning, since it is used for the very contrary of life, yet the monument representing the person guarantees, at any rate for a limited time, the continuation of his presence (*Theology of the Old Testament*, 161; compare Johnson, *Vitality*, 26, n. 2; Robinson, *The Christian Doctrine of Man*, 17).

If *nepeš* can stand for the "dead body" or corpse of a person or animal who has died, does the Old Testament say anything else about what happens to the *nepeš* at death? We will discuss this matter more fully under the subject of death. However, the Old Testament does speak of the *nephesh* being breathed or poured out at death (Job 11:20; Isa. 53:12; Lam. 2:12), departing (Gen. 35:18), and in some instances as returning after a dead person is revived (1 Kings 17:21-22). Wheeler Robinson said that the inhabitants of Sheol are not *nepheshim* "souls" but *repha'im* "shades" (*The Christian Doctrine of Man*, 17-18; compare Johnson, "Jonah II 3-10," 86-87; Jacob, *Theology of the Old Testament*, 299; Wolff, *Anthropology of the Old Testament*, 99-118; Eichrodt, *Theology of the Old Testament II*, 214).

lēb, lēbab, "heart" are two related terms with the same meaning, *lēb* occurring 598 times and *lebab*, 252 times, making "heart" the most frequently used anthropological term in the Old Testament. "Heart" refers to animals only 5 times (2 Sam. 17:10; Job. 41:24; Dan. 4:16; 5:21; Hos. 7:11). The first four of these uses may be metaphorical. The "heart of God" is mentioned 26 times (Wolff, *Anthropology of the Old Testament*, 40,

55-58). The remainder of the references (814) refer to the human heart.

Although the people of the Old Testament knew the heart as a physical organ, they did not understand its significant physical function of circulating the blood. Few Old Testament references point to the heart as a physical organ. Hosea spoke of the "enclosure" (*segôr*) or lock of the heart (Hos. 13:8), probably referring to the ribcage that protects the heart. Abigail told David that her husband's heart died "within him" and he became like a stone, although he continued to live ten more days (1 Sam. 25:37). The expression "within him" *qereb* is an indication of Israel's awareness of the inward location of the heart (1 Sam. 25:37; Pss. 39:3; 64:6; Jer. 23:9).

Other Old Testament passages indicate the inward location of the heart. Jehu shot Joram between the arms so that the arrow pierced his heart (2 Kings 9:24). Aaron wore the breastplate on his chest over his heart (Ex. 28:29). Two passages may refer to the heart beating (Ps. 38:10; Jer. 4:19). (However, neither verb properly means "beat." The first, *hōmĕh*, is a participle from *hmh*, "to make a noise," and the second, *sĕharhar*, is an onomatopaeic word meaning "to rove around.")

The people of the Old Testament attached little emphasis to the heart's physical aspect. The same is true of the other eighty different parts of the human body mentioned in the Old Testament. The Old Testament is concerned with the psychical qualities of the parts of the body more than with their physical functions.

"Heart" in the Old Testament primarily refers to a person's psychical powers. The Old Testament ascribed to the heart everything that we ascribe to the head and the brain—the power of perception, reason, thinking, understanding, insight, consciousness, conscience, memory, knowledge, feeling, will, and judgment.

Heart can be used as a synonym of *nepeš*, "soul," and *rûah*, "spirit," in the areas of feelings and emotions. Joy and sorrow can be described equally well by the expressions "strengthening the heart" or "refreshing the soul" (Gen. 18:5; Judg. 19:5,8; Ps. 104:15); "pouring out the heart" or "pouring out the soul" (Ps. 62:8; Lam. 2:19). Similarly, the uses of heart and spirit overlap. The Old Testament speaks of a "broken heart" or of a "broken spirit" (Ps. 34:18; 51:17); of pride as the lifting up either of the heart or the spirit (Ps. 131:1; Prov. 18:12; Ezek. 28:2,5,17). Like *nepeš* and *ruJah*, "heart" can stand for the whole person and be translated with a personal pronoun (Prov. 3:1; 10:8; compare Johnson, *Vitality*, 82-83).

The unique significance of "heart" in the Old Testament is not in its expression of feelings of fear, courage, joy, or sorrow, but in its expression of intellectual and volitional processes. Wheeler Robinson assigned 20 occurrences of "heart" in the Old Testament to the intellectual category and 195 occurrences to the volitional category (*The Christian Doctrine of Man*, 22). The use of "heart" in the intellectual and volitional sense seems concentrated in Wisdom Literature and in Deuteronomy. "Heart" is used 99 times in Proverbs, 42 times in Ecclesiastes, and 51 times in Deuteronomy.

Plato distinguished sharply between reason and emotion. The Stoics often made morality equal to the suppression of passion and the control of desire by reason. "Passion and vice, emotion and weakness were often treated as synonyms and it was assumed that reason and ruthlessness, knowledge and evil were mutually exclusive (Heschel, *The Prophets*, 255). The heart, according to Heschel, is the seat of all inner functions. Passions are not disturbances or weaknesses of the soul. Asceticism was not the ideal of biblical individuals, and the source of evil was not in passion but in the callousness, insensitivity, and hardness of the heart. The ideal state in the Old Testament is not apathy, like the Stoics, but sympathy, like Yahweh (Hos. 11:8-9).

The heart as the center of knowledge or reason is often associated with the ear in the Old Testament (Deut. 29:4; 1 Kings 3:9-12; Prov. 2:2; 18:15; 22:17; 23:12; Isa. 6:10; 32:3-4; Jer. 11:8; Ezek. 3:10; 40:4; 44:5). The intelligent person in the Old Testament was a person of heart (Job 34:10,34), but the fool lacked heart (Prov. 10:13) or said in the heart, "There is no God" (Pss. 14:1; 53:1). Memory is also related to the heart (Deut. 4:9,39; Ps. 31:12; Isa. 33:17; 65:17; Jer. 3:16; 51:50).

Conscience is associated with the heart. David's heart smote him on two occasions: after he cut off the corner of Saul's garment (1 Sam. 24:6) and after he took a census of his fighting forces (2 Sam. 24:10; compare 1 Kings 2:44; Eccl. 7:22). True love has its seat in the heart (Judg. 16:15), nevertheless, the heart is not used in the "romantic" or affective sense in the Old Testament as it is in our conceptions and language (Jacob, *Theology of the Old Testament*, 165).

When the Old Testament says, "You shall love the LORD your God with all your heart, and with all your soul, and with all your might" (Deut. 6:5), "heart" takes first place and carries primarily the meaning of "mind"—but not in a narrow sense. One is to love God with all of one's intellect, feelings, emotions, and will—with the total being.

The heart is the source of thoughts, words, and actions (Prov. 4:23), both good and bad. The heart can be soft (2 Chron. 34:27), clear (Ps. 24:4), pure (Ps. 51:10), upright (Deut. 9:5), whole (1 Kings 8:61), perfect (Gen. 20:6), strong (Ps. 57:7), and faithful (Neh. 9:8). It can also can be hard (Ex. 7:3), corrupt and deceitful (Jer. 17:9), wicked (Isa. 32:6), sinful (Prov. 6:18), crooked or perverted (Ps. 101:4; Prov. 11:20; 12:8; 17:20), and evil (Gen. 6:5; 8:21; Deut. 15:9; 1 Sam. 17:28). The Old Testament speaks of a divided heart (Ps. 12:2), of fat hearts (Ps. 119:70; Isa. 6:10), and of hard hearts. Heschel said that what we call the irrational nature of people, the prophets called hardness of the heart (Isa. 46:12; Jer. 9:26). "The opposite of freedom is not determinism, but hardness of the heart. Freedom presupposes openness of heart, of mind, of eye and ear" (*The Prophets*, 189, 191). The Old Testament also speaks of the heart as having an imagination or a bent toward evil (Gen. 6:5; 8:21). However, we should not assume that *yeṣer* "imagination" is always directed toward evil. It is used in the Old Testament and in rabbinic literature of an "impulse" toward good as well as evil (compare Simpson, "Genesis," 538; Johnson, *Vitality*, 86). In Isaiah 26:3 (RSV) *yeṣer* is "mind" and is used in a positive fashion: "Thou dost keep him in perfect peace, whose mind (*yeṣer*) is stayed on thee, because he trusts in thee."

If the heart is evil, God knows it because He looks on the inward parts (1 Sam. 16:7). He "tests" (Jer. 12:3), "weighs" (Prov. 21:2), and "circumcises the heart" (Lev. 26:41; Deut. 10:16; 30:6; Jer. 4:4; 9:26; Ezek. 44:7,9). When one's heart becomes hard, God can give a new heart (Jer. 32:39; Ezek. 18:31; 36:26).

A study of the four primary words related to human nature (*bāsār* "flesh," *rûaḥ* "spirit," *nepeš* "soul," "life," and *lēb* "heart") reveals that a person is a multi-faceted creature. In some aspects people are like other creatures, but in other ways they are totally different. Each of these four terms has various shades of meaning. Each has physical and psychical implications. The context of every use of each term must be carefully considered. Each term can be used in some sense almost as a synonym of the others, and each term can stand for the whole person.

Eichrodt said that Hebrew thought was not interested in a theoretical analysis of psychical phenomena. "A strict dualism, which feels that flesh and spirit, body and soul, are irreconcilable opposites, is completely unknown" (*Theology of the Old Testament II*, 147). However, it is nevertheless impossible to comprehend *nepeš* and *rûaḥ* "as two component parts of the spiritual nature of Man." They are excellent descriptions of the differing qualities of psychical events, but they are not in any way suitable terms for special capacities or areas of the psyche. Instead, they always represent the whole life of the person from a particular point of view. "A trichotomistic human psychology is therefore as little to be based on the Old Testament concepts as a dualistic one" (*Theology of the Old Testament II*, 148).

This holistic view of persons has implications for many areas of life. For example, if the body (flesh) has psychical as well as physical powers, it is not merely an object we possess standing outside our real being. It is a vital part of our self. It cannot be despised or regarded lightly. It is a part of the image of God. Again, in light of the holistic view of persons, sin cannot be explained one-sidedly as *concupiscent*, the desire of the flesh, but must be understood as the act or condition of the whole person. Redemption also must be understood as including the physical as well as the psychical aspects. Life after death will include a resurrected body and soul.

7

Sin and Redemption

Sin is a major theme in the Old Testament. It is easy to find Old Testament passages referring to sin. De Vries said, "There are few chapters which do not contain some reference to what sin is or does" ("Sin, Sinners," 361). C. R. Smith pointed out that the Old Testament has more terms denoting "evil" than terms denoting "good"; while there is only one way of doing right, there are many ways of doing wrong (*The Biblical Doctrine of Sin*, 15).

The Bible takes sin seriously. "In contrast to many modern religionists who seek to find excuses for sin and explain away its seriousness, most of the biblical writers were keenly aware of its heinousness, culpability, and tragedy" (de Vries, "Sin, Sinners," 361). The seriousness of sin in the Old Testament is seen in the estrangement it brings between a person and God; a person and the world; a person and society; and within a person. Even though the Bible assumes human dignity and worth, human need is the Bible's primary concern. The Bible is full of human tragedy, with the misery, guilt, and alienation that is humanity's lot. A person's need is even more vital to the Old Testament than its conception of human nature. "He is not alone a creature of dignity and high estate; he is a creature of deep need. And his need is salvation from sin" (Rowley, *The Rediscovery of the Old Testament*, 217).

In the Old Testament, sin shatters the unity of human nature and destroys the harmony of the world. "Sin is not fun; it is tragedy" (de Vries, *The Achievements of Biblical Religion*, 156). One of the tragedies of sin is that humans cannot overcome it by themselves. The biblical writers knew that apart from God, humans are lost sinners unable to save themselves or find happiness (de Vries, "Sin, Sinners," 361). If rightness is to be restored, it must come as God's generous gift and not by human accomplishment. Pannenberg agreed that we cannot overcome sin by ourselves. "The conflict between self-centeredness and openness to the world is not to be overcome on our own. The harmony between the ego and the whole of reality can be received only from God" (*What Is Man?*, 62).

Some writers make sin the central issue in the Old Testament. Edward J. Young, writing on the state of Old Testament theology in 1958, criticized von Rad's work for not taking the Genesis account of the fall seriously. Young wrote, "Von Rad completely avoids mention of the fact that man is a fallen creature and that a promise of salvation has been made" (*The Study of Old Testament Theology Today*, 70). He further argued that von Rad, G. Ernest Wright, Mowinckel, Gunkel, and K. Barth were blind to the fact that the Bible is concerned primarily with sin (*The Study of Old Testament Theology Today*, 18, 20, 44, 70, 74, 82).

While Young and his colleagues made sin the central issue in Old Testament theology, primarily because of their adherence to Federal theology, some Old Testament theologians seem to ignore the subject. Many recent Old Testament theologies do not have a separate treatment of sin. This may be due in part to the methodologies that current scholars use. It may also reflect a modern attitude that sin is part of human nature (Westermann) or that it should be treated under different terminology, such as crime, threat, guilt, or mental instability. Some time ago Karl Menninger lamented the loss of the word and the concept "sin" from our modern vocabulary. He said,

> The very word "sin," which seems to have disappeared, was a
> proud word. It was once a strong word, an ominous and serious
> word. It described a central point in every civilized human

being's life plan and life style. But the word went away. It has almost disappeared—the word along with the notion (*Whatever Became of Sin?*, 14).

Bruce Milne began his Tyndale Biblical Theology lecture in 1975 by quoting William Law's famous saying, "The whole nature of the Christian religion stands upon these two great pillars, namely, the greatness of our fall and the greatness of our redemption" ("The Idea of Sin in the Twentieth Century," 3). Milne said that one looks almost in vain during this century for a major discussion of sin. Four new factors have contributed to the modern dilemma concerning the nature of sin: (1) the rise of the theory of biological evolution; (2) Karl Marx's all embracing socio-economic account of behavior and values; (3) the whole psycho-analytical approach associated with the work of Freud, Jung, and others; and (4) the radical and ever-deepening pessimism of the secular world.

Milne examined in some depth the views of K. Barth, R. Niebuhr, and Norman Pittenger with reference to sin. He finds all three scholars' views on sin unsatisfactory when measured by the biblical view. According to Milne, the biblical view of sin still needs to be enunciated to modern people.

Our primary concern here is not with the modern world, but with the Old Testament's view(s) of sin. One of the problems of presenting the Old Testament view of sin is the vastness and variety of the material. How does one deal with the prophetic and priestly views of sin? Is the view of sin the same in the early and later parts of the Old Testament? Does one make an exhaustive study of the words for sin in the Old Testament? Should one consider Israel's view of sin in light of the concepts of her neighbors? Should one raise such questions as: What is the nature of sin? What was the origin of sin? Is sin universal?

A Czechoslovakian priest, Stefan Porubcan, published a huge volume (631 pages) on *Sin in the Old Testament* in 1963. He dealt with all of the major Hebrew words for sin along with their opposite terms for cleanness, righteousness, forgiveness, and salvation. The book did not receive wide distribution or use in the United States, but Rolf Knierim wrote a twenty-page review of it for *Vetus Testamentum* ("The Problem of an Old Testament Hamartiology," 366-385).

Knierim criticized Porubcan's work, claiming that it represents the theological conception of the author rather than a theology of the Old Testament witnesses (Knierim, 384). Such a criticism might be made of most doctrinal studies. Knierim also faulted Porubcan for a failure to use "sufficient literary criticism and traditio-historical methods" (Knierim, 384). Knierim concluded his review by saying that "the task of an Old Testament hamartiology, adequate to our needs, remains a hope which is unfulfilled up till now" (Knierim, 385).

Knierim should be qualified to judge a hamartiology of the Old Testament because he published a major work on the subject based on his doctrinal dissertation at Heidelberg University in 1965 (*Die Hauptbegriffe für Sünde im Alten Testament*). What follows is no hamartiology but an attempt to portray honestly some of the views of sin presented in the Old Testament. We will discuss the nature of sin, the source of sin, the effects of sin, and the removal of sin.

31. The Nature of Sin

No definition of sin appears in the Old Testament. One should not expect such a definition, considering the fact that the Scripture is always dealing with actual life and presenting rules for conduct or passing judgment upon it. "What we find is concrete designations of actual evil in various spheres" (Davidson, *The Theology of the Old Testament*, 209). "The Bible has no single comprehensive definition of sin. The latter is described in every sort of act, condition and intention" (Wright, *The Biblical Doctrine of Man in Society*, 40).

Is sin in the Old Testament an act or a state? Most Old Testament scholars answer that it is both. Eichrodt said individual actions point to a perverted direction of the human will. "Behind the sin stands sin, in the sense of a wrong condition of human nature" (*Theology of the Old Testament II*, 387). Wright claimed that sin in the Old Testament is

> both voluntary and constituent. Sin is the result of man's free will; it is his free act. But it is also imparted as an objective quantity. When it is one it is at the same time and immediately the other also. Where there is transgression, there is also material dislocation, a state of sinfulness. . . . Sin as an act of the will has integral physical and social concomitants including the cor-

ruption of the will itself (*The Biblical Doctrine of Man in Society*, 40).

The essence of sin is rebellion against God. It is not simply moral evil, but moral evil regarded religiously. A. C. Knudson said:

> Sin is a positive act or state of hostility to God. It is not an "unreality or an illusion" as Spinoza would have us believe; nor is it as Hegel teaches an essential moment in the progressive or eternally realized life of God; nor is it as some evolutionists tell us simply a relic of the animal nature which we have inherited. Not even Kant's conception of evil as "the perversion of the right relation between reason and sense, the false subordination of the rational to the sensuous," fills out the biblical idea of sin. Sin, as it is conceived both in the Old and the New Testament, carries with it the thought of a defiant attitude of the soul toward God and . . . comes to be thought of as an objective power (*The Religious Teachings of the Old Testament*, 255-256).

In the Old Testament, sin is the violation of "a gracious and righteous Divine will, a rebellion which destroyed personal communion" (Wright, *God Who Acts*, 20). Israel, unlike her neighbors, analyzed the problems of life over against the will and purpose of the God who chose one people to be the instruments of His universal redemptive purpose (Gen. 12:3).

Sin in the Old Testament is not a disturbance of the "status quo" in nature or an aberration which destroyed the harmony of affairs in the cosmic state. It is the violation of communion, the betrayal of God's love, and a revolt against His lordship.

A. The Vocabulary of Sin

What is sin, according to the Old Testament? Some Hebrew words for sin might supply part of an answer, but we must not take each word out of context or overemphasize its etymology to get its meaning. Von Rad pointed out that Israel had many varied terms for sin, but that any statistical review of these terms would come far short of disclosing the heart of the matter for theology (*Old Testament Theology I*, 264).

G. Ernest Wright said that it is a common practice to attempt to comprehend the nature of sin by an etymological study of the words used for it, but this practice is not very helpful. "The fact is that the vocabulary for sin is almost identical, for the most part, with that used in Egypt, Babylon and

Greece. Hence the nature of sin is to be understood from the vocabulary employed only when the terms are studied in the total context of faith. The context differs from that given them in paganism only because of the radical difference in the content of the faith" (*The Biblical Doctrine of Man in Society*, 40).

Davidson noted that the terms the Old Testament employs for "good" or "evil" are popular, figurative, common sense language and should not be considered scientific or philosophical terms expressing the principle or essence of "good" or "evil" (*The Theology of the Old Testament*, 204-206).

The basic term for sin, *hata^c* means "to miss the mark" as a stone slinger misses the target (Judg. 20:16) or a traveler misses the way (Prov. 19:2). The word *ʾawôn* means "to pervert" or "to make crooked" (1 Sam. 20:1). Sin is that which is crooked, not "straight," "upright," or "smooth." "Sin is of the nature of failing to reach a mark; it is of the nature of what is crooked compared with what is straight; of the nature of what is uneven contrasted with what is smooth; of the nature of what is unclean compared to what is clean" (Davidson, *The Theology of the Old Testament*, 207).

Some writers have tried to get at the meaning of the Old Testament words for sin by classifying them by groups. C. R. Smith classified the Hebrew words for sin in the Old Testament into three groups: (1) generic terms (*ra^c* "bad," *rašac* "wicked," and *ʾāšām* "guilty"); (2) metaphors (*hataʾ*, *ʾawôn*, and *ʾawla* "to miss the mark, *ʿābār* "to cross over," *šāgāh*, and *tāʾāh* "to err," "to go astray," *pesac*, *marah*, *marad*, *sārar*, "to rebel," *mā^{c}al*, *bāgad*, "to act treacherously," *hānap*, "to lean away from" as a renegade or apostate, *ʾāven*, "trouble," *bĕliyac al* "worthless," *šiqqûs*, *to^{c}ebah* "abomination," "that which nauseates"; (3) opposites—that is, terms opposite to the main words used to describe God: "righteous," "holy," "pure," "wise," and "glorious." Words opposite to these are: *rašac* "wicked," *hālel* "profane," *tāmeʾ* "unclean," *kesel* "folly," and *bōset*, *hārap*, *kālam*, "shame." In addition to these general terms, other terms denote specific sins such as murder and theft (*The Biblical Doctrine of Sin*, 15-22).

Wheeler Robinson said that the value of any classification of the Hebrew terms for sin was only introductory. "The revelation of the Old Testament is not philological, but historical;

the mere term is a locked drawer until we have opened it with the key of history" (*The Christian Doctrine of Man*, 43). Robinson classifies the principal words for sin in four groups: (1) deviation from the right way (*ḥataʾ, ʾāwon, sāgah, sûr, śaṭâ*); (2) the changed status (guilt) of the agent (*rāsāʿ, ʾāšam*); (3) rebellion against a superior or unfaithfulness to an agreement (*pesaʿ, mārad, sārar, maʿal, begad, mermâ*), and (4) some characterization of the quality of the act itself (*rāʿah, ḥāmas, šāgâ, hebel, ʾwôn šewaʾ*).

S. J. de Vries said it is no accident that the Bible is rich in its vocabulary for sin. This is especially true of the Old Testament. The Old Testament writers were not interested in offering a theoretical definition of sin, but they reflected in their rich and vivid terminology "the profundity and the widespread effects of sin as they experienced it" ("Sin, Sinner," 360).

De Vries arranged the Hebrew words for sin in the Old Testament into six groups: (1) formal words indicating a deviation from what is good and right; (2) theological terms, indicating sin as defiance against God; (3) terms describing a sinner's inner state; (4) terms in which the ethical aspect is prominent; (5) terms indicating the baneful results of sin; and (6) terms for guilt.

In addition to these groups, de Vries noted that the Old Testament uses many other terms to express sin: obstinacy, pride, backsliding, folly, deceit, uncleanness, and others. "In addition there is a name for every particular sin and crime" ("Sin, Sinners," 362). De Vries also classified the language of sin as formal terms, relational terms, psychological words, and qualitative words (*The Achievements of Biblical Religion*, 164).

The lists of Porubcan and Hermann Schultz should be added to the lists of C. R. Smith, Wheeler Robinson, and de Vries. A study of these lists of words for sin shows that sin in the Old Testament is error, failure, rebellion against God. It is disobedience, folly, unfaithfulness. It is greed, oppression, violence, pride, and immorality. Sin is wrongdoing, bad deeds, and evil.

For the most part, sin in the Old Testament is personal. It is the result of a conscious decision. Animals or things do not sin because they are not free to choose "good" or "evil." Sin in the Old Testament is individualistic and corporate. Sinners are responsible for their choices, attitudes, and actions. One way to get a "feel" for the Old Testament's view of sin is to read some of its own lists of the sins of Israel and of individuals (compare Deut. 9:6-24; Ps. 106:6-39; Isa. 59:1-8; Jer. 2:4-28; 7:9-11; 29:23; Ezek. 16:14-58; 18:5-13; Amos 2:6-8; 5:10-12; 8:4-6; Mic. 2:1-2; 7:2-7).

E. W. Heaton said that in addition to the formal and technical Hebrew words for sin, the Hebrew prophets ransacked their experience and vocabulary to bring home to Israel the meaning of their unrighteousness. In the language of the laundry, they were filthy and needed cleansing (Jer. 2:22); in the language of the physician, they were desperately sick and needed Yahweh's healing (Isa. 1:5-6); in the idiom of the shepherd, Israel was a lost sheep who had strayed from the fold (Jer. 23:3); in the farmer's language, they were grain full of chaff which Yahweh would winnow (Amos 9:9); for the miner, they were full of dross and would be given to the smelter (Ezek. 22:18-19); in the language of the builder, Israel was a leaning wall (Amos 7:8); in the language of the home, they were a littered floor which would be swept clean (Isa. 14:23); in the language of the potter, they were marred clay (Jer. 18:1-4); in the jargon of the marketplace they had been sold as slaves because of their iniquities and transgressions (Isa. 50:1) (see Heaton, *His Servants the Prophets*, 84).

B. Categories of Sins

Sin may be categorized in four ways: (1) personalistic, as rebellion against God; (2) moralistic, as deviation from an external norm; (3) monistic, as somehow equated with human creatureliness or physical nature; and (4) dynamistic, in which sin is the transgression of a taboo (de Vries, "Sin, Sinners," 362; de Vries, *The Achievements of Biblical Religion*, 157-160).

The Old Testament view of sin is primarily personalistic, although examples or illustrations of other views may occur. The moralistic view could easily develop in a society which made the law or Torah the external norm by which conduct and attitudes were judged. Perhaps some of the ritual transgressions or unexplained judgments in the Old Testament (compare Ex. 4:24-26; 2 Sam. 6:6-7) may be "carryovers" from an earlier dynamistic view of sin (see Eichrodt, *Theology of the*

Old Testament II, 382-384; de Vries, *The Achievements of Biblical Religion*, 165). Some writers have pointed to a few Old Testament passages (Job 4:17-21; 13:4; Pss. 78:38-39; 103:14-16; Isa. 40:6-8) to argue that at least the relics of a monistic view of sin may be found in the Old Testament, but the precise meaning of these passages is debatable.

The Bible acknowledged evil in its most important personalities. Fromm said, "Adam is a coward; Cain is irresponsible; Noah is a weakling; Abraham allows his wife to be violated because of his fear; Jacob participates in the fraud against his brother Esau; Joseph is an ambitious manipulator; and the greatest of the Hebrew heroes, King David, commits unforgivable crimes" (*You Shall Be As Gods*, 127).

Near the close of the Old Testament, Israel's personal sense of sin was dulled by a failure to emphasize its inwardness and its corrupting influence on the human heart (Jer. 17:9). Emphasis was placed instead on observing the external rules of the law.

Postbiblical Judaism took a different view of sin from that of the Old Testament. S. J. de Vries said that in the postbiblical period, sin was defined as the breaking of the Mosaic law. "To assure the righteous that they could overcome sin by keeping the law a notion of a good and evil impulse (*yeṣer*), inside of man but not a part of him, supplanted the prophetic concept of the depraved heart" (de Vries, *The Achievements of Biblical Religion*, 169; see S. Rosenblatt, "Inclination, Good and Evil," 1315). The crisis of enslavement to sin no longer appeared impossible of human resolution. From the time of Ben Sirach, the doctrine of an evil impulse innate in people was given striking expression, but this evil impulse is not invincible. A person can and should master it. In fact, God gave the law as a means of salvation. "Thus Judaism never acknowledged a *servum arbitrium* (slave will), and on this point refused to be a disciple of the prophets" (Eichrodt, *Theology of the Old Testament II*, 392).

The rabbis also taught the existence of a good impulse in people. They held sinlessness to be entirely possible. Even though every person submits at least once to an evil impulse, "yet in the righteous there are only a few sins to be found, and these do not in fact, essentially challenge their righteousness"

(Eichrodt, *Theology of the Old Testament II*, 393; compare Cohen, *Everyman's Talmud*, 33-93; K. Köhler, *Jewish Theology*, 215, 223, 239-245).

Modern Judaism, for the most part, takes a very optimistic view of human nature and the possibility of self-reformation. "The modern Jew does not believe . . . that he needs to be 'saved' by any act of Christ or of any other mediator in earth or heaven. There is no place for the fall in his interpretation of his own literature. . . . Man, says the modern Jew, is essentially good at birth, and is therefore able to rise to the heights of God; but it is a gulf that can be bridged by man's prayers and study, by his thought and by his actions" (Knight, *A Christian Theology of the Old Testament*, 356). Kaufman Köhler said, "The Jewish idea of atonement by the sinner's return to God excludes every kind of mediatorship. Neither the priesthood nor sacrifice is necessary to secure the divine—grace; man need only find the way to God by his own efforts" (*Jewish Theology*, 247).

Whereas rabbinic Judaism took an optimistic view of humans and sin in the sense that it is possible for a person to overcome sin alone (or without outside help), the New Testament and Christianity have taken a pessimistic view of sin (de Vries, *The Achievements of Biblical Religion*, 156). The New Testament uses essentially the same terms and concepts for sin as the Old Testament, but it broadens and deepens them.

Jesus went beyond anything the scribes and Pharisees imagined in His statements about sin (Matt. 5:21-48; Mark 7:21-23). Paul went beyond the law as a standard for sin and righteousness. No one can keep the law. The law points out a person's failures and shows the depths of personal sinfulness (Rom. 3:20; 5:20; 7:7-24; Gal. 3:19-24). "The doctrine of sin in the New Testament is dominated by the assurance that Christ has come to conquer it" (de Vries, "Sin, Sinners," 371; compare de Vries, *The Achievements of Biblical Religion*, 171).

C. The Essence of Sin

Sin in the Old Testament is more than wrong or harmful acts or wrong attitudes. It involves the whole person (flesh, spirit, heart, and soul). In light of the holistic view of human nature set out at the end of chapter 6, sin cannot be explained

one-sidedly as concupiscence or as a psychological disturbance. Sin has a spiritual as well as a physical and mental
dimension in the Old Testament. People do not sin with just
one part of their nature (mind or body), but the total self is
involved in every sin (Matt. 5:27-28).

De Vries said that sin in its grosser forms makes a person
lower than the animals because animals only sin with their
flesh. They lack the higher qualities of self-understanding,
self-consciousness, memory, imagination, and a sense of meaning and purpose in earthly activity. "It is misleading to use the
term 'animalism' for immoral and sensuous human behavior.
When we human beings abandon ourselves to unrestrained
fleshliness, whether that be drunkenness or gluttony or fornication, we are not behaving like animals, for we have become
lower than animals" (de Vries, *The Achievements of Biblical
Religion*, 155).

Humans were created with higher capabilities than the animals (Ps. 8:5-8). Misusing those higher capabilities, we often
make wrong choices and act in ways that result in failure,
frustration, suffering, and alienation from God and others. We
sin!

32. The Source of Sin

"Whoever reflects on the doctrine of sin in the light of God's
Word is struck very early with the question of sin's origin"
(Berkouwer, *Sin*, 11). When one recognizes a problem, the natural course of action is to try to find the primary cause, source,
or origin of the problem. The Old Testament recognizes a problem in nature and humanity. "A profound and abnormal disorder exists in both. So pervasive is this disorder that not only
is true life and a just society not to be found among the kingdoms of this earth, but the beneficence of an orderly nature is
likewise disturbed" (Wright, *The Biblical Doctrine of Man in
Society*, 35).

Humans are not the "good" creatures God created. Human
"existence-in-opposition" to God openly manifests itself in particular acts of rebellion and disobedience. "Every inclination
(*yeṣer*) of the thoughts of their hearts was only evil continually"
(Gen. 6:5). Nature is under a curse because of human sin (Gen.
3:17-19). We do not live in an ideal world or a world of serene

communion and beatitude. Our human experience is not a matter of constant blessings. Appalling evidences of disturbances can only call forth the question of *unde* (whence?).

Christoph Barth spoke of "the Scandal of Human Rebellion." The world is distorted and depraved by human rebellion. God created everything perfect. Humanity revolted against its Creator at the very outset. The record in Genesis 3—11 interweaves confessions of sin into the story of achievement. In Genesis 3 rebellion is a bold attempt to make God's commandment a means of repression. If the man and his wife ate of the "forbidden fruit," they thought they would be like God, no longer subject to His supremacy. In the story of the flood the whole of humanity was corrupt (Gen. 6:5). "The people of Sodom were wicked, great sinners against the Lord" (Gen. 13:13; compare 18:20). "Violence and sexual perversion gave evidence of the incurable decay of humanity" (*God With Us*, 32).

According to Barth, "Human rebellion is a baffling event" (*God With Us*, 33). Biblical accounts do not try to explain it. "Rebellion against the Creator will always be unexpected, unfounded, unreasonable, inexcusable, and unjustified. If God created all things perfectly, there can be no explanation, no acceptable reason, for sin" (*God With Us*, 33]. If we ask whether the Creator could have prevented this human fiasco of revolt against God, we should answer that God purposed to create voluntary partners and not robots that must respond automatically to His will and command.

If the creation of nature and humanity originally were good and now are "bad" or "evil," how and when did the change come? How did nature and humans move from "good" to "evil"? The classical answer of the Christian church to that question is "the fall" or "original sin," but the Old Testament never uses these terms. Actually, the Old Testament seldom speaks of sin in theoretical or theological terms. It refers to sins committed at some particular place, at some particular time, and by some particular person. "But we seldom find theological reflection on 'sin' as a religious phenomenon of the utmost complexity" (von Rad, *Old Testament Theology I*, 154). Eichrodt said that when the Old Testament speaks of sin, the chief emphasis falls on the current concrete expression of it in individual acts.

Therefore "the question of the origin of sin is forced into the background" (*Theology of the Old Testament II*, 401).

The Old Testament contains one narrative (Gen. 3) that tells of a decisive turning point in the lives of the first human couple, by which the history of mankind became the history of sin. Von Rad said that in the great hamartiology in Genesis 3—11 "sin broke in and spread like an avalanche." The Old Testament tells how sin began and continued to increase within the human race, generation after generation. However, it does not pinpoint the source of the entrance of sin into the world other than in the free choice of Eve and Adam to disobey God at the prompting of a snake. The Old Testament does not say that the snake was the devil, Satan, or the source of sin. It does not blame God for human sin, although Adam seems to have had some thoughts along those lines (Gen. 3:12). The ultimate source of sin in the Old Testament remains a riddle (a mystery).

Although the Old Testament does not call the snake (or serpent) the devil or Satan, the New Testament does. Twice the Book of Revelation speaks of "the great dragon . . ., that ancient serpent, who is called the Devil and Satan" (Rev. 12:9; 20:2). It seems that the writer combined the roles of the serpent in Genesis 3 and the role of the sea monster (Leviathan), chaos (Ps. 74:14; Dan. 7:19-22). The beast, monster, or devil makes war on the saints and is cast down to do his destruction on earth (Rev. 11:7; 12:1-9) (see the discussion of Leviathan and the sea monsters in chap. 5).

Zimmerli said that the Old Testament gives no answer to the basic question of how evil came into the world. "In common with the rest of the Old Testament, it does not make the slightest attempt to take refuge in a dualistic or pluralistic universe. Guilt is left to stand unexplained as guilt, in all its harshness" (*Old Testament Theology in Outline*, 169). Two essential statements on the subject are utterly clear from the Old Testament story in Genesis 3: (1) evil does not come from God; and (2) evil is subject to God's power. Therefore dualism is ruled out as an explanation for the source of sin (Eichrodt, *Theology of the Old Testament II*, 406; Hamilton, "The Book of Genesis 1-17," 188; G. Wenham, *Genesis 1-15*, 72-73).

Brevard Childs noted that Old Testament scholars are divided on how to interpret the canonical function of Genesis 1—11. Von Rad interpreted the function of these chapters as portraying a history of increasing alienation from God or "an avalanche." A turning point is reached with the call of Abraham. For von Rad, "the election of Israel provides the perspective from which the universal history of divine judgment and mercy toward human sinfulness is viewed in Genesis" (Childs, *Old Testament Theology in a Canonical Context*, 225).

Claus Westermann argued that these chapters (1—11) do not move on a horizontal plane, with an increasing intensity of sin until the election of Abraham. They move on a vertical God-humans axis. They treat the universal reality of human existence as under threat and limitation. "For Westermann there is no primeval age of innocence, nor a 'fall,' but only a portrayal of the ontological problem of human existence as one of frailty and limitation" (Childs, *Old Testament Theology in a Canonical Context*, 226; Westermann, *Elements of Old Testament Theology*, 94-98, 118-119).

Childs agreed that Israel's primeval history (Gen. 1-11) should not be read as merely an aetiology of Israel's election, but he asserted that Westermann's attempt to substitute an ontological interpretation of Genesis 1-11 raises a host of theological questions.

There is no biblical basis for interpreting the threat in these chapters as "the result of being human." Rather, the point of Genesis 1-3 is to contest the ontological character of human sinfulness. "Mankind was not created in alienation from God, his fellows, or himself. The theological function of a period of innocence is to testify to a harmony in God's creation at the beginning which overcame the threat of non-being in the presence of God. It also bears witness to the eschatological restoration of God's new creation in which all threats will have been conquered" (Childs, *Old Testament Theology in a Canonical Context*, 226).

33. The Effects of Sin

A. The Effects of Adam's Sin

A discussion of sin in the Old Testament should include the effects of Adam's sin and the effects of the sins of individuals and societies. The Old Testament says nothing about how Adam's sin affected his descendants. In fact, Adam is only mentioned four times in the Old Testament after Genesis 5 (Deut. 32:8; 1 Chron. 1:1; Job 31:33; Hos. 6:7). Two of these references probably should be read "men" rather than "Adam" (Deut. 32:8; Hos. 6:7).

Although nothing is said about how Adam's sin affected his descendants, Genesis 3 does speak of consequences of the first sin for the participants. The serpent is cursed because of its part in humanity's sin. Consequences (not a curse) also ensue for the woman and the man as the result of their sin. Shame, guilt, and fear come on both Adam and Eve after their sin (Gen. 3:11).

The specific consequences of sin for the woman were pain in childbirth and a desire for and subjection to her husband. Lifelong toil in order to make a living from the cursed ground was the consequence of sin for the man. All of nature is cursed because of the first sin. God drove the first man and woman from the garden of Eden. Their return to that paradise was forever blocked by a divine power (Gen. 3:24). Now life, not only for Adam and Eve but for every person, must be lived outside the garden. Since the garden furnished the only access to the tree of life, human life must end inevitably in death (Gen. 3:22-23).

Victor Hamilton noted that death is not listed as one of the consequences of Adam's sin in Genesis 3:17-19. The consequences of Adam's sin is the theme of the larger context of 3:17-19, but in these verses the consequences for Adam's sin is toilsome work for a lifetime. "The penalty for Adam's disobedience and Cain's fratricide is not death but expulsion and wandering" ("The Book of Genesis 1—17," 203-204; compare G. Wenham, *Genesis 1—15*, 83, 89-91).

The Old Testament has no dogmatic or philosophical explanation of how the sin of the first couple affected their descendants. It simply tells the story of succeeding generations as a story of sin. The first son of Adam and Eve murdered his brother (Gen. 4:8). Scripture contains some indications that Cain's sin did not consist merely of his outward act of violence; the locus of sin was found in his anger against his brother (Gen. 4:5-7). The word *chata'* "sin" occurs here first in the Old Testament. The consequence of Cain's sin is seen in his fear of and alienation from his fellows. Lamech added bigamy to the growing lists of sins (Gen. 4:19).

By the time of Noah, God saw that "every inclination (*yeṣer*) of the thoughts of their hearts was only evil continually" (Gen. 6:5). The earth was corrupt and filled with violence (Gen. 6:11-12). God sent the flood to destroy the human race as judgment on human sins, but that did not solve the sin problem. After the flood He again saw that "the inclination of the human heart is evil from youth" (Gen. 8:21), implying that sin is universal. Noah and his family were not without sin; they were not spared because they were sinless. Noah is called "perfect" (Gen. 6:9), but the word *tāmîm* "perfect" or "blameless" does not mean "sinless." It means "to be whole."

A number of Old Testament passages have been used as "proof-texts" for the universality of sin and even for the dogma that sin is hereditary (for example, 1 Kings 8:46; 2 Chron. 6:36; Job 14:4; 25:4; Pss. 51:5; 58:3; Prov. 20:9; Eccl. 7:20; Isa. 48:8). Wheeler Robinson said, "To speak of inherited sinfulness in the case of any of these passages, including Ps. 51:5, is not justified by historical exegesis; probably no more is intended than what Isaiah says (6:5): 'I am a man of unclean lips'" (*The Christian Doctrine of Man*, 58).

H. J. Kraus probably had it right: "The prayer in Psalm 51 speaks of the original primeval tendency to sin, 'Behold, I was brought forth in iniquity, and in sin did my mother conceive me' (Ps. 51:5). Statements of this sort cannot be understood either causally as biologically inherited sin, nor in terms of sexual morality. . . . They recognize the power of evil to corrupt humans from the very beginning (compare Gen. 8:21; Job 14:4; 15:15f.; 25:4; Ps. 143:2; John 3:6)" (*Theology of the Psalms*, 156-57; see Marvin Tate, *Psalms 51-100*, 18-19, for a discussion of different possible interpretations of Ps. 51:5).

Although the Old Testament says nothing about a doctrine of original sin in the sense of guilt transmitted from Adam, it is well aware of a native human bias toward evil. Some passages indicate that during certain periods of Old Testament history, children were punished for the sins of their father (Ex. 20:5; 34:7; Lev. 26:39; Num. 14:18; Josh. 7:24; 2 Sam. 21:1-6). Perhaps these passages can be best explained on the basis of Israel's view of "corporate personality" or social solidarity. In a sense, the individual in ancient Israel was subordinate to this group. However, the individual was never subordinated to a group to the extent that the person was not responsible for personal acts. Other passages emphasize the independence of the individual from the group (see Deut. 24:16; 2 Kings 14:6; Jer. 31:29; Ezek. 18).

A. C. Knudson said that the uncleanness of the people or race to which one belonged was regarded as permeating one's own life. How this was done is not explained. Nowhere in the Old Testament is there any account of the origin of the native human inclination to evil. "This inclination is simply accepted as a fact, a fact revealed by observation and introspection" (*The Religious Teachings of the Old Testament*, 265).

Later Jewish and Christian writers developed many theories about how Adam's sin affected the human race. Second Esdras (written sometime before A.D. 100) makes several references to Adam's sin and its effect on his descendants.

"For the first Adam, burdened with an evil heart, transgressed and was overcome, as were also all who were descended from him. Thus the disease became permanent; the law was in the hearts of the people along with the evil root; but what was good departed, and the evil remained" (2 Esdras 3:21-22).

"For a grain of evil seed was sown in Adam's heart from the beginning, and how much ungodliness it has produced until now—and will produce until the time of threshing comes!" (2 Esdras 4:30).

"O Adam, what have you done? For though it was you who sinned, the fall was not yours alone, but ours also who are your descendants" (2 Esdras 7:48, 118). (Verses 36-105 formerly missing, have been restored to the text. Verse 48 is numbered 118 in the restored version.)

The New Testament view of sin is essentially the same as that of the Old Testament. All of the old terms are here (de Vries, *The Achievements of Biblical Religion*, 17-71). The terms "fall" and "original sin" do not occur in the New Testament. Paul did say that sin and death came into the world through Adam (Rom. 5:12-14; 1 Cor. 15:21-22).

Hamilton suggested that Paul drew on the Adam-Christ typology because it provided material in debating three mis-

understandings of resurrection: (1) death does not mean extermination, for there will be a resurrection; (2) death does not
mean, as the Greeks claimed, the release of the immortal
soul—the body will be resurrected; (3) the resurrected body
will be a spiritual body (1 Cor. 15:45-49). (See Hamilton, "The
Book of Genesis 1-17," 217.)

Paul claimed that sin is universal (Rom. 3:23; 5:12); that all
have sinned and are "without excuse" (Rom. 1:20; 2:1; compare
1 John 1:8). James 1:13-15 says, "No one, when tempted,
should say, 'I am being tempted by God'; for God cannot be
tempted by evil and he himself tempts no one. But one is
tempted by one's own desire, being lured and enticed by it;
then when that desire has conceived, it gives birth to sin, and
that sin, when it is fully grown, gives birth to death."

The doctrines of the "fall" and "original sin" were developed
fully by Patristic scholars in the eastern and western branches
of the early church. In the East, Adam's sin was explained as
the primary type of human sin. In the West it became its foun-
tainhead (Robinson, *The Christian Doctrine of Man*, 165).
Both Irenaeus and Tertullian stressed "the unity of the race,
in some sense, in Adam." Ambrose was the first to speak of
humans "having incurred guilt in Adam" (Robinson, *The
Christian Doctrine of Man*, 168).

Augustine said, "Thus the fall of man is also understood as
a sliding down to a lower level of being, so that sin must not
be understood as a lack, but as a degradation in existence"
(cited by Westermann, *Elements of Old Testament Theology*,
95). Augustine's words express a full-blown doctrine of the
"fall" and its effects on the human race. Augustine's statement
says more than do the Old Testament and New Testament on
the subject (Zimmerli, *Old Testament Theology in Outline*,
168).

Wheeler Robinson said that Genesis 3 gives no suggestion
that human nature is changed by the act of disobedience—still
less, that Adam handed on a corrupted nature to his children.
The disobedience of a divine command through desire for that
which God withheld from him contains a clear, deep, ethical
meaning. "Man gains what he desires, and passes from the
naked innocence of the child to the knowledge and powers of
maturity; but the price he has paid makes his civilization

accursed since progress in civilization proves to be progress also in evil" (*The Christian Doctrine of Man*, 59).

Eichrodt understood that Genesis 3 speaks of a decisive event, by which God's plan for humanity was frustrated and human history came to be stamped with the brand of enmity toward God.

> *This event has the character of a 'Fall,' that is, of a falling out of the line of development willed by God*, and, as the subsequent narrative shows, exerts a determining influence on the spiritual attitude of all men. The teaching of the Church on the subject of original sin has rightly fixed on this passage to show that the real seriousness of enslavement to sin consists in the fact that sin is not simply an "occasional act . . . always arising out of the wrong decision of the moment, but . . . a perverted tendency of our nature" (*Theology of the Old Testament II*, 406-407).

Vriezen said that the Christian interpretation of the Paradise narrative as the story of the fall of humanity, already taught by Paul in Romans 5 and afterwards elaborated into the doctrine of original sin, is not unsound. Once a person admits sin into his life, "it spreads rapidly and is transmitted from one generation to the rest. He has, therefore, come very close to the conception of original sin" (*An Outline of Old Testament Theology*, 416).

G. Ernest Wright indicated that the Christian treatment of the "fall" of humanity has continually been in danger of losing the active, living, and vital relationship between God and individuals, substituting instead a static view of human nature as totally depraved and alienated from God. This substitution is not totally wrong, but it turns our attention away "from vital and responsible self-understanding and active decision to intellectual cogitation and rational argument" (*God Who Acts*, 92).

Is humanity totally or only partially depraved? Is the difficulty due to an innate moral corruption and tendency to sin, or is it due to a person's misuse of free choice in following the bad example of Adam? (Augustine vs. Pelagius). Is a person predestined to salvation or destruction, the recipient or nonrecipient of irresistible grace? (Calvinism vs. Armenianism). Wright said that the Bible gives no clear, distinct, and incontrovertible answers to these questions because they represent an intellectual cogitation on a person as a "substantive" and make the dynamic movement of the Bible a formalized ratio-nal paradox which the mind naturally tries to resolve by tak-ing one side or the other (*God Who Acts*, 92-93).

The nature of humanity can be seen in what a person does. Many human acts, beginning with Adam, are acts of rebellion against God. The culminating act of rebellion can be seen in the crucifixion of Christ. "The sin and death in Adam have placed a barrier between man and God which Christ as medi-ator has removed. It is this act of God's grace which restores the original creation (e.g. Rom. 8:29; Col. 3:10; 1 Cor. 15:49; 2 Cor. 3:18). Consequently, the Cross is the only adequate sym-bol of Biblical faith" (Wright, *God Who Acts*, 91).

Many church creeds and confessions have addressed the question of the "fall" and "original sin." Most Protestant state-ments absolve God of any blame and put the onus on human-ity. The Belgic Confession, for example, states that nothing happens in this world without God's appointment; neverthe-less, "God neither is the Author of nor can be charged with the sins which are committed" (Berkouwer, *Sin*, 29).

The New Hampshire Confession of Faith says about the fall of man: "We believe that man was created in holiness, under the law of his maker; but by voluntary transgression fell from that holy and happy state; in consequence of which all man-kind are now sinners, not by constraint, but by choice; and by nature inclined to evil; and therefore under just condemnation to eternal ruin, without defense or excuse" (H. Leon McBeth, *A Sourcebook for Baptist Heritage*, 503-504).

B. Consequences of Sin for the Individual

What are the consequences of sin for the individual in the Old Testament? The first consequence or result of sin is guilt. Guilt can be a sense of inner disturbance, alienation, and estrangement. This was the experience of Adam and Eve (Gen. 3:10). They were ashamed and hid themselves. David's heart smote him after he numbered the people (2 Sam. 24:10). The psalmist said;

> While I kept silence, my body wasted away
> through my groaning all day long.
> For day and night your hand was
> heavy upon me;

> my strength was dried up as
> by the heat of summer.
> Selah
> (Ps. 32:3-4)

This sense of guilt comes only to those who are personally aware of their sins. The Old Testament speaks of "unwitting sins" which people may commit without being aware of them at the time (Lev. 4; 6). However, the Old Testament makes it very clear that the sinner is guilty and is held responsible for any and all offenses, even without being aware of a personal sin (Lev. 5:17).

A person may sin and not have a sense of shame or guilt because of a basic flaw in one's character brought on by a rejection of God.

> Fools say in their hearts,
> "There is no God."
> They are corrupt, they do
> abominable deeds;
> there is no one who does good.
> (Pss. 14:1; 53:1)

> (Woe to) you who call evil good
> and good evil.
> (Isa. 5:20)

> They have held fast to deceit,
> they have refused to return.
> I have given heed and listened,
> but they do not speak honestly;
> no one repents of wickedness,
> saying, "What have I done!"
> All of them turn to their own course,
> like a horse plunging headlong
> into battle.
> (Jer. 8:5b-6)

The Old Testament does not have a special word for guilt. It often uses the same word for the act of sin and for the penalty of sin. Hebrew thought, for the most part, did not distinguish between the sin act and the penalty involved (Eichrodt, *Theology of the Old Testament* II, 413). Von Rad explained this phenomenon as a part of the "synthetic view of life," since personal action and ensuing personal results were not yet understood as two separate and independent things. Instead, the Old Testament presupposes the closest possible correspondence between action and fate. This means that "there is absolutely nothing in the thought of the Old Testament which by and large corresponds to the separation which we make between sin and penalty. The best proof of this is that both *chata'* and *'awôn* can stand for sin as act and for the consequences of sin, that is, for penalty" (*Old Testament Theology I*, 265-66).

It is true that some words can refer to evil acts and punishment, sin and judgment, but that is not true of all Hebrew words for sin. The root *'wl* in all its forms is not such a word. It always refers to acts of injustice or iniquity and never to calamitous events, consequences, or punishment in the way that such words as *'awôn*, *'awen*, or *ra'* can. In several contexts it is explicitly stated that God never does 'evil,' *'awel* or *'awlâ* (Deut. 32:4; 2 Chron. 19:7; Job 34:10).

Although Hebrew had no special word for guilt, the term *'āšam*, is often translated "guilt" and "guilt-offering." It and its cognates are translated "guilt" or "guilty" less than twenty times in the Old Testament (C. R. Smith, *The Biblical Doctrine of Sin*, 16). The term *'awôn* which is most often translated "guilt," implies the element of "a perverted attitude" (Eichrodt, *Theology of the Old Testament* II, 416).

The first result of an individual's sin is guilt or shame. A second result is punishment or judgment. "Every fault brings punishment." This is necessary because "the offense against God must be repaired, the contagious poison of sin must be eliminated, and the sinner must be penalized" (Jacob, *Theology of the Old Testament*, 287). Yahweh is presented in the Old Testament as a God "who will by no means clear the guilty" (Ex. 34:7; Num. 14:18) and who will "never forget any of their deeds" (Amos 8:7). At least in premonarchical times, Israel believed that sin always entailed consequences, some of which came visibly on the sinner. Some consequences involved a "radiation of evil" which, when set in motion, would sooner or later inevitably turn against the sinner and the community (see Amos 1:3,6,9,11,13).

Many Old Testament scholars agree that God's judgment on sin is a major element in the Old Testament, but considerable recent discussion concerns the method of that judgment. Is God's judgment direct or dynamic, immanent or transcendent?

Does God bring judgment on the sinner in a unique, unexpected transcendent manner, or does He confront the sinner through a series of effects and consequences, "built in" to the natures of sin and personhood?

Klaus Koch in a now-famous essay, "Gibt es ein Vergeltungsdogma im Alten Testament?" argued that the Old Testament contains no doctrine of retribution. Yahweh does not function as judge in this context. No judicial norms or prescribed punishments determine the punishment. Judgment or punishment is rooted directly in the sin in a relationship of deed and its consequence. Koch spoke of the fate one creates for himself by his action ("menschlicher Tat entspringendes Schicksal"). This does not mean that Koch considered the process to be purely immanental or mechanical. "Yahweh is actively involved in the process. He is the one who makes the connection" (Patrick Miller, *Sin and Judgment in the Prophets*, 5).

Vriezen noted that Koch opposed the idea of a religious concept of retribution and said that von Rad largely agrees with him. Vriezen does not deny that the Old Testament often suggests that sin carries its own punishment, but this view is not the predominant note in the Old Testament. "The views of the two scholars (Koch and von Rad) mentioned above leave the law of the covenant out of account too much" (Vriezen, *Outline of Old Testament Theology*, 309, n. 1).

Berkouwer criticized Koch's theory that the Old Testament has no doctrine of retribution. Koch's view of the Old Testament accent on a "fate-determining sphere of action" rather than a stress on the retributive act of God, as we find in the Septuagint, is forced. This is evident, according to Berkouwer, in Koch's own article, particularly in his discussion of the several texts from Proverbs. "The fact that he finds the 'age-old view' also in Paul's 'sowing and reaping' (p. 36) cannot possibly support his conception. His construction is unsatisfying because of its exclusive emphasis on the 'fatalizing act'" (Berkouwer, *Sin*, 39-40, n. 41).

Berkouwer said that total inadequacy in Koch's view is his posing a dilemma: either reprisal *or* an immanent dynamic, transcendent *or* immanent. It is simply impossible to set the dynamic activity of sin and God's judicial activity alongside each other in an attitude of competition (Berkouwer, *Sin*, 375).

Marion Frank Meador said the question of the relation of sin and punishment has taken on new vigor since Klaus Koch raised the issue (1955) of whether there is a doctrine of retribution in the Old Testament. Koch did not find the doctrine there. Rewards and punishment are not given according to some previously established norms. Rather, the consequences of an action are built in to the flow of the action itself, in a kind of *Tun-Ergehen* such as "sowing and harvesting" (Prov. 11:18; Hos. 8:7; 10:12-13). (See Meador, "The Motif of God as Judge," 166.) Meador said that Koch's thesis is not supportable and opted for a modified retribution model for the relationship between sin and punishment. However, he insisted that "God is the Supreme Judge and his judgments are always appropriate" ("The Motif of God as Judge," 172).

Many Old Testament scholars have observed the *correspondence* between the sin and its punishment in the Old Testament. Eichrodt called attention to "the profound thought . . . that *offence and punishment ought to correspond to one another*" (*Theology of the Old Testament II*, 426). He said that the prophets made it their business to convey to their audiences that punishment is the annulment of a wholly personal relationship between God and humanity, "thus replacing an external consonance of transgression and retribution with *an inner correspondence*, and enabling them for the first time to understand, and inwardly affirm, punishment as the necessary consequence of sin" (*Theology of the Old Testament II*, 452).

Patrick Miller, after discussing many Old Testament passages dealing with the "correspondence" pattern of sin and judgment, concluded his study with a section on the "theology of judgment." He said that no single monolithic notion of judgment dominates the Old Testament. On the contrary Israel's experience of judgment was multifaceted and multi-dimensional. Miller noted that the passages he had dealt with showed a widespread correspondence between sin and punishment. "But many passages do not demonstrate such correspondence" (*Sin and Judgment in the Prophets*, 121).

Miller argued that Koch's view must be modified. Punishment growing out of a crime can be understood within a judicial context. The Old Testament often speaks of God as Judge. Even though correspondences and even causal aspects exist between the sin and judgment, the link is made by Yahweh's decision to punish because of disobedience. The dimension of correspondence "sets at the center of Yahweh's judgment the affirmation of *appropriate justice*. What Yahweh requires in all human beings is *mispat*, "justice" (Miller, *Sin and Judgment in the Prophets*, 136).

The purpose of the judgment of God in the Old Testament is more than punishment. It has a purifying purpose like a refining fire (Mal. 3:2-3); a correcting purpose like the use of a plumbline (2 Kings 21:10-12); and a renewing purpose like the wiping of a dish (2 Kings 21:10-12). God is always free to extend mercy. Mercy is not the cancellation of punishment, but it removes from it the aspect of irrevocable condemnation. The pain of childbirth gives way to the promise of a new life. The mark on Cain is a protective symbol to guard his life from those who might seek to do to him what he did to Abel.

Punishment or judgment is intended to set right again and within, to bring back to the right road those who have turned aside. Jacob said, "What Yahweh seeks to obtain by punishment is the sinner's return and the possibility of a new life. Conversion is the indispensable condition of forgiveness; without it all of the means of forgiveness which God has made available run the risk of being inoperative" (*Theology of the Old Testament*, 289).

34. The Removal of Sin

The Old Testament language for the removal of sin is as rich and varied as its vocabulary for sin. Much of the language is concerned with what God does with sin.

What does God do with sin?

1) He removes it, turns it aside, puts it off like dirty, filthy clothes.

> Now that this has touched your lips,
> . . . your sin is blotted out."
> (Isa. 6:7)

> "Take off his filthy clothes . . .
> See, I have taken your guilt away.
> (Zech. 3:4; compare 2 Sam. 12:13)

2) He lifts it up and/or takes it away.

> The LORD, the LORD, a God merciful and gracious . . . ,
> forgiving iniquity and transgression and sin.
> (Ex. 34:6-7)

3) He blots it out.

> I, I am He/who blotts out your
> transgressions for my own sake.
> (Isa. 43:25; compare Pss. 51:1,9;
> 109:14; Isa. 44:22; Jer. 18:23)

4) He washes and cleanses it.

> Wash me thoroughly from my iniquity,
> and cleanse me from my sin.
> (Ps. 51:2; compare 51:7; Jer. 33:8)

5) He unsins, de-sins, or purges it.

> Purge me with hyssop.
> (Ps. 51:7)

6) He covers it.

> "Happy are those whose transgression is forgiven,
> /whose sin is covered.
> (Ps. 32:1; compare Ps. 85:3)

7) He expiates it.

> I will establish my covenant with you,
> and you shall know that I am the LORD,
> in order that you may remember and be confounded,
> and never open your mouth again because of your shame,
> when I forgive for all that you have done,
> says the LORD God.
> (Ezek. 16:62-63; compare Isa. 6:7; Pss. 65:3; 79:9)

8) He forgets sins or does not remember them.

> I will not remember your sins.
> (Isa. 43:25)

9) He casts them behind his back and into the sea.

> For you have cast all my sins behind your back.
> (Isa. 38:17)

> You will cast all our sins/into the depths of the sea.
> (Mic. 7:19)

10) He tramples them.

> He will tread our iniquities under foot.
> (Mic. 7:19)

11) He forgives them.

> "Bless the Lord, O my soul,
> and forget not all his benefits,
> who is always forgiving your iniquity.
> (Ps. 103:2-3; compare Neh. 9:17; Ps. 130:4;
> Isa. 55:7; Jer. 5:1; 31:34; 33:8; 50:20)

These are some of the many ways God dealt with sin in the Old Testament.

The Old Testament presents many ways people tried to get rid of sin, none of which were completely successful. The earliest attempts to get rid of sin in the Old Testament may be called "primitive," or "relics" of an earlier dynamistic age (Eichrodt, *Theology of the Old Testament II*, 443). Here the removal of sin is accomplished by purely external procedures which operate automatically. Sometimes the sinful condition is removed by washing with water (Num. 8:7; 19:9,21; 31:23; Lev. 14:5-6); sometimes it is burned away by fire (Num. 31:22-23; Isa. 6:6). Sometimes an animal or a bird carries away sin (Lev. 14:7,53; 16:21-22); in the most serious conditions, the sinner is cut off from the community or put to death (Lev. 20:6,10,11,14). These "primitive" methods of getting rid of sin show the people's awareness of sin and their attempt to find a solution for it.

Certain passages in the Old Testament speak of the need for God's anger to be "turned aside." The most striking example is 1 Samuel 26:19, where sacrifice becomes the means to avert divine anger. David says, "If it is the LORD who has stirred you up against me, may he accept an offering; but if it is mortals, may they be cursed before the LORD, for they have driven me out today from my share in the heritage of the LORD, saying, 'Go, serve other gods.'" Vriezen noted that the word "atonement" is not used in the text, "but the idea is present" (*Outline of the Old Testament*, 267). The idea of sacrifice turning away the wrath of God may be seen in the words, "When the Lord smelled the pleasing odor, he said in his heart, 'I will never again curse the ground because of humankind'" (Gen. 8:21).

Mesha, the king of Moab, sacrificed his eldest son (presumably to Chemosh) to turn away what he interpreted to be the wrath of the god of Moab (2 Kings 3:27). Human sacrifice was not unknown in the Old Testament. Abraham was told to sacrifice Isaac before God substituted a ram for him (Gen. 22:12-13). Some scholars understand Exodus 22:29-30 to say that at one time the firstborn son was to be sacrificed. Jepthath sacrificed his daughter to fulfill his vow to the Lord (Judg. 11:30-35). Heil of Bethel may have sacrificed two of his sons when he built Jericho (1 Kings 16:34). Although the law made it clear that child sacrifice was wrong (Ex. 34:20; Deut. 18:10), two kings in Judah, Ahaz and Manasseh, offered their sons as sacrifices and were condemned for that pagan act (2 Kings 16:3; 21:6).

Sometimes the Old Testament uses the idea of propitiation-expiation to speak of removing God's anger. This is a very difficult subject to interpret in the Old Testament. The Hebrew word *ḥāllâ* is used sometimes to mean "to stroke the face" (of God), "to entreat" (Him), thus to "soften Him" and make Him favorable (1 Sam. 13:12; 1 Kings 13:6).

The word seems to mean "propitiate" in three places in the Old Testament (Zech. 7:2; 8:22; Mal. 1:9). C. H. Dodd said that in these three passages in the Septuagint, we meet for the first time unmistakable examples of ordinary classical meaning of *exhilaskesthai*, "to propitiate." In every other use of the term the translators used some other Greek word. Dodd thought that something exceptional about these three verses accounted for the use of this Greek word.

The first and third passages (Zech. 7:2; Mal. 1:9) have a distinct tone of contempt: it is useless to think of "placating" Yahweh! Thus it seems clear that the translators have deliberately used the term *exhilaskesthai* with a note of contempt for its standard meaning in pagan usage, as unworthy of the God of Israel. In the second passage (Zech. 8:22) it is pagan peoples (not Israel) who come to "propitiate" Yahweh (Dodd, *The Bible and the Greeks*, 86-87). In any case, Vriezen was probably right in seeing these passages as using simple and very human concepts of atonement with the belief that God could be swayed with gifts and personal favors. If that is the case, people who held that idea in Israel must have been a small minority (*Outline of the Old Testament*, 268).

A second way humans attempt to get rid of sin is through the cult (sacrifices). The sacrifices, however, could not atone for all sins. No sacrifice could atone for some murders (Num. 35:31-32), sins against the covenant (Ten Commandments), or sins of a high hand (Num. 15:22-31; 1 Sam. 3:14). Unwitting sins and less serious sins could be atoned on the conditions that they were confessed when they became known and that appropriate restitution was made (Lev. 5:14-19; 19:20-22; Num. 5:5-8). It may not be correct to use the word "atone" for "unwitting sins" (Jacob, *Theology in the Old Testament*, 293).

Hartmut Gese said that "atonement does not mean forgiveness of sin and errors that can be made good. Everyone should look out for themselves in such cases. Restitution, where it is possible, must obviously be made. To atone does not mean to bring reconciliation, to accept forgiveness for what can be made good again. It means to snatch one away from a death that is deserved" (*Essays on Biblical Theology*, 99).

The word "atonement" is one of the few theological terms which derives basically from Anglo-Saxon. It means "a making at one" and points to a process of bringing those who are estranged into a unity (Morris, "Atonement," 107). Frank Stagg notes that the biblical idea of atonement is more than a meeting of the minds. It is the restoration of a relationship (*New Testament Theology*, 162-63). The words "atone" or "atonement" occur several times in the Old Testament in the King James Version and Revised Standard Version, but only one time in the New Testament (Rom. 5:11, KJV) although the idea is constantly present. W. T. Conner said that "atonement" is not a proper translation of any word found in the Greek New Testament (*The Gospel of Redemption*, 76).

"Atonement" translates the Hebrew root *kpr*. The root *kpr* occurs as a verb ninety-one times in the Old Testament, sixty of those occurrences related to sacrifice in the priestly materials. Scholars do not agree as to the precise etymology of *kpr*. Although Old Testament sacrifices served as "gifts" and/or avenues of communion with God, "the whole sacrificial cult is dominated by the idea of atonement" (Vriezen, *Outline of Old*

Testament Theology, 261). The sacrificial act is in miniature the actual renewal of a relationship.

During much of her history Israel had a day—the Day of Atonement (Lev. 16:1-34; Num. 29:7-11; Ezek. 45:18-21)—in which atonement was made for priests, people, and the sanctuary. Only on this day was the high priest (and only the high priest) permitted to enter the holy of holies. He was to offer for himself a sin offering (Lev. 16:6); confess the sins of the people on the head of a scapegoat (vv. 7-10); and cleanse the sanctuary (vv. 18-19). Much of this ritual gives evidence of being "an extremely ancient practice" (Clements, *Leviticus*, 45).

The Day of Atonement had a special place in Israel's religion. "More than any other festival of the year it affirmed a profound sense of sin and a realization that only God could deal with this. In a special way it demonstrated that God's ministers were in no way exempt from the power of sin" (Clements, *Leviticus*, 46).

The writer of Hebrews said that the outer part of the tabernacle proper symbolized that the way into the holy of holies had not yet been opened (Heb. 9:8). When Christ came as high priest, He entered the holy of holies—not with the blood of bulls and goats, but with His own blood securing an eternal redemption (Heb. 9:11-12).

In Christian theology the term "atonement" has been used almost exclusively to refer to the death of Jesus Christ on the cross "to atone" for human sins and to reconcile sinners to God. A sharp distinction is often made between "reconciliation" or "propitiation" (*Versohnung, katallage*) and "expiation" or "cover" (*Suhne, hilasmos*). This distinction can be found in places in the Old Testament, but not with the word *kipper*. God is always the subject of the verb *kîppēr*, never the object when it is used in relation to Him. He is the "atoner" and not the "atonee" in the Old Testament (Whale, *Christian Doctrine*, 92).

According to Whale, there is no vicarious suffering, no penal substitution in Old Testament sacrifices. "The key-word is not the misleading word 'propitiation,' nor even the difficult and ambiguous word 'expiation.' There is no thought of propitiating an angry God or of paying him compensation for wrong done to him. God is never the object of the Hebrew verb meaning 'to propitiate' or 'to expiate.' God himself 'expiates' sin by purging or covering it in this his appointed way" (*Christian Doctrine*, 81).

C. H. Dodd noted that the "stock rendering" of *kîppēr* in the Septuagint is *hilaskesthai* or *exhilaskesthai* and their corresponding nouns. In classical and *koine* Greek outside the New Testament, *hilaskesthai* regularly has the meaning "placate," "propitiate," "appease," "make joyous or happy" with a personal object (*The Bible and the Greeks*, 82; compare Morris, *The Apostolic Preaching of the Cross*, 125-126). As a secondary meaning, *exhilaskesthai*, may mean "to propitiate," but in the Septuagint and New Testament the primary meaning is "to expiate." Morris said,

> It is a relief to know that we have solid grounds for our conviction that the God of the Bible is not a Being who can be propitiated after the fashion of a pagan deity. . . . The Bible writers have nothing to do with pagan conceptions of a capricious and vindictive deity, inflicting arbitrary punishments on offending worshippers, who must then bribe him back to a good mood by the appropriate offerings. Dodd's important work makes this abundantly clear (*The Apostolic Preaching of the Cross*, 129).

Dale Moody said that propitiation is a pagan religious concept that became a part of Christian vocabulary through the Latin translation of Romans 3:25; 1 John 2:2; 4:10. The Old Testament view of the holy love of God and the New Testament view of the work of God in Christ so modified the pagan term that the idea of reconciliation in the New Testament "is confined to man alone. God as the father of our Lord Jesus Christ is never described as either propitiated or reconciled. The problem is exclusively in man, and the solution is in God" (Moody, "Propitiation=Expiation," 14).

Other religions apart from Judaism and Christianity take it for granted that God is the one who by His nature requires to be reconciled. If we allow the consensus of other religions to influence us at this point, we shall most certainly be wrong. "This is one of the points where the danger of parallelism comes out very clearly. Christianity is not to be understood by the analogy of any other faith whatever. . . . It is God who reconciles, man who is reconciled" (Stewart, *Man in Christ*, 210-11).

The prophets had little confidence in sacrifice as a means of getting rid of sin. They spoke primarily of the necessity of "repentance" and "forgiveness" as the way to remove sin (Isa. 1:11; Hos. 6:6; Amos 5:23-24; Mic. 6:8). The prophets expressed disappointment over the people's unresponsiveness to appeals to repent.

What is repentance? What is forgiveness? Is repentance a necessary prerequisite for forgiveness? Many modern Old Testament scholars have minimized the place of the repentance motif in the preaching of the great prophets. Thomas Raitt said that although many scholars have affirmed that the call to repentance had a place of pivotal importance in the role of the prophet and in his theology, surprisingly few paid attention to the speech-form "call to repentance" in the words of the prophets ("The Prophetic Summons to Repentance," 30-48).

Twenty-four passages in the Old Testament may be classified as "announcements of judgment" because of a failure to repent (Isa. 6:10; 9:13-14; 30:15-16; Jer. 3:1,7,10; 5:3; 8:4-7; 9:5; 13:22; 15:7; 23:14; 25:3-4; 34:16; 45:5; Ezek. 3:19; Hos. 5:4; 7:10; 11:5; Amos 4:6,8,9,10,11), and twenty-eight passages as "summons to repentance" (2 Kings 17:13; 2 Chron. 30:6-9; Neh. 1:8-9; Isa. 1:19-20; 55:6-7; Jer. 3:12-13,14,22; 4:1-2,3-4,14; 7:3-7; 15:19; 18:11; 22:3-5; 25:5-6; 26:13; 31:21-22; 35:15; Ezek. 18:30-32; Joel 2:12-13; Amos 5:4-5,6-7,14-15; Jonah 3:7-9; Zeph. 2:1-3; Zech. 1:2-6; Mal. 3:7). The "call to repentance" is simply the call of the prophets for Israel to turn back to God.

In addition to the "call to repentance" speech-form, the repentance motif forms part of a number of narrative forms and the entreaty portion of prayers (Lev. 26:40; Deut. 4:30; 30:2,10; 1 Kings 8:33,35,47,48; 2 Kings 23:25; 2 Chron. 7:14; Neh. 9:26,29,35; Job 22:23; Pss. 7:12; 22:27; 78:34; Jer. 3:7,10; 26:4-6; 36:2-3,7-10; Zech. 1:6; Mal. 2:6).

In one place Raitt said that salvation is sometimes an act which creates repentance ("The Prophetic Summons to Repentance," 47; compare Isa. 44:22; Jer. 31:31-34; Ezek. 27:22-36) and that salvation comes at times without reference to the need for repentance (see Isa. 40:2; 43:25; Jer. 30:14-17; 33:8; Mic. 7:18-19). However, he concluded "Under the influence of the prophets, repentance came to great theological prominence, and down to the present it is theologically normative in both Judaism and Christianity that repentance necessarily precedes and often is followed by forgiveness" ("The Prophetic Summons to Repentance," 48).

What is repentance according to the Old Testament? Several Hebrew words express a variety of ideas, including a change of mind, a feeling of regret or remorse, and a "turning away from sin and back to God" (Quanbeck, "Repentance," 33). William Holladay made an exhaustive study of the Hebrew root *šûb* "turn." This root occurs unambiguously 1054 times in the Masoretic text, with both God and/or humans as the subject. Most uses are "secular" and simply mean "to turn back to or from something, someplace, or someone." Holladay insisted that the root means "to move all the way back to the point of departure" (*The Root Subh in the Old Testament*, 53).

Holladay believed that 164 of the 1054 occurrences of this root *šûb* may be classified as "covenant usages." By covenant uses he meant the expression of a change of loyalty on the part of Israel or God, each for the other (1 Kings 8:33; Jer. 4:1) (See *The Root Subh*, 116.) As with most themes, the Old Testament does not present us with the generalizations that can become a systematic doctrine of "repentance." One reason for this is that classic Hebrew has no noun for "repentance," and "where there is no vocabulary there can be no concepts. . . . The word *mĕšûba* 'repentance' is an abstraction from a later time" (*The Root Subh*, 157). Other Hebrew terms could be considered synonyms or parallels to *šûb*, such as *sûr* "turn aside," *pānâ* "to turn the face," and *nāḥam* "to be sorry" (*The Root Subh*, 155-156).

The noun *šûbâ* occurs one time in the Old Testament (Isa. 30:15), and the noun *tĕšûbâ* is used in the Old Testament (but only in the temporal sense). A noun form of *nāḥam* also occurs one time in the Old Testament, "repentance" or "compassion" (Hos. 13:14).

Jeremiah used the word *šûb* 111 times and illumines all the meanings of the root, "turning away," "turning back," "inward conversion and renewal." Repentance is a painful process: a circumcision of the heart, a plowing up of the fallow ground, a complete renunciation of idolatry, and a total return to God (Jer. 4:1-4). This means a radical transformation of life. The only alternative is ruin. Even when Jeremiah addressed the nation, he directed his strongest appeal to the individual: "Let each one of you" (Jer. 25:5; 26:3; 36:3,7). Jeremiah knew that the possibility of redemption would not remain open forever, and conversion "is *solely the work of God*, who makes the new heart in which inward obstinacy is overcome by obedient receptiveness" (Eichrodt, *Theology of the Old Testament II*, 468-469).

In the Old Testament people repent, and God forgives. A part of repentance is confession. Confession of sin in the Old Testament indicates that the sinner is aware of personal sins (Lev. 5:5) and is willing to turn away from them (Prov. 28:13; Dan. 9:4).

> Then I acknowledged my sin to you,
>   and I did not hide my iniquity;
>   I said, "I will confess my
>   transgressions to the LORD,"
> and you forgave the guilt of my sin.
>   *Selah*
>   (Ps. 32:5)
>
>   I confess my iniquity;
>   I am sorry for my sin.
>   (Ps. 38:18)

Since sin is an offense against God which results in a person's separation from God and a life of evil (Isa. 59:1-15), "sin can only be effaced by an act of forgiveness" (Jacob, *Theology of the Old Testament*, 290). What, then, is forgiveness, and how is it accomplished? Can forgiveness be bought with sacrifices or by a reformed life?

Three Hebrew words are translated "pardon" and/or "forgiveness" in the English versions of the Bible. They are *kipper*, *nāsaʾ* ("to lift up"), and *sālaḥ* (possibly "let go"). All three words are metaphors for the removal of sin. The first and third words are used only for God's forgiveness (Deut. 21:8; 2 Chron. 30:18; Ps. 78:38; Jer. 18:23).

Forgiveness is conditioned upon repentance, but repentance is no guarantee that God must or will forgive (Amos 5:15; Jonah 3:8; Zeph. 2:3). Norman Snaith said the modern attitude is that the restoration to full fellowship with God, which is the meaning of forgiveness, is a direct consequence of human repentance. God's forgiveness, however, is not auto-

matic upon human action. It is the "actual and personal immediate work of God" ("Forgiveness," 86).

Harry Emerson Fosdick said that when you hear someone
talking about forgiveness light-heartedly, as an easy matter,
you may be sure that the person is not forgiving sin but is con-
doning it. "To say that sin does not matter, to make light of it,
to take it easily, to be gracious and tolerant about it . . . is not
forgiveness. That is moral looseness. Sin does matter—tre-
mendously! To condone sin is easy; to forgive it is hard" ("Forgiveness of Sins," 192-193; see Moberly, "Punishment and
Forgiveness," 244).

W. A. Quanbeck emphasizes the freedom and sovereignty of
God in forgiveness in saying that the burning of the sacrifices
symbolized the transformation of the gift and its acceptance
by God. "This emphasized the fact that sacrifice is not a barter
transaction in which God forgives for a consideration, but that
sacrifice is effectual because God in his mercy chooses to
accept the offering as the offering of the worshiper's life. Sacrifice is not the purchase of forgiveness but the claiming of
God's promise of mercy" ("Forgiveness," 316; see Sakenfeld,
"The Problem of Divine Forgiveness in Numbers 14," 317-330).

Only God can forgive sins, but how and on what basis does
He forgive them? Eichrodt noted that the mechanical putting
away of sin by magic excludes forgiveness as a free act of God.
Also a legalistic understanding of guilt and punishment nar-
rows and externalizes it. "Where punishment is regarded as
compensation fitted to the offence, and may possibly even be
circumvented by voluntary works of supererogation, *forgiveness* is comprehensible *only as reduction or total remission of
punishment.* In this way God's action is bound up with God's
right to compensation" (*Theology of the Old Testament II*, 453).
Does God forgive because of human remorse over sins, or at a
person's confession of sins? Does God forgive with baptism?
Does God forgive as humans forgive?

The people of the Old Testament believed that God would
forgive—indeed, had forgiven—their sins (Pss. 65:3; 85:2,3;
106:6-47; Ezek. 16:63; 20:9,14,22). What did Israel understand
"the forgiveness of sins" to mean? How should we understand
it? R. C. Moberly said that when a child comes to a parent for
punishment and the parent refrains from penalty or reproach,

forgiveness means the remission of a penalty. This is the first and simplest form of forgiveness.

However, Moberly said that although the remission of penalty may be the first step in understanding forgiveness, it is not the last step. "The theology which allows itself to be entangled in a theory of forgiveness of which the leading character is remission of penalty, will by and by (as not a few attempts to explain the doctrine of atonement have shown) be landed in insoluble perplexities. Indeed. . . forgiveness cannot really mean as much as this without meaning more . . . the simple idea of not punishing is too negative and external to touch the real core of the matter" ("Punishment and Forgiveness," 243).

To define forgiveness as remission of penalty would blur all distinction of right and wrong. Remission of penalty requires an explanation and a justification. Remission of penalty can be good or bad. If it has no justification, it is immoral. God forgives iniquity, transgression, and sin; but He will not clear the guilty" (Ex. 34:6-7). God has His reasons and justification for forgiving sin.

Forgiveness is not the remission of a penalty; it is the restoration of a relationship. If we say that forgiveness is the remission of all penalty for every offense, then we must try to harmonize that with the operation of rigid natural law, cause and effect, sowing and reaping, acts and consequences. Forgiveness does not merely mean "letting off." Pardon does not mean escaping all the consequences or penalty of sin. Part of the penalty of sin is the irreparable harm some sinful acts cause, such as the death of another caused by a drunken driver. All the repentance in the world cannot make a dead person alive.

Is forgiveness right? If God passes over sin, if He pardons freely and unconditionally, is He not encouraging sin? Some may say that He is (Rom. 6:1-4). Is it right to help people in trouble? Is it right to save people from burning buildings or sinking ships? Psalm 107 admonished the redeemed of the Lord to say so. In this psalm people in four kinds of danger (wanderers in a desert, prisoners sitting in darkness and gloom, some who are sick because of their sins and iniquities, and some in a shipwreck) are delivered. They all thank the Lord for His steadfast love and wonderful works. Saving people from the consequences of sin is listed along with salvation from physical evils. God never takes sin lightly, but He can set the prisoner free (Ps. 107:10-14; Isa. 61:1-3).

Some people try to understand God's forgiveness on the analogy of human forgiveness. William J. Wolf said that laudable motives probably lead to forgiveness on the human level. Genuine contrition on both sides and a mutual feeling of deep penitence may flower into genuine forgiveness. However, such instances are often the fruit of religious insight and spring from minds that have been opened to God's forgiveness. More often the human situation that leads to reconciliation is based on mutual self-interest. Business partners "patch up their differences," and husbands and wives try "to make a go" of their marriage for the benefit of the children.

"It is difficult to project this element into the rationalized claim that God has only to forgive as men do. One reason that prompts man to forgive is that he knows he himself needs to be forgiven. The absurdity of saying that God needs to patch up his differences with man, or is prompted to forgive because he needs forgiveness, effectively unmasks the 'argument from human forgiveness.' We do not forgive God!" (Wolf, *No Cross, No Crown*, 190).

The ultimate basis for God's forgiveness remains a mystery in the Old Testament. Yet the Old Testament contains signs, gleams, and pledges of an ultimate solution to the problem of sin. The ultimate basis of God's forgiveness in the Old Testament comes to clearest expression in Isaiah 52:13—53:12. The idea of vicarious suffering of a Redeemer was broached. The note of Isaiah 53 echoes in the shepherd parable of Zechariah 11, though the detailed references of the latter are veiled in even thicker darkness. The great penitential lament of Zechariah 12:10-11 strikes the same chord as Isaiah 53:1-6, so that here, too, the background may be the atoning death of the shepherd God sent.

The closing section of Psalm 22 links the victory of the kingdom of God with the suffering of the righteous and His redemption. God's servant experiences undeserved oppression and affliction, pain and suffering, attack and rejection. These are not to be shrugged off or avenged. They are the means of bringing healing and forgiveness to "many" (Isa. 53:5,11).

Through the servant's suffering "the arm of the Lord will be revealed," not in military power or might but in weakness, suffering, and death.

Who indeed could have recognized this in the Old Testament (53:1)? God can do all this because it is in His power. "In some sense even in the Old Testament Yahweh is the 'crucified God'" (Goldingay, "The Man of War and the Suffering Servant," 101; compare Moltmann, *The Crucified God*; Kaufman, *Systematic Theology*, 219-222; R. L. Smith, "The Messiah in Zechariah," *Micah-Malachi, WBC* 28, 175-180).

Sin is a serious problem in the Old Testament that is never solved satisfactorily. Some people try to deny they have sinned (Gen. 4:9). Some try to hide their sin or cover it up (Gen. 3:8-11). Sin was no surprise for God. He had anticipated it and made provision for dealing with sin on a temporary basis in the Old Testament. But the means of ultimate forgiveness came in the New Testament, in Christ, through His atoning death and the power of His resurrection.

Worship

Worship seems to be as old as mankind. The early chapters of Genesis tell about sacrifices offered by Cain, Abel, and Noah. No explanation is given for these sacrifices, and none seems to have been needed. Cain and Abel's sacrifices probably were the response of gratitude to God for the gift of fertility of the animals and the land (firstborn and firstfruits), along with an implied petition for further blessings. Noah's sacrifice (Gen. 8:20-22) was a gift to God for saving him from mortal danger. Westermann noted that these two motifs (saving and blessing) have remained determinative for worship until the present (*Elements of Old Testament Theology*, 188).

Traditionists tell us that there has never been a human community void of something like worship. "Worship is a universally human phenomenon. This has in the meantime been confirmed by the history of religions" (Westermann, *Elements of Old Testament Theology*, 188). According to Walter Harrelson, writing about worship in a "secular age," some say that God moves and works in the complex, technological, and urbanized culture of today. They say our task is to discern God's presence there and not to continue the merely religious functions of the past.

However, Harrelson saw a profound lack in this way of viewing our new situation. What is overlooked is the human need to celebrate. Human beings, by virtue of their humanity, are evoked to praise by the very process of living their lives. "While I would not insist that, in terms of some historians of religion, man is incurably religious, I would insist that man cannot live a fully human life without acts of celebration" (Harrelson, *From Fertility Cult to Worship*, xi).

35. The Terms for Worship

G. Henton Davies said that worship is homage—the attitude and activity designed to recognize and describe the worth of the person or thing to which the homage or worship is addressed. "Worship is thus synonymous with the whole of a reverent life, embracing piety as well as liturgy" ("Worship in the Old Testament," 879). Wheeler Robinson said, "Worship is essentially, as well as etymologically, the recognition of God's worth. It has no direct reference to the edification of the worshipers. It is an offering to God, acceptable to Him and incumbent on man. All other aspects of worship are subordinate to this primary emphasis" ("The Old Testament Background," 19).

The word "worship" comes from the English word "worthship" and means "the acknowledgment made by finite man of God's infinite worth, and also the aesthetic representation or dramatic expression, by symbolic acts, attitudes, and words of this recognition" (Terrien, *The Psalms and Their Meaning for Today*, xi). Terrien noted that worship does not aim primarily at edifying, elevating, purifying, or consecrating the worshipers. It should bring about these results as by-products. The purpose of worship is to glorify God.

The psalmists' concept of worship was "theocentric," not "anthropocentric." They held that nothing on earth is worthwhile unless it is properly related to the Creator of the universe, the Giver of life, Master, Judge, and Savior. "But they did not lose themselves in the godhead, and their preoccupations with things divine and eternal did not prevent them from remaining flesh and bones, living on earth, and concerned with the world of human life and its manifold realities. There was no trace of Hindu pantheism in them, no deluding mysticism of the type which seeks to evade the self and the responsibilities of social existence" (Terrien, *The Psalms and Their Meaning for Today*, xi).

To emphasize that worship is the attribution of highest worth to God, Harry Buck quoted the prayer of Rabia, a woman Muslim mystic about A.D. 800.

> O God! if I worship Thee in fear of Hell,
> burn me in Hell;
> and if I worship Thee in hope of Paradise,
> exclude me from Paradise;
> but if I worship Thee for Thine own sake,
> withhold not Thine Everlasting Beauty.
> (Buck, "Worship, Idolatry, and God," 67)

Buck pointed out that the woman's prayer is correct. If one worships God for fear of hell or hope of heaven, that would make hell or heaven of greater "worth" than God, "and hence the object of worship" (Buck, 69).

A. S. Herbert said that worship is an end in itself. "Worship may well lead man to a recognition of his need for forgiveness, but the prayer of penitence rightly follows the recognition of the absolute worth of God; forgiveness is sought in order that worship may be worthily offered" (*Worship in Ancient Israel*, 10).

The English word "worship" carries a little different emphasis than the Old Testament words for worship. The English word stresses a value judgment on the part of the worshiper characteristic of Western internalization of ideas. The Hebrew terms for worship describe an action or response to the Holy One. The Old Testament often calls God the "Holy One of Israel" and frequently asserts that He is "with" or "in the midst of" His people.

A little reflection will make clear the paradoxical nature of these words. "Holy" (*qādoš*) emphasized the otherness, transcendence, inaccessibility, mystery, unapproachableness of God. Yet He is spoken of as the "Holy one in the midst (*qereb*) of you" (Isa. 12:6; Hos. 11:9). To be in God's presence was an awesome, even terrifying experience. It awakened a consciousness of sin (Isa. 6:5) and a strong desire for worthy living (Lev. 19:2). Israel's hope for forgiveness and blessing individually and collectively lay in the Holy One (Isa. 41:14; 54:5).

Herbert said that this factor of God's holiness "determines the nature and direction of Israel's worship as far back as we can trace it, and underlies the changing forms of worship from its beginnings to the developed form of post-exilic Judaism"

(*Worship in Ancient Israel*, 5). Harrelson made the same point in defining worship as "an ordered response to the appearance of the Holy in the life of individuals and groups" (*From Fertility Cult to Worship*, 16).

Three Hebrew words are translated "worship" in our English versions: (1) *šāḥaḥ* "to bow down," "to prostrate oneself"; (2) *ʿābad* "to serve"; and (3) *sāgad* "to bow down." *sāgad* is used in the Old Testament only in the context of bowing to a person (Daniel, Dan. 2:46) or to an idol (Isa. 44:15,17,19; Dan. 3:5,7,10,12,14,18,28).

ʿābad means "to work," "to act as a slave" for the owner. It is used of a household slave and of the subject and vassal of an overlord. However, the emphasis is not so much on the servile status of the worshiper as on the function to carry out the will of the Lord. The vassal is a member of the household or kingdom of the Lord. In the context of worship, the word refers to a humble relationship and a faithful discharging of the work given to the worshiper.

The Hebrew term *ʿăbôdâ* means "service" or "worship." The Old Testament uses the word to refer to the service of the king (1 Chron. 26:30), of God (Ex. 3:12; 4:23; 12:25, 27; Deut. 6:13; Josh. 22:27), or of the temple (Ezek. 44:14). Actually the term "serve" is used in two clusters in the Old Testament: (1) in Exodus where it designates the goal of leaving Pharaoh's domain to go into the wilderness to serve Yahweh (Ex. 3:12; 4:23; 7:16; 8:1; 10:26); and (2) in Deuteronomy where it connotes "service" of Yahweh over against other gods (Deut. 7:16; 8:19; 11:16; 12:2).

The terms "serve" and "service" may be political language. In Exodus the choice seems to be to serve either Pharaoh or Yahweh. In Deuteronomy it is to serve Yahweh or "other gods." James L. Mays said that these two clusters in Exodus and Deuteronomy show that to serve God is conduct which "excludes slavery to human government or subjection to the power of the gods" ("Worship, World and Power," 322).

The expression "serve Yahweh" occurs twice in the Psalms: "Serve the Lord with fear" (2:11*a*) and "Worship the Lord with gladness;/ come into his presence with singing" (100:2). Mays said that the invitation to serve the Lord is a summons to join others in the formation of a congregation as the people of Yahweh. It can be called worship because its focus is God. "The psalm [100] belongs at the point where men publicly assemble to recognize the power to which they will submit their living. It means opting for one 'power structure' as decisive, and therefore it ought to be the most significant social action that men can take" ("Worship, World and Power," 322).

Unlike their neighbors, Israel did not view worship or "service" as a means of cajoling, coercing, or influencing God to give them something He would not otherwise give them. Worship in the Old Testament was not like the occult, devised to open up the will of the gods to the worshiper. There was no magic in Old Testament worship or service (Harrelson, *From Fertility Cult to Worship*, 3, 6). H. J. Kraus said that in the covenant, the Old Testament worshipers meet the Lord whom they serve (*ʿābad*) in all their cultic activity. "Worship in the Old Testament is *ʿābôday*, and whenever man aspires in any way 'to bestow power' upon Yahweh, to affect him or influence him by means of cultic institutions the *ʿābodâ* is destroyed" (*Worship in Israel*, 124).

The Hebrew word most frequently translated "worship" is *sāḥaḥ* "to bow down" or "to prostrate oneself" (see Nakarai, "Worship in the Old Testament," 282-284). It is comparable to other Semitic words for worship. It is something done, whether felt or not. It need not be used with an object. "And Moses quickly bowed his head toward the earth and worshiped" (Ex. 34:8). Are "serve" and "worship" identical? The terms do appear together frequently. "Serve" refers to doing the will of God in human affairs. "Worship" is more closely related to cultic ritual.

Actually, that which English speakers call "worship" is usually referred to as "cult" in European countries. The word "worship" seldom appears in the major works of Old Testament theologians such as Eichrodt, von Rad, Jacob, Vriezen, Zimmerli, and Westermann. The word "cult" appears frequently (see Nakarai, "Worship in the Old Testament," 285).

What does "cult" mean? Norman Gottwald said that cult is one of those vexed jargon words in biblical studies which, more often than not, biblical scholars use without giving any clear content to it (*The Tribes of Yahweh*, 67). A. R. Johnson said that "cult" may and should be used to include all those reli-

gious exercises which form the established means used by any
social group to: (1) secure right relations with the realm of the
"sacred" or "holy," and (2) to enjoy those benefits, including
having guidance in the various crises of life (*The Cultic
Prophet in Ancient Israel*, 29-30, n. 3).

Sigmund Mowinckel said that religion appears in three
main aspects: cult, myth, and ethos or as worship, doctrine,
and behavior (morals). The three terms signify forms of
expression of the same phenomenon—the whole living content
of a religion. The picture will appear differently to each
observer, depending on the perspective from which one views
religion. "In the cult both doctrine and morals are expressed,
and both draw power and new life from the cult."

The cult appears in all religions, even in the most "anti-cul-
tic" Protestant sects and groups. Mowinckel defined cult as
"the socially established and regulated holy acts and words in
which the encounter and communion of the Deity with the congregation is established, developed, and brought to its ultimate goal. . . . The cult is . . . the visible and audible expression
of the relation between the congregation and the deity" (*The
Psalms in Israel's Worship I*, 15-16).

Roland de Vaux defined "cult" as all those acts by which
communities or individuals give outward expression to their
religious life by which they seek and achieve contact with God.
"Man's action in cultic worship is basically the response of a
creature to his Creator" (de Vaux, *Ancient Israel*, 271). In his
famous definition of worship, Martin Luther emphasized its
reciprocal exchange between God and His people "that God
may speak to us and we to him in prayer and song of praise"
(see Westermann, *Elements of Old Testament Theology*, 187).

What is worship according to the Old Testament? It is service, doing the will and work of God. It is prostrating oneself
before God in public assembly. It is recognizing and acknowledging Yahweh's infinite worth.

36. The Times and Places of Worship

Holy time is more important in the Old Testament than holy
space, and the seasons for worship are more important than
the places set aside for such worship (Harrelson, *From Fertility Cult to Worship*, 16). The Greeks lived and thought prima-

rily in the world of space, while Israel more often lived and thought mainly in the world of time (Muilenburg, "The Biblical View of Time," 32-33).

This does not mean that Israel ignored or rejected the world of space, nor that Greece did not take time seriously. Time and space are interrelated, but space is not in control. Israel differed radically from their neighbors at this point. Israel did not appeal to the cosmic world of space, as did their neighbors, to resolve the mystery and meaning of time. The neighbors deified the heavenly bodies and saw life moving in circles with the changing seasons of nature. Israel resolved the mystery of time by recognizing Yahweh as the Lord of time, nature, and history. Israel did not know the way of her history, only God knew it (Muilenburg, "The Biblical View of Time," 36). The psalmist cried, "My times are in your hand" (31:15).

A. A History of Worship in the Old Testament

It would be difficult to write a history of worship in the Old Testament. That worship had a history in Old Testament times is clear. Striking changes in times, places, and procedures for worship occurred from the time of the patriarchs to the Babylonian exile. In the patriarchal period worship was simple, individual, and periodic. It occurred at mountains, streams, rocks (Bethel), or trees (Oak of Moreh)—wherever God appeared to the worshiper. Worship had no mediator, no idol, and no stated times.

H. H. Rowley noted that some scholars suggest that the patriarchs were animists or polytheists, but we do not find the patriarchs worshiping material objects or the spirits which some suppose reside in them. Rowley quoted Henton Davies with approval: "It is no longer possible to state that worship in the days of the founding fathers of Israel can be described in terms of animism and the like" (Rowley, *Worship in Ancient Israel*, 16-17).

Rowley also noted that Abraham might have gone to the shrine of Melchizedek, although there is no reference to this or to the shrine itself in the biblical account. "There is no reason to suppose that Abraham shared in any ritual ceremony at Melchizedek's shrine or offered any worship to El 'Elyon. For the study of Abraham's worship it is safer to rely on the recorded evidence rather than on what we reconstruct out of silence. We nowhere find the Patriarchs possessing or worshiping idols" (*Worship in Ancient Israel*, 19).

Nothing is said in Genesis about Joseph or his family worshiping. Joseph does say that God (Elohim) sent him into Egypt to preserve life or a remnant (Gen. 45:5,7,8; 50:20), and his brothers refer to "the God of your father" (50:17).

Worship in the Mosaic period begins with the theophany at the burning bush and Moses' call to lead Israel out of Egypt (Ex. 3:12,18; 4:23; 5:1,3). The worship of Yahweh is a part of the purpose of the exodus. "When you have brought the people out of Egypt, you shall worship (*ʾabad*) God on this mountain" (Ex. 3:12). "The LORD, the God of the Hebrews has met with us, let us now go a three days' journey into the wilderness, so that we may sacrifice (*zebaḥ*) to the LORD our God" (Ex. 3:18). "Let my son go that he may worship (*ʿābad*) me" (Ex. 4:23). "Let my people go, so that they may celebrate a festival (*ḥag*) to me in the wilderness" (Ex. 5:1).

Free of Egypt, Israel was to hold a feast, make *sacrifices*, and *serve* Yahweh. A great change occurred in Israel's worship at Sinai (Ex. 19—24). Worship became corporate. The whole "nation" was to take three days to prepare themselves for the theophany. This implies a stated time. The mountain may represent a stated place. The lawgiver (Moses) is the mediator of the holy. A fourth element in the worship at Sinai is the response of the people.

Actually, it was not three days but three months after leaving Egypt that Israel made a sacrifice to God. Then Moses and the elders made the sacrifice to seal the covenant between God and Israel (Ex. 24:4-8). God gave the Ten Commandments as the basic covenant document. He added a list of laws called the Covenant Code to implement or to add sanctions to the covenant. The first two commandments of the Decalogue deal directly with worship: (1) Israel was not to worship any god other than Yahweh, and (2) Israel was to make no graven image to represent Yahweh. Both these commands are unique in the ancient world.

Nothing is said in the Ten Commandments about stated times, places, and forms of worship. However, in the Covenant Law Codes, provisions are made for the altar to be made only of earth or unhewn stones, without steps, and to be set up in every place where God causes His name to be remembered (Ex. 20:24-26). The firstfruits of the ground and firstborn of the animals and humans were to be consecrated to God (Ex. 22:29-30; 23:19). The seventh day was to be a rest day (Ex. 23:12), and all males were to appear before God to keep the three major feasts: unleavened bread, harvest, and ingatherings (Ex. 23:14-17).

Although the Old Testament text indicates that the Ten Commandments and the Covenant Law Codes were given at Sinai, many Old Testament scholars such as Wellhausen, Stade, Budde, Smend, and Karl Marti have argued that the whole pericope of Exodus 19—24 is a much later reconstruction (compare Stamm and Andrew, *The Ten Commandments in Recent Research*, 22-35; John I. Durham, *Exodus*, 259-260). However, a growing number of scholars, including Gressmann, Hans Schmid, Aalders, Neher, Martin Buber, Rowley, Eichrodt, and Stamm argue that the earliest form of the Ten Commandments was Mosaic and that some of the laws in the Covenant Code may be pre-Mosaic (compare Stamm and Andrew, *The Ten Commandments in Recent Research*, 24-26, 39, 69).

Exodus 25—Numbers 10 is an extensive and detailed account of: the building of the tabernacle with its elaborate furniture; the types of sacrifices; the consecration of the priests; and the inauguration of congregational worship. Views concerning the historicity of this section differ widely. Brevard Childs reviewed the various scholarly viewpoints and suggested that a growing consensus among scholars sees that ancient material underlies the priestly tabernacle account. Still, a wide difference of opinion remains regarding both the nature of the early traditions and the process by which they took shape (Childs, *The Book of Exodus*, 532).

Casuto, a conservative Jewish author, acknowledged the historical problems involved in the biblical account of the tabernacle. But he noted that there is "an increasing tendency, particularly on the part of scholars engaged in studying the archaeology of the Ancient East, to assume that we have here, at least in its essential features, an ancient and trustworthy tradition" (*A Commentary on the Book of Exodus*, 320).

No doubt the tribes of Israel did have a portable sanctuary (*mîqdeš*) "holy-place," or a "dwelling place" (*šākan*) for God during their wilderness journeys. Whether or not sacrifices were actually offered in the wilderness may be debated. Jeremiah 7:22 and Amos 5:25 were used by Wellhausen to argue that sacrifices were not offered in the wilderness. But Rowley believed that these two verses say that Yahweh required obedience in the wilderness, not sacrifice. Obedience is defined in the Decalogue and in the prophets "in terms of conduct and not of ritual" (Rowley, *Worship in Ancient Israel*, 42).

Worship in Israel entered a new phase during the period of the monarchy. A temple was built, and eventually all communal worship involving the offering of sacrifice was centralized in the new temple. The temple was a royal chapel, and the king probably played a significant role in its operation. (See Solomon's dedication of the temple, 1 Kings 8.) However, Westermann noted that although kingship gave splendor and luster to temple worship, dependency on royal politics produced serious syncretistic threats (see accounts of the reigns of Ahaz and Manasseh). This worship collapsed with the monarchy (see Westermann, *Elements of Old Testament Theology*, 191).

During and after the exile a new type of worship emerged. It emphasized prayer, reading of Scripture, and singing psalms. Eventually the synagogue was founded, and family worship was renewed.

B. The Times of Worship

A glance at the brief history of worship in the Old Testament reveals the changes that occurred. A pattern of set times, places, and personnel of worship began to emerge. The times of worship can be seen most clearly in the four accounts of the cultic calendars (Ex. 23:10-19; Lev. 23:4-44; Num. 28—29; Deut. 16:1-17).

The cultic calendar in Exodus 23:10-19 is probably the earliest and the shortest. It begins with sowing in the fall and indicates that the land was to lie fallow every seven years. The seventh day was to be a day of rest. The word "sabbath" does not occur in this passage. Three times a year the men were to appear before God to keep a feast. No specific time or place is given for such an "appearance before God." The names of the three feasts are Unleavened Bread (Passover is not mentioned); Harvest, when the firstfruits of the ground were offered; and Ingathering, "at the end" of the year.

It seems that the year began in the fall, according to the earliest Old Testament evidence. The oldest calendar discovered in Palestine was found at Gezer and may be the most ancient inscription in early Hebrew writing. It dates from about 1000 B.C. The year began with the fall sowing and ended with the harvest of the autumn fruits (see D. Winton Thomas, *Documents from Old Testament Times*, 201-203). About 700 B.C. the time for the new year was shifted from the fall (seventh month) to the spring (first month, *Abib*), probably under Assyrian influence to conform to the Assyrian practice. This practice continued through the Babylonian and Persian periods. Then a secular calendar appeared in Israel which began in the spring and a sacral calendar in which the New Year was still celebrated at the beginning of the seventh month (Kraus, *Worship in Israel*, 44-45; Harrelson, *From the Fertility Cult to Worship*, 17).

The second cultic calendar appears in Deuteronomy 16:1-17. The year begins in the spring in the month Abib. Passover is connected with the feast of Unleavened Bread and is a communal affair to be observed at the central place of worship, rather than in the home by the family as it was in Exodus 12. The Passover sacrifice is to be boiled or "cooked" (NRSV) in Deuteronomy 16:7. Exodus 12:9 expressly commands that the meat not be eaten raw or boiled but roasted. The name of the fall feast is changed in Deuteronomy from "Ingathering" to "Booths" (Deut. 16:13).

The third cultic calendar in the Old Testament is in the Holiness Code (Lev. 23:1-44). This calendar begins with the sabbath, which is called "a holy convocation." This is the first calendar to mention the sabbath by name and the first to call it holy. The three appointed feasts are also called "holy convocations" here. The definite day for Passover is given as the fourteenth day of the first month. Passover is followed by the seven day feast of Unleavened Bread, and that is followed by the wave offering (Lev. 23:14). The directions for observing the feast of Harvest are greatly expanded. A provision for helping the poor is added to these directions in Leviticus 23:22.

For the first time the fall festival is divided into three parts. The first day of the seventh month was to be a holy convocation; the tenth day was the Day of Atonement; and the feast of Booths was held from the fifteenth to the twenty-third days.

The fourth cultic calendar in the Old Testament is in Numbers 28—29. This calendar begins with the daily burnt offerings (compare Ex. 29:28; Ezek. 46:13). The offerings and sacrifices for the sabbath are described in Numbers 28:9-10 (compare Ezek. 46:4-5). Offerings for the first day of every month (the new moon) are stipulated in 28:11-15. The rites of the Passover and Unleavened Bread are described in 28:16-25, and the details for the Feast of Weeks are given in 28:26-31. Numbers 29 describes the observance of the first day of the seventh month (New Year), the Day of Atonement, and a detailed description of the required sacrifices on the various days of the feast in the seventh month.

How well were all of these cultic calendars followed during Israel's history? We read of the observance of Passover in the time of Joshua (Josh. 5:10); in the time of Hezekiah, in the second month rather than the first (2 Chron. 30:1-3); and in the time of Josiah (2 Kings 23:21-23). The last passage says, "No such Passover had been kept since the days of the judges who judged Israel, or during all the days of the kings of Israel or of the kings of Judah; but in the eighteenth year of King Josiah this passover was kept to the LORD in Jerusalem" (2 Kings 23:22-23).

Evidently the passover was not kept regularly through much of Israel's history. The Old Testament also provides evidence that the sabbatical year, in which the land was to lie idle every seventh year, was not kept. In the list of curses for not keeping the covenant is the warning that Israel will be removed from her land. Then the land will be able to "enjoy" its sabbaths, which it was not able to do while Israel dwelled in the land (Lev. 26:34-35). That the sabbath was not always observed properly in Israel can be seen in Nehemiah 13:15-18.

The origins of the sabbath are still obscure (Zimmerli, "The Place and Limit of Wisdom," 90-91; Kraus, *Worship in Israel*, 78-88). Some have tried to explain the origin of the sabbath in terms of its similarity with the Babylonian word, *shabattu/shapattu*. At first it was argued that the Babylonian word, like the Hebrew *šābbat*, meant "rest," but that view was quickly abandoned (see Andreasen, *The Old Testament Sabbath*, 1-2; compare Köhler, and Baumgartner, *Dritte Auflage Lieferung* IV, 1310-1311). Then it was suggested that the Babylonian word meant "evil days," which occurred approximately every seven days. But it is very difficult to find any connection between the Hebrew celebration of the sabbath and the evil, gloomy taboo days of Assyria and Babylonia (Stamm and Andrew, *The Ten Commandments in Recent Research*, 91).

In 1904 Theophilus Pinches discovered a Babylonian tablet that identified *shapattu* as the fifteenth day of the month. On the basis of this discovery, Johannes Meinhold argued that the Old Testament sabbath was originally a full-moon day and became a weekday only under the influence of Ezekiel (Andreasen, *The Old Testament Sabbath*, 4). Instead of the sabbath being a lunar day, Edmond Jacob thought it more likely that the sabbath was given to Israel for the very purpose of turning them away from the lunar cults (*Theology of the Old Testament*, 265).

Abraham Kuenen argued that the idea of the week could be traced back to the worship of the seven planets in the time of Moses. Eerdmans, Budde, Köhler, and Rowley have developed this idea into the "Kenite hypothesis." This hypothesis sees the Kenites as a tribe of metalsmiths who worshiped Yahweh. This theory makes much use of Exodus 35:3, "You shall kindle no fire in all your dwellings on the sabbath day," and Numbers 15:32-36 which tells of the stoning of a man who picked up sticks on the sabbath—evidently with the intention of making a fire. This hypothesis has not gained wide support.

Various other theories have been advanced to explain the origin of the sabbath, including the idea that it was a market day (Kraus, *Worship in Israel*, 81) or an agricultural rest day (Morgenstern, "Sabbath," 135-140). None of these theories is convincing, although there may be an element of truth in many of them.

Actually, the sabbath in Israel cannot be tied to the movement of the heavenly bodies or to the natural rhythms of life. Walter Harrelson concluded, "The commandment to observe one day of rest in seven seems to me very probably to go back to Moses. And this rest is not merely a humanistic institution;

it aims at ever deeper devotion to God. It provides time in which Israelite spirituality can flower" (*From Fertility Cult to Worship*, 26).

Some evidence indicates that the sabbath was a distinctively Israelite observance (Rowley, *Worship in Ancient Israel*, 91). The sabbath was observed in Israel from an early date, although there is no mention of it in the time of the patriarchs. The command to keep the sabbath is in both versions of the Decalogue (Ex. 20; Deut. 5), whose origins can be traced to the Mosaic period. The eighth-century prophets accused their hearers of violating the sabbath (Isa. 1:13; Hos. 2:11; Amos 8:5). The primary purpose of the sabbath was rest. Its observance did not require a sacrifice, a mediator, or attendance at a holy place. For its proper observation, this law was incumbent on every member of society.

By the time of Ezekiel, sabbath observance had become a badge of orthodoxy or a sign of the covenant. The Lord says, "Moreover I gave them my sabbaths, as a sign between me and them, that they might know that I the LORD sanctify them. But the house of Israel rebelled against me in the wilderness; they did not observe my statutes but rejected my ordinances, by whose observance everyone shall live; and my sabbaths they greatly profaned" (Ezek. 20:12-13; compare 20:16,18-21). Exodus 31:12-17 makes the sabbath the sign of the perpetual covenant between Yahweh and Israel.

Samuel Terrien remarked that the sabbath, whatever its prehistoric origins, became for the Jews a sacrament of presence. When the temple was destroyed, "sacred space became obsolete." The sabbath now became their temple. In the exile the uniqueness of the holy place, through the sabbath, became an interior and universal reality (*The Elusive Presence*, 392). The creation accounts of Israel's neighbors (*Enuma Elish* and Canaanite creation poems) ended with temple building. The first creation account in the Old Testament ends not with a temple but with the sabbath, which took the place of the temple in the exile. "Yahweh's residence in the *hagios topos* ('holy place') was transfigured into Yahweh's presence in the *hagios kairos* (holy time)."

The idea of divine rest on the seventh day should not be understood as referring to lethargic passivity. The seventh day did not call for a withdrawal of God's activity but for a "refreshment" of His being (Ex. 31:17). In a sense, the seventh day was "open-ended." There was no "evening and morning" at the end of the account of the seventh day. "God blessed the seventh day and hallowed it" (Gen. 2:3). Terrien said that by observing the sabbath, people participate in the divine rest. "Not only his work but also his rest is transfigured into an act of presence, which is the basis of all worship" (*The Elusive Presence*, 394).

C. The Places of Worship

In the Old Testament, a place was holy because God had appeared there. God appeared to Abraham at the Oak of Moreh in Shechem, and Abraham built an altar there (Gen. 12:6-7). He built another altar at Bethel (Gen. 12:8). God appeared to Isaac at Beer-sheba, and Isaac built an altar there (Gen. 26:23-25). God appeared to Jacob at Bethel, and Jacob set up a stone to mark the place of his vision. He called the stone a *māzzebâ*, "pillar," and said the pillar would be God's house (Gen. 28:18-22). God appeared to Moses at Sinai (Horeb) (Ex. 3) and to Joshua at Gilgal near Jericho (Josh. 5:13-15). These and other sites of God's appearances became "holy places" in early Israel.

At first these holy places did not seem elaborate and were not attended by priests. Harrelson suggested that when cultic personnel were assigned to holy places, they were there to protect the worshiper as much as to provide access to the holy. "Holy sites are dangerous" (*From Fertility Cult to Worship*, 27).

In addition to these altars built by the patriarchs and other leaders of Israel, the land of Palestine was filled with altars, sacred stones, pillars, and trees which the Canaanites had built and/or planted. Most of these altars, pillars, and sacred trees were on the tops of hills called "high places" (*bamôt*). Some of the "high places" were open-air or roofed sanctuaries with altars on raised platforms. Israel was commanded to destroy such places of worship when they came into the land (Num. 33:52; Deut. 12:2-3). Instead of destroying the high places, Israel often forsook Yahweh and served the Baals and the Asherahs (Judg. 2:12; 3:7; 6:25-26,30; 8:33; 10:6; 17:4-6; 18:14; compare Josh. 4:9).

Samuel offered sacrifices on the high place at Ramah (1 Sam. 9:12). Solomon received his inaugural vision at the high place of Gibeon (1 Kings 3:2-14). Solomon built high places for his wives to worship other gods (1 Kings 11:7). Jeroboam's temples are called "high places" by Hosea (10:8) and Amos (7:9). The kings of Israel built high places, and the people worshiped there (2 Kings 17:9,11). In Judah Rehoboam (Solomon's son) built high places, pillars, and asherahs on every high hill and under every green tree (1 Kings 14:23).

Only Hezekiah and Josiah tore down the high places (2 Kings 18:4; 23:5). Hosea charged, "They sacrifice on the tops of the mountains, and make offerings upon the hills" (4:13). Jeremiah said, "For your gods have become as many as your towns, O Judah; and as many as the streets of Jerusalem are the altars you have set up to shame, altars to make offerings to Baal" (Jer. 11:13; compare Jer. 2:28).

All of the sacred places in Israel were not Canaanite altars, nor was all of Israel's worship syncretistic. As the tribes of Israel came into the land, they set up altars at certain sites and returned to some of them over and over to celebrate and commemorate what Yahweh did for them there. At Gilgal Joshua took twelve stones from the bottom of the Jordan and built an altar at the crossing point (Josh. 4:1-7). Later Israel would visit the stones, perhaps annually; and the children would ask, "What do those stones mean?" The answer was, "the waters of the Jordan were cut off in front of the ark of the Covenant" (Josh. 4:6,7). Gilgal continued to be a sacred site through much of Israel's history.

1) *Shechem*—Perhaps the most significant historical and religious center in ancient Israel was not Jerusalem but Shechem. Shechem is located forty-one miles north of Jerusalem in a valley between Mount Ebal on the north and Mount Gerizim on the south, in almost the exact center of western Palestine, by the most important mountain pass in the country. Highways radiated out from Shechem in every direction. Near the ancient mound of Shechem is the modern village *Tell Balatah* with the traditional tomb of Joseph and Jacob's well nearby.

The city is mentioned in two early Egyptian texts so that the beginning of Shechem's glory should be dated about 1900 B.C.

(Wright, *Shechem*, 15-17). Its strongest period, from about 1800 to 1100 B.C., would include both the patriarchal period and the Exodus (compare Gen. 12:1-6; 33:18-20,34; 25—31; Josh. 24:32; Acts 7:16). The Bible makes no reference to any Israelite "conquest" of Shechem, but Joshua did set up an altar at Shechem and read the blessings and curses according to the law of Moses (Josh. 8:30-35; compare Deut. 11:29-30; 27:4-13). Joshua also called all the tribes of Israel to Shechem to renew the Sinai covenant (Josh. 24:1-28).

In the time of the Judges (about 1100 B.C.) Canaanites seem to control Shechem (Judg. 8:31; 9:1-6,17-25, 31, 41, 45). The Canaanite influence in the city shows itself in a temple dedicated to Baal-berith (Judg. 9:4). Reference is also made to an oak, a pillar (9:6), and a fall harvest festival (9:27).

Shechem is not mentioned in the Old Testament during the period of the united monarchy, but when Solomon died "all Israel" went to Shechem to make Jeroboam king. When Solomon's son and successor Rehoboam followed the bad advice of his young advisers, Jeroboam set up his own kingdom in Shechem, taking ten of the twelve tribes of Israel with him (1 Kings 12:25). He changed the cultic calendar of Israel, appointed two new worship centers (Dan and Bethel), and consecrated priests for the high places (1 Kings 12:26-33).

Shechem did not serve as the capital of the Northern Kingdom very long. Jeroboam had his residence at Tirzah (14:17). The third king of Israel, Baasha, made Tirzah his capital (15:21,33). Omri besieged Tirzah, defeated Zimri, and burned the palace, whereupon he built a new capital at Samaria (15:17,24).

After the exile Shechem experienced a revival of cultic importance. A Samaritan temple was built on Mount Gerizim, probably about 300 B.C. Much debate has centered on who the Samaritans actually were and when the schism came between them and the Jews. The word "Samaritans" is only found once in the Old Testament (2 Kings 17:29). There it refers to the inhabitants of Samaria, not Shechem. "The Samaritans themselves make a clear distinction between their own forebearers and the inhabitants of Samaria" (Coggins, *Samaritans and Jews*, 9).

H. J. Kraus said that the founding of the Samaritan temple on Mount Gerizim was not merely the outcome of a particular religious and political schism, but was at the same time the

revival of very ancient traditions. "The newly founded community, basing itself on the authority of the Pentateuch and
rejecting as a matter of principle the whole cultic history of
Jerusalem, thought of itself as the original Israel. It was this
purist tendency that brought about this return to the place of
origin of the people of God" (*Worship in Israel*, 145-146). A
small group of Samaritans still worship on Mount Gerizim.

2) *Shiloh*—Shiloh seems to have been the religious center of
the tribes of Israel and the site of the tabernacle after the initial conquest. Located about midway between Bethel and
Shechem, it is not mentioned in the times of the patriarchs,
but was the site of the casting of lots for the division of the land
of Canaan among the tribes (Josh. 18:1,8,9,10; 19:51). It was
also the gathering place of the tribes in times of crises (Josh.
22:12). It was the site of an annual pilgrimage in the time of
Samuel (1 Sam. 1–3).

The ark was removed from Shiloh, and the Philistines captured it in battle (1 Sam. 4:11,19). Evidently the Philistines
destroyed the sanctuary at Shiloh (see Ps. 78:60; Jer. 7:12-14;
26:6). A priest was still serving in Shiloh in the time of Saul (1
Sam. 14:3). A prophet named Ahijah still lived in Shiloh at the
beginning of the divided kingdom (1 Kings 11:29; 12:15; 14:2,4;
15:29).

3) *Jerusalem*—Other "sacred places" abounded in Israel,
including Bethel, Beersheba, Mount Tabor, Hebron, and Miz-
pah. None of these places compared to Gilgal, Shechem, Bethel,
Shiloh, or Jerusalem as places of worship. The story of Jerusalem and its significance in the worship of Israel is too lengthy
and too familiar to tell here. Under one name or another, it
appears in about two-thirds of the books of the Old Testament.

The name occurs first in the Egyptian execration texts soon
after 1900 B.C. (Burrows, "Jerusalem," 843). Abraham paid
tithes to Melchizedek at "Salem" (Gen. 14:18-20). David conquered Jerusalem and made it his capital (2 Sam. 5:6-9).
Solomon built the temple in Jerusalem (1 Kings 6). The Babylonians destroyed Jerusalem along with the temple in 587
B.C., and the Romans destroyed it again in A.D. 70.

Jerusalem was more than a geographical and political
entity in the Old Testament. It became a theological symbol of
the universal kingdom of God (Porteous, "Jerusalem-Zion," 93-

111]. The Bible seems to create a word play on the idea of peace (*šālom*) in the name Jerusalem. Scattered evidence in the Old Testament also links the two ideas of righteousness (*ṣedeq*) and peace (*šālom*) with Jerusalem (compare Pss. 72:1,3,7; 122:6-8; Isa. 1:21,26; 28:16).

Jerusalem began to assume unusual significance from the time David chose it to be his own city and the capital of the united monarchy. Jerusalem was David's choice for a dwelling place. It was also God's choice (2 Sam. 24:16-25; 1 Chron. 21:16-27; Pss. 76:2; 132:13; Isa. 14:32).

The prophets identified Jerusalem as a future city of peace and its coming ruler as the prince of peace and righteousness (Isa. 9:7; 16:4-9; 54:10,14; Jer. 29:10-11; Ezek. 37:24-26; Mic. 5:5). Jerusalem is spoken of in the Old Testament as the center (navel) of the world (Ezek. 5:5-6; 38:12); as a city set on a hill or mountain (Isa. 2:1-5; Ezek. 40:1-2; Mic. 4:1-4); and as the light of the world (Isa. 60:1-7). Von Rad said that Isaiah 60:1-7 is probably behind Jesus' statement in Matthew 5:14 that His disciples were to be the eschatological congregation of the faithful who were to make their light visible to the world ("The City on the Hill," 242).

Some Old Testament scholars speak of "a Zion theology" (Kraus, *Theology of the Psalms*, 78-83). The same psalms that refer to Jerusalem as the city of God have a remarkable Zion theology (see Pss. 46; 48; 76). Zion is spoken of as being located in the far north (Ps. 48:2) and in the center of the earth (Ezek. 38:12). The temple, God's earthly dwelling place, is there. A river—a life-giving stream—flows from underneath the temple (Ps. 46:4; Isa. 33:20-21; Ezek. 47; Joel 3:18; Zech. 14:8). Enemies threaten the city of God (Pss. 46:6; 48:4; 76:5-6), but the city is unconquerable (Ps. 46:8-10; Ezek. 38—39; Zech. 12; 14) (see von Rad, *Theology of the Old Testament II*, 293-94). In the end there will be peace (Isa. 9:6; Ezek. 36:36; Mic. 5:5). (For very good discussions of "Zion theology" see H. J. Kraus, *Theology of the Psalms*, 78-83; Jon D. Levenson, *Sinai and Zion*, 89-184; Porteous, *Living the Mystery*, 93-112.)

A. M. Fairbairn, compared the views of Augustine, Abraham, and John about living in the last days of great empires while looking for a city whose Maker and Builder is God. Fairbairn said, "In these so dissimilar and distant men a similar faith stands expressed. There *is* a city of God invisible, spiritual, which knows no place or time, which embodies God's ideal of society, the ordered and obedient life of man" (*The City of God,* cited in Fisher Humphreys, *Nineteenth Century Evangelical Theology,* 370). A vision of the city of God has a practical value. It furnishes a hope of a nobler future.

> Without this vision, earth, even where most full of material wealth, can be a galley and the man a galley slave . . . when out of the future the light of the eternal city gleams it glorifies the meanest moments of the present. . . . The city, in order to fulfil the hopes of its citizens, must have throughout two qualities, it must be of God and eternal as God. . . . To be of God is the source and spring of the city's perfection; to be eternal, the condition of its realization. The ideal is God's . . . but it can be translated into reality only through obedience (see Humphreys, *Nineteenth Century Evangelical Theology,* 376-377).

The place of worship varied from time to time in the Old Testament. At times, Israel had only one legitimate place to offer sacrifice—in the temple in Jerusalem. Some evidence points to other Jewish temples in Israel, perhaps on Mount Gerizim, at Lachish, and at Arad. (For a discussion of other Israelite temples at Arad, Lachish, and Hazor, see P. D. Miller, "Israelite Religion," in *The Hebrew Bible and Its Modern Interpreters,* 227.) Even Jerusalem eventually ceased to be only the site for the earthly temple. Before the Old Testament was completed, it became the transcendent symbol of the presence of God.

The times and places of worship varied in the Old Testament. The time of worship was sporadic in the beginning. Near the end of the Old Testament, worship was highly structured as to times and places.

37. Forms of Worship

The Old Testament only occasionally gives glimpses of forms of worship, and those are "given quite incidentally" (Robinson, "The Old Testament Background," 22). During much of Israel's history each day began and closed with the sacrifice of a lamb on the altar (Ex. 29:38; Num. 28:3-8). Ezekiel 46:13 mentions only a morning sacrifice. It seems the daily sacrifice was doubled on the sabbath (Num. 28:9-10). Wheeler Robinson graphically described the morning sacrifice.

In the darkness before the dawn a solitary priest entered the inner enclosure where the altar stood, to remove the ashes of the ever-burning altar fire. We are told in the *Mishnah* that "none went in with him and he carried no lamp, but he walked in the light of the altar fire." What a scene for a Rembrandtesque painting—the dimly seen outline of altar and building, the flickering flames lighting up that solitary figure! ("The Old Testament Background," 23-24).

Joining these daily sacrifices were three great festivals lasting seven or eight days with processionals (Pss. 43:4; 48:12; 68:22-27); entrance liturgies (Ps. 24; Isa. 33:13-16; Jer. 7); the priestly blessings (Num. 6:22-27); ceremonies for offering firstfruits and tithes (Deut. 26:1-15); and the reading of covenant curses and blessings (Deut. 27:9-26; compare Lev. 26; Deut. 28; Josh. 24).

Major events in an individual's life often were times of worship. Soon after the birth of a child, the mother was to offer a sin offering. Males were circumcised on the eighth day. (See "Excursus: Circumcision and Baptism," following.) Some children were dedicated to the Lord at birth (Samuel, Jeremiah). The Nazirite vow could be made at any age by a male or female (see Num. 6). A worshiper charged with a crime or falsely accused could take an oath of innocence (Job 31; Ps. 7:3-5). In sickness or danger a person often prayed for help and vowed a thanksgiving offering if God would save him or her (Pss. 6; 116; Jonah 2).

Harrelson said that in the matter of death, the Old Testament is most astonishing for that which it does not provide. When the great among Israel died, they were mourned and buried, but their burial place never became a place of veneration or pilgrimage. Cult places are always distinguished from burial places (*From Fertility Cult to Worship*, 33).

Excursus: Circumcision and Baptism

Circumcision was a religious act in the Old Testament. The Old Testament practice of circumcising male babies has often been cited as the basis for infant baptism in the church, but there is no positive evidence in the New Testament that infant baptism was practiced in the first century A.D. A. H. Strong said, "Infant baptism was established neither by Christ nor by his apostles. Even in later times Tertullian opposed it" (*Systematic Theology*, 953).

Infant baptism was practiced as early as the second century according to the witness of Origin and Cyprian. It became widespread in the fourth century and was defended with great energy by all the Reformers. The Roman Catholic Church viewed infant baptism in the context of its doctrine of original sin. If sin is hereditary, babies are sinners and need "forgiveness" and "regeneration." Baptism became the sacrament of grace for infants and adults.

Is infant baptism biblical? Can it be related to the Old Testament practice of circumcision? Oscar Cullmann and J. Jeremias are two modern scholars who defend infant baptism on the bases of the Old Testament practice of circumcision and Jewish proselyte baptism (see Cullman, *Baptism in the New Testament*, 45-65; compare Jeremias, *Hat die Urkirche die Kindertaufe geübt?*). In an article on baptism, W. F. Flemington traced some "indirect" evidence in the New Testament that might support infant baptism ("Baptism," 352).

H. H. Rowley, writing about a possible connection between infant baptism and Jewish proselyte baptism, said,

> No Jew could possibly confuse circumcision with ordinary lustrations, or with proselyte baptism, nor could it be confused with John's baptism. It is surely one of the unsolved mysteries of Christian scholarship why the leap should be made to what is a completely different and unrelated rite. Circumcision was a rite which all male Jews had to undergo. . . . It did not apply to females. . . . Judaism had no sacramental rite (*The Unity of the Bible*, 155-156).

Rowley denied that Colossians 2:11-12 teaches an analogy between Old Testament circumcision and New Testament baptism. "Here there is no suggestion that the subjects of baptism and the subjects of circumcision are the same, or that the two rites are in any way parallel in their significance. Indeed Paul mentions faith, which was not required of infants who were circumcised" (*The Unity of the Bible*, 157).

Since Rowley was a Baptist, he confessed that his readers might expect such a position from him (*The Unity of the Bible*, 149). Reservations about infant baptism are not confined to the Baptist "communion." Emil Brunner said, "The contemporary practice of infant baptism can hardly be regarded as anything short of scandalous" (*The Divine-Human Encounter*, 132). Karl Barth said that the church's teaching on infant baptism has in it not a mere chink but a hole.

> The baptism practice found in use on the basis of the prevalent teaching is arbitrary and despotic. Neither by exegesis nor from the nature of the case can it be established that the baptized person can be a merely passive instrument (*Behandelter*). Rather it may be shown by exegesis and the nature of the case, that in this action the baptized is an active partner (*Handelnder*) and that at whatever stage of life he may be, plainly no infant can be such a person (*The Teaching of the Church Regarding Baptism*, 41).

Barth pointed out that in the New Testament "one is not brought to baptism; one comes to baptism" (*The Teaching of the Church Regarding Baptism*, 42). He acknowledged that baptism is compared to circumcision in Colossians 2:11-12 but insisted that "from this it no ways follows that baptism like circumcision is to be carried out on a babe" (*The Teaching of the Church Regarding Baptism*, 43).

Infant baptism is a well-entrenched practice in many churches. Even some Baptists do not rule it out completely. Walter Harrelson (a Baptist) said that "in Christian practice the act of Christian baptism of children before they are able to say a word lays upon the community and the family the awesome responsibility to identify the child as God's child. If we can live with such responsibility, we have a perfect right to practice infant baptism" (*From Fertility Cult to Worship*, 32).

G. A. F. Knight (a Presbyterian) is one modern Old Testament scholar who tries to justify infant baptism by the use of typology. Pointing to Paul's comparison of the crossing of the Red Sea to baptism (1 Cor. 10:1-2), Knight said that Paul, using the rabbinical typological method, interprets God's action in the life of Israel in terms of what he knew to be God's action recently in Christ. "So he parallels the life of Israel with the life of Christ. No sooner had God brought his son to birth . . . than God baptized him 'in the cloud and in the sea'. He did so before Israel was able to take the promise of loyalty to him. God's action in baptizing his 'infant' Son was thus an act of prevenient grace" (*A Christian Theology of the Old Testament*, 216).

H. H. Rowley disagreed with Knight's analogy. Rowley said that in this passage Paul was really concerned with stressing the contrast between the crossing of the sea and baptism and with urging that the example of the Israelites who came out of Egypt is not to be followed by the church, since the example was one of disobedience (*The Unity of the Bible*, 149, n. 1; compare Craig, "First Corinthians," 107-108).

A. H. Strong said that if the church followed the analogy of circumcision in the Old Testament, it would be a hereditary body in which fleshly birth rather than the new birth qualifies for membership. If the analogy were true, circumcision followed the natural birth; therefore, baptism should follow the new birth (*Systematic Theology*, 954; see the interesting discussion of infant baptism in Trutz Rendtorff, *Ethics* II, 117-20).

Priests and worshipers expressed their worship in physical acts and postures. They prostrated themselves on the ground in humility and lifted their hands to receive the blessing for which they had prayed. "Worship was full of color, noise and movement" (Robinson, "The Old Testament Background," 20; compare Rowley, *Worship in Ancient Israel*, 206-207). The smell of blood and burning meat often accompanied worship in the temple. The music consisted largely of clanging cymbals and blaring trumpets and horns. Some singing was antiphonal, accompanied by stringed music, and probably was melodious at times.

The Old Testament gives almost no details about what went on during the major festivals. All males were required to attend, but most of them never went to Jerusalem for the feasts. "It is probably fair to say that the majority of the Israelites never saw the temple" (Herbert, *Worship in Ancient Israel*, 26-27). Leviticus 16 gives some details of the observance of the Day of Atonement, but this still leaves blank places in our understanding of what occurred.

Many scholars have tried to reconstruct the forms of the festivals from their study of the Old Testament and comparative religions, without much agreement. Sigmund Mowinckel saw the fall festival primarily as an "enthronement festival for Yahweh." His hypothesis is based on many of the psalms, including 29, 47, 93, 95—99 (Mowinckel, *The Psalms in Israel's Worship*; compare Kraus, *Worship in Israel*, 108-122). Kraus argued that the fall festival was primarily a Royal-Zion festival in which God's covenant with David was renewed. Artur Weiser believed that the covenant renewal was the celebration of the Sinai covenant (see *The Psalms*).

Israel's worship was dramatic at times. They lived in booths during the fall festival. They put blood on their doorposts at Passover. They marched around Jerusalem and counted its towers (Ps. 48) and bound the festal branches to the horns of the altar (Ps. 118:27). They danced (Ex. 32:19; Judg. 21:21; 2 Sam. 6:14; Pss. 87:7; 149:3; 150:4), lit candles (1 Kings 7:49), and poured out water (1 Sam. 7:6). Most Old Testament forms of worship did not last. After A.D. 70 Israel's worship had to be expressed without sacrifice, altar, and priests. Herbert said that this fact suggests a certain impermanence and inadequacy of worship to meet total human needs in worship (see *Worship in Ancient Israel*).

The sacrificial system was inadequate. The prophets recognized that God required obedience and not merely rote, external, detached offerings of sacrificial animals (1 Sam. 15:22; Hos. 6:6; Mic. 6:8). Old Testament sacrifices were gifts to God, but people, not God, needed help (atonement). If a person furnished the sacrifice, how could anything a human might bring absolve a person of guilt?

H. H. Rowley said that the highest word on sacrifice in the Old Testament is not in the priestly code and does not involve an animal. The highest word on sacrifice in the Old Testament concerns the future sacrifice of the Suffering Servant, a man without sin. That is a voluntary, vicarious sacrifice on behalf of Israel and the nations and will be accomplished through the suffering, death and "resurrection" of the servant (see Rowley, *The Faith of Israel*, 97; Rowley, *The Unity of the Bible*, 55-59).

The term "resurrection" does not occur in Isaiah 53, but some kind of life beyond death is intended in 53:10-11: "He shall see his offspring, and shall prolong his days. . . . Out of his anguish he shall see light; /he shall find satisfaction through his knowledge." Some understand this to refer to the nation after the exile. Muilenburg said, "If the servant is the community, we have ample precedent for the idea, but it would be striking if Second Isaiah referred to the resurrection of an individual, since this represents a late development. . . . The great surprise of the nations reflected in vs. 1 and 52:13 need not imply that an individual is meant" (*Isaiah 40—66*, 629).

On the other hand, Westermann said that two things are made clear in 53:9. First, the report has in view one single man, an individual. Second it shows "perfectly plainly that the one about whom the report is made had actually died and been buried" (*Isaiah 40—66*, 266).

About Isaiah 53:10 Westermann said that in spite of all appearances, now we are told that all along Yahweh was on the side of the servant and has revived, restored, and healed him. Westermann was quite sure that the servant's resurrection is reported here. The text does not actually say this, but "there is no doubt that God's act of restoring the Servant, the latter's exaltation, is an act done upon him after his death and on the far side of the grave" (*Isaiah 40—66*, 267).

The Old Testament sacrificial system came to an end in A.D. 70 when the temple was destroyed. The New Testament indicates that Jesus' death on the cross was the ultimate sacrifice which fulfilled the Old Testament sacrifices (Heb. 9:23—10:14).

Not only were Old Testament sacrifices inadequate, the temple as the dwelling place of God was inadequate. The Old Testament itself recognized its own inadequacy at this point. God could not live in a temple made with human hands (1 Kings 8:27). Worship at the temple in the Old Testament was exclusive. Certain groups could not enter. A disfigured person, an illegitimate person, a Moabite, or an Ammonite could not enter the place of worship (Deut. 23:1-3). A leper or unclean person could not enter the camp (Num. 5:1-4). Isaiah 56:3-8 indicates that in the future, foreigners, eunuchs, and outcasts would be allowed to come into the temple, since it was to become a house of prayer for all people.

To say that Old Testament worship was inadequate to meet all human needs in worship is not to say that Old Testament worship was without value. Muilenburg said that when we inquire, "What is the supreme good for man, the Old Testament answers, 'it is supremely good for man to worship God'" (*The Way of Israel*, 107). Worship in the Old Testament is not "a flight into the dim unknown, to timelessness, or to a presence that disturbs and elates one in ecstasy. It is a holy meeting in which God grants forgiveness, comfort, and guidance, and where the worshiper responds in praise, often reciting God's great redemptive acts" (*The Way of Israel*, 107-108). The life of worship was rescued from otherworldliness and irresponsible ecstasy by the repeated insistence on moral obedience.

Why does the Old Testament say it is good to worship God? Because in worship Israel discerned the source of their existence and the destiny to which they were called; because in worship Israel heard the word of forgiveness; because behind and in their life there was "an ultimate love which comprehends all, judges all in wrath yet is merciful" (Muilenburg, *The Way of Israel*, 126).

In their worship Israel realized they were free. In Old Testament hymns, laments, confessions, thanksgivings, songs of trust, blessings, and curses we have the words of released, liberated people. In the sanctuary these people feel free to speak, free to pray, free to confess and disclose the awful secrets of the heart, free to sing and praise and adore. In this last freedom they are free indeed, for they have been delivered from the egocentricities and self-obsessions which lay people low and make them trivial and caviling.

"Israel is liberated in her acknowledgment of her relation to a transcendent God, who cannot be fettered by the work of man's hands nor by the sophistries of their thoughts. The true Israel is free in the only freedom available to man" (Muilenburg, *The Way of Israel*, 127).

The Good Life

38. The Good Life and Religion in the Old Testament

The good life or "ethics" in the Old Testament is closely related to worship and religion. Most ethical rules and regulations in the Old Testament are in the cultic materials. Muilenburg said, "When we . . . inquire what is the supreme good for man, the answer of the Old Testament is plain for all to hear. It is supremely good for man to worship God" (*The Way of Israel*, 107). Christopher Wright said that "theology and ethics are inseparable in the Bible" (*An Eye for An Eye*, 19).

Did all of Israel's ideas of the good life or "ethics" come from their idea of God and His commands, or were some drawn from the culture? Walther Eichrodt believed that both sources are evident in the Old Testament. Israel knew little about a morality apart from religion. The Old Testament confirms the idea that moral conduct is derived from the all-ruling will of God. "From the earliest to the latest periods it is God's demand, . . . vested with absolute authority, which is the strongest and the dominating motive of human conduct. The power of the good rests entirely on the recognition of God as the One who is good. Of moral behavior for the sake of an abstract good there is none" (*Theology of the Old Testament II*, 316).

Nevertheless, even within a morality so strongly determined by religious factors, norms possess a certain independent validity, an unconditional "ought," which is absolutely
valid in itself because it is an imperative not only for Israel but
for all people. Gerhard von Rad warned that one should not be
misled as to the actual significance of such norms as the Decalogue, the Sermon on the Mount, and the divine imperative
in determining the conduct and decisions of individuals in
society.

As a rule, the call to ethical behavior comes to the individual
from quite a different direction. Every individual possesses a
family, tribe, or town—some specific form of community life.
The community has its own ethical standards. It compels all
individuals to live up to specific communal expectations. It
provides them with long established examples and values.

It would be unrealistic, therefore, to understand the behav-
ioral rules of a community as the expression of specific absolute ethical convictions of principle or divine imperative. "The
role which a man has to play in the community into which he
is born is to be [sic] great extent conditioned and determined
by community considerations" (von Rad, *Wisdom in Israel*, 75).
Examples of such peer pressure in society in Israel may be
seen in such expressions as "folly in Israel" (Gen. 34:7; Deut.
22:21; Judg. 19:23,30; 2 Sam. 13:12; Jer. 29:23) and "It is not
so done in our country" (Gen. 29:26; Deut. 25:9).

Vriezen said that it is one-sided and incorrect to insist, as
some biblical scholars have, that the whole of religious and
moral ideas spring from only one of these two sources (revelation or society). When the ethical values in the Old Testament
are simply looked upon as inspired of God, the morality of the
Old Testament is made into something completely absolute.
"In this way it seems possible to solve all moral problems, even
those of our day, with the help of the Old Testament, a point of
view that must be considered extremely dangerous to Christian ethics" (*Outline of Old Testament Theology*, 377). On the
other hand, when the ethical values in the Old Testament are
said to come from society alone, "morality becomes an entirely
fortuitous social phenomenon that has only historical importance and can no longer have any fundamental meaning for
us" (*Outline of Old Testament Theology*, 378).

Bruce Birch said that our moral character is shaped by many different influences on our lives. If our identity is to be Christian, the Bible must be primary but not self-sufficient. "It [the Bible] can never be the sole source of authoritative influence in the shaping of Christian character and conduct" (*Let Justice Roll Down*, 34). Birch said the Bible plays a key role in our *decision making*, but it never makes moral decisions for us or lays out strategies or courses of action. "The Bible cannot be used as a prescriptive code book. Many issues requiring moral decision were never imagined by the biblical communities (e.g.: bio-ethical issues)" (*Let Justice Roll Down*, 32). For Birch, the Bible's authority is inescapable without being absolute.

Old Testament morality does not come from society alone. It is not autonomous. In this sense it is diametrically opposed to Greek and modern philosophical ethics, which attempt to build a morality on the basis of human reason, starting with an *idea of the good*. Human conscience is not the starting point of the knowledge of good and evil in the Old Testament. The Word of God is. "Conscience, in the meaning of the autonomous sense of justice inherent in man, is the product of an a-religious humanism. . . . In later times the Jews do not know the concept of conscience in the Western sense of the word" (Vriezen, *Outline of Old Testament Theology*, 379, n. 2).

The Old Testament does not contain a system of ethics. The word "ethics" does not occur in the Old or the New Testament (Lofthouse, "Biblical Ethics," 350). Muilenburg said that anyone who speaks of the "ethics" of ancient Israel uses the term with considerable latitude. If by "ethics" we mean the *theory* or *science* of right conduct, the *principles* of morality, or the *systematic analysis* of the "good," then we will look in vain in the pages of the Old Testament for such formulations. We find there no unified and coherent body of ethical principles (Muilenburg, *The Way of Israel*, 15; compare Trutz Rendtorff, *Ethics* II, 3). Instead the Old Testament offers pictures of various states of society and ideas of right and wrong obeyed and disobeyed. The main interest of the writers is not with humanity but with God; His will, purposes, commands, pleasure, and displeasure (Lofthouse, "Biblical Ethics," 350).

People in the Old Testament knew that they had been addressed, that they had been told what was required of them

(Mic. 6:8). They knew what demands were incumbent upon them and who exacted such demands. "What is good is what God requires, what is evil is what God forbids" (Muilenburg, *The Way of Israel*, 15).

If the term "ethics" does not occur in the Old Testament and no "system" of ethics can be found there, we may ask whether it is appropriate to discuss Old Testament ethics or morality in a study of Old Testament theology. Scholarly opinion has been divided on this question. Few full-length studies have been devoted to a study of Old Testament ethics.

39. A Review of the Literature on the Good Life or Old Testament "Ethics"

Brevard Childs wrote in 1970 that in spite of the great interest in ethics, no outstanding modern work written in English attempts to deal adequately with biblical ethics (*Biblical Theology in Crisis*, 124). Ronald Clements concluded:

> The subject of Old Testament ethics has proved to be a most difficult one and has in fact generally been treated as a subsidiary part of the wider study of Old Testament theology. The literature devoted to it has been surprisingly sparse, and the complex interaction of historical, sociological and religious factors has made it a subject in which it has been difficult to avoid the merely superficial (*One Hundred Years of Old Testament Interpretation*, 107).

One of the first books on Old Testament ethics in English was written by a strong conservative Landmark Baptist, W. A. Jarrel. In the third edition of his book (1890), Jarrel noted that the "subject of this volume—Old Testament Ethics—in the field of apologetics has been almost totally ignored or neglected" (*Old Testament Ethics Vindicated*, iii). The fact that Jarrel took an apologetic approach to this subject is emphasized by the title of his book, *Old Testament Ethics Vindicated*: "Being an Exposition of Old Testament Morals; a Comparison of Old Testament Morals with the Morals of Heathen—so-called—'Sacred Books,' Religions, Philosophers, and Infidel Writers; and a Vindication of Old Testament Morals against Infidelity."

Jarrel quoted Professor H. B. Smith's *Apologetics* as saying, "One thing is certain, that infidel science will rout everything excepting thorough-going orthodoxy. All the flabby theories, and the molluscous formations, and the intermediate purgatories and speculations will go by the board. The fight will be between a stiff, thorough-going orthodoxy and a stiff, thorough-going infidelity."

Jarrel did recognize that Old Testament ethics are germinal and preparatory to New Testament ethics and are accommodated to the Old Testament age. But he maintained that from first to last, Old Testament ethics are "as *pure* as the New, as spotless as the throne of God" (*Old Testament Ethics Vindicated*, iii).

Old Testament Ethics Vindicated contains fourteen chapters on such subjects as: Old Testament ethics germinal and preparatory to New Testament Ethics; Indispensable rules to Old Testament interpretation (The Old Testament lays the only Ethical basis); The Sabbath essential to Old Testament laws and regulations; Revelation essential to Old Testament ethics; the Ten Commandments the constitution to Old Testament ethics; Ethical nature and design of Old Testament ceremonies; Some of the miscellaneous Hebrew laws relating to Ethics; Old Testament care and tenderness for animals; Old Testament laws concerning treatment of enemies, heathen and strangers; Old Testament and servants; women, marriage, the family and chastity; answer to infidel objections; Old Testament ethics in basis and structure morally faultless, spotless and holy. Jarrel was well acquainted with the leading theologians and the theological currents of his day. In a circular printed at the end of his book *The Gospel in Water*, he quotes eighty-four denominational and theological leaders recommending his book. Among those quoted are: Methodist Bishop Wilson; Baptist scholars John R. Broadus, J. R. Graves, Alexander McLaren, C. H. Spurgeon, J. P. Boyce, A. H. Strong, W. R. Harper, B. H. Carroll. Other leading scholars quoted are Geo. P. Fisher, and J. A. Dorner (Berlin). Perhaps the best evaluation of this book comes from the secular *Cincinnati Daily Gazette* (from the flyleaf of *Old Testament Ethics Vindicated*, 1882 edition):

> The author is well up on the literature of the subject and cites freely from writers of every variety of opinion and battles valiantly for the Old Testament. . . . Mr. Jarrel can hardly be

denominated an apologist, for he carries the war into the ene-my's camp and hews about him without mercy. It is decidedly refreshing in these times of timid compromise to find one who is so firm in his opinions and who gives so much good reason for the fact. . . . No one can object when Ingersoll and his imitators are slayed alive with their own weapons.

Although he was not the first to venture into this field, W. S. Bruce (1846-1933), a pastor of the Church of Scotland at Banff, wrote the only major book in English on Old Testament ethics in the first half of the twentieth century. Bruce was edu-cated in Aberdeen, Edinburgh, and Tübingen. At Tübingen he studied with G. F. Oehler who influenced his views on the Old Testament and ethics. He published the first edition of *The Ethics of the Old Testament* in 1895. The aim of the book is "to exhibit in a short compass the Ethics of the Old Testament in its historic growth and development" (*The Ethics of the Old Testament*, 1). For Bruce, the ethics of the Old Testament do not start with an abstract theory of virtue, but represent a morality "designed by God for a people at a rudimentary stage of religious education." Bruce wrote when Old Testament crit-icism was in a period of transition. He was aware of the docu-mentary hypothesis for the composition of the Pentateuch but chose not to deal with it. He said, "The battle of the critics regarding the authenticity and literary features of these ancient writings is not yet ended. The grain is still upon the threshing floor of Araunah the Jebusite, and vigorous arms ply the flail. . . . If we should ultimately have to give up some old and revered traditions that have come down to us regarding the growth of the canon of the Old Testament, yet the laying aside of these will only the more reveal the intrinsic beauty and perennial freshness of the Scriptures. The loss will prove a gain. The soil will be the better for the critics' sifting, and where weeds once stood, flowers and fruit will grow" (*The Eth-ics of the Old Testament*, 4-5).

Bruce recognized that there should be some general charac-teristics or principles for the study of Old Testament ethics. His enunciation of these principles is not very distinct. The reader may be able to detect some of the principles as: (1) the Old Testament is unscientific and unsystematic in form, yet with a great moral purpose running through the whole history of Israel; (2) a person in the Old Testament is free to choose; (3) because of the Fall, the Highest Good is thrown forward into the Messianic hope; (4) the Highest Good became a universal not a national goal; (5) the good is sometimes defined in material terms and sometimes in ethical terms; (6) sometimes the goal is expressed in outward symbols and sometimes in inward symbols; (7) the Highest Good is never that of the *individual* good; (8) the ultimate basis of ethics in the Old Testament is the will of God (*The Ethics of the Old Testament*, 26).

One strength of Bruce's book is that he saw that Old Testament ethics must be viewed in the context of election and covenant (*The Ethics of the Old Testament*, 63). Bruce said that the Old Testament's idea of election is a much grander and higher conception than the narrow individualistic one, common to Calvinistic theology. It is an election to service (*The Ethics of the Old Testament*, 65). He gave much attention to the law as a covenant law and devoted two chapters (6, 7) to the Ten Commandments.

Bruce noted that the Ten Commandments stand at the head of the Book of the Covenant. The Ten Commandments have a moral eminence of their own, unrivaled in comprehensiveness, excellency, and simplicity. They sum up in a pregnant form Israel's duties as a people of God. Many Old Testament laws were temporary, but "the Decalogue had been retained unchanged in the Christian church. . . . There is nothing in it that is not valid for mankind. It is a universal code of morals. No compendium of morality among ethnic religions can be compared with it" (*The Ethics of the Old Testament*, 95).

In chapters 9 and 10 Bruce discussed Old Testament laws dealing with relevant ethical issues including the land, slavery, sanitation, the poor, women and children, and worship and ethical conduct. Chapters 11-13 are devoted to the future life and a development of Old Testament ethics through Mosaism, Prophetism, Wisdom, and later Judaism.

At the end of his book Bruce discussed the moral difficulties in the Old Testament under three classes. Class 1 included difficulties connected with the character or actions of God such as the destruction of the Canaanites. Class 2 discussed the imperfect character and actions of some Old Testament "saints" such as Abraham, Jacob, Moses, David, and some psalmists. Class 3 consisted of difficulties arising from moral defects of the law, such as the permission of slavery (*The Ethics of the Old Testament*, 283).

Bruce's book was the last major book on Old Testament ethics until Johannes Hempel published his *Das Ethos des Alten Testaments* in Berlin in 1938 (rev. ed. 1964) and H. van Oyen published his *Die Ethik des Alten Testaments* in 1967. In the 1960s articles and books on "Biblical Ethics" or on some ethical issues began to appear, but very little work was done in the area of Old Testament ethics alone. In 1961 James Muilenburg published *The Way of Israel: Biblical Faith and Ethics*. T. B. Maston published a survey of *Biblical Ethics* in 1967 in which he devoted 108 pages to Old Testament ethics. James Crenshaw and John T. Willis published *Essays in Old Testament Ethics* in 1974.

Edmond Jacob said that Old Testament theology should deal "only with God and his relationship with man and the world. Piety, religious institutions and ethics are not part of Old Testament theology's domain" (*Theology of the Old Testament*, 32). Although Jacob made no room in his major work for a fully developed treatment of ethics in the Old Testament, he did say that a summary of obligations like that of Micah 6:8 shows that the *imitation* of God is the mainspring of all the religion and *ethics* in the Old Testament (*Theology of the Old Testament*, 105, 173).

Whereas most Old Testament theologies treat the subject of ethics in sporadic ways, Eichrodt, Vriezen, and Rowley devoted separate sections or chapters to it. The title of chapter 22 in Eichrodt's *Theology of the Old Testament* is "The Effect of Piety on Conduct" (Old Testament Morality). The chapter contains more than sixty pages. Eichrodt traced an ethic "of different colors" through the different periods of Old Testament history. He saw the true ethic of Yahwehism struggling against the popular morality. The popular morality gradually gives way to the higher ideas of Yahwehism.

Vriezen discussed Old Testament ethics in two sections: Motives and Limitations. Under Motives he asserted that the religious nature of morality is the foundation of all action, and the two guiding principles of ethical action are a sense of community and individual responsibility. Under Limitations,

Vriezen discussed historically oriented limitations such as slavery and polygamy, national limitations, legal limitations, casuistry in ethics, and eudaemonistic ("happiness") traits.

H. H. Rowley called his discussion of ethics in the Old Testament "The Good Life." He said, "In the faith of Israel the good life consists in doing the will of God" (*The Faith of Israel*, 124). This statement is of little significance until the will of God is defined. Rowley noted that Allah is represented in the Koran as a slave-owner whom the slaves are to obey implicitly. He also noted that the Old Testament refers to the people of Israel as servants or slaves of Yahweh *'abde*. The Hebrew and Islamic ideas of obedience are not the same.

The Suffering Servant (slave) in Isaiah 53 is a title of honor rather than dishonor. While some passages in the Old Testament understand the will of God in ritual terms, the essence of Israel's faith claims that His will is conceived in moral and spiritual terms. Rowley believed that the strong moral and ethical emphasis of Old Testament faith began long before the eighth century prophets, probably with Moses (*The Faith of Israel*, 126).

Rowley concluded that the good life, as the Old Testament presents it, is the life lived in harmony with God's will. It expresses itself daily in reflecting the character of God. It draws its inspiration and strength from communion with God and the fellowship of His people in public worship and private experience.

Perhaps Georg Fohrer, more than any other modern Old Testament scholar, has tried to integrate Old Testament ethics and Old Testament theology. In his *Theologische Grundstrukturen des Alten Testaments*, "Theological Foundations of the Old Testament," the former editor of *ZAW* gave great attention to Old Testament ethics. He did not devote a separate chapter to ethics, but he saw ethics as inherent in the "ground-structures" in the Old Testament. The central or primary "ground-structures" are the lordship of Yahweh and communion with Yahweh.

God is presented in the Old Testament in personal terms. Yahweh addresses individuals in apodictic (unconditional) laws and calls them to decide to obey or disobey. Fohrer said the Old Testament history should not be called *Heilsgeschichte*, "salvation history," but *Entscheidungegeschichte*, "decision history." Faith and conduct are inseparable. Yahweh is "a God of ethical will, a God of morals and morality" (*Theologische Grundstrukturen*, 164). Fohrer's last chapter (7) on "applications" is an attempt to apply the ethical principles of the Old Testament to the state, social life, humanity and technology, and the future. Ricky L. Johnson's review of Fohrer's book drew a number of conclusions from Fohrer's discussion of the state: (1) The state is secondary in importance to the community of families. The state is not an order of creation but an earthly human institution. (2) A person can serve the state only by loving God with all one's might. (3) The state has no absolute claims on its people. (4) The Old Testament maintains the right of individuals to disobey a state that pursues evil ends. (5) The Old Testament speaks of people as brothers and sisters. Therefore, people are not to be subjects but partners in rulership, and the ruler is to serve the people (Johnson, "The Place of Ethics in Old Testament Theology," 60). Fohrer lived during Hitler's regime in Germany, a fact that probably explains his concern with ethics and the state.

In 1978 John Barton analyzed Hempel's and Eichrodt's works on Old Testament ethics. He agreed that both works continue to have great value and are fundamental for modern study ("Understanding Old Testament Ethics," 44). Both also have shortcomings. Barton said that the picture the reader is likely to get from these works will probably be an artificial construct whose coherence and system is purchased at a price of historical objectivity and verifiability. Barton believed that it is virtually impossible to write "The Ethics of the Old Testament." However, treatments of particular areas of Old Testament morality might be made easier by removing this ideal ("Understanding Old Testament Ethics," 44).

Barton criticized both Hempel and Eichrodt for supporting so strongly a development in Old Testament ethics. Barton believed that different ethical ideas and actions in the Old Testament probably come from different groups present in Israel at the same time rather than from the same group at different periods in Old Testament history. "Talk of development is idle when there are so many variables" ("Understanding Old Testament Ethics," 49). Barton argued against Hempel and Eichrodt that models other than that of obedience to the will of God may be found in the Old Testament as the basis of ethics ("Understanding Old Testament Ethics," 51). Barton objected to Hempel's and Eichrodt's rationale for ethics in the Old Testament, "obedience to the will of God," saying that their presupposition was their starting point.

Barton enumerated three possible starting points:

(1) admission of obedience to God's revealed will;

(2) a conformity to a pattern of natural order or a belief that creation somehow works according to moral principles;

(3) a notion of the imitation of God.

Barton quoted both Buber and Eichrodt in support of the third viewpoint. He then invited others to join him in an invigorating exploration of the ethics of the Old Testament. Barton took up his own challenge in an article called "Natural Law and Poetic Justice" and in a chapter entitled "Approaches to Ethics in the Old Testament" (see *Beginning Old Testament Study*, edited by John Rogerson, 113-130).

In "Approaches to Ethics in the Old Testament" Barton quoted two Old Testament passages (1 Sam. 15:32-33; Mic. 6:8) which may represent the low and high points of Old Testament ethics. These two passages show the variety and extremes of "ethical" conduct or morality found in the Old Testament. As a way to get a handle on the subject, Barton suggested two ways to understand the term "Old Testament ethics." First, it may refer to a study of the historical development of ideas about morality in ancient Israel. Second, it may refer to a system which recognizes the Old Testament as a part of Christian Scripture and asks what the Old Testament has to say to us about ethical issues. He discussed the first under the heading "Ethics in Ancient Israel" and the second as "The Ethics of the Old Testament." The "Ethics in Ancient Israel" reflected in the Old Testament were extremely variable. Time and different social groups were the primary factors responsible for such variable ethical ideas and conduct. In "The Ethics of the Old Testament" the Old Testament is approached as a finished work and as a part of Christian Scripture. The variety is not as noticeable, and it is possible to speak of moral norms and the basis of morality in the Old Testament (see Rogerson, *Beginning Old Testament Study*, 123, 127).

Henry McKeating took up Barton's distinction between "The Ethics of the Old Testament" and "Ethics in Ancient Israel" in a study of the sanctions against adultery in ancient Israelite society. He showed that in the ethics of ancient Israel, although the law (Torah) required the death penalty for adulterers, the actual practice of dealing with adulterers in the Old Testament was much less harsh. One cannot always tell what the law of a society is by observing the behavior of the people. Laws may express an ideal or desirable behavior, but society might permit or tolerate lower levels of behavior.

McKeating said that Old Testament ethics is "a theological construction, a set of rules, ideals and principles theologically motivated throughout and in large part religiously sanctioned" ("Sanctions Against Adultery," 70). The study of that theological construct is important, but so is the study of the actual ethical norms of what was supposed to be done. These were supported by a whole battery of sanctions from religious obligations, cultural behavior patterns, and courtesy or etiquette to criminal law. In relation to any given offense the Law, Prophets, and Wisdom Literature may use different sanctions, but this fact does not mean that these materials support different ethical standards. "It simply means that they are concerned with operating different bits of the machinery of social control" (McKeating, "Sanctions Against Adultery," 68).

John Goldingay addressed the problems of Old Testament ethics in his *Approaches to Old Testament Interpretation*. He noted that Judaism uses the word *halakah*, "walk" or "way," in discussing questions of behavior. Goldingay suggested that an ethicist might distinguish five ways in which the Scriptures direct this "walk" or "way": (1) by explicit commands; (2) by examples of behavior; (3) as a source of values or principles; (4) by its influence on one's overview of reality; and (5) by the way its stories, images, paradigms, and beliefs shape character.

However, each of these five ways the Scriptures influence conduct requires interpretation. Which Old Testament commands are still binding? Which examples of Old Testament character are to be imitated and which avoided? How are principles for proper behavior to be deduced from the Old Testament? Is one's view of reality primarily that of a Redeemer or

Creator, or both? How is character shaped by Old Testament materials?

On the basis of his study of "law" in the Old Testament and New Testament, Goldingay concluded that a Christian ethicist will not take Old Testament law as the last word on behavior, but neither will he ignore it as a possible source of guidance for decision-making as to the way God expects His people to live. "The Christian Ethicist will not become a legalist, an antinomian, a strict contextualist, nor a prescriptionist" (*Approaches to Old Testament Interpretation*, 50-51).

One problem Goldingay found in using the Old Testament as a guide to ethical behavior is its specificity. Most Old Testament laws and "ethical" materials are expressed in specific historical, cultural, and social terms designed to function in specific situations. One specific example may be seen in the Old Testament admonition of "not boiling a kid in its mother's milk" (Ex. 23:19; 34:26; Deut. 14:21). Many of those concrete situations present in the Old Testament no longer exist. New situations have arisen, raising questions about such things as euthanasia. How can the Old Testament help in such times of decision-making?

Goldingay suggested that the specificity of God's commands in the Old Testament may be the concrete expression of some principle. Cultural changes are real, but cultural continuity is also real. "God remains consistent, and the conditions of human life today are not totally discontinuous with those of biblical cultures" (*Approaches to Old Testament Interpretation*, 53).

Some Old Testament passages may have priorities in serving as the basis of Old Testament ethics: (1) the Decalogue; (2) the principle of holiness as a way of imitating God (Lev. 11:44-45; 19:1-2); and (3) the covenant framework of the Old Testament laws (Deut. 5—11). Old Testament laws were given to ordinary, sinful people. If the people of Israel had not sinned, laws may not have been necessary. Therefore, laws regulating war, slavery, and economics were aimed to draw society back toward God's ideal (Goldingay, *Approaches to Old Testament Interpretation*, 59).

Are biblical ethics sufficient for today, or have twentieth-century citizens progressed so far that they no longer need Old or New Testament principles of conduct? Goldingay said that some may think so because the Bible does not make explicit all of the implications of its own theology (*Approaches to Old Testament Interpretation*, 61). It is true that both the Old and the New Testaments accepted the institutions of monarchy and slavery because the ideal had not been realized. But systems of injustice, oppression, and abuse were already being modified by the biblical faith.

A limitation of Old Testament ethics which twentieth-century theologians do not understand is the fact that "ethics" are not distinguished from "custom," "Law," and "religion" in the Old Testament. In some contexts the religious may seem to have priority over the ethical. To follow Yahweh's direction may take a person to the very verge of the "unethical" (Gen. 22). Israel's ideal heroes—including Abraham the liar, Moses the murderer, and David the adulterer—were heroes because they followed in Yahweh's way rather than accepting the way of another god (*Approaches to Old Testament Interpretation*, 64).

Again, a different approach from our own can be instructive. The Bible says that all of life is to be lived before God. It does not compartmentalize God's concerns or declare that ethics are more important than worship, even though some prophets come close to saying that. Hosea, Amos, Isaiah, and Micah say that ethics are more important than corrupt worship (Isa. 1:10-14; Hos. 6:6; Amos 5:23-24; Mic. 6:1-8).

The Old Testament does not divide its laws into moral, civil, and ceremonial types. All laws recognize the lordship of one Yahweh. All Old Testament laws were given to one specific cultural community. Since Jesus is the fulfillment of the promises to Israel, all Old Testament laws must be interpreted in light of the person, work, and teaching of Christ; and all may be instructive today in light of the principles they embody (*Approaches to Old Testament Interpretation*, 65).

Walter Kaiser's very conservative background is evident throughout his work, which shows familiarity with the latest Old Testament scholarship and excellent summaries of many of the latest contributions to this field of study. However, two old works seem to have had the greatest influence on Kaiser's views. These are an article on Old Testament ethics by William B. Greene, Jr., in the *Princeton Theological Review* in 1929, and the 1909 edition of W. S. Bruce's book on Old Testament ethics (Kaiser, *Toward Old Testament Ethics*, 22).

Kaiser's book has five major sections: (1) Definition and method; (2) summary of moral texts in the Old Testament, including the Decalogue, book of the covenant, and Holiness Code; (3) content of Old Testament ethics, including such topics as family, war, capital punishment, marriage, sex and divorce, wealth, lying, and motives; (4) moral difficulties in the Old Testament; and (5) conclusions regarding Old Testament ethics and New Testament applications. Kaiser said that his work is intended to suggest and probe rather than to stand as a *fait accompli*, therefore, he used the word "Toward" in the title of the book.

Christopher J. H. Wright took a fresh approach to the field of Old Testament ethics in his *An Eye for an Eye*, published in 1983. The subtitle is "The Place of Old Testament Ethics Today." In a very "popular" way (few footnotes and technical terms), Wright said that the way to understand and apply Old Testament ethics is not to plunge into the Old Testament and seize whatever appears relevant (*An Eye for an Eye*, 19). Instead, we must put ourselves in Israel's position. Then we can understand how they experienced their relationship with God and how that relationship affected their daily relationships.

Wright believed that an "ethical triangle" drawn from the Old Testament can provide the framework for our understanding. The three angles of the triangle are represented by God, Israel, and the land.

God represents the theological angle, which is most important. All Old Testament ethics are God-centered in origin, history, content, and motivation. Wright said that ethical teaching in the Old Testament presupposes God's initiative in grace and redemption; it is framed by what God has done and will do in history; it is shaped by His character and action; and it is motivated by personal experience of God's dealing with His people (*An Eye for an Eye*, 31).

The social angle in the framework of Old Testament ethics, according to Wright, is represented by Israel as the redeemed, chosen people of God who were to serve as a model or paradigm for other peoples' behavior. Israel's role was visible and tangible, not just verbal. They were to be holy as God was holy; to demonstrate in their "flesh" the great chords of freedom, justice, love, and suffering. Ultimately these qualities were "enfleshed" in Jesus and were to be reflected in the life of the new Israel (*An Eye for an Eye*, 45).

The third angle in the triangular framework of Old Testament ethics is the land promised to Abraham and his descendants. That land becomes one of the most prominent features of the entire story of the Old Testament (*An Eye for An Eye*, 46).

Wright's rapid review of the story of the land in the Old Testament leads from promise to conquest to use and abuse to loss and recovery. This shows that the land was a dominant theological, ethical, and economic theme in the Old Testament. Israel was to remember always that the land was theirs only as a gift of God. They were to be stewards of the land. The land served as a spiritual and economic thermometer to reveal the spiritual and social health of Israel's relation to God and to one another.

This three-angled approach to Old Testament ethics shows that the study of Old Testament ethics must be covenantal, canonical, and comprehensive. C. J. H. Wright demurred on the questions of Old Testament criticism. He said that we have to see the whole sweep of Scripture to ensure that our ethical constructs are consistent with the whole.

Wright recognized the validity of studying traditions underlying the finished books and of isolating, comparing, and contrasting the varying ethical emphasis of different authors, editors, and schools within the living kaleidoscope of the Old Testament document. Such a task would be appropriate in a large-scale analytical work on Old Testament ethics. "But . . . if our aim is a coherent biblical ethics, then our final authority must be the completed text in its canonical form" (*An Eye for an Eye*, 64).

In part 1 of his book Wright reconstructed the framework for a study in Old Testament ethics. In part 2 he discussed themes in Old Testament ethics. Most of his themes are community oriented, such as "economics and the land," "politics and the world of nations," "righteousness and justice," "law and the legal system," and "society and culture." The last chapter is devoted to the ethics of the individual.

Wright wrote out of a conviction that the Old Testament "when properly understood and applied as a part of the whole canon of Scripture, has a vital relevance for the whole range of our ethical concerns" (*An Eye for an Eye*, 10). His aim was to point out ways and suggest directions for proper application of ethical principles drawn from Old Testament materials.

He did not attempt to make final ethical constructs. He left that to modern economists, politicians, lawyers, and sociologists. This may be a "dream" rather than a viable hope that professional "secular" laypeople in these vital areas will take the time and interest to understand and apply Old Testament ethical principles. (Bernard S. Jackson has a very useful article on "Ideas of Law and Administration" in *The World of Ancient Israel*, ed. Ronald E. Clements, 185-202.)

Kaiser and Wright speak for the conservative view of Old Testament ethics. Walter Harrelson and Bruce Birch speak for the moderate or "liberal" view. However, Harrelson is very concerned about the loss of moral values in Western society and is willing to attribute most of the loss to an abandonment of the use of Ten Commandments and other ethical passages from the Bible in the moral education of our people. Harrelson says, "Young men and women learned the Ten Commandments by heart as a part of the catechism in many Christian communities during the past centuries. The practice has now been abandoned. . . . Many people in the Western world must surely believe that the loss of the Ten Commandments from our common life threatens to sweep away something vital" (*The Ten Commandments*, 3).

Harrelson contends that the societies of the Western world have indeed suffered a great and almost numbing loss now that these prohibitions no longer have a vital place. He cites various reasons why this loss occurred: (1) the prohibitions are a part of the *Old* Testament; (2) they were looked on as *law*; (3) they were considered *irrelevant* to life; and (4) they were viewed as *negative* and *legalistic*.

Harrelson sees a deeply felt need in Western societies today for absolute norms and prohibitions. "Men and women today do have a profound longing for set norms that can be relied upon. What kinds of conduct are simply not possible to the Christian man or woman? What is 'the good life' for the Christian family today? How can we teach our children anything that we claim to be absolutely right and binding for all of life? Is there really any such thing as a set of basic, concrete guidelines for the Christian community today?" (*The Ten Commandments*, 9-10).

Harrelson calls our moral situation "desperately grave." We have clearly gone too far in sentimental lawlessness in the name of love and mercy. We have let slip away from us the biblical picture of a God who cares fiercely about justice and will not allow injustice to continue. The religious community must maintain its social and personal ethics. Some ways must be found to describe in credible ways "the absolutely binding claim of the God of biblical faith upon the religious community and the individual. . . . We need norms that are credible and durable. Perhaps we will find that these ancient norms that have been of great value to past generations do in fact continue to have great value" (*The Ten Commandments*, 10).

In his closing chapter Harrelson points out that the Old Testament always keeps together the idea of bondage and freedom under God and the idea that the Ten Commandments are the charter of human freedom. The only way a person can find true freedom is to say no to the things that enslave and destroy. Harrelson believes that the Ten Commandments were given by Moses and exerted great influence on every aspect of Israel's life. The Ten Commandments are the negative counterpart ("You shall not . . .") of the commandment to love God and neighbor. Both are essential for human beings, and their neglect can be catastrophic. "Without such crisp prohibitions that point unmistakably to the path that leads to death, who can hold fast to the freedom under God that these bonds entail? None of us has sufficient moral energy to make decisions on all matters of moral activity one by one, as the occasions arise. A well-ingrained habit must govern most actions" (*The Ten Commandments*, 186-187).

As an example, Harrelson says that when a person is committed to not having sexual relations with anyone other than one's spouse, a commandment such as "Thou shalt not commit adultery" engenders trust, freedom from anxiety, and proper consideration of persons who otherwise might be objects of sexual exploitation. "Such a commandment is not an enslavement but a liberation, not a threat to freedom but a means to freedom, not a thwarting of life's flowering but an incentive to the flowering of human relations" (*The Ten Commandments*, 187).

Bruce Birch is most active in the field of biblical ethics. He begins his book *Let Justice Roll Down* by noting that a number of important works in the field of Christian ethics have appeared recently. He says his volume tries to relate the testimonies and stories of Israel's faith, recorded in the Hebrew canon, to the character and conduct of Christians and the Christian community in our time. It tries to bridge the gap between the Old Testament and today concerning ethical issues. The task in this volume is not to discuss those ethical issues as such but "to select and focus elements of the Old Testament traditions that can inform and undergird the task of Christian ethics related to any set of specific issues" (*Let Justice Roll Down*, 18).

In the introduction Birch lists four things this volume is not:

(1) a descriptive book on Old Testament ethics;

(2) an attempt to write the ethics of the Old Testament;

(3) an introductory text or an attempt at the comprehensive survey of the subject;

(4) intended to address topical issues in the life of the church.

Following these disclaimers, Birch turns to his positive intentions for this volume. It is consciously Christian and confessional in character. It treats the Old Testament as a portion of the canon of Scripture of the church. The volume is committed to the critical method, but not to objectivity. Birch does not believe it is possible or desirable to achieve objectivity in exercising the critical method. He describes himself as an "ecumenical Protestant Christian," concerned that the Old Testament be in dialogue with the New Testament, and as one committed to values of inclusivity with regard to gender, race, class, and age. These are admirable traits, but the book is more about how to do biblical or Christian ethics than about doing them.

40. How to Do Old Testament Ethics

A. Definition of Ethics and Old Testament Ethics

Perhaps enough has been said about how others have done and proposed to do Old Testament ethics. Do we have a better way? Any valid approach to a study of Old Testament ethics should start with a definition of ethics and Old Testament ethics and make use of proper principles of interpretation.

We said earlier that the word "ethics" is not a biblical word. It does not appear in the Old or New Testament as a list of rules or principles for living or as a theory for the conduct of human life. Our term "ethics" comes from a classical Greek term, *êthos*, or a variant of that word, *êthikos*, meaning "habit" or "custom (see Aristotle, *Natural Science, Psychology, The Nicomachean Ethics*, 134). *Ethos* appears in the New Testament several times, usually translated "custom" (Luke 1:9; 22:39; Acts 6:14; 15:1; 16:21; 26:3; 28:17) or "as usual" (Luke 2:42). The verb form occurs at least twice and is translated "accustomed" or "was customary" (Matt. 27:15; Luke 2:27). Almost all uses of êthos come from the only Greek Gentile New Testament writer, Luke, in the Books of Luke and Acts.

The idea that "ethics" means "habit" or "custom" is in line with Aristotle's philosophy. He classified ethics and state craft (politics) as practical sciences. A practical science deals with objects that (1) are alterable and (2) lie within human power. They involve deliberation and purposive choice, which can refer to what lies outside human power. Humans have within themselves the power of reason to steer their own course (Aristotle, *Natural Science, Psychology, The Nicomachean Ethics*, xxxix).

Aristotle said, "Moral excellence is the product of habit (*êthos*), and in fact has derived its name by a slight variation of that word." Aristotle taught that none of the moral virtues is implanted in us by nature, for no natural property can be changed by habit. A stone cannot be habituated to rise rather than to fall; fire cannot be habituated to move downward. The virtues are not engendered in us by nature or in opposition to nature, "rather nature gives us the capacity for receiving them—and this capacity is developed through habit" (*Natural Science, Psychology, The Nicomachean Ethics*, 134; the name

Nicomachean comes from Nicomachus, Aristotle's father, a physician of some renown).

One can easily see that Old Testament "ethics" and Nicomachean ethics are quite different in philosophy. "Ethics" or proper human conduct in the Old Testament was not the result of a habit. "Ethics" came from the revelation of God's will. George Foot Moore said:

> Right and wrong were for them [the Jews] not defined by the reason and conscience of men, naïve or reflective, nor by national custom or the *consensus gentium*, but by the revealed will of God; and constituted a distinctive Jewish morality which as a whole was different from that of other people (*Judaism in the First Centuries of the Christian Era*, Vol. 2, 79).

Many would sum up biblical ethics in the words of the two great commands: love God and your neighbor (see Luke 10:27). Love is the foundation for proper conduct, but "ethics" deal primarily with outward acts.

Millar Burrows said that essentially what Jesus taught was "the ethics of the Old Testament, with some shift of emphasis, but with no change of substance" ("Ethics of Jesus," 242). Burrows distinguished the ethics of the Old Testament, Judaism, and Jesus from modern or classical philosophical ethics. He said that the fundamental difference is that philosophical systems are secular and anthropocentric. The *summum bonum* of the philosopher is what a human considers best for humans. The Old Testament, Judaism, and Jesus are also concerned with human welfare, but in strict subordination to the will of God. What God wills is best for humans, "but it is not to be found by human reason; it is revealed" (Burrows, "Ethics of Jesus," 228).

B. Proper Principles of Interpretation

Some important things to remember in dealing with Old Testament ethics are:

1. The Old Testament is an historically and culturally conditional document. The twenty-four (Hebrew) or thirty-nine (Greek and English) books of the Old Testament were written by divinely inspired persons who lived in particular time frames and cultural milieu. Their ethical concepts and actions reflect the influence of and relation to the "customs" of their times.

2. Ethics in the Old Testament are not clearly distinguished from religion. Therefore, Old Testament laws are not divided into groups of moral, cultic, and criminal laws.

3. Old Testament ethics did not "develop" or evolve naturally. Some ethical ideals are early (see Ahlström, "Some Remarks on Prophets and Cults," 114-115). Diversity of ethical conduct is largely due, however, to the actions of different contemporary groups.

4. Ethics in the Old Testament are primarily group or community centered rather than concerned with the individual alone. The strong community emphasis in Old Testament is due largely to the concept of the covenant. This does not mean, however, that the individual was forgotten or was absorbed by the group in the Old Testament. The Ten Commandments are addressed to the individual, even though they stood as the basic covenant document.

5. The ethics of the Old Testament were primarily the ethics of the common, ordinary sinful person. Human sinfulness, frailties, and weaknesses in the moral realm are recognized. No attempt is made to hide the sins of heroes.

6. Old Testament ethics find their fulfillment or completion in Christ and in His Sermon on the Mount. W. D. Davies said, "The ethical aspirations of the Old Testament and Judaism, the Prophets and the Law were not annulled in the Christian dispensation; they were fulfilled. The early church consciously accepted the moral concern of Israel as it was illumined and completed in the light of the life, death and Resurrection of Jesus" ("The Moral Teaching of the Early Church," 311).

Christopher Wright emphasized the fulfillment of the Old Testament ethical themes in the New Testament and specifically in Christ. For example, "Economics and the Land" is the first ethical theme Wright considered in *An Eye for an Eye*. Near the end of this section Wright asked, "What happens to the Land in the New Testament?" Wright said there is no doubt that the New Testament writers regarded Jesus as the Messiah who fulfilled and embodied the mission of Israel. Therefore, the church as the organic continuation of Old Testament Israel was the spiritual seed of Abraham and the heir to the covenant and promise. The land was a major constituent of the Old Testament promise. How was that part of the promise fulfilled?

Christopher Wright stated, "The *physical territory* of Jewish Palestine is nowhere referred to with any theological significance in the New Testament. The land as a holy *place* has ceased to have relevance, partly because Christianity rapidly spread beyond its borders to the rest of the 'profane' world, but more importantly because its holiness was transferred to Christ himself. The spiritual presence of the living Christ sanctifies any place where believers are present. . . . For the holiness of place Christianity has fundamentally . . . substituted the holiness of the person" (*An Eye for an Eye*, 92-93; compare Davies, *The Gospel and the Land*, 367-368).

The use of proper principles of interpretation will go a long way in eliminating pejorative references to Old Testament ethics. The practice of disparaging Old Testament ethics is almost as old as the church. Marcion, who was born in Asia Minor and came to Rome about A.D. 140, was a "Christian" who believed, largely on moral and philosophical grounds, that the God of the Old Testament was not the same as the God of the New Testament. The Manichaeans were the followers of Mani, a Persian who was crucified about A.D. 277 (Newman, *A Manual of Church History I*, 195). Manichaeanism was a syncretistic religion with a strong gnostic and ascetical bias. The Manichaeans rejected the Old Testament and the parts of the New Testament that did not fit their views. Augustine of Hippo was a Manichaean for nine years. In more recent times, skeptics such as Thomas Paine and Robert Ingersoll coarsely selected the most shocking stories from the Old Testament and said to Christians, "That is your God—a God who approves of slavery and vengeance."

More recently, Old Testament scholars have been willing to acknowledge the imperfections in the lives and the understanding of Old Testament people. Many scholars are saying that it is time to stop emphasizing the moral and ethical problems and get on with pointing out the positive strengths of Old Testament ethics. John Bright said that Old Testament heroes are not always heroes and very seldom are saints.

> Call the roll of the heroes of faith as given in Heb. 11: not one is depicted as perfect, and many are not even admirable. Even Abraham, that paragon of faith, passed off his wife as his sister in

the interest of his own safety. Jacob, to put it bluntly, was a cheat and a crook, whose duplicity was proverbial. Moses took life in anger, Rahab was a harlot. . . . Of all these heroes of faith here listed, not one is depicted as a saint. And it is time we took this fact of biblical history seriously. It is time that we stopped combing the Bible for these dreary moral lessons of ours and tut-tutting whatever in its story displeases us. It is time that we stopped evaluating its characters from the pinnacle of some lofty Christian idealism and patronizing them for their spiritual and moral shortcomings (*The Authority of the Old Testament*, 231-232).

Edmond Jacob indicated that anyone attacking the Old Testament in the name of ethics would do well to remember that the Old Testament does not set out to give general principles of behavior without taking into "account the concrete circumstances in which they were promulgated" (*Theology of the Old Testament*, 200). Jacob asserted that the dependence of Israel's cult (worship) on history "invested it with an ethical character unparalleled in other religions" (*Theology of the Old Testament*, 268).

F. C. Eiselen emphasized the positive contributions of Old Testament ethics. He asked, "Will we ever get beyond the moral duties, according to the Old Testament, obligatory upon man? Purity of thought, sincerity of motive, singleness of purpose, truthfulness, honesty, justice, generosity, love. . . . Indeed the Old Testament emphasizes the loftiest ideals of human life and society." Eiselen cited an editorial from the *Expository Times* (Nov. 1908, 54-55), commenting on a paper read at the first International Moral Education Congress: "It is when the teaching of the Old Testament is simple, frank, and historical that it becomes the best text-book of ethics in the world" (*The Christian View of the Old Testament*, 259).

The ultimate irony of criticizing the Old Testament for its low moral standard can now be seen in the two-volume work of Friedrich Delitzsch, *Die grosse Tauschung*, "The Great Deception." John Goldingay noted that Delitzsch was particularly offended by the carnage described in books such as Joshua and by the nationalism that runs through the Prophets and the Psalms. Delitzsch's two volumes were published in Germany in 1920 and 1922, barely a decade before the beginning of the Third Reich and the rule of Adolf Hitler in 1933. Hitler's rule was marked by perhaps the greatest carnage and the strongest views of nationalism ever experienced in human history. It may be that Friedrich Delitzsch's unjust and intemperate criticism of the Old Testament helped pave the way for Adolf Hitler.

C. Methods for Doing Old Testament Ethics

Any attempt to deal with the "ethics" of the Old Testament must give at least a passing nod to the terminology of ethics in the Old Testament. James Muilenburg said, "The Old Testament is rich in ethical terminology, but it is striking that many of the words most congenial to modern man are absent. Such terms as morality, experience, conscience, personality, virtue, history and nature are not to be found although the reality they are designed to describe may . . . be present" (*The Way of Israel*, 16).

Some of the most significant ethical terms in the Old Testament are: ʾemet, "truth"; mišpāṭ "justice"; ṣedeqâ, "righteousness"; tob "goodness"; kābôd, "honor"; and šālôm "peace. Each of those terms has a wide range of meanings, and it cannot be assumed that Hebrew terms had the same connotations or association as our English words. To understand the precise meaning of each Hebrew term, one should consult a comprehensive Hebrew lexicon or a reliable modern Bible dictionary and exegete every passage in which the term occurs. Obviously we cannot do that for all of these "ethical" terms here.

We will try to capture the basic meaning(s) of three major Hebrew words vital to an understanding of Old Testament ethics: ʾemet, mišpāṭ, and ṣedeq. The basic meaning of the root ʾmn from which we get the word ʾemet is faithfulness, reliability, dependability, trustworthiness, truthfulness.

ʾemet is used of God's truth (Pss. 117:2; 146:6) and human truth (Ps. 15:2; Zech. 8:16), or the lack of it (Isa. 59:14; Hos. 4:1). God's word is truth, believable, and reliable (1 Kings 17:24). People should speak the truth (Zech. 8:16). Two of the Ten Commandments deal with telling the truth (Ex. 20:7,16; Deut. 5:11,20). The psalmist said, "You desire truth in the inward being;/ therefore teach me wisdom in my secret heart" (51:6).

The word mišpāṭ primarily means "justice." It comes from the root šāpat "to judge," but it often means "law," "custom," "ordinance," or "social justice." The word should not be understood in the modern sense of a judge rendering a decision or handing out a judgment or sentence. It is a broad term that includes all of the actions and the whole process that took place when two parties came before the proper authority to claim his or her rights. The prophets shifted the meaning of the word from its legal sense to an ethical and religious significance (see Epzstein, *Social Justice in the Ancient Near East*, 46-47; Birch, *Let Justice Roll Down*, 155).

Justice is a chief attribute of God's activity in the world (Isa. 5:16). God does not act according to some abstract legal norm. He acts in behalf of the poor, the needy, and the oppressed (Deut. 10:18; Ps. 10:18; Jer. 5:28). He acts in judgment against those who deny or withhold the rights of others (Amos 2:6-7; Mic. 2:2,8-10).

Some people in Micah's day were moral and religious relativists. They said, "One should not preach of such things;/ disgrace will not overtake us" (Mic. 2:6). Micah said such people abhor justice, pervert all equity, and build Zion with blood. They take bribes and divine for money, yet lean on the Lord and say, "Surely the LORD is with us! No harm shall come upon us" (Mic. 3:9-11). The Lord spoke through Jeremiah: "Will you steal, murder, commit adultery, swear falsely . . . and then come and stand before me . . . and say, 'We are safe!'—only to go on doing these abominations?" (Jer. 7:9-10). Micah asked Israel's leaders, "Should you not know justice (*mišpāṭ*)?—you who hate the good and love the evil,/ who tear the skin off my people,/ and the flesh off their bones" (Mic. 3:1-2).

Perhaps the greatest passage concerning God's requirements is in Micah 6:8:

> He has told you, O mortal, what is good;
> and what does the LORD require of you
> but to do justice, and to love kindness
> and to walk humbly with your God.

God told *Adam*, "mortal" (all mankind), what is good. The Old Testament has no treatise on the nature of goodness. The people of Israel had been addressed concerning what God required, and that was "good." They knew that good is what God requires, and evil is what God forbids (see Smith,*Word Biblical Themes: Micah—Malachi*, 16). Several times we read in the Old Testament that "God is good" (Pss. 100:5; 136:1). The good is part of God's essence. It has no existence apart from God. "What God wills, that is good" (R. Mehl, "Good," in *A Companion to the Bible*, 152).

God requires "goodness" from humanity. According to Micah, goodness includes three things: "justice," "kindness," and humble walk with God. Disraeli said, "Justice is truth in action." Raymond Calkins said that real religion consists in something higher than religious observances (*The Modern Message of the Minor Prophets*, 62-63).

> It is not sacrificing animals, ourselves or others. It is not a creed to believe, a feeling we experience, or something we cannot do. Justice is fair mindedness in action. It encompasses every area of life: play and business, capital and labor, buyer and seller. Justice is a badge of character. At home or away, it rules out harsh, unfair treatment of others, faultfinding and conclusions not founded in fact. Someone said, 'To build on injustice is to build on a time bomb. No permanent social order or lasting organization is built without justice" (R. L. Smith, *Word Biblical Themes: Micah—Malachi*, 17).

Justice alone is not all God requires. *Goodness* and *justice* are not synonyms. *Justice* connotes external acts. God requires our actions to be expressions of an internal love for kindness, "mercy," "loyalty." The Hebrew word is *hesed*, a great covenant word sometimes translated "devotion" (Jer. 2:2), suggesting "devoted to," committed to that person regardless of what happens.

No one can "do justice" or "love kindness" by themselves. Where is the power for people to do justice and to love mercy? It is in a humble walk with God (Mic. 6:8). When people see God in His holiness (purity and power) as Isaiah did (Isa. 6:1-2), they see themselves as they are (sinful and finite). Their relationship with other people is profoundly changed. They know all people need divine patience, pardon, and restoration. That is what Micah 6:8c means. We are to walk before God "abased in absolute humility . . . renewed in the gratitude that springs from the Divine forgiveness" (W. A. L. Elmslie, "Ethics," in *Record and Revelation*, ed. H. Wheeler Robinson, 291).

The word *ṣedeqâ* basically means "righteousness." To the modern Western mind, righteousness often connotes a legalistic, narrow concept. Actually, the primary meaning in the Old Testament is that of a proper relationship with God or with other people. In the Old Testament, a righteous person was one who "preserved peace and wholeness in the community because . . . he fulfilled the demands of communal living" (Job 29:12-16). (See Elizabeth Achtemeier, "Righteousness in the Old Testament," 81.) The "righteous" are often contrasted with the wicked *rāsāʿ*, "the evildoer," not because the latter violates a norm of ethical action but because such a person destroys the community itself by failing to fulfill the demands of community relationship.

The Old Testament often proclaims that God is righteous (2 Chron. 12:6; Neh. 9:8; Pss. 7:9; 103:17; 111:3; 116:5; Jer. 9:24; Dan. 9:14; Zeph. 3:5; Zech. 8:8). Yahweh's righteousness is never solely an act of condemnation. No verse in the Old Testament equates God's righteousness with His vengeance on the sinner. God's righteous judgments are His saving judgments (Ps. 36:6; Isa. 45:21) or deliverance (1 Sam. 12:7; Pss. 22:31; 51:14; 65:5; Isa. 46:12-13; 51:1,5-6,10; 62:1-2).

In recent years the works of H. H. Schmid have sparked a whole new approach to Old Testament theology, including the ideas of righteousness (*ṣedeq*) and ethics. For Schmid "righteousness" was a part of the created proper world order of salvation (*Heil*). Schmid argued that the idea of creation was early and central in the religions of the Ancient Near East and that Israel was familiar with this fact. Schmid claimed Israel basically shared this thinking, but expressed it "in her own way" ("Creation, Righteousness, and Salvation," 102-117).

Schmid saw the legal order and the ethical-social order as part of the universal world order. He understood the announcement in Isaiah 40:1-2 that Israel's debt has been doubly paid and salvation is close at hand against this "judgment" background. Once the marred order is restored by punishment (exile), the world returns to its order and becomes whole and healthy (*Heil*) again. In numerous passages salvation (*Heil*) is described with the word *ṣedeqâ*. In these passages "righteousness" is not described as a narrow legal matter but as the universal world order, as comprehensive salvation (Isa. 45:8,23; 46:12-13; 51:6; 54:14,17). (See "Creation, Righteousness, and Salvation," 107.)

It is true that in the New Testament "righteousness" has several meanings. In the sermon on the Mount Jesus (according to several of the best manuscripts) said, "Beware not to do your 'righteousness' (*dikaiosuné*) before men to be seen of them" (Matt. 6:1). He was speaking of almsgiving (*elemosuné*). Giving to charity was a part of "righteousness" for rabbinical Judaism.

Paul made it clear in Romans 1 and 3 that he considered the "righteousness of God" God's power to save everyone who has faith (Jews and Gentiles alike). It was not part of the world order. James Denny said the great subject of Romans and the gospel is (*dikaiosune Theou*) "the righteousness of God" ("*dikaiosune Theou,*" *The Expositor's Greek Testament III*, 589). Paul said the reason he was not ashamed to preach the gospel anywhere, even in Rome, was because of God's power to save anyone, anywhere.

Why should Paul be ashamed of the gospel? Perhaps because it meant identifying himself with a message that had for its subject a person who had been put to death as a criminal. The cross was a stumbling block to the Jews and foolishness for Gentiles, but to anyone who had faith (believed) it was the power of God. Paul quoted Habakkuk 2:4 to back up his claim. He could have cited Genesis 15:6, "And he [Abraham] believed the LORD; and the LORD reckoned it to him as righteousness." A full-length book on Old Testament ethics could deal with other major terms for ethics such as *tôb* "good" and *šālôm* "peace."

There are three common ways of doing Old Testament ethics. The first method is to examine the primary "ethical" passages in the Old Testament, including critical exegesis and word studies. The second method is to select primary ethical themes and exegete certain Old Testament passages which relate to those themes. The third approach is to use a history of Israel's religion approach, emphasizing the growth, development, or advancement of Israel's ethical ideas period by period.

The *problem with the first method* is with deciding which Old Testament passages are "the primary ethical" ones. Almost all scholars would begin with or at least include the Ten Commandments in this list. One recent writer has argued that the laws in Deuteronomy 12—26 are based on and arranged according to the Ten Commandments as given in Deuteronomy 5 (see Kaufman, "The Structure of Deteronomic

Law," 105-158; Kaiser, *Toward Old Testament Ethics*, 127-137). Other chief passages would include the Book of the Covenant (Ex. 20:22—23:33); the Holiness Code (Lev. 18—20); the Deuteronomic Code (Deut. 12—26); Job 31; Psalms 15; 24; Proverbs; Isaiah 33:13-16; Ezekiel 18:5-9; 22:6-12).

The *problem with the second method* is how to select the major ethical themes. In 1968 C. Freeman Sleeper saw signs of attempts to bridge the gap between biblical scholars and Christian ethicists. Yet no clear or consistent rationale for studying the Bible in relation to ethical questions has yet emerged. Sleeper proposed that contemporary ethical issues provide a vital context for pursuing biblical studies. He wanted to approach the Bible in a way that would not compromise the integrity of either exegesis or ethics but would exploit their interdependence ("Ethics as a Context for Biblical Interpretation," 443-460).

The *problem with the third* method is our inability to trace the growth and development of Israel's religious and moral ideas. (One who uses the "history of growth of Israel's ethics" is W. A. L. Elmslie, "Ethics," in *Record and Revelation*, ed. H. W. Robinson, 275-302.)

One should select the major ethical themes of the Old Testament by examining such passages as the Decalogue, the Book of the Covenant, the Holiness Code; Job 31; Psalms 15; 24; Isaiah 33; Ezekiel 18; 22. One could follow the suggestion of Sleeper by selecting the major ethical concerns of society, then going to the Old Testament to find what it says about them. Many of the ethical concerns of the Old Testament Laws, Prophets, and Wisdom Literature are essentially the same as many concerns in our society: the land (property), honesty, justice, truthfulness, sexual purity, war, government, the place of women. Each theme deserves a separate monograph. Much diversity appears in the Old Testament about each of these themes, but the highest word on each theme in the Old Testament would compare favorably with New Testament teachings on the subject.

D. Views of Ethical Purity in the Old Testament

Probably the highest word on ethics in the Old Testament emerges in Job 31. In his "oath of innocence" Job swore that he was innocent of twelve sins which, no doubt, his "friends" had accused him of committing. These sins are lasciviousness, falsehood, covetousness, adultery, disregard for the rights of servants, hardheartedness against the poor, trust in riches, superstition, hatred of enemies, inhospitality, hypocrisy, and exploitation of land. "Crimes" mentioned in Job 31 may not be actual or public crimes. Job was concerned about attitudes that cannot be controlled by the law ("looking on a virgin" (v. 1), "deceit" (v. 5), "heart" (vv. 7,9,27), "trusting in gold" (v. 24), "rejoiced in the ruin of an enemy" (v. 29), "concealed and hidden sins" (v. 5). Only religious and ethical sins are mentioned. Cultic sins are not included. The denial of sun-worship is religious and not cultic.

Fohrer said "it cannot be disputed that the Job who utters the oath of purity in chapter 31 stands almost alone upon an ethical summit" ("The Righteous Man in Job 31," 19). Some would say that Job attained the loftiness of the Sermon on the Mount. T. H. Robinson said, "In ch. 31 we have the highest ethical standard which the Old Testament contains" (*Job and His Friends*, 64).

Even though Job's claim of righteousness, innocence, and purity are undisputed, a fatal flaw could be found in his attitude. He boasted about his "goodness" and tried to use it as a "cudgel" to force God to acknowledge his innocence, therefore to triumph over God. Job was guilty of the original sin of Adam—that of wanting to be "like God" or of wanting to take God's place. "His ethically perfect behavior would lead him into the worst kind of sin" (Fohrer, "The Righteous Man in Job 31," 20).

Job's purpose in reciting his virtues may have been to prove that God was guilty. Yahweh asked, "Shall a faultfinder contend with the Almighty?/Anyone who argues with God must respond. . . . Will you even put me in the wrong?/Will you condemn me that you may be justified?" (Job 40:2,8).

Yahweh's question shows that ethical purity alone is not enough to please God. A person must also trust the Lord. "He has told you, O mortal what is good;/and what does the LORD require of you/but to do justice, and to love kindness,/and to walk humbly with your God?" (Mic. 6:8; compare H. W. Robinson, *Inspiration and Revelation*, 83; R. L. Smith, *Micah—Malachi,WBC,* 49-51).

If the Old Testament makes it clear that ethical purity alone is not enough to please God, it also emphasizes the fact that ritual without righteousness is worthless in the sight of God. The eighth-century prophets severely condemned nonethical religions. Today the temptation is of a different kind. People are disposed to turn away from religious observance as a waste of time and effort and to rely on their own strength and understanding.

Norman Porteous said, "Morality without religion appeals to the modern mind." Porteous saw this as a legacy of Greek thought. Early Greek religion was immoral and childish. Homer and Hesiod ascribed to the gods all that humans hold "shameful and blameworthy: theft, adultery, and deceit" (Aubrey Moore, "The Christian Doctrine of God," 51). The collision between the early immoral mythology and moral philosophy came in the times of Xenophanes. His scathing satire reminds one at times of the way Isaiah spoke about the idolatry of his day. Plato criticized the received theology of Greece on moral grounds. God cannot lie or deceive. He cannot be the cause of evil. He is good, and the only source of good. He is true in word and deed. If not, we cannot reverence Him. When we pass from Plato to Aristotle the last trace of religion in morals disappears. Theology becomes metaphysics and has no place in the world of practical life (Porteous, *Living the Mystery*, 61).

Moderns, as the heirs of Greek thought, have become accustomed to the idea of ethics and religion being considered separate autonomous disciplines, each resting on its own axioms and operating on its own independent principles. However, we should consider the pronouncements of the Hebrew prophets on ethics at least as worthy of modern ethical consideration as statements in Aristotle's *Nicomachean Ethics*. Modern moral philosophers would probably consider such a claim as overenthusiasm of the religiously naive. They are apt to look on the Hebrew prophetic writings as a primitive mixture of elements which must be kept separate. Porteous said, "Thus it comes about that a student taking Moral Philosophy at the university may never or seldom encounter the biblical teaching on the subject of morality either in the lectures or in the prescribed readings" (*Living the Mystery*, 61).

In the Bible, religion and ethics are inseparable. Worship acceptable to God must be moral. The moral side of life requires the support of regular worship. Religion and morality are not synonymous in the Old Testament. One could be religious and not be moral. Few in that day tried to be moral without being religious.

The terms "religious" and "moral" have broad meanings. What is religion? What is morality? Were Israel's neighbors religious and moral? Israel shared countless points of common culture, social norms, and conventions with her contemporaries. Yet, Israel rejected and prohibited certain practices prevalent at that time. Cultic prostitution and homosexuality, along with a variety of other sexual perversions, were outlawed in the Holiness code (Lev. 18—20). On the grounds of God's sovereignty each series of commands ended with the solemn expression "I am the Lord." All kinds of occult practices such as spiritism, mediums, witchcrafts, necromancy, and divination were prohibited. Child sacrifice was most severely condemned as an abominable practice (Deut. 12:31).

Israel tolerated some practices of the ancient world without explicit divine command or sanction. These included polygamy, divorce, and slavery. However, these practices were regulated by legal safeguards to soften or eliminate their worst effects (Wright, *An Eye For an Eye*, 176).

Some practices were accepted and affirmed with value added. One socio-cultural pattern Israel shared with her neighbors was the idea of kinship and family. The extended family concept of Israel and her neighbors included a strong tie of lateral kinship or "brotherhood." It also had a vertical effect on respect for parents, ancestors, and children. The land was tied to the family and tribal concept, thus guaranteeing an economic undergirding of the family. Israel's view of the family had a significant "value added" dimension above that of her neighbors. Although practices varied at different periods in Israel's history, monogamy was more common than polygamy. It seems that Lamech was the first to break the practice of monogamy (Gen. 4:19). Isaac had one wife, Rebekah. With the exception of the royal harems Elkanah, Samuel's father, is the only man named in Samuel and Kings with more than one wife.

Like Israel's neighbors, parents in Israel usually arranged the marriages of their children. Isaac and Rebekah's marriage and Samson's wedding were arranged (Gen. 24; Judg. 14:1-9). However, Ruth and Abigail, both widows, made their own choices of husbands (Ruth 3:7-13; 1 Sam. 25:40).

Some scholars claim the Old Testament indicates that husbands "owned" their wives as "property" or "bought" them for a *môhār* marriage present or "brideprice." (See the earlier discussion in chapter 6, Sect. 29, A.) However, the word *môhār* only occurs three times in the Old Testament (Gen. 34:12; Ex. 22:16-17; 1 Sam. 18:25), and it is by no means certain that the word meant "to buy or sell." Brevard Childs said, "The content of the Hebrew law shows remarkable transformation in respect to the other Ancient Near Eastern codes. . . . The seduction of an engaged maiden was no longer simply viewed as property damage" (*Exodus*, 476-477). Grace I. Emmerson marshaled evidence to show that wives were not considered chattel of their husbands, but ideally were to be considered equal to their husbands ("Women in Ancient Israel," *The World of Ancient Israel*, ed. R. E. Clements, 383-385, 389-391).

Two prominent ethical issues today, abortion and homosexuality, do not figure prominently in the Old Testament. Neither term appears in the Hebrew Bible. Children were considered "gifts of God." Large families were the norm. Barrenness of the womb seemed to be a larger problem than abortion. Hosea spoke of a miscarrying womb as a curse of God (Hos. 9:14). In Exodus 23:26 God promised Israel that in the land of Canaan, "no one shall miscarry or be barren."

When Elijah was "taken up" in a chariot of fire at Gilgal (a city north of Bethel), the people told Elisha the location of the city was good but the water was bad. Evidently the water was thought to cause miscarriages. Elisha went to the spring, threw salt into it, and said, "Thus says the LORD, I have made this water wholesome; from now on neither death nor miscarriage shall come from it" (2 Kings 2:19-21).

Today miscarriage or abortion is often used as a tool for family planning or general birth control. Trutz Rendtorff said, "The termination of a pregnancy is the rejection of parenthood and in principle is also the negation of the specific responsibilities that children bring" (*Ethics II*, 85; 161-167).

The word "homosexuality" does not appear in the Old Testament, but the practice was well known. Two famous incidents of widespread homosexuality in the Old Testament caused great danger and catastrophies. One incident at Sodom (Gen. 18) caused the destruction of five cities. The other incident at Gibeah (Judg. 19) led to civil war among the tribes of Israel and almost decimated the tribe of Benjamin. After the battles were over, Benjamin had only six hundred men left (Judg. 20:47). Leviticus 18:22; 20:13 called homosexuality a perversion and assigned it the death penalty.

Today homosexuality is a large social issue. Trutz Rendtorff said that homosexuality constitutes a conflict in people's self-understanding and their relationship to persons of the same sex. Some portray homosexuality as an alternate of equal value to heterosexuality and promote it as a marriage-like partnership. Homosexual practice is not in the best interests of the homosexual and "imposes general expectations that cannot be resolved" (*Ethics II*, 60).

Brevard Childs said it was not by chance that the Old Testament portrays human sexuality as the mirror of disruption. Sex is introduced in Genesis 2 as part of God's gracious acts of a good creation. The Lord said, "It is not good that the man should be alone" (Gen. 2:18). God escorts Eve to Adam, and great joy and celebration break out because of their unity and fulfillment. Shortly after that, the world is filled with violence, and Lamech boasts before his wives of his savagery (Gen. 4:23).

> The gift of human sexuality has been twisted to become a major threat to both faith and life. The rest of the Old Testament is filled with stories of sexual abuse as the once creative drive for good is unleashed with demonic power to destroy. . . . Even when the distortion of the human self through homosexuality is submerged into the narrative of the biblical text (Gen. 19:1) it continues to function as a dark shadow enveloping its characters" (Childs, *Old Testament Theology in a Canonical Context*, 225).

Recent attempts to find an opening or warrant for the practice of homosexuality go far beyond interpreting occasional texts condemning the practice. Homosexuality turns on the divine structuring of human life as male and female with the potential of greatest joy or deepest grief. "The Old Testament continually witnesses to the distortion of God's intention for humanity. . . . The Old Testament views homosexuality as a distortion of creation which falls into the shadows outside the blessing" (Childs, *Old Testament Theology in a Canonical Context*, 194).

We cannot deal with all ethical issues in the Old Testament, but we can learn some basic principles for our ethical conduct. One is that Israel put God first. The First Commandment is the foundation of biblical ethics. Israel had a scale of values expressed in the Decalogue which began with God and ended with the inner thoughts of humans. Two particular features of Israel's scale of values are significant: Life has priority over property, and persons have priority over punishment.

Regarding the relationship of the people of God to culture today, perhaps we can use the same principles that Israel used. Although we must not be too simplistic in our application of Old Testament truths and principles to the customs and practices of today, some things must be prohibited, such as idolatry, sexual perversion, exploitation, the abuse of power, and the mistreatment of the unfortunate. Since our culture is a fallen society and has not yet reached the ideal of being holy as God is holy, some practices, such as divorce, are necessary. Perhaps God's people can take some aspects of modern culture and affirm them as positive: but these aspects need to be examined thoroughly and carefully to assure they are "good."

10

Death and Beyond

The subject of this chapter is part of the larger topic "eschatology," the doctrine of last things. Eschatology usually includes both the final destiny of the individual and also the future of the universe (Bertholet, "Eschatology in the History of Religion," 215). This chapter will treat the final destiny of the individual as the Old Testament materials present it, and in the last chapter will discuss the idea of the future of the universe or the culmination of history.

Eschatology is a relatively recent term. It does not appear in the Old or New Testament. Apparently Abraham Calovius coined it for use in his dogmatic theology, *Systema locorum Theologicorium Tomus duodecimus et ultimus ESCHATOLOGIA SACRA* (1677). (See Westermann, *Prophetic Oracles of Salvation in the Old Testament*, 266.) George Bush used the term in a book called *Anastasis* ("Resurrection") published in 1845. In 1858 James Martineau published a paper called "The Eschatology of the Apocalypse and the Epistles" in *The Studies of Christianity*. In 1909 Shalier Matthews, writing in *Hastings' Dictionary of the Bible,* defined eschatology as "that department of theology which is concerned with 'last things,' with the state of the individual after death, and with the course of human history when the present order of things has been brought to a close" (compare Rist, "Jesus and Eschatology," 193).

Van der Ploeg noted that at first Catholic and Protestant theologians avoided the term *eschatology*, but now it has even crept into some texts of the second Vatican Council ("Eschatology in the Old Testament," 89). He said that *eschatology* has become a popular term used by the media and journalists to mean a "quality of the period of the end"—a definition that the Greek word *eschatos* never had. Van der Ploeg wanted to limit the meaning and use of the term to its literal meaning, "the end" ("Eschatology in the Old Testament," 98).

Lindblom said, "All events that refer to the age to come are to be designated as eschatological, even when they form part of the historical process" (*Prophecy in Ancient Israel*, 361). Old Testament passages that describe the new age may express either a positive or negative eschatology. Those referring to Israel speak of a national eschatology. Those referring to death and beyond, speak of an individual eschatology (*Prophecy in Ancient Israel*, 362). Westermann thought the term should not be used in an Old Testament theology, although most writers use the term freely (*Prophetic Oracles of Salvation in the Old Testament*, 266-277).

In the Old Testament, death is a stark reality. It never takes a holiday. Death comes to everyone (Num. 16:29; Josh. 23:14; 2 Sam. 14:14; 1 Kings 2:2; Job 14:1-2; 16:22; 30:23; Ps. 49:10; Eccl. 9:5; Isa. 51:12). Humans are like God in many ways, but differ from God in one glaring way. God is everlasting (Ps. 90:2; Hab. 1:12); persons are mortal. Alan Richardson said that the Bible "never for one moment allows men to forget their mortality; man is akin to God, he is 'visited' by God, yet he differs from God in that he shares their mortality with the beasts that perish (Ps. 49:10-12,20, *passim* [throughout]). The illusion of natural or inherent immortality is the Serpent's lie (Gen. 3:4)" (*A Theological Word Book*, 60).

Although from first to last the Old Testament is full of references to death, dying, destruction, and perishing, the problem of life and death for the individual does not seem to be "a pressing question in the Old Testament" (Zimmerli, *The Old Testament and the World*, 108). Perhaps Israel's strong emphasis on the group, family, or community took some of the sting out of the death of the individual. A person who died and was buried in the family grave was thought of as being at rest with the ancestors (Gen. 25:8-10,17; 35:29; 49:33; Num. 20:24; Deut. 32:50). God's promise of an heir to Abraham (Gen. 12:1-3) may counterbalance the curse on the ground and the announcement that a person must return to dust (Gen. 3:17-19). After the promise to Abraham was verified in the birth of Isaac, Abraham "died in a good old age, an old man and full of years, and was gathered to his people" (Gen. 25:8). The same was said of Isaac and Jacob (Gen. 35:29; 49:33).

Although humans are like animals in that both are mortal, people differ from the animals in that they are consciously aware of their approaching death (de Vries, *The Achievements of Biblical Religion*, 388). However, people do not know the time, place, or circumstance of death (Gen. 27:2,7,10; Deut. 31:27,29; Judg. 13:7; Job 21:23-26; 34:20; 36:14; Pss. 39:4-6; 49:10-12; 88:3-7,15; 90:3-6; Eccl. 3:2,19-20; 9:3-5; Isa. 40:6-8; 51:12).

41. What Is Death?

Death is the opposite of life. In the final sense, death refers to the cessation of breathing and the end of life (Job 34:14-15; Pss. 104:29; 146:4). Life is a gift of God. God controls the birth process (Job 10:10-12; Ps. 103:13-16) and the dying process (Ps. 31:15). In the Old Testament, death is more than the cessation of physical life. It could refer to anything that threatens or weakens life or vitality such as sin, disease, darkness, waters, or the sea Jacob, *Theology of the Old Testament*, 299).

Hartmut Gese noted that the ancient mind did not share our biological concept of life. We divide the world into the dead realm of minerals and the living realm of plants, animals, and humans. For ancient Israel life was more alive than our life, and what was dead was not as dead as our dead. For them life was always whole and healthy, and the severely ill person had already entered the underworld, the sphere where death was at work. According to this way of thinking, a dead person was never thought of as nonexistent (see Ps. 6:4-5; Isa. 14:4-20; Gese, "Death in the Old Testament," 37).

Beliefs about life and death are expressed everywhere in the Old Testament. The root *ḥāyâ* "live" occurs approximately eight hundred times in the Old Testament, and the root *mût* "death" occurs more than a thousand times (Knibb, "Life and Death," 395).

Lloyd Bailey said that *death* is used in the Old Testament in at least three senses: (1) as a metaphor for those things which distract from life as Yahweh intends it (illness, persecution, despair); (2) as "power" in opposition to the created order; and (3) as biological cessation in the sense of the end of a given individual's historical existence (*Biblical Perspectives on Death*, 39).

Westermann agreed that in many places in the Old Testament, death is understood as a power invading life. It attacks the sick person and robs strength. Saving one from "death" can mean saving one from sickness or enemies (Ps. 116:3-4,8). Thus death may not always refer to "that moment when things are 'done,' the exit, but rather the power encountered in the life of the individual which is after that individual's life" (*Elements of Old Testament Theology*, 162; compare von Rad, *Old Testament Theology I*, 387-389).

Still, the Old Testament was very aware of biological death. With few exceptions, everyone in the Old Testament dies a physical death. "Who can live and never see death?/ Who can escape from the power of Sheol?" (Ps. 89:48; compare Ps. 49:12,20).

The Old Testament pictures few death bed scenes. Only reports of deaths appear in the Old Testament, much like today's obituaries. These reports are not very emotional. People die at all ages: the old, the youth, and the infants. They die of all causes: in war, of disease, or by accident, murder, suicide, or capital punishment.

There are some gruesome death scenes in the Old Testament:

> "And Samuel hewed Agag in pieces before the LORD in Gilgal."
> (1 Sam. 15:33)

> "So Saul took his own sword and fell upon it. . . . when the Philistines came to strip the dead . . . they cut off his head, stripped off his armor. . . ."
> (1 Sam. 31:4,8-9)

> "Abner struck him in the stomach with the butt of his spear, so that his spear came out at his back. He fell there, and died

> where he lay. And all those who came to the place
> where Asahel had fallen and died, stood still."
>
> (2 Sam. 2:23)

> "Absalom was riding on his mule, and the mule went under the
> thick branches of a great oak. His head caught fast in the oak,
> and he was left hanging between heaven and earth. . . . [Joab]
> took three spears in his hand, and thrust them into the heart of
> Absalom, while he was still alive in the oak. And ten young
> men, Joab's armor-bearers, surrounded Absalom
> and struck him, and killed him."
>
> (2 Sam. 18:9,14-15)

The Old Testament does not explain what actually happens to a person at death. The Old Testament views a person in "holistic" terms. The various aspects of a person's nature (body, spirit, breath, heart) are so integrated and interrelated that any one aspect can stand for the whole. Obviously Old Testament people realized that physical death was marked by the lack of breathing (1 Kings 17:8-23) and, in some cases, by the loss of blood. For them life was in the blood (Lev. 17:11).

One Old Testament passage has often been used to support the Christian doctrine that at death a person's soul goes immediately to God, and the body returns to the dust of the ground (Eccl. 12:7). This passage may not be saying anything other than that death is the result of God's withdrawal of His "spirit" or "life-force" from a person. A. B. Davidson affirmed that to say the "spirit" returns to God, who gave it, is to say very little. "For that may mean nothing more than that the vitality which flowed from God is withdrawn by God, and the living person falls into weakness and death" (*Theology of the Old Testament*, 201; compare Eichrodt, *Theology of the Old Testament II*, 214). W. H. Schmidt said, "What leaves man at death is not the immortal soul, but the life-force sent by God" (*The Faith of the Old Testament*, 272; compare Bailey, *Biblical Perspectives on Death*, 44-45).

Some Old Testament passages seem to indicate that death is the end of humans; their life-force is "poured out" so that it can never be recovered (Job 7:21; 14:7-10; Pss. 39:13; 146:4). These may only be strong expressions of despondency and regret over a life so soon ended, never to be lived on this earth again (Davidson, *Theology of the Old Testament*, 425).

However one interprets these pessimistic Old Testament passages about death, such ideas are counterbalanced and dominated by the point of view that the individual does not cease to exist at death, but continues in a shadowy attenuated form of the former self in Sheol (Jacob, *Theology of the Old Testament*, 301). Eichrodt said, "What survives, therefore, is not a *part* of the living man but a shadowy image of the *whole* man" (*Theology of the Old Testament II*, 214). Otto Kaiser asserted that it would be a mistake to conclude from Old Testament texts that Israel believed persons were utterly annihilated at death. "What survived down there below therefore was not simply nothing, but a shadowy, ghostly double of the living" (*Death and Life*, 34).

When a person died in the Old Testament, the relatives would close the eyes (Gen. 46:4), weep, kiss the body (Gen. 50:1), and prepare it for burial. Usually the body was not placed in a coffin (see 2 Kings 13:21) but was carried on a bier (2 Sam. 3:31). Embalming or cremation was never practiced in ancient Israel (de Vaux, *Ancient Israel*, 56-57). Anyone who touched a dead body was ceremonially unclean (Num. 19:11). The Old Testament did not allow a cult of the dead or ancestor worship (Eichrodt, *Theology of the Old Testament II*, 216-220).

Tombs were not monuments of honor to the deceased (except in Isa. 22:16). Moses' tomb was never found (Deut. 34:6). Tombs belonged to the realm of the dead and were unholy and a source of defilement (Isa. 65:4). (Compare Wolff, *Anthropology of the Old Testament*, 101-102; Harrelson, *From Fertility Cult to Worship*, 33-34.)

42. The Grave and Sheol

The burial of a dead person in the family grave was the norm for much of the Old Testament (Gen. 25:8-10; 35:29; 49:33; Josh. 24:30,32; Judg. 8:32; 16:31; 2 Sam. 2:32; 17:23; 19:37; 21:12-14). Family graves were located on the familial land or on property purchased for a burial site. Landless people and the poor were usually buried in graves for the common people (2 Kings 23:6; Jer. 26:23). To be left unburied was the worst of all curses (1 Kings 14:11; Jer. 16:4; 22:19; Ezek. 29:5). To burn a body was an outrage except in the case of a notorious criminal (Gen. 38:24; Lev. 20:14; 21:9; Josh. 7:25) or of an enemy to be annihilated (1 Sam. 31:12; Amos 2:1). A special fate awaited fetuses, the uncircumcised, the executed, orphans, and unwanted slaves (Job 3:16; Jer. 36:30; Ezek. 28:10; 31:18; 32:19; see Kaiser, *Death and Life*, 52).

We do not know the reason(s) for Israel's emphasis on proper burial—perhaps out of respect for the dead. Originally the reason might have been the fear of retaliation from the "departed spirits." W. O. E. Oesterley believed that it was the latter. Proper burial was the effort of the community to protect itself against the restless souls of the unburied "which would wander about harming men" (*Immortality and the Unseen World*, 178). In the same vein Martin-Achard said, "A dead man without a grave is like a man without a home, he is condemned to perpetual wandering, he haunts the places that he has known and becomes a danger to the living" (*From Death to Life*, 29).

The Old Testament seems to preserve a popular belief that the presence of the deceased can be discerned in the vicinity of his or her burial place. Jeremiah refers to Rachel's voice still being heard weeping for her children from her tomb in Ramah (Jer. 31:15). This could be metaphorical language. Nothing is said about Rachel being a disinterred spirit. Samuel is reported to have been recalled from the dead by the witch of Endor (1 Sam. 28), but he is certainly not depicted as a "ghost" running around scaring people. Bailey said that the purpose of the story is not to attest to or deny the effectiveness of the necromancer's art, "but to relate another tragic episode in the decline of King Saul" (*Biblical Perspectives on Death*, 33).

Some evidence indicates that Israel's neighbors believed in ghosts. In the twelfth tablet of the Gilgamesh Epic, Enkidu, Gilgamesh's friend, comes up from the underworld to report on the status of the inhabitants below:

> Him whose corpse was cast out upon the plain . . .
> His ghost finds no rest in the nether world.
> Him whose ghost has no one to care for (it) . . .
> It eats what is left in the pots and other
> scraps of food that are thrown into the streets
> (Bailey, *Biblical Perspectives on Death*, 10).

H. C. Brichto agreed with Fustel de Coulanges that "the most ancient generations, long before there were philosophers, believed in a second existence after the present. They looked upon death not as a dissolution of our being, but simply as a change of life" ("Kin, Cult, Land and Afterlife," 3).

According to Brichto, de Coulanges studied the laws and literature of Greece and Rome, the Vedas, and the laws of Manu. He concluded that before there was a notion of a universal abode of the dead, the dead were buried in the family homes or graves. The dead were dependent upon their descendants for food-offerings to rest their "souls." "The spirit, deprived of these necessities, wanders wretchedly and endlessly, turns malevolent and uses its considerable powers to afflict the living" (Brichto, "Kin, Cult, Land and Afterlife," 4). Brichto said that de Coulanges' findings can serve as a model for understanding some of the Old Testament materials.

The idea of an afterlife is old even in the Old Testament. Israel had an idea similar to that of some of their neighbors, that sons were to "call the name" of their ancestors—that is, to perpetuate the family line (Brichto, "Kin, Cult, Land and Afterlife," 22). Brichto saw such expressions as "you shall be cut off from your people" (Lev. 17:10; 20:3,5,6; 1 Sam. 2:31; 24:21; 1 Kings 21:21; Pss. 37; 109:13-14; Isa. 14:22; Mic. 2:4) as a total annihilation of one's family line, therefore a failure to survive in the afterlife.

Brichto argued, contrary to most Old Testament scholars, that the dead in their afterlife depended on their posterity for survival. Offerings for the dead were sanctioned but not prescribed in ancient Israel, according to Brichto. The two references to offerings for the dead in the Old Testament (Ps. 106:28; Deut. 26:14) condemn the practice, but Brichto argued that in Psalm 106:28 offerings for the dead were condemned because they were being eaten with worshipers of Baal of Peor. The Deuteronomy passage (26:14) is proscribing only the offering of the third tithes as sacrifices for the dead. According to Brichto, the implication is that the passage "constitutes a sanction of the offering to them [the dead] of other food" ("Kin, Cult, Land and Afterlife," 28-29).

Undoubtedly, Israel's neighbors believed in ghosts, disembodied spirits which came out of the tombs or the underworld. Eichrodt noted that the idea is still prevalent in parts of the world. Among the Batak of Sumatra it is the custom to make a clamor at the interment and, if possible, to remove the body through a hole in the wall rather than through the door so that the spirit of the dead might not find its way back again. (*Theology of the Old Testament II*, 215).

In *Folklore in the Old Testament*, Frazer suggested in his discussion of the mark of Cain that the deity decorated Cain with red, black, and white paint so that the first "Mr. Smith" would not be recognized by his victim's ghost (cited by Hooke in *The Siege Perilous*, 66).

The people of the Old Testament were prohibited from consulting the dead (Lev. 19:31; 20:6,27; Deut. 18:11) but mediums, spiritualists, and necromancers were apparently common in Israel and presented a continual temptation to the people of the Old Testament (1 Sam. 28:3,7,9; 2 Kings 21:6; 23:24; 1 Chron. 10:13; 2 Chron. 33:6; Isa. 8:19; 19:3). Isaiah portrayed Jerusalem (Ariel) as being destroyed, yet able to speak.

> Then deep from the earth you shall speak,
> from low in the dust your words shall come;
> your voice shall come from the
> ground like the voice of a ghost,
> and your speech shall whisper
> out of the dust.
> (Isa. 29:4)

Many scholars interpret some signs of mourning, such as tearing one's clothes and cutting the hair or flesh, as efforts to disguise one's appearance in order to be unrecognizable by the ghosts. (See Noth, *Leviticus*, 143; Wolff, *Anthropology of the Old Testament*, 105; Eichrodt, *Theology of the Old Testament II*, 215. Also see the discussion of mourning customs in the Old Testament in an unpublished Ph.D. dissertation by Paul Armes, *The Concept of Dying in the Old Testament*, 150-160.)

Otto Kaiser said that "ghost stories are not to be expected in the Old Testament, by the very nature of the literature" (*Death and Life*, 167, n. 152). Lloyd Bailey believed that the dead in the Old Testament do not dwell in a demonic realm, and "they are not able to roam the earth and terrorize the living even if offerings of food and drink are not made to them" (*Biblical Perspectives on Death*, 35-36).

Yahweh's demand for exclusive worship was incompatible with the idea that the dead could in any way affect the fate of the living. Thus the living were freed from time-consuming and economically burdening incantations for the dead and from the preoccupation with death itself. Eichrodt said the unimportance of the dead for the normal life of the Israelite is an incontrovertible fact. "In Israel a grave was a grave and nothing more!" (*Theology of the Old Testament II*, 218).

Overlapping or parallel with the idea that the dead are in the grave is the idea that they are in Sheol. *Sheol* is a Hebrew word that has taken on the properties of a proper noun. Its etymology is uncertain. It is used sixty-five or sixty-six times in the Old Testament and does not occur in any other Semitic language except as a loan word from Hebrew (Gaster, "The Abode of the Dead," 787). Sometimes it seems that the dead are in the grave and Sheol at the same time (Jacob, *Theology of the Old Testament*, 302). The KJV translates Sheol "grave" thirty-one times and "hell" thirty-one times. The RSV and NRSV transliterate the word Sheol every time it occurs except in Song of Solomon 8:6. The NIV regularly translates *Sheol* "grave."

It is clear from the way the word is used in the Old Testament that Sheol was located in the depths of the earth. Twenty-one times the expressions "go down" or "brought down" are used in connection with Sheol (Gen. 37:35; 42:38; 44:29,31; Num. 16:30,33; 1 Sam. 2:6; 1 Kings 2:6,9; Job 7:9;17:16;21:13; Prov. 1:12;5:5; Isa. 14:11,15;57:9; Ezek. 31:15,16,17; 32:27). The "depths of Sheol" are mentioned six times (Deut. 32:22; Ps. 86:13; Prov. 9:18; 15:24; Isa. 7:11; 14:15). Four times Sheol is described as the farthest point from heaven (Job 11:8; Ps. 139:8; Isa. 7:11; Amos 9:2). Six times Sheol is parallel with the "Pit" (Job 17:13-14; Ps. 16:10; Prov. 1:12; Isa. 14:15; 38:18; Ezek. 32:21).

Sheol is said to be synonymous with *ăbaddôn*, "destruction" (Job 26:6; Prov. 15:11; 27:20). Nine times Sheol is parallel with death (2 Sam. 22:6; Pss. 18:4-5; 49:14; 89:48; 116:3; Prov. 5:5; Isa. 28:15,18; Hos. 13:14; Hab. 2:5). Sheol is described in terms of overwhelming floods, water, or waves (2 Sam. 22:6; Ps. 18:4-5; Jonah 2:2-6). Once it is called a place of dust (Job 17:16).

Sometimes Sheol is pictured as a hunter setting snares for its victims, binding them with cords, snatching them from the land of the living (2 Sam. 22:6; Ps. 116:3). Sheol is a prison with bars, a place of no return (Job 7:9; 10:21; 16:22; 21:13; Ps. 49:14; Isa. 38:10). Some people go to Sheol alive (Num.

16:30,33; Ps. 55:15; Prov. 1:12). Sheol is an insatiable monster, always wanting more (Prov. 1:12; 27:20; 30:16; Isa. 5:14; Hab. 2:5). Sheol is a place where all people go when they die (Job 3:11-19; Ps. 89:48). (See Russell, *The Method and Message of Jewish Apocalyptic*, 355). It is a place of silence, forgetfulness, inactivity, and no praise of God (Ps. 6:5; Eccl. 9:10; Isa. 38:10).

Even though everyone (rich-poor, good-bad, old-young) goes to Sheol when they die, some Old Testament passages imply that the wicked and sinners may be snatched away sooner and the righteous may be spared from Sheol longer (Job 24:19; Pss. 9:17; 16:10; 31:17). Sheol is open to God. He is in charge of it (Job 26:6; Ps. 139:8; Amos 9:2).

Although Sheol is not an attractive place in the Old Testament, at least it carried the belief that death was not the absolute end of existence. The dead continued to exist as the *rephāîm*, "shades" (Job 26:5; Prov. 2:18; 9:18; 21:16; Isa. 26:14). This idea of Sheol closely resembles the Babylonian concept of the place of the dead, called *Aralü* (Robinson, *Inspiration and Revelation*, 96, 99).

One of the surprising things about the Old Testament from the Christian perspective is its inadequate view of death and the afterlife. Vriezen said the fact that the Old Testament speaks very little about life after death is "one of the important elements where the Old Testament clamors for its 'fulfillment' by the New Testament" (*Outline of Old Testament Theology*, 409).

Perhaps one reason Israel's view of life after death was inadequate was her struggle with her neighbors' concepts of death and beyond, particularly those of Egypt and Ugarit. In Egypt death was masked as life, at least for the wealthy and powerful. In Ugarit the worship of the god *Mot*, "death," was part of the fertility cult or the cult of the dying and rising god. Any concept that nature was divine or that the dead were to become gods or "the knowing ones" was prohibited in the Old Testament (Lev. 19:31; Deut. 18:10-11; Isa. 8:19-20; 65:4).

What happens to a person after death in the Old Testament? The dead is buried and goes to Sheol. Is there a judgment to determine a person's place in Sheol? The Old Testament speaks often of judgment, but usually the judgment concerns groups, the nation, or the nations; and it usually takes place within history. Very little in the Old Testament resembles the words of Hebrews 9:27: "And just as it is appointed for mortals to die once, and after that the judgment. . ." Most Old Testament references to the dead suggest that they continue to exist in an attenuated form in Sheol.

Some Old Testament references imply that there is no difference in Sheol between the righteous and the wicked (Job 3:17-19; 9:20-23; Pss. 6:4-5; 88:3-7; Isa. 14:9-11). Other passages may imply at least the beginning of a distinction of the just and unjust after death (compare Isa. 66:24; Ezek. 32:23; Mal. 4:1-3). The idea of world judgment is approached only a few times in the Old Testament (Isa. 24—27; Dan. 7:9-10; 12:2; Zeph. 3:8-10).

Ancient Israel seemed to have had little or no understanding of a judgment after death (Eichrodt, *Theology of the Old Testament II*, 511). However, ancient Egypt had a highly developed concept of such a judgment. The Egyptian Book of the Dead is best preserved in the Papyrus of Ani (seventy-eight feet long and fifteen inches wide) now in the British Museum. Chapter 125 of the Papyrus of Ani has an illustration of Ani, followed by his wife Tutu, bowing humbly in the great Hall of Judgment. In the middle is a scale (balance) operated by the jackal-headed Anubis. Ani's heart is on the left scalepan, and a feather representing truth is on the other. Other gods appear in the picture along with a scribe and Amemit, the devourer of the dead, who stands ready to devour Ani's heart if it does not pass the test. Above are twelve gods who are judges, and at the right is the sentence of acquittal.

The text of Chapter 125 is Ani's denial of forty-two sins before forty-two judges. Each judge was responsible for one specific crime. Among the crimes denied are murder, blasphemy, stealing, mistreatment of cattle, and having sexual relations with a boy. Although much of the Book of the Dead deals with the use of magic, it reveals a belief in a judgment after death to determine one's fate in the afterlife (see de Vries, *Achievements of Biblical Religion*, 237-238; Finegan, *Light From the Ancient Past*, 101-102; Steindorff and Seele, *When Egypt Ruled the East*, 144-148). The idea of God weighing the heart or spirit is reflected in the Old Testament (Prov. 16:2; 21:2; 24:12). Dahood saw these references as evidence that the wise man knew the Egyptian doctrine of judgment after death (*Psalms 3*, xliv).

43. The Grave and Beyond

"Mortal, can these bones live?"
I answered, "O Lord GOD, you know."
(Ezek. 37:3)

"If mortals die, will they live again?"
(Job 14:14*a*)

Is there life after death? From time immemorial people have buried their dead in ways which suggest their belief in a continued existence after death. Many philosophers have supported the claim for a universal desire for an extension of life beyond the grave. Immanuel Kant said such hope "arises from the feeling, which exists in the breast of every man, that the temporal is inadequate to meet and satisfy the demands of his nature" (*Critique of Pure Reason*, 35).

Plato argued for the immortality of the soul on the basis that the true essence of the soul was the perceptive spirit of the person. The human spirit participated in the eternal archetypes of things or general concepts. These general concepts are not perishable. If a person's spirit or soul participates in these concepts, the soul must be imperishable (see Pannenberg, *What Is Man?*, 46). Plato distinguished between the soul and body. Pannenberg said that modern anthropology has removed this common conception that soul and body represent two completely different realms of reality (*What Is Man?*, 47).

Pannenberg himself made "hope beyond death" or "the resurrection" the key to his theological system. All other creatures except people live entirely in the present. Humans can predict (to some degree) and anticipate the future. People can anticipate their own death. People are never satisfied with their achievements or failures. They are always pressing forward to something else. "It is inherent to man to hope beyond death, even as it is inherent to know about his own death" (*What Is Man?*, 44). Hope beyond death may be inherent in persons, but only the biblical promises have made the new thing of the future significant and reliable. "The power and faithfulness of the biblical God stand behind the promises" (Pannenberg, *What Is Man?*, 43).

The Old Testament has no systematic or organized presentation of life after death. Bits and pieces or glimmers of truth on this subject must be gleaned from various parts of the Old Testament and studied together. By no means do all Old Testament scholars and readers agree on the interpretation of many passages that may relate to life after death.

It is generally agreed that the "doctrine" of life after death was very slow in developing in the Old Testament. F. B. Huey said, "A historical development of the doctrine of life after death can be justified on the basis that the doctrine of a resurrection of the body, the pinnacle of faith, was not fully delineated until New Testament times. The pagan accretions had to be shed by Israel in order to arrive at a resurrection doctrine, a process which took many years" ("The Hebrew Concept of Life After Death," 55).

Several reasons may explain Israel's slowness in developing a doctrine of life after death. The ideas of death and future life played a major role in the religions of Israel's pagan neighbors: Egyptians, Canaanites, and Babylonians. Their ideas concerning death and future life were false and misleading. They made death a god and deified some humans at death. The cult of the dead exerted great influence over the lives of many people in the Ancient Near East, and the idea of the dying and rising god was tied very closely to the fertility cult with its glorification of sex. Inquiry of the dead was prohibited in Israel (Lev. 19:31; 20:6,27; Deut. 18:10; 2 Kings 21:6; 23:24). The whole realm of death was unclean in the Old Testament (Lev. 11:24; Num. 19:11).

Israel's slowness in developing a satisfactory view of life after death may have been due to her strong emphasis on "corporate personality" rather than on "pure individualism"; on the unitary view of humanity rather than the dichotomy of soul and body; or on the significance of life here and now rather than in the hereafter.

Bruce Vawter noted that because Israel excluded necromancy as a superstition and discouraged inquiry about the dead, they were compelled to examine the meaning of earthly existence to a depth and degree seemingly without parallel in the thinking of their contemporaries. Israel's Wisdom Literature stresses a high morality, a healthy materialism, and a reverence for the dignity of the body. Without a strong emphasis on "this world," it is unlikely that the prophetic doctrine of social justice would have been strong. "When life is valued so much, long life inevitably comes to be accounted the greatest of blessings (Ps. 21:4)" ("Intimations of Immortality and the Old Testament," 170).

Where does the idea of a life after death begin in the Old Testament? Some writers see the references to the "tree of life" and "the tree of the knowledge of good and evil" (Gen. 2:4*b*— 3:24) as evidence of an idea of life after death. But there is certainly no reference to resurrection here. Rather than referring to life after death, the trees in the garden of Eden may represent a way to avoid dying. The "translation" of Enoch in Genesis 5:24 had a great influence on later parts of the Old Testament; however, no general doctrine of life after death can be based on Enoch's translation. Again, there is no reference to resurrection here. When David said that at death he would go to be with his son who had died (2 Sam. 12:23), he may have been saying no more than what had already been said about being "gathered to one's fathers" in the grave or in Sheol (Gen. 25:8,17; 35:29; 49:33; Num. 20:24; 27:13; Judg. 2:10).

The Old Testament reports three cases of resuscitation. The first two were the raising of the widows' sons by Elijah and Elisha, and the third was the resuscitation of an unnamed man whose dead body was thrown into Elisha's grave and came into contact with Elisha's body in his grave (1 Kings 17:17; 2 Kings 4:29; 13:21). All three of these people died again as far as we know.

Many scholars make the Babylonian exile a dividing line between earlier and more advanced religious concepts in the Old Testament. The collapse of the nation shifted the emphasis in Judah from the nation to the individual. Questions of suffering and justice became more intense. What had once been sporadic gleams in the darkness or a momentarily expressed hope of life after death now became "an unshakable conviction that whatever befell the righteous man in this life, the one thing that meant more to him, his fellowship with God, would never be taken from him in this life or in the life to come" (Huey, "The Hebrew Concept of Life After Death," 136-137).

In 1966 Mitchell Dahood caused a stir in the circles of biblical scholarship when he challenged the statement of Sigmund Mowinckel that "neither Israel nor early Judaism knew of a faith in any resurrection nor is such a faith represented in the Psalms" (Dahood, *Psalms 1*, xxxvi). Dahood said that the most significant contribution to biblical theology his translation of Psalms 1—50 had made concerned the subjects of resurrection and immortality. He asserted that if his interpretation of certain passages ranging from Psalms 1—73 bears up under criticism, "the treatment of these topics in standard biblical theologies will need drastic revision" (*Psalms 1*, xxxvi).

Dahood finished his commentary on the Psalms in 1970. In the third volume he noted that he had said in his first volume that "the psalmists gave much more thought to the problem of death and the afterlife than earlier commentaries had suspected. The psalmists' preoccupation with death becomes evident from the numerous names of the nether world in the Psalter" (*Psalms 3*, xli). In the same place Dahood spoke of "his insistence that a deep and steady belief in resurrection and immortality permeates the Psalter."

To support his argument that the ideas of resurrection and immortality permeate the Psalter, Dahood listed at least forty texts from the psalms, along with others from Proverbs, Ecclesiastes, Isaiah, and Daniel. His evidence is built largely on the use of Hebrew words with Ugaritic or Canaanite meaning and is very questionable. For example, he translated the Hebrew word *hayyîm* "life" as "eternal life" (Pss. 16:11; 21:4; 27:13; 30:5; 36:9; 56:13; 69:28; 116:8,9; 133:3; 147:6). In another questionable procedure Dahood translated the word *'aharît* "last" as "the future" or "future life" (Pss. 37:37-38; 109:13). (See *Psalms 3*, xlv-lii). Dahood's theories have been widely discussed, but few scholars have defended his views (Vawter, "Intimations of Immortality," 158-171).

Perhaps some literary genres in the Old Testament offer a clue to Israel's view of life after death. The laments in the Old Testament suggest a dissatisfaction with one's lot in life. Old Testament laments are concerned with many different problems of the individual and the nation. Suffering, sickness, oppression, false accusations, foes, invasions, and death are all themes of Old Testament laments. Claus Westermann distinguished between the "lament of affliction" and the "lament of the dead." The lament of the dead looks backward; the lament of affliction looks forward. A lament of the dead on the

lips of one who mourns bewails the death of another (2 Sam.
1:18-27; 18:33). Different Hebrew words are used for the two
kinds of lament. The lament of affliction is addressed to God;
the lament of the dead is addressed to Israel or to others (Westermann, "The Role of the Lament," 20-38).

Walter Brueggemann saw the difference between "the
funeral song," the lament of the dead, and the lament of affliction as the difference between the "tragic reversal" from glory
to shame and a "saving reversal" which moves from distress to
wholeness. Israel's normal expectations might see tragic
reversal as the pattern of historical experience; their "normative faith is exactly the opposite. It insists that saving reversal
and not tragic reversal is the pattern of their experience. Thus
we suggest that the lament form, as contrasted with the
funeral song, gives expression to Israel's most fundamental
conviction, namely that Yahweh is sovereign over the present
situation and can work good out of it" ("From Hurt to Joy," 13).

Brueggemann concluded that the structure of cry-response
which is expressed as petition and praise dramatizes the
moment which the early church experienced as crucifixion-res-
urrection. "The psalms of lament in their two principal parts of
before/after reflect precisely the experience of death and gift of
new life" ("From Hurt to Joy," 19). In a footnote Brueggemann
suggested that it would be useful for the practice of ministry to
study the movement of the form "from distress to affirmation"
in relation to the grieving process as outlined by Granger Westberg in *Good Grief*, and the dying process suggested by Elisabeth Kubler-Ross in *On Death and Dying*.

In 1977 Brueggemann developed his own suggestion when
he compared the formfulness of grief from the work of Kubler-
Ross to that of the Old Testament laments ("The Formfulness
of Grief," 267-275). Kubler-Ross observed that the grief and
death process tends to follow a fairly regular form. She suggested that the process included five elements: denial and isolation; anger; bargaining; depression; and acceptance.

These five elements may be correlated with the movement
in Israel's laments discerned by Westermann and Brueggemann. The first four stages are part of a plea, and the last
stage is an affirmation. However, Brueggemann said that
Israel and Kubler-Ross begin at very different places. Israel

places little emphasis on denial of death, but often protests, especially against an early death. Brueggemann attributed this difference to the modern sense of loneliness over against Israel's sense of covenant. Israel did express anger in the face of death; but, again, Israel had the context of the covenant in which it could be received and dealt with.

Kubler-Ross observed that family and medical staff were not equipped to cope with death. Bargaining may be considered a minor motif in both Israel's and Kubler-Ross's systems. Depression grows out of a sense of worthlessness, impotence, and insignificance. Some of this can be seen in the Old Testament in the "worm" theme (Job 25:6; Ps. 22:6; Isa. 41:14). However, Kubler-Ross's sufferer has no one to address and so will be finally depressed. Israel always by form has a Partner with whom to speak. Depression is never full blown in Israel. In place of depression, Israel's form has petition.

In both systems the last stage is acceptance. However, for Kubler-Ross acceptance of death may be no more than resignation to one's fate. That may have been true for some in Israel, but all of Israel's canonical laments end with or contain an element of praise with the possible exception of Psalm 88.

Perhaps because of Israel's sense of covenant with its vertical and horizontal dimensions, Israel was able to overcome the limitations of death which bound them. Certainly the breaking up of the nation at the fall of Jerusalem (586 B.C.), the rise of the responsibility of the individual, and the apparent failure of justice in this life led to some serious reflections on the possibility of an adequate concept of life after death. At first there were sporadic gleams of hope and leaps of faith until near the close of the Old Testament, when more meaningful expressions of hope appeared. However, the Old Testament never developed a full or systematic doctrine of life after death.

Walther Eichrodt said that the idea that death might be overcome even in the case of an individual came to be at home in Israel's faith in two different ways. On one hand, the conquest of death was seen as an eschatological event in which the victory and the glory of God will be recognized universally over all powers in heaven, on earth, and below the earth (*Theology of the Old Testament II*, 509-510). On the other hand, Israel arrived at an assurance of the conquest of death by the individual through the realization that life acquires an indestructible content in direct encounter with God. Eichrodt called this second way "the way of faith-realism," believing that this way was open only to those who had previously been engaged in a severe struggle for assurance (*Theology of the Old Testament II*, 517).

One example of those coming to an assurance of life after death along the way of "faith-realism" is Job, who depicts the distress of one brought near death. Job was stripped of the support of family and friends, but his biggest problem was his misconception that God was his enemy. Timidly at first, then with increasing boldness, he maintained his own integrity (13:1-19). He asserted by faith that his witness was in heaven; the one who would vouch for him was on high (16:19). Audaciously he proclaimed that his living Redeemer would vindicate him (19:25-27). When God spoke to him through the whirlwind, Job acknowledged not only God's wisdom and sovereignty, but also His personal concern and presence with the individual. In such an experience, death has no more terror.

Two of the Psalms (49 and 73) seem to include a "leap of faith" beyond death into the arms of God. Psalm 49 is a Wisdom psalm in which the writer reflected on the fate of the rich and poor. Both die along with the wise man (Ps. 49:5-6,10,12,20). If all go to the same place at death, they take their inequities with them. H. H. Rowley said that in using the expression "he will receive (*lāqaḥ*) me" (v. 15), the psalmist was saying that "the inequalities of this life will be rectified in the next" (*The Faith of Israel*, 171; compare A. A. Anderson, *The Book of Psalms*, Vol.1, 379-381).

In Psalm 73 the psalmist faced the problem of the prosperity and well-being of the wicked (vv. 3-12). The psalmist ultimately came to understand that the wicked may seem to prosper, but God sets them in slippery places and makes them fall to their ruin (v. 18). Conversely, the psalmist went through life at God's right hand with his foot on the solid rock. "In all trials and tribulations he knows what it is to be with God, to be held by his hand, and to be guided by his counsel, and thus his life has a content which cannot be endangered by any outward event. God himself has become his portion" (Eichrodt, *Theology of the Old Testament II*, 521). This relationship continues beyond death. How can this happen? The only word accessible to the psalmist was *lāqaḥ*, "taken" or "translated" (Ps. 73:24).

Although these and other psalms (see 16:10-11) seem to anticipate the idea of the righteous spending eternity in heaven in the presence of the Lord, such an "otherworldly" view never replaced the thought that the future was related to life on the earth. Eichrodt said, "The fundamental feature of the Old Testament hope, that history should issue in the consummation of God's sovereignty, and the establishment of his kingdom over Israel, has not been replaced by an otherworldly god of salvation for the righteous individual, divorced from all relation to things earthly" (*Theology of the Old Testament II*, 514).

Wheeler Robinson said we must look elsewhere than to Sheol for the possibility of real advance in the idea of human destiny. The new hope springs from the belief in a continued life on the earth, "not a life beneath it, or even above it" (*Inspiration and Revelation*, 100). G. A. Cooke, in his commentary on Ezekiel 37 and 47:1-12, said, "According to O.T. ideas of the blessed future, man is not translated to dwell with God, but God comes down to dwell with man, and His presence transforms earth into heaven" (*Ezekiel*, 404).

The other way in which the people of Israel were able to conceive of overcoming death was through an eschatological event (Eichrodt, *Theology of the Old Testament II*, 509). For the most part this included references to the culmination of history, to universal judgment, and to the resurrection of some of the dead. Scholars are divided as to possible foreign influence on Israel's thinking at this point. Dahood, von Rad, and Otto Kaiser thought that such ideas originated in Canaan or Persia. Eichrodt and E. Jacob believe that "internal reasons alone account for the arrival at the doctrine of resurrection" (Jacob, *Theology of the Old Testament*, 314; compare Eichrodt, *Theology of the Old Testament II*, 516).

44. Resurrection

In the Old Testament, the final word on life after death is "resurrection." The technical Hebrew term for resurrection, *tehiyat hammetim*, does not occur in biblical Hebrew, but is attested four times in the Mishnah and forty-one times in the

Talmud. It is quite common in the Hebrew literature of the middle period and is listed in all of the dictionaries of modern Hebrew (Sawyer, "Hebrew Words for Resurrection," 220). Although "resurrection" is not found in the Old Testament, the idea may be expressed with the use of eight verbs: *ḥāyâ* "to live"; *qûm* "to arise"; *heqis* "to awake"; *lāqaḥ* "to take"; *ʿālâ* "to go up"; *sûb* "to come back"; *ʿāmad* "to stand"; *neʿor* "to arouse."

It is difficult to determine precisely the earliest Old Testament reference to resurrection. Scholars disagree on the date and interpretation of many passages that might refer to the resurrection. D. S. Russell said, "The historical occasion marking the beginning of this resurrection is hidden from us, but it may well have arisen by reason of the martyrdom of certain righteous people in Israel" (*The Method and Message of Jewish Apocalyptic*, 367). Walther Zimmerli said that it is quite possible to see the beginnings of a radical hope for life beyond death in some of the psalms and in the Book of Job. We must try to determine precisely where this hope began because it is different from the hope which Israel's neighbors had of regaining life after death (Zimmerli, *The Old Testament and the World*, 134).

Sawyer tried to circumvent the question of the date of the earliest reference to resurrection in the Old Testament by saying that the final form of the Hebrew text comes to us from the "middle period" of the Hebrew language, which began about 200 B.C ("Hebrew Words for Resurrection," 218, 299). Sawyer believed that the meaning of a particular Hebrew word in the Masoretic text was colored by its original context and by the context of the period when the text was finalized.

Almost twenty Old Testament passages may relate to resurrection in the final form of the text (Deut. 32:39; 1 Sam. 2:6; 1 Kings 17:22; Job 14:12; 19:25-27; Pss. 1:6; 16:10; 17:15; 49:15; 71:20; 73:24; 88:10; Isa. 26:14,19; 53:11; 66:24; Ezek. 37:10; Dan. 12:2; Hos. 6:2). These passages do not prove an early belief in resurrection in Israel, according to Sawyer, but an Old Testament theology based on the final form of the text would have to include a substantial section on the subject. These passages are not just vague foreshadowings of the New Testament, but they are "clear expressions of belief in God's power to create out of the dust and decay of the grave a new humanity where good lives do not end in suffering and justice prevails" ("Hebrew Words for Resurrection," 230).

Strictly speaking, probably only two passages in the Old Testament clearly assert "a second life after death. It is a life on earth, however new in its conditions, and it is a resurrection life, involving the restoration of the dead body" (Robinson, *Inspiration and Revelation*, 101-102). Those passages are Isaiah 26:19 and Daniel 12:2. Other passages may be understood as oblique references to bodily resurrection (compare Ps. 22:29; Job 19:25-27; Isa. 53:10-12).

The first clear reference to the resurrection in the Old Testament is Isaiah 26:19.

> Your dead shall live, their
> corpses shall rise.
> O dwellers in the dust, awake
> and sing for joy!
> For your dew is a radiant dew,
> and the earth will give birth to
> those long dead.

The date of this passage has been widely debated. Some writers place it as late as the second century B.C., while others assign it to Isaiah of Jerusalem. H. Ringgren thought that the reference to dew is an influence from Canaanite thought. The Ras Shamra texts seem to associate dew with the resurrection of the dying and rising god (Ringgren, *Israelite Religion*, 247; for a review of various theories concerning the date, nature, and content of Isaiah 24—27 see B. Otzen, "Traditions and Structures of Isaiah XXIV-XXVII," 196-206).

Undoubtedly Isaiah 24—27 is eschatological but not yet apocalyptic. In connection with the "feast of the kingdom," it is said that God will swallow up death forever. He will wipe away tears from all faces and will remove the reproach from all faces (Isa. 25:8). Resurrection is not, however, explicitly mentioned in this text.

Isaiah 26:19 does underscore the idea of resurrection. All of the significant terms are there. "Your dead shall live" (*ḥāyâ*); "their corpses shall rise" (*qûm*); "dwellers in the dust, awake" (*heqis*); and "the dew of light shall fall on the land of shades." Sawyer said, "This is a reference to the resurrection of the dead which no one but a Sadducee, ancient or modern, could possibly misconstrue" (*Hebrew Words for Resurrection*, 234).

There is little doubt about Daniel 12:2 referring to the resurrection: "Many of those who sleep in the dust of the earth shall awake, some to everlasting life, and some to shame and everlasting contempt." Again, significant terms are used: "awake" (*yeqis*); "life everlasting" (*hayye ʿōlām*); and "many" (*rabbîm*).

The term "many" is not clear. Does it mean "many" as over against "a few" or against "all"? Or is it a religious symbolism referring to the "righteous remnant" or the "wise"? F. F. Bruce noted that the general assembly of the Qumran community was called "the session of the many" (*Second Thoughts on the Dead Sea Scrolls*, 105). Ringgren said that the "many" may relate to the Servant (Isa. 53:11) and to the eschatological community (Matt. 26:26; Mark 10:45; 14:24; see Ringgren, *The Faith of Qumran*, 211-212; compare Cross, *The Ancient Library of Qumran*, 174-176).

Sometimes the words "resurrection" and "immortality" are used interchangeably, but they are not synonyms. "Resurrection" in Hebrew means "the dead shall live again," and the Greek word *anastasis* ("resurrection") means "to stand again." Immortality carries a Greek concept—athanatos, "without death." William LaSor said that the concept of resurrection cannot be of Hellenistic origin because "for the Greeks resurrection was an impossibility" (*The Truth About Armageddon*, 167).

Perhaps more changes occurred in the concept of life after death in the period between the Testaments than any other Old Testament concept. The idea of the separation between the righteous and the wicked after death is clarified (Russell, *The Method and Message of Jewish Apocalyptic*, 364-365). The idea of an intermediate state between death and resurrection is enunciated (2 Esdras 7:75; 1 Enoch 5:5-9), and the concept of the last judgment is established (2 Esdras 7:70). Russell said that "the doctrine of the last judgment is the most characteristic doctrine of Jewish apocalyptic. It is *the* great event towards which the whole universe is moving and which will vindicate once and for all God's righteous purpose for men and all creation. On that day all wrongs will be set right" (*The Method and Message of Jewish Apocalyptic*, 280). Russell noted evidence for belief in a general resurrection of all people in five apocalyptic books (Testament of XII Patriarchs, the Sibylline Oracles IV, the Apocalypse of Moses, 2 Esdras, and 2 Baruch). (See *The Method and Message of Jewish Apocalyptic*, 371-372.)

The clearest and most poignant statement of faith in bodily resurrection before New Testament times comes from 2 Maccabees 7. This chapter tells the story of the martyrdom of seven brothers and the steadfastness of their mother. Seven brothers and their mother were arrested, and the king tried to compel them by torture to eat unlawful swine flesh. Their spokesman asked the king, "What do you intend to ask and learn from us? For we are ready to die rather than transgress the law of our fathers."

The king was enraged and commanded that pans and caldrons be heated. The spokesman's tongue was cut out; he was scalped. His hands and feet were cut off, and he was taken to the fire, still breathing, and fried in a pan before his mother and brothers. Still they encouraged each other to die nobly.

One by one the brothers were put to death. The fourth son said, "One cannot but choose to die at the hands of mortals and to cherish the hope God gives of being raised again by him. But for you there will be no resurrection to life!" (2 Maccabees 7:14). The mother said after the death of her seven sons, "Therefore the Creator of the world, who shaped the beginning of humankind and devised the origin of all things, will in his mercy give life and breath back to you again, since you now forget yourselves for the sake of his laws" (2 Maccabees 7:23).

This is not quite the same as the New Testament concept of resurrection. Resurrection in the New Testament is related to the Savior, the Messiah, and not to the individual martyr (Eichrodt, *Theology of the Old Testament II*, 517). Eric Rust said that the fuller vision came beyond the Old Testament canon. In the intertestamental period, the assurance grew that the righteous should not descend to the gray half-lights of Sheol.

> At long last, on a land still lying under the shadow of death, the glory broke on the first Easter morning with its assurance the Christ had conquered death. So the cry of Habakkuk was answered: "Thou that art of purer eyes than to behold iniquity,

and that cannot look on perverseness, wherefore lookest thou upon them that deal treacherously, and holdest thy peace when the wicked swalloweth up the man that is more righteous than he? Art not thou from everlasting, and Jehovah my God, mine Holy One? We shall not die" (Hab. 1:12*a*, 13, Rust, "The Destiny of the Individual in the Thought of the Old Testament," 311).

11

In That Day (National Eschatology)

The details of Old Testament eschatology often seem to lack organic coherence. The various elements were never systematically arranged; and any attempt to present them systematically will probably result, to some degree, in an artificial picture. Nowhere is the ambiguity of Old Testament "eschatological" language seen more than in the various uses of the terms "in that day," "in the latter days," "the day of the Lord," "in those days," "behold, days are coming," and "the end." Some of these expressions may refer to a past event or any future event, not necessarily one that is eschatological. (Compare LaSor, *The Truth About Armageddon*, 11-18; Mowinckel, *He That Cometh*, 145-147, 267; Kosmala, "At the End of the Days," 302-312; Beasley-Murray, "The Day of the Lord," *Jesus and the Kingdom of God*, 11-16.)

Scholars do not agree on the definition of Old Testament eschatology. P. R. Davies defined eschatology as a "dimension of belief that history moves in a direction, that this direction is set by God, and that God acts within history to insure this direction" ("Eschatology in the Book of Daniel," 33; compare Hubbard, "Hope in the Old Testament," 34).

Von Rad spoke of the expression "eschatological element" in the Old Testament as "controversial but unavoidable." He attributed the rediscovery of eschatology as an element of research to H. Gressmann, even though Gressmann's idea of eschatology as a body of ideas taken from the environment was mistaken (von Rad, *Old Testament Theology II*, 113). Von Rad said the message of the prophets was "eschatological wherever it regards the old historical bases of salvation as null and void" (*Old Testament Theology II*, 118).

Some scholars are prepared to use *eschatology* only in connection with the end of this world's time (compare Van der Ploeg, "Eschatology in the Old Testament," 93; von Rad, *Old Testament Theology II*, 114). To define the term so narrowly, however, would rule out much of what the Old Testament says about the future.

What is Old Testament eschatology? The prophets expected something to happen soon, involving such a deep break with the past that the situation beyond the break could not be understood as part of what had gone before. A "vacuum" separated the past and future. The new act of God's saving work could be described in terms analogous to God's former saving acts, such as a new entry into the land (Hosea), a new David (Isaiah), a new covenant (Jeremiah), and a new exodus (Isaiah 40—66).

Claus Westermann took a slightly different approach to Old Testament eschatology. In the Bible, the future is not primarily *what* is coming but *who* is coming. From Exodus (3:8) to Revelation 3:11; 22:7,12 runs a line of talk about God's coming. Georges Pidoux began his *Le dieux qui Vient* ("The God Who Comes") affirming that "The faith of the Old Testament rests on two certainties equally profound and indissolubly bound together. The first is God has come in the past, and that He has intervened in favor of His people. The other . . . is the hope that God will come anew in the future" (*Le dieux qui Vient*, 7; see G. R. Beasley-Murray, "Theophany in the Old Testament," *Jesus and the Kingdom of God*, 3).

Many "appearances" of God, theophanies or epiphanies in worship or history, are for revelation and/or deliverance. From the exile onward many references point to the advent of God in the future (Ps. 96:1-2; Isa. 40:9; Zech. 9:9; Mal. 3:5). Westermann acknowledged the profusion of statements about that which is coming in the Old Testament, but God's coming is more than

> all utterable futurity; . . . God precedes all alterable futurity in his coming; he remains the coming one. . . . The entire future is contained in God's coming, the future of the individual person, of the people of God, the future of humanity and of the world. The only absolute certain thing we can say about the future is that we are going towards God and God is coming towards us, just as the final sentence in the New Testament says: "Behold, I am coming soon" (*Elements of Old Testament Theology*, 60).

Even though Westermann may be correct in defining Old Testament eschatology as "a new saving act of God" or as "the coming of God," we cannot limit our study of the Old Testament view of the future to these concepts. The inspired writings refer to a complex of eschatological expectations or a profusion of statements about *what* is coming. These complex eschatological expectations about *what* and *who* are coming concern us here. We will take a broad definition of Old Testament eschatology which includes happenings before, during, and after the "end" of this age.

G. A. F. Knight observed that Israel, unlike her neighbors, looked forward and backward. "Other ancient nations looked back alone" (*A Christian Theology of the Old Testament*, 294). Israel looked both ways because they alone believed in the living God, but they did not identify the end time (*endzeit*) with the primeval time (*urzeit*) as a return to Eden. H. H. Schmid came close to saying that Israel did make such an identity when he spoke of a new world order. B. S. Childs said that those German scholars (Gunkel, Winckler, and Gressmann) who coined the phrase *urzeit ist endzeit* and applied it to Old Testament eschatology were mistaken. The Old Testament view of the end time is not merely a return to paradise, Eden, or the primeval age. It is new. Something vital has occurred between the beginning and the end (*Myth and Reality in the Old Testament*, 73-81).

Knight suggested that the Old Testament concept of the end is portrayed on a vast canvas. In doing this the Old Testament employs the language of imagery, just as the New Testament does in picturing the New Jerusalem with its gold and precious stones. The multifaceted eschatology of the Old Testament may be compared to a many-stranded rope.   Each strand of the "eschatological" rope represents an important element of hope. However, Knight observed that when one holds the *middle* of a rope, it is not easy to see the many separate strands or to see how each strand contributes to the function of the whole rope. "So it is with Israel's eschatological hope" *(A Christian Theology of the Old Testament*, 296). What are some of the strands of the Old Testament eschatological hope?

45. The End or Culmination of History

Did ancient Israel expect an end to or a culmination of history? James Muilenburg noted that Israel's religion is a historical religion. "Only historical religions are susceptible of eschatological formulation, for where history has meaning there the question of the future, of its resolution is paramount" ("Biblical Understanding of the Future," 99). History is deeply lodged within Israel's self-understanding so that "the question of its outcome is the preoccupation of the sacred writers from very early times" (Muilenburg, *The Way of Israel*, 128).

God never permitted security in the present. Israel never found their "rest." No present was ever the intended consummation. Every present is stamped with the seal, "not yet." Israel's existence was always tentative and preliminary to what was still to come. Even the temple and worship celebrations were often subject to corruption and compromise by those who sought to exploit religious services for their own purposes. Jeremiah said to the people who wept over the destruction of the temple: Hear the word of the LORD, all you people of Judah, you that enter these gates to worship the LORD. Thus says the LORD of hosts, the God of Israel: Amend your ways and your doings, and let me dwell with you in this place. Do not trust in these deceptive words: "This is the temple of the LORD, the temple of the LORD, the temple of the LORD."

People must have been shocked when they heard Micah say, "Therefore because of you [corrupt leaders]/Zion shall be plowed as a field/. . . and the mountain of the house a wooded height" (Mic. 3:12). Equally surprising, when the temple lay in ruins, Haggai told his people that "the latter splendor of this house shall be greater than the former" (Hag. 2:9). The preposition "until" is inscribed over the whole Old Testament. The orientation of Israel's faith is to the future. The past is prologue to what is yet to come. History culminates in the coming of God. "He who came at the beginning to call a people into history and for history will come in the decisive hour of 'the end'" (Muilenburg, *The Way of Israel*, 128).

Von Rad spoke of the Old Testament as a history book which tells of God's history with Israel, the nations, and the world from creation to the "last things—that is, until dominion over the world is given to the Son of Man" (*Old Testament Theology II*, 357).

Von Rad said the Old Testament can only be read as a book of ever-increasing anticipation. It began with that huge amalgam of expectations surrounding the promise of the land to the patriarchs and continued through the conquest, the promise to David, and the Zion traditions. Scarcely did Israel come to terms with one situation before a new act of God startled them. This shows how Israel's religious ideas were completely different from those of their neighbors. The neighbors had to return to the primordial sacred orders expressed in myth and in the cycle of festivals for any hope of salvation. But Israel was always on pilgrimage, traveling a road that could not be retraced, with expectations mounting up to vast proportions (von Rad, *Old Testament Theology II*, 321).

Israel's history with God thrusts forward into the future until, in the New Testament, it appears in a new light. There, "following upon the numerous new saving beginnings, it reaches its last hermeneutic modification and its full and final interpretation" (von Rad, *Old Testament Theology II*, 332).

The historical and critical scholars who regard the Old Testament as a body of independent religious documents (without the New Testament) interpret it in its own light and that of its environment (history of religions). Scholarship that takes the Old Testament to be an independent religious document cannot give a certain answer to the question of whether the Old Testament is to be read as a book which foretells Jesus Christ (von Rad, *Old Testament Theology II*, 321). A traditio-historical reading of the Old Testament, on the other hand, leads directly to the Christ of the New Testament. "Such a transformation of the traditional material in the light of the new saving event was as proper for early Christians as were many other such transformations which had already taken place in the Old Testament" (von Rad, *Old Testament Theology II*, 333).

For von Rad the "end" of Israel's history is found in Jesus Christ in the New Testament. Not all scholars agree. In 1972 J. Coert Rylaarsdam wrote that the Old Testament has two primary covenants which are so different they can never be synthesized. One was the covenant with Israel at Sinai. The other was God's covenant with David (2 Sam. 7). The former was historical. The second was eschatological or trans-historical. In the first "God is accomplishing the redemption of the world, and of mankind, in, through, and by means of the processes of nature and history. That is the meaning of creation. Therefore genealogy and chronology are so important in the Hebrew Bible; and that is also why it takes the form of a history" (Rylaarsdam, "Jewish-Christian Relationships," 84).

Rylaarsdam said that the Christian community in the New Testament interpreted the Christ event eschatologically.

> Jesus Christ, the event of redemption, becomes the foundation of a new Creation that is neither historical nor temporal. He is the eschatological End of history, an absolute whose meaning cannot be synthesized with the temporal world, not even with its salvation history. . . . This event cannot simultaneously be added to the series of events celebrated in Jewish Salvation History ("Jewish-Christian Relationships," 84).

Rylaarsdam's philosophical presuppositions have caused him to see too great a difference between the two major covenants in the Old Testament (Sinai and Davidic) and to overlook the New Testament explanation of how the new covenant announced by Jeremiah (Jer. 31) has been ratified by the death of Christ for the church (Heb. 8:6-13). Thomas McComiskey said that the reference to Israel (Jer. 31:33) is applied to the experience of all the people of God, not simply national Israel. "The new covenant is now in force—it is in no way bifurcated. There is one new covenant. It was ratified by the death of Christ and it mediates the gracious blessings of justification and holiness for all who are under that covenant" (*The Covenants of Promise*, 160).

46. Creation and Eschatology

Is creation, the universe, or nature involved in eschatology in the Old Testament? Wheeler Robinson said, "Nature is an essential part of eschatology, and indeed supplies many of its principal ingredients" (*Inspiration and Revelation*, 28). In the Old Testament creation has a beginning, a history, and an end. Creation is part of a history characterized by figures and dates. The motive of this arithmetic may be to answer the question: How long will the world last? The Book of Daniel clearly announces the end of the world (Dan. 9:27; 11:40; 12:13). Ludwig Köhler said:

> Creation is the first in a series of events which together make up a definite world age, so that at any point in the process one can ask when will the end come? To the beginning there corresponds an end, to creation there corresponds a consummation, to the "very good" here a "perfectly glorious there." They belong together. *Creation in Old Testament theology is an eschatological concept* (*Old Testament Theology*, 88; compare Jacob, *Theology of the Old Testament*, 141-142).

Nothing suggests any intrinsic moral evil in nature as in the gnostic view of matter. The Old Testament indicates that nature or the world stands under a curse because of human sin (Gen. 3:14-19). "When sin breaks the *šālôm* God intended for creation, it is not just a human matter." Created material that is nonhuman participates in the brokenness that results from sin (Birch, *Let Justice Roll Down*, 95). Moral evil comes from humans alone, but nature and humans are so closely interlinked that what happens to one affects the other.

The great prophets were aware of the connection between human sin and the "curse" on the land. Hosea 4:1-3 says, "Hear the word of the LORD, O people of Israel; /for the LORD has an indictment against the inhabitants of the land. / There is no faithfulness or loyalty, /and no knowledge of God in the land./Swearing, lying, and murder, /and stealing and adultery break out; /bloodshed follows bloodshed. /Therefore the land mourns, /and all who live in it languish; /together with the wild animals /and the birds of the air, /even the fish of the sea are perishing."

The earth dries up and withers because the people "have transgressed laws, violated the statutes, broken the everlasting covenant" (Isa. 24:4-5; compare 33:8-9). One of the most graphic poems in the Old Testament describes the earth as waste and desolation, dark, peopleless, and creatureless. The fruitful land lay ruined, and cities stood without inhabitants before the Lord's fierce anger. "I looked on the earth, and lo, it was waste and void;/ and to the heavens, and they had no light. /I looked on the mountains, and lo, they were quaking,/and all the hills moved to and fro. /I looked, and lo, there was no one at all,/and all the birds of the air had fled. /I looked, and lo, the fruitful land was a desert, /and all its cities were laid in ruins/ before the LORD, before his fierce anger" (Jer. 4:23-26).

Israel knew that the present world was coming to an end. Descriptions of earthquakes, droughts, and darkness, reminiscent of original chaos, were often used to describe the coming destruction of the world (Isa. 24:4-6,19-20,23; 33:8-9; 54:10; Jer. 4:23-26; Hos. 8:7; 10:8). The day of the Lord is described as a day of darkness and not light (Joel 1:10—2:2; 2:10-11,30-31; 3:14-15; Amos 5:18; 8:9-10; Zeph. 1:14-18). The coming judgment includes not only the earth but also the heavens (Isa. 24:21,23; 34:4; 65:17; 66:22).

If the day of the Lord is marked by earthquakes, drought, and darkness, the new age will be characterized by renewal, transformation, the cleansing of the world, and *šālôm* "peace" among people and animals (Isa. 11:6-9; 65:25; Joel 2:18-19,24; 3:18; Amos 9:13-14; Zech. 8:4-5,12).

H. H. Schmid saw a close relationship between creation and consummation in the Old Testament. The salvation (*Heil*) expected at the end of history corresponds to what the entire Ancient Near East considered an orderly (*heil*) world. Schmid said that the "so-called" messianic prophecies attributed to the king of the end time is expressed *materialiter* in the thought of what the Ancient Near East expected of the reigning king.

God's enthronement as King in Zion will be celebrated with a pilgrimage to Zion. "Then all who survive of the nations that have come against Jerusalem shall go up year after year to worship the King, the LORD of hosts, and to keep the festival of booths" (Zech. 14:16).

An ever-increasing awareness grew of the "difference between the world of creation and that which can be realized in history. Consequently the period of salvation was postponed into an ever-receding future and eventually was expected to be the in-breaking of a completely new eon" (Schmid, "Creation, Righteousness, and Salvation," 110). Schmid did not make clear how this new eon will come. Will it be empowered by nature or by the Lord? Wheeler Robinson said, "This unity of land and people for weal and woe derives from their common dependence on God as their creator, upholder, and future transformer" (*Inspiration and Revelation*, 32).

47. The Restoration of the Nation and God's Universal Reign

In the Old Testament, much of Israel's future hope is tied to the national and political fortunes of the nation. Israel hoped for the restoration of freedom from foreign domination and the recovery of her land and prosperity lost in battles with Assyria and Babylon. Some prophets and people looked for a moral and religious purification and a future with happiness, glory, and perfection. Between 760 and 700 B.C. prophets Amos, Hosea, Isaiah, and Micah announced God's judgment on Israel and Judah. They also understood that God was bound up with His people and could not let them go. Amos admonished his hearers, "Seek the LORD and live" (Amos 5:6). Hosea said, "Return, O Israel, to the LORD your God" (Hos. 14:1). Isaiah and Micah spoke often of a remnant that would be saved (Isa. 4:3; 7:3; 10:20; 11:11,16; 38:5; Mic. 2:12; 4:7; 5:7,8; 7:18). Isaiah and Micah also spoke of a time in the latter days when the mountain of the house of the Lord would be established as the highest of the mountains and peoples would flow into it (Isa. 2:2; Mic. 4:1).

The hope for national and political restoration of Israel included the defeat of the oppressors (Isa. 9:3; 10:27; 14:25; 52:2; Jer. 30:8; Ezek. 34:27); the restoration of the dynasty and kingdom of David (Isa. 9:7; Jer. 3:18; Ezek. 37:15-28; Hos. 2:20; Amos 9:8; Obad. 19; Mic. 5:1-4; Zech. 9:9-10); the reunion of the two kingdoms (Isa. 11:13-14; Jer. 3:18; 31:27; 33:7; Ezek. 37:15-22; Hos. 1:11; 3:5; Zech. 8:13; 10:6-12); the return from the exile (Isa. 11:11-16; 14:1; 27:12-13; 35:10; 43:5; 48:20; 49:17; 52:8; 56:7; 57:13; 60:4; 66:20; Jer. 3:18; 23:3; 30:3; 31:7-12; 32:37; 33:7,11; Ezek. 11:17; 20:34,41; 27:25; 34:11-12; 36:24; 37:12; Hos. 11:10-11; Mic. 2:12-13; 4:6-7; Zeph. 3:19-20;

Zech. 8:7-8; 9:11-12; 10:8-10); religious and moral cleansing (Isa. 1:18-20; 2:20; 4:2-6; 17:7; 27:9; 30:22; 31:6-7; 58:6-12; Mic. 5:9-13; Zeph. 1:2-6; 3:11-13; Zech. 13:2-6; Mal. 2:10-13; 3:2-5); the rebuilding of the temple and a cleansed priesthood (Ezek. 40—48; Hag. 1:7; Zech. 1:16; 3:4-5; 4:6-9; Mal. 3:2-3); paradisiacal fertility of the land, people, and cattle (Isa. 7:21-22; 35:1-2; 60:19-22; Ezek. 36:33-38; Joel 3:18; Amos 9:13); transformation of wild beasts (Isa. 11:6-9; Ezek. 34:25; Hos. 2:18); exaltation of Zion (Pss. 46; 48; 76; 84; 87; 122; Isa. 2:4; 49:14-18; 51:3; 60:4-14; 62:1-4; Mic. 4:1-4); a new king (Isa. 7:10-14; 11:1-4; Jer. 23:5-6; 30:9,21; 33:17; Ezek. 17:22-24; 34:23; 37:22-24; Hos. 3:5; Amos 9:11; Mic. 4:8; 5:1-4; Zech. 9:9-10); universal knowledge of God (Isa. 11:9; Jer. 31:34; Joel 2:28-29; Hab. 2:14); and universal peace (Ps. 46:10; Isa. 2:4; 9:4-7; Mic. 5:9; Zech. 10:10).

These Old Testament expectations probably did not include any that could not be fulfilled in this world. The Old Testament never distinguished "this world" or "this age" (*hāʿōlām hazzeh*) from "the world (age) to come" (*hāʿōlām habbaʾ*). However, Jews between the Testaments developed such a concept. The earliest occurrence of the expression "the world to come" (*hāʿōlām habbaʾ*) seems to be Enoch 71:15 (LaSor, *The Truth About Armageddon*, 21).

The expression "this age or in the age to come" is used in the New Testament (Matt. 12:32). Undoubtedly most Jews and early Christians in the first century looked for the kingdom of God to be established on earth. Even the disciples asked after Jesus' resurrection when He would restore the kingdom to Israel (Acts 1:6). (Some people still ask this question, but the concept that the restored kingdom would be an earthly kingdom of Israel seems too small and mundane.) The idea of the restored kingdom as the kingdom of God had to be reinterpreted.

The term "kingdom of God" does not appear in the Old Testament. However, nine passages refer to "the kingdom God rules" or "God's kingdom" (1 Chron. 29:11; Pss. 22:28; 103:19; 145:11,12,13; Dan. 4:3 [Aramaic 3:33] 32; Obad. 21). Yahweh is called "King" forty-one times in the Old Testament (Eissfeldt, "Jahwe als König," 89; compare G. R. Beasley-Murray, "The Kingdom of God in the Old Testament," *Jesus and the*

Kingdom of God, 17). Ludwig Köhler said, *"God is the ruling Lord*: that is the one fundamental statement in the theology of the Old Testament" (*Old Testament Theology*, 30).

We do not know when Israel first conceived of God as king, but according to the canonical shape of the Old Testament Yahweh was the Creator of heaven and earth from the beginning (Gen. 1:1). The idea of God as king is seen in the "theocracy" before the monarchy. When the people requested a king from Samuel, the thing displeased him (1 Sam. 8:6). It also displeased the Lord. The Lord said to Samuel, "Listen to the voice of the people . . . for they have not rejected you, but they have rejected me from being king over them" (1 Sam. 8:7).

The Lord did not abandon the people when they asked for and received a king other than Yahweh. He participated in the selection of Saul, the first king. He commanded Samuel to anoint Saul (1 Sam. 10:1). However, Saul showed little religious sensitivity. He left the ark at Kiriath-jearim for twenty years after it had been returned by the Philistines (1 Sam. 6:20—7:2). He did not consult the Urim or Thummin for a word from God except when he was in dire trouble. Then he consulted the witch of Endor, in violation of his own sanctions against the occult (1 Sam. 28:3-7). Saul was displaced as king because of his presumption. He assumed the role of priest to offer a sacrifice to begin a battle with the Philistines (1 Sam. 13:8-14), and he broke the law of the "ban" [*herem*] in failing to kill Agag the Amalekite (1 Sam. 15:9).

The idea of the kingdom of God in the Old Testament was tied to David's kingdom. David's throne is called God's throne (1 Chron. 28:5; 29:3; perhaps Ps. 45:6). The Lord chose David and anointed him (1 Sam. 13:14; 16:12-13). The psalmist said:

> You said, "I have made a covenant
> with my chosen one,
> I have sworn to my servant David;
> I will establish your descendants forever,
> and build your throne for all
> generations."
> (Ps. 89:3-4)

> Then you spoke in a vision to your
> faithful one, and said:
> "I have set the crown on one
> who is mighty,

> I have exalted one chosen from
> the people.
> I have found my servant David;
> with my holy oil I have anointed him;
> My hand shall always remain with him;
> my arm shall strengthen him."
> (Ps. 89:19-21)
>
> He shall cry to me, "You are my Father,
> my God, and the Rock of my salvation!"
> . . . .
> I will establish his line forever,
> and his throne as long as the
> heavens endure.
> (Ps. 89:26,29)

Hartmut Gese said, "We must understand divine sonship in terms of God's choosing and dwelling with Israel, and of the relationship of Zion and David's clan" ("The Messiah," *Essays on Biblical Theology*, 144). Gese pointed out that only God speaks of the king as His son in the Old Testament. The term "son of God" is rarely used for the messianic king outside the Old and New Testaments. The New Testament refers to Jesus as *ho huios tou theou* ("the Son of God"), following the Old Testament tradition of the role of the Davidic king. "Any other origin of the designation, from the non-Jewish world . . . is excluded" ("The Messiah," 146).

David made a great effort to tie his kingdom to the old sacral wilderness and theocracy traditions. When he first became king, he conquered Jerusalem, the place where Abraham had paid tithes to Melchizedek (2 Sam. 5:6-10). He searched for the ark of the covenant, God's footstool, and found it still in the house of Abinadab (2 Sam. 6:3; 1 Chron. 13:5-8; Ps. 132:4-10). He moved the ark to Jerusalem with one mishap and much fanfare.

The king ruled according to the decree and authority of Yahweh (Ps. 2:6-9). However, as time went on, strong secular influences took control of most of the affairs of the kingdom. David himself was caught up in the expansion of the territory through military conquest and in amassing a huge private fortune (1 Chron. 27:25-31).

Solomon won the bitter struggle to succeed David, largely through the influence of Bathsheba and Nathan, but he squandered the wealth of the nation and mismanaged the nation into disruption. Revolt was rampant before Solomon died (1 Kings 11). When Solomon died, the kingdom was divided, never to be reunited. Only one tribe (Judah) remained as a kingdom for the descendants of David (1 Kings 11:11-13). Revivals and renewals occurred under Jehoshaphat, Hezekiah, and Josiah, but with little lasting effects. After God sent the prophets to warn the king and people many times that they must turn back to Him, they refused. He expelled the people of Jerusalem and Judah because they angered Him so much (2 Kings 24:20; 25:8-21). The earthly king in Israel failed to bring in the kingdom of God and to achieve the goals of righteousness and justice for all (Ps. 72:1-2,4), but kingship was not a total failure. Bruce Birch said, "Kingship in Israel becomes the context through which some of the most important and perennial theological and ethical themes are introduced in the Old Testament" (*Let Justice Roll Down*, 206).

The anointing of kings opened the door for the idea of a "Messiah," an ideal anointed one who would come and perform the functions of an ideal king (von Rad, *Old Testament Theology II*, 169). The important step from the king to Messiah was made in Isaiah 7:10-17. God rejected the reigning house of David. The concept of the son of God is transformed. The true Son, with whom God is present, will now be born. Somewhere in the great Davidic clan "God will choose the bearer of the dynastic promise of eternal lordship on Zion. Even the reference of Ephrathah in Micah 5:2-4 provides a broad framework for the origin of the Messiah" (Gese, "The Messiah," 146-147).

48. The Messiah

The word *Messiah* is a transliteration of the Greek word *Messias*, or the Aramaic word *meshiha*, or the Hebrew word *māšiaḥ*. The word means "the Anointed One." Objects as well as people could be "anointed" in the Old Testament. Jacob anointed a pillar at Bethel (Gen. 31:13). The tabernacle was anointed (Ex. 30:26) as well as the altar and vessels (Lev. 8:11). Persons anointed in the Old Testament included the priests (Ex. 29:7), some prophets (1 Kings 19:16; Ps. 105:15; Isa. 61:1), and the patriarchs (Ps. 105:15). In a special sense the king was "Yahweh's anointed." "In the Old Testament the primary sense of the expression 'Yahweh's anointed' is *the king*, the earthly king who at any given time is reigning over Yahweh's people" (Mowinckel, *He That Cometh*, 5). The Old Testament did not speak as much of crowning a king as anointing him. "Anointing" implies a special relationship, a commission, a sacral character of office and person, and perhaps an endowment of holy power. Kings were anointed in the Old Testament until the fall of Jerusalem in 586 B.C. After that Israel did not have another king until the Maccabean period (1 Maccabees 14:41-47).

In later Judaism and in New Testament times Jews were expecting "an Anointed One," a Messiah. Franz Delitzsch said, "Messianic prophecies in the narrowest signification are accordingly such prophecies, as connect the hope of salvation and the glory of the people of God with a future king, who, proceeding from Israel, subjects the world to himself" (*Messianic Prophecies*, 17). A political and perhaps a military figure, he would come and "save" them from their enemies and restore the kingdom to Israel.

Most modern writers point out that the word "Messiah" in this technical sense of a coming eschatological king does not occur in the Old Testament (see Mowinckel, *He That Cometh*, 7; Delitzsch, *Messianic Prophecies*, 17). According to David Hubbard, "Messianism in the technical sense of the expectation of an anointed king from David's house, consequently, is not the controlling motif of Old Testament hope" ("Hope in the Old Testament," 53). "The word (*Mesiah*) as a technical term developed in the Intertestamental Period" (LaSor, *The Truth About Armageddon*, 74).

The early church did believe that the Old Testament was a book of prophetic promises which foretold an age of salvation that was to come (see especially Acts 3:24; 1 Cor. 10:11; 1 Pet. 1:10-12; compare Clements, *Old Testament Theology*, 131-133). Jewish writers in the Apocrypha (Ecclesiasticus 49:10) and at Qumran also assumed that the prophets foretold the coming days of salvation in a distant future. The major difference between Christian and Jewish interpretation of prophecy is that Christians regarded the prophecies as fulfilled. Jewish interpreters still waited for their fulfillment.

The early church, in its desire to show that Jesus was the long-awaited king, searched the Old Testament for prophecies fulfilled by Jesus. W. C. Kaiser said that 456 Old Testament passages refer to the Messiah or messianic times, attested in 558 separate quotations from the rabbinic writings ("Messianic Prophecies," 75; compare LaSor, *The Truth About Armageddon*, 86, note F).

The historical-critical approach to the Old Testament in the 1800s changed the way scholars interpreted Old Testament prophecy. Rather than starting with the New Testament fulfillment and seeing the prophets as precise predictors of significant events across many centuries, scholars started with the Old Testament prophecies and tried to understand the oracles from their historical setting.

R. E. Clements said that to understand the prophets as having referred to events that were to take place many centuries later raises serious problems about the nature of God's provisional control of history and stands at variance with what we find in much of the prophetic literature of the canon. The prophets addressed their contemporaries "about the meaning and outcome of events which were taking place at that time, or which were shortly expected to take place" (*Old Testament Theology*, 133). The prophets, according to the historical method of interpretation, were primarily preachers of righteousness and denouncers of social injustice. They called their people back to life under the covenant with God and exposed the hollowness of worship that was not accompanied by a righteous lifestyle and faith in God.

LaSor argued for the use of the historical method in interpreting messianic passages.

> A more reasonable approach is to ask first what the prophecies meant, that is, how they were understood, *at the time they were given*, and then discover how later generations of the people of God came to understand them. Prophecy, I am convinced, is *not* "history written in advance," but rather it is revelation of truth from God that has immediate and continuing relevance to God's people until it attains its fullness. When it is filled full, it is fulfilled (*The Truth About Armageddon*, 77).

Franz Delitzsch defended the historical and exegetical approach to Old Testament prophecy. He said, "It is true that our doctrinal material does not consist merely in predictions in the strict sense of the term, but the promises and hopes which have reference to the future salvation may be included under the conception of prophecy" (*Messianic Prophecies*, 9).

The messianic hope in the Old Testament is usually associated with the king in Jerusalem because he was the primary anointed figure in Israel, at least in the pre-exilic period.

The account of Yahweh's covenant with David in 2 Samuel 7 is parallel in many ways with God's promise to Abraham. The following chart illustrates the similarities between God's covenants with Abraham and David.

Promise to Abraham	Promise to David
Genesis 12; 17	2 Samuel 7
1. Great name (12:2)	1. Great name (7:9)
2. Great nation (12:2)	2. Great kingdom (7:16)
3. Kings as descendants (17:6,16)	3. Kings as descendants (7:12-16)
4. A blessing (12:2)	4. A blessing (7:19)

Still, God's covenant with David–not the one with Abraham—became the starting point of Israel's messianic hope and expectation (Vriezen, *Outline of Old Testament Theology*, 66).

Several royal psalms (2; 72; 110) were called messianic psalms in the past as if they only referred to the coming messianic king and had no reference to the contemporary setting or the current reigning king. To call them royal psalms rather than messianic psalms does not mean that all eschatological perspective is absent from these psalms. Psalm 2 was no doubt used as a coronation hymn for many kings of the line of David, but its view goes beyond that of the present ruler, who is called "God's anointed" (*Messiah*). The coronation day was the king's birthday as "the son of God." For the psalmist, the present king became a "sign of the coming king who alone will be able to carry out the mission of victory and universalism" (Jacob, *Theology of the Old Testament*, 334).

Peter Craigie said Psalm 2 reflects the joint kingship between the Lord, the enthroned one (v. 4) as the universal king, and the earthly king as His "son," a representative (v. 7). The Davidic kings never exercised worldwide dominion. Jesus spoke of the kingdom of God which would include all nations. Psalm 2 is quoted often in the Book of Revelation to refer to the "ultimate rule and triumph of the man born to be King in the language and imagery of Ps. 2 (Rev. 1:5; 2:27; 4:2; 6:17; 12:5; 19:5 and others)" (*Psalms 1-50*, 68-69).

Psalm 72 is a prayer for a new Davidic king on his coronation day. The king is highly idealized, and some have suggested that he is a messianic figure (Briggs, *Psalms*, *ICC*). Marvin Tate said the king does not rule the messianic kingdom because there are still oppressors of the poor, and nowhere else do we find the people interceding for the messianic king. "The idealization apparent in the psalm is the result of the hope attendant at every new beginning" (*Psalms 51-100*, 222). The psalmist prayed that God's justice and righteousness would characterize the rule of his king; that the king would have long life; and his reign would be from sea to sea and to the ends of the earth; that his foes would be put down; and that peace (*šālôm*) would prevail. No king in Israel ever matched the hopes of this psalm. At least in part, it was the frustrations of these hopes that led to the development of the messianic idea in Israel.

Psalm 110 holds the record for being "the Old Testament text most frequently cited or alluded to in the New Testament" (Leslie C. Allen, *Psalms 101-150*, 87). The original psalm probably was an enthronement psalm for one or more of the Davidic kings. Leslie Allen said that one respects the worthy motives of those who seek to restrict the psalm to a messianic intent from the beginning (see D. Kidner, *Psalms 73-150*, 392). "But it hardly accords with the pattern of historical and theological development discernable in the royal psalms in general and with the ancient cultural and historical royal references within Ps. 110" (Allen, *Psalms 101-150*, 83-84).

Old Testament prophets recognized the positive values of the Davidic monarchy, but they also regarded it as too narrow a basis for the coming of the kingdom. It is improbable that a prophet like Isaiah, who lived in close proximity to the kings, ever thought that the Davidic dynasty was enough to establish Yahweh's kingship on earth. Isaiah viewed the reigning king as "only a sign, positive or negative, of the king whom the prophet was awaiting in accordance with the most ancient tradition of his people" (Jacob, *Theology of the Old Testament*, 336).

Isaiah contrasted the weak, hesitant Ahaz, who sought salvation in foreign alliances, with Immanuel, the child of mysterious origin, who, as far as we know, was not the son of Ahaz or the prophet, and who represented a new age which would put an end to the old order of things (Isa. 7). Immanuel was the name of a baby to be born. The name means "God with us." He was not God, and he was not a king—at least, not like Ahaz. But he embodied the presence and the power of God among his people.

Immanuel's mission is described in some detail in chapters 9 and 11. A new king would be born whose reign would be marked by wisdom and light. He would reign with justice and righteousness. Wars would cease. Universal peace and knowledge of God would prevail. Micah 5:1-4 and Zechariah 9:9-10 also speak of a new Davidic king. Jeremiah envisaged the messianic kingdom as a contrast to and not as a continuation of the earthly kingdom of David (Jer. 23:5-6; 33:15-16).

The role of a personal Messiah is not very clear or strong in the Old Testament. The word does not occur in the technical sense. The strong feeling about the sovereignty of God and the sacral role of the king left little room in between for a personal Messiah. Most of the time it was Yahweh who was to come to deliver His people. The Davidic king was the adopted "son of God" to rule in God's name on the earth. Beasley-Murray said we should not check through the books of the Old Testament to see where the Messiah is not mentioned and then declare that the authors of those works did not look for a Messiah (*Jesus and the Kingdom of God*, 24). A Messiah is often tacitly assumed where it is not mentioned.

In Isaiah the Messiah is pictured as a "shoot from the stump of Jesse." The spirit of the Lord shall rest upon him. He will have the spirit of wisdom and understanding, of counsel and might, of knowledge and fear of the Lord. His judgments will be true and righteous. He will bring *šālôm* "peace," "wholeness" to all creation (Isa. 11:6-9). In other Old Testament passages,

deliverance and salvation will come through the messianic figures of the Suffering Servant and One like the Son of Man.

49. The Suffering Servant

Many people are called "the servant of God" in the Old Testament, including Abraham (Gen. 26:24); the patriarchs (Ex.
32:13; Deut. 9:5); Moses (Ex. 4:10; 14:31); David (2 Sam. 7:5,8);
the prophets (2 Kings 24:2); and Nebuchadnezzar (Jer. 25:9).
The term "servant" takes on a special significance in Isaiah
40—66. Bernard Duhm in his commentary on Isaiah (*Das
Buch Jesaja*, 1892) called attention to four separate servant
songs in Isaiah 40—55 which he said were not a part of their
context, nor were they written by the author of the chapters
surrounding them. In Duhm's view, these four "Servant
Songs" (Isa. 42:1-4; 49:1-6; 50:4-11; 52:13—53:12) portrayed
the career of a historical individual earlier than or contemporary with the prophet. Duhm's views were widely accepted by
Old Testament scholars.

Now a growing consensus rejects Duhm's idea of isolating
these songs from their context. One such scholar, John W.
Miller, has attempted to interpret the songs in light of their
context. Miller argued that the songs refer to the prophet himself and that their context reveals the conflict the prophet had
with some of his fellow countrymen and with the leaders in
Babylon ("The Servant Songs in the Light of Their Contexts,"
77-85).

The word *servant* occurs twenty times in Isaiah 40—53,
always in the singular. It appears ten times in Isaiah 54—66,
always in the plural. Sometimes the "servant" plainly is Israel
(42:8) or Jacob (44:1). Sometimes the servant is chosen for a
mission to Israel and/or the world (42:1-4; 44:1-2; 49:1-6).
Sometimes the servant is a great sufferer (50:4-6; 52:13—
53:12). Who was this servant?

In addition to the traditional view that the songs are direct
predictions of the suffering, death, and resurrection of Jesus,
four main theories have been advanced as to the identity of the
servant. One theory holds that the servant was some historical
individual such as Moses, Jeremiah, Job, Zerubbabel, or the
prophet himself. A second theory, the collective theory, makes
the servant Israel personified or a remnant of Israel. A third

view is that the servant represented the king in a cultic celebration of the new year's festival in which the king portrayed the dying and rising God.

The fourth theory is the "messianic" or the "fluid" theory. The messianic view sees the servant as a future individual representative (perhaps of the Davidic line) who by suffering, would save his people. The "fluid" view starts with the idea that the servant is Israel and develops, or fluctuates, between the nation and a future savior who suffers vicariously for his people and the world. H. H. Rowley did not believe that Jews ever had any idea of a suffering Messiah until Jesus came (*The Servant of the Lord and Other Essays*, 15-16, 61-72). Mowinckel said that the Servant far surpasses everything in the Old Testament message about the Messiah as a future king (*He That Cometh*, 247).

Let us examine the four "servant songs" of Isaiah 40—55 separately. This is necessary to understand each song, not because we believe they have no connection with their context. Both in diction and theological subject matter "they have much in common with the rest of Deutero-Isaiah" (von Rad, *Old Testament Theology II*, 251-252). They do stand in a certain isolation from the rest of their material, and they certainly are the "highwater mark" of Old Testament prophecy and perhaps of the whole Old Testament. H. H. Rowley noted that the highest word on Old Testament sacrifice is here in Isaiah 53. It is not that of an unblemished animal but of a sinless human being. (See this book's section on sacrifice, chapter 7, sect. 37; H. H. Rowley, *The Changing Pattern of Old Testament Studies*, 29-30; Page Kelley, *Isaiah*, 343.)

> Here is my servant, whom I uphold,
> my chosen, in whom my soul delights;
> I have put my spirit upon him;
> he will bring forth justice to the
> nations.
> He will not cry or lift up his voice,
> or make it heard in the street;
> a bruised reed he will not break,
> and a dimly burning wick he
> will not quench;
> he will faithfully bring forth justice.
> He will not grow faint or be crushed

until he has established justice in
the earth;
and the coastlands wait for his
teaching.
(Isa. 42:1-4)

In this first song the Lord speaks throughout. He introduces
His chosen servant, whom He upholds and who delights Him.
God empowers him by His spirit (*charisma*) to bring forth justice (*mišpāṭ*) to the nations. "Justice" occurs three times in this
song and is the key to the servant's mission. *mišpāṭ*, "justice,"
is a broad term that has many connotations in the Old Testament. Here it probably has a very general sense and means the
God-given orders for life and worship. In this instance it may
be equated with true religion (see 2 Kings 17:27; Isa. 58:2).
The servant was to perform his work without fanfare, noise,
or street demonstration (42:2). His approach was soft, tender,
and caring. "A bruised reed he will not break, /and a dimly
burning wick he will not quench" (3). He will gently save that
which could easily be snuffed out. He is interminably patient
and faithful. He will not give up until justice is established in
the remotest corner of the world (see Matt. 12:18-21).

Listen to me, O coastlands,
pay attention, you peoples
from far away!
The Lord called me before I was born,
while I was in my mother's
womb he named me.
He made my mouth like a sharp sword,
in the shadow of his hand he hid me;
he made me a polished arrow,
in his quiver he hid me away.
And he said to me, "You are my servant,
Israel, in whom I will be glorified."
But I said, "I have labored in vain,
I have spent my strength for
nothing and vanity;
yet surely my cause is with the LORD,
and my reward with my God."
And now the LORD says,
who formed me in the womb to
be his servant,
to bring Jacob back to him,
and that Israel might be

<blockquote>
gathered to him,
for I am honored in the sight of the LORD,
and my God has become my strength—
he says,
"It is too light a thing that you
should be my servant
to raise up the tribes of Jacob
and to restore the survivors of Israel;
I will give you as a light to the
nations,
that my salvation may reach to
the end of the earth."
(Isa. 49:1-6)
</blockquote>

The servant speaks in the second song. He addresses the coastlands and peoples of the world. He tells them that the Lord called him and named him before he was born (49:1). The word of his mouth was to be a sharp sword and a polished arrow to penetrate the hearts and ears of his hearers. Before he began his ministry, while he was in the shadow of the Lord's hand hidden in His quiver, the Lord confided to him His plan. "You are my servant, Israel, in whom I will be glorified" (49:3). "Israel" is often regarded as a later addition to the text. (See Mowinckel, *He That Cometh*, 462-463.)

The servant complained that his labor had been in vain, even though the Lord was with him (49:4). The Lord said that He formed the servant in the womb "to bring Israel back," a mission not yet accomplished. In addition to the mission to Israel, the servant is now given a new mission: to be a light to the Gentiles so that God's salvation might reach the ends of the earth (49:6).

<blockquote>
The Lord GOD has given me
the tongue of a teacher,
that I may know how to sustain
the weary with a word.
Morning by morning he wakens—
wakens my ear
to listen as those who are taught.
The Lord GOD has opened my ear,
and I was not rebellious,
I did not turn backward.
I gave my back to those who struck me,
and my cheeks to those who
pulled out the beard;
</blockquote>

I did not hide my face
from insult and spitting.
The Lord GOD helps me;
therefore I have not been disgraced;
therefore I have set my face like flint,
and I know that I shall not be
put to shame;
he who vindicates me is near.
Who will contend with me?
Let us stand up together.
Who are my adversaries?
Let them confront me.
It is the Lord GOD who helps me;
who will declare me guilty?
All of them will wear out like a garment;
the moth will eat them up.
Who among you fears the LORD
and obeys the voice of his servant,
who walks in darkness
and has no light,
yet trusts in the name of the LORD
and relies upon his God?
But all of you are kindlers of fire,
lighters of firebrands.
Walk in the flame of your fire,
and among the brands that you
have kindled!
This is what you shall have from
my hand:
you shall lie down in torment.
(Isa. 50:4-11)

The servant speaks in verses 4-9. Someone else, perhaps the Lord, speaks to the servant's hearers in verses 10-11. The servant says that God gave him the tongue of a teacher so that he could sustain the weary with a word of encouragement (50:4). He was obedient, not rebellious, even though his obedience brought suffering, humiliation, insults, disgrace, and shame (50:6-7). Still, he did not give up. He set his face like flint because he knew that God, who would vindicate him, was near (50:7-8a).

The servant challenges his abusers: "Who will contend with me? Who are my adversaries?" This is courtroom language, not that of the boxing ring or the battlefield. The servant, like the apostle Paul centuries later, said, "Who will bring any charge against God's elect? It is God who justifies" (Rom. 8:33). In Isaiah 50 it is the servant who is being charged and spit upon. In Romans it is Christians who, as God's elect, have been charged. They have been justified by Christ Jesus, who died, who was raised, and who intercedes for them (Rom. 8:34).

Isaiah 50:10-11 expands the meaning of the end of verse 9 that God's and the servant's adversaries will wear out like garments. Moths will consume them. No one who fears the Lord and obeys the voice of His servant walks in darkness (50:10). All those in darkness who try to kindle their own light and walk in it rather than in God's light (see Isa. 8:16—9:2) will lie down in torment (Isa. 50:11).

> See, my servant shall prosper;
> he shall be exalted and lifted up,
> and shall be very high.
> Just as there were many who were
> astonished at him
> —so marred was his
> appearance, beyond human semblance,
> and his form beyond that of mortals—
> so he shall startle many nations;
> kings shall shut their mouths
> because of him;
> for that which had not been told
> them they shall see,
> and that which they had not
> heard they shall contemplate.
>
> Who has believed what we have heard?
> And to whom has the arm of
> the LORD been revealed?
> For he grew up before him like a young plant,
> and like a root out of dry ground;
> he had no form or majesty that
> we should look at him,
> nothing in his appearance that
> we should desire him.
> He was despised and rejected by others;
> a man of suffering and
> acquainted with infirmity;
> and as one from whom others
> hide their faces
> he was despised, and we held
> him of no account.

Surely he has borne our infirmities
and carried our diseases;
yet we accounted him stricken,
struck down by God, and afflicted.
But he was wounded for our transgressions,
crushed for our iniquities;
upon him was the punishment that made us whole,
and by his bruises we are healed.
All we like sheep have gone astray;
we have all turned to our own way,
and the LORD has laid on him
the iniquity of us all.

He was oppressed, and he was afflicted,
yet he did not open his mouth;
like a lamb that is led to the slaughter,
and like a sheep that before its
shearers is silent,
so he did not open his mouth.
By a perversion of justice he was taken away.
Who could have imagined his future?
For he was cut off from the land of the living,
stricken for the transgression of my people.
They made his grave with the wicked
and his tomb with the rich,
although he had done no violence;
and there was no deceit in his mouth.

Yet it was the will of the LORD to
crush him with pain.
When you make his life an
offering for sin,
he shall see his offspring, and
shall prolong his days;
through him the will of the LORD shall prosper.
Out of his anguish he shall see light;
he shall find satisfaction through his knowledge.
The righteous one, my
servant, shall make many righteous,
and he shall bear their iniquities.
Therefore I will allot him a
portion with the great,
and he shall divide the spoil
with the strong;
because he poured out himself to death,
and was numbered with the transgressors;
yet he bore the sin of many,
and made intercession for the

transgressors.
(Isa. 52:13—53:12)

The fourth servant song has been described as "the most influential poem in any literature." If the entire song were to disappear from the Book of Isaiah, it could be almost completely reconstructed from quotations from it in the New Testament. Page Kelley noted that of the twelve verses in chapter 53, only one does not reappear in whole or in part somewhere in the New Testament. "The wide use of the passage in the New Testament shows that they [the writers] considered it to be vital to the understanding of the gospel" (*Isaiah*, 340-341).

This fourth and final servant song is the longest and the apex of the series. It is made up of five almost equal stanzas of three verses each. The Lord speaks in the first (52:13-15) and the last stanzas (53:10-12). The three middle stanzas (53:1-3,4-6,7-9) seem to be the words of the prophet and his people. The first stanza (52:13-15) announces the servant's surprising victory over suffering and death. He will surprise and startle (or sprinkle) many nations. Kings will shut their mouths at him. They will be speechless, for they will see and hear that which has never happened.

The second stanza (53:1-3) says people will not believe that which has been revealed and heard (v. 1). The servant grew up in an unpretentious place, with nothing in his form or appearance that would attract people. Actually, he was despised and rejected by others. His suffering and infirmities were repulsive, and people turned their eyes away from looking at him (vv. 2-3).

The third stanza is surprising because the speaker and those who despised the servant—and possibly contributed to his suffering—realized and confessed that the servant was not suffering for his own sins. He was suffering voluntarily and vicariously for others. The speakers said:

> All we like sheep have gone astray;
> we have all turned to our own way,
> and the LORD has laid on him
> the iniquity of us all.
> (Isa. 53:6)

The fourth stanza (53:7-9) describes how the servant suffered submissively, unresistingly, deliberately. By a perversion of justice (53:8) he was taken away to prison, executed, and given a degrading burial, even though he did no violence or spoke any deceit.

Finally, in the fifth stanza (53:10-12) we are told that it was the plan of God to bruise the servant so that his life and death could become an offering for sin.

Who was this servant? Gerhard von Rad said the expressions in this poem go "far beyond the description of anyone who might have existed in the past or the present. The picture of the servant of Jahweh, of his mission to Israel and to the world, and of his expiatory suffering, is prophecy of the future, and . . . belongs to the realm of pure miracle which Yahweh reserved for Himself" (*Old Testament Theology II*, 260). In Jesus Christ the Old Testament prophecies of the Suffering Servant were fulfilled in ways beyond anything the prophet ever imagined.

50. The Son of Man

The term "son of man" in a messianic sense only occurs one time in the Old Testament, and even that reference is now questioned.

> As I watched in the night visions,
> I saw one like a human being (son of man)
> coming with the clouds of heaven.
> And he came to the Ancient One
> and was presented before him.
> (Dan. 7:13)

In a generic sense, the expression "son of man" means "a human being in contrast to a divine or animal-like being" and occurs approximately 108 times in the Old Testament. In the Book of Ezekiel God addresses the prophet ninety-three times as "son of man." The term is used fifteen times in other books as a lofty designation for "humanity" (Num. 23:19; Job 16:21; 25:6; 35:8; Pss. 8:5; 80:18; 146:3; Isa. 51:12; 56:2; Jer. 49:18,33; 50:40; 51:43; Dan. 8:17; 10:16). (See Hartman and DiLella, *The Book of Daniel*, 85.)

The expression "son of man" or "human being" in Daniel 7:13 is used in contrast to four great beasts, which represent four world kingdoms arising out of the sea. The "son of man" or "human being" represents the fifth kingdom or the kingdom of heaven. Daniel 7 is similar in many ways to Daniel 2. Both chapters are written in Aramaic. Both describe a vision of Daniel about four world kingdoms, followed by a fifth kingdom which is the universal and eternal kingdom of God. In chapter 2 the fifth kingdom is represented by a stone cut out of the mountains without hands. The stone destroys the four earthly kingdoms and fills the whole earth (Dan. 2:34-35,44-45). In chapter 7 the four kings, kingdoms, or horns are represented by four beasts coming up out of the sea (Dan. 7:3). The fifth kingdom is represented by one "like a human being" coming with the clouds of heaven to the Ancient One seated on a judgment throne (Dan. 7:13).

> To him was given dominion
> and glory and kingship,
> that all peoples, nations, and languages
> should serve him.
> His dominion is an everlasting dominion
> that shall not pass away,
> and his kingship is one
> that shall never be destroyed.
> (Dan. 7:14)

From Daniel 7:13-14 it seems that the "son of man" or "human being" is an individual completely different from the animals which came up from the sea. He is king of all peoples, nations, and languages; and they will "serve" or "worship" him (v. 14). Daniel asks for help in interpreting what he has seen (v. 16). The interpreter tells him that the four great beasts are four kings who shall arise out of the earth (v. 17), but the holy ones of the Most High shall receive the kingdom "and possess the kingdom forever—forever and ever" (v. 18). In verse 21 the holy ones are identified as those who were attacked by a representative of the fourth beast. The court gave the kingdom to the holy ones of the Most High (v. 22).

What does this mean? In 7:14 the Ancient One gave the world kingdoms to the son of man or the human representing the fifth kingdom, but in verse 18 the saints or "holy ones" receive the kingdom. The son of man is represented as a human being coming from the clouds to contrast his kingdom from those of the beasts coming out of the sea. His kingdom will come from the clouds (or heaven), but theirs (the beasts') from the regions of chaos. The son of man or human being who comes with the clouds of heaven is more than an ordinary human. Von Rad said "There can be no doubt that the son of man described in Daniel 7:13 is initially presented as a Messianic figure in the wider sense of the term" (*Old Testament Theology II*, 312).

G. R. Beasley-Murray said, "Elsewhere in the Old Testament the rider on the clouds is Yahweh [Ps. 18:10-11], not a symbol for a group. It is to be expected, then, that in this vision the cloud rider should denote the representative of the rule of God and (in light of the interpretation) the representative of the people to whom the rule is given" (*Jesus and the Kingdom of God*, 33). In the prophetic tradition, the Messiah holds just such a position, the representative of Yahweh and the people privileged to be included in His rule. "This concept is sometimes referred to without use of the term *Messiah*, as we see in the Servant Songs of Deutero-Isaiah, in which the concepts of servant leader and servant people flow together" (Beasley-Murray, *Jesus and the Kingdom of God*, 33).

Many scattered threads in the Old Testament point to a new, coming kingdom of God. Ideas such as a son of David, son of God, son of man, and suffering servant appear at different times and circumstances. They are never put together or related in any systematic form in the Old Testament. The New Testament brings all of these ideas together and says that Jesus Christ is the fulfillment of all of them.

51. The Old Testament and the New: Christians and Jews

Where and when does the Old Testament end? Does it have a sequel? Has it been "fulfilled" and we are now living in the eschaton? Do we need the Old Testament any longer? Does it still have religious significance, relevance, and value?

Two great living religions, Judaism and Christianity, regard the Old Testament (Hebrew Bible) as Scripture. However, they do not interpret this Scripture in the same way. Maimonides said, "The Christians believe and confess, as do we, that the Bible is of divine origin and was revealed to our teacher Moses; only in interpretation of Scripture do they differ" ("Pe'er ha-Dor," 50, cited by Schoeps, *The Jewish-Christian Argument*, 15). Jews see themselves as the heirs and the continuation of the Old Testament faith. Christians claim that they are heirs and, through Christ, are the fulfillment of the promises of God. Their mission is the mission God gave to Israel in the Old Testament—that is, to proclaim His salvation and peace (*šālôm*) to the ends of the earth.

The mainstreams of Christianity and Judaism add to the Old Testament. Judaism adds the Mishnah and the Talmud as aids in interpretation and application of the Hebrew Scriptures. Christianity adds the New Testament as the definitive and authoritative interpretation of the Old Testament. For Christians the New Testament is more than an interpretation of the Old Testament. It is the record of the last great saving act of God in human history as seen in the life, death, resurrection, and ascension of Jesus Christ (Heb. 1:1-3).

Jesus was a Jew. The twelve apostles were Jews. The first Christians were Jews. Jesus' ministry of teaching and healing was for the most part limited to Jews. Early Christians in Jerusalem continued to frequent the temple (Acts 2). The Old Testament was the only Scripture of the early church. It was perfectly natural and normal for the first Jewish Christians to consider the Old Testament as their own. They began to search the Old Testament for passages which they believed referred to or were "fulfilled" in the life, death, and resurrection of Jesus (1 Cor. 15:3-5). Evidently early Christians had a list of Old Testament passages which served as "messianic proof-texts" before any part of the New Testament was written (see Dodd, *According to the Scriptures*, 25-26).

Disagreements, disputes, and acts of violence occurred during Jesus' lifetime between Himself, His followers, and groups of Jews and their leaders. After Jesus' crucifixion and resurrection, persecution arose among some Jews against Jewish Christians. Stephen was stoned to death (Acts 7:54-60). The persecution of the church in Jerusalem resulted in the scattering of Christians throughout the region (Acts 8:1). As Jewish Christians moved out of Jerusalem, they carried with them the Great Commission of the risen Christ to go into all the world and "make disciples of all nations baptizing them in the name of the Father and of the Son and of the Holy Spirit, and teaching them to obey everything that I have commanded you" (Matt. 28:19-20).

More and more the early church became Hellenized, due in part to the antagonism that arose between the Jewish church and the synagogue and in part to the rapid growth of believers among the Gentiles in the Roman Empire. The center of the early church moved first from Jerusalem to Antioch of Syria. The disciples were called "Christians" first in Antioch (Acts 11:26). Antioch became the base for Paul's missionary movement to the Gentiles.

As the church became Hellenized, the Hebrew Scriptures presented some problems in understanding and application. One Gentile, Marcion (about 145 A.D.), rejected the Old Testament as Christian Scripture. He chose only the Gospel of Luke and ten of Paul's letters as his Bible. Other Gentile Christian leaders felt an ambivalence between the Old Testament and the New Testament, but chose to retain the Old Testament and reinterpret it by using typological and allegorical principles of interpretation.

Through the centuries Christians have for the most part considered the Old Testament to be an integral part of their Bible. Certain groups and individuals have attempted to remove it. The Socinians and Anabaptists had a very low view of the Old Testament. Friedrich Nietzche called it "a monstrous farce: to pull the Old Testament out from under the Jews with the contention that it contains nothing but Christian doctrine" (see Schoeps, *The Jewish-Christian Argument*, 93). In his book on Marcion, Adolf Harnack suggested that the Old Testament should be "deposed from canonical rank and placed at the head of the Apocrypha." Harnack said:

> To have cast aside the Old Testament in the second century was an error which the church rightly rejected; to have retained it in the sixteenth century was a fate which the Reformation was not yet able to avoid; but still to keep it after the nineteenth century as a canonical document within Protestantism results from a religious and ecclesiastical paralysis (*Marcion, Das Evangelium vom fremden Gott*, 217; see Bright, *The Authority of the Old Testament*, 65).

Harnack's objection to the Old Testament as a part of the Christian canon was based in part on its offensive elements to moral sensitivities, such as murder, cheating, immorality of leaders, and war. To remove the Old Testament on these grounds is to deny the historical nature of revelation and to imply that neither the New Testament church nor contemporary Christians have these problems. John Bright argued that the Old Testament must be retained in the Christian Bible precisely because it is impossible to be true to the New Testament faith while getting rid of the Old Testament. Jesus came, lived, died, and rose again "according to the Scriptures" (*The Authority of the Old Testament*, 78). Von Rad said the new faith actually needed the Old Testament for its own self-expression, to guard it against mythology, speculation, and a narrow cult mentality; to preserve the universalism of the Old Testament doctrine of creation, and "to prevent Christians from being a group of esoterics to whom the world is foreign" (*Old Testament Theology II*, 335, 386-387).

Does the Old Testament lead directly to the Christ and the church of the New Testament? Since New Testament times, most Christians have not doubted that the Old Testament is filled with "complex expectations" of the culmination of history, and these were fulfilled in Jesus of Nazareth. Peter said on the day of Pentecost, "This is what was spoken through the prophet" (Acts 2:16). Augustine said, "In the Old Testament the New lies concealed; in the New Testament the Old lies revealed." In 1899 Bishop Westcott wrote, "The teaching of the Old Testament as a whole is a perpetual looking forward" (*The Epistle to the Hebrews*, 485). John Paterson said, "Those prophets seem to be standing on the tiptoe of expectation waiting for 'Him who is to come'" (*The Goodly Fellowship of the Prophets*, 284).

Old Testament prophecy was no premature unrolling of history to satisfy an idle curiosity. It was never separated from its ethical (*telos*) end. The bulk of prophetic preaching was directed toward current ethical and religious crises. However, it also pointed to some future divine event toward which the history of Israel and the world were moving. The hopes of Old Testament prophets were not completed in the Old Testament. The study of the Old Testament prophets by themselves leaves one with a keen sense of disappointment "as one who might find in some lonely desert the foundations of a vast building laid, and costly materials prepared in abundance, with plans and sketches suggestive of majestic perfection, but all abandoned, unused, forgotten" (Kirkpatrick, *The Doctrine of the Prophets*, 519).

When the curtain falls on the stage of Old Testament prophecy, the riddle waits for its answers; the drama lacks its denouement. In the fullness of time Jesus came, gathering to Himself and uniting in His person all lines of prophecy which had seemed "so strangely inconsistent and irreconcilable, filling them with a new meaning, vivifying them with a new energy" (Kirkpatrick, *The Doctrine of the Prophets*, 521). People could not have drawn from the Old Testament prophecies "the portrait of Him who was to come." The style of His coming caused some not to recognize Him or to refuse to acknowledge Him. The church recognized in Him the union of the various elements which had been foreshadowed in many fragments and fashions and welcomed Him as the coming priest, prophet, king, and Lord. In more recent times F. F. Bruce commented on the way the whole Old Testament finds its fulfillment in Jesus.

> This note of fulfillment is struck throughout, yet not so much one note as a harmony of notes. In Jesus promise is confirmed, the covenant is renewed, the prophecies are fulfilled, the law is vindicated, salvation is brought near, sacred history has reached its climax, the perfect sacrifice has been offered and accepted, the great priest over the household of God has taken his seat at God's right hand, the prophet like Moses has been raised up, the Son of David reigns, the kingdom of God has been inaugurated, the Son of Man has received dominion from the Ancient of Days, the Servant of the Lord, having been smitten to death for his people's transgression and borne the sin of many, has accomplished the divine purpose, has seen light after the travail of his soul and is now exalted and extolled and made very high (*The New Testament Development of Old Testament Themes*, 21).

The foundations of Christianity rest on the Old and New Testaments together. The "preparation" for the coming of Jesus Christ began with the very first revelation of the secret of Yahweh's person. Von Rad said that we should go back there to clarify the relationship between the two Testaments. Jesus could appeal to the God of the Old Testament without having to give any special explanations or preparations. This means that all Old Testament witnesses are, in the last analysis, to be seen and understood as pointing directly to Christ's coming. "The

Old Testament witnesses express insights which could only have been produced in the context of a particular saving activity. This precedes the New Testament one in time, yet it only reaches its goal with the coming of Christ. What is described in the New Testament as his own (John 1.11), to which he came, is already heralded in clearly recognizable terms in the Old Testament" (*Old Testament Theology II*, 355-356).

Many Old Testament scholars, especially those who use the traditio-historical method of interpretation, agree with von Rad. Claus Westermann wrote:

> One thing can now be said for certain: those who work on the text of the Bible can no longer ignore the fact that the *traditions-geschichtliche* aspect of their work points them inevitably to the church, its doctrine, its confessions, and its worship. . . . In the Old as in the New Testament, it appears as a history . . . the history of God with his people which continues in the history of the church until it comes to that consummation toward which the Bible points (*Essays on Old Testament Hermeneutics*, 13).

Some scholars claim it points to a "quite different tradition on a different level, that of halakah and aggada, which led to the Talmud and Midrash" (Gese, *Essays on Biblical Theology*, 14; see this book's Introduction and chap. 1's Excursus). B. W. Anderson affirmed that it is no exaggeration to say that on this question of the relation of the Old Testament to the New hangs the meaning of the Christian faith (*The Old Testament and the Christian Faith*, 1).

The New Testament regards the Old Testament as Holy Scripture, and its validity is by no means regarded as limited. The Christian cannot regard the Old Testament as a second-rate Scripture which found its legitimate continuation only in a later Judaism without rejecting "a priori the New Testament's interpretation as forced and tendentious, or unimportant" (Gese, *Essays on Biblical Theology*, 11).

Gese asserted that God's revelation of Himself is neither timeless nor restricted to one point in time. It begins in a historical time (*kairos*) and travels a historical path. The path has a goal, and revelation reaches its end, *telos*. The starting point is the revelation at Sinai, where God reveals himself by saying, "I am Yahweh" (*Essays on Biblical Theology*, 25). The end of the Old Testament took place in grandiose fashion. The three great streams of tradition—Torah, Prophets, and Wisdom—came together to present in terms of content the many-sided Christology of the New Testament, "which is no less than the theology of the Old Testament" (*Essays on Biblical Theology*, 29).

In the fullness of time Jesus of Nazareth entered into that historical realm which had been prepared by the history of revelation. In His life He accomplished the messianic establishment of the kingdom of God. In His death Jesus plumbed the final depths of human existence, the holy united with the extreme suffering of death. "Through this death of the Son of God the light of a new creation shines forth. According to the New Testament then, the *telos* is reached, the path of revelation is at an end. The so-called Old Testament is completed by the events of the New Testament; it is brought to its goal" (Gese, *Essays on Biblical Theology*, 29).

The early Brevard Childs spoke about the forward look of the Old Testament and the proper relationship of the Testaments as leading to a "new Israel," who turned out to be Jesus Christ. Childs' doctoral dissertation at Basel, written under the direction of Baumgartner and Eichrodt in 1954, was on "Myth in the Old Testament." A revised edition of that thesis was published in 1960 with the title *Myth and Reality in the Old Testament*.

Childs argued that both myth and the Old Testament have as their ultimate concern an understanding of reality. The Old Testament conflicted with myth because of its new understanding of the redemptive activity of God. Myth's view of reality is that nature or the world is alive with divine or demonic power. Through the cult, humans must maintain world order. The Old Testament view of reality is that God created and controls the world. Because of sin (Gen. 3:1-6), humans and their world are under the judgment of God (Gen. 3:16-19). But God will send a new ruler who will establish a new order in a new age (Isa. 11:1-9).

Childs said that "the reality of which the Bible speaks took form within the life of historical Israel, but what is the reality? In our opinion, the message of the Old Testament is that the reality is the new Israel" (*Myth and Reality in the Old Testa-*

ment, 97). Old Testament Israel rejected the new way of life. The Old Testament is a history of Israel's rejection of the new way.

> It is a story of the manner in which the old forms of existence fought to extinguish the new. There is no "upward sloping line" of gradual perfection, but the Old Testament ends in dissidence. Because of the inability of the new existence to maintain itself within Israel, the Old Testament is theologically meaningless apart from the New Testament (*Myth and Reality in the Old Testament*, 97).

Perhaps one can see an influence of Barth on Childs' thinking at this point. Barth defined history in terms of God's execution of His purpose through His word (which is Jesus Christ) in bringing to completion His covenant of Grace (*Dogmatics III*, 63—64; Childs, *Myth and Reality in the Old Testament*, 101).

Childs asked how the new Israel can be distinguished from the old Israel. He said that there are no ethical principles or right doctrines by which the new existence can be measured. The ultimate criterion does not lie with the Old Testament.

> In Jesus Christ *the* new reality has appeared as the self-authenticating "New Israel." As the truly obedient man Jesus is the new existence in its fullest and most concrete form . . . 'an Israelite in whom there is no guile.' Not just in his teachings or in particular actions, but in the total existence of the Jew, Jesus Christ, the entire Old Testament receives its proper perspective. It is fulfilled in its obedience, but judged in its disobedience (*Myth and Reality in the Old Testament*, 104).

Norman Porteous took exception to Childs' strong statement that "the Old Testament is theologically meaningless apart from the New Testament" on the grounds that the Jew may interpret the Old Testament theologically in an altogether different way (*Living the Mystery*, 141). Evidently Childs changed his mind after 1960 to agree with Porteous against von Rad, Westermann, and Gese that the Old Testament does not point inevitably to the New Testament and Jesus Christ ("Interpretation in Faith," 444-449). Childs profoundly recognized the right of Judaism to interpret its Scripture in ways appropriate to Jewish faith commitment, even though his own faith commitment affirmed that a common purpose of God is witnessed to in both Testaments—a position undoubtedly unacceptable to Judaism.

In his later years Childs abandoned the traditio-historical approach of von Rad and Gese and developed his "canonical" approach. This approach takes the Old Testament as Scripture, but it also devalues the importance of the history of the Old Testament traditions. The final form of the canon as we have it in the Masoretic text is the sole form of the text for studying its theology. This deemphasizes the process or movement in the Old Testament that leads inevitably to Christ. Childs chose von Rad's "faith-construed" approach rather than Hesse's "scientific history" approach to the Old Testament, but he differed from von Rad in not assigning theological value "to a traditio-historical trajectory which has been detached from the canonical form of the text" (*Old Testament Theology in a Canonical Context*, 16).

Childs wanted to keep the two Testaments separate to allow their differences to appear, but he also wanted to emphasize the common purpose of God when the two Testaments are seen together. James Wharton asked,

> Is this sense of the "independence" and "duality" of the two Testaments derived from the character of the New Testament usage of the Old Testament, or is it more nearly governed by a concession to the historical-critical scruple against relating the theological substance of the Old Testament to the theological substance of the New Testament? ("Splendid Failure or Flawed Success?", 275).

Wharton saw little support in the New Testament for keeping the two Testaments separate. Rather, the New Testament expresses the astonished affirmation that all that has gone before in the story of God with Israel and the world from creation has fully reached its goal in the life, death, and resurrection of Jesus Christ. God has now brought his whole great work to a decisive conclusion (Heb. 1:1-4).

Here Jewish and Christian claims diverge most sharply, with disastrous consequences whenever either group construes that divergence with arrogance and pride. The New Testament claim to the Old Testament witness is ineradicable, but it must not be understood to imply that the followers of Jesus Christ are superior to other people, privileged in relationship to God, or morally and spiritually infallible. Rather, it should give them an overwhelming sense of gratitude, humility, and responsibility. The New Testament's claim to the Old Testament must be affirmed as the integral and indispensable framework of the Christian gospel.

Epilogue

The present state of Old Testament theology, like that of many other disciplines, is confused. Nathan O. Hatch said:

> The modern intellectual world is adrift, incapable or unwilling to allow any claim of certainty to set the coordinates by which others are to be judged. The dominant forces work toward fragmentation, the limitations of reason, and a breakdown of verities—what Charles Krathammer has called the Balkanization of American education. Examples can be found in virtually every scholarly discipline and every area of intellectual life ("Christian Thinking in a Time of Academic Turmoil," 9).

Hatch mentioned three disciplines where extreme relativism has been rampant in recent years: literary criticism, history, and law. We could add the areas of academic Bible study, religion, and theology.

Hatch said no discipline reveals the present state of disjointedness more than literary criticism. The new deconstructionist school undermines the idea that literary texts have any objective meanings intended by their authors or inherent in the texts. Barbara Hernstein Smith, former president of the Modern Language Association, contended in her work *Contingencies of Value* that the meaning of any work of literature is to be found in the understanding of the individual reader. Naturally, one reader's interpretation is as good as another. By the end of her book Barbara Smith pushed her reasoning to its logical conclusion that radical relativism is the only appropriate standard for moral questions as well as aesthetic questions. Her final conclusion: "There is no *bottom* bottom line anywhere." (See Nathan O. Hatch, "Christian Thinking," 9. For a discussion of the influence of new literary criticism on recent biblical studies see John Barton's "Reading the Old Testament," 141.)

Hatch said that historical studies went through its first crisis of authority in the 1930s when a group of influential American historians began to poke holes in the pretentions of those who aspired after total objectivity. In biblical studies the problem of history has been one of the chief enigmas. Scholars today have almost ceased talking about history. Instead, they speak of "salvation-history" (*Heilsgeschichte*), story, narrative, and imagination.

In recent years constitutional law has been eroded and diluted by political and institutional influences. Hatch said a school of thought calling itself critical-legal scholarship has challenged the assumption that law is based on the attempt to approach an absolute standard of justice. "This school argues instead that law is merely an extension of politics, constantly changing as the goals of those who make and enforce the law change. The result of both these shifts in direction has been to leave legal scholars groping in confusion as the profession lurches toward thorough going relativism" ("Christian Thinking," 10).

Are there signs that biblical studies are moving toward relativism? James Barr said that scholarship is moving away from Old Testament theology because agreement about the subject is too difficult to achieve; new paradigms are not "theological"; and the new Jewish biblical theology brings a whole new dimension to the subject. (See James Barr, "Are We Moving Toward an Old Testament Theology or Away From It?" 20; and G. Hasel, *Old Testament Theology: Basic Issues,* 37, 95.)

The study of Old Testament theology has problems, but it is not dead. Gerhard Hasel said the subject is "more alive today than at any time in its history despite the pessimistic view of some scholars" ("The Future of Old Testament Theology: Prospects and Trends," *The Flowering of Old Testament Theology,* 373). The issues occupying the minds of scholars in the future concerning Old Testament theology will be many and complex. Is it strictly descriptive, objective and scientific, or confes-

sional and normative? Bruce C. Birch said in the introduction
to *Let Justice Roll Down*:

> This volume is committed to the critical method, but not to
> objectivity. It will be amply clear that my work is informed by
> the exegetical approaches which have developed from the his-
> toric-critical method. However, I no longer believe that it is pos-
> sible or desirable to achieve objectivity in the exercise of this
> method (*Let Justice Roll Down*, 21-22).

What should be the name of this discipline? Should we call
it Old Testament theology, the theology of the Hebrew Bible,
or Tanakh theology? Is it to be built on the final canonical form
of the Massoretic Text or on the traditio-historical reconstructions and actualizations behind the texts? Should we search
for the intentions of the original writers, or should we let the
literary form or the understanding of each reader determine
its meaning?

How should we try to bridge the gap between the Old Testament and the New and our own time? Can we bridge that gap
by simply reading the texts of the Old and New Testaments?
James Barr insisted that "theology cannot simply be read off
from the text as it stands: . . . theology *does* stand behind the
text" ("The Literal, the Allegorical, and Modern Scholarship,"
114).

The writer of the Book of Hebrews and the apostle Paul had
no trouble reading "Old Testament theology" off the texts of
the Old Testament. Of course, they were looking back after
they had experienced the fulfillment of the Old Testament
promises in Christ. For them, the theology of the Old Testament was Christological.

Near the end of the Book of Hebrews the writer called the
roll of Old Testament heroes and heroines of faith (Heb. 11:1-
31). He spoke of Abel, Enoch, Noah, Abraham, Sarah, Isaac,
Jacob, Joseph, Moses (and his parents), and Rahab. Then he
asked:

> And what more should I say?
> For time would fail me to tell of Gideon, Barak, Samson,
> Jephthah, of David and Samuel and the prophets—
> who through faith conquered kingdoms,
> administered justice, obtained promises,
> shut the mouths of lions, quenched raging fire,
> escaped the edge of the sword,

won strength out of weakness. . . .
Others were tortured, refusing to accept release. . . .
Yet all these, though they were commended for their faith,
did not receive what was promised,
since God had provided something better
so that they would not, apart from us, be made perfect.
Therefore, since we are surrounded
by so great a cloud of witnesses,
let us also lay aside every weight
and the sin that clings so closely,
and let us run with perseverance
the race that is set before us,
looking to Jesus the pioneer and perfecter of our faith,
who for the sake of the joy that was set before him
endured the cross, disregarding its shame,
and has taken his seat at the right hand of the throne of God.
(Heb. 11:32—12:2)

The apostle Paul, quoting a hymn of the early church, said of Jesus:

And being found in human form,
he humbled himself
and became obedient to the
point of death—
even death on a cross.

Therefore God also highly exalted him
and gave him the name
that is above every name,
so that at the name of Jesus
every knee should bend,
in heaven and on earth and under
the earth,
and every tongue should confess
that Jesus Christ is Lord,
to the glory of God the Father.
(Phil. 2:7c-11)

For Christians, Old Testament theology should be Christological. Edmond Jacob said, "A theology of the Old Testament which is founded not on certain isolated verses, but on the Old Testament as a whole, can only be a Christology, for what was revealed under the old covenant, through a long and varied history, in events, persons and institutions, is, in Christ, gathered together and brought to perfection" (*Theology of the Old Testament*, 13). Others may understand the Old Testament some other way. That is between them and the Lord. Christians should not superimpose the New Testament on the Old. The Old Testament must be allowed to speak on its own terms. But, as Gerhard Hasel has said, there is "a forward flow in the Old Testament that reaches its climax in the New Testament" ("The Future of Old Testament Theology," 383).

Of course, "holy history" is not yet complete. We are living "between the times." The final consummation is still to come.

Bibliography

Abbot, Walter M., S. J., ed. *The Documents of Vatican II.* New York: Guild Press, 1966.

Achtemeier, Elizabeth R. "Overcoming the World." *Interpretation* 38 (1974): 75-90.

_____. "Righteousness in the Old Testament." *IDB* 4. New York: Abingdon, 1962: 80.

Ahlström, G. W. "Some Remarks on Prophets and Cults." *Transitions in Biblical Scholarship*, edited by J. C. Rylaarsdam. Chicago: University of Chicago Press, 1968: 112-130.

Albrektson, Bertil. "On the Syntax of אהיה אשר אהיה in Exodus 3:14." *Words and Meanings*, edited by P. R. Ackroyd and B. Lindars. Cambridge: Cambridge University Press, 1968: 15-28.

Albright, W. F. *From the Stone Age to Christianity.* Garden City: Doubleday, 1957.

_____. *History, Archaeology, and Christian Humanism.* New York: McGraw-Hill, 1964.

Allen, Leslie C. *Psalms 101—150. Word Biblical Commentary* 21. Waco: Word Books, 1983.

Anderson, A. A. *The Book of Psalms.* 2 vols. New Century Bible. Grand Rapids: Eerdmans, 1981.

Anderson, B. W. "The Book of Hosea." *Interpretation* 8 (July 1954): 301.

_____. *The Old Testament and the Christian Faith.* New York: Harper, 1963.

_____. "The Old Testament View of God." *IDB* 2. New York: Abingdon, 1962: 419.

Anderson, B. W., ed. *Creation in the Old Testament.* Philadelphia: Fortress, 1984.

Anderson, G. W. "Israel: Amphictyony: '*Am; Kahal; `Edah*." *Translating and Understanding the Old Testament*, edited by Harry Thomas Frank and William L. Reed. Nashville: Abingdon, 1970.

_____, ed. *Tradition and Interpretation*. Oxford: Clarendon Press, 1979.

Andreasen, Niels-Erik. *The Old Testament Sabbath*. Atlanta: SBL Dissertation Series, 1972.

Aristotle. *Natural Science, Psychology, The Nicomachean Ethics*, translated by Philip Wheelwright. New York: The Odyssey Press, 1935.

Armes, Paul. "The Concept of Dying in the Old Testament." Ph.D. diss., Southwestern Baptist Theological Seminary, 1981.

Baab, Otto J. "Old Testament Theology: Its Possibility and Methodology." *The Study of the Bible Today and Tomorrow*, edited by H. R. Willoughby. Chicago: The University of Chicago Press, 1943.

_____. *The Theology of the Old Testament*. New York: Abingdon-Cokesbury, 1949.

Bailey, Lloyd R. *Biblical Perspectives on Death*. Philadelphia: Fortress, 1979.

Ballentine, Samuel E. "A Description of the Semantic Field of Hebrew Words for 'Hide,'" *VT* 30 (1980): 137-153.

_____. *The Hidden God*. Oxford: Oxford University Press, 1983.

Baly, Denis. "The Geography of Monotheism." *Translating and Understanding the Old Testament*, edited by H. T. Frank and W. L. Reed. Nashville: Abingdon, 1970: 253-278.

Barr, James. "Are We Moving Toward an Old Testament Theology or Away From It?" *Abstracts of the American Academy of Religion*, edited by James B. Wiggins and D. J. Lull. Atlanta: Scholars Press, 1989: 2.

_____. "Biblical Theology." *IDBS*. New York: Abingdon, 1976: 104-111.

_____. *Biblical Words for Time*. London: SCM, 1962.

_____. "The Image of God." *BJRL* 51 (1968): 11-26.

_____. "The Interpretation of Scripture, II: Revelation Through History." *Interpretation* 17 (1963): 193-205.

_____. "The Literal, the Allegorical, and Modern Scholarship." *JSOT* 44 (1989): 114.

_____. *Judaism: Its Continuity with the Bible*. Southampton: The Camelot Press, 1968.

_____. *Old and New in Interpretation*. New York: Harper and Row, 1966.

_____. "The Old Testament Case Against Biblical Theology." *Canon, Theology and Old Testament Interpretation*, edited by Gene Tucker, David Petersen, and R. R. Wilson. Philadelphia: Fortress, 1988: 3-19.

_____. "Some Semantic Notes on the Covenant." *Beitrage zur alttestamentlichen Theologie*, edited by H. Donner and others. Göttingen, 1977.

_____. *The Semantics of Biblical Language*. Oxford: Oxford University Press, 1961.

Barth, Christoph. *God With Us*. Grand Rapids: Eerdmans, 1991.

_____. *Introduction to the Psalms*. New York: Scribners, 1966.

Barth, Karl. *Church Dogmatics III*. Edinburgh: T. and T. Clark, 1958.

_____. *Dogmatics in Outline*. New York: Harper Torchbooks, 1959.

_____. *The Humanity of God*. Atlanta: John Knox Press, 1963.

_____. *The Teaching of the Church Regarding Baptism*. London: SCM, 1954.

Barton, John. "Natural Law and Poetic Justice." *JTS* 30 (1979).

_____. "Reading the Old Testament." *Method in Biblical Study*. Philadelphia: Westminster Press, 1984.

_____. "Understanding Old Testament Ethics." *JSOT* 9 (1978): 44-64.

Beasley-Murray, George R. *Jesus and the Kingdom of God*. Grand Rapids: Eerdmans, 1986.

Begrich, Joachim. "*Berit*, Ein Beitrag zur Erfassung einer altestamentlichen Denkform," *ZAW* 60 (1944): 1-11.

Berger, Peter L. *A Rumor of Angels*. Garden City: Doubleday, 1969.

Berkouwer, C. G. *Sin*. Grand Rapids: Eerdmans, 1971.

Bertholet, Alfred. "Eschatology in the History of Religion." *Twentieth Century Theology in the Making*, edited by Jarslav Pelikan. New York: Harper, 1969.

Bikerman, E. "Couper une alliance," *Archives d'histoire du droit oriental* 5 (1950-1951): 133-156.

Birch, Bruce C. *Let Justice Roll Down*. Louisville: Westminster/John Knox Press, 1991.

Blaike, R. J. *Secular Christianity and God Who Acts*. London: Hodder and Stoughton, 1970.

Blenkinsopp, Joseph. "Old Testament Theology and the Jewish-Christian Connection." *JSOT* 28 (1984): 3-11.

_____. *A Sketchbook of Biblical Theology*. New York: Herder and Herder, 1968.

Braaten, Carl E. *History and Hermeneutics. New Directions in Theology*, vol. 2. Philadelphia: Westminster, 1966.

Bratsiotis, N. P. *'ish. TDOT* I. Grand Rapids: Eerdmans, 1966.

Braybrooke, M. *Time to Meet*. London: SCM; Philadelphia: Trinity International, 1990.

Brichto, H. C. "Kin, Cult, Land and Afterlife." *HUCA* 44 (1973): 1-54.

Briggs, C.A. *The Study of Holy Scripture*. New York: Scribners, 1899.

Briggs, C. A and E. G. Briggs. *A Critical and Exegetical Commentary on the Book of Psalms*. 2 vols. *ICC*. Edinburgh: T. and T. Clark, 1906.

Bright, John. *The Authority of the Old Testament*. Nashville: Abingdon, 1967.

_____. "An Exercise in Hermeneutics: Jeremiah 31:31-34," *Interpretation* 20 (1966): 188-210.

_____. *The Kingdom of God*. Nashville: Abingdon-Cokesbury, 1953.

_____. *Covenant and Promise*. Philadelphia: Westminster, 1976.

_____. *Jeremiah*. Anchor Bible. Garden City: Doubleday, 1965.

Brooks, Roger, and John J. Collins, eds. *Hebrew Bible or Old Testament*. Notre Dame: University of Notre Dame Press, 1990.

Brown, Charles R. *Jeremiah*. Philadelphia: American Baptist Publication Society, 1904.

Brown, Francis, S. R. Driver, and Charles A. Briggs (BDB). *A Hebrew and English Lexicon*, Oxford: Clarendon Press, 1907.

Brownlee, W. H. "Anthropology and Soteriology in the Dead Sea Scrolls." *The Use of the Old Testament in the New*. Edited by James M. Efird. Durham, NC: Duke University Press, 1972: 210-240.

_____. "The Ineffable Name of God." *BASOR* 226 (1977): 39-45.

Bruce, F. F. *Biblical Exegesis in the Qumran Texts*. London: Tyndale Press, 1960.

_____. *The New Testament Development of Old Testament Themes*. Grand Rapids: Eerdmans, 1968.

_____. *Second Thoughts on the Dead Sea Scrolls*. London: Pater Noster, 1956.

_____. "The Theology and Interpretation of the Old Testament." *Tradition and Interpretation*, edited by G. W. Anderson. Oxford: Clarendon Press, 1979: 385-416.

Bruce, W. S. *The Ethics of the Old Testament*. Edinburgh: T. and T. Clark, 1909.

Brueggemann, Walter. "The Formfulness of Grief." *Interpretation* 31 (1977): 267-275.

_____. "From Hurt to Joy." *Interpretation* 28 (1974): 3-19.

_____. *Genesis. Interpretation Commentary*. Atlanta: John Knox Press, 1982.

_____. "The Kergma of the Deuteronomistic Historian." *Interpretation* 22 (1968): 387-402.

Brunner, Emil. *The Divine-Human Encounter*. Philadelphia: Westminster, 1943.

_____. *Man In Revolt*. Philadelphia: Westminster, 1947.

Buck, Harry M. "Worship, Idolatry, and God." *A Light to My Path*, edited by Howard N. Bream, Ralph D. Heim, Carey A. Moore. Philadelphia: Temple University Press, 1974.

Burrows, Millar. *The Basis of Israelite Marriage. American Oriental Series* 15. New Haven: American Oriental Society, 1938.

_____. "Ethics of Jesus." *Essays in Old Testament Ethics*, edited by James L. Crenshaw and John T. Willis. New York: KTAV, 1974.

_____. "Jerusalem." *IDB* 2. New York: Abingdon, 1962.

Butler, Trent C. *Joshua. Word Biblical Commentary* 7. Waco: Word Books, 1983.

Calkins, Raymond. *The Modern Message of the Minor Prophets*. New York: Harper, 1947.

Campbell, E. F. "Moses and the Foundations of Israel." *Interpretation* 29 (1975): 141-154.

Carroll, Robert P. *Jeremiah. The Old Testament Library*. Philadelphia: Westminster Press, 1986.

Casuto, U. *A Commentary on the Book of Exodus*. Jerusalem: Magnes Press, 1961.

Cate, Robert L. "The Development of Monotheism." *Biblical Illustrator* 15.4 (1989): 30-32.

Childs, Brevard S. *Biblical Theology in Crisis*. Philadelphia: Westminster, 1970.

_____. *Exodus. The Old Testament Library*. Philadelphia: Westminster Press, 1974.

_____. "Interpretation in Faith." *Interpretation* 18 (1964): 444-449.

_____. *Myth and Reality in the Old Testament*. Naperville, IL: Alec R. Allenson, 1960.

_____. *Old Testament Theology in a Canonical Context*. Philadelphia: Fortress Press, 1985.

Clements, Ronald E. *Abraham and David: Genesis 15 and Its Meaning for Israelite Tradition. SBT* Second Series 5. London: SCM Press, 1967.

_____. "Claus Westermann: On Creation in Genesis." *SWJT* 32 (1990): 24.

_____. *Leviticus. Broadman Bible Commentary* 2. Nashville: Broadman Press, 1970.

_____. *Old Testament Theology: A Fresh Approach*. Atlanta: John Knox, 1978.

_____. *One Hundred Years of Old Testament Interpretation*. Philadelphia: Westminster, 1976.

_____, ed. *The World of Ancient Israel: Sociological, Anthropological and Political Perspectives*. Cambridge: Cambridge University Press, 1989.

Clines, D. J. A. "The Image of God in Man." *Tyndale Bulletin* 19 (1968): 53-103.

Coats, George W. "Theology of the Hebrew Bible." *The Bible and Its Modern Interpreters*, edited by D. A. Knight and Gene M. Tucker. Philadelphia: Fortress Press, 1985: 239-262.

Coggins, R. J. *Samaritans and Jews*. Atlanta: John Knox, 1975.

Cohen, A. *Everyman's Talmud*. New York: E. P. Dutton, 1949.

Collins, John J. "Is a Critical Bible Theology Possible?" *The Hebrew Bible and Its Interpreters*, edited by W.tt. Propp, Baruch Halpern, and D. N. Freedman. Winona Lake, IN: Eisenbrauns, 1990: 10-17.

Conner, W. T. *The Gospel of Redemption*. Nashville: Broadman Press, 1945.

Cook, James. "The Old Testament Concept of the Image of God." *Grace Upon Grace*. Grand Rapids: Eerdmans, 1975.

Cooke, G. A. *Ezekiel. ICC*. Edinburgh: T. and T. Clark, 1936.

Corley, Bruce. "The Jews, the Future and God." *SWJT* 19 (1976): 42-56.

Craig, C. T. "First Corinthians." *IB* 10 (1953): 107-108.

Craigie, Peter C. "The Book of Deuteronomy." *NICOT*. Grand Rapids: Eerdmans, 1976.

_____. *Psalms 1-50. Word Biblical Commentary* 19. Waco: Word Books, 1983.

Creager, Harold L. "The Divine Image." *A Light to My Path*, edited by H. N. Bream, Ralph Heim, C. A. Moore. Philadelphia: Temple University Press, 1974.

Crenshaw, James L. *Gerhard von Rad*. Waco: Word Books, 1978.

_____. *Studies in Ancient Israelite Wisdom*. New York: KTAV Press, 1976.

Crenshaw, James L., ed. *Theodicy in the Old Testament*. Philadelphia: Fortress Press, 1983.

Crim, Keith. *The Royal Psalms*. Richmond: John Knox, 1962.

Cross, Frank Moore. *The Ancient Library of Qumran*. Garden City: Doubleday, 1958.

_____. *Canaanite Myth and Hebrew Epic*. Cambridge: Harvard University Press, 1973.

_____. "Creation and History." Lecture at Southwestern Baptist Theological Seminary, February 14, 1961. Roberts Library tapes, TC3281.

_____. "The Song of the Sea and Canaanite Myth." In *God and Christ. Journal for Theology and the Church* 5, edited by Robert W. Funk. New York: Harper Torchbooks, 1968.

_____. "Yahweh and the God of the Fathers." *HTR* (1962): 225-259.

_____, Lemke, and Miller, eds. *Magnalia Dei*. Garden City: Doubleday, 1976.

Cullman, Oscar. *Baptism in the New Testament*. London: SCM, 1950.

_____. *Christ and Time*. London: SCM Press, 1962.

Culver, Robert D. *Daniel and the Latter Days: A Study in Millenialism*. Westwood, NJ: Fleming H. Revell, 1954.

Dahood, Mitchell. *Psalms*. 3 vols. Anchor Bible. Garden City: Doubleday, 1970.

Davidson, A. B. *The Theology of the Old Testament*. New York: Scribners, 1910.

Davidson, Robert. "Covenant Ideology in Ancient Israel." *The World of Ancient Israel*, edited by R. E. Clements. Cambridge: Cambridge University Press, 1989: 323-348.

Davies, Alan T. *Anti-Semitism and the Christian Mind*. New York: Herder and Herder, 1969.

Davies, G. Henton, *Genesis. Broadman Bible Commentary* 1. Nashville: Broadman Press, 1969.

_____. "Worship in the Old Testament." *IDB* 4. New York: Abingdon, 1962.

Davies, P. R. "Eschatology in the Book of Daniel." *JSOT* 17 (1980): 33.

Davies, W. D. *The Gospel and the Land*. Berkeley: University of California Press, 1974.

_____. "The Moral Teaching of the Early Church." *The Use of the Old Testament and Other Essays*, edited by James M. Efird. Durham, NC: Duke University Press, 1972: 310-322.

Davis, P. R. "Daniel." *Old Testament Guides*. Sheffield: JSOT Press, 1985.

Day, John. "Asherah in the Hebrew Bible and Northwest Semitic Literature." *JBL* 105 (1986): 385-408.

de Geus, C. H. J. *The Tribes of Israel*. Assen/Asterdam: Van Gorum, 1976.

de Vaux, Roland. *Ancient Israel*, translated by John McHugh. New York: McGraw-Hill, 1961.

_____. "Is It Possible to Write a 'Theology of the Old Testament'?" *The Bible and the Ancient Near East*, translated by Damian McHugh. Garden City: Doubleday, 1971.

_____. *The Early History of Israel*. London: Darton, Longman & Todd, 1978.

_____. "The Revelation of the Divine Name YHWH." *Proclamation and Presence*, edited by J. I. Durham and J. R. Porter. Richmond: John Knox, 1970.

de Vries, S. J. *The Achievements of Biblical Religion: A Prolegomenon to Old Testament Theology*. Lanham, MD: University Press of America, 1983.

_____. "Sin, Sinners." *IDB* 4. New York: Abingdon, 1962: 361-376.

De Wette, W. M. L. *Biblische Dogmatick*. Berlin: Realschulbuchhandlung, 1913.

Delitzsch, Franz. *Messianic Prophecies*. New York: Scribners, 1891.

Delitzsch, Friedrich. *Die grosse Tauschung.* 2 vols. Stuttgart: n.p., 1920, 1922.

Denny, James. *"Sikaiosune Theou." The Expositor's Greek Testament,* vol. 3. Grand Rapids: Eerdmans, n.d.

Dentan, Robert C. *The Knowledge of God in Ancient Israel.* New York: Seabury Press, 1968.

_____. *Preface to Old Testament Theology.* Rev. ed. New York: Seabury Press, 1963.

der Leeuw, G. Van. *Religion in Essence and Manifestation,* vol. 1. New York: Harper and Row, 1963.

Dever, William G. "Asherah, Consort of Yahweh?" *BASOR* 255 (1984): 21-29.

_____. "Iron Age Epigraphic Material from the Area of Khirbet El Kom." *HUCA* 40-41 (1969-1970): 139-204.

Dockery, David S. "Monotheism in the Scriptures." *Biblical Illustrator* 17.4 (1991): 27-30.

Dodd, C. H. *According to the Scriptures.* London: Nisbet and Co., 1953.

_____. *The Bible and the Greeks.* London: Hodder and Stoughton, 1954.

_____. *Moffatt New Testament Commentary: The Epistle of Paul to the Romans.* London: Hodder and Stoughton, 1954.

Driver, S. R. *The Book of Genesis.* London: Methuen, 1911.

Dubarle, A. M. "La signification du nom de Jahweh." *RSPhTH* 35 (1951): 3-21.

Duhm, Bernard. *Das Buch Jesaja.* Gottingen: Vandenhoeck & Ruprecht, 1968.

Durham, John I. *Exodus. Word Biblical Commentary* 3. Waco: Word Books, 1987.

_____. "Is There an Old Testament Theology?" *The Outlook, SEBTS Bulletin* (1969): 3-12.

_____. *Psalms. Broadman Bible Commentary* 4. Nashville: Broadman Press, 1971.

Dumbrell, W. J. *Covenant and Creation: An Old Testament Covenantal Theology.* London: Pater Noster Press, 1984.

Dyrness, William. *Themes in Old Testament Theology.* Downers Grove, IL: InterVarsity Press, 1979.

Efird, James M. *The Use of the Old Testament in the New.* Durham: Duke University Press, 1972.

Eichrodt, Walther. "Does Old Testament Theology Still Have Independent Significance Within Old Testament Scholarship?" *The Flowering of Old Testament Theology,* edited by B. C. Ollenburger and others. Winona Lakes, ID: Eisenbrauns, 1992: 30-42.

_____. *Man in the Old Testament*. London: SCM, 1951.

_____. "Review: A Guide to Understanding the Bible, By H. E. Fosdick." *JBL* 45 (1965), 205.

_____. *Theology of the Old Testament I*. Philadelphia: Westminster, 1961.

_____. *Theology of the Old Testament II*. Philadelphia: Westminster, 1967.

Eiselen, F. C. *The Christian View of the Old Testament*. New York: Eaton and Maens, 1912.

Eissfeldt, Otto. "The History of Israelite-Jewish Religion and Old Testament Theology." *The Flowering of Old Testament Theology*, edited by B. C. Ollenburger and others. Winona Lakes, ID: Eisenbrauns, 1992: 20-29.

_____. "Jahwe als König." *ZAW* 5 (1928): 89.

Emerton, J. A. "New Light on Israelite Religion: The Implications of the Inscriptions from Kuntillet 'Ajrud." *ZAW* 94 (1982): 1-20.

_____. "The Origin of the Son of Man Imagery." *JTS* 9 (Oct. 1958): 225-242.

Emmerson, Grace I. "Women in Ancient Israel." *The World of Ancient Israel,* edited by R. E. Clements. Cambridge: Cambridge University Press, 1989: 383-91.

Epzstein, Leon. *Social Justice in the Ancient Near East*. London: SCM Press, 1986.

Fairbairn, A. M. *The City of God*. London: Hodder and Stoughton, 1883.

Farris, T. V. *Mighty to Save*. Nashville: Broadman Press, 1993.

Finegan, Jack. *Light From the Ancient Past*. Princeton, NJ: Princeton University Press, 1959.

Finger, Thomas. "Humanity." *Holman Bible Dictionary*. Edited by Trent C. Butler. Nashville: Holman Bible Publishers, 1991.

Flemington, W. F. "Baptism." *IDB* 1. Nashville: Abingdon, 1962.

Fohrer, Georg. "Altes Testament-'Amphiktyonie' und 'Bund'?" *ThLZ* XCL (1966): 801-806, 893-904.

_____. "The Righteous Man in Job 31." *Essays in Old Testament Ethics,* edited by James L. Crenshaw and John T. Willis. New York: KTAV, 1974.

_____. *Theologische Grundstrukturen des Alten Testaments*. Berlin: de Gruyter, 1972.

Fosdick, Harry Emerson. "Forgiveness of Sins." *The Protestant Pulpit,* edited by A. W. Blackwood. New York: Abingdon, 1947.

Francisco, Clyde T. *Genesis. Broadman Bible Commentary* 1 (rev. ed). Nashville: Broadman Press, 1973.

Frankfort, Henri. *Kingship and the Gods*. Chicago: University of Chicago, 1948.

Freedman, David Noel. "Divine Commitment and Human Obligation." *Interpretation* 18 (1964): 419-431.

———. "The Name of the God of Moses." *JBL* 79 (1960): 155-156.

Freedman, R. David. "Woman, A Power Equal to Man." *BAR* 9 (1983): 56-58.

Fretheim, Terence E. "The Repentance of God." *HBT* 10: 47-70.

Friedman, Richard Elliot, and H. G. M. Williamson, eds. *The Future of Biblical Studies: The Hebrew Scriptures*. Atlanta: Scholars Press, 1987.

Fromm, Erich. *You Shall Be As Gods*. New York: Fawcett Books, 1966.

Frost, S. B. "Eschatology and Myth." *VT* 2 (1952): 70-80.

Galling, K. "Die Erwählungstraditionen Israels." *BZAW* 48 (1928).

Gammie, John G. "Behemoth and Leviathan." *Israelite Wisdom*, edited by John G. Gammie and others. Atlanta: Scholars Press, 1978.

———. *Holiness in Israel*. Minneapolis: Fortress Press, 1989.

Gaster, T. H. "The Abode of the Dead." *IDB* 1. New York: Abingdon, 1962.

Gese, Hartmut. "Death in the Old Testament." *Essays on Biblical Theology*. Minnesota: Augsburg, 1981: 34-59.

———. "The Messiah." *Essays on Biblical Theology*. Minneapolis: Augsburg, 1981: 141-166.

Giesebrecht, F. *Die Geschichtlichkeit des Sinaibundes*. Königsberg: n.p., 1900.

Goitien, S. T. "Yahweh the Passionate." *VT* 6 (1956): 1-9.

Goldingay, John. *Approaches to Old Testament Interpretation*. Downers Grove, IL: InterVarsity Press, 1981.

———. "The Man of War and the Suffering Servant." *TB* 27 (1976): 79-113.

———. *Theological Diversity and the Authority of the Old Testament*. Grand Rapids: Eerdmans, 1987.

Goshen-Gottstein, Moshe H. "The Religion of the Old Testament and the Place of Jewish Biblical Theology." *Ancient Israelite Religion*, edited by Patrick Miller and others. Philadelphia: Fortress, 1987: 617-644.

———. "Christianity, Judaism and Modern Bible Study." *SVT* 28 (1975): 77.

Gottwald, Norman K. *The Tribes of Yahweh*. Maryknoll, New York: Orbis Books, 1979.

———. *The Hebrew Bible: A Socio-Literary Introduction*. Philadelphia: Fortress Press, 1985.

Gray, G. B. *Numbers. ICC*. Edinburgh: T. and T. Clark, 1903.

Green, James Leo. *Jeremiah. Broadman Bible Commentary* 6. Nashville: Broadman Press, 1971.

Gunkel, Hermann. *Genesis*. Göttingen: Vandenhoeck & Ruprecht, 1964.

Hamilton, Victor P. "The Book of Genesis 1—17." *NICOT*. Grand Rapids: Eerdmans, 1990.

Hanson, Paul D. "War and Peace." *Interpretation* 38 (1984): 341-362.

_____. *The People Called.* San Francisco: Harper and Row, 1986.

Harnack, Adolf. *Marcion, Das Evangelium vom fremden Gott,* 2nd ed. Leipzig: J. C. Hinrichs Verlag, 1924.

Harrelson, Walter. *From Fertility Cult to Worship.* New York: Anchor, 1970.

_____. "Life, Faith and the Emergence of Tradition." *Tradition and Theology,* edited by Douglas A. Knight. Philadelphia: Fortress, 1977.

_____. *The Ten Commandments and Human Rights.* Philadelphia: Fortress, 1980.

Hartman, Louis F., and Alexander A. DiLella, *The Book of Daniel.* The Anchor Bible, vol. 23. Garden City, NY: Doubleday, 1978.

Hasel, G. F. "A Decade of Old Testament Biblical Theology." *ZAW* 93 (1981): 165-184.

_____. "The Future of Old Testament Theology: Prospects and Trends." *The Flowering of Old Testament Theology,* edited by Ollenburger, Martens, and Hasel. Winona Lake, IN: Eisenbrauns, 1992.

_____. "The Identity of the 'Saints of the Most High' in Daniel VII." *VT* 26 (1976): 173-192.

_____. *Old Testament Theology: Basic Issues in the Current Debate.* 4th ed. Grand Rapids: Eerdmans, 1991.

_____. "The Polemic Nature of the Genesis Cosmology." *Evangelical Quarterly* 46 (1974), 81-102.

Hatch, Nathan O. "Christian Thinking in a Time of Academic Turmoil." *The Southern Baptist Educator* 56 (Aug. 1992): 9.

Hayes, John H., and Frederick Prussner. *Old Testament Theology: Its History and Development.* Atlanta: John Knox Press, 1985.

_____ and J. Maxwell Miller. *Israelite and Judean History.* Philadelphia: Westminster Press, 1977.

Heaton, E. W. *The Book of Daniel. Torch Bible Commentaries.* London: SCM, 1956.

_____. *His Servants the Prophets.* London: SCM, 1950.

Heidel, Alexander. *The Babylonian Genesis.* 2nd ed. Chicago: University of Chicago Press, 1963.

Hempel, Johannes. "Das Ethos des Alten Testaments." *BZAW* (1938): lxvii.

Herbert, A. S. *Worship in Ancient Israel.* Richmond: John Knox, 1959.

Heschel, Abraham J. *The Prophets.* New York: Harper and Row, 1962.

Higgins, Jean. "Anastasius Sinaita and the Superiority of Women." *JBL* 97 (1978): 253-256.

Holladay, William. *Concise Hebrew-Aramaic Lexicon*. Grand Rapids: Eerdmans, 1971.

_____. "Jer. XXXI 22b Reconsidered." *VT* 16 (1966): 236-239.

_____. *The Root Subh in the Old Testament*. Leiden: E. J. Brill, 1958.

Hooke, S. H. *The Siege Perilous*. London: SCM, 1956.

Hubbard, D. A. "Hope in the Old Testament." *TB* 34 (1983): 34-53.

Hubbard, Robert L., Jr., Robert K. Johnston, and Robert P. Meye. *Studies in Old Testament Theology*. Dallas: Word, 1992.

Huey, F. B. "The Hebrew Concept of Life After Death in the Old Testament." Th.D. diss., Southwestern Baptist Theological Seminary, 1962.

Huffmon, Herbert B. "The Treaty Background of Hebrew *Yada'*. *BASOR* 181 (1966): 31-37.

Humphreys, Fisher, ed. *Nineteenth Century Evangelical Theology*. Nashville: Broadman Press, 1983.

Hyatt, J. Philip. *Exodus*. New Century Bible. London: Oliphants, 1971.

_____. "Was Yahweh Originally a Creator Deity?" *JBL* 86 (1967): 369-377.

Jacob, Edmond. "Feminisme ou Messianisme?" *Beitrage zur Alttestamentlichen Theologie*. Göttingen: Vandenhoeck and Ruprecht, 1977.

_____. *Theology of the Old Testament*. New York: Harper and Row, 1958.

Jarrel, W. A. *Old Testament Ethics Vindicated*. 3rd ed. Dallas: privately published, 1890.

Jenkins, David E. *What Is Man?* Valley Forge: Judson, 1971.

Jenni, E. "Das Wort *'Olam* im Alten Testament." *ZAW* 64 (1952): 246-247.

Jepsen, Alfred. "Berith, Ein Beitrag zur Theologie der Exilszeit." *Verbannung und Heimkehr, Wilheim Rudolph Zum 70. Geburtstag*, edited by A. Kusshke. Tübingen, 1961: 161-179.

Jeremias, J. *Hat die Urkirche die Kindertaufe geübt?* Göttingen: Vanderhoeck and Ruprecht, 1949.

Johnson, Aubrey R. *The Cultic Prophet in Ancient Israel*. 2nd ed. Cardiff: University of Wales Press, 1962.

_____. "Jonah II 3-10." *Studies in Old Testament Prophecy*, edited by H. H. Rowley, Edinburgh: T. and T. Clark, 1950.

_____. *The Vitality of the Individual in the Thought of Ancient Israel*. Cardiff: University of Wales, 1949.

Johnson, Ricky L. "The Place of Ethics in Old Testament Theology." Ph.D. diss., Southwestern Baptist Theological Seminary, 1983.

Kaiser, Otto. *Death and Life*. Translated by John E. Steely. Nashville: Parthenon, 1981.

Kaiser, Walter C. "Messianic Prophecies in the Old Testament." *Dreams, Visions and Oracles*, edited by C. E. Amerding and W. W. Gasque. Grand Rapids: Baker, 1977.

_____. *Toward Old Testament Ethics*. Grand Rapids: Zondervan, 1983.

_____. *Toward an Old Testament Theology*. Grand Rapids: Zondervan, 1978.

Kant, Immanuel. *Critique of Pure Reason*. New York: P. F. Collier and Son, 1900.

Kapelrud, A. S. "The Role of the Cult in Old Israel." *The Bible in Modern Scholarship*, edited by J. Philip Hyatt. Nashville: Abingdon, 1965: 44-56.

Kaufman, Gordon. D. *Systematic Theology: A Historicist Perspective*. New York: Charles Scribner's, 1968.

Kaufman, Stephen A. "The Structure of Deuteronomic Law," *Maarav* 1 (1979).

Kelley, Page H. *Isaiah. Broadman Bible Commentary* 5. Nashville: Broadman Press, 1971.

_____. "The Repentance of God." *Biblical Illustrator* 9. Nashville: The Sunday School Board, 1982: 13.

Kelm, George M. *Escape to Conflict*. Fort Worth: IAR Publications, 1991.

Kidner, Derek. *Proverbs. TOTC*. Chicago: InterVarsity Press, 1964.

_____. *Psalms 73—150. TOTC*. London: InterVarsity Press, 1975.

Kiessling, Nicolas K. "Antecedents of the Medieval Dragon in Sacred History." *JBL* 89 (1970): 167-177.

Kirkpatrick, A. F. *The Book of Psalms*. 1902; reprinted Cambridge: Cambridge University Press, 1951.

_____. *The Doctrine of the Prophets*. London: Macmillan, 1912.

Kittel, Rudolph. "Die Zukunft der altestamentlichen Wissenschaft." *ZAW* 84 (1921): 84-99.

Kleinknecht, H. J. Fichtner, and others. "Wrath." *Bible Key Words* 4. New York: Harper, 1964.

Knibb, Michael A. "Life and Death in the Old Testament." *The World of Ancient Israel*, edited by R. E. Clements. Cambridge: Cambridge University Press, 1989: 395-415.

Knierim, Rolf. *Die Hauptbegriffe für Sünde im Alten Testament*. Gütersloher Verlagshaus, 1965.

_____. "The Problem of an Old Testament Hamartiology." *VT* 16 (1966): 366-385.

Knight, Douglas A., ed. *Tradition and Theology in the Old Testament*. Philadelphia: Fortress Press, 1977.

Knight, D. A., and G. M. Tucker. *The Hebrew Bible and Its Modern Interpreters*. Philadelphia: Fortress Press, 1985.

Knight, G. A. F. *A Christian Theology of the Old Testament*. London: SCM, 1959.

_____. *Deutero-Isaiah*. New York: Abingdon, 1965.

_____. "Eschatology in the Old Testament." *SJT* 4 (1951): 355-362.

_____. *Psalms*. 2 vols. Philadelphia: Westminster, 1982.

Knudson, A. C. *The Religious Teachings of the Old Testament*. New York: Abingdon, 1918.

Koch, Klaus. "Gibt es ein Vergeltungsdogma im Alten Testament?" *ZTK* 52 (1955): 1-42.

_____. "Is There a Doctrine of Retribution in the Old Testament?" *Theodicy in the Old Testament*. Translated from the German; edited by James L. Crenshaw. Philadelphia: Fortress, 1983.

Köhler, Kaufman. *Jewish Theology: Systematically and Historically Considered*. New York: KTAV Publishing House, 1968.

Köhler, Ludwig. *Old Testament Theology*. Translated by A. S. Todd. Philadelphia: Westminster, 1957.

_____, and Walter Baumgartner. *Hebraisches und Aramaisches Lexicon, Dritte Auflage*. 4 vols. Leiden: E. J. Brill, 1953.

Kosmala, H. *geber*. *TDOT* II. Grand Rapids: Eerdmans, 1975.

_____. "At the End of the Days." *Messianism in the Talmudie Era*. Edited by Leo Landman. New York: KTAV, 1979: 302-312.

Kraeling, Emil G. *The Old Testament Since the Reformation*. New York: Harper and Brothers, 1955.

Kraus, H. J. *Theology of the Psalms*. Minneapolis: Augsburg, 1986.

_____. *Worship in Israel*. Richmond: John Knox, 1966.

Kubler-Ross, Elisabeth. *On Death and Dying*. New York: Macmillan, 1969.

Kuntz, J. Kenneth. *The Self-Revelation of God*. Philadelphia: Westminster, 1967.

Kutsch, Ernst. "berit." *Verpflichtung, THAT* I (1971): 339-353.

_____. *Verheissung und Gesetz*. BZAW 131. Berlin: Walter de Gruyter, 1973.

Kuyper, Lester J. "Grace and Truth." *Interpretation* 18 (1964): 3-19.

Labuschagne, C. J. *The Incomparability of Yahweh in the Old Testament*. Leiden: E. J. Brill, 1966.

Lacocque, Andrew, *The Book of Daniel*. Atlanta: John Knox, 1979.

Landes, George M. "Creation Tradition in Proverbs 8:22-31 and Genesis 1." *A Light to My Path*, edited by Howard N. Bream, Heim, and Moore. Philadelphia: Temple University Press, 1974.

Lane, W. R. "The Initiation of Creation." *VT* 13 (1963): 63-73.

LaSor, William S. *The Truth About Armageddon*. San Francisco: Harper and Row, 1982.

Latourette, Kenneth Scott. *Nineteenth Century in Europe*. New York: Harper and Brothers, 1959.

Laurin, Robert. "The Concept of Man as a Soul." *ET* 72 (1961): 131-134.

Laurin, Robert, ed. *Contemporary Old Testament Theologians*. Valley Forge: Judson Press, 1970.

Lehman, Chester K. *Biblical Thelology I: Old Testament*. Scottdale, PA, 1971.

Lemaire, A. "Les inscriptions de Khirbet El Qom et l' Asherah de Yahweh." *Revue Biblique* 84 (1977): 597-608.

Lemke, Werner E. "Revelation Through History in Recent Biblical Theology." *Interpretation* 36 (1982): 34-45.

Levenson, Jon D. *Sinai and Zion*. New York: Harper and Row, 1985.

Lindblom, J. *Prophecy in Ancient Israel*. Philadelphia: Fortress, 1963.

Lofthouse, W. F. "Biblical Ethics." *A Companion to the Bible*, edited by T. W. Manson. Edinburgh: T. and T. Clark, 1942.

Ludwig, Theodore M. "The Traditions of the Establishing of the Earth in Deutero-Isaiah." *JBL* 92 (1973): 345-357.

Luyster, Robert. "Wind and Water: Cosmogonic Symbolism in the Old Testament." *ZAW* 93 (1981): 1-10.

Lys, Daniel. "The Israelite Soul According to the LXX." *VT* 16 (1966): 226-228.

Maass, Fritz. *'adam*. *TDOT* I. Grand Rapids: Eerdmans, 1974.

_____. *'enosh*. *TDOT* I. Grand Rapids: Eerdmans, 1974.

Mace, David R. *Hebrew Marriage: A Sociological Study*. London: Epworth; New York: Philosophical Library, 1953.

Margalit, Baruch. "The Meaning and Significance of Asherah." *VT* 49 (1990): 264-297.

Marsh, John. "Numbers." *IB* 2 (1953).

Martens, Elmer A. *God's Design: A Focus on Old Testament Theology*. Grand Rapids: Baker, 1981.

Martin-Achard, Robert. *From Death to Life*. Edinburgh: Oliver and Boyd, 1960.

Maston, T. B. *Biblical Ethics*. Cleveland: World, 1967.

Mayes, A. D. H. *Israel in the Period of the Judges*. Naperville, IL: Alec R. Allenson, 1974.

Mayo, S. M. *The Relevance of the Old Testament for the Christian Faith*. Washington, D.C.: University Press of America, 1982.

Mays, James L. "Worship, World and Power." *Interpretation* 23 (1969): 322.

McBeth, H. Leon. *A Sourcebook for Baptist Heritage*. Nashville: Broadman Press, 1990.

McBride, S. D. "The Yoke of the Kingdom, An Exposition of Deuteronomy 6:4-5." *Interpretation* (1974): 296-297.

McCarthy, Dennis. *Old Testament Covenant*. Atlanta: John Knox, 1972.

_____. "Treaty and Covenant." 2nd ed. *Analecta Biblica* 21a. Rome: Pontifical Biblical Institute, 1978.

McCasland, S. V. "The Image of God According to Paul." *JBL* 69 (1950): 85-86.

McComiskey, Thomas E. *The Covenants of Promise: A Theology of the Old Testament Covenants*. Grand Rapids: Baker, 1985.

McCullough, W. S. "Israel's Eschatology from Amos to Daniel." *Studies on the Ancient Palestinian World*, edited by F. S. Winnet, J. W. Wevers, and D. B. Reford. Toronto: University of Toronto Press, 1972.

_____. "Psalms." *IB* 4. Nashville: Abingdon Press, 1955: 442.

McKeating, Henry. "Sanctions Against Adultery in Ancient Israelite Society." *JSOT* 11 (1979): 68-70.

_____. "Vengeance is Mine." *Expository Times* 74 (1963): 239-245.

McKenzie, John L. *A Theology of the Old Testament*. Garden City: Doubleday, 1974.

Meador, Marion Frank. "The Motif of God as Judge." Ph.D. diss., Southwestern Baptist Theological Seminary, 1986.

Mehl, R. "Good." *A Companion to the Bible*. New York: Oxford University Press, 1958.

Mendenhall, George E. *Law and Covenant in Israel*. Pittsburgh: n.p., 1955.

_____. *The Tenth Generation*. Baltimore: John Hopkins University Press, 1973.

Menninger, Karl. *Whatever Became of Sin?* New York: Hawthorn, 1973.

Mesel, Ze'ev. "Did Yahweh Have a Consort?" *BAR* 5 (1979): 24-35.

Michaelis, John David. *Commentaries on the Laws of Moses I*. London: F. C. and J. Revington, 1814.

Millard, A. R., and Pierre Bordrevil. "A Statue from Syria with Aramaic and Assyrian Inscriptions." *BA* 45 (1982): 135-143.

Miller, J. Maxwell. "In the Image and Likeness of God." *JBL* 91 (1972): 289-301.

_____ and John H. Hayes. *A History of Ancient Israel and Judah*. Philadelphia: Westminster Press, 1986.

Miller, John W. "The Servant Songs in the Light of Their Context." *Wort-Gebot-Glaube* (Eichrodt's Festschrift), edited by J. J. Stamm, E. Jenni, and H. J. Stoebe. Zurich: Zwingli Verlag, 1970.

Miller, Patrick D. "The Blessing of God." *Interpretation* 29 (1975): 240-251.

_____. "Israelite Religion." *The Hebrew Bible and Its Modern Interpreters*, edited by D. A. Knight. Philadelphia: Fortress, 1985: 201-238.

_____. *Sin and Judgment in the Prophets*. Chico, CA: Scholars Press, 1982.

Milne, Bruce A. "The Idea of Sin in the Twentieth Century." *TB* 26 (1975): 3-33.

Miskotte, K. H. *When the Gods Are Silent*. New York: Harper and Row, 1967.

Mitton, C. L. "Atonement." *IDB* 1. New York: Abingdon, 1962.

Moberly, R. W. L. *The Old Testament of the Old Testament*. Minneapolis: Fortress Press, 1992.

Moberly, R. C. "Punishment and Forgiveness." *Nineteenth Century Evangelical Theology*, edited by Fisher Humphreys. Nashville: Broadman Press, 1983.

Moltmann, J. *The Crucified God*. London: SCM, 1974.

Moody, Dale. "Propitiation = Expiation." *Biblical Illustrator* 9, 1982: 14-16.

Moore, Aubrey. "The Christian Doctrine of God." *Lux Mundi*, edited by Charles Gore. London: John Murray, 1904.

Moore, George Foot. *Judaism in the First Centuries of the Christian Era*. 3 vols. Cambridge: Harvard University Press, 1927.

Morgenstern, J. "Sabbath." *IDB* 4. New York: Abingdon, 1962: 135-140.

Morris, Leon. *The Apostolic Preaching of the Cross*. Grand Rapids: Eerdmans, 1956.

_____. "Atonement." *The New Bible Dictionary*, edited by J. D. Douglas. London: InterVarsity, 1962.

Mowinckel, Sigmund. *He That Cometh*. Nashville: Abingdon, 1954.

_____. *The Psalms in Israel's Worship*. 2 vols. New York: Abingdon, 1962.

Muilenburg, James. "Biblical Understanding of the Future." *Journal of Religious Thought* 19 (1962): 99.

_____. "The Biblical View of Time." *Grace Upon Grace*, edited by James Cook. Grand Rapids: Eerdmans, 1975.

_____. "Isaiah 40—66." *IB* 5 (1956).

_____. *The Way of Israel*. New York: Harper, 1961.

Murphy, Roland E. "History, Eschatology and the Old Testament." *Continuum* 7 (1969/70): 583-593.

Murray, John. "Covenant." *The New Bible Dictionary*, edited by J. D. Douglas. London: InterVarsity, 1962.

Nahveh, J. "Graffiti and Dedications." *BASOR* 235 (1979): 27-36.

Nakari, Toyozo W. "Worship in the Old Testament." *Encounter* 34 (1973): 282-286.

Neusner, Jacob, and others, eds. *Judaic Perspectives of Biblical Studies*. Philadelphia: Fortress Press, 1987.

_____. *Formative Judaism*. 2 vols. Decatur, GA: Scholars Press, 1982, 1983. Brown Judaic Studies.

Newman, A. H. *A Manual of Church History I.* Philadelphia: American Baptist Publication Society, 1903.

―――. *A Manual of Church History II.* Philadelphia: American Baptist Publication Society, 1933.

Nicholson, Ernest W. *God and His People: Covenant and Theology in the Old Testament.* Oxford: Clarendon Press, 1986.

―――. "Israelite Religion in the Pre-exilic Period." *A Word in Season,* edited by James D. Martin and Philip R. Davies, *JSOTS* 42. Sheffield: JSOT Press, 1986: 3-34.

North, C. R. *The Suffering Servant in Deutero-Isaiah.* London: Oxford University, 1948.

Noth, Martin. "Das System der zwölf Stamme Israels." Stuttgart: *BWANT* IV:1 (1930).

―――. *The History of Israel.* New York: Harper and Brothers, 1958.

―――. "The Holy Ones of the Most High." *The Laws in the Pentateuch and Other Essays.* Edinburgh: Oliver and Boyd, 1966.

―――. "God, King, and Nation." *The Laws in the Pentateuch and Other Essays.* Edinburgh: Oliver and Boyd, 1966.

―――. *Leviticus.* Old Testament Library. Philadelphia: Westminster, 1965.

Oehler, G. F. *Theology of the Old Testament.* New York: Funk and Wagnalls, 1883.

Oesterley, W. O. E. *Immortality and the Unseen World.* London: SPCK, 1921.

Ollenburger, Ben C., Elmer A. Martens, and Gerhard F. Hasel, eds. *The Flowering of Old Testament Theology.* Winona Lake, IN: Eisenbrauns, 1992.

―――. *Zion the City of the Great King.* JSOTS 41 (Sheffield: JSOT Press, 1987).

Otto, Rudolph. *The Idea of the Holy.* Oxford: Oxford University Press, 1924.

Otzen, B. "Traditions and Structures of Isaiah XXIV-XXVII." *VT* 24 (1974): 196-206.

Outler, Albert. *Who Trusts in God.* New York: The Oxford Press, 1968.

Pannenberg, Wolfhart. *What Is Man?* Philadelphia: Fortress, 1970.

Paterson, John. *The Goodly Fellowship of the Prophets.* New York: Scribners, 1950.

Payne, D. F. "The Everlasting Covenant." *Tyndale Bulletin* 7-8 (1961): 10-16.

Payne, J. Barton. *The Theology of the Older Testament.* Grand Rapids: Zondervan, 1962.

Peake, A. S. "Jeremiah." *The Century Bible*, 2 vols. Edinburgh: T. and T. Clark, 1910, 1912.

Perlitt, Lothar. *Bundestheologie im Alten Testament. WMANT* 36. Neu-kirchen-Vluyn: Neukirchener Verlag, 1969.

Pidoux, George. *Le dieux qui Vient*. Neuchatel, 1947.

Pope, Marvin. *Song of Songs. The Anchor Bible*. New York: Doubleday, 1977.

Porteous, Norman W. *Daniel*. Old Testament Library. Philadelphia: Westminster, 1976.

———. "Jerusalem-Zion: The Growth of a Symbol." *Living the Mystery*. London: Blackwell, 1967.

———. *Living the Mystery*. London: Blackwell, 1967.

———. "Man." *IDB* 3. New York: Abingdon, 1962: 243.

———. "Old Testament Theology." *The Old Testament and Modern Study*, edited by H. H. Rowley. Oxford: Clarendon Press, 1951.

Porubcan, Stefan. *Sin in the Old Testament*. Roma, 1963.

Preuss, H. D., ed. *Eschatologie im Alten Testament*. Darmstadt: Wissenschaftliche Buchgesellschaft, 1978.

Pritchard, James B., ed. *Ancient Near Eastern Texts*. Princeton: Princeton University Press, 1955.

Pussey, E. B. *The Confessions of St. Augustine*. New York: E. P. Dutton, 1907.

Quanbeck, W. A. "Forgiveness." *IDB* 2. New York: Abingdon, 1962.

———. "Repentance." *IDB* 4. New York: Abingdon, 1962.

Raitt, Thomas. "The Prophetic Summons to Repentance." *ZAW* 83 (1972): 30-48.

Reed, W. L. *The Asherah in the Old Testament*. Fort Worth: Texas Christian University Press, 1949.

———. "Some Implications of *Hen* for Old Testament Religion." *JBL* 73 (1954): 36-41.

Rendtorff, Rolf. "The Concept of Revelation in Ancient Israel." *Revelation as History*, edited by Wolfhart Pannenberg. New York: Macmillan, 1968.

Rendtorff, Trutz. *Ethics*, vol. 2, translated by Keith Crim. Philadelphia: Fortress Press, 1989.

Reventlow, Henning Graf. *The Authority of the Bible and the Rise of the Modern World*. Philadelphia: Fortress Press, 1984.

———. "Basic Problems in Old Testament Theology." *JSOT* 11 (1979): 2-22.

———. "Grundfragen der alttestamentlichen Theologie im Lichte der neueren deutschen Forschung." *TTZ* 17 (1961): 81-98.

_____. *Problems of Old Testament Theology in the Twentieth Century.* London: SCM, 1985.

Richardson, Alan. "Salvation, Savior." *IDB* 4. New York: Abingdon (1962): 168-169.

_____. *A Theological Word Book.* London: SCM, 1954.

Ringgren, Helmer. *The Faith of Qumran.* Philadelphia: Fortress, 1963.

_____. *Israelite Religion.* Philadelphia: Fortress, 1963.

_____. *The Messiah in the Old Testament.* London: SCM, 1956.

Rist, Martin. "Jesus and Eschatology." *Transitions in Biblical Scholarship,* edited by J. C. Rylaarsdam. Chicago: University of Chicago Press, 1968.

Roberts, Alexander, and James Donaldson, eds. *Anti-Nicene Christian Library.* 20 vols. Edinburgh: T. and T. Clark, 1886.

Robinson, H. Wheeler. *The Christian Doctrine of Man.* Edinburgh: T. and T. Clark, 1952.

_____. *Corporate Personality in Ancient Israel.* Philadelphia: Fortress, 1964.

_____. *Inspiration and Revelation in the Old Testament.* Oxford: Clarendon, 1946.

_____. "The Old Testament Background." *Christian Worship,* edited by Nathaniel Micklem. Oxford: The University Press, 1959.

_____. *Redemption and Revelation.* London: Nisbet and Co., 1947.

_____, ed. *Record and Revelation.* Oxford: Clarendon Press, 1938.

Robinson, T. H. *Job and His Friends.* London: SCM, 1954.

Rogers, A. K. *A Student's Handbook of Philosophy.* New York: Macmillan, 1935.

Rogerson, J. W. *Anthropology and the Old Testament.* Atlanta: John Knox, 1978.

Rogerson, John, ed. *Beginning Old Testament Study.* Philadelphia: Westminster, 1982.

Rosenblatt, S. "Inclination, Good and Evil." *EJ* 8: 1315.

Rowley, H. H. *The Biblical Doctrine of Election.* London: Lutterworth Press, 1950.

_____. *The Changing Pattern of Old Testament Studies.* London: The Epworth Press, 1959.

_____. *The Faith of Israel: Aspects of Old Testament Thought.* Philadelphia: Westminster, 1956.

_____. "Papyri from Elephantine." *Documents from Old Testament Times,* edited by D. Winton Thomas. New York: Harper's Torchbooks, 1958.

_____. *The Rediscovery of the Old Testament.* London: Clarke, 1946.

_____. "The Samaritan Schism in Legend and History." *Israel's Prophetic Faith*, edited by B. W. Anderson and Walter Harrelson. New York: Harper, 1962.

_____. *The Servant of the Lord and Other Essays*. London: Lutterworth, 1952.

_____. *The Unity of the Bible*. London: Carey Kingsgate, 1953.

_____. *Worship in Ancient Israel*. Philadelphia: Fortress, 1967.

Rowley, H. H., ed. *The Old Testament and Modern Study*. Oxford: Clarendon, 1951.

Rubenstein, Richard L. *After Auschwitz*. Indianapolis: Bobbs-Merrill, 1966.

_____. *My Brother Paul*. New York: Harper Torchbooks, 1972.

Russell, D. S. *The Method and Message of Jewish Apocalyptic*. Philadelphia: Westminster, 1964.

Rust, Eric C. "The Destiny of the Individual in the Thought of the Old Testament." *Review and Expositor* 58 (1961): 296-311.

Rylaarsdam, J. C. "Jewish-Christian Relationships: The Two Covenants and the Dilemmas of Christology." *Grace Upon Grace*. Grand Rapids: Eerdmans, 1975: 70-84.

Sakenfeld, Katharine D. "The Problem of Divine Forgiveness in Numbers 14." *CBQ* 37 (1975): 317-330.

Sanders, James A. "First Testament and Second." *BTB* 17 (1987): 47-49.

Sandmel, Samuel. "Reflection on the Problem of Theology for Jews." *JBR* 33 (1965): 111.

Sawyer, F. A. "Combating Prejudices About the Bible and Judaism." *Theology* 94 (1991): 269-278.

Sawyer, J. F. A. "Hebrew Words for Resurrection." *VT* 23 (1973): 218-234.

Scherer, Paul. *Event in Eternity*. New York: Harper and Brothers, 1945.

Schild, E. "On Exodus 3:14—'I am that I am.'" *VT* 4 (1954): 296-302.

Schmid, Hans Heinrich. "Creation, Righteousness, and Salvation." *Creation in the Old Testament*, edited by B. W. Anderson. Philadelphia: Fortress, 1984.

_____. *Gerechtigkeit als Weltordnung*. Beiträge zur historischen Theologie 40. Tubingen: Mohr, 1968.

Schmidt, Werner H. *The Faith of the Old Testament*. Philadelphia: Westminster, 1983.

Schoeps, Hans Joachim. *The Jewish-Christian Argument*. New York: Holt, Rinehart and Winston, 1963.

Schultz, Hermann. *Old Testament Theology*. 2 vols. Edinburgh: T. and T. Clark, 1895.

Sebass, Horst. *bachar*. *TDOT* II, edited by Johannes Bötterweck and Helmer Ringgren. Grand Rapids: Eerdmans, 1975.

Shafer, Byron E. "The Root bhr and Pre-exilic Concepts of Chosenness in the Hebrew Bible." *ZAW* 20 (1977): 20-52.

Shires, Henry M. *Finding the Old Testament in the New.* Philadelphia: Westminster Press, 1974.

Simpson, C. A. "Genesis." *IB* 1 (1952): 538.

Skinner, John. *Genesis. ICC.* New York: Scribners, 1910.

_____. *Isaiah. The Cambridge Bible.* Cambridge: The University Press, 1951.

_____. *Prophecy and Religion.* London: Cambridge, 1936.

Sleeper, C. Freeman. "Ethics as a Context for Biblical Interpretation." *Interpretation* 22 (1968): 443-460.

Smart, James. "The Death and Rebirth of Old Testament Theology." *Journal of Religion* 23 (1943): 1-11; 124-136.

_____. *The Interpretation of Scripture.* Philadelphia: Westminster, 1961.

_____. *The Past, Present, and Future of Biblical Theology.* Philadelphia: Westminster, 1979.

Smith, C. R. *The Biblical Doctrine of Sin.* London: Epworth, 1953.

Smith, J. M. P. "The Chosen People." *ASJL* 45 (1929): 73-82.

Smith, Ralph L. *Amos. Broadman Bible Commentary* 7. Nashville: Broadman Press, 1972.

_____. "Major Motifs in Hosea." *SWJT* 18 (1975): 27-28.

_____. *Micah—Malachi. Word Biblical Commentary* 32. Waco, Tx: Word Books, 1984.

_____. *Word Biblical Themes: Micah—Malachi.* Waco: Word Books, 1991.

Snaith, Norman. *The Distinctive Ideas of the Old Testament.* London: Epworth, 1944, 1983.

_____. "Forgiveness." *A Theological Wordbook of the Bible,* edited by Alan Richardson. London: SCM, 1954.

_____. "Righteous, Righteousness." *A Theological Wordbook of the Bible,* edited by Alan Richardson. London: SCM, 1954.

_____. *The Seven Psalms.* The Epworth Press, 1964.

Soggin, A. "Approaches to Old Testament Theology Since Von Rad." *SWENSK Exegetisk Arsbok* 47, edited by H. Ringgren. Gleerup: Lund, 1982.

Speiser, E. A. *Oriental and Biblical Studies.* Philadelphia: University of Pennsylvania, 1967.

Stacey, W. D. "Man as a Soul." *ET* 72 (1961): 349-350.

Stagg, Frank. *New Testament Theology.* Nashville: Broadman Press, 1962.

Stamm, Johann Jakob, and Maurice Edward Andrew. *The Ten Commandments in Recent Research.* London: SCM, 1967.

Steindorff, George, and Keith C. Seele. *When Egypt Ruled the East*. Chicago: University of Chicago, 1963.

Stek, John H. "What Says the Scriptures." *Portraits of Creation*, edited by Howard van Till. Grand Rapids: Eerdmans, 1990.

Stewart, James S. *A Faith to Proclaim*. New York: Scribners, 1953.

_____. *Man in Christ: The Vital Elements of St. Paul's Religion*. New York: Harper, 1935.

Stott, John R. *Our Guilty Silence*. Grand Rapids: Eerdmans, 1967.

Streane, A. W. *Jeremiah. Cambridge Bible*. Cambridge: Cambridge University Press, 1899.

Strong, A. H. *Systematic Theology*. Philadelphia: Judson, 1943.

Tasker, R. V. G. "Wrath." *The New Bible Dictionary*. London, 1962.

Tate, Marvin E. *Psalms 51—100. Word Biblical Commentary* 20. Waco: Word Books, 1990.

Taylor, F. J. "Save, Salvation." *A Theological Word Book of the Bible*, edited by Alan Richardson. London: SCM, 1954.

Terrien, Samuel. *The Elusive Presence: Toward a New Biblical Theology*. San Francisco: Harper, 1978.

_____. *The Psalms and Their Meaning for Today*. Indianapolis: Bobbs-Merrill, 1952.

Thomas, D. Winton. *Documents from Old Testament Times*. New York: Harper Torchbook, 1958.

Thompson, J. A. *Deuteronomy. TOTC*. London: InterVarsity Press, 1974.

Toy, Crawford H. *Proverbs*. ICC. Edinburgh: T. and T. Clark, 1914.

Trible, Phyllis. *God and the Rhetoric of Sexuality*. Philadelphia: Fortress, 1978.

Tsevat, Matitiahu. "God and the Gods in Assembly." *HUCA* 40 (1969): 123-137.

_____. "Theology of the Old Testament—A Jewish View." *HBT* 8/2: 33-50.

Van der Leeuw, G. *Religion in Essence and Manifestation*, vol. 1. New York: Harper and Row, 1963.

Van der Ploeg, J. P. M. "Eschatology in the Old Testament." *The Witness of Tradition. Oudtestamentische Studiën* 17. Leiden: E. J. Brill, 1972: 89-99.

van Till, Howard J., ed. *Portraits of Creation*. Grand Rapids: Eerdmans, 1990.

Vawter, Bruce. "Intimations of Immortality and the Old Testament." *JBL* 91 (1972): 158-171.

von Rad, Gerhard. "The City on the Hill." *The Problem of the Hexateuch and Other Essays*. Edinburgh: Oliver and Boyd, 1966.

_____. *Genesis*. Old Testament Library. Philadelphia: Westminster, 1961.

_____. *God at Work in Israel*. Nashville: Abingdon Press, 1980.

_____. *Old Testament Theology I*. New York: Harper and Row, 1962.

_____. *Old Testament Theology II*. New York: Harper and Row, 1965.

_____. *Wisdom in Israel*. Nashville: Abingdon, 1972.

Vos, Geerhardus. *Biblical Theology*. Grand Rapids: Eerdmans, 1948.

Vriezen, Th. C. "Die Erwählung Israels." Zurich: Zwingli Verlag, 1953.

_____. *An Outline of Old Testament Theology*. 2nd ed. Newton, MA: Chas. T. Branford, 1970.

_____. "Prophecy and Eschatology." *SVT* I (1953): 199-229.

Watts, John D. W. *Isaiah 1—33. Word Biblical Commentary* 24. Waco: Word Books, 1985.

_____. *Isaiah 34—66. Word Biblical Commentary* 25. Waco: Word Books, 1987.

Weatherhead, Leslie D. *The Significance of Silence*. Nashville: Abingdon, 1945.

Weber, Alfred, and Ralph B. Perry. *A History of Philosophy*. New York: Scribners, 1925.

Weinfeld, Moshe. "The Covenant of Grant in the Old Testament and in the Ancient Near East." *JAOS* 90 (1970): 189-192.

Weiser, Artur. *The Psalms*. Old Testament Library. Philadelphia: Westminster, 1962.

Wellhausen, Julius. *Prolegomena to the History of Israel*. Meredian Books, 1957.

Wenham, Gordon J. *Genesis 1—15. Word Biblical Commentary* 1. Waco: Word Books, 1987.

Wernberg-Möller, P. "Is There an Old Testament Theology?" *Hibbert Journal* 59 (1960-1961): 21.

Westberg, Granger. *Good Grief: A Constructive Approach*. Philadelphia: Fortress, 1962.

Westcott, B. F. *The Epistle to the Hebrews*. London: Macmillan, 1899.

Westermann, Claus. *Blessing in the Bible and the Life of the Church*. Philadelphia: Fortress, 1978.

_____. *Creation*, Translated by John J. Scullion. Philadelphia: Fortress, 1974.

_____. *Elements of Old Testament Theology*. Atlanta: John Knox, 1982.

_____. *Essays on Old Testament Hermeneutics*. Richmond: John Knox, 1963.

_____. *Genesis 1—11*. Minneapolis: Augsburg, 1984.

_____. *Isaiah 40—66*. Philadelphia: Westminster, 1969.

_____. *Prophetic Oracles of Salvation in the Old Testament.* Louisville: Westminster/John Knox Press, 1991.

_____. "The Role of the Lament in the Theology of the Old Testament." *Interpretation* 28 (1974): 20-38.

Whale, J. S. *Christian Doctrine.* London: Fontana, 1961.

Wharton, J. A. "Splendid Failure or Flawed Success?" *Interpretation* 29 (1975): 275-276.

Whybray, R. N. "Proverbs 8:22-31 and Its Supposed Prototypes." *Studies in Ancient Israelite Wisdom*, edited by James L. Crenshaw. New York: KTAV, 1976.

_____. "Old Testament Theology—A Non-Existent Beast?" *Scripture, Meaning and Method* (A. T. Hanson's festschrift), edited by Barry P. Thompson. Hull University, 1987: 168-180.

Wildberger, Hans. "Auf dem Wege zu einer biblischen Theologie." *Evangelische Theologie* 19 (1959): 70-90.

_____. "bhr, *erwählen.*" *THAT*, vol. 1, edited by Ernst Jenni and Claus Westermann. Zurich Theologischer Verlag, 1971: cols. 275-300.

Williamson, C. M., and R. S. Allen. *Interpreting Difficult Texts: Anti-Judaism and Christian Preaching.* Philadelphia: Trinity International, 1989.

Wolf, William J. *No Cross, No Crown.* Garden City: Doubleday, 1957.

Wolff, Hans Walter. *Anthropology of the Old Testament.* Philadelphia: Fortress, 1974.

_____. "Das Thema 'Umkehr' in der altestamentlichen Prophetie." *ZTK* 48 (1951).

_____. "The Kerygma of the Yahwist." *Interpretation* 20 (1966).

Woudstra, Martin H. "The Everlasting Covenant in Ezekiel 16:59-63." *Calvin Theological Journal* 6 (1971): 22-48.

_____. "The Old Testament in Biblical Theology and Dogmatics." *Calvin Theological Journal* 18 (1983): 47-60.

Wright, Christopher J. H. *An Eye for an Eye.* Downers Grove, IL: InterVarsity, 1983.

_____. *God's People in God's Land.* Grand Rapids: Eerdmans, 1990.

Wright, G. Ernest. *The Biblical Doctrine of Man in Society.* London: SCM, 1954.

_____. *The Challenge of Israel's Faith.* Chicago: University of Chicago Press, 1944.

_____. "Deuteronomy." *IB* 2 (1953): 372-373.

_____. "The Faith of Israel." *IB* 1 (1952): 349-390.

_____. *God Who Acts.* London: SCM Press, 1952.

_____. "History and Reality." *The Old Testament and The Christian Faith*. New York: Harper and Row, 1963.

_____. *The Old Testament Against Its Environment*. London: SCM, 1950.

_____. *The Old Testament and Theology*. New York: Harper and Row, 1969.

_____. "Reflections Concerning Old Testament Theology." *Studia Biblica et Semitica*. (Vernman, 1966): 376-388.

_____. "Review of Jacob's Old Testament Theology." *JBL* (1960): 81.

_____. *The Rule of God*. New York: Doubleday, 1960.

_____. *Shechem: The Biography of a Biblical City*. New York: McGraw-Hill, 1965.

Young, Edward J. *The Study of Old Testament Theology Today*. Westwood, NJ: Revell, 1959.

Zevit, Zion. "The Khirbet el-Qom Inscription Mentioning a Goddess." *BASOR* 255 (1985): 30-47.

Zimmerli, Walther. "The History of Israelite Religion." *Tradition and Interpretation*, edited by G. W. Anderson. Oxford: Clarendon Press, 1979.

_____. *The Old Testament and the World*, translated by J. J. Scullion. Atlanta: John Knox, 1976.

_____. *Old Testament Theology in Outline*. Atlanta: John Knox, 1978.

_____. "The Place and Limit of Wisdom in the Framework of Old Testament Theology." *SJT* 17 (1964): 165-181.

Zobel, Hans-Jürgen. *galah*. *TDOT* II, edited by G. Johannes Bötterweck and Helmer Ringgren. Grand Rapids: Eerdmans, 1975.

Subject Index

Author Index

Old Testament Index

Psalms

New Testament Index

Classic Author Index

Early Literature Index

Hebrew Index